THE PHILOSOPHY OF
W. V. QUINE

THE LIBRARY OF LIVING PHILOSOPHERS

Lewis Edwin Hahn and Paul Arthur Schilpp, Editors

Already Published:

THE PHILOSOPHY OF JOHN DEWEY (1939)*
THE PHILOSOPHY OF GEORGE SANTAYANA (1940)
THE PHILOSOPHY OF ALFRED NORTH WHITEHEAD (1941)*
THE PHILOSOPHY OF G. E. MOORE (1942)
THE PHILOSOPHY OF BERTRAND RUSSELL (1944)*
THE PHILOSOPHY OF ERNST CASSIRER (1949)
ALBERT EINSTEIN: PHILOSOPHER-SCIENTIST (1949)
THE PHILOSOPHY OF SARVEPALLI RADHAKRISHNAN (1952)*
THE PHILOSOPHY OF KARL JASPERS (1957; aug. ed., 1981)
THE PHILOSOPHY OF C.D. BROAD (1959)
THE PHILOSOPHY OF RUDOLF CARNAP (1963)
THE PHILOSOPHY OF MARTIN BUBER (1967)
THE PHILOSOPHY OF C. I. LEWIS (1968)
THE PHILOSOPHY OF KARL POPPER (1974)
THE PHILOSOPHY OF BRAND BLANSHARD (1980)
THE PHILOSOPHY OF JEAN-PAUL SARTRE (1981)
THE PHILOSOPHY OF GABRIEL MARCEL (1984)
THE PHILOSOPHY OF W. V. QUINE (1986)
THE PHILOSOPHY OF GEORG HENRIK von WRIGHT (1986)

In Preparation:

THE PHILOSOPHY OF CHARLES HARTSHORNE
THE PHILOSOPHY OF A. J. AYER
THE PHILOSOPHY OF PAUL RICOEUR

*Available only from University Microfilms International.

W. V. Quine

THE LIBRARY OF LIVING PHILOSOPHERS
VOLUME XVIII

THE PHILOSOPHY OF
W. V. QUINE

EDITED BY

LEWIS EDWIN HAHN

AND

PAUL ARTHUR SCHILPP

SOUTHERN ILLINOIS UNIVERSITY—CARBONDALE

LA SALLE, ILLINOIS • OPEN COURT • ESTABLISHED 1887

THE PHILOSOPHY OF W. V. QUINE

Printed in the United States of America.

First printing 1986.
Second printing 1987.

FIRST EDITION

Library of Congress Cataloging-in-Publication Data

The Philosophy of W.V. Quine.

(The Library of living philosophers ; v. 18)
"A bibliography of the publications of W.V. Quine": p.
Includes index.
1. Quine, W.V. (Willard Van Orman) 2. Philosophers—United States—Biography. I. Quine, W.V. (Willard Van Orman) II. Hahn, Lewis Edwin, 1908- III. Schilpp, Paul Arthur, 1897- IV. Series.
B945.Q54P48 1986   191   86-17980
ISBN 0-8126-9010-9
ISBN 0-8126-9012-5 (pbk.)

The Library of Living Philosophers is published under the sponsorship of Southern Illinois University—Carbondale.

GENERAL INTRODUCTION*
TO
THE LIBRARY OF LIVING PHILOSOPHERS

According to the late F. C. S. Schiller, the greatest obstacle to fruitful discussion in philosophy is "the curious etiquette which apparently taboos the asking of questions about a philosopher's meaning while he is alive." The "interminable controversies which fill the histories of philosophy," he goes on to say, "could have been ended at once by asking the living philosophers a few searching questions."

The confident optimism of this last remark undoubtedly goes too far. Living thinkers have often been asked "a few searching questions," but their answers have not stopped "interminable controversies" about their real meaning. It is nonetheless true that there would be far greater clarity of understanding than is now often the case if more such searching questions had been directed to great thinkers while they were still alive.

This, at any rate, is the basic thought behind the present undertaking. The volumes of the Library of Living Philosophers can in no sense take the place of the major writings of great and original thinkers. Students who would know the philosophies of such men as John Dewey, George Santayana, Alfred North Whitehead, G. E. Moore, Bertrand Russell, Ernst Cassirer, Karl Jaspers, Rudolf Carnap, Martin Buber, et al., will still need to read the writings of these men. There is no substitute for first-hand contact with the original thought of the philosopher himself. Least of all does this Library pretend to be such a substitute. The Library in fact will spare neither effort nor expense in offering to the student the best possible guide to the published writings of a given thinker. We shall attempt to meet this aim by providing at the end of each volume in our series as nearly complete a bibliography of the published work of the philosopher in question as possible. Nor should one overlook the fact that essays in each volume cannot but finally lead to this same goal. The interpretative and critical discussions of the various phases of a great thinker's work

---

*This General Introduction, setting forth the underlying conception of this Library, is purposely reprinted in each volume (with only very minor changes).

and, most of all, the reply of the thinker himself, are bound to lead the reader to the works of the philosopher himself.

At the same time, there is no denying that different experts find different ideas in the writings of the same philosopher. This is as true of the appreciative interpreter and grateful disciple as it is of the critical opponent. Nor can it be denied that such differences of reading and of interpretation on the part of other experts often leave the neophyte aghast before the whole maze of widely varying and even opposing interpretations. Who is right and whose interpretation shall he accept? When the doctors disagree among themselves, what is the poor student to do? If, in desperation, he decides that all of the interpreters are probably wrong and that the only thing for him to do is to go back to the original writings of the philosopher himself and then make his own decision— uninfluenced (as if this were possible) by the interpretation of anyone else— the result is not that he has actually come to the meaning of the original philosopher himself, but rather that he has set up one more interpretation, which may differ to a greater or lesser degree from the interpretations already existing. It is clear that in this direction lies chaos, just the kind of chaos which Schiller has so graphically and inimitably described.[1]

It is curious that until now no way of escaping this difficulty has been seriously considered. It has not occurred to students of philosophy that one effective way of meeting the problem at least partially is to put these varying interpretations and critiques before the philosopher while he is still alive and to ask him to act at one and the same time as both defendant and judge. If the world's great living philosophers can be induced to cooperate in an enterprise whereby their own work can, at least to some extent, be saved from becoming merely "desiccated lecture-fodder," which on the one hand "provides innocuous sustenance for ruminant professors," and on the other hand gives an opportunity to such ruminants and their understudies to "speculate safely, endlessly, and fruitlessly, about what a philosopher must have meant" (Schiller), they will have taken a long step toward making their intentions more clearly comprehensible.

With this in mind, the Library of Living Philosophers expects to publish at more or less regular intervals a volume on each of the greater among the world's living philosophers. In each case it will be the purpose of the editor of the Library to bring together in the volume the interpretations and criticisms of a wide range of that particular thinker's scholarly contemporaries, each of whom will be given a free hand to discuss the specific phase of the thinker's work that has been assigned to him. All contributed essays will finally be sub-

---

1. In his essay "Must Philosophers Disagree?" in the volume of the same title (London: Macmillan, 1934), from which the above quotations were taken.

mitted to the philosopher with whose work and thought they are concerned, for his careful perusal and reply. And, although it would be expecting too much to imagine that the philosopher's reply will be able to stop all differences of interpretation and of critique, this should at least serve the purpose of stopping certain of the grosser and more general kinds of misinterpretation. If no further gain than this were to come from the present and projected volumes of this Library, it would seem to be fully justified.

In carrying out this principal purpose of the Library, it is planned that (as far as is humanly possible) each volume will contain the following elements:

First, an intellectual autobiography of the thinker whenever this can be secured; in any case an authoritative and authorized biography;

Second, a series of expository and critical articles written by the leading exponents and opponents of the philosopher's thought;

Third, the reply to the critics and commentators by the philosopher himself; and

Fourth, a bibliography of writings of the philosopher to provide a ready instrument to give access to his writings and thought.

The editors have deemed it desirable to secure the services of an Advisory Board of philosophers to aid them in the selection of the subjects of future volumes. The names of ten prominent American philosophers who have consented to serve appear on the next page. To each of them the editors are most grateful.

Future volumes in this series will appear in as rapid succession as is feasible in view of the scholarly nature of this Library. The next volume in this series will be devoted to the philosophy of Georg Henrik von Wright.

Throughout its forty-eight years, the Library of Living Philosophers has, because of its scholarly nature, never been self-supporting. The generosity of the Edward C. Hegeler Foundation has made possible the publication of many of the volumes, but for the support of future volumes additional funds are needed. On 20 February 1979, the Board of Trustees of Southern Illinois University contractually assumed all responsiblity for the Library, which is therefore no longer separately incorporated. Gifts specifically designated for the Library may be made through the University, and inasmuch as the University is a tax-exempt institution, all such gifts are tax-deductible.

P.A.S.
L.E.H.
Editors

DEPARTMENT OF PHILOSOPHY
SOUTHERN ILLINOIS UNIVERSITY—CARBONDALE

ACKNOWLEDGEMENTS

The editors hereby gratefully acknowledge their obligation and sincere gratitude to all the publishers of W. V. Quine's books and publications for their kind and uniform courtesy in permitting us to quote—sometimes at some length—from Professor Quine's writings.

LEWIS E. HAHN
PAUL A. SCHILPP

---

*Deceased.
#Added to Board after the subject of this volume was chosen.

✓=readed

TABLE OF CONTENTS

PREFACE

For more than thirty years W. V. Quine has been a dominant figure in logical theory and philosophy of logic. Few, if any, have done more than he to bring the science of mathematical logic to full growth. His clear, accurate, and elegant expositions have helped set standards for the field, and his innovations in notations and techniques have paved the way for much solid work on the part of others. Nor have his contributions been limited to theory. Many generations of students of elementary logic have benefited from his strong pedagogical motivation, and, perhaps even more importantly, a host of graduate students, or budding professionals, have also learned from him about logic and what is involved in a sound philosophical attitude toward it.

If he had to choose between being a great philosopher or a great teacher, I suspect he would choose the latter; but, fortunately for us, we do not have to choose between his being one or the other; for he is both. With his technical work in logic, moreover, he has combined an impressive array of philosophical insights in methodology, theory of language, epistemology, and ontology. His special brand of empiricism or pragmatic naturalism has helped blur the supposed boundaries between speculative metaphysics and natural science and generated a sizable literature on such topics as the distinction between analytic and synthetic truths, synonymy and its explication, meaning holism and the underdetermination of theory by particular experiences, reference and its roots, inscrutability of reference, and indeterminacy of translation and multiple translatability. Accordingly, his philosophical views have been increasingly the center of attention, discussion, and controversy. And whether or not "to be is to be the value of a variable," we have learned much from him about theories and things, statements and translations, words and their objects, and what there is as well as how to express what there is.

In view of the many years this volume has been in the making and the number of delays which have plagued it, Professor Schilpp and I wish to express our heartfelt thanks to Professor Quine and each of the other contributors for their co-operation, patience, and understanding. We are grateful also, of course, for their substantive contributions. In a gratifyingly large number of instances they effect a fruitful joining of issues, and in each case they shed fresh light on various features of Quine's views. Unhappily, however, one contributor as well as two additional long-term members of the Advisory Board did not live to see the volume in print. Herbert G. Bohnert passed away on 2 March 1984; and we lost Herbert W. Schneider on 15 October 1984 and Richard P. McKeon on 31 March 1985.

My special thanks go to Paul A. Schilpp for advice and counsel. I am grateful also for help in diverse ways on many matters from Dawn Boone, Loretta Smith, and the Philosophy Department secretariat as well as from my colleagues, especially David S. Clarke, Jr., Elizabeth R. Eames, Matthew J. Kelly, and G. K. Plochmann.

In addition, my grateful appreciation goes to the staff of the Morris Library and especially to Alan M. Cohn and his associates for bibliographical aid.

I am also appreciative of the support, encouragement, and co-operation of our publisher, Open Court Publishing Company of La Salle, Illinois.

To the administration of Southern Illinois University I am happy to extend warm thanks and appreciation for much needed support and encouragement. In this connection, moreover, perhaps attention should again be directed to the fact that since 20 February 1979 Southern Illinois University—Carbondale has been contractually responsible for the Library.

LEWIS EDWIN HAHN
EDITOR

DEPARTMENT OF PHILOSOPHY
SOUTHERN ILLINOIS UNIVERSITY—CARBONDALE
MARCH 1985

PART ONE

AUTOBIOGRAPHY OF
W. V. QUINE

Preface

Each volume of the Library of Living Philosophers begins with an intellectual autobiography. Writing ~~are~~ seventy odd pages for that purpose got me ~~started in~~ triggered this more inclusive chronicle. ~~This one~~ It is laced still with professional memoirs, and I have cribbed ~~the ~~ scraps ~~equivalent of thirty pages from~~ the more austere piece, ~~But~~ I have tried to render ~~som passages~~ them intelligible to lay readers, if read in order, ~~and~~ I even encourage the more ~~frivolous~~ of my ~~lay readers~~ to skip ~~them The dogs~~ Readers who are drawn to the book by friendship or kinship rather than ~~by~~ philosophy or logic, can easily ~~spot~~ pass those passages ~~and pass them~~ by.

I have ~~been~~ true my account to the truth.

I have undertaken in this ~~book~~ to tell the truth; not the whole truth, which would tax everyone's patience, ~~but~~ to tell nothing but the truth, to the best of my knowledge and belief. It has not been easy. For example, in the bit about Stern I wanted to report my little barside exchange with an habitué along the following lines.

    "I first met Peter Garrett at the Troc."

    "The Troc?"

    "The Trocadero, in Bangkok. We old Thai hands always think of it as the Troc."

    "Something very elegant, no doubt."

    "Well, it wasn't the Erawan."

    "Oh, good heavens. no. It never occured to me to

1. Origins and Early Concerns

I was born 25 June 1908 in Akron, Ohio, six blocks from my father's birthplace and twelve miles from my mother's. My father's parents had come from Europe by separate ways. His father, Manx-speaking, had left the Isle of Man in 1866 at age sixteen as a sailor. He ranged from the Faeroes to the Falklands under sail. By 1870 he had settled in Akron as a mechanic. My father's mother, née Motz, had moved in childhood with her parents from the Palatinate to a farm near Akron. My own mother's forebears all were American for some generations back, but of Dutch descent on her father's side, with the puzzling name Van Orman, and on her mother's side British.

My mother attended the local college, stopped short of graduation, and taught school. My father's formal education ended with high school, but he studied law, accounting, and engineering on his own. He worked his way up in the heavy industry of tiremold manufacture, founding his own firm in 1917. He lived to see it prosper. An energetic and thoughtful man, he made hobbies of local history and fruit farming.

We were two sons, I somewhat the younger. Bob and I have shared a penchant for foreign travel that recalls our Manx grandfather, not our father; for in all his 85 years our father could never be lured farther beyond our borders than a fringe of Canada.

My concern with maps and far places dates from the dawn of my memory, when, sprawled at my mother's nineteenth-century geography book, I would ponder Servia, the Turkish Empire, Tibesti, Bornu, Ashantee. I would skip the maps of America as dull, and the map of Asia because I did not know the word. Then one luxurious morning I looked at the map of Asia, and a world of myth became real: Jerusalem, Arabia, India, Persia, China, Japan. I had not associated these storied places with actual modern geography. Two realms were integrated into one—an early taste of scientific discovery.

I was six when we drove our Ford to Niagara Falls and crossed to Canada. I asked how we could still be in America, having left the country. This was when I learned the word 'continent'.

I was younger when, not yet having a car, we travelled six miles by street car and train to visit some country relatives, a distance of three miles as the crow flies. While there I amused myself below a grassy bank, pretending to dig a tunnel to Europe. By evening, I am told, I was so inconsolably homesick as to cause an untimely end to our visit; Uncle Dan hitched up his horse and drove us home.

This early incident illustrates a tension between the lure of the remote and the drive for the familiar. On later occasions this tension has been good for an agreeable thrill: I am in an unfamiliar place and choose an unfamiliar road toward familiar territory, intent on seeing just where it joins up. I have dreamed this of Akron, and I have contrived it in other places. This thrill of the strange way home is a paradigm of the thrill of discovery in theoretical science: the reduction of the unfamiliar to the familiar.

The continuing charm of geography was due not only to the exotic, but to structure. I was interested in boundaries, and in where you get to when you proceed thus and so. I savored the specification of street ends in the city directory. I relished a proposed revision of Akron street names, for it was a revision toward elegance, minimization.

In my teens I drew a map of a chain of lakes near Akron and peddled blueprints of it by canoe. My parting cartographic fling came just between college and graduate school in 1930, turning a spare week to gainful use at the end of my summer employment. I mapped Mogadore, Ohio, under the title "Meet the Merchants of Mogadore," and surrounded the map with paid advertisements, and put a copy of this printed broadside on every doorstep.

That proved not to be my last geographic publication. A third of a century later Robert Silvers pressed me to review a philosophy book for his *New York Review of Books*. I read the book and found it ill suited to a lay review. To console me for wasted time, Silvers sent me the new *National Geographic Atlas;* someone had told him I liked maps. He said he would be glad if I felt moved to write about it, and as I idled away the hours over the rich pages his hint took hold. It was a fun review, gaily outside my field. More followed: I reviewed another atlas and a history of cartography for Silvers and an atlas for the *Washington Post.* Someone told Silvers that I also liked words, so he had me review two dictionaries and a posthumous edition of Mencken's *American Language.* Presently these excursions from my main business lost their novelty and I stopped.

My childish concerns—to get back—were not all geographical. My main recreation for seven years was elaborate make-believe. Adventurous history, planned and acted, evolved over the years. Thornton Burgess, Wild West movies, and the serial movie thrillers contributed inspiration. I recruited neighborhood children to the roles when I could, and my mother showed indulgent interest. I compiled lists, maps, house plans, and records implementing this fictitious life. In time Joe Weller became my constant companion in this activity, and the plot became more ingenious and convincing thanks to his bookish mind and his seventeen months of seniority. As high school approached we felt obliged to put away these childish things; stamps, less disreputable, became heir to the enthusiasms. Still, my frequent hikes with Joe and others in the woodlands northwest of Akron were given an air of purpose by a continuing project of mapping and facetious naming.

I had no early literary bent. My brother was the avid reader. There was attention to plot in my organized make-believe, but none to expression. I undertook small journalistic ventures, but there the urge was editorial rather than literary. Between my ninth and thirteenth years I published my weekly *Grove Gazette,* summers at the lake. Early issues I produced by pencil and carbon paper; later ones by typewriter and carbon paper. My other journalistic venture, occupying my fifteenth and sixteenth years, was my little monthly *O.K. Stamp News*—a house organ for my stamp business. This miniature mail–order business, with customers in perhaps eighteen states and seven countries, had grown out of my stamp collecting. I found comfort in the trivial details of this business, and joy in the sight of my professionally printed paper; but it was not joy in *belles lettres.* I felt similarly eight years later on seeing my first published logic paper.

2. *Thoughts of a Career*

There is that which one wants to do for the glory of having done it, and there is that which one wants to do for the joy of doing it. One can want to be a scientist because one wants to see oneself as a Darwin or an Einstein, and one can want to be a scientist because one is curious about what makes things tick. The crackpot is motivated in the first way. He extols some shabby idea which he has conceived for the purpose not really of clarifying the world to himself, but of shaking it. Such being his purpose, he is not his idea's severest critic. In more normal cases the two kinds of motivation are in time brought to terms. In early youth one aspires to be president and millionaire and cowboy, independently of any interest in state or business or cows. Later, substantive interests contribute increasingly.

In me the glory motive lingered sufficiently to prevent contemplating a career as cartographer or stamp dealer, despite those substantive interests. In school I was doing well in mathematics, a domain with more scope for ambition; so there was thought of engineering. The insides of machines bored me, but there remained, I was told, civil engineering. No one thought of an academic career.

So, when at West High School the time came to choose the Classical or Scientific or Technical or Commercial Course, I chose the Scientific. I did intend to go to college.

The Scientific Course meant stopping Latin after Caesar. It meant laboratory work, which I disliked. Mathematics went nicely, but still, in reaction perhaps to the main trend of my Course, I began to look to writing. Here I was moved more by the glory motive than by taste or talent. My reading had been meager, and my style was labored and pretentious. However, I worked on the school paper and became editor of the senior annual. I even won the school poetry contest.

My mother revered her brother, after whom I was named. I never saw him, but grew up believing that what he stood for was good. He had taught mathematics at the local college. He had liked Poe, from whose stories my mother recoiled with a tolerant shudder; so it was commendable and indeed manly to like Poe. I read all of Poe. I was enthralled by some of his poems, but I suspect that my taste for his tales was somewhat self-induced. Anyway a summer midway in high school found me effortfully writing, trying to evoke a mood of horror in a style yet more pompous and circumstantial than Poe's.

A more authentic interest began to engage me: philosophy. Poe's "Eureka" helped to spark it. But I also had an early philosophical concern apart from reading: I was worried, already before high school, by the implausibility of the home religion. In my third year of high school I walked often with my new Jamaican friends, Fred and Harold Cassidy, trying to convert them from their Episcopalian faith to atheism. I had previously directed similar efforts toward other friends, and I may vaguely remember a parental repercussion.

Late in high school I acquired two philosophy books through my brother, who was studying at Oberlin. They were Max Otto's *Things and Ideals* and William James's *Pragmatism*. I read them compulsively and believed and forgot all. Also I read Swami Vivekananda's *Raja Yoga*. It was not a notably philosophical phase; I was also doing other pretentious reading, including Ibsen, Edward Young, Samuel Butler.

Thus when I finished high school in January, 1926, my interest in philosophy was partly spurious and partly real. "Eureka," for all its outrageousness, fostered the real thing: the desire to understand the universe. So did the antireligious motive.

But I conceived a new interest at about the end of high school: word origins. It did not issue from school; my enthusiasms seldom did. My source was George H. McKnight, *English Words and their Background,* which I borrowed from the public library, I do not know why. Naturally the subject proved fascinating. An interest in foreign languages, like an interest in stamps, accorded with my taste for geography. Grammar, moreover, appeals to the same sense that is gratified by mathematics, or by the structure of boundaries and road networks. Etymology, more particularly, was a bonanza. Here you can pursue scientific method without a laboratory, and check your hypotheses in a dictionary. Each etymology is a case, in miniature, of the strange road home.

I entered Oberlin College in September 1926, after working some months in a bank. I still vaguely pictured creative writing as my likeliest career, with journalism as the entering wedge. I contributed trifles to the college magazine, and with a misguided sense of tongue in cheek I wrote a horrid thriller for the pulps, no one of which was undiscriminating enough to accept it. But my authentic interest was not literary; it had struck root in linguistics. I claim credit for encouraging this interest in Fred Cassidy, who, with his brother Harold (today an eminent chemist), did me the great good of following me from Akron to Oberlin. In odd hours Fred and I collaborated on an etymological and semantical tabulation of English suffixes, for our amusement. The project came of my having upbraided him for a hybrid coinage. Now he is a prominent linguist and lexicographer. He might otherwise have been a notable poet and illustrator; he had a fine wit and resourcefulness in verse, along with a gift for quick and telling pen sketches.

In choosing a field of concentration I was torn three ways. Literature I had put aside, but there remained mathematics, philosophy, and what I called philology, which would have meant a Classics major. The glory motive intruded a little: I could not invest philology, or linguistics, with the profundity of philosophy or mathematics.

The decision was eased by Bill Bennett, a knowledgeable senior in English whom I knew through poker. He told me of Russell, who had a "mathematical philosophy". It promised a way of combining two of my three competing interests. Majoring in mathematics had some added appeal because of a certain awe that those majoring in mathematics seemed to inspire in others; mathematics was the hardest subject. It was a dry subject, and one that stopped short of most that mattered; but the link with philosophy promised wider possibilites. So I majored in mathematics with honors reading in mathematical philosophy.

Bill's father later ran for mayor of New York. Bill became a broker. Evidently his interest in philosophy continued and grew, for he lately made a gift of books to the Stanford philosophy department.

3. Induction into Logic

Having thus decided that Russell was going to be important for me, I turned to him for leisure reading. *Marriage and Morals* disposed me kindly to my new master. I read *Skeptical Essays, Philosophy, Our Knowledge of the External World, A.B.C. of Relativity,* and *Introduction to Mathematical Philosophy*. It was these books, and not my two survey courses in philosophy, that further whetted my appetite for cosmic understanding. I expounded my new lore interminably to my roommate, Clarence Loesch, when, stealing rides on freight trains and hitch–hiking, we crossed the continent in the summer of 1928.

In our Oberlin rooming house, renamed Ἄρθρον at my suggestion, life was a rich blend of intellectuality and high spirits. Three fellow 'Arthrites' contributed incalculably: besides the Cassidy brothers there was Ed Haskell, a polyglot polymath whose subsequent career has been devoted to social reform and the unification of science. It was an ideal setting in which to wax articulate.

My linguistic drive did not subside. I took a year of Greek and a year of German and more French. The mathematics courses, to which my mathematics major committed me, brought high marks but often imperfect understanding. I got more pleasure from Stetson's course in psychology, where we read Watson on behaviorism, and from Thornton's in Old French.

Much contentment with my mathematics major came with my honors reading, however, which began in 1928. Nobody at Oberlin knew modern logic; however, William D. Cairns, the department chairman, made inquiries and got books. I read Venn's *Symbolic Logic*, Peano's *Formulaire de Mathématiques*, Couturat's *Algebra of Logic*, Keyser's *Mathematical Philosophy*, Russell's *Principles of Mathematics*, Whitehead's *Introduction to Mathematics*, and half of *Principia Mathematica*. I would see Cairns and explain what I had been learning.

I was shocked by a chapter in Keyser on "Korzybski's Concept of Man", in which the theory of types was misused. Cairns pointed Korzybski out in a group photograph and told of his buttonholing mathematicians and holding forth on time-binding. This was before *Science and Sanity*.

Reading in Russell of Sheffer's stroke function and Wittgenstein's doctrine of tautology, I tried some computations in hopes of finding, as possible content of Wittgenstein's doctrine, that equivalent truth-functional formulas become alike when expanded by the definitions into stroke notation. It is salutary for teachers to recall foolish ideas of their youth.

The summer of 1929 brought the glorious fulfillment of my persistent dream, a trip to Europe. By cheapest ways I visited twelve sovereign states, including the four smallest. That summer brought also, in its later portions, my immersion in *Principia Mathematica*. A formula in Couturat,

$$(x \cap y) \cup (x \cap z) \cup (y \cap z) = (x \cup y) \cap (x \cup z) \cap (y \cup z),$$

gave me an idea for an instructive exercise. I educed the more general law, that the union of all intersections of m classes out of n is the intersection of all unions of $n - m + 1$, and proved it within the system of *Principia*. Since this theorem treats of number, its proof depended on most of the first volume and a half of *Principia*. Working backwards in *Principia* from requisites to prerequisites, I gained a functionally structured understanding of that work; such was the value of the exercise. It kept me busier, through the fall term, than I had ever been. The proof took eighteen pages of symbols; such was my honors thesis. Three years later in Vienna I got the proof down to three pages for the *Journal of the London Mathematical Society*.

My four-year average at Oberlin was under A $-$, for my seriousness had not been unflagging. However, thanks to my thesis and some eighteen hours of general examinations, I was graduated *summa cum laude*. In that final spring, 1930, Cairns invited me to review Nicod's *Foundations of Geometry and Induction* for the *American Mathematical Monthly*. I wrote a respectful and ignorant review, and I was so callow as to give back the book. Still it was a proud moment when I saw the review in print, my first professional publication.

Whitehead, co-author of the great *Principia*, was in philosophy at Harvard.

So I applied for a scholarship in that department. I was awarded $400, which was tuition. I got a summer job in Akron instructing in the use of the dial telephone—a job done mostly by women, but with men for the dives and speakeasies.

With my Oberlin fiancée, Naomi Clayton, I hitch–hiked to Boston. We dropped from a fish truck into Scollay Square. I petitioned Harvard for permission to marry without forfeiting the $400. We married and moved into furnished rooms at 8 Howland Street, Cambridge.

I studied hard, unsure of my adequacy to Harvard standards. My four mid-year grades, ranging from A − to A +, reassured me, but there remained another reason for intense work: if I could pass the preliminary examinations in that first year I might get my doctorate in the next. I was moved by financial insecurity. The two-year Ph.D. is rare, but C. I. Lewis suggested I try. I had to grind hard for an even chance at the prelims, for my previous philosophy was meager. The chore courses for me were the historical ones: Woods on Plato, Prall on Leibniz, and especially Lewis on Kant. Lewis required a written synopsis of a chunk of the *Critique of Pure Reason* each week, with a limit on the number of pages. It made for grotesquely crowded pages.

Whitehead was not teaching logic. Sheffer was. He talked of Oswald Veblen and of E. V. Huntington, who was on the Harvard mathematics faculty, and he assigned a piece by J.W.A. Young. He mentioned Hilbert, if only to protest his doctrine that mathematics was the manipulation of meaningless marks. "I am not a marksian," he said, "but only a symbol-minded logician." He talked of the elements of *Principia,* and of his own notions. He was emphatic on propositions and their neutrality in respect of assertion. He had a theory of formal systems about which he was proprietary and conspiratorial. It suffered, I thought, from confusion of sign and object.

American philosophers associated Harvard with logic because of Whitehead, Sheffer, Lewis, and the shades of Peirce and Royce. Really the action was in Europe. In that year Gödel's first papers were just appearing, but there were already other notables to reckon with: Ackermann, Bernays, Löwenheim, Skolem, Tarski, von Neumann, and, by a narrow chronological margin, Herbrand. Their work had perhaps not reached any American classrooms, nor had even the Wiener-Kuratowski definition of the ordered pair. E.L. Post worked alone in New York, little heeded. America's logical awakening was still to come, through Alonzo Church in the Princeton mathematics department. I was unaware of these lacks. The logic that was offered ran thinner than I had hoped, but I assumed that *Principia* was still substantially the last word.

Whitehead lectured on Science and the Modern World and on Cosmologies Ancient and Modern. I responded little to these courses, even after accustoming myself to his accent. What he said had little evident bearing on problems that

I recognized. His hours were mercifully short, but his speech exasperatingly slow. My notes were crowded with doodles. For a term paper I took refuge in his relatively mathematical material on "extensive abstraction." But I retained a vivid sense of being in the presence of the great.

The Whiteheads were at home Sunday evenings, in their flat on Memorial Drive, to graduate students in philosophy and their wives. His salon was one room and hers another, and at mid-evening he and she would change places. The talk, largely monologous, ran to history, education, literature, and politics. Their political talk punctiliously avoided American politics and was mostly reminiscent, peopled with personages. The young were awed and fearful of gaffes. Spontaneity would rekindle as we emerged into the little streets behind the building.

The preliminary exams were the great hurdle. They ran to twelve hours and were failed by about two students out of five. I passed them in the spring of 1931, as well as the language exams. I could consequently have been excused from final exams in courses, but I took them so as to qualify for the A.M. This again was an economic precaution, since I might still miss the Ph.D. in my second year. That summer I began my dissertation, "The Logic of Sequences: A Generalization of *Principia Mathematica*".

4. The Year of the Dissertation

In retrospect the touted generalization is unimpressive; it was merely the simultaneous coverage of classes and relations of all degrees, as contrasted with the separate handling of classes and dyadic relations in *Principia*. What is rather to be commended in the dissertation is its cleaning up of *Principia*. It resolved confusions of use and mention of expressions. Propositional functions, in the sense of attributes, ceased to be confused either with open sentences or with names of attributes. One effect of sorting these matters out was the recognition of *predication* as a primitive operation of the system. Another effect was justification of Ramsey's proposal that ramified types and the axiom of reducibility be skipped. I rewrote this bit later for *Mind, 1936*.

Full control of the distinction between use and mention seems little to ask. A little clarity of mind suffices for the purpose, one would suppose, without special training. In my case it did suffice. I had not read Frege and I knew nothing of Carnap or the Poles; and certainly the authors and teachers that I had been reading and hearing had no tendency to bring out the distinction. In the thirties at Harvard, notably in arguments with Lewis and Huntington over modal logic, I had ever and again to recur to the theme of use versus mention. A little clarity of mind proves not always to suffice for the purpose after all.

My system was extensional. Predication was membership. Partly for continuity with *Principia* and partly, I fear, to keep peace with my professors, I retained *assertion* as a primitive operation. I admitted the ordered-pair operation as a further primitive, because I did not know about Wiener or Kuratowski. I assumed also an ugly binary operation called superplexion, and in effect I assumed abstraction. The truth functions and quantifiers emerged by definition.

It was while I was writing the dissertation (1931) that Tarski and Gödel, unbeknownst to me and to each other, published the now classical thumbnail formulation of these matters. Aware not perhaps of Wiener but of Kuratowski, they knew how to derive the ordered pair; moreover they appreciated that class abstraction was reducible to quantification, e.g., via Russell's contextual definition of description. They could make do with just truth functions, quantification, and class membership, and they could settle for a single hierarchy of types based on single individuals. They were past masters *de facto;* I a master *de gradu* and a doctor *in spe.*

I saw fit to prove that my eight inelegant axioms, my rules of inference, and my sixty definitions sufficed for deriving *Principia.* The dissertation ran to 290 pages, with appalling masses of symbols. I got my typewriter altered for the purpose. Long sleepless and with a week's beard, I took the dissertation to Whitehead's flat at 9 p.m. on 1 April 1932, with three hours to spare.

During the preceding months I had gone to him fortnightly to report my progress and problems, for he was my dissertation advisor. He would listen until I reached a point suited to a philosophical tangent on his part. The sessions impressed me but yielded little logic. I did carry away two technical terms. I wanted one for the length of a sequence x (why not 'length'?) and one for the class $\ni x$ of all classes to which x belongs. He suggested the *cardinal* of x and, aptly, the *essence* of x. I recall also his reminiscence of *38 of *Principia*—a section that had tickled him because of how it simplified later sections.

In October 1931 Russell came and gave a lecture, introduced by Whitehead—a dazzling juxtaposition. Afterward Whitehead introduced me to Russell, and I told him of my thoughts on polyadic relations.

Perhaps my fortnightly sessions with Whitehead were what moved him to offer a logic seminar that spring. In it he developed the material that appeared later in *Mind* under the title "Classes, Propositions, Number, Validation." I thought it poor.

A few weeks before my 24th birthday I received my Ph.D. A two-year Ph.D. is inadvisable, apart from strong financial motives such as I felt in those depression years. It precludes the unclocked reflection that best suits scholarship. But my reprieve was in store: four untrammeled years of postdoctoral fellowships. The first of these, 1932–33, was Harvard's Sheldon Traveling Fellowship. Two friends advised me to start the year at Vienna. One was Herbert Feigl, who had come from Vienna to Harvard on a postdoctoral fellowship. The other was my fellow graduate student John Cooley, who had discovered Carnap's *Logischer Aufbau der Welt.*

I was desperately eager to start my year abroad, but I had reason to delay into August. The department shared my exalted evaluation of my dissertation and undertook to subsidize its publication by Harvard Press. I had ideas for its improvement, which the April deadline had forced aside. I worked from April into August revising it, so that C.I. Lewis might start it through the press during my absence.

In Jørgensen's *Treatise of Formal Logic,* the previous winter, I had found a fallacy in the derivation of truth-function logic from Nicod's single axiom. I had sent an article to *Mind,* my first, setting matters right. It appeared, to my delight, just as we were leaving for Europe in August 1932. In Warsaw later I learned that in 1931 Łukasiewicz had published in Polish on the same matter, correcting the error and also improving the axiom. Łukasiewicz insisted on imputing the fallacy to Nicod's own paper of 1916, but I held that Nicod's fault lay only in exposition.

5. *Wiedergeburt in Mitteleuropa*

My Wanderlust did not abate. During the year abroad Naomi and I made our frugal way to 27 countries. We slept in hammocks on the Baltic and on a load of goat skins in the Aegean. We touched Asia and Africa. Even so, logic and philosophy retained the upper hand. We spent five months in Vienna. I attended Schlick's lectures; also some meetings of the Vienna Circle. At one of these I summarized the revised version of my dissertation, and at another Waismann reported on Bridgman's *Logic of Modern Physics.* I came to know Ayer; newly graduated from Oxford, he was setting out on the Viennese path that was to lead to *Language, Truth and Logic.* I met Gödel, Menger, and Hahn, and at a party in Schlick's flat I met Reichenbach. I gained a firm command of German, and that was a boon. It prepared me for what proved to be the intellectually most rewarding months I have known, namely, my six weeks in Prague and six in Warsaw.

Carnap had just moved to Prague, and I followed him there. I regularly attended his lectures and I read his *Logische Syntax der Sprache* as it issued from Ina Carnap's typewriter. Sometimes Naomi and I took the trolley to the west edge of Prague and spent the day at the Carnaps' house while he and I discussed his exciting doctrines. As I since wrote in a memoir of Carnap,

> It was my first experience of sustained intellectual engagement with anyone of an older generation, let alone a great man. It was my first really considerable experience of being intellectually fired by a living teacher rather than by a dead book. I had not been aware of the lack. One goes on listening respectfully to one's elders, learning things, hearing things with varying degrees of approval, and expecting as

a matter of course to have to fall back on one's own resources and those of the library for the main motive power. One recognizes that his professor has his own work to do, and that the problems and approaches that appeal to him need not coincide in any very fruitful way with those that are exercising oneself. I could see myself in the professor's place, and I sought nothing different. I suppose most of us go through life with no brighter view than this of the groves of Academe. So might I have done, but for the graciousness of Carnap.[1]

While in Prague I sampled the lectures of Oskar Kraus on metaphysics and Philipp Frank on hydrodynamics. Frank told me that I was the first American he had met. He became one himself six years later.

In Prague I reaped philosophy, in Warsaw logic. My hosts and tireless interlocutors in Warsaw were Tarski, Leśniewski, and Łukasiewicz. I went regularly to Tarski's vigorous, high-level seminar, in which for my sake he banned Polish in favor of German and French. I went to Leśniewski's lectures, which consisted in filling the blackboard with formulas; no language problem there. I went to Łukasiewicz's lectures, which were two hours long with a recess. Formulas helped; for the rest, he would brief me in German before and after the lecture and during the recess.

So much time went into discussion with these three generous men, and into studying the articles in French and German with which they plied me, that I had no time to study Polish. With Leśniewski I would argue far into the night, trying to convince him that his quantification over all syntactic categories carried ontological commitment.

I met Kotarbiński, Ajdukiewicz, Kuratowski, Sobociński, Jaśkowski. Sobociński, thin and frail, spoke only Polish and Russian. Leśniewski interpreted him for me into German. Today Sobociński is a robust American professor. Jaśkowski chose to write his pioneer paper on natural deduction in English, and I helped him.

In Vienna the preceding December I had been desperately disappointed by a letter from Lewis saying that he had decided not to start my book through the press, because of the complex typographical decisions involved; that I would be happier deciding everything myself next year. I bitterly resolved to put the book out of my mind meanwhile. But in Warsaw I had come abreast of contemporary logic, and thoughts of the book came rushing in. On the train out of Warsaw in June 1933, bound for the Baltic states, I happily began outlining drastic revisions. I could look ahead to boundless freedom for the project, for I had received in Prague a cable from Whitehead saying that I had been elected to the Society of Fellows that they were just establishing at Harvard.

---

1. *Boston Studies in the Philosophy of Science* 8 (1971): xxiv, *by permission.*

6. Society of Fellows

It means three years of good stipend and no duties. We began as six; two were
B.F. Skinner and Garrett Birkhoff. The distinguished governing board, called
Senior Fellows, outnumbered us: Whitehead, A. Lawrence Lowell, John Liv-
ingston Lowes, L. J. Henderson, Charles P. Curtis, Jr., and the university
president and dean. We would all meet Mondays in the Society's rooms for
good dinners and conversation. After two years the number of Junior Fellows
reached its quota of twenty-odd. The Society has maintained its ways these
forty years and more. As Junior Fellow, as ex-fellow, and since 1948 as Senior
Fellow, I have gained pleasure and casual instruction from a thousand Mondays.

My book went to press in March 1934: *A System of Logistic*. Propositional
functions had become unequivocally classes. Superplexion gave way to mere
inclusion. Class abstraction became forthrightly primitive; it is definable
through quantification, but I was getting quantification conversely from inclusion and abstraction. My primitives were just these two, nearly enough, and
the old ordered-pair operation. I made the latter do double duty as predication,
or membership, by construing a proposition as a pair comprising the predicated
class and the thing or sequence of which it is predicated. The axioms were
improved, and there was a compact proof notation adapted from Łukasiewicz.
Truth-function logic was derived from class theory with help of vacuous abstraction. I reported Wiener and Kuratowski on ordered pairs, but made ex-
cuses for not using their idea: my new version of predication saved a primitive
anyway, and I liked thus reifying propositions in extensional terms. I was
aware that propositions *could* be dispensed with, as witness my "Ontological
Remarks on the Propositional Calculus," 1934; there already, terminology
aside, was the doctrine of schematic letters. But I had not quite outgrown my
dissertation.

Discussions with Huntington elicited my other little 1934 paper, "A
Method of Generating Part of Arithmetic without Use of Intuitive Logic". I
wanted to exhibit an extra-logical calculus with private rules of inference. I
like its simplicity and its kinship to the recursiveness algorithm that was about
to emerge.

Already in 1932 and 1933 in Vienna and Prague, while my book was in
abeyance, I had been pondering broader objectives. I felt a nominalist's discon-
tent with classes. Also I was discontented with Russell's theory of types where
it imputed meaninglessness; I should have liked to base the theory of types
upon contextual definitions of abstraction and membership in such a way as to
be able to account the purportedly meaningless formulas meaningless in the
straightforward sense of not getting defined. I adopted as primitive a substitution operator '$x \in y \ni$', expressing substitution of 'x' for 'y' in the appended

sentence; thus the incomplete symbol 'y ∍ (. . .y. . .)' behaved as a name of what I have since called a virtual class. I then sought in vain a definition of the parallel idiom in the next higher type: a definition of '[y∍ (. . .y. . .)] ∈ α ∍ (. . .α. . .)' with 'α' acting as a bound class variable.

I returned to that problem on finishing my book in 1934. "A Theory of Classes Presupposing No Canons of Type", 1936, presented a language with two letters and five words. One word was a predicate tantamount to 'predicate'. One was a semantic functor of subsumption, applicable to predicates. Others yielded names of the letters, and concatenation. A truth predicate was defined on this basis. Quantification over nominalistically simulated classes of all types was defined, along with membership. For brevity I phrased the paper in terms unreservedly of classes, but my *arrière pensée* was nominalistic.

The paper stopped short of axiomatization. I worked on that. Nominalism was threatened by the need of inscriptions without limit of length. Worse, my rationalization of the theory of class types came to naught, since I needed to assume a theory of semantic types to restrain the semantic functor that underlay my truth predicate. Just then Tarski's "Wahrheitsbegriff"* appeared and put an end to the fumbling.

My ill-starred project brought fringe benefits. It involved me in what I later called protosyntax, the elementary theory of concatenation. Embedded in "A Theory of Classes Presupposing No Canons of Type" there is a protosyntactical definition of substitution, which in another 1936 paper I extricated and clarified in terms of sequences. The essential trick is the framed ingredient: a means of coding sequences of sequences in simple sequences, and so of reducing inductive definitions to direct definitions without Frege's recourse to classes or Gödel's to number theory. It recurs in my 1937 paper "On Derivability", and in the last chapter of *Mathematical Logic,* and in my 1946 paper on concatenation.

For me another abiding feature of "A Theory of Classes Presupposing No Canons of Type" was its innocence of variables. They entered only through contextual definition. To my mind such elimination of variables, first achieved by Schönfinkel, was a major step of conceptual analysis. I had tinkered with his combinators in 1933, and late in 1934 I had tried adapting his idea to the elimination of variables from *A System of Logistic.* This meant reinterpreting the combinators. My note on that move appeared in 1936.

The project of thus reworking *A System of Logistic* wavered and dissolved into the inaugural article of the *Journal of Symbolic Logic:* "Toward a Calculus

---

*"Der Wahrheitsbegriff in den formalisierten Sprachen," *Studia Philosophica* 1 (1936): 261–405; separately printed in 1935; first published in Polish in 1933. For an English translation see "The Concept of Truth in Formalized Languages" in his book *Logic, Semantics, Metamathematics* (Oxford: Clarendon Press, 1956)., essays collected and translated by J. H. Woodger—ED.

of Concepts''. It was what I would now describe as a predicate logic using no variables but only schematic predicate letters. Unlike Schönfinkel's scheme with its runaway ontology, this was even weaker than ordinary predicate logic: weaker in not fixing the degrees of predicates (the numbers of places). It thus rather foreshadowed Tarski's cylindrical algebras, but without presupposing, like Tarski's, an underlying logic. However, I presented no proof procedure for it; only the primitive ideas and definitions. In another 1936 paper I showed that the primitives could be simplified by imagining negative degrees.

I resumed this sort of logic decades later, when I was elected to the American Philosophical Society and needed a theme for a lay audience. It was "Variables Explained Away''. This apparatus is exactly intertranslatable with ordinary predicate logic. After yet another decade I improved it and called it predicate-functor logic; this late revival of my interest in it came of a talk with Davidson about Tarski's theory of truth.

I had reviewed six books for various journals by the time the *Journal of Symbolic Logic* began, 1936. My reviewing of books and articles for the *Journal* then became a steady background activity for six years, until I joined the Navy. I reviewed more than anyone else except the prime mover, Church himself. It was burdensome, but it kept me posted. Since I stopped reviewing, the mounting activity in logic has left me far behind.

As Junior Fellow I worked mostly in logic. But I did other philosophy too. I had been expounding Carnap to Henderson and Curtis in the Society of Fellows. This led to Carnap's honorary degree at the tercentenary, and meanwhile it led to my being asked to give three lectures on him. I saw this occasion approach with growing anxiety. I had lectured before, in German, to the Vienna Circle. I had written that out and read it, and had been nervous. But this home occasion in 1934 was far worse, because I no longer felt shielded by the allowances that are extended to a foreigner. I felt it would no longer be fitting to read my lectures; yet I had to write them out, or I should be speechless; and so I tried memorizing, pacing, memorizing. The typescript went with me to the podium even so, a vital precaution. On the podium my panic promptly subsided, for a lifetime.

The three lectures were uncritical. "Truth by Convention'', which I wrote shortly afterward for the Whitehead *Festschrift*, drew upon the lectures but showed already the beginnings of my misgivings over analyticity: the seeds of my apostasy.

7. Faculty Instructor

During my Junior Fellowship, I was offered teaching positions at Oberlin, Michigan, and Princeton. All would have meant curtailing my fellowship. When at length I was told I could count on something however modest at

Harvard after my fellowship, I dismissed the alternatives—out of preference not for Harvard but for the rest of my fellowship. Thus it was that in 1936 I came into a three-year Faculty Instructorship, not to be confused with the lowlier annual instructorship. My post was in philosophy, but two of my four semester courses that year were graduate courses in mathematical logic in the mathematics department.

It was with a view to these courses that I tried to settle on a sanest comprehensive system of logic—or, as I would now say, logic and set theory. One venture was "Set-Theoretic Foundations for Logic", 1936; a second was "New Foundations for Mathematical Logic". In these at last I settled down to the neo-classical primitive notation that Tarski and Gödel had settled on in 1931: just truth functions, quantification, and membership. But I was intent on avoiding the theory of types.

A problem then arises of distinguishing the null class from the individuals. One way is to add a primitive name for it. Another costly way is to use a distinctive style of variables for classes. A third way, Fraenkel's, is to repudiate individuals. A fourth, mine in "Set-Theoretic Foundations", is to let the null class get lost among the individuals. A fifth, mine in "New Foundations" and after, is to accord members to individuals by making them unit classes of themselves.

In "Set-Theoretic Foundations" I took Zermelo's set theory as point of departure. But instead of assuming with Zermelo the class of all those *members* of any given class that satisfy a given condition, I assumed the class of all those *subclasses* that satisfy a given condition. This already suffices, all by itself, for all of Zermelo's existence axioms, except those of infinity and choice. Still, the null class is lost among the individuals. By way of making up this loss I proved that the neo-classical or Tarski-Gödel theory of types, complete with null classes of all types, could be modeled in my system and derived from my axioms. Practically my system was not ideal, since it left us either with the theory of types or without the null class.

"New Foundations" was an invited address at a meeting of the Mathematical Association of America, in Chapel Hill late in 1936. Here I tried dispensing with the substance of the theory of types while preserving its restraining effect upon the axiom schema of class existence, where paradoxes come from. This effect is preserved by requiring only that the membership condition be "stratified," i.e., that its bound variables not be linked by epsilons in patterns that would have violated the theory of types. Stratification ceases to be a condition of meaningfulness. Moreover the distasteful type ontology is banished, with its reduplication of numbers and null classes and universe classes from type to type. The curious relation of this system to Cantor's theorem on the cardinality of power classes elicited a paper a few months later.

In the leisure of the following summer I brought my enhanced standards to bear retrospectively on *A System of Logistic,* thinking what might have been. I saw that by accepting Kuratowski's definition of the ordered pair I could make do with just two of the three primitive ideas of that book: inclusion and abstraction. I published the resulting system that same year, 1937. I liked its elegance, but I disliked its retention of the theory of types. Since abstraction was primitive, I could bar paradoxical abstracts only by some irreducible canon of meaninglessness like the theory of types; the freedom enjoyed in my two preceding papers was not here available. But I did presently find ("On the Theory of Types") that I could relax the theory of types even here, limiting the stigma of meaninglessness to unstratified abstracts. I could drop stratification requirements elsewhere, and the type ontology. The resulting system was close kin to "New Foundations", and had the added charm of economy of primitives: inclusion and abstraction. Still I continued to prefer the three primitives of "New Foundations", the Tarski-Gödel triad, because of the neat program of treating first the truth functions, then quantification, and then classes.

My courses in mathematical logic began with few students. In the second term of my first year there were two in the class: an undergraduate in mathematics, George Brown, who got A+, and a graduate student in philosophy, who failed. In contrast my elementary logic course in the philosophy department ran to about sixty. No text was available along modern lines. I coped with Eaton, with Chapman and Henle, with Cohen and Nagel, even with old Jevons. I tried to clarify and simplify the techniques of quantification theory so that they could reasonably be acquired in full by the general student. By the third year my assistant John Cooley had produced for us a mimeographed text, the forerunner of his *Primer of Formal Logic.* I taught also a philosophy course along Carnap's lines, and a logic seminar, and did my quota of tutoring.

Midway in 1938 there dawned a semester's glorious leave for writing. We wanted to spend it in a cheap and picturesque place with a mild climate and a foreign language, preferably Romance. It should be more hygienic than Mexico and Haiti, for our Elizabeth and Norma were babies. We sublet our Cambridge flat to Morris Raphael Cohen and sailed to Ponta Delgada, where we stayed from September through January 1939. I nearly finished writing *Mathematical Logic* and learning Portuguese.

Back on the job during the spring of 1939, I was asked by my friend Frederick Fassett at M.I.T. to write a popular article on logic for his *Technology Review.* I wrote one, and his cartoonist transformed it into a delight. Two years later I wrote a brief bit for him on paradoxes, anticipating an observation of James Thomson's.

8. *Still Faculty Instructor*

I was to have been considered for assistant professor for 1939, after my three years as faculty instructor. But the rules were changed: the rank of assistant professor was abolished, and the faculty instructorship was redefined as quinquennial. I had published a book and nineteen articles, was vice president of the Association for Symbolic Logic, and had been seven years a doctor; so I resented my lowly rank and vainly wished for offers.

Korzybski's *Science and Sanity* had been gaining an uncritical following among our students. Naturally I could rate it low on the strength of small samples; and naturally the enthusiasts could protest the smallness of my samples. Partly because of this challenge and partly out of restlessness and curiosity, I accepted Korzybski's invitation to spend a week of August 1939 in his intensive seminar as guest of his Institute just off the Chicago campus. He addressed his motley audience seven hours a day, swaying them visibly. I argued with his bright young disciple S.I. ('The Heathen') Hayakawa, who defended the canon with creative imagination beyond its deserts. He subsequently wrote *Language in Action,* behaved courageously as president of the University of San Francisco, and became a senator.

In the following month Harvard was the scene of a Conference for the Unity of Science. Basically this was the Vienna Circle, with accretions, in international exile. Woodger, Ernest Nagel, Charles Morris, and I pressed Tarski to accept an invitation, and funds were found to bring him. We hoped that once here he might find a better post than what he had in somewhat anti-Semitic Warsaw. Reluctantly he came, and his life was saved; for the Germans then invaded Poland. Their massacre of the Jews included Tarski's parents.

The papers of the conference were preprinted from an intended volume of the *Journal of Unified Science,* successor to *Erkenntnis,* that was subsequently stopped at press by the German invasion of Holland. Mine was "A Logistical Approach to the Ontological Problem". A better expression of the same sentiments appeared presently under the title "Designation and Existence".

Tarski spent the year at Harvard on a meager makeshift appointment. Carnap, who had moved from Prague to Chicago, was at Harvard for the year as visiting professor. Russell came for the second half of 1940 as William James Lecturer. Halcyon days. Carnap, Tarski, and I met for discussion from time to time, together perhaps with I.A. Richards, Nelson Goodman, or John Cooley. By way of providing structure for our discussions, Carnap proposed reading the manuscript of his *Introduction to Semantics* for criticism. Midway in the first page, Tarski and I took issue with Carnap on analyticity. The controversy continued through subsequent sessions, without resolution and without progress in the reading of Carnap's manuscript.

Because of its negativity, my repudiation of analyticity was nothing I felt impelled to write about. Still, the issue would come up. Morton White became interested and launched a triangular correspondence with Goodman and me. By the end of a decade the issue was widely aired, and I was asked to address the American Philosophical Association on it. Thus came "Two Dogmas of Empiricism", 1951, and a spate of controversial literature in its train.

Nelson Goodman and I were meeting for discussion at intervals in 1939 and after. Much of it focussed on Carnap's *Aufbau* and on Goodman's related project, which was to issue in his *The Structure of Appearance*. A spin-off was our somewhat playful "Elimination of Extra-Logical Postulates". Decades later I tightened and modernized our result, in the sardonically entitled paper "Implicit Definition Sustained". In those terms the result is that any finite set of true axioms can be rendered arithmetically true by defining the predicates. Definitions to this purpose are effectively discoverable and they preserve coextensiveness with the originally intended interpretations. We felt that our theorem cast further doubt on analyticity.

In the summer of 1939 I talked with W. W. Norton about *Mathematical Logic,* which I hoped soon to finish. For wide circulation I wanted to keep the price under four dollars. He said I could do so by waiving royalties on the first thousand and accepting, instead, a higher rate on succeeding thousands. I submitted the manuscript in April 1940 and settled down with his printer to a painstaking collaboration on styles and spacing of symbols. The book came out at four dollars after all, because it had grown. Still, I had waived royalties on the first thousand. Furthermore my collaboration with the printer got all charged to author's corrections, taking the royalties on the second thousand. Then the type was distributed; no second printing. I made $80.64.

In *Mathematical Logic* I was emphatic on use versus mention and punctilious about ontology. I presented the logic of truth functions and predicates metalogically, lest there be any thought that the sentence letters and predicate letters took propositions and attributes as values. I did not trust my readers to take those letters as schematic, though I had ventured the schematic line already in "Set-Theoretic Foundations" and earlier. I was fussy, furthermore, about having only closed sentences as axioms and theorems. There were infinitely many axioms and a single weak rule of inference: *modus ponens* for closed sentences.

Today the separation of use and mention is better heeded, and I think I helped. My crusade against confusing implication with the conditional has succeeded to some degree. I see surface evidence of the book's impact in the recurrence of my neologisms: 'biconditional', 'singular', 'metatheorem', 'quasi-quotation', 'alphabetic variant', and indeed 'use versus mention'.

In the set-theoretic chapters I had meant at first merely to follow "New Foundations", but I disliked the failure of mathematical induction for unstratified conditions; so, taking a leaf from von Neumann, I threw in ultimate classes (as I now call them). His ultimate classes had been predicative only; that is, their membership conditions did not quantify over ultimate classes. Mine were not thus restricted; my line was the line taken later by Kelley and Morse.

I was influenced still by *Principia*. My hierarchy of definitions, like that in *A System of Logistic,* was a conscious simplification of that in *Principia*. In a final chapter I developed protosyntax and proved Gödel's incompleteness theorem by showing protosyntactical truth protosyntactically indefinable. This development was novel in by-passing number theory and in dispensing with singular terms other than variables. Substitution of numerals, so central to Gödel's proof, was thus doubly precluded, and gave way to a method of what I called identity matrices.

The need to acknowledge sources, in *Mathematical Logic,* issued in historical paragraphs in small print throughout the text. My search for sources led me to examine Frege, whose slim *Begriffsschrift* I soon recognized as the real beginning of mathematical logic. Not that I saw it. Frege's later books were at Harvard, but there was no discoverable copy of the *Begriffsschrift* in America. I recovered its content from old published accounts by P.E.B. Jourdain.

My celebration of Frege in *Mathematical Logic* and in the classroom must have helped to bring people to see Frege as the father of modern logic. Russell had introduced him to us long ago, but we remained unaware of how many of the good things of logic had been done first by Frege. I think Church first learned from my small print that his operation of functional abstraction was in Frege. At any rate he returned the favor three years later, pointing out that my notion of referential position and even my example of the Morning Star and the Evening Star were in Frege. I had missed Frege's "Ueber Sinn und Bedeutung", and may have got his example through Russell.

When I had seen *Mathematical Logic* through the press I turned my attention to my immediate teaching need: an *Elementary Logic.* The manuscript reached Ginn in January 1941. Times have since changed; in 1973, complimentary copies of fifty-five modern introductory American logic texts adorned the cornice of my office.

From *Elementary Logic* I turned to the essay that I had consented to write for the volume on Whitehead in this Library of Living Philosophers. The invitation came in February 1941, and I submitted my essay July 5. It was inevitably a study of both Whitehead's and Russell's contributions, but these proved to be fairly separable in the light of the separately signed articles that preceded *Principia.* Already in writing *Mathematical Logic* I had been probing the history of modern logic; in this essay I profited by those inquiries and carried them farther.

9. Tenure

The summer of 1941 was bright with memorabilia. I toured Mexico with two students, Donald Davidson for one. My third book came out, and my twenty-third article. I became associate professor, with tenure.

The fall was memorable too in its way. Barkley Rosser phoned me that he had derived Burali-Forti's paradox of ordinals, affectionately known to Rosser as B40, from my *Mathematical Logic*. I was surprised, having taken precautions against the analogous paradox of cardinals. It was less analogous than I thought.

The set theory of *Mathematical Logic* had been fashioned from "New Foundations" in two moves: I had reconstrued the stratification condition for class existence as a condition for sethood, and I had provided unrestrictedly for classes of sets. To cut off Rosser's proof of B40, now, I might either restrict this unrestricted provision for classes, which was so luxuriously simple and productive, or I might cut back on the sets. Better the latter. So in "Element and Number" I dropped the stratification condition and cut back to finite sets. I switched from Frege's version of natural numbers to von Neumann's in order to exploit the finite sets. I went on to develop von Neumann's infinite ordinals, noting that their existence would depend on adding further sethood axioms as desired.

Also I indicated less drastic restitution: drop the stratification condition of sethood but keep as axioms seven of its proved consequences. A correction slip bearing these instructions was inserted in the unsold copies of the book. After five years had passed and Norton had sold his two thousand, the Harvard Press reprinted the book; and they printed the correction in an available space near the scene of the disaster. They did their reprint edition by offset, and I rejoiced in making numerous incidental emendations by scissors and paste on the reproduction proofs. Paul Weiss, for instance, had pointed out to me that Paul was not one of the twelve disciples; so I substituted a 'John' snipped from elsewere in the proofs.

But it was three years later still when my student Hao Wang showed what should have been done about B40. He saw that one of the two moves noted above, by which I had fashioned the set theory of *Mathematical Logic* from "New Foundations", was not what it seemed. I had not really taken just the classes of "New Foundations" as the sets of *Mathematical Logic;* I had taken more. The stratified membership conditions in the two systems differed in force, because in *Mathematical Logic* the bound variables ranged over both sets and ultimate classes. If the sets of *Mathematical Logic* were really not to exceed the classes of "New Foundations", the bound variables in their stratified membership conditions should be limited to sets for their values. Such, then, was Wang's neat repair of *Mathematical Logic,* occasioning the revised edition, 1951. Other improvements then gained access too, notably a welcome reduction by my old student George Berry of my rules for quantification theory.

Wang's repair is curious historically. In moving from "New Foundations" to *Mathematical Logic* I had followed von Neumann in adding ultimate classes. In the membership conditions of his classes, von Neumann had limited the values of the bound variables to sets; I did not. Yet the cure has not consisted in reverting to von Neumann's plan of thus limiting the bound variables of the membership conditions of classes; it consisted in thus limiting the bound variables of the membership conditions of sets.

This pursuit of the vicissitudes of *Mathematical Logic* has brought us nine years past my first year of tenure, to which let us return. It was a desperate year. Germans massacred Jews, Germans swarmed over France, Japanese bombed Hawaii. Logic seemed off the point, and I put in for a commission in the Navy. Meanwhile I was invited by the office of the Coordinator of Inter-American Affairs to go to São Paulo as visiting professor. I flew to Brazil in May, 1942, leaving my assistant George Berry to examine my students in mathematical logic. I flew back in September and was sworn into the Navy.

The plane to Rio via the Antilles took four days and made fourteen stops. We flew low, always by daylight, and familiar maps came alive. I came home via the Andes on a similar schedule. Surely these were travel's greatest thrills. I foresaw in subsequent travel only anticlimax.

In preceding months I had worked on my Portuguese, for I was resolved to lecture in that language. I wrote out my first lectures for want of linguistic confidence. Then I continued to write them out for another reason: it struck me that I could have more impact on Brazilian philosophers and mathematicians by leaving them my lectures in book form. The lectures were spoken in my uncorrected Portuguese, but Vicente Ferreira da Silva helped me correct them before publishing. When I left Brazil, *O Sentido da Nova Lógica* was in the publisher's hands.

I produced it so quickly because it had been pent up. Ideas for a new logic book had been occurring to me for a year, and I had kept suppressing them because of the German conquests. I wondered whether there would be a place for further logic in our time. So, when I was called upon to prepare a course for São Paulo, the suppressed ideas came welling forth and flowing into place.

Having started with symbols for negation and conjunction, why go on to define 'v' and '⊃'? Not for brevity; the gain there is negligible. Not for heuristic links with ordinary language; they are better forged by defining the actual words 'or' and 'if' in terms of negation and conjunction. Similar remarks apply to universal and existential quantifiers: one kind is enough. This was my line in *Elementary Logic* the year before, and I held to it in *O Sentido*. There results a saving in algorithm, there being fewer symbols to interrelate.

My proof procedure for predicate logic in *O Sentido* differed from my previous books and was more convenient in deducing consequences from premisses. I added a transparent decision procedure for monadic predicate logic, which proves to have been anticipated by Herbrand. I pressed on through identity and singular descriptions and into set theory, which I handled as in "Element and Number."

I added a section on what I called the virtual theory of classes and relations, in which I showed the scope and limits of a simulated set theory built upon predicate logic by contextual definition. R. M. Martin was writing concurrently in this vein, and Gödel's 1940 notion of 'notion' is the same. It was foreshadowed, we saw, in my 1936 paper ''A Theory of Classes Presupposing No Canons of Type''. Decades later it assumed a central role in my *Set Theory and Its Logic*. Today, however, I prefer to drop the pretense of classes and read the virtual class abstracts as ontologically innocent predicates, in the form of 'such that' clauses.

Parts of *O Sentido* were more philosophical than my previous books. In ''Whitehead and the Rise of Modern Logic'' I had touched on the failure of substitutivity of identity in modal contexts, but in this book I discussed it at length, distinguishing purely referential occurrences from others. I was unaware of my anticipation by Frege; on the other hand I went beyond Frege in challenging quantification into opaque contexts. Eager to put these bits of *O Sentido* before English readers, I dictated a translation of my Portuguese to an English stenographer in São Paulo under the title ''Notes on Existence and Necessity''. It is a theme that I pressed further in later years.

I sent also a lesser offshoot of *O Sentido:* ''On Existence Conditions for Elements and Classes.'' It points out that my impredicative extension of the von Neumann existence schema for classes—the line taken later by Kelley and Morse—is logically equivalent to Zermelo's *Aussonderung* plus existence of the union of all classes.

Noting my admiration for Frege, Ferreira da Silva gave me a little halftone portrait of the great man. He had torn it from the frontispiece of a book. The suitcase containing it got lost in transit, and I especially regretted the loss of the picture. Behmann's little *Mathematik und Logik* bore on its cover an inchsquare reproduction of a line drawing of Frege, so I copied it large in pen and ink to redeem my loss. I was so pleased with the result that I tried drawing faces from life—surreptitiously for the most part, at jazz concerts and philosophy meetings. The uneven results encouraged me just often enough so that I continued the practice intermittently down the years.

10. War and Peace

I began naval duty as lieutenant in October 1942 and ended it as lieutenant commander late in 1945. I worked in Washington at radio intelligence in the Atlantic anti-submarine campaign. My group worked closely with the cryptanalysts, who would pass the deciphered intercepts to us for translation and analysis. We would pass the digested information to the high command and back to the cryptanalysts. It was a bright and congenial group of scholars and mathematicians.

I had little leisure for the arts of peace. I devoted some of it to trying to make sense of sameness of meaning in terms of linguistic behavior. Eventually

I realized that after a most inconclusive sketch of an approach to the hard problem, I had taken refuge in busywork. I had got to tinkering with techniques for handling the overlapping of synonymy classes caused by homonyms. So I stopped. Years later I reported this to Jerrold Katz in a letter criticizing something similar of his.

Late in the war I wrote a paper "On the Logic of Quantification". It begins by stressing the difference between schematic letters and variables. Schemata had been the medium already of my *Elementary Logic,* 1941, under the name of "frames"; but here I called them schemata. In *Elementary Logic* also I had introduced under the name of "stencils" a notation using circled numerals to facilitate substitution for predicate letters; but here I called them predicates. The style for *Methods of Logic* was by then established. Lately I dropped that notation of circled numerals in favor of the notation of class abstraction, ontologically deactivated. Such, now, are my predicates.

The core of "On the Logic of Quantification" was a monadic decision procedure, less transparent but more efficient than the Herbrand method in *O Sentido;* more like Behmann's. Then I systematized polyadic schemata as follows. Those obtainable by substitution in valid monadic schemata I called *monadically valid,* noting that the decision procedure for validity of monadic schemata afforded a decision procedure for monadic validity generally. I showed that the rest of the valid schemata could be inferred from the monadically valid ones by universal generalization and *modus ponens.* I recount this because I can now prove more. Let us now count as monadically valid rather the universal closures of the schemata obtainable by substitution in valid monadic schemata. Monadic validity in this sense is still decidable; and from these closed schemata we can derive all valid closed schemata by *modus ponens* alone. This follows from *Mathematical Logic* as improved by Berry, since the axioms of quantification there are all monadically valid and *modus ponens* is the only rule.

My note "On Ordered Pairs", of the same season, was elicited by Goodman's interest in diminishing the difference in type between a pair and its components. I devised a definition that equalized these types, but required numbers of next lower type. This equalization was relevant not only to the theory of types but to "New Foundations", because of the appeal to stratification in that system; and in that system the requirement regarding numbers was no limitation. Hence Rosser used the definition in his *Logic for Mathematicians,* which is based on "New Foundations". I noted later that my definition simplifies the theory of relations by making every class a relation as well as vice versa.

I resumed my Harvard duties in February 1946. A notable company of graduate students in logic began to gather: John Myhill from England, Henry Hiż from Poland, William Craig from Germany via California,

Hugues Leblanc from Canada. Hao Wang joined the group in the fall; we had
corresponded when I was in the Navy and he was still in China. I had also my
tutorial responsibilities; one was a sophomore of Zionist proclivities named
Burton Dreben, interested in philosophy and politics. Presently he was moving
with the graduate students, chopping logic with the best of them.

My resumed teaching from *Mathematical Logic* rekindled my interest in
protosyntax and led to "Concatenation as a Basis for Arithmetic". The concatenate of two numbers *m* and *n* is the number whose Arabic numeral is the
concatenate of those of *m* and *n*. In *Mathematical Logic* I had defined this in
terms of elementary number theory; I now showed, conversely, that concatenation suffices as sole operation of elementary number theory. Elementary number theory *is* protosyntax.

I was also teaching and pondering the philosophy of logic and language.
Misgivings over quantified modal logic that I had expressed in Brazil in 1942,
and in "Notes on Existence and Necessity", gained in relevance as the challenge was taken up. Ruth Barcan (Marcus)'s pioneer venture in quantified
modal logic appeared in the *Journal of Symbolic Logic* in 1946. Presently so
did Carnap's, and an abstract by Church. I was arguing by mail with Carnap,
whose *Meaning and Necessity* I had in manuscript, and he included one of my
letters in that book. "The Problem of Interpreting Modal Logic" was a further
expression of my misgivings.

My other philosophical theme was ontological commitment, dating from
"Designation and Existence" and indeed from my arguments with Leśniewski.
On this theme there appeared in 1947–48 my Yale lecture "On What There
Is" and my paper "On Universals". The latter was based on an oral presentation to the Association for Symbolic Logic which had included also a compact formulation of the predicative theory of types. I restored this eventually,
in *From a Logical Point of View*.

Renewed sessions with Goodman led to "Steps Toward a Constructive
Nominalism", an effort to get mathematics into an ontology strictly of physical
objects. We settled for a formalist account of mathematics, but still had the
problem of making do with an inscriptional proof theory in a presumably finite
universe. Our project was good, I think, and well begun. But our paper created
a stubborn misconception that I am an ongoing nominalist. Readers try in the
friendliest ways to reconcile my writings with nominalism. They try to read
nominalism into "On What There Is" and find, or should find, incoherence.

Nominalism was our position in "Steps toward a Constructive Nominalism". It was the statement of our problem. It would be my actual position if I
could make a go of it. But when I quantify irreducibly over classes, as I usually
do, I am not playing the nominalist. Quite the contrary.

An urgent occupation in those years was the preparation of a new text for
my basic logic course. I produced a mimeographed draft in 1946 under the title

A *Short Course in Logic,* and a fuller mimeographed draft in 1948 called *Theory of Deduction.*

We saw reasons a few pages back for minimizing logical notations, as was my way in *Elementary Logic* and *O Sentido.* But there are reasons also to the contrary, if certain algorithms are used. If we are to exploit duality, we need alternation as the dual of conjunction and we need both kinds of quantification. If we are to use alternational or conjunctional normal forms, in which the negation signs are driven inward so as to govern only atoms, then again we need both alternation and conjunction. If we are to prove implications by proving chains of conditionals, then a conditional sign is perspicuous. In my mimeograms of 1946 and 1948, for such reasons, I reverted to the redundant notation of *Mathematical Logic* and other literature.

The algorithm for general predicate logic in both mimeograms was natural deduction. Natural deduction was in the air. I had toyed with it earlier because of Jaśkowski and Gentzen, and had moved toward it in *O Sentido.* Cooley had used it in his *Primer of Formal Logic,* 1942, at the suggestion of Saunders MacLane. Rosser, unbeknownst, had been using it in mimeographed teaching aids of his own.

Since Jaśkowski used only existential quantification, not universal, there was for him no question of symmetry of rules for the two kinds of quantification. Gentzen used both kinds of quantification, and his rules were uncomfortably asymmetrical. Cooley brought more symmetry, and this required increased delicacy in framing the rules lest they conflict. I worked at this problem.

11. Professor

In July 1948 I became a full professor. I became also a Senior Fellow of the Society of Fellows. My first marriage had subsided *pari passu,* roughly, with the war. Late in 1948 I married Marjorie Boynton, formerly a lieutenant in my command. A sabbatical semester opportunely began, and we drove through Mexico and flew around Central America. At Oaxaca we settled down for weeks of intensive work, and at Tuxtla and Taxco. I was writing *Methods of Logic,* the outgrowth of my mimeograms, and Marge was typing it.

Truth tables gave way in *Methods* to quicker ways. Monadic predicate logic proceeded by an accelerated variant of the decision procedure in my 1945 paper. General predicate logic proceeded by my best brand of natural deduction. Then came identity, descriptions, and a modicum of set theory.

From Mexico we continued to California, where I spent the summer of 1949 unaccustomedly well paid as consultant at Rand. In the Navy I had had top-secret clearance, but fresh clearance was required for Rand. It came too late, so I was put onto innocuous projects. One of them concerned Kenneth Arrow's monograph on social reconciliation of individual preferences. My resulting memoranda included two theorems about Boolean functions, ultimately published in *Selected Logic Papers*. The other project was in game theory. My memorandum on this was subsequently incorporated by McKinsey and Krentel into an article under our three names. We saw something of the Reichenbachs while we were in California, and on our way home we visited the Carnaps in New Mexico.

The Fulbright committee solicited my application for a grant to teach at Oxford during the next academic year, at Oxford's request. The financial arrangements were still vague, but I was told to expect neither gain nor loss. I compromised on a half year. Harvard granted me, despite my recent sabbatical, a semester's leave without pay. By June 1950 the Fulbright committee still had not notified me of my award, despite having asked me to apply. Marge and I were already leaving for a summer in Europe. My department chairman phoned Washington and determined that I had the award; then he phoned Goodman, my intended stand-in at Harvard, and got his acceptance. On reaching Paris I received at last the Fulbright papers and found that they demanded a heavy financial sacrifice. I refused; better to live frugally for a term and write, unpaid and unencumbered. I wrote to Oxford and to the dean at Harvard explaining my refusal. To my pleased surprise the Harvard administration volunteered to cancel my leave and restore my pay; and we had Goodman as well.

The Oxford philosophers had invited me to give the first John Locke Lectures during the period that I was expected there, and also they organized a symposium "On What There Is" for the meeting of the Aristotelian Society scheduled for Edinburgh in that interval. I had to decline the lectureship and to participate only by proxy in the symposium. My "Reply to Mr. Geach on What There Is", bewilderingly misprinted, was read and ably defended by Dreben at the meeting. My disappointment over missing Oxford was lavishly compensated three years later with the George Eastman Visiting Professorship.

Methods of Logic had gone to the publisher in April 1950, whereupon I resumed my philosophical reflections on meaning and ontology. From afar I envisaged a book, but what I wrote were pieces for occasions. "Two Dogmas" was one such, and the rejoinder to Geach; "Semantics and Abstract Objects" and "On Mental Entities" were for Philipp Frank's Boston symposia; "Identity, Ostension, and Hypostasis" was my Delaguna Lecture at Bryn Mawr; "On Carnap's Views on Ontology" was my part of a debate with Carnap in his Chicago seminar; "Ontology and Ideology" was a response to Bergmann solicited by the editors; "Three Grades of Modal Involvement" was an invited address at an International Congress; and "The Problem of Meaning in Linguistics" was my contribution to a linguistics meeting in 1951 at Ann Arbor.

This last was the one wholly fresh essay in *From a Logical Point of View;* some in that collection were slightly revised reprints of articles, others were patchworks of old bits and new. I published the volume as a stopgap when I saw that my major work in progress would take years to finish. Henry Aiken suggested the title; we had just heard Harry Belafonte sing the words in a calypso.

I was doing logic too. The revised edition of *Mathematical Logic,* touched on above, came out in 1951, and various logic papers were called forth by occasions. "On Decidability and Completeness" and "The Ordered Pair in Number Theory" were called forth by Festschriften. "On a So-Called Paradox" was called forth by a flurry of papers in *Mind* concerning a puzzle that had circulated years earlier in the Navy; I published the answer that I had originally written for my Navy friends. "On an Application of Tarski's Theory of Truth" was sparked by a query from Leblanc. It shows how narrowly the system of *Mathematical Logic* escapes the fate of affording a definition of its own truth predicate. The gap is alarmingly narrowed by a technique of relational images that circumvents, in effect, the requirement that values of functions be sets.

Other logic papers issued from my concurrent seminar efforts. "On ω-Inconsistency and a So-Called Axiom of Infinity" resolves some anomalies by rectifying terminology. "On the Consistency of 'New Foundations' " shows that "New Foundations" is consistent if a certain innocent-looking variant of *Principia* is consistent. In the ensuing twenty-five years a remarkable lot of relative consistency theorems for "New Foundations" have been produced by Specker, Jensen, Boffa, Gumin, and others, but the system has still not been shown consistent relative to Zermelo's or *Principia*.

Something I thought I proved in my seminar was found by Church to be wrong. His disproof led to a theorem, which in turn led to five more. The outcome was our joint paper "Some Theorems on Definability and Decidability". My student Craig pushed one of these theorems further, whence our joint note "On Reduction to a Symmetric Relation". I touched up this result later in "Reduction to a Dyadic Predicate".

Late in 1951 James Willard Oliver, once my top-notch teaching assistant in logic, phoned me in desperation from his post in Florida to say that as program chairman of the Association for Symbolic Logic he had been let down by his main speaker. Groping for something to offer, I remembered my vain efforts in 1948, when, working toward *Methods of Logic,* I had sought an algorithm for reducing truth-functional formulas to their simplest equivalents. Clearly a practical routine to this purpose would generally expedite truth-function logic. I had at length stopped trying, having convinced myself that any such algorithm would be too elaborate for the beginning of an introductory text. But I knew also, from Claude Shannon's observations, that simplification of truth-functional formulas could serve computer engineers in simplifying electric circuits. So I prepared for Oliver's program a paper on "The Problem of Simplifying Truth Functions". Many subsequent contributors to engineering journals cited my paper and took up my terminology. I gave three lectures on the subject to the engineers at Ann Arbor in 1958. At intervals I have drifted back to the subject for refreshment, for it is clean work. Hence "Two Theorems about Truth Functions", "A Way to Simplify Truth Functions", and "Cores and Prime Implicants".

We spent the summer of 1952 in Taxco with our infant Douglas. There I began *Higher Logic*, a proof-theoretic sequel to *Methods of Logic*. My deepened insight into Gödel's proof of the completeness of quantification theory was due partly to Dreben, whose first paper on the subject appeared that summer. As I reflected on this debt I was moved to drop the project and leave him a clear field. One residue of my project was "Interpretations of Sets of Conditions", and another was the completeness proof in later editions of *Methods of Logic*.

My term as department chairman, from February 1952, was mercifully curtailed midway in 1953 by my Eastman chair at Oxford. Meanwhile I had been weighing an offer from the West; and what kept me at Harvard, besides a raise, was a provision that I would not be chairman again. I dislike administration. For the same reason I had twice declined the presidency of the Association for Symbolic Logic, remembering Curry's industrious presidency when I was vice president. Now, however, I was president: 1953–55. I had tried to excuse myself by citing Oxford, and the excuse was overruled.

12. Oxford and After

In 1952 I stopped reviewing for the *Journal of Symbolic Logic*, feeling that I had done my share. Years earlier I had stopped accepting other review assignments, with rare exceptions such as Goodman. But when Ryle asked me to review Strawson's *Introduction to Logical Theory*, I envisaged the review as a manifesto to start my Eastman year at Oxford. Entering into the spirit, Ryle published it as the lead article in *Mind*, October 1953.

The Eastman flat was at 8 Merton Street, but the numeral hung at a side door in Logic Lane; so 8 Logic Lane was the address I used in presiding over the Association for Symbolic Logic.

I gave a lecture course each term. One was on the philosophy of language. I was struggling to find the right structure for my work in progress, what was to become *Word and Object* in later years. My other courses were on logic and set theory. One in which I compared various systems of set theory pleased me by the neatness of interconnections. I thought of making a short book of this forthwith, since my philosophical work in progress moved so slowly. However, I subdued the impulse and kept to the opposite priorities. *Word and Object* proved to take six more years, and the set-theory book followed three years later still, swollen beyond expectation. More of that in its place.

Three of my eagerest auditors at Oxford were a Junior Fellow of All Souls, a scholar from New Zealand, and a Privatdozent on leave from Innsbruck: Michael Dummett, Jonathan Bennett, and Wolfgang Stegmüller. The three would compare notes, prepare questions, and then meet with me for discussion. I frequented a seminar by Strawson and Grice; also Austin's Saturday meetings of dons. I had good talks with Kreisel and Geach, who were readers at Reading and Birmingham. Marge and I dined happily in many homes and I in thirteen colleges. Marge bore a daughter, Margaret.

Early in 1954 I gave the Shearman Lectures at University College in London, on ontology. In them I pondered the Skolem-Löwenheim theorem, and also Carnap's expedient of spatiotemporal coordinates, as possible avenues to a Pythagorean ontology of natural numbers. I was not deeply stirred by such a prospect, and ten years later I argued in "Ontological Reduction and the World of Numbers" that the Skolem-Löwenheim theorem bore no such Pythagorean implications. Twelve years later still, however, in "Whither Physical Objects?", I recognized that developments in particle physics itself lent some support to a wholly abstract ontology.

During my Oxford year I fared forth for single lectures at Cambridge, Bristol, Aberystwyth, Leicester, and Manchester, and for a five-day symposium with Ayer, Ewing, McKeon, and others in the Great Park at Windsor. Also there were some solicited writings. I had declined to write the general article on logic for the Encyclopedia Americana, but I rose to their subsequent invitation to write "Logic, symbolic." I wanted to see how much logic I could render generally intelligible within their prescribed limits of space. My efforts at maximization brought some novelties in the way of decision procedures and proof procedures. Further there was "Carnap and Logical Truth", requested by Schilpp for Carnap's volume in the Library of Living Philosophers. It met the May 1954 deadline, though the rest of his volume took nine more years. And then there was "On Frege's Way Out", elicited by Scholz. He had urged in his review of Geach and Black's translation of Frege that I assess Frege's response to Russell's paradox.

I had known Heinrich Scholz by correspondence since Nazi times, when he had worked courageously to save Poles. At last I met him, that summer of 1954, in Münster, as well as Hermes and Hasenjaeger. Dummett came along, so that I might help him gain entrée to the Frege Archives. Marge and I went on to visit the Conants at Bonn, where he was High Commissioner. The academic year ended as it had begun, with an international congress: philosophy at Brussels the one summer, mathematics at Amsterdam the other.

Another paper of that year, "Quantification and the Empty Domain", was sparked by a paper of Hailperin's. He and others had been extending quantification theory to allow an empty universe. My paper included a more concise system to that purpose. But John P. Burgess has shown me, sixteen years later, that my system was incomplete—my sketch of a proof to the contrary notwithstanding. Let me now offer a corrected system. Its axioms comprise the closures of tautologies and of $\ulcorner(\alpha)(\phi \supset \psi) \supset . (\alpha) \phi \supset (\alpha) \psi\urcorner$ and $\ulcorner(\alpha) f \supset (\beta)$ $f\urcorner$; also the closures of formulas $\ulcorner(\alpha) \phi \supset \phi \dfrac{\beta}{\alpha}\urcorner$ where α is free in ϕ, and of formulas $\ulcorner\phi \supset (\alpha) \phi\urcorner$ where α is not. Inference proceeds still by *modus ponens*.

I was invited to participate in the Columbia bicentennial celebrations that fall, 1954. I wrote "The Scope and Language of Science", in which *Word and Object* begins visibly to emerge. Editorial tampering made hash of crucial distinctions between use and mention when the essay appeared in the bicentennial volume. J.O. Wisdom kindly published the correct text later in the *British Journal for the Philosophy of Science*.

In that same fall I wrote "A Proof Procedure for Quantification Theory", a by-product of my resumed teaching of logic at Harvard. Dreben found later that my Method A was anticipated by Skolem in a 1928 paper unavailable at Harvard. But for the most part, in that year and succeeding ones, I was groping toward *Word and Object*. "Quantifiers and Propositional Attitudes" was an interim report on one aspect of the project, elicited by queries of Donald Quimby. Late in 1955, however, I was drawn back for a while to my deferred project of a little book on comparative set theory; for this was the theme of my retiring presidential address to the Association for Symbolic Logic, "Unification of Universes in Set Theory".

In the summer of 1956 I became Edgar Pierce Professor. That same summer I was sent as delegate to an inter-American philosophical congress in Chile. It enabled Marge and me to make a memorable tour of Peru and Bolivia. Then came a duty-free year at the Institute for Advanced Study at Princeton, a year serenely devoted to *Word and Object*. My good company that year included again Kreisel, who undertook to tell me a new result each day at tea, weekends excepted.

That winter I gladly became president of the Eastern Division of the American Philosophical Association, the office being mainly titular. My presidential address a year later was "Speaking of Objects," which clearly foreshadows *Word and Object*, sometimes verbatim.

For me 1957–58 was an isolated Harvard year, for I was already booked for another duty-free year on *Word and Object:* the year 1958–59 at the Center for Advanced Study in the Behavioral Sciences at Stanford. Even the intervening Harvard year was broken by an invitation to the week-long Colloque de Royaumont in April 1958. The topic that year was *philosophie analytique,* and the participants from outside France were mostly friends of mine from Oxford. Our papers were translated into French, mimeographed, and distributed. The translator was a stylist and innocent of philosophy. I corrected my paper, "Le mythe de la signification,'' before mimeographing. But in the discussions, with our stylist as interpreter, communication languished. At the final session, despairing, I burst extempore into French. I held forth at length and communicated. I learned anew what I knew in Brazil sixteen years before: speak, if you can, the local language, even if badly.

We had just moved into our 1820 row house in Beacon Hill, downtown Boston. Thirty miles inland, in a town confusingly named Harvard, we had bought some woodland along a lake and a carpenter had built us a summer cottage of my designing. I did much writing in both places in those years and after. But the summer of 1958 was crowded: there were my lectures to the engineers at Ann Arbor, mentioned above, and there was our move to Stanford, which we combined with a drive across Mexico. I caught hepatitis and began my Stanford year in the hospital.

Mario Bunge, the star of the Chile congress two years before, had proposed translating *O Sentido* into Spanish. A microfilm of his typescript arrived and I corrected it while convalescing. It was the first translation of any of my books. There are now forty, and more coming.

The year brought also the delayed second edition of *Methods of Logic*. Already in 1954 I had had plans for an easier soundness proof and for an appendix perspicuously proving completeness and Löwenheim's theorem. The editor at Holt was to alert me when a new printing was foreseeable. Two years later I drew up these revisions and others and sent them along to await the day, only to learn that the book had been inadvertently reprinted in the editor's absence. The publisher made partial amends by printing the appendix as a pamphlet for insertion in the unsold books. I never knew it to turn up in a copy of the book, but I distributed it privately. By 1958, at last, the inadvertent reprinting had dwindled and proofs of the revised edition came to Stanford.

It was another idyllic year, in a glorious setting and a congenial group. I saw much of Davidson, Roman Jakobson, and the ubiquitous Kreisel. I devoted the year to finishing *Word and Object*.

13. Beyond Word and Object

The six years last sketched were years to be grateful for, what with Oxford, Princeton, Stanford, and the various travels intervening. There were the two presidencies, and there was further glory: I was elected to the American Philosophical Society and the British Academy and was awarded my first two honorary doctorates.

More excitement lay just ahead. I left Stanford in June 1959 and flew to South Australia to give the Gavin David Young Lectures—a résumé of *Word and Object*. On the way I had a taste of Hawaii, Fiji, and New Zealand. From Australia I proceeded to Tokyo to give two summer courses, and on the way I hurriedly prowled Singapore, Bangkok, Angkor Wat, Saigon, Hong Kong, Macao, and Taipeh.

At Tokyo I lectured of course in English, though at Stanford I had worked some at Japanese. My philosophy lectures—*Word and Object* again—were interpreted a paragraph at a time, at an irreducible ration of three minutes to one. My other course, for the mathematicians, was on comparative set theory, reaching toward my next book. Aided by formulas, it went uninterpreted.

My Japanese friends wanted me represented in a volume of theirs. I gave them "Posits and Reality", a superseded first section of *Word and Object*. Over the years I had persisted in cutting and rewriting *Word and Object* so as not to harp unduly on the obvious. Dreben tells me that I overdid those precautions, and that he and others have found both "Posits and Reality" and "Speaking of Objects" helpful in orienting to the book.

Marge joined me in Japan, which we delightedly toured. By the time we returned to Boston in September 1959, we had added Korea and northern Alaska. Then came a sequence of five unbroken years at Harvard.

During the first three of them my working time apart from teaching went mostly into *Set Theory and Its Logic*. I intended a thin book comparing various axiomatic set theories. But I needed first to brief the reader on central themes, on the infinite ordinals and cardinals and transfinite induction, if he was to appreciate the objectives and advantages of the various axiom systems. Such briefing needs some deductive structure, moreover, to lend plausibility to unintuitive properties. But deduction from mere uncodified plausibles is ill suited to this domain, for it leads to paradox; we need the constraints of explicit axioms. Thus we are caught up, expositorily, in a circle.

I coped with the predicament by beginning with weak axioms, valid in most of the systems eventually to be compared. In order to keep them weak I exploited the virtual theory of classes and relations (§9 above), which I integrated with the real theory of classes as a continuing source of virtual supplementation. In the same parsimonious spirit I based number theory on finite classes by inverting the inductive structure, as if to count downward. As the preliminary matter developed, parsimony and perspicuity jostled as rival objectives. Incidentally I made rather a game of the definitions of rational, real, and complex numbers; the ratios are reals and the reals are complex, as in olden times, and they are all classes of natural numbers.

The comparison of systems that was to have been the substance of the book came to be outweighed by this general introduction to set theory. The thickening book came to stress the logic at the bottom no less than the axiom systems at the top. Logic was doing double duty in the virtual theory, which is just set theory logically simulated.

April 1960 elicited "Variables Explained Away" (see §6) for the American Philosophical Society and "Logic as a Source of Syntactical Insights" for a

New York meeting on more or less mathematical linguistics. In June 1960 I went to Geneva as a guest kibitzer at Piaget's week of research reports. It was a quick trip, but I was able to include some walks in Santa Maria, Lisbon, Copenhagen, and Reykjavik, and a brief tour of southern Norway.

My efforts in set theory were interrupted again in the fall of 1961 by an invitation to speak at the University of Akron. In loyalty to the home town it was a command performance. I had to be intelligible to non-specialists, so the natural topic was paradox. Later in the year my turn came to address our Shop Club at Harvard, and again I had to be intelligible to nonspecialists; so I repeated my talk. Months afterward my fellow Shopclubman Jacob Fine was still praising that talk and advising me to publish it. The season for polite response had passed, so I took him seriously and sent it to the *Scientific American*. Two years later I was invited to participate in a mathematics issue of that journal. Both papers reappeared in my collection *The Ways of Paradox* and in a book by *Scientific American*. Such were the consequences of a sentimental journey home.

There were further interruptions to *Set Theory and Its Logic*. In February 1962 the Boston Colloquium for the Philosophy of Science drew me back into the controversy over modal logic to comment on a paper by Ruth Barcan Marcus. My contribution subsequently appeared in *Synthese* for 1961, an odd anachronism. Also I wrote two radio talks, "On the Application of Modern Logic" and "Necessary Truth", for vicarious delivery abroad. In the summer of 1962 I gave a series of lectures at Bowdoin on the history of logic.

Set Theory and Its Logic went to the publisher in January 1963, and my next writings were sparked by further invitations. Yale launched a series of lectures on Frontiers in Philosophy, and France launched a journal *Etudes Philosophiques;* and invitations from these two quarters combined to elicit "Frontières dans la théorie logique". Woodger's Festschrift elicited "On Simple Theories of a Complex World". My first merry review of an atlas (see §1) dates from those days, and it drew other reviews in its train. Still, two papers welled forth unbidden: "Implicit Definition Sustained" and "Ontological Definition and the World of Numbers" (see §§8, 12).

14. Plus ça Change

In the middle of 1964 a sabbatical began. I went traveling with my wife, son, granddaughter, and two of my daughters. We crossed Europe and pressed on to Nubia and the Levant. There were reunions in Oxford and days with the Davidsons and John Wallace in Greece. In January we sailed back to America and settled for the spring term at the Center for Advanced Studies at Wesleyan.

I worried about the idioms of propositional attitude: they are conspicuously unsatisfactory in logical ways, yet not readily dispensable. How might their purposes be served in more scientific terms? Such was my preoccupation in writing "Propositional Objects" that spring. I took the paper on a lecture circuit: Amherst, Ann Arbor, Chicago, Urbana.

Dover Publications proposed reprinting *Elementary Logic,* and this set me to thinking rather of a revised edition. In the truth-functional part I relaxed my old adherence to negation and conjunction and admitted alternational normal forms. In the quantificational part I gave up the unintuitive proof procedure of the first edition in favor of a transparent procedure that I had used for the completeness proof in the appendix to *Methods;* namely, *reductio ad absurdum* by universal and existential instantiation. The revised edition, half new, went off to Harper's that same spring.

My old student and former colleague Føllesdal wanted to include many papers of mine in an anthology that was under consideration by Random House. This set me to thinking that the time was ripe rather for some collecting on my own part. I prepared *Selected Logic Papers* and *The Ways of Paradox.* It seemed only fair to offer them to Random House, and I got them off that same spring.

By June, after these few months in America, I was back in England for a week-long symposium of Popper's. It was a heart-warming revival of old times, for along with Kreisel and others of his generation there were Tarski, Bernays, Kalmár, and, in admirable form, Carnap.

Harvard again in September 1965 for two years and a half, a period much punctuated by outside engagements. I presented an Arnold Isenberg Memorial Lecture on "Stimulus and Meaning" at Michigan State, and pieces on Russell and Austin in symposia of the American Philosophical Association. I produced at short notice a pedestrian paper on "Existence" for a curiously hybrid symposium on logic, physics, and history at Denver that included Kreisel, Popper, Bethe, and Bondi. I responded to Father Owens on ontology at a congress at Quebec. I contributed "Philosophical Progress in Language Theory" to a colloquium in the ambitious International Philosophical Year at little-known Brockport. At Brooklyn and at Storrs I lectured from the essay "Natural Kinds" that I was writing for Hempel's Festschrift.

"Existence and Quantification" was meant for a colloquium in London, Ontario, but the plane that was bearing James and Judy Thomson and me thither was grounded at Rochester by a blizzard. The airline sent us on in a taxi, which ran out of gas. We hitchhiked down the icy road to Buffalo and got no farther. Margolis read my paper to the colloquium, having had the foresight to ask for a copy.

In that period also I wrote introductory notes for van Heijenoort's monumental source book *From Frege to Gödel,* and reviewed Russell's autobiography for a Boston newspaper.

I got unpaid leave from Harvard for the spring of 1968 and spent a pleasant term as visiting professor at Rockefeller University. I wanted to see how I might like moving to Rockefeller if the Harvard administration failed to contain the mounting disorders. Half the term went to finishing the inaugural pair of John Dewey Lectures, "Ontological Relativity", which I gave at Columbia in March. Columbia had publication rights, but a forty-page monograph is unappealing, so I suggested adding other essays; it seemed a reasonable precedent for future Dewey Lecturers. Hence *Ontological Relativity and Other Essays*. One of these other essays, "Epistemology Naturalized", was destined for the congress of Vienna, where I was to represent the American Philosophical Association. In writing it I borrowed portions from my Arnold Isenberg Lecture, having awaited overlong the volume in which that was to appear. The theme, naturalism versus phenomenalism in a historical perspective, fitted my mood of reminiscence in returning to Vienna after thirty-five years. Also I wrote a technical paper "On the Limits of Decision" for the congress, because I was expected to contribute something of my own to the logic session which I was to chair.

15. Seventh Decade, First Half

The summer of 1968 was enriched by three weeks of lecturing and listening at a Summer Institute of Philosophy on Long Island. Fifty teachers from obscure colleges came on fellowships to hear Sellars, Chisholm, Plantinga, and me in those weeks and others in other weeks. We four lectured, conducted discussions, and attended one another's lectures. Sellars and his wife lived away; Chisholm, Plantinga, and I shared a college house and made merry. I relished their lectures for their acuteness, despite disapproving of *necessitas de dicto et de re;* it is a game one can be drawn into.

After the September congress of Vienna, which gave occasion for family travels in Italy and Dalmatia, I returned to Harvard duties and to a new array of outside projects. I wrote a lecture "Grades of Theoreticity" for a series at Amherst. I studied the critical essays that my generous friends Donald Davidson and Jaakko Hintikka had elicited with my sixtieth birthday in mind. I wrote replies to these, and thus *Words and Objections* was in the mill.

Then I turned to the little *Philosophy of Logic* that Prentice-Hall had asked me to write. By coincidence the Collège de France invited me to give a course of lectures on that same subject during the following May and June, 1969. By April I finished a draft in English and proceeded to convert it to French lectures. Having helped Mondadori with his Italian translation of *Word and Object,* I knew I was hard to translate; so now in doing my own French version I luxuriated in the freedom that a self-translator enjoys. If a sentence is sticky, he is free to say something else to the same long-run purpose. There were other changes, too, to suit the material to the lecture hall, and there were substantive afterthoughts. The French text was an improvement all in all, and when I got home from Paris I used it as basis for reworking the English manuscript for Prentice-Hall.

My six weeks in Paris, living and writing in the handsome rue des Beaux Arts and walking to the Collège, are a bright memory. Vuillemin helped to brighten it, and so, again, did Kreisel.

Late that summer, 1969, I participated in a tight little colloquium on linguistics and logic at Stanford, organized by Davidson and Harman. Geach, David Kaplan, and seven others were there, half from linguistics. My piece was "Methodological Reflections on Linguistic Theory". The colloquium was a fiasco at bridge building. Devices of Geach's that ought to delight structural linguists fell on deaf ears. The chatter of two of the linguists crowded Davidson's paper off the program altogether.

By then my old student Joseph Ullian and I were well embarked on a collaboration by mail that was presently to issue in our slight *Web of Belief*. Dushkin at Random House had asked me to write such a thing for a series meant for freshman English. When I protested that I had lost touch with the freshman mind, he suggested that I think of a former student who might still have the touch; hence Ullian. Ullian sent me a rough draft of part; I reacted with a revision of this and free association of further matter; and so we alternated.

Our slender volume proved over the years to serve not so much freshman English as beginning philosophy courses. In 1976 the publishers urged us to undertake a revised edition, slanted more to philosophy. For our possible guidance they engaged two anonymous critics who had been teaching from the book. One of them, who proved to be Douglas Stalker, provided page-by-page criticism and shrewd advice. It affected me to see our too casual product so thoughtfully treated by so clearly dedicated a teacher of philosophy. I was moved to rewrite the book in large part and to expand it. I passed my effusions to Ullian, and so the revision proceeded.

But let us regain our footing back in 1969, for there is more to say. Holt had approached me for a third edition of *Methods of Logic*. Years of teaching had brought me many ideas for improving the book and supplementing it with omissibilia. Friends at Columbia had pooled their suggestions while I was at Rockefeller. By the end of 1969 I was getting on with it. Ullian gave it a productive reading, and it went to the publisher in September 1970, emerging in 1972.

Nor let me elide the spring and summer of 1970, for they were extraordinary. In May I lectured at Calgary and Edmonton and waded in the snow at Lake Louise. Then I went to an American Philosophical Association meeting at St. Louis, where I commented on Belnap, discussed with Davidson and Harman, and introduced one of Hempel's three Paul Carus Lectures. My next stop was Notre Dame, for a week of lecture and discussion. A week of this kind had proved so helpful in clarifying my ideas for the philosophers at Ohio State a few years earlier that I have tended since to accept similar invitations despite the strenuousness; thus Notre Dame, and in the next three years Bloomington, Princeton, Wayne.

The spring and summer of 1970 were extraordinary, I said, but I have only begun to say why. In June I went to three commencements: to Columbia for a gold medal and to Temple and Oxford for my seventh and eighth honorary doctorates. (The earlier ones were from Oberlin, Ohio State, Akron, Washington, Lille, and Chicago.) Oxford meant going to Europe, so Føllesdal suggested adding an Arctic jaunt and Davidson a safari. Føllesdal met me at Helsinki and we drove to the Arctic Ocean. Marge, Douglas, and Margaret joined us in the Arctic and we zigzagged through scenic Norway to a logic meeting at Oslo, where I spoke on predicate-functor logic. After Oxford we made rendezvous with the three Davidsons in Ethiopia and prowled East Africa seven strong, mostly in rented microbusses. The Davidsons had done complex and masterly prearranging.

My Oslo paper underwent two expansions, along different dimensions. One was "Algebraic Logic and Predicate Functors", which includes a historical background. It went to Goodman's Festschrift, but the publisher kindly issued it also in advance as a monograph when he saw that the Festschrift would be delayed. The other expansion was "Truth and Disquotation", which compares truth definitions for predicate-functor logic and other logics.

The American Philosophical Association appointed me Carus Lecturer for December 1971. My main task for the fall of 1970 and after, apart from teaching, was thereby set: writing the book whereof my three Carus Lectures should be a resumé. Such is *The Roots of Reference*. In it I pursue further the theme of Chapter 3 of *Word and Object,* the ontogenesis of reference.

In the summer of 1971 I flew twice to California. There was the Tarski festival at Berkeley, where I read "Truth and Disquotation". Then there was a Summer Institute of Philosophy, this time at Irvine, where I again lectured and listened for three weeks. Davidson, Harman, David Kaplan, and Strawson were active, and briefly Kripke. Thanks to some stretching of mandate, the stipendiaries were not all from obscure faculties. They included Richard Thomasson, Oswaldo Chateaubriand, Stephen Stich, Robert Vogelin, Peter Unger, James McGilvary, John King-Farlow, Edwin Martin, Michael Levin, Herbert Bohnert, Helen Cartwright, Jack Nelson, Gareth Evans. We lecturers attended not only one another's lectures but also one another's discussion sessions, such was the level. My lectures were a first draft of *The Roots of Reference,* and my brilliant audience worked wonders in deflecting me from error. I went to Irvine hoping to get by with substitutional quantification over abstract objects, and I came away disabused.

The fall of 1971 began another sabbatical, my last. We stayed home and I worked at *The Roots of Reference,* but for sporadic trips. The longest of these took in Madeira, the Canaries, and the western Sahara, and ended at Valencia in April 1972, where I lectured for the first time in Spanish: "Reflexiones sobre el aprendizaje del lenguaje." The ideas were from *The Roots of Reference.*

In June 1972 I addressed a lexicography conference in New York on definition, by invitation of Fred Cassidy (see §2), after which he and I went hiking in his native Jamaica. In November I talked on levels of abstraction at another New York meeting: a conference on unified science under the auspices of Ed Haskell (see §3). Old Ἄρθρον lives.

In January 1973, between Harvard commitments, I gave the Hägerström lectures at Uppsala: again *The Roots of Reference,* by then in the publisher's hands. Further outside engagements punctuated my Harvard spring: lectures at New Orleans, Nashville, and Evanston, a colloquium at Storrs, a radio talk "On the Limits of Knowledge", and the week at Wayne.

16. Oxford Again

I spent the academic year 1973–74 at Merton College, Oxford, as the first incumbent of the generous Sir Henry Savile Fellowship. Merton's sixteenth-century library with its gambrel ceiling and its chained books was Sir Henry's doing. The magic proportions of Merton's squat square tower and the mellow richness of its bells awakened vivid feelings of twenty years before, when we had lived across the street. I had admired Merton for its ancient buildings, dating in part from 1280. Belonging now, I divided my working time between my rooms in college and the narrow seventeenth-century house that was provided for Marge and me in Holywell Street.

Davidson was in Oxford for the year, and Føllesdal for a term. Freddie Ayer's Play Group, as Ann Strawson called it, met Thursdays in the college rooms of one or another member. A paper would be read and followed by drinks and discussion. Ayer, Strawson, Dummett, Pears, Mackie, Parfit, Wiggins, Evans, Mc Dowell, and Foster were regulars.

Wolfson College at Oxford sponsored six public lectures on Mind and Language that drew vast audiences. I wrote a lecture "Mind and Verbal Dispositions" for the series, but then I observed that other speakers were dwelling so much on my work that I might do better to present a more central statement of my philosophical position. So I wrote and presented a different lecture, "The Nature of Natural Knowledge"; but both were printed in the volume of lectures. A session for discussion of my lecture was arranged, based on written questions that were solicited and edited for me by Dana Scott and Christopher Peacocke.

I lectured to the Moral Science Club in Cambridge, to the philosophers of science in London, and to the philosophers in Aberystwyth, Edinburgh, St. Andrews, Manchester, and Leeds. The symposium at Leeds included Hintikka, Davidson, Føllesdal, and Geach. Also I discussed my philosophy with my readers in Birmingham and participated informally in a colloquium in the Great Park at Windsor.

A typescript by Imre Lakatos on empiricism in mathematics reached my hands, and I liked it. I could see that he did not know my *Set Theory and Its Logic,* and that he would find parts of it congenial; so I tried to send him a copy. It proved to be unobtainable in Oxford, despite the fact that the Oxford University Press was the agent for it in Britain. It took them ten days to get a copy for me from London. On the day I mailed it I read of his death.

Soon I was telephoned from Utrecht, where Imre had been scheduled to address a group of philosophically minded scientists. I went over and lectured in his place.

Another group of philosophically minded scientists invited me to address them in Florence. They would have expected to hear English, but I decided to try my hand at an Italian version of "The Nature of Natural Knowledge". Presenting papers in the auditor's native language is desirable where possible. When one hears a paper in a language other than one's own, even a familiar one, one's attention to the content is not undivided: some attention goes to the language. If on the other hand the speaker takes the trouble to prepare his paper in the auditor's own language, he gets the linguistic considerations out of the way on his own time and thus frees the auditor for his brief hour of philosophy unalloyed. Foreign accent, within limits, is no impediment.

But it was a venture. I had lectured in five languages, but Italian was for me a weak sixth, mainly a reading language. So I deployed the manuals. The excessive time spent was not wasted, for I was not only putting my lecture into Italian; I was learning more Italian. When my best effort was complete I got a young Italian-American philosopher at Oxford named Ronald Laura to correct the mistakes, and so it went. The text appeared later in the *Rivista di Filosofia.*

In June 1974 my Savile Fellowship terminated in another foreign involvement: a colloquium on my philosophy at Cullera in Spain under the direction of Manuel Garrido. I alone, of the eight, was not a native speaker, and I was the one who had to hear all and respond appropriately; so these were tiring days. The papers were sent to me in America subsequently in their publishable form and I wrote up my replies. The volume has appeared: *Aspectos de la filosofía de W.V.Q.*

True to form, we turned to non-professional travel during the generous vacations between Oxford terms. In December 1973 we enjoyed northwestern Spain with the Garridos and then Portugal with our son and daughter, who flew over from the States. In April 1974 we toured Persia.

17. Four More Years

Retirement at Harvard is normal at 66 and mandatory at 70. I was invited to stay on till 70.

Each year something calls us abroad. In the summer of 1975 we were given five weeks of residence at the Rockefeller Foundation's idyllic Villa Serbelloni on the Lake of Como. It is a luxurious life in a breathtaking setting, amid bright academic company with varied interests. While there I wrote replies to such essays as had thus far been received for the present volume.

In the spring of 1976 we had two weeks in Israel. The occasion was a colloquium on Language and Philosophy in memory of Bar-Hillel. Participants included Strawson, Davidson, Dummett, Putnam, and Kripke. "Use and its Place in Meaning" was my contribution. A week later I gave a public lecture there: "Facts of the Matter".

In the summer of 1977 we were off again to Uppsala. This time it was a colloquium on Logic and Grammar in connection with the fifth centenary. My paper was "Grammar, Truth, and Logic". Later we proceeded to London, where I was taped for an hour's television dialogue with Bryan Magee. We visited my daughters Elizabeth and Norma, who live in London, and cruised on Elizabeth's newly outfitted river boat. Between Uppsala and London we had some days on Gotland and a visit to Leningrad. It was our first time in Russia, and it leaves me having been in every country in Europe. My worldwide count of countries touched now stands at 113, six of which (Danzig, Latvia, Lithuania, Newfoundland, South Vietnam, Spanish Sahara) are countries no longer.

Between times there was frivolous foreign travel: to Venezuela at the end of 1975 and to Yucatan shortly after. There was domestic travel as usual, lecturing. It was for a conference at Oklahoma under the flattering title "Two Hundred Years of American Philosophy: Edwards to Quine" that I wrote "Facts of the Matter". I read the same paper at Rockefeller University and, as mentioned, Jerusalem. A paper on identity, which in its evolving phases had stood me in good stead on several occasions in Britain and earlier, served me still in 1975 at Dallas and Tucson. One on "Ontology and Truth", used twice in Britain, served again in Oklahoma. One on "The Mentalistic Foundations for Physicalism" served at West Chester, Pa., at Boston, and at Oberlin. "On Empirically Equivalent Systems of the World" emerged in 1975 and was heard at Iowa, Salt Lake, and Princeton. In Denton, Texas, and Columbia, Mo., I spoke on "Physical Objects." At South Carolina I contributed to a colloquium on pragmatism, and in Chapel Hill and New York I commented on other speakers. At Dartmouth I made a trial run of my Uppsala paper.

My published writings in this interval have been brief and numerous. Some of them are recognizable among the foregoing lecture headings. Some— "Whither Physical Objects?", "On the Individuation of Attributes", "On the

Nature of Moral Values"—were written for Festschriften. "Symbols" was commissioned for an Oxford reference volume. Others came of more inward promptings.

18. Modus Operandi

Mostly I have worked alone. For years my work in logic was almost necessarily a lone venture, there being little appropriate company in easy reach. But I think the causes run deeper. This is suggested by my reactions to lectures, to reading, and to discussion.

Generally I have found it hard to sit through lectures; hard to keep my mind on them. As a boy I would sit long hours bored in school, dreaming of slipping down through a trap door into the cool basement and running to freedom. This impatience has persisted.

Books serve me better, but still imperfectly. I can escape contentedly into books of linguistics or popular science or into the encyclopedia, but I study writings in my professional sphere with less patience, preferring evidently to get on with it on my own. Thus it was that my early work with *Principia Mathematica* suited me so well: I was using the book as a tool rather than passively reading it. Often in my later logical efforts I have tried to prove something anew rather than search and study a book that I knew must contain a proof of it. Both in logic and in philosophy I have tended to write first and search the literature only afterward for anticipations to acknowledge. Sometimes I have stopped searching too soon. This indocile habit of mind has obvious drawbacks. Surely it has led to inefficiency and duplication of effort.

What then of oral discussion? Take first the mathematico-logical side. If someone makes or challenges a technical point, the matter can usually be settled in short order and I am always then gratified, except perhaps for chagrin at having erred indelibly in print. If on the other hand someone raises a technical problem that takes long pondering, I do better to go away and think alone.

Within philosophy proper, I find private discussion wasteful and frustrating except with persons of kindred outlook and purpose. Worse still is private argument with one who is motivated by vanity or *parti pris;* I withdraw when I sense motives other than desire for truth. But not so in public discussion, oral or written. Public discussion even with someone with unworthy motives or a very alien outlook can be of value in clarifying matters for receptive third parties. If the defining feature of debate is the desire to win, then private debate is folly but public debate can still have its uses.

Philosophical discussion with persons of kindred outlook has been valuable to me, though I have rarely sought it. It can be valuable in four ways. First, and least frequently, my interlocutor communicates an attractive new idea. Second, and more frequently, he shows me a fault in my idea. Third, and more frequently still, he causes me to relate my own ideas in rewarding new ways in my effort to explain. Fourth, and most frequently, he shows by the error of his ways that I am writing to good purpose. If for a long period I write philosophy in a vacuum, I feel increasingly that I am belaboring the obvious, and so I begin to doubt the urgency of my task, or, at best, to overdo the succinctness (see §13).

Writers have been generous to me with their books, reprints, and duplicated typescripts. Some of this I read and annotate, also writing to the author if I have a point to make. Other items I decide not to read. But I file most of it, alphabetically by author. There must be three thousand reprints, and my retrieval of relevant items by subject is haphazard. Haskell Curry used to summarize his technical reading on cards, exhaustively indexed; but this takes time and discourages reading. I have only my memory to go by, or references in other literature; and both are woefully inadequate. My piece "On a Suggestion of Katz" is a case in point. Katz had suggested an experiment to determine whether people have fairly uniform intuitive standards of analyticity. In my reply I acknowledged that a positive result would be interesting. I forgot that Apostel and others had made that very experiment at Geneva with indifferent results and that I owned their little book and had even reported on it in *Word and Object*. I am hardly the one to blame Katz for missing or forgetting that passage in *Word and Object*.

From 1933 until the war I kept a logic notebook, not of my reading but of my ideas. Many of my published papers began in that book. I dropped the practice when I turned increasingly to discursive philosophy, which goes less readily into discrete memoranda; but I would still occasionally write out a short item and put it in a general file. Over the years my correspondence with readers and distant colleagues became increasingly heavy, so that now a large part of my unpublished logical and philosophical writing consists of copies of my letters. Filed alphabetically by addressee as they are, these letters again present a retrieval problem. All too recently I thought of the easy expedient of keeping a daily log of professional correspondence and other writing. This proves helpful not only in reporting my use of grants in aid, but also in finding letters; for I can often recover a correspondent's name by scanning likely dates. I wish I had started it long ago.

I do not work on schedule. Mostly I have simply worked, unless some social engagement intervened, or an attractive opportunity for travel. In my seven-by-ten-foot retreat at our summer place, intent on some absorbing project such as *Set Theory and Its Logic*, I sometimes worked nearly a hundred hours in a week.

I try to make short work of irrelevancies. Thus I am apt to write a check on opening the bill, or scribble an answer immediately on reading some easily answered inquiry, so as not to have to pick the thing up twice. My desk is usually pretty tidy, for the sight of a tangle of agenda makes me nervous. It is not to be wondered that my chairmanship of the department was distasteful. I then took to keeping a tally of the time spent in various categories—administration, teaching, research and writing—so as to be able to turn to my chosen work with a clear conscience when I had done my day's quota of the other.

Research and writing and reviewing can have boring phases too, and at times I have indeed taken refuge in leisure reading on irrelevant subjects for a time. Sometimes also I have escaped from some boring task into logic, thinking up a logical idea for no other purpose, deep down, than the escape itself. This is a sly escape, for it deceives the conscience. I think a couple of my little logic papers probably began thus.

I have never learned to use an assistant, except in teaching. I have hardly ever used a stenographer or a dictaphone. I write everything by hand, both letters and essays, and pass them to the department secretary for typing. In harder times I typed my own writings, but first I composed them in handwriting. I like the freedom for emendations. I write on the blank backs of the shoals of administrative reports and superseded Xeroxes.

Logic is easy to write. Once the theory is worked out, the organization is virtually determined. The writing proceeds as a straightforward exposition of antecedently determined matter. Philosophy is another affair. I find philosophical thought hardly separable from its expression. Consequently a full outline cannot very well be drawn up in advance of some pretty full writing. Usually I begin by noting down, as I think of them, points that want covering. I group them tentatively and start writing, in complete sentences and paragraphs as if it were a final version—which it is not. At the foot of the page I jot further agenda as they occur to me. I think of improvements in organization as I go along, and I execute them by permutations and new transitions. This used to mean much crossing out and various insertion instructions. Nowadays I use scissors and paste, thus maintaining a more easily readable copy, which facilitates my continued critical rereading of what has gone before.

I reread searching out repetitions of content, which can be remedied by permuting and condensing. I search out obscurities, of course, and ambiguities. Also I reread for style. I dislike clashing etymologies. "Stirring up tensions" and "at the height of the Depression" are two striking examples from newspapers, and there are also less striking ones that I avoid when I can. I have come to see moreover that in my writing I have tried all along for rhythm and flow. It disturbs me to read something like "in ignorance of, or without regard to, the regularity principle" where one could have written "in ignorance of the regularity principle or without regard to it." What price the saving of a two-letter pronoun?

I have another latter-day insight worth noting. Sometimes, struggling with an idea that proved hard to expound, I have found myself trying novel literary turns and figures of speech. But I have come to see that the better strategy in such a case is to go for a walk and try recasting not the mode of expression but the whole idea. It had not been adequately thought through, and there was a flaw in it.

A concluding reflection on the *bon mot*. It is a pleasure to hit upon a clever and amusing way of making some point that wanted making. Then, as revision proceeds, one may find that the point no longer wants making; it gives the wrong emphasis, or it does not advance the main theme. One is torn. If the work in progress is one of my fun reviews for the *New York Review of Books*, I am apt to keep the *bon mot*. If it is a professional piece, I bite the bullet and excise the *mot*. Here I see a boundary mark between *belles lettres* and science.

Postscript, 1985

I began these memoirs a dozen years ago, when the plan for this volume was first laid. The sections last added are nearly eight years old. It seems pointless to append a chronicle of these eight further years, since my full-width auto-biography, *The Time of My Life,* is now being brought out by the M. I. T. Press. It was sparked by the present more specialized narrative, whereof approximately one fifth recurs sporadically in its five hundred pages.

PART TWO

DESCRIPTIVE AND CRITICAL ESSAYS ON THE PHILOSOPHY OF W. V. QUINE, WITH REPLIES

1

William P. Alston

QUINE ON MEANING

It is, or should be, a mere truism that meaning is essential to languagehood. Linguistic items, above a certain level of complexity, *have meanings,* and the simplest meaningful items enter into complexes the meaning of which is some function of the meanings of their constituents and the structure of the complex. This semantic side of language is essential to its distinctive functions, to its serving as a vehicle of thought and communication. Focusing on the latter, it is because a sentence means what it does that it is standardly usable to say something, to perform illocutionary acts[1]—remark that the weather is warming up, predict that the needle will move, or ask someone for a cup of coffee. It is because a word, e.g., 'bell', means what it does that its insertion in a sentence frame, e.g., The———is ringing' will yield a sentence that is usable to say one thing rather than another. Mastery of a language involves knowing the meanings of elementary meaningful units of the language and knowing how the meaning of a complex is a function of that.[2] It is by virtue of this knowledge that a fluent speaker of the language is (1) able to construct a sentence that is standardly usable for saying what he wants to say, and (2) able to understand what another speaker of the language is saying.

This being the case, an essential part of the description of a language is the depiction of its semantic structure—a listing of the meanings of its elementary meaningful units and a specification of the principles by which the meanings of complexes are determined by the meanings of elementary constituents plus structure. Likewise a crucial part of the psychology of speech communication will be the investigation of the processes by which a hearer determines the meaning of what is said. And a central task for philosophical reflection on language is the explication of semantic concepts.

In preparing this paper I have profited greatly from comments by my colleagues, José Benardete, Jonathan Bennett, Thomas McKay, and Philip Peterson, however unsuccessful they have been in their attempts to dislodge me from some of the positions I take therein.

Let's call all this the Standard Picture (SP). SP has been widely accepted by linguists, philosophers, and others who think about language, though sharp divergencies appear when we begin to put flesh on this innocuous looking skeleton. And I believe that SP is deeply rooted in our commonsense picture of language. Against this background Quine stands out as an iconoclast. The details have varied somewhat over the years, but throughout Quine has persistently maintained that there is something fundamentally wrong with the above picture of language and that it will have to be replaced with something better.

In this paper I want to examine Quine's opposition to SP and to assess its force. I want to decide whether his criticisms show the whole edifice to be fundamentally unsound, or whether, at most, they exhibit the need for some remodeling or the removal of unsightly excrescences. I find it useful to class Quine's arguments against SP under five headings: (1) Hypostatization; (2) Explanation; (3) Analyticity; (4) Intensionality; and (5) Indeterminacy. When I first set out to write this paper I expected to give roughly equal treatment to all five, but as things turned out the last demanded such extended discussion that the tail wound up wagging the dog. I have had to curtail the consideration of the first four, and, quantitatively, this has pretty much turned into a paper on semantic indeterminacy. However the ground plan remains as just indicated. It is still a consideration of Quine's opposition to traditional views on meaning, with the indeterminacy thesis given a large (not, I hope, disproportionately large) place.

I

Hypostatization

The first phase of the attack is the rejection of *meanings* as a special realm of entities, and the consequent restriction of semantic concepts to those that do not involve reference to any such entities. This line is more prominent in the late 40s and early 50s, though we find later echoes in, e.g., "Ontological Relativity" (1969, 27).

> The explanatory value of special and irreducible intermediary entities called meanings is surely illusory. (1953, 12.)

> For the theory of meaning a conspicuous question is the nature of its objects: what sort of things are meanings? A felt need for meant entities may derive from an earlier failure to appreciate that meaning and reference are distinct. Once the theory of meaning is sharply separated from the theory of reference, it is a short step to recognizing as the primary business of the theory of meaning simply the synonymy of linguistic forms and the analyticity of statements; meanings themselves, as obscure intermediary entities, may well be abandoned. (1953, 22.)

Sometimes there is a more specific objection to taking meanings to be ideas or other "mental entities".

> An object referred to, named by a singular term or denoted by a general term, can be anything under the sun. Meanings, however, purport to be entities of a special sort: the meaning of an expression is the idea expressed. Now there is considerable agreement among modern linguists that the idea of an idea, the idea of the mental counterpart of a linguistic form, is worse than useless for linguistic science. I think that the behaviorists are right in holding that talk of ideas is bad business even for psychology. The evil of the idea is that its use, like the appeal in Molière to a *virtus dormitiva*, engenders an illusion of having explained something. (1953, 47–8.)

If the meaningfulness of a word consists in its *having a meaning,* what are those meanings words thus have? Since all attempts to answer this question are unsatisfactory in one or another way, we must abandon the supposition that being meaningful consists in being related in a certain way to a special kind of entity called a meaning. We can still, so far as these considerations are concerned, apply semantic concepts to language but only those that can be construed as not involving any reference to meanings.

> What happens in this maneuver is that we fix on one important context of the baffling word 'meaning', namely the context *'alike* in meaning', and resolve to treat this whole context in the spirit of a single word 'synonymous', thus not being tempted to seek meanings as intermediary entities. . . . Does the word have other contexts that should concern linguists? Yes, there is certainly one more—the context 'having meaning'. Here a parallel maneuver is in order: treat the context 'having meaning' in the spirit of a single word, 'significant', and continue to turn our backs on the suppositious entities called meanings. (1953, 48. See also 1953, 11–12)

Elsewhere Quine mentions *analyticity* (1953, p. 22), and *knowing the meaning of an expression* (1975. p. 86) as terms that can be used apart from reference to a realm of meanings.

Now I am wholly in sympathy with Quine's repudiation of a special realm of meanings.[3] But I don't agree as to what we are left with in the way of (applicable) semantic concepts. As the above quotations and others[4] make explicit, Quine supposes that the abandonment of quantification over meanings leaves us only with what we might call "content-free" semantic concepts and facts. We can speak of an expression's being meaningful, of its meaning more or less the same as another, and of someone's knowing what the expression means, without presupposing a realm of meanings. But he thinks that we can no longer speak of *what* a word means, except in the indirect way of specifying another expression that is semantically equivalent to it. The "entitative" style of semantics is the only way of giving substance to the idea that each meaningful constituent of a language means something(s) that can in principle be specified as such.[5] There is no fact of the matter as to *what it is that an expression,*

E, means. It is as if, having forsaken a separate ontological realm of *uses,* one
supposed that all one can say about the use of a tool is that (1) it is useful, (2)
it has the same use as, or a different use from, another tool, and (3) a certain
person does or doesn't know its use. There is no room left for saying what its
use is.

It seems to me, on the contrary, that this central notion of *what E means*
can be dissociated from commitment to a realm of meanings just as surely as
the notions of *having the same meaning* and *having a meaning.* How? By the
same kind of maneuver. Quine cuts 'x and y have the same meaning' loose
from 'x has M_1 and y has M_2, and $M_1 = M_2$'; and he searches for an alternative
construal. In the same spirit, we can cut 'x means . . .'' loose from 'x has
M_1' and search for an alternative construal. Just what construal? This is, I
think, the most central issue in the philosophy of language. To provide an
alternative would be to spell out a theory of my own, and this is not the place
for that. However, just by way of indicating that there are alternatives, let me
suggest the following. Having a certain meaning on the part of a sentence
consists in having a certain illocutionary act potential, being standardly usable
to perform illocutionary acts of a certain type, e.g., predicting that a certain
strike will soon be over or asking someone for a spoon. A word's having a
certain meaning consists in its being usable to affect sentence-meaning (i.e.,
illocutionary act potential) in a certain way. The psycho-social substance of
illocutionary act potential consists in the fact that rules are in force in a lan-
guage-community that specify the conditions under which a sentence may be
uttered.[6] There is no quantification over meanings in any of this. Gricean[7] and
truth-condition accounts[8] can also satisfy this condition. The renunciation of a
realm of meanings does not require abandonment of SP. It merely forecloses
certain elaborations of that picture.[9]

II

Explanation

Another strand in Quine's attack on SP is the claim that it entrusts meaning
with an explanatory responsibility it cannot successfully discharge. Gilbert Harman in his well known "Quine on Meaning and Existence" (1967) takes this
to be *the* central Quinean objection to meaning. Though I take Harman to have
overstated his case, there is no doubt that such charges are to be found in the
corpus. The quotations already given provide a sample. There, and elsewhere,
the charge is directed against meanings as special sorts of entities; and if that
construal of meaning is abandoned the charge, taken *au pied de la lettre,* will
have to be dismissed. But Quine may still feel that SP, even on a non-entitative
construal, supposes the semantic aspect of language to furnish explanations that
are not forthcoming. Let's explore that possibility, taking as our text some

passages from "Mind and Verbal Dispositions" (1975), where the hypostatization issue is not prominent.

> . . . there is an age-old persistent tendency to try to explain and analyse the physical phenomenon of speech by appealing to mind, mental activity, and mental entities: by appealing to thoughts, ideas, meanings. (1975, 83)

> People persist in talking thus of knowing the meaning, and of giving the meaning, and of sameness of meaning, where they could omit mention of meaning and merely talk of understanding an expression, or talk of the equivalence of expressions and the paraphrasing of expressions. They do so because the notion of meaning is felt somehow to *explain* the understanding and equivalence of expressions. We understand expressions by knowing or grasping their meanings; and one expression serves as a translation or paraphrase of another because they mean the same. It is of course spurious explanation, mentalistic explanation at its worst. (1975, 86–7)

This calls for quite a bit of sorting out. Different applications of that protean term 'explanation' are lumped together here. The explanation of speech in terms of mental activity is a sort of causal explanation, or at least it is explanation as an answer to a why–question, a search for a *because*. Whereas explaining understanding E as knowing or grasping the meaning of E, and explaining the correctness of F as a translation of E as amounting to the fact that E and F have the same meaning, is explanation as an answer to a what-question, explanation as saying what something consists of. For reasons that will appear shortly, it is the latter sort of explanatory claim that is essential to SP rather than the former; and so I will start with it.

Since SP takes each word, phrase, and sentence to have one or more meanings, it naturally supposes that equivalence of meaning is to be understood in terms of each expression having the same meaning. And, similarly, to understand an expression is to have a working grasp of what it means. Likewise, to understand what a speaker says I must have a practical, working grasp of what his sentence means in the language, though I must also know in what sense he is using various words, as well as following his references. Thus Quine really is denying some basic commitments of SP. But the grounds he adduces are irrelevant. He objects to these, as we may say, 'analytic' explanations, as 'mental'. But that is to conflate two targets: (1) the account of synonymy in terms of having the same meaning, and (2) a mentalistic account of the latter. SP is committed to the first but not to the second. As I construe the traditional picture, it is neutral between various accounts of what it is for an expression to have a certain meaning. If, contrary to what I believe, a purely behavioral account of this could be given, SP would remain standing, although the form it would thereby take would be surprising to many of its devotees. I myself favor an account of meaning that involves mentalistic concepts, though not in the Lockean form that Quine is thinking of when he condemns meaning as mentalistic. The central mentalistic factors in my illocutionary-act-potential account of meaning are recognitions that a certain utterance is impermissible or out-of-order, more general recognitions that a particular utterance falls under a certain rule, and the intention to be performing an illocutionary act of a certain type. But it is no part of my task here to argue the merits of one account of the nature of meaning over another. The immediate point is that one could accept (1) without being committed to (2).

In fact, there are arguments for (1) that are quite independent of the mentalism-behaviorism squabble. The conceptual priority of *what E means* over *E is synonymous with F* can be seen by noting that a word means something whether or not there is another expression, in that language or elsewhere, with which it is synonymous. It is at least possible that there are meaningful expressions that have no even approximate synonyms. Hence the semantic status of meaningful expressions is not adequately represented by the synonymy relations in which they stand.

In the light of the above, we can see why the question of whether speech is to be explained mentalistically is not crucial for SP. No doubt, SP is committed to the thesis that speech is to be explained in terms of what the speaker means, what the speaker intends to say, and so on. But that leaves open the question whether speaker meaning and intentions can themselves be analysed in terms of behavioral dispositions.

III

Definition

The remaining arguments are explicitly directed by Quine at the kinds of semantic concepts he takes the earlier arguments to have left standing—particularly synonymy, translation, paraphrase, or other putative semantic equivalences. They are designed to cast doubt in one way or another on the viability of such concepts—on the intelligibility, objectivity, or determinacy of these relationships. However if these arguments are cogent they would have equal force against the concept of what an expression means, and I shall feel free to interpret them as so directed.

In the first part of "Two Dogmas of Empiricism", one of the most widely discussed philosophical writings of this century, Quine argues that the concept of cognitive synonymy, which he took to be the somewhat more respectable survivor of the concept of meaning, cannot be adequately defined except in other semantic terms, 'analytic', 'definition', 'semantic rule', or the like. The general suggestion is that this shows some unsuitability, unusability, or even unintelligibility of these terms. They are represented as having failed to pass some test that thoroughly respectable terms would pass.

I won't spend much time on this. Quine should be the last person to expect reductive definition as a ticket of admission for a concept. Such a demand runs directly counter to the attitude he, in company with other 'post-positivist' thinkers, have taken toward the theoretical concepts of science. Perhaps what we have here is another example of the "double standard" for physical science and for semantics, which we shall see exemplified in the arguments for semantic indeterminacy.

IV

Extensionality

Quine's dislike of intensional contexts is well documented. As Chapter VI of 1960 makes abundantly clear, he takes the fact that a certain way of talking involves referential opacity to be a good reason for foreswearing it. We don't find Quine bringing this consideration directly to bear on non-entitative meaning talk, for he doesn't recognize the possibility of such talk. And as for synonymy, other doubts having to do with definability and indeterminacy have dominated the discussion. The objection to the intensional aspect of meaning has been directed, e.g., at propositions, construed as the meanings of eternal sentences (1960, secs. 40–43). Nevertheless, it is clear that meaning–talk, even where it avoids commitment to meanings as a special sort of entity, exhibits referential opacity. Thus 'instructor' means *a person who teaches a course of study,* but 'instructor' does not mean *a person over one year of age who teaches a course of study,* even if the underlined phrases have the same extension. Hence if language is to be purified of referential opacity, meaning-talk will have to go.

For purposes of this paper I will not contest Quine's complaints about intensional contexts. I will agree that, for the reasons he gives, we would be better off if we could get along without them. But this gives us only a motivation to avoid traditional meaning-talk; it gives us no reason to suppose that we can. It gives us no reason for denying that the meaning-aspect of language is among the facts of the world that we must recognize and seek to understand. In this paper I am concentrating on Quine's reasons for that denial.

V

Indeterminacy

A

We come now to the final beast, Quine's most substantial objection to SP, the argument for the indeterminacy of translation, an argument that, if successful, would also establish the indeterminacy of linguistic meaning. This is another of the most widely discussed claims in twentieth century Anglo-American philosophy; but since it has rarely been viewed from the present perspective, we may hope to add something to the already immense literature.

Let's begin by reminding ourselves of the argument. In Chapter II of *Word and Object* Quine explores what there is of objective fact in such relations as synonymy by envisaging a situation of "radical translation", one in which an investigator sets out to translate a wholly unknown language into his native tongue, without any reliance on bilinguals. Quine takes it that this extreme situation will reveal what empirical basis there can be for interlingual synonymy claims, bases that get obscured in more ordinary situations by our unthinking acceptance of traditional alignments. According to Quine, "all the objective data he has to go on are the forces that he sees impinging on the native's surfaces and the observable behavior, vocal and otherwise, of the native" (1960, p. 28). In other terms, "What is before us is the going concern of verbal behavior and its currently observable correlations with stimulation". *(Ibid.)* Quine imagines his jungle linguist as succeeding somehow in identifying native assent and dissent.[10] With these tools he can look for the "stimulus meaning" of various whole utterances by presenting them under various stimulus conditions and noting the conditions under which the informant will assent or dissent; "the *affirmative stimulus meaning* of a sentence such as 'gavagai', for a given speaker" is "the class of all the stimulations . . . that would prompt his assent". (1960, 32) Some sentences can be discovered to possess distinctive stimulus meanings for a given informant, and in some cases these will hold up pretty well throughout the community. These latter may be called observation sentences, and for these we have a firm objective basis for translation; simply pick sentences in the home language that have the same stimulus meaning. On this basis we can also determine how to translate truth-functional connectives. But all the rest of our translational manual will lack adequate evidential basis. The linguist will make projections from his empirical basis in ways that seem intuitively satisfying, but there will always be many alternative ways of doing it that equally well fit the observed or observable facts, equally well conform to the totality of dispositions to speech behavior.[11]

In his presentations of this point Quine has stressed two areas in which translation is underdetermined by the observable facts. First, even with observation sentences, as well as elsewhere, when we come to analyze the sentence into terms we will be confronted with a variety of alternatives, all equally compatible with the data. Given the stimulus meaning of 'gavagai', the linguist is likely to translate it as 'There's a rabbit', and to take some part of 'gavagai' to be the term for rabbits. But the stimulus meaning of 'gavagai' is equally well accounted for by translating it as 'There's a rabbit-stage', 'There's an undetached rabbit part' or 'There's an instance of rabbithood'. We could try to settle this by determining under what conditions the native would make a judgment of same or different gavagai. But the trouble with this is that, lacking independent constraints on the translation of the putative identity connectives, we are free to translate them in a way that supports any of the alternative translations of the term, 'gavagai'. If the native says 'Ik gavagai em ok gavagai' where, as we would say, the native points successively to two different parts of the same rabbit (and assuming that 'ik' is 'this' and 'ok' 'that'), then if we translate 'em' as 'is the same as', then 'gavagai' will be rendered as 'rabbit'. But if we translate 'em' as 'belongs to the same thing as', then 'gavagai' will go into 'undetached rabbit part'. Whereas if 'em' is rendered as 'is a different stage of the same thing as', then 'gavagai' will be 'rabbit-stage'. And the claim is that, with further compensatory adjustments, these alternatives, and more, will equally well fit the whole range of speech dispositions.

The other main example has to do with non-observation sentences that do not have a distinctive stimulus–meaning. In 1970 Quine fastens on an extreme example, the sentences of physical theory. "Insofar as the truth of physical theory is underdetermined by observables, the translation of the foreigner's physical theory is underdetermined by translation of his observation sentences". (1970, 179) It is clear that this argument can be generalized to all non–observation sentences. Here the indeterminacy of translation affects sentences and not just sentence-constituents.

Quine is not content with an epistemological or methodological point about the possibilities of support for translation. He insists that the impossibility of deciding between alternative translations on the basis of observation shows that there is really nothing to be decided. ". . . there is not even. . . an objective matter to be right or wrong about". (1960, 73) "It is indeterminate in principle; there is no fact of the matter." (1969, 38) It is not that the native really does mean 'rabbit' rather than 'rabbit-stage' by 'gavagai', though we can never find this out. His meaning really is indeterminate as between the various alternatives mentioned. Moreover there is nothing special about our (imagined) denizen of the jungle. Why should we suppose that we are capable of more determinate meaning and reference than he? Not only is there the presumption of universal human liability to the indeterminacy here illustrated; the very same arguments can be applied to one's own language, and even to oneself, to one's own idiolect.

On deeper reflection, radical translation begins at home. Must we equate our neighbor's English words with the same strings of phonemes in our own mouths? . . . we can systematically reconstrue our neighbor's apparent references to rabbits as really references to rabbit stages, and his apparent references to formulas as really references to Gödel numbers and vice versa. We can reconcile all this with our neighbor's verbal behavior, by cunningly readjusting our translations of his various connecting predicates so as to compensate for the switch of ontology. In short, we can reproduce the inscrutability of reference at home.

But if there is really no fact of the matter, then the inscrutability of reference can be brought even closer to home than the neighbor's case; we can apply it to ourselves. If it is to make sense to say even of oneself that one is referring to rabbits and formulas and not to rabbit stages and Gödel numbers, then it should make sense equally to say it of someone else. After all, as Dewey stressed, there is no private language. (1969, 46–7)

Thus Quine's argument leads to the conclusion that no one means anything determinate either by any of his terms or by any of his non-observation sentences. And since the constitution of language is ultimately derivative from the speech activity of its users, it follows that no term or non-observation sentence in a language means anything determinate. It is this aspect of the indeterminacy thesis which hits directly at SP and with which I shall be concerned.[12]

Before setting out to defend SP on this point I should say that I do not take it to hold that meanings are perfectly determinate. Semantic indeterminacy has long been recognized in the form of vagueness of degree. As the term 'city' (in contrast to 'town' or 'village') is ordinarily used there is no precise answer to the question, "How many inhabitants does it take to make a city?". More recently other forms of indeterminacy have been explored. Wittgenstein's "family resemblance" is exemplified when there are a number of features that count toward something's being a P, though there is no definite answer to the question, "How many of these features must X possess (to what degree) in order to be a P?". This kind of indeterminacy is a marked feature of many concepts, particularly concepts of cultural forms like 'religion' and 'game'.[13] Waismann (1945) has made us aware of still another form, which he termed 'open texture'. Moreover, SP, as I conceive it, is compatible with what Michael Dummett (1978, 377–8) calls Quine's "inextricability thesis", the view that there is no sharp line between what belongs to the meaning of a word and what belongs to widely shared and firmly held beliefs about what the word denotes. One can still maintain the crucial role of meaning in language, while recognizing that the boundaries of the meaning of an expression are fuzzy in this way too.

Where then is the issue between Quine and SP? It lies in the fact that Quine's indeterminacy argument is designed to establish a degree of indeterminacy that goes far beyond all of the above. The above forms have to do with fuzzy edges or with uncertainty in certain special circumstances. At the core everything is clear cut. But with Quinean indeterminacy there is never any central determinate core. In what would ordinarily be regarded as the most clear-cut and uncontroversial cases, it is still radically indeterminate what is meant. It is this claim that is subversive of the traditional conception of the semantic structure of languages.[14]

B

In discussing Hume's scepticism Thomas Reid wrote:

> A traveller of good judgement may mistake his way, and be unawares led into a wrong track; and while the road is fair before him, he may go on without suspicion and be followed by others; but when it ends in a coal-pit, it requires no great judgement to know that he hath gone wrong, nor perhaps to find what misled him. (1764, Ch. 1, sec. 8.)

Where, then, did Quine lead us astray?

Various critics have challenged Quine's claim that the public data to which he confines himself leave translation as undetermined as he supposes.[15] I myself think that Quine has failed to explore ways in which we might use such data to decide between alternatives of the sorts he considers. But rather than add my bit to the criticisms just mentioned, I shall pursue a different tack. It seems to me that there are considerations of a sort quite different from those Quine allows that radically alter the prospects for semantic determinacy. Let me explain.

Here is the skeleton of the indeterminacy argument, construed as an argument for indeterminacy of meaning. 'E_1' stands for an expression to which Quine applies his indeterminacy thesis.

1. There will be a large number of alternative translations of expression E_1 of language L_1 into expressions of language L_2, all of which equally well account for the speech dispositions of all speakers concerned, as well as any other relevant observational data.
2. Therefore there can be no sufficient reason for regarding one of these translations as correct.
3. Therefore there is no objectively correct translation.
4. Therefore it is impossible to determine what E_1 means.
5. Therefore there is no fact as to what E_1 means.
6. Therefore E_1 does not mean anything determinate.

I shall initially attack the move from 3. to 4., suggesting that it looks plausible only if we ignore other resources for determining what E_1 means.[16] Later I will argue that a recognition of these resources will also enable us to break the link between 1. and 2. But the resources in question can best be introduced in connection with the move from 3. to 4.

Let's reflect for a moment on why it seems so absurd to say that because we are irretrievably stumped in fastening on a unique translation for 'gavagai' by observing the native's behavior and its circumstances, we must therefore conclude that the native doesn't mean anything definite by 'gavagai', and, by extension, that we don't mean anything definite by 'rabbit'. Clearly, it is because it seems obvious that *I* know what I mean by 'rabbit' and other words in my language.[17] *I* know that, e.g., I use 'rabbit' to denote complete enduring organisms like that, rather than the parts or stages of such organisms or the kinds to which they belong.[18] My assurance as to what I mean by 'rabbit' does not rest on what I or anyone else is able to do in translating one language into another, much less on what is possible by way of radical translation. Even if everything Quine says about that were correct, I would still know what 'rabbit' means in my language. I know this just by virtue of being a master of my language. Knowing this is an essential part of what it is to *have* that language; knowing this is required for being able to use that language as a vehicle of thought and means of communication. If I didn't know such things as that 'rabbit' denotes complete organisms rather than parts or stages of complete organisms, I wouldn't be able to engage in communication in the way I do. I wouldn't know what sentence to use to remark that a rabbit just ran across the front lawn, and I wouldn't know whether another speaker had just remarked that rather than something else. A natural language is, *inter alia,* a system for performing acts of these sorts, and mastery of a language involves knowing how to use it to do so. And how could my mastery of the language put me in a position to do these things unless it involved my knowing what various expressions mean in the language, to a degree of determinacy far above that allowed for by the indeterminacy thesis? The resource Quine has ignored is the knowledge of the semantics of the language one has just by virtue of being a fluent speaker of the language. Since there is this kind of knowledge, the possibility of determining *what* 'rabbit' means cannot depend solely on what can be gleaned from the observation of behavior and the circumstances of behavior.

Before dealing with a Quinean retort to all this, let me make more explicit just what I am and am not claiming. For this purpose I will need two distinctions. First there is the distinction between speaker meaning, what someone means by what she says, and linguistic meaning, what expressions mean in the language. Second there is the distinction between an 'implicit' and an 'explicit' knowledge of meaning or of anything else.

(A) Let's begin with speaker meaning. What is clearest and most indubitable is the kind of "practical" or "working" knowledge of what one means by what one says when in the heat of action. Reporting that a rabbit ran across the lawn is normally an intentional action, one that I meant to perform. But I couldn't be deliberately and intentionally making *that* report without, in an important sense, knowing what I am saying, which includes knowing what I meant by the words I am speaking. I couldn't be making a normal report of that sort, in uttering 'A rabbit ran across the lawn', without realizing that by 'rabbit' I mean the complete organism, rather than parts or stages thereof, any more than I can be intentionally using a hammer to knock in a nail without realizing what I am using the hammer for. If I didn't know what I was doing,

I wasn't doing it intentionally. This *implicit*, "agent's" knowledge must be distinguished from the reflective *explicit* knowledge of what one is saying or what one means, where the latter is, paradigmatically, formulated in so many words. Obviously, intentionally saying something does not necessarily involve my saying, even to myself, what it is that I am saying. If it did, an infinite regress would ensue and we would never get anything said. Hence, I don't want to claim that in every intentional illocutionary act there is an explicit, reflective knowledge of what is said and of what one means by the linguistic resources deployed. However I do wish to claim that it takes only a moment's reflection to convert the implicit into the explicit. For the knowledge of what I mean is already "conceptualised". No extra intellectual labor is required to schematize a manifold of experience. I have already wielded the concept of a rabbit in reporting that a rabbit ran across the lawn. All that is needed is to direct attention to what is already there. It is not like motor skills, where I may totally lack the linguistic-conceptual equipment to specify what I am doing. I can execute complicated manuevers on skates without having the conceptual resources to characterize them; but I can't mean something (express a certain concept) by 'rabbit' without having the conceptual resources to specify *what* is meant. That is not to say that I will necessarily be in a position to say in other words what I mean; perhaps 'rabbit' is the only term I have to formulate this. Still less am I suggesting that fluency carries with it an ability to answer philo-sophical questions about the concepts expressed or about the items satisfying those concepts. The kind of knowledge of the meaning of 'rabbit' I am ascrib-ing to the fluent speaker does not include knowledge of how physical object concepts are related to phenomenal concepts; and one can have this kind of knowledge of the meaning of 'true' without being able to tell whether sen-tences, propositions, or statements, are bearers of truth–value. But the fluent speaker *will* be able to choose between alternatives of the sorts presented by Quine. My working grasp of what I mean will enable me to be quite sure, and justifiably so, that I was talking about a whole organism of the sort so called rather than about one of its parts.

(B) However we are not yet home free. The knowledge we appealed to in criticizing the step from (3) to (4) in the indeterminacy argument is not just knowledge of what A meant by a particular utterance of 'rabbit', not just speaker meaning, but linguistic meaning, knowledge of what 'rabbit' means in the language. Here I wish to claim that this further knowledge is equally avail-able to the fluent speaker on reflection. As a fluent speaker of the language I am, normally, making use of the resources the language provides, semantic as well as phonemic and syntactic. Therefore I only have to reflect on one or more typical performances with 'rabbit' to become explicitly aware of one thing 'rabbit' means in the language.[19] To deny that I can become explicitly aware of what words mean in English by reflecting on my typical employments of those words in communication, is to deny that I am a fluent speaker of English. If I do enjoy that status I *ipso facto* possess that capacity.

(C) The *explicit* knowledge of linguistic meaning that, according to (B), is available to the fluent speaker as such, will undoubtedly be unsatisfactory for various theoretical purposes. I may not be able to say in any revealing way what 'rabbit' means; I may not be able to supply an exact synonym. I am not guaranteed an adequate vocabulary for talking about meanings. Moreover this knowledge is piecemeal, dealing with particular expressions one at a time. It does not carry with it knowledge of the *structure* of the language, semantic or otherwise.[20] But it does suffice to decide between the sorts of alternatives Quine poses; it does serve to resolve radical Quinean indeterminacy.

(D) These various levels of knowledge afford ample scope for mistake in particular cases. Even if one can't be mistaken in one's practical knowledge of what one means while in the act of speech, this by no means implies that the speaker is infallible when he makes this explicit on reflection. Still less am I immune to error when I reflect on what a word means in the language. (I may make an unfortunate choice of a supposedly normal employment.) But the occasional error is quite compatible with the normal felicitous operation of the cognitive faculties in question.

What can I say to one, like Quine, who will doubt the existence of this kind of knowledge? I can ask him to look within his own breast, but I daresay that when Quine enters most intimately into what he calls himself, he will always stumble on some particular behavioral disposition. I can allege, correctly as I believe, that knowing the meanings of words in the language (to a degree of determinacy far beyond what Quine's thesis allows) is essentially involved in the very concept of knowing a language. He might agree, but then contend that such a concept has no application to the way actual human beings are situated vis-a-vis actual languages. And, indeed, Quine's conception of a language as ''the complex of present dispositions to verbal behavior'' (1960, 27) is quite different from the one that underlies the above claim.

Faced with such an impasse I am inclined to go transcendental. Implicit knowledge of what one is saying, and of what one means by the words one is using to say it, is necessarily presupposed whenever one sets out to say anything significant. This can be verified by trying to preface a putative saying with a denial of the alleged presupposition; that denial will nullify any claim to be saying something in what follows. Consider: ''I don't know what I'm saying, but your premises really presuppose the conclusion''. Or ''I don't know what I mean by 'premises', but . . .'' Or ''I don't know whether by 'premises' I mean the propositions expressed by the sentences you uttered at t_1, or the propositions expressed by the sentences derived from those by the following permutations, ... but . . . .''. Clearly those initial disavowals make hash out of any pretensions to be making any comment on the argument under discussion. When Quine writes "In 'I saw the lion', the singular term 'the lion' is presumed to refer to some one lion, distinguished from its fellows for speaker and hearer by previous sentences or attendant circumstances" (1960, 112), intending to make a reasonably definite assertion, he presupposes that he means something fairly definite by 'singular term', 'sentence', 'speaker', and so on; and he presupposes that he knows what he means by these terms. Since I can't say anything without presupposing that I know what I mean by the words I use, I can't suppose that I, from time to time, make significant statements without committing myself to the proposition that I, from time to time, know what I mean by the words I use. More boldly, one can't suppose that human beings make reasonably definite statements from time to time without thereby committing oneself to the proposition that human beings, from time to time, know what they mean by the words they use. Thus one who is prepared to accept the existence of intelligible discourse is in no position to deny that speakers frequently know what they mean by the words they use. This shows that everyone is, in practice, committed to the reality of the first level of semantic knowledge I distinguished, viz., one's implicit knowledge of what one means when in the act of speech. I can then use the considerations deployed earlier to argue that since we are all committed to the first step, we should all recognize that explicit knowledge of what words mean in one's language is available to the fluent speaker on reflection.[21]

A realist like myself will not suppose that the practical necessity of a presupposition renders it true. It is logically possible that we are always mistaken in supposing that we know what we mean by the words we use. The point of noting the presupposition is that none of us who speak, i.e., none of us, is in a position to take this possibility seriously. Furthermore the necessity of the presupposition obtains only in the heat of the moment. Today I am free to question whether I knew what I meant by 'rabbit' yesterday; and I am always free to question whether my colleagues know what they mean by, e.g., 'abstract entity'. It would be capricious to doubt these things without specific reason for doing so, but we sometimes have such reasons. In any event, the basic point is that our position does not imply that speakers *always* know what they mean by the words they use.

D

Now let's turn to what Quine might say about these claims. He may well level the charge of "mentalism". Let's consider that for a moment. If to say that my position is "mentalistic" is simply to say that it recognizes semantic facts that are not facts about behavioral dispositions, and knowledge of semantic facts that is not knowledge of behavioral dispositions, then this is indeed a correct characterization of my position, but it remains to be shown that it is a defect. I cannot be charged with the weakness of mentalistic explanations, for I have proffered no explanations. Nor can I be charged with explicating meaning in terms of "ideas" bouncing around in the "field of consciousness", nor with explicating knowledge of meaning in terms of introspective awareness of such "mental entities". My conception of the knowledge of meaning that is the speechright of every fluent speaker is not like that at all. My practical knowledge of what I mean by the words I use is like the practical knowledge of whatever I am doing intentionally, e.g., opening a jar. There is little temptation to suppose that my knowledge that I am opening a jar, knowledge that accrues to me just by virtue of doing so rather than by virtue of watching myself doing it and trying to figure out what I am doing, consists in introspective awareness of ideas, images, feelings, or the like. I don't want to suggest that I agree with Quine in decrying mentalistic explanations, introspective knowledge, and so on; quite the contrary. However we need not go into that. The charge of "mentalism", levelled against my claims for the fluent speaker's knowledge of his own language, is simply a red herring.

A charge deserving of more serious discussion is that the commitment to knowledge of meaning that is not knowledge of behavioral dispositions conflicts with the facts of language learning.

> Language is a social art. In acquiring it we have to depend entirely on intersubjectively available cues as to what to say and when. Hence there is no justification for collating linguistic meanings, unless in terms of men's dispositions to respond overtly to socially observable stimulations. (1960, ix)

> Meanings are, first and foremost, meanings of language. Language is a social art which we all acquire on the evidence solely of other people's overt behavior under publicly recognizable circumstance. Meanings, therefore, those very models of mental entities, end up as grist for the behaviorist's mill. (1969, 26–27)

Here Quine is seeking to show what can be learned in learning a language. But is the conclusion (a) that the upshot is the *acquisition* of behavioral dispositions, or (b) that the upshot is *knowledge* of behavioral dispositions? Quine certainly thinks that learning a language is, most basically, the *acquisition* of behavioral dispositions, and he presumably does not think that fluent speakers always, or typically, have even implicit knowledge of those dispositions. But, presumably, he would allow that it is possible for a speaker to acquire such knowledge. So, since the issue is as to the most that can be learned in learning a language, let's work with (b). Then the argument can be set out as:

1. In acquiring a language, one has nothing to go on but the overt speech of others and observable features of the situation of utterance.

2. Therefore, all one can come to know, in learning a language, is what utterances speakers of the language are disposed to make under what observable circumstances.

3. Therefore, by virtue of having learned a language one has no knowledge of meanings or anything else that goes beyond knowledge of speech dispositions.[22]

The vulnerable transition is from (1) to (2). There Quine makes a strong and questionable assumption as to what human beings can come to know from a given body of data. It assumes that the most one can learn from observing behavior under certain circumstances is a set of truths about dispositions, the actualization of which involves behavior of that sort in circumstances of those sorts. That is, it assumes the impossibility of justifiably going from the observed data to a system of explanatory hypotheses that posits entities quite different from those observed and that attributes to those entities features quite different from those observed entities. That is, it assumes that nothing like what goes on in the most highly developed sciences can be involved in learning a language. In the absence of further reasons for making this assumption I think that it can be safely ignored.[23]

E

My criticism, based on an appeal to the fluent speaker's knowledge of his own language, was originally directed at the transition from 3. to 4. of the indeterminacy argument as formulated above:

3. There is no objectively correct translation of S_1.
4. Therefore, it is impossible to determine what S_1 means.

The claim has been that even if an outsider cannot, in principle, determine a correct translation of S_1, it doesn't follow that there is no way for anyone to determine what S_1 means. On the contrary, a fluent speaker of the language *ipso facto* knows what S_1 means. This response, if adequate, blocks the move from the indeterminacy of translation to the impossibility of determining what an expression means; but it leaves the former standing. Now I can point out that the same appeal to inside knowledge can defeat the claim of indeterminacy of translation as well. More specifically, it can block the move from

1. Except for observation sentences, there will be a large number of alternative translations of expression E_1 of a language L_1 into expressions of language L_2, all of which equally well account for the speech dispositions of all speakers concerned, as well as for other relevant observational data.

to

    2. Therefore there can be no sufficient reason for regarding one of these translations as correct.

The point is that what 1. says is that no such reason is available to the outsider, to one who must decide on the basis of observing the behavior of fluent speakers of L_1, without being one himself, without himself being in a position to use L_1 as a vehicle of thought and communication. A particular speaker of L_2 suffers from this incapacity just because of the contingent fact that he is not a master of L_1. But he can learn L_1, and then he is master of both; and others can join him in this enterprise. Persons who satisfy this hardly extravagant condition possess resources for settling the translation question that are lacking to those who do not. They can use their insider's knowledge of what expressions in each language mean. If they have this insider's grasp of the meaning of both 'gavagai' and 'rabbit', they can use that grasp to determine whether they mean the same, or if fastidiousness dictates, to determine whether they mean approximately the same. How can it be maintained that A knows both what 'gavagai' means and what 'rabbit' means but can't determine whether they are at least approximately the same in meaning? If he has the capacity to use both expressions as vehicles of thought and communication, and has the capacity to reflect on how he is using them, he can surely determine, by reflection, whether he is making the same use of both.[24] More specifically, he will be in a position to answer Quinean questions about both—whether it denotes the complete organism or a part or a stage thereof, and so on. If all relevant questions were answered in the same way for each, it would have been determined that the one can be used to translate the other. The indeterminacy argument at most establishes indeterminacy of translation for so long as it remains radical.[25]

VI

We are now in a position to delineate the most fundamental opposition between Quine's perspective on language and the one developed in section V. For Quine there can be no facts about a language that cannot be established by an outside investigator, formulating hypotheses and testing them against publicly observable data, whether or not the investigator is a fluent speaker of the language in question. For the position I was developing in section V, on the other hand, a fluent speaker's mastery of a language gives him special access to certain features of the language, including semantic features. Whether or not all these features could be ascertained by an outside investigator, the fluent speaker has a different way of ascertaining them, a way that does not involve consciously formulating hypotheses and testing them against observed data. From this perspective one cannot show that there can be no such objective fact about language as F just by showing that F could not be established by an outside investigator.

Thus at the deepest level the opposition is not between mentalism and behaviorism, private and public, or rationalism and empiricism. It is rather a methodological issue between inside and outside, between a participant stance and a spectator stance. Quine requires that any fact about a language be available to an investigator who approaches the language purely as a spectator (albeit an active inquiring spectator). Being *au courant* with the social form in question is to count as nothing, epistemically. It gives one no edge in principle over the non-participant investigator,[26] though, of course, it makes one an indispensable source of data. This opposition is a special case of the familiar opposition in the methodology of the social sciences between those who hold that, e.g., there is a certain knowledge or understanding of a culture that is available only to participants, and those who regard such a view as ''unscientific''.

What should we say about this opposition? Of course I have already provided some reasons for supposing that we do all have special access to semantic facts about languages in which we are fluent. And since Quine's ''spectator'' methodology, and especially its use to determine what there is, presupposes that this is not the case, these are also reasons for rejecting his position. But apart from all that, is there anything we can say to recommend or condemn one or the other of these methodological stances? I shall conclude by making one suggestion.

One aspect of Quine's position is what might be called Explicitism, a get-it-all-out-in-the-open attitude. Remember that Quine's basic principle is that there can be no facts that could not be discovered by the use of a method of empirical hypothesis testing in which everything is consciously and explicitly formulated: observed data, alternative hypotheses, background theories, reasons for regarding one alternative as superior to another, and so on. Whatever is hidden can be revealed. Nothing can properly command our assent unless we can fully spell it out and make a conscious judgment on its worth. Now there are various indications that we human beings are just not constructed in such a way as to make this a reasonable attitude. Much of our knowledge is acquired by implicit unconscious processes that we are not capable of making fully explicit. Much of our perceptual knowledge of the environment, e.g., is the fruit of unconscious information processing, and although we can envisage a being that would do all that by conscious inference, it is very dubious that *we* are capable of that. If we were to renounce all this, on methodological principle, we would be much the poorer and, perhaps, unable to survive.

An analogous point can be made at a higher level. We can critically examine a certain method of hypothesis testing, or a certain practice of belief formation, only by using some other practice to do so, a practice that either has not itself passed a critical scrutiny, or has done so by our use of still another practice. It is clear that unless we argue in a circle or have carried out an infinite number of such critical examinations, we can't carry out an injunction to use no method that has not survived a critical scrutiny. At any point we must be using methods that we simply acquiesce in. We can achieve a reflective justification of some of our methods only on condition of using others without any such explicit checking of credentials. If this process is going to work, it must be that we are endowed with tendencies to engage in certain reliable practices without explicit reasons for doing so.[27]

Finally, to come closer to home, it appears that we each learn our first language by unconscious processes which there is no reason to think we human beings, constituted as we are, could make fully explicit. Even if Quine is right in supposing that no one meaning assignment or translation schema is best supported by behavioral evidence in a process of explicit hypothesis testing, still the unconscious cognitive processes by which we acquire our first languages might involve procedures for reaching unique results from behavioral data.

In any event, considerations of the sort illustrated in the last three paragraphs strongly suggest that Quine's explicitism is unsuited to the human condition, and that if anyone really could succeed in foreswearing any knowledge that could not be acquired and validated by explicit conscious processes, he might suffer the traditional penalty for overweening pride, perishing in proud isolation from the surrounding nature that offers him succor, but not on those terms.

WILLIAM P. ALSTON

DEPARTMENT OF PHILOSOPHY
SYRACUSE UNIVERSITY
APRIL 1982

NOTES

1. For an indication of the way in which I am using the term 'illocutionary act' see Alston (1977).

2. This is practical, working knowledge. It does not include an ability to say what words mean, much less the ability to articulate a systematic account of the semantic structure of the language.

3. For a general critique of the "entitative" way of construing meaning see Alston (1963).

4. 1953, 11–12, 49, 56 ff.; 1978.

5. This has to be qualified somewhat in the light of the notion of stimulus meaning developed in *Word and Object* (1960, 31–46). This gives Quine, in principle, a way of saying something about what an observation sentence means. But, as Quine notes, "stimulus meaning as defined falls short in various ways of one's intuitive demands on 'meaning' as undefined". (1960, 39) And in any event, this device extends only to observation sentences. With respect to the full scope of linguistic expressions, the judgment in the text holds.

6. For a sketch of such a theory see Alston (1977). I am completing a book-length presentation of the theory.

7. See Grice (1957, 1968, 1969); Schiffer (1972); Bennett (1976).

8. Davidson (1967); Platts (1979).

9. In holding that we can recognize objective semantic facts as to what an expression, E, means, without construing them in terms of a relation between E and a meaning, I do not mean to suggest that there are no unsolved problems as to how to specify or articulate these facts. I hope that progress will be made on this in the course of the development of linguistic science, the quarter to which one should look for such progress.

10. In Davidson and Hintikka (1969, 312) Quine acknowledges that this identification is itself underdetermined by the empirical evidence, and hence that what depends on it, e.g., assignment of stimulus meanings, is itself indeterminate, relative to the evidence. In my discussion I shall follow the original exposition in (1960), where indeterminacy is represented as entering at a later stage. There will be troubles enough with that version.

11. Although Quine does not make this sufficiently explicit, the "totality of speech dispositions" includes dispositions to utter S_1 upon hearing S_2 uttered by oneself or another, where other sensory stimulation is playing no role. The question of whether dispositions of this sort place significant constraints on translation deserves much more discussion than Quine gives it.

12. Since, by the time he came to develop the indeterminacy thesis, Quine had already disposed of "meaning" to his own satisfaction, he formulates his thesis in terms of translation (paraphrase or synonymy), and in terms of reference. But it is quite clear that if one takes the concept of meaning to be otherwise in order, the arguments, insofar as well grounded, do support a thesis of indeterminacy of meaning.

13. See the discussion in Alston (1964, 87–90), where this is called "combination-of-conditions vagueness".

14. Quine seeks to mitigate the paradoxicality of this conclusion by allowing that even though 'rabbit' does not have any unique correct translation *absolutely,* it may be ascribed a unique translation, *relative* to a certain scheme of translation into another language. (1969, 48–55.) I cannot see that this is of much help. Considering the facts that (a) the choice of scheme is arbitrary and (b) the term that is chosen as the translation is itself equally indeterminate in meaning, this does nothing to reduce the semantic indeterminacy of the original term.

15. See, e.g., J. Hintikka, "Behavioral Criteria of Radical Translation", in Davidson & Hintikka (1969); Bennett (1976, 257–264).

16. I will not challenge the verificationist move from 4. to 5., vulnerable though I consider it to be, since SP is committed not just to there being reasonably determinate semantic facts, but also to our being able to ascertain them.

17. Let me remind the reader that I am not claiming that what I mean by 'rabbit' is completely determinate in *every* respect. There are borderline cases, there is the kind of indefiniteness Waismann called 'open texture', and so on.

18. Quine will no doubt say that this amounts only to the point that the sentence 'Rabbits are complete enduring organisms' is stimulus-analytic for me and 'Rabbits are parts of complete enduring organisms' is stimulus-contradictory for me. But, as will appear more explicitly in the sequel, I am not talking about relations between expressions in my idiolect. I am using these words to bring out to anyone who understands them (as we all do really) some of what I know about what I mean by 'rabbit'.

19. We would be grievously oblivious to the social character of language were we to suppose, as some thinkers do, that the only thing available to me on reflection is the semantics of my "idiolect", facts about what *I* mean by words; and that to find out anything about what words mean in the language, the language of many others as well as myself, I must rely on additional evidence garnered from observation of the behavior of other speakers. The knowledge I have by virtue of my mastery of my language is knowledge of a socially shared system, not just knowledge of some private possession of mine. This contention must be balanced by the point that the knowledge of my language I possess just by virtue of being a fluent speaker does not, in itself, enable me to know which other persons share that language, what its geographical, historical, or political extent is, and so on. To know whether you are also a master of my language I will have to observe you in action. My account of this observation would be very different from Quine's. It would feature, e.g., my noting whether or not we can successfully communicate in my language. But that is a further problem.

20. I am neither denying nor affirming the Chomskyan thesis that a fluent speaker *ipso facto* possesses a complete *implicit* knowledge of the grammar of the language. I am merely pointing out that we do not have the capacity to make all that explicit just on reflecting, though we do have the capacity to become explicitly aware of various features of what various expressions of the language mean.

21. To keep our bearings straight, let's note that the thesis of the last paragraph (M) is to be distinguished from the thesis (N) that a reasonably determinate meaning of the words used is a necessary condition of saying something reasonably determinate. (N) was implicitly appealed to in pointing out earlier that the indeterminacy thesis implies that no one is ever saying anything determinate. (N) is, I would judge, too obviously true to need argument or even explicit notice. (M) goes beyond (N) by bringing in considerations of the speaker's *knowledge* of his meanings. It makes the bolder claim that in supposing myself to be saying something fairly definite, I *ipso facto* suppose myself to *know* what I mean by the words I use. (M) is (N) in second intention.

22. My position will not be incompatible with 3. *if* it is possible for a speaker to have a special, "agential" access to her own speech dispositions, *and* it is possible for the knowledge of meaning speakers actually possess to be construable as knowledge of speech dispositions. But even if the first conjunct is true, the second is dubious at best. At least this much is clear. If Quine is right as to the degree of determinacy of meaning on a behavioral interpretation, and if I am right as to the degree of determinacy with which fluent speakers know what they mean, then what they know cannot be their own speech dispositions. Hence I shall proceed on the assumption that 3. does contradict my position.

23. This judgment is reinforced by the existence of a powerful challenge to this assumption in the work of Noam Chomsky and people influenced by him. See, e.g., Chomsky (1965, 1969, 1972).

24. This is not to say that it is impossible for two bilinguals to disagree on a translation. I find it hard to imagine them exhibiting so radical a disagreement as that between 'rabbit' and 'rabbit stage' as a translation of 'gavagai'; but my thesis should not be taken to rule out the possibility even of that. The general availability of knowl-

edge of a certain kind is quite compatible with disagreement, and even with the occasional radical disagreement. All normal human beings get quite a lot of perceptual knowledge about their immediate physical environment, but sometimes there is even radical disagreement between people about what transpired right under their noses.

25. To be sure, Quine, in his initial presentation of the argument in *Word and Object,* acknowledged that the linguist might "go bilingual", but denied that this would put him in an epistemically superior position.

> Thus suppose, unrealistically to begin with, that in learning the native language he had been able to simulate the infantile situation to the extent of keeping his past knowledge of languages out of account. Then, when as a bilingual he finally turns to his project of a jungle-to-English manual, he will have to project analytical hypotheses much as if his English personality were the linguist and his jungle personality the informant; the differences are just that he can introspect his experiments instead of staging them, that he has his notable inside track on non-observational occasion sentences, and that he will tend to feel his analytical hypotheses as obvious analogies when he is aware of them at all. Now of course the truth is that he would not have strictly simulated the infantile situation in learning the native language, but would have helped himself with analytical hypotheses all along the way; thus the elements of the situation would in practice be pretty inextricably scrambled. (1960, 71)

This is, no doubt, the way the bilingual situation looks from a Quinean perspective on language. Since a language is just a set of dispositions to verbal behavior under external stimulation, the bilingual has essentially the same task as does the monolingual of matching one set of behavioral dispositions with the other, and building airy castles out beyond that. His advantage is only that of being investigator and investigated inside one skin. But from the perspective I have been developing things look quite different. The bilingual has the unique advantage of being able to set two pieces of inside knowledge of meaning side by side and determining how well they match. This is radically different from anything that is possible from the outsider's standpoint, to which Quine confines even the insider.

26. To be fair to Quine, we must stress the *"in principle"*. Quine does recognize that being a fluent speaker of a language involves knowledge of the language, or at least involves being in a favorable position to get knowledge of the language. It is just that he thinks one still acquires this knowledge by basically the same processes that are available to the non-participant.

27. For more on this point see my articles, "The Role of Reason in the Regulation of Belief", in *Rationality in the Calvinian Tradition,* ed. H. Hart, J. Van Der Hoeven, and N. Wolterstorff (Lanham, MD: University Press of America, 1983) pp. 135–170, and "Epistemic Circularity", forthcoming in *Phil. Phen. Res.*

REFERENCES

Alston, W.P. (1963) "The Quest for Meanings," *Mind* 72.
———. (1964) *Philosophy of Language.* Englewood Cliffs, NJ: Prentice-Hall.
———. (1977) "Sentence Meaning and Illocutionary Act Potential," *Phil. Exchange* 2.

Bennett, J. (1976) *Linguistic Behavior*. Cambridge: Cambridge University Press.

Chomsky, N. (1965) *Aspects of the Theory of Syntax*. Cambridge, MA: MIT Press.

———. (1969) "Linguistics and Philosophy," in S. Hook (ed), *Language and Philosophy*, New York: New York University Press.

———. (1972) *Language and Mind*. New York: Harcourt, Brace, Jovanovich.

Davidson, D. (1967) "Truth and Meaning," *Synthese* 7.

———. (1979) "The Inscrutability of Reference," *Southwestern Journ. Philos.* 10.

Davidson, D. & Hintikka, J. (eds.) (1969) *Words and Objections: Essays on the Work of W.V. Quine*. Dordrecht: Reidel.

Dummett, M. (1978) *Truth and Other Enigmas*. Cambridge MA: Harvard University Press.

Field, H. (1974) "Quine and the Correspondence Theory," *Phil. Rev.* 83.

———. (1975) "Conventionalism and Instrumentalism in Semantics," *Nous* 9.

Grice, H.P. (1957) "Meaning," *Phil. Rev.* 66.

———. (1968) "Utterer's Meaning, Sentence-Meaning, and Word-Meaning," *Found. Lang.* 4.

———. (1969) "Utterer's Meaning and Intentions," *Phil. Rev.* 78.

Harman, G. (1967) "Quine on Meaning and Existence, " *Rev. Metaph.* 78.

Platts, M.B. (1979) *Ways of Meaning*. London: Routledge and Kegan Paul.

Quine, W.V. (1953) *From a Logical Point of View*. Cambridge MA: Harvard University Press.

———. (1960) *Word and Object*. Cambridge MA: MIT Press.

———. (1969) *Ontological Relativity and Other Essays*. New York: Columbia University Press.

———. (1970) "On the Reasons for the Indeterminacy of Translation," *Journ. Philos.* 67.

———. (1975) "Mind and Verbal Dispositions," in Samuel Guttenplan (ed), *Mind and Language,* Oxford: Clarendon Press.

———. (1978) "Use and Its Place in Meaning," *Erkenntnis* 13.

Reid, T. (1764) *An Inquiry into the Human Mind*. Chicago: University of Chicago Press, 1970.

Schiffer, S. (1972) *Meaning*. Oxford: Clarendon Press.

Tolman, E.C. (1932) *Purposive Behavior in Animals and Men*. New York: Appleton-Century-Crofts.

Waismann, F. (1945) "Verifiability," *Proc. Arist. Soc. Suppl. Vol.* 19.

REPLY TO WILLIAM P. ALSTON

Hypostasis of meanings is a red herring. I keep urging that we could happily hypostasize meanings if we could admit synonymy. We could simply identify meanings with the classes of synonyms. Ayer made the same point long ago, and so did Russell. What then of the three quotations in which Alston takes me to be opposing the hypostasis of meanings? The point of each of those passages is that the *prior* assumption of an *unexplained* domain of objects called meanings is no way to explain synonymy or anything else. Synonymy, not hypostasis, is the rub. Given synonymy, a domain of meanings is trivially forthcoming for whatever good it may do.

Alston proposes that we "cut 'x means . . .' loose from 'x has M_1' and search for an alternative construal." If he feels he can make sense of synonymy prior to that search, then there is no point in searching or in cutting loose; M_1 is already forthcoming as an equivalence class of synonyms. Therefore let us assume rather that he does not feel that he can make prior sense of synonymy, and that he seeks a construal of 'x means . . .' instead of that. What he comes up with, in his present brief allusion to his work in progress, is "the conditions under which a sentence may be uttered."

I can go along with this. I am strong for translation, in which I have been much involved in a practical way; strong also for lexicography; and strong for theoretical semantics, when responsibly pursued. The "conditions under which a sentence may be uttered" constitute the proper focus, in my opinion, of all these pursuits. It would be reasonable even to refer to those conditions collectively as the *meaning* of the sentence; and I would be the last to complain on the score of hypostasis.

The synonymy relation gains no support from *this* notion of meaning. The reason is that, on this version of meaning, no two sentences can have the same meaning; for no two sentences are wholly alike in their conditions of utterance. A sentence can be uttered only to the exclusion of all other sentences, and hence only under conditions not totally shared, if we grant determinism. To make sense of synonymy we would have to say which of the conditions is to count as semantically relevant; and this is the whole of the synonymy problem.

Abandoning synonymy as a will-o'-the-wisp, I recognize with Alston that the business of semantics is the exploration and analysis of "the conditions under which a sentence may be uttered." Such studies may be expected to proceed the better when not burdened with the preconception of an undefined synonymy relation, or of meanings of a kind relevant to synonymy.

The preconception of synonymy springs, indeed, from the uncritical old ontology of ideas, the museum myth; hence my protest against the *prior* assumption of an *unexplained* domain of meanings. But synonymy is the operative side of the confusion, and it is what my thesis of the indeterminacy of translation is all about.

Essential features of what Alston calls the Standard Picture survive the scouting of synonymy. The meanings of the wholes may still be said, metaphorically, to be built from the meanings of the parts. In soberer phrase, the lexicographer's word-by-word entries are clauses in a recursive characterization of the conditions of utterance of sentences. This outline needs filling in, and I have done so to some extent in "Vagaries of Definition", "Use and its Place in Meaning", and "Cognitive Meaning".

I have been celebrating my agreement with Alston, but to my regret it abruptly terminates. Not content just to define meaning as "the conditions under which a sentence may be uttered," and leave it at that, he goes on to explain synonymy as sameness of such meaning. He thereby slurs over the problem of settling what conditions to count as semantically relevant and what ones not, which is the whole substance of the synonymy problem.

He wrongly ascribes my doubts about synonymy to an irreducible aversion to the mental. My aversion, within its limits, has a reason: the want of intersubjective checkpoints. It is Wittgenstein's rejection of private language. It is this, and not mentality as such, that disqualifies any irreducibly intuitive notion of meaning or synonymy or semantic relevance. Just give me checkpoints; I ask but little here below.

Alston notes an asymmetry in my attitudes toward physics and semantics; I assume "that underdetermination is compatible with truth in the case of physics but not in the case of semantics." My position amounts to no more, he thinks, than saying "that lexicography is not part of physics, hardly startling news to the practitioners of either discipline."

In my view, as in his, the underdetermination of both disciplines is quite on a par methodologically. The asymmetry lies elsewhere than in methodology, as I shall try to explain. It may be helpful to forget about theoretical physics; I can express my point in another way.

We can agree, I hope, that one's command of language, one's understanding of language, one's dispositions to respond, indeed one's very thoughts, cannot differ from one moment to another without some difference, however undetectable, in the states of one's physical organism. Call the doctrine materialism or psychophysical parallelism; either will do. Now the relation between the interchangeable but incompatible manuals of translation that I have postulated is that they accord with exactly the same states of human organisms, however minutely modulated; all the same hidden states of nerves. This is the sense in which I say there is no fact of the matter. I am talking not of criteria, but of nature.

Alston goes on to delineate the fearful consequences of the indeterminacy of translation. These consequences are couched in the very terms or concepts that the indeterminacy thesis challenges, and so are apt to strike fear only into unregenerate hearts. It is reassuring to reflect that any discrepancies of translation within the limits of indeterminacy will fall innocuously between objective checkpoints, *ipso facto*. Who is to say to what degree we talk past one another between checkpoints? Or, better, who would there be to say, if there were a fact of the matter?

On ontological relativity, which Alston finds especially distressing, I would cite the first essay of my recent *Theories and Things* as a more succinct and conclusive presentation than what had gone before. I see no gainsaying the proxy functions.

W.V.Q.

2

Herbert G. Bohnert

QUINE ON ANALYTICITY

In his war on analyticity, Quine is fond of stressing the transitory character of linguistic conventions (especially such as might be invoked to distinguish analytic from synthetic), and to argue that defenders of the distinction overestimate their importance. For example, noting that adjustment of a scientific theory to new facts may take place by changing a definition as readily as by changing a postulate, Quine likes to argue that the two procedures are essentially the same. Defenders of the distinction, including the present writer, stress the methodological importance of keeping the two procedures distinct, holding that blurring the distinction makes it difficult to keep track of exactly what a theory consists of at a given moment.

The definition issue (to which we shall return) might be said to lie somewhere between natural language and fully formalized language. Although the analytic-synthetic distinction arose in natural language, and still has some value there, some feel, its application is well known to be obscure in the large areas where convention is not explicit. The crucial arena, then, is at the opposite extreme, namely, with respect to formalized languages. Such languages, after all, were intended to illustrate the clarity which natural language lacked. To be sure, Quine has dismissed natural unclarity as the source of trouble with analyticity. But it is his case against analyticity in formalized languages that is crucial to defenders of the distinction.

Accordingly, let us begin by examining Quine's conception of formalized languages, and his arguments stemming from his evaluation of their rules as conventional, arbitrary, true-by-fiat, and transitory.

Before refining the issues it will be helpful to have before us an example of Quine's. It concerns "the imaginary case of a logical positivist, say Ixmann".[1] I quote *in extenso* but with minor omissions and paraphrases. Ixmann shows

> in detail how people (on Mars, say) might speak a language quite adequate to all of our science but, unlike our language, incapable of expressing the alleged meta-

physical issues. . . . Now how does Ixmann specify that . . . language? By telling us, at least to the extent needed for his argument, what these Martians are to
be imagined as uttering and what they are thereby to be understood to mean. Here
is Carnap's familiar duality of formation rules and transformation rules (or meaning
postulates), as rules of language. But these rules are part only of Ixmann's narrative
machinery, not part of what he is portraying. He is not representing his hypothetical Martians themselves as somehow explicit on formation and transformation
rules. Nor is he representing there to be any intrinsic difference between those
truths which happen to be disclosed to us by his partial specifications (his transformation rules) and those further truths, hypothetically likewise known to the Martians of his parable, which he did not trouble to sketch in.

The threat of fallacy lurks in the fact that Ixmann's rules are indeed arbitrary
fiats, as is his whole Martian parable. The fallacy consists in confusing levels,
projecting the conventional character of the rules into the story, and so misconstruing Ixmann's parable as attributing truth legislation to his hypothetical Martians.

The case of a non-hypothetical artificial language is in principle the same. Being
a new invention, the language has to be explained; and the explanation will proceed
by what may certainly be called formation and transformation rules. These rules
will hold by arbitrary fiat, the artifex being boss. But all we can reasonably ask of
these rules is that they enable us to find corresponding to each of his sentences a
sentence of like truth value in familiar ordinary language. There is no (to me)
intelligible additional decree that we can demand of him as to the boundary between analytic and synthetic, logic and fact, among his truths.

Quine refers back to this parable at the end of "Carnap and Logical Truth"
as illustrating the first of four possible causes for Carnap's attitudes toward
analyticity ("Mis-evaluation of the role of convention in connection with artificial languages").

It may be granted that much theorizing by Carnap and others was indeed
carried on with reference to such an idealized situation, that is, with reference
to an imagined community using a formalized language. It may further be
granted that in the pictured situation with the rules formulated not in the Martians' language but in Ixmann's metalanguage, it would be a confusion of levels to suppose the Martians able to characterize any of their sentences as analytic, or to suppose the Martians to be "somehow explicit" on the rules. But
no such confusion is necessary for nonMartians to characterize Martian sentences as analytic or to be explicit about rules. (Nor is confusion necessary, of
course, to suppose the Martians to be speaking a language characterized by
rules of which they are unaware.) But without such confusion, what is the point
of Quine's parable? Quine says that he is not accusing Carnap of making such
a confusion, but "has no doubt that (it has) worked on his readers." One
wonders whether Quine is not suggesting that such a confusion would be required in *some* way to justify talk of analyticity. In any case, Quine overdraws
the confusion he is pointing to. He characterizes it as "projecting the conventional character of the rules into the story, and so misconstruing Ixmann's parable as attributing truth legislation to his hypothetical Martians". That is, he

seems to suggest that talk of analytic Martian sentences requires that the Martians not only conform to the rules of Martian, and be explicit as to what they are, but even to have legislated them! Though it seems unlikely that even Carnap's most incautious readers would have supposed any such things, there appears here and elsewhere in Quine's arguments the suggestion that truth–by–convention implies knowledge of the convention, and knowledge of its conventionality, perhaps even participation in making the convention(s).

In the last sentence I am using Quine's phrase "truth–by–convention" to refer extensionally to the class of sentences under debate, of course. But the debate labors under a difficulty because the phrase already carries some of the suggestions mentioned. The phrase suggests, for example, that to defend a truth so characterized one must show how convention *can* make something true. The suggestion has already prompted at least one elaborate analysis of the concept of convention with just such an objective.[2] But to undertake such an enterprise is to take Quine's phrase in just the sense in which it is indeed absurd—to try to show that convention could literally make something true. The absurdity is evident if we envision an attempted demonstration of truth ending triumphantly: ". . . and that, in turn, is true because it is a convention!"

There is, of course, some sense in which linguistic rules may be said to be conventions, and also some sense in which linguistic rules may be said to enter into the determination of which sentences are true. There is also a sense in which one might combine these remarks to conclude that conventions play a role in determining truth. But however worth analyzing each of these ways of speaking may be, none could be taken to add up to a proposal to amend a semantical truth definition by inserting one or more clauses specifying that some or all of its own clauses be conventions. The semantics of a language specify the conditions, respectively, under which each sentence of the language is true. Those conditions, though specified conventionally in some sense, will not involve the conventionality of rules, unless the sentence happens to be about such conventionality. An attempt to carry talk of the truth–determining role of convention into semantics would itself, indeed, be a confusion of levels. Here first sounds the basic theme of the present essay, to be sounded again in other keys, namely, that Quine's evaluation of linguistic rules as conventional, transitory, and so on, in any sense in which such appellations are intelligible, is irrelevant to his case.

The preceding mention of semantics prompts notice of another feature of Quine's Ixmann parable. Quine's reference to "Carnap's familiar duality of formation rules and transformation rules" harks back to the purely syntactical conception put forward in Carnap's *Logical Syntax of Language*. Though perhaps unimportant to the parable, it may seem odd in view of the fact that Quine had already explicitly attacked Carnap's later, Tarski-inspired, semantical formulations. It may seem especially odd in view of the remark that Ixmann's language is specified "by telling us what these Martians are to be imagined as uttering and what they are thereby understood to mean." Though strictly inappropriate, the remark may find some motivation in recalling that Carnap's view in *Syntax* was that a full syntactical characterization of a language almost provides an interpretation. The reason was that Carnap envisioned a syntactically specified "language of science" (or of an imagined, scientifically oriented community) as containing a vast network of defined terms whose meaning inter–relationships were reflected syntactically by the system of definitions (syntactical interchangeability rules). This permitted a term's "meaning" to correspond in many ways to what was syntactically derived from its various occurrences. The only thing that this deductive network did *not* say about meaning, Carnap thought, concerned the *use* of the language (later termed pragmatics), a fleeting flux of psychological phenomena of concern to the psychologist perhaps, but not to the logician. It will be observed that Quine's present behavioristic attitude toward meaning is thus not entirely unlike the attitude of the Carnap of *Syntax,* despite familiar disagreements. And it may dispose him, as it did Carnap, to view language primarily as a syntactical system, though used by humans to express "meanings", in some unformalizable, psychological sense.

On the other hand, the remark in the Ixmann parable about lack of "any intrinsic difference between those truths which happen to be disclosed to us by Ixmann's partial specifications (his transformation rules)" and other truths, suggests that Quine's operant conception of a formalized language may sometimes be narrower still. It may be merely that of a formalized language as the set of well-formed formulas specified by its formation rules. But this purely formational conception no longer does justice to the supposition that the Martians are speaking the language not merely in accord with the formation rules but with the fuller set of rules provided by Ixmann. Bearing in mind that speaking Martian would be simply a kind of behavior—behavior in accord with the rules of Martian, but not necessarily caused by knowledge of the rules—one may suppose it spoken in accord with transformation rules as easily as with formation rules. Speaking in accord with the transformation rules then, Martians might be expected sometimes to make the interchanges allowed by the definitions. Such an interchange might change a sentence like "Bachelors are unmarried" to "Unmarried men are unmarried". If we suppose them to be using the language meaningfully, either in the informal way contemplated in *The Logical Syntax of Language* or in accord with semantical rules specified by a later Ixmann, it seems in keeping with the idealization to expect "Bachelors are unmarried" to be treated differently from "Bachelors are irritable", despite their lack of "intrinsic difference" formation-syntactically.

I have dwelt this long on Quine's predilection for syntactical conceptions in the Ixmann parable only because I feel it to reveal tendencies which will be useful to refer back to. The more questionable aspects of this parable have been already mentioned—the suggestion of level-confusion in talk of analyticity, and the ways in which the need for explicit conventionality are overdrawn. These aspects would still mar the parable even if it were rephrased for a formalized language in the semantical sense.

But the parable is, after all, poorly chosen to illustrate anything at all about the functioning of explicit rules of a language by users of that language. By hypothesis, they are not available to Ixmann's Martians. It is perhaps understandably tempting to suppose that a Carnapian theorizer, an advocate of the use of metalinguistic terminology, would theorize only about a community of Martians possessing proper metalinguistic equipment. He would not, one might suppose, theorize about a "meta-linguistically naked" use of language. Indeed, it might seem almost paradoxical to talk of using a formalized language without any reference to its formalization.

Nevertheless, as already admitted, Carnapian theorizers did at times contemplate an Ixmann–like idealization. But it should be born in mind that only very limited points would be involved in discussing an Ixmann–like idealization. For such purposes it would suffice to suppose linguistic change to be temporarily held in abeyance, or metalinguistic rules could be thought of as describing only a momentary stage of a changing language. It would strain the utility of the idealization to think of unchanging use of language over any length of time. It may lead toward a more realistic view of the role of rules if we imagine what would happen over a longer period of time—as a kind of counter-parable. What the theorist might wish to say about using Martian could be taken to hold only as long as the rules were conformed to. This would not be long, of course, if the Martians had no better memories than humans. Once the theorist's scaffolding were removed, so to speak, meanings and usages would begin to drift. The language would change as natural languages do. Sooner or later one might expect some Martian genius to perceive that disagreements often arose from discrepancies in understood meanings, and seek to make some rule or distinction about one or more expressions. Soon, we might foresee, the Martians would slowly be led to their own growth of explicit rules, conventions, definitions, etc. (not necessarily those of Ixmann, of course), and to the development of metalinguistic capabilities needed for their formulation. With such metalinguistic resources, it would be possible to single out linguistically those sentences which were felt as somehow trivially true. Such feelings would begin to be backed up by appeals to explicit definitions, new, suggested, or imagined. In short, the analyticity issue would begin to take shape among the Martians themselves, and a Martian Quine and a Martian Carnap might appear, to take up the cudgels.

Perhaps one may conjecture that such a sequel to the Ixmann parable might occur more readily to a Carnap than to a Quine. Carnap was always alert to the possibility of disagreements arising from differences of meaning, advocating the systematization of linguistic conventions as a safeguard, while Quine holds himself prepared to write off persistent disagreement as mere stubbornness, so that for him the accretion of explicit rules might never be supposed to get started.

So far, linguistic rules have been spoken of simply. But they have appeared in varying roles in the Ixmann parable and its suggested sequel. A difficulty in discussing linguistic rules is the inescapable interplay of their normative, descriptive, and definitional aspects. For example, when linguistic rules are understood by a speaker, they can act normatively to guide and correct his linguistic behavior. If he follows rules of which he is unaware, the rules can not be regarded as normative, but may be regarded as descriptive. On the other hand, if linguistic rules are taken as definitional of a language, i.e., as defining what a certain language is to consist of, the definition may be used descriptively or normatively, as well as definitionally. Descriptively, the rules spell out what is meant by describing a certain group as speaking the language. Normatively, they may guide speakers who wish to speak the language. In the Ixmann parable, the rules of Martian will appear to Ixmann as clauses in a definition of a formalized language which he dubs "Martian". At the same time the rules can be said to *describe* the linguistic behavior of the hypothetical Martians. Ixmann's Martians 'obey' the rules only in the sense that planets obey the law of gravity. On the other hand, in the sequel to the parable, rules explicitly understood by the Martians may act normatively.

It is when rules of language are explicitly used and regarded normatively that Quine's talk of them as conventions may appear most appropriate. The word "convention" carries among its principal meanings "a rule or usage based upon general agreement", "a practice generally adhered to", "an arbitrary or inflexible rule . . .", "an agreement, contract, or convenant, enforceable by law". Such senses may tend variously to support Quine's phrases, "arbitrary fiats", "truth legislation", "the artifex being boss." They may also support his evaluation of rules as temporary, if we conceive a rule as enduring only as long as it is adhered to.

By contrast, if rules of language are viewed definitionally, it is hardly appropriate to view the definer as an "artifexboss", or as exercising "arbitrary fiat". While the definition and its clauses may be regarded as conventional, in the sense in which all use of words is conventional as opposed to "natural", nothing urges conformity with them, or says that anyone conforms.

Conceivably, Carnap might have avoided some of Quine's criticisms by not choosing to use the word "rule". After all, Tarski drew no fire from Quine when he showed how a truth predicate could be *defined* for various formalized languages. But when Carnap used the phrase 'semantical rule' for clauses in his definitions of truth (which were only technical variants of Tarski's), Quine made a stinging attack—concluding that "semantical rules are distinguishable, apparently, only by the fact of appearing on a page under the heading 'Semantical Rules'; and this heading is itself then meaningless". The difference between Quine's treatment of Carnap and Tarski may well be related to the fact that he presents Carnap's semantical rules only as being used to define analyticity. But Carnap's most typical procedure with semantical rules was to define truth first, whereupon a sentence was defined to be analytic if the statement that the sentence was true was a logical consequence of the definition of truth. Thus, although the notions involved in Carnapian procedures were Tarskian ones, which Quine accepted then and now, Quine was led to read Carnap as doing something more questionable.

In any case, Carnap's use of "rule" was deliberate, though he may not have foreseen the controversy it would aggravate. Among his motivations was his awareness that to someone who was using the language the clauses of the definition of the language could indeed function as rules in the normative sense. The prospect of such functioning, though excluded from an Ixmann–like idealization, was a basic incentive in Carnap's preoccupation with formalized languages. He saw the increasing use of agreed–upon rules as an essential ingredient in mankind's progress in science, philosophic understanding, and communication in general. Accordingly, an Ixmann-like idealization of a "metalinguistically deprived" community, once the limited purpose of such an idealization were served, could for other Carnapian purposes, be better replaced by one which supposed possession of metalinguistic resources.

For example, it may be questioned whether the normative use of linguistic rules, in Carnap's definitional sense, justifies anything of what Quine's various epithets suggest. The points are best talked of in terms of a more elaborate idealization of the sort just mentioned; namely, a community using a language *with* the help of metalinguistic formulations. The community may be thought of as historically continuous with our previously mentioned Martians, but at a more advanced state of development. And let us suppose further as follows.

Our more advanced Martians use a language L*, which by now possesses means suitable for metalinguistic reference. L* has been used to formulate a Carnapian definition of language L, which is in fact a commonly used sublanguage of L*. The definition of L is the culmination of a sequence of definitions, syntactical and semantical, providing Martians with systematic terminology to refer intelligibly to sentences of their sublanguage L as true, false, self–contradictory, etc. Before getting to deeper questions about such a picture, it will be well first to dispel certain surface misapprehensions. It might be suspected that the above assumptions would have to be accompanied by further, highly unrealistic ones, such as that all Martians know all of L, or L*; that they speak always correctly; that they speak always in conscious accordance with pertinent rules, or that their linguistic knowledge is gained through a knowledge of the rules. But Carnap's conception of linguistic behavior, was not unrealistically "formalistic", even in the connection with use of a formalized language. Martian children would be supposed to learn language as we do, not beginning with rules, but with pointings, imitated sounds, and corrections. Explicit metalinguistic reference would be learned secondarily. Nevertheless, such reference enters early, even in the acquisition of natural language (as in the early use of the word 'word'). Logicians from Frege, through Carnap and Church, who have maintained the speakability in principle of formalized languages, have all acknowledged the practical importance of metalinguistic reference in language acquisition.[3] Metalinguistic methods, then, may be supposed to be presented gradually, as pedagogy might recommend, though with the advantage of being based ultimately on a full syntax and semantics.

Leaving behind such preliminary misapprehensions, more serious Quinean questions might focus on the relationship of the definition to convention. How would the definition of L be conceived to acquire its normative function or to determine linguistic convention. As a mere definition, might it not be simply ignored, an item in a scholar's drawer? Are we to suppose a process of publication and gradual acceptance, or some step of genuine legal convention 'adopting' it? In any case, was sublanguage L not spoken prior to the definition? If it was, would its definition not have to be formulated first as a *description* of L? Would a Carnapian definition–description of L not have to use syntactical and semantical terminology not hitherto applied (or applied with any exactness) to L. Could such a definition–description be said to be true in any exact sense? Could it be "*made* true by convention"?

Quine has given a vivid word-picture of how some such questions might arise in reflecting about the inception of linguistic convention:

> When I was a child I pictured our language as settled and passed down by a board of syndics, seated in grave convention along a table in the style of Rembrandt. The picture remained for a long while undisturbed by the question of what language the syndics might have used in their deliberations, or by the dread of vicious regress.[4]

The questions which disturbed Quine about his imagined syndics (as well as the others mentioned) become less challenging if account is taken of the gradual, evolutionary character of language and growth. For example, there is little strain involved in supposing the syndics to be speaking much the same language as the one whose more explicit rules were being "settled and passed down", though we should not be surprised if that language underwent some informal changes in metalinguistic terminology in the course of their deliberations. And we can further suppose their language to have evolved from one "passed down" from an earlier board of syndics, though again we should not be surprised if such an earlier characterization were less adequate in various ways. And if in imagination we pursue the specter of an infinite regress further, we can readily imagine it to vanish after disintegrating into increasingly fragmentary and more primitive rule specifications.

Such imaginings do not yet answer any 'in principle' questions about infinite metalinguistic regress, but they show that they need pose no practical difficulty to be faced in contemplating such a conclave of syndics. Accordingly, we could envision the Martians' formalization of L to be only the latest revision of many, produced by periodic official sessions of an organization like the French or the Spanish Academy. From a Carnapian standpoint each revision would effect a definition of a separate new language whose names should be distinguished—perhaps by subscripting according to year of the session. Linguistic behavior need be little altered. For practical purposes, indeed, it should not be, ordinarily. This could lead the new definition to be drawn up almost so closely to existing usage that it might be thought of as a description. But questions of its truth as description, insofar as they can be made clear, would have no necessary effect on the definition. Indeed, the definition might deliberately be made at variance with existing usage for some purposes.

Though Quine presented his board of syndics as illustration of an abandoned conception, the foregoing remarks suggest that it is not an impossible one. Indeed, Carnap would have regarded it as an attractive one for the future. And he would certainly not ban it from our present Martian parable.

A board of syndics is not essential to the parable, however. While a definition can function normatively only insofar as it is known and accepted, it does not need an official decree to become so. As with a dictionary, unofficial publication can suffice. (Although linguists criticized Merriam-Webster's second edition, for acquiring a normative function, they were criticizing a natural tendency.)

Thus it seems that Quine's truth–by–convention epithets are not warranted by linguistic rules, when definitionally conceived, whether or not such rules are used normatively, and whether or not concomitant convention arises spontaneously or by legislative action. What renders such epithets inappropriate is the fact that the truth of a sentence of a certain language depends only upon whether what the rules defining the language interpret the sentence to be saying is so. It does not depend upon convention, fiat, or artifex in any way relevant to Quine's arguments.

The same independence of convention is shown by the legality of a move in a game. The legality of the move is determined by the rules of the game, but is unaffected by whether the rules are conventions in any particular sense. It is similarly unaffected by whether the rules are laid down by arbitrary fiat of an artifex or by an official panel of players. It is unaffected by whether the rules are followed by many, by few, or by none, by conscious rule-following or by habit. It is unaffected by whether the rules are norms, descriptions, or clauses in the definition of the game. The game analogy is limited. As Quine has remarked, since games are not languages, the rules of a game can not be formulated in another game. Nevertheless, the analogy is appropriate to the present point.

The definition of analytic (sentences) of the Martian language L may be pictured as proceeding in a straightforward way (by a non-Quinean). It would be defined so as to include logical truths, truths-by-definition, perhaps a list of meaning postulates, and logical consequences of these. John Kemeny has ably criticized Quine's special attention to definition, holding that definition is not an exceptionally important kind of meaning postulate.[5] However, Quine's special attention to definition makes it rewarding to focus here also on definition.

Quine is an expert in the use of definitions, but his views about them have varied. While often coinciding with those of formalized language theorists, they are at times influenced by other conceptions, in which they are viewed as reports of pre–existing synonymies, explications of pre–existing usages, or simply postulates of a certain universal, biconditional form.

In "Truth by Convention", he treats them much as Carnap would. A definition is a "license for rewriting". A statement inferred through definition is "shorthand for another statement". A similar account is given in both "Two Dogmas of Empiricism" and "Carnap and Logical Truths". In the latter he says that "formulas of definition which appear in connection with formal systems . . . are best looked upon as correlating two systems, . . . one of which is prized for its economical lexicon and the other for its brevity or its familiarity of expression".

As for analytic truth by definition, he is content in "Truth by Convention" to allow definitions a responsibility "only for transforming truths, not for founding them" (since sentences which are held to be true by definition are only shorthand for logical truths, and logical truths are neither true by definition nor, Quine would say, analytic).

In "Two Dogmas of Empiricism", however, after characterizing definitions in formal systems as described, he goes on to a discussion of explication, and concludes that "In formal and informal work alike, thus, we find that definition—except in the extreme case of the explicitly conventional introduction of new notations—hinges on prior relations of synonymy".[6] It is hard to see that a case has been made, however, since no way of "hinging" on prior relations of synonymy, or on explicative intent, is shown which makes a definition logically dependent thereon, or which otherwise affects its logical role.

In "Carnap and Logical Truth", Quine makes a more explicit distinction between "legislative" and "discursive" definitions. Discursive definitions "set forth a preexisting relation of interchangeability or coextensiveness . . . .".[7] Legislative definitions introduce new notations. The distinction figures in a discussion of conventionality in which Quine reveals once again his unwanted preoccupation with conventionality. Thus he says "It is only legislative definition, and not discursive definition . . . that makes a conventional contribution to the truth of the sentences''. Only legislative definition ''finally, affords truth by convention unalloyed''.

Truth by convention so afforded is then disparaged by observing that distinction between the two types of definition is only one ''between particular acts of definition, and not germane to the definition as an enduring channel of translation'' and that ''conventionality is a passing trait, significant at the moving front of science, but useless in classifying the sentences behind the lines. It is a trait of events and not of sentences''. But the issue of truth by convention, even if it were a passing trait in Quine's sense, is hardly the issue of truth by definition. A truth by definition is as easily obtainable from a long familiar definition, far behind the lines, as from one still glowing with transitory conventionality. Even an unarguably discursive one, which accurately describes a pre–existing relation of interchangeability, can by the described interchange, convert a logical truth to a truth by definition, whether conventional or not.

In other discussions, one comes to suspect that it is not just conventionality that Quine regards as a passing trait, but the status of definition altogether. One seems at times almost presented with the following scenario. A sentence (in an interpreted, formalized language) wins admission to the corpus of truths (belonging to a theory formulated in that language) through definitional substitution in a logical truth (in the vocabulary of that theory). The sentence then acquires synthetic status when its definitional origin is forgotten. Then it becomes a postulate, on a par with other postulates of the theory. (That is, it may be found to be false or to participate in the collective, Duhemian falseness of the whole.) When such straying of meaning from definitional moorings is taken for granted, one is easily led to the pronouncement that definition is postulation. The danger in such a scenario, of course, is that when definitional meanings become blurred, the meanings of synthetic sentences become blurred as well.

To be sure, the foregoing scenario, hinging on forgetfulness, is not invoked by Quine quite that baldly. But, something not too distant from it underlies his view that amending a scientific theory by changing a definition is not a fundamentally different procedure from that of changing a postulate. This view was mentioned at the outset and it is time to examine it more carefully.

Quine provides a vivid example in ''Necessary Truth''. A physicist is pictured who makes a ''neat repair'' to a physical theory by ''revising slightly the law that momentum is proportional to velocity''.[8] Quine then asks ''Will his colleagues protest that he is flying in the face of logical necessity? . . . that he is departing from the meaning of 'momentum' and so depriving his theory of meaning? . . . that he is redefining momentum and so merely playing with words? I think they will do none of these things. His modification . . . will strike them in no other way than a modification of any other time-honored proposition of physics might strike them. And this, I feel, is as it should be''.

The situation pictured by Quine is common enough in science, to be sure. Not only does definitional status of a given law recede from attention, but it may have another status in other axiomatic systematizations. Making such systematizations, indeed, is often regarded as a separate activity, ancillary to the catch–as–catch–can advance of science. Moreover, even when the definitional status of a given law is widely accepted, as it is for the momentum law, the physicist's colleagues would be too familiar with the process of revising a definition to protest.

Familiarity with the process of revising a definition, however, is not the same thing as regarding it as basically the same process as changing a postulate of a theory. If the definitional status of the momentum law is not really forgotten, the physicist's colleagues would hardly say that a sentence that was a definitional truth (i.e., a logical truth in disguise) was now to be rejected as false. Furthermore, the physicist's new definition using the same term in an incompatible way could hardly be accepted as true unless at least some words were assumed to be meant differently. Revising a postulate, by contrast, involves neither of these considerations. Calling the two procedures basically the same would therefore seem to call for the forgetting scenario, or for something with a similar effect.

Before considering what alternatives Quine might have in mind, it will be well to stress an obvious but sometimes forgotten difference between revising a definition and revising a postulate of a scientific theory. Revising a definition is never forced in the way that revision of a postulate of a scientific theory is forced. Strictly indeed, it is never forced at all. Let us suppose that Quine's physicist was right in his new discrepant observations, and that he was right that if a word which was defined by a definiens which differed slightly from that for 'momentum' were to replace 'momentum' in the accepted statements of the science, the statements so formed would remain true, while not all could continue to be accepted as true unchanged. Nothing would then really force the physicist or his colleagues to make the proposed word be 'momentum'. Normal definitional procedure, indeed, would bar defining a word twice. The only 'force' behind a decision to use 'momentum' nevertheless, and to 'redefine', is the desire to avoid labor. With definition unchanged, the word 'momentum' and its many useful associations, would fall into disuse, of course, but the definition would remain true, if only as a logical truth in a no longer useful 'disguise'.

To avoid labor, and other inconveniences, we do 'redefine' the same word, of course. And the impression over time may well be one of transitoriness, not to say chaos. Both impressions are discounted, however, if we are careful to relativize talk of definition to particular language systems. The original momentum law can then be said to be true by definition in such and such a system without reference to time and concern for transitoriness.

To use the physicist's new definition, to be sure, would be to use a different system. But no puzzles arise over whether a given sentence is a definition eternally or only transitorily when it is a question of whether a given sentence is a definition in a certain system.

Not relativizing definitional status to a system, Quine is sufficiently puzzled by the question of transitoriness that it may affect his basic views. The "passing trait" passage is immediately followed by a rejection of a suggested way in which definition, or rather truth by convention, might gain desired "eternal" status: "Might we not still project a derivative trait upon the sentences themselves, thus speaking of a sentence as forever true by convention if its first adoption as true was by convention? No; this, if done seriously, involves us in the most unrewarding historical conjecture." But one feels that Quine's acceptance of transitoriness may stem from an unnecessary, and equally unrewarding, historical conjecture about the fate of an (unrelativized) definition. (Transitoriness, here, of course, is still confused by the idea that the conventionality of an act of writing a rule is essential to a sentence's being true according to the rule. But the same considerations would apply if the remark were rephrased so as to concern the eternality of definition.)

Changing a definition of a word, then, involves a change of system or language, while, changing a postulate does not. (Quine speaks of the physicist's repair as "neat"—an adjective appropriate to redefinition, in view of the trouble it spares, but not to revision of a postulate. Even while arguing for the sameness of the two processes, Quine recognizes their formal difference.)

If the definitional status of the momentum law were genuinely forgotten by the physicist's colleagues, definitions and postulates would, of course, have to be treated alike, and the theory would have to be treated as having one more primitive term than it had at some earlier time. Quine does not quite follow the forgetting scenario, however. Following the momentum example, he says instead that "we unduly exalt the act of definition" and that definitions are related at best only to the order in which we learn the terms of a theory and not "as making for an enduring difference in status between the variously interlocking laws of the theory itself".[9]

It may not be unreasonable to interpret this in a more general way, as viewing definitional status as pertaining only to a theoretically unimportant choice among many possible axiomatic presentations. A given theory may be seen as axiomatically systematizable in various ways. A sentence that is definitionally true in one system may be a consequence of postulates in another. Quine's attitude toward the possibility of alternative axiomatizations seems at times to be that if something can be done in either of two ways no distinction can be drawn between the ways. But of course even if either of two systematizations would do, it would be chaotic to use both. Traffic will be equally orderly if all keep to the right or all keep to the left. Even if the choice were arbitrary, it could nevertheless be important to make.

There is a sense, however, in which the choice between systems cannot be fully arbitrary when the systems involve definitions. Let us consider two theories T_A and T_B with distinct vocabularies (possibly, but not necessarily, disjoint) and such that a certain definitional extension, T_A^*, of T_A (i.e., the deductive closure of the union of a certain set of definitions with T_A) and a certain definitional extension, T_B^*, of T_B each contains exactly the same sentences as theory T. T_A^* and T_B^* would then usually be regarded as possible axiomatic systematizations of T. However in the ordinary conception of definition, a theory says exactly the same thing as a definitional extension of the theory. Therefore, although T may be held to be axiomatically systematizable as T_A^* or as T_B^*, the definitional reducts, T_A and T_B will in general not be equivalent to each other, or to T, since theories with differing vocabularies are equivalent only in trivial, exceptional cases.

When we change a definition in an axiomatization of a scientific theory, even when we do not simply engage in the make believe that we had been operating with a theory having one more primitive term than we had, it is difficult not to cause some other change in the use of the primitive vocabulary. Let us suppose the following. After developing a certain scientific theory K, two groups of scientists, C and D, separate, both continuing work with K. In the process of their separate developments, they form two definitional extensions, K_C^* and K_D^*, of K. Group C finds facts contrary to theory and revises by changing a definition in K_C^*, obtaining $K_C^{*'}$. The facts are not now discordant with $K_C^{*'}$, and since $K_C^{*'}$ is only another definitional extension of K, $K_C^{*'}$ can be reexpressed in the vocabulary of K, as K itself. So the facts are not discordant with K. But for this to be so, K must have changed its interpretation. If now Group D resumes communication with Group C, they may for a while appear to be using the common vocabulary of K in the same interpretation. And confusion may be expected—when Group D encounters the discordant facts, if not before.

The foregoing assumes the traditional view of definitions, of course. But the alternative is not clear. One might feel it liberating simply to cast the distinction between definition and postulate aside for good. But then every minor coinage in every scientific circle would have to be regarded in principle as the birth of a new scientific theory, different from those aborning in other circles. One would quickly wish to reinvent purely abbreviational definitions, providing they could be distinguished from other kinds. But that is the distinction that formalized language theorists have been using all along. All definitions are handled logically as abbreviational (whatever purpose they may be said to serve). And the formalists' distinction is exactly what Quine would have us reject.

It will have been noticed that nothing has been said about empirical content, and it may be argued that if we assume that if theory K is formulated in theoretical terms it is inappropriate to speak formalistically about its original interpretation. Nevertheless, according to the supposition, Group C found enough empirical content in K to find certain facts discordant with it—facts which were no longer discordant for K as the definitional reduct of K_A^*. It seems clear that if a theory is understood to make contact with experience even in a not well formalized way, it is methodogically important to keep track of what its primitive terms are, and when a previously defined term begins to be treated as a new primitive term.

Quine has made his case against analyticity formidable by tying the analytic–synthetic distinction to some form of empiricist reductionism. While there is an undeniable historical and motivational relationship, the logical relationship is not as clearcut as he would have us believe. Philosophers such as Frege and Grice and Strawson, not to mention Kant, have expounded or defended views of analyticity without simultaneously being proponents of empiricism. To be sure, Carnap wished to be able to demonstrate for his languages that a sentence which was not empirically meaningful was analytically determinate (i.e., analytically true or analytically false). But it was more important for him to show that the sentences which were classed as analytically determinate in his languages were without significant content. Kant's claim for mathematics, for example, would be refuted if mathematics could be shown to be analytic in only the latter sense, whether or not sentences were exhaustively partitioned between those which were analytically determinate and those which were empirically meaningful. And exhaustiveness is of course not a crucial demand for non–empiricist defenders of analyticity.

Furthermore, many of Quine's most characteristic arguments, such as the unclarity of analyticity, linguistic regress, the arbitrariness, inessentialness, transitoriness of linguistic convention, etc., are directed at analyticity alone, not at difficulties with the concept of empirical meaningfulness, or with being synthetic *per se*. It is suggested, therefore, that there is value in considering the two "dogmas" separately (without necessarily forgetting the possible relations). In view of the difficulties of Quine's purely analyticity-directed arguments, herein discussed, it is hoped that such separate consideration will hasten the reinstatement of analyticity as a valued instrument in philosophical analysis. Debates as to whether any predicates can be usefully spoken of as observational, or as to whether a meaning postulate involving a Ramsey sentence will produce the exact cleavage desired, should not impede speaking of a definitional truth as analytic, whether the terms involved are empirical, theoretical, mathematical, or metaphysical.[10]

HERBERT G. BOHNERT

DEPARTMENT OF PHILOSOPHY
MICHIGAN STATE UNIVERSITY
JULY 1977

NOTES

1. "Carnap and Logical Truth", in P. A. Schilpp (ed.), *The Philosophy of Rudolf Carnap* (La Salle, Illinois: Open Court, 1963), pp. 385–406. Reprinted in W. V. Quine, *The Ways of Paradox* (New York: Random House, 1966), pp. 100–125. Page numbers of specific passages, here pp. 401–402, 119–120 respectively, will henceforth refer to the earlier publication.

2. David K. Lewis, *Convention: A Philosophical Study* (Cambridge: Harvard University Press, 1969).

3. See Alonzo Church, *Introduction to Mathematical Logic* (Princeton: Princeton University Press, 1956), p. 47, n108. An account of Carnap's class discussions of this point is given in the author's "Carnap's Logicism" in J. Hintikka (ed.), *Rudolf Carnap: Logical Empiricist* (Dordrecht: Reidel, 1975), pp. 195–197. Quine's not incompatible accounts in *Word and Object* and *Roots of Reference* are well known.

4. From the Foreword, p. xi, of Lewis's *Convention*.

5. *John Kemeny, "Analyticity versus Fuzziness"*, in J. Gregg and F. Harris (eds.), *Form and Strategy in Science* (Dordrecht: Reidel, 1964).

6. *From a Logical Point of View*, p. 27.

7. Ibid., p. 394.

8. The Ways of Paradox, pp. 54–55.

9. Ibid., p. 55.

10. Other criticisms of Quine's views on analyticity, some more deepgoing, are given in my defense of Carnap's view on analyticity in the earlier Carnap volume in this series. These criticisms have had an already-said status in my mind during the present writing, and should in some sense be regarded as forming a whole with the present. I am indebted to Michael Levin for pointing out several errata in the Carnap volume paper, including especially: p. 426, line 4 from bottom: Add a prime sign to the second *t*. Line 8 from bottom: insert a single small letter 'e' before 'which'.

REPLY TO HERBERT G. BOHNERT

It appears that Bohnert missed the point of my parable of Ixmann and the Martians. It is to be expected, accordingly, that others will have missed it too. I shall try again.

Terms were L–equivalent for Carnap, and sentences analytic, if their coextensiveness or truth followed from the semantical rules of the language. The notion of there being such rules, intrinsic to a language, was fostered by the circumstance that in specifying an artificial language we are indeed bound to state explicit semantical rules. Their inconspicuousness for everyday language was put down to everyday lack of precision. Now the purpose of my parable was to illustrate why we are bound to state semantical rules for an artificial language and why, properly viewed, they have nothing to do with the case.

Ixmann, in my parable, gave a partial sketch of an imaginary language to prove some philosophical point—perhaps that a language could accommodate natural science without harboring a term for cause, or without quantifying over abstract objects. He sketched the imaginary language by paraphrasing some expressions into ordinary language or giving truth conditions, but only so far as needed in proving his philosophical point. Such were his semantical rules; but the traits thus compiled were not meant to be somehow essential to the imaginary language, and any others accidental. They were merely the fragment needed for his argument.

This parable typified the role of semantical rules in imaginary or artificial languages, insofar as such rules make sense to me. They are a casual selection from the totality of sentences descriptive of the language. They are selected from that totality not on essentialist grounds, but only for some particular purpose for which the language is being cited at the moment, or perhaps as one among various possible points of entry in the teaching of the language.

Relativity to the context or circumstances of the moment—this is for me the keynote. Bohnert and others have remarked on the utility of the notion of analyticity for studies of methodology; and it is just in this occasion–dependent status, I hold, that its utility is to be found. Such is my view regarding analyticity and, more broadly, necessity and essence. When we enter upon any particular investigation or debate, we bring to it a fund of unstated beliefs, together perhaps with some working hypotheses. All this is shared, we suppose, by our collaborators or interlocutors, and in contrast to this shared matter there are the moot statements that are the objects of inquiry or debate. The adverb 'necessarily' commonly serves to introduce a statement of the first sort, or a logical consequence of such statements, in contrast to the moot ones. The utility of the distinction is evident, but its dependence upon the circumstances of the moment should be borne in mind. The utility is comparable to the undeniable utility of personal pronouns and other indexical locutions.

Similarly for essence. Certain properties of a thing or substance are under investigation, against a background of others that are not being questioned. The utility of this contrast, dependent again on the project of the moment, has doubtless nurtured the age-old belief in an eternal distinction between essence and accident. I part company with the essentialists and the modal logicians only when they accord these modes a place in the austere and enduring description of reality. Once we abstract from the passing concerns of the moment, I can recognize only gradations of obviousness, gradations of consensus, gradations of platitude, rather than any intelligible demarcation between the necessary and the contingent.

Thus I see the necessity idiom, like the indexicals, as intelligible and useful only as relativized to the passing occasion. Something remains to be said, however, of analyticity as a notion of natural semantics: the notion of a sentence true solely by virtue of meaning. There are strong reasons for viewing some sentences in that way.

First, there are sentences to which virtually any speaker of the language will unhesitatingly assent. If someone denies such a sentence, we try to restore communication by paraphrasing so as to avoid a suspected word. If someone translates a foreigner's assertion in such a way as to deny such a sentence, we suspect the translator. Thus it is that such sentences are forcibly linked in our minds with considerations of meanings of words. Observe, however, that they were just any sentences to which virtually all speakers will unhesitatingly agree. Is *this* all that 'analytic' or 'true by meaning' means?

We can do better. There are sentences that we learn to recognize as true in the very process of learning one or another of the component words. 'No bachelor is married' is a paradigm case. Anyone who learned English as his first language, rather than through translation, will have learned 'bachelor' through a paraphrase in which manhood and the exclusion of marriage are explicit. Similarly for sentences of the forms 'If p then p', 'p or not–p', 'not both p and not–p'; to have learned to use the particles 'if', 'or', 'and', and 'not' in violation of such sentences is simply not to have learned them.

Here, I suggested in *The Roots of Reference,* is the germ of an intelligible and reasonable notion of analyticity. However, I see little use for it in the epistemology or methodology of science. It contributes one worthwhile general insight: that some truths are learned by learning words. Which ones are thus learned, however, and by whom, is scarcely to be determined, apart from a few clear cases of the sorts just noted. What is more, we need not care; for beliefs, however acquired, are fitted into a system without regard to individual pedigree. My old point about legislative definition and postulation, that it is episodic only and confers no enduring distinctive trait, applies equally to analyticity in the psychogenetic sense just now proposed. (See further my reply to Hellman.)

There is still a distinction, heedlessly and needlessly linked to analyticity, that is indeed important both daily and enduringly for the methodology of science. It is the distinction between verbal and substantive issues. Verbal issues are the ones that can be bypassed by some paraphrase. But no synonymy relation is presupposed here; what matters is just that the paraphrase be acceptable to all parties for purposes of the continuing investigation.

W. V. Q.

3

Dagfinn Føllesdal

ESSENTIALISM AND REFERENCE

1. A Disturbing Remark

Quine developed his view on the modalities during the twenty years from 1941 ("Whitehead and the Rise of Modern Logic") to 1961 (the second edition of *From a Logical Point of View*). Since this later date it seems that Quine has rested satisfied that the situation was well understood and that there was little need for further arguments or clarification.

I, too, was of this opinion when I wrote "Quine and Modality" for the *Words and Objections* volume in 1969. There I summarized Quine's arguments against the modalities and indicated how they require us to look at reference in a new way. What Quine calls essentialism is a consequence of this new view of reference. Little did I know that my paper would need a sequel. This became apparent to me only when I read "Intensions Revisited" (1977), the only place where Quine has addressed these issues at any length in later years.

On the face of it, this article recapitulates Quine's position from 1961. However, there is an important difference. The article brings to the surface a conflation which seems to me to be shared by Quine and his opponents as to exactly what was achieved through Quine's arguments against modal logic in the years up to 1961 and what the situation is with regard to quantification into modal contexts, essentialism, and reference. Quine notes that in order to make sense of quantified modal logic one needs a kind of singular term 'a' for which one can establish '$(\exists x)\Box(x = a)$'. He then goes on to say:

> A term thus qualified is what Føllesdal called a genuine name and Kripke has called a rigid designator. It is a term such that $(\exists x)\Box(x = a)$, that is, something is necessarily a, where 'a' stands for the term.

I am grateful to David Kaplan, Ruth Marcus, Joseph Almog, Howard Wettstein, John Etchemendy, Julius Moravcsik, and David Smith for helpful remarks.

. . .

A rigid designator differs from others in that *it picks out its object by its essential
traits*. It designates the object in all possible worlds in which it exists. Talk of
possible worlds is a graphic way of waging the essentialist philosophy, but it is
only that; it is not an explication. *Essence is needed to identify an object from one
possible world to another.*[1]

2. *Two Conceptions of Essentialism*

What is the conflation here? Is not this exactly what Quine has argued for
throughout his writings on modal logic, that essentialism is required in order
to make sense of quantification into modal contexts? My claim is that we must
distinguish between two different notions of essentialism. The first, weak notion was developed in response to Carnap, Lewis, and others, who championed
quantified modal logic while at the same time rejecting as metaphysical nonsense the traditional Aristotelian view that necessity inheres in things and not
in language. In *From a Logical Point of View* Quine says that quantification
into modal contexts requires Aristotelian essentialism, in the following sense:

> An object, *of itself and by whatever name or none,* must be seen as having some
> of its traits necessarily and others contingently, despite the fact that *the latter traits
> follow just as analytically from some ways of specifying the object as the former
> traits do from other ways of specifying it.*
> . . .
> Essentialism is abruptly at variance with the idea, favored by Carnap, Lewis, and
> others, of explaining necessity by analyticity.[2]

Quine saw that Carnap and Lewis's linguistic conception of necessity was untenable if one wants to quantify into modal contexts, and that their position
therefore was incoherent.

The second, strong notion of necessity is evoked by a very different historical situation: the discussion amongst modal logicians in the seventies concerning how one should identify objects from one possible world to another, how
one should draw what David Kaplan appositely dubbed "trans-world heir
lines". One proposal that sometimes was made, was that each object had an
individual essence, a set of properties that it had by necessity and that no other
object had. It is clear from the last italicized clause in the quotation I gave
from Quine that it is this issue Quine addresses here, and no longer those raised
by Carnap and Lewis. It seems to me that Quine in 1961 was satisfied that he
had refuted Carnap and Lewis's views on the modalities and had shown that
quantified modal logic requires what he then called 'essentialism'. He also acknowledged that the formal difficulties that he had brought to light in his writings on quantified modal logic could be overcome if one introduced a notion
of "genuine" singular terms. When some modal logicians in the seventies argued that there was a problem of identifying an object from one possible world

to another and appealed to a notion of essence for this purpose, Quine seems to have regarded this as just another manifestation of his old claim that quantified modal logic requires essentialism. However, in my view, Quine was wrong here. The problem of trans-world identification is an ill-conceived problem. It is based on a misconception of how genuine singular terms work, and the strong notion of essence that has been introduced in order to take care of such identification is not required for modal logic, while the weaker kind, which Quine discussed in his earlier writings, is needed.

Although I think that Quine was in his full right when in 1977 he expressed his misgivings about trans-world identity and about the strong notion of essence invoked to account for it, I find the quoted passage unfortunate in two ways: First, it may make the reader confuse the subtle arguments concerning quantified modal logic and essentialism that Quine gave in the forties and fifties and that refuted Carnap and Lewis, with the trifling claim that essences are needed to identify objects from one possible world to another. Secondly, the passage gives a wrong view on the nature of reference, as epitomized by the behavior of genuine singular terms. In the rest of this paper I shall attempt to put straight these two points, first Quine's arguments and the insights they give, and secondly the nature of reference.

3. Quine's Arguments Concerning Quantified Modal Logic and Essentialism

I have discussed these arguments before, in my dissertation *Referential Opacity and Modal Logic* (Harvard 1961) and in "Quine on Modality." I shall therefore be brief here.

Most of Quine's arguments turn on there being fundamental difficulties concerning what the objects are that one refers to in modal contexts, difficulties that become especially apparent when one quantifies into such contexts. Quine's example concerning the number of planets illustrates this. Consider

$$(\exists x)\Box(x > 7)$$

"Would 9, that is, the number of planets, be one of the numbers necessarily greater than 7?" Quine asked in "Notes on Existence and Necessity"[3], pointing out that such an affirmation would be true in the form

$$\Box(9 > 7)$$

and false in the form

$$\Box(\text{the number of planets} > 7)$$

Alonzo Church, in his review of "Notes on Existence and Necessity,"[4] claimed that these difficulties could be overcome if one restricted the universe over which one quantifies to intensional objects. Church may have had in mind here his later logic of sense and denotation, where the universe is thus restricted, but where the crucial feature that saves the system is that there is a Fregean reference shift within the scope of the modal operators. Instead of referring to their ordinary reference, singular terms within such contexts refer to their ordinary sense, to use Frege's terminology. Barring such an interpretation, one can easily show that merely restricting the universe to intensional objects or in fact any other kind of objects does not put an end to the difficulties.

Quine brought out the new difficulties in three successively stronger stages. First, in letters to Carnap in 1945–46, he pointed out that excluding extensional entities altogether from the range of values of one's variables is a more radical move than one might think, as becomes apparent when one tries to reformulate in intensional language the two statements:

> The number of planets is a power of three.
> The wives of two of the directors are deaf.

It can be done, but the examples "give some hint of the unusual character which a development of it (an intensional language) adequate to general purposes would have to assume."[5]

Secondly, in "Reference and Modality" in *From a Logical Point of View* (1953) Quine shows that if, in order to overcome the difficulties, one were to retain within one's universe of discourse only objects x such that any two conditions uniquely determining x are analytically equivalent, that is, such that

$$(y)(Fy \equiv . y = x) \cdot (y)(Gy \equiv . y = x) \cdot \supset \Box (y)(Fy \equiv Gy))$$

then one can prove that all identities are necessary, that is:

$$(x)(z)(x = z \cdot \supset \Box (x = z)).$$

However, this is a conclusion which most modal logicians accept. In fact, they have to accept it, I have argued; it is a consequence of the view on variables and reference that we shall come to later in this paper.

However, in *Word and Object* Quine brings his argument into its third and final stage. He draws the following, disastrous consequence of the requirement that any two conditions that uniquely determine an object within the universe of discourse should be analytically equivalent, viz. the consequence that every true sentence is necessarily true:

$$p \supset \Box p$$

Since the converse holds, too, this means that modal distinctions collapse; the whole point of the modalities vanishes.[6]

This might seem to clinch Quine's case against modal logic. However, Quine's conclusion is too disastrous to be true. For although the argument in *Word and Object* is directed against the logical modalities, it can be paralleled for any type of nonextensional construction. In fact it would show that any attempt to build up adequate theories of causation, counterfactuals, probability, preference, knowledge, belief, action, duty, responsibility, rightness, goodness, etc. must be given up, since, presumably, any such theory would require quantification into non-extensional contexts.

4. Singular Terms in Traditional Semantics

The mere fact that Quine's conclusion has these disastrous consequences indicates that there must be a way of avoiding it. The way to take is to focus on one's *language,* not one's *objects.* Regardless of what kind of context we are dealing with and what kind of objects we are quantifying over, our variables of quantification have to keep on referring to the same objects irrespective of what changes and modifications these objects are supposed to undergo. In order to make sense of such quantification, we have to make sense of talking of an *it,* which is said to have various properties, undergo various changes etc. In fact, I regard reference as more basic than explicit predication: in order to predicate something of an object, we have to be able to refer to the object without explicit use of any predicates. We will return to this later.

In traditional semantics, as developed by Frege, Carnap and Quine, the variables behave in this orderly manner, but other singular terms may relate to different objects from time to time and from "possible world" to "possible world". These other singular terms behave basically like general terms; their reference depends upon their sense, and the sense fits now one object or set of objects, now another.

Only where the subject matter does not change, or cannot be otherwise, as in mathematics, do our general terms keep their extensions from time to time and from "world" to "world". In such discourse, the singular terms, which in traditional semantics are "parasitic" on the general ones, do likewise. These terms do not cause difficulties for us in modal logic. Those that do, are those singular terms that feed on general terms from more mutable and accidental areas, like 'the number of planets'. They may happen to refer to an eternal object, like a number, but what determines their behavior, is their sense, not their reference.

5. Taking Reference Seriously

All that is needed in order to interpret quantified modal logic, is to take reference seriously and notice that there is at least one category of singular terms—namely, the variables, or their natural-language counterpart, the pronouns—

that behave quite differently from the general terms. Once this has been observed, it does not take long to see that several expressions, in addition to variables, belong in the former group—notably, most proper names. These expressions are intended to keep on referring to the same object throughout all its changes and throughout our changing opinions and theories concerning the object. When used in modal contexts, these expressions are intended to relate to the same object in all "possible worlds" where that object occurs. In worlds where their objects do not occur, the terms relate to nothing. These terms that are perfectly faithful to their objects, I call 'genuine singular terms'. Other terms—for example, definite descriptions in most of their uses—are in many ways much more like general terms that happen to be true of just one object. They have this object as their extension, but they do not refer; reference should be looked upon as a peculiar relation holding between the genuine singular terms and objects.

I prefer to confine the notion of reference to the relation that the genuine singular terms bear to their objects. Others may use the word 'reference' in a wider sense and say that also non-genuine singular terms refer, and perhaps even general terms and sentences, as Frege would have it. I will not quarrel over terminology. The relation between genuine singular terms and their objects has, however, very special properties, and it is this relation I shall discuss in the rest of this paper under the label 'reference'. If one wants to keep the old, broad, usage of 'singular terms' and 'reference', one is of course free to do so, but one should be aware that one is then lumping together terms and relations that are of very different kinds.

There is a main dividing line in semantics between the genuine singular terms on the one hand, and all other terms and sentences on the other. Genuine singular terms relate to their reference in a quite different way from the way in which general terms and sentences relate to their extension or truth value. Instead of assimilating these expressions to one another and treating them all on a par with singular terms (Frege) or general terms (Carnap), one comes to emphasize the difference between reference and extension, and one becomes able to distinguish two notions of opacity: referential opacity, where substitutivity of co-referential singular terms breaks down, and extensional opacity, where substitutivity of co-extensional general terms and sentences breaks down. For the exact definitions I refer to my dissertation, pages 4–8, or to my article "Quine on Modality," pages 152–153. In these two places I also give proofs that only some combinations of referential transparency or opacity and extensional transparency or opacity are possible. What is important, is that the combination of *referential transparency* and *extensional opacity,* which is required for quantified modal logic, is possible. This means that quantified modal logic can be interpreted in a coherent way.

Quantified modal logic requires both referential transparency and extensional opacity. The referential transparency part is required by the quantifiers:

whatever is true of an object is true of *it* regardless of how it is referred to. The extensional opacity part reflects the non-extensional character of the modal operators: we are not free to substitute co-extensional general terms or sentences for one another everywhere.

6. Essentialism

This combination of referential transparency and extensional opacity is just what Quine means by 'essentialism' in his writings between 1941 and 1961. Recall his definition, which I cited at the beginning of Section 2 above:

> An object, *of itself and by whatever name or none,* must be seen as having some of its traits necessarily and others contingently, despite the fact that *the latter traits follow just as analytically from some ways of specifying the object as the former traits do from other ways of specifying it.*

In other words: if a trait is necessary of an object, it is necessary of the object *regardless of the way in which the object is referred to.* This definition expresses the exact combination of extensional opacity and referential transparency which I have just explained: We distinguish between necessary and contingent traits (extensional opacity), and the objects over which we quantify have these traits regardless of the way in which the object is referred to (referential transparency). However, is 'essentialism' a well-chosen label for this feature?

7. What is Meant by 'Essentialism'?

The 'essentialism' to which quantified modal logic is committed, is a very weak notion, and no doubt many philosophers who have advocated essentialism, including perhaps Aristotle, have had a much stronger notion in mind. Many stronger notions of essentialism have been proposed in discussions of Quine's view. Thus, when Ruth Marcus and Terence Parsons argue against Quine, by showing that most systems of quantified modal logic have anti-essentialist models, they use a stronger notion of essentialism.[7] There is no conflict between their results and the argument from Quine that we just went through. The only form of essentialism that Quine's argument shows modal logic to be committed to, is essentialism in the weak sense of the above definition. This is the sense in which Quine consistently uses the word in his writings on the modalities of 1941–61. I will quote two more of his definitions of essentialism. First, in "Three Grades of Modal Involvement," which in my view is his most careful and penetrating discussion of the modalities, he characterizes essentialism in the following way:

> This is the doctrine that some of the attributes of a thing *(quite independently of the language in which the thing is referred to, if at all)* may be essential to the thing, and others accidental.[8]

And Quine ends his reply to Marcus as follows:

> This is how essentialism comes in: the invidious distinction between some traits of an object as essential to *it* (by whatever name) and other traits as accidental.[9]

Quine's basic point, early and late, is that quantified modal logic requires necessity to reside in things and not in the way in which we talk about things. (See e.g. the last paragraph of "Three Grades of Modal Involvement."[10]) This is the key feature of what Quine calls essentialism and this is what is expressed in his various definitions of this notion. As I noted in Section 2 above, we should keep in mind that both of the philosophers who loomed large in Quine's criticism of modal logic, Carnap and C. I. Lewis, championed quantified modal logic while at the same time they rejected as metaphysical nonsense the traditional Aristotelian view that necessity inheres in things and not in language. Quine's admonition to these and other modal logicians therefore is that if one quantifies into modal contexts, one has to pay the price: one must accept this "invidious distinction". Read in this context, one sees that for Quine, essentialism is a matter of the *meaningfulness* of this distinction. If, like Carnap and Lewis, one regards the distinction as meaningless, one must reject quantification into modal contexts as meaningless. Strictly speaking, those who quantify into modal contexts need therefore not hold that there *are* any non-trivial necessary properties, only that one can meaningfully discuss whether there are any. One might, however, wonder what the point would be of quantified modal logic if one does not think that there are any necessary properties. This is probably the reason why Quine, in the first of the three definitions of essentialism that I have quoted, includes in his definition that there be such properties. The second definition is more careful; Quine there requires only that there *may* be such properties.

In my opinion, this weak form of essentialism is no more objectionable than the modal operators themselves, when applied to closed formulae. In the case of other types of nonextensional contexts, for example, those of counterfactuals or probability, the corresponding notions are required in order to permit quantification into such contexts. So, in this extended sense of 'essentialism', we are all essentialists.

8. The Most Important Misunderstandings Concerning Essentialism and Quantified Modal Logic

I will now pass on to the misunderstandings concerning essentialism which have vitiated some discussions of quantified modal logic as well as some approaches to reference.

The argument I have outlined shows that *if* an object has a necessary property, it has to have this property regardless of how the object is referred to. The argument does not show that any object in our universe of discourse has to have some nontrivial essential property, far less that it has to have a unique essential property, by which it can be identified. Unfortunately, this view has slipped into the discussion because one has mixed up Quine's carefully argued view on "weak" essentialism with the further, misconceived, idea that essential properties are required in order to "keep track of the objects over which one quantifies as one moves from one possible world to the next".

It must no doubt have confused some readers that Quine himself in 1977 suddenly started talking about essentialism in this way, without noting that this is a different and much stronger notion than the one that is required by quantification into modal contexts. I hope that I have succeeded in making it clear that Quine is here mixing together two different notions of essentialism, and that he is thereby obfuscating his very valuable insights concerning the modalities.

The second misgiving I have over Quine's statement is that it gives the wrong impression that genuine singular terms refer to their objects in virtue of an essence that these objects have.

Quine's statement expresses a widespread, but misleading view concerning the identification of objects. Quine puts this view forth in order to reject it, but he seems to take for granted that if one tries to interpret modal logic, essences are called for in order to identify objects from world to world.

There is no doubt that many modal logicians have had eccentric views on the individuation and identification of objects. An extreme case is David Lewis's counterpart theory, where objects do not recur from world to world, but are only correlated with counterparts in other worlds.[11] This idea violates many basic features of identity and reference, and the fact that Lewis makes the correlation depend on similarity relations, multiplies the difficulties. A less extreme and more common version of the view lets the same object recur from world to world and then introduces essences in order to solve the problem of how to identify the object from world to world. This is the view that Quine criticizes in the passage in question.

In my view, the notion of a genuine singular term is not fundamentally a modal notion; it is not a notion that requires appeal to necessity or essentialism for its definition or clarification. That genuine singular terms refer to the same object "in all possible worlds"—to use modal jargon—is not definitive of such terms. It merely follows from the fact that these terms are *referring* expressions. Preservation of reference is basic to our use of language even outside of modal logic, for example in connection with our talk of an object as changing over time and in predicating different properties of an object at different times.

9. *Quantification and Substitution*

Before we turn to this topic and go more deeply into the notions of reference and genuine singular terms, let us first note in passing an important point that Quine has made repeatedly and which in "Quine on Modality" I called

"Quine's thesis". It concerns the following connection between quantification and substitution:
Whatever context '. . . x . . . .' stands for, if it makes sense to quantify into it,

$$(x)(y)(x = y. \supset . . . . x . . . \equiv . . . y . . .)$$

must be true.
Similarly, when *a* and *b* are genuine singular terms, then:

$$a = b. \supset . . . . a . . . \equiv . . . b . . .$$

must be true.
    This is just what we should expect of genuine singular terms, but the thesis highlights a general principle, of which Quine's "weak" essentialism is an instance: quantification is inseparable from a "pure" notion of reference which is such that whatever is true of an object, whether accidentally or by necessity, is true of it regardless of how it is referred to. The variables of quantification are *referring* expressions *par excellence*. In order to lay bare our semantics, we should let the only expressions that flank identity signs and are used in universal or existential instantiation be expressions that, like the variables, refer in this "pure" way—that is, we should use only genuine singular terms for these purposes.

10. Reference

Let us now leave the formal arguments and and look more closely at the genuine singular terms and the reference relation. I am particularly eager to do this in this paper because Quine usually has expressed a relatively Fregean view on reference, although the notion of genuine singular terms seems to fit more naturally in with his philosophy.
    The notion of genuine singular terms may seem somewhat mysterious, especially to a philosopher who has grown up in the tradition of Frege, according to which every singular term has an associated sense and refers to whichever object this sense happens to fit uniquely, if there is one.
    However, genuine singular terms are not at all mysterious. If one reflects a little on how we conceive of the world and its objects and how they matter to us, we should expect to find such terms in our language and expect them to play an important role. As has been pointed out by philosophers of all varieties, from Husserl to Quine, conceiving of the world as consisting of *objects* helps us to systematize our theories and thoughts and helps us to predict and cope with our surroundings.
    Objects have *three* features that are crucial for reference:

First: They are the bearers of a (usually) large number of properties and relations. Normally we know only a small number of these, but the object is conceived of as having numerous *further properties* that we do not know yet, but which are there to be explored. They transcend our knowledge, to use Husserl's phrase.

Secondly: Objects, except mathematical ones and a few others, *change* over time. One and the same object can have a property at one time and lack it at another time. The *object* remains identical through changes. Modalities come in at this point; not only are there the actual changes, there are also possible ones, there are accidents and there are necessities. Or, at least, so we say when we talk about modalities.

Finally: There is our *fallibility*. We may have false beliefs about objects. We may seek to correct these beliefs, but all the while our beliefs, true or false, are *of* the objects in question. A belief, or set of beliefs, is not about whichever object happens best to satisfy our beliefs. A semantics that just would seek to maximize our set of true beliefs would reflect poorly the role that objects play in epistemology.

Similarly, the *world* itself, the collection of all objects, is conceived by us as having more objects in it than we know about, the supply of objects changes over time, and we often go wrong concerning what objects there are and what there are not and whether in different situations we deal with the same object or different ones.

Given that objects play an important role in our attempts to explore and cope with the world, and given that objects have these features, we should expect these features to be reflected in our language. We should expect a language to have a category of expressions that is especially designed to refer to these objects and stay with them through all these changes that they and our beliefs about them undergo. And this, as you will remember, is just what genuine singular terms are supposed to do. Genuine singular terms are hence inseparably tied up with the notions of change and fallibility and not just with the modal notions.

11. Reasons for Introducing Genuine Singular Terms

Genuine singular terms comprise, as I have argued, the *variables* of quantification and correspondingly the *pronouns* of ordinary language. But also, *proper names* are usually used as genuine singular terms, and sometimes so are even *definite descriptions*. What is decisive, is that the expression in question is used in order to keep track of the same object through changes, etc. Given our concern with objects and other constancies in the world, we should in fact expect a lot of expressions to have this feature. For example, we should expect this to be the case for mass terms, natural kind terms, properties, etc., as has been pointed out by Kripke and Putnam. Even terms that refer to events will have these features. Events, in spite of their often short duration, are objects that we commonly want to say several things about, and find out more about.

Fregeans tend to look upon proper names as short for definite descriptions (although in some cases the sense might be embodied in perception and not expressed in language). According to them, names save us from repeating the whole descriptions. They could be called '*names* of laziness', just as Geach talked about *pronouns* of laziness.

There does not seem to be any other role for names for the Fregean. I think that names, like pronouns, are not usually introduced for reasons of laziness. If I am right in what I have been saying so far, names are normally introduced for the following three purposes:

(i)   When we are interested in *further features* of the object beyond those that were mentioned in the description that was used to draw our attention to the object.

(ii) When we want to follow the object through *changes*.

(iii) When we are aware that some or many of our beliefs concerning the object are *wrong* and we want to correct them.

If we are not interested in any of the above, we will normally not introduce names or pronouns.

Let me illustrate this by an example. Compare the three descriptions:

the balance of my bank account,
the person with the glasses,
the ratio between the circumference and the diameter of a circle.

Here, the first of the descriptions may be by far the most frequently used. On the Fregean view it would therefore be likely to be replaced by a name. However, I doubt that any of you have ever introduced a name instead of this description which you use so often. The third of the descriptions was, however, replaced by a name a long time ago, viz 'π'. The explanation for this on my view is that π, but not the balance of my bank account, is an object that has lots of interesting features beyond that mentioned in the description, features that we may wish to explore further. The first description, 'the balance of my bank account', focuses on the *only* feature of its object that we are interested in, namely that it is the balance of my account. It philanders from object to object, and we do not have any deeper or recurring interest in any of these objects. If I am right, we would normally not introduce a name for this description. We *might* devise a name, e.g. 'Darling', but this would be a name of laziness, it would not be a genuine singular term, but an attempt to be cute.

The second description is also likely to be replaced by a name, if we are interested in the person and want to find out more about her or him, with or without glasses, and as she or he changes from day to day. The second and third descriptions illustrate different of the abovementioned characteristics that prompt us to introduce names. The third description picks out an object with lots of interesting features besides those mentioned in the description, and concerning which we may have some wrong beliefs. The object picked out in the second description has both of these characteristics and in addition is susceptible to change.

12. The Tie Between Word and Object

So far, there is little difference between Kripke and myself. We both urge the need for genuine singular terms, or rigid designators as Kripke calls them. There has been a difference in emphasis: I have focused on the formal arguments for such a category of terms, while Kripke has focused on how to account for the tie between these terms and their objects, and proposed his causal approach to reference.

It is important to keep these issues apart, for while I agree with Kripke on the need for such a class of terms, I disagree with his causal approach.

Let me sketch my view on the tie between genuine singular terms and their objects. My view is much closer to Frege's than to Kripke's. This may seem odd, in view of all the short-comings I have pointed out in Frege's theory, and the many more Kripke has pointed out.

In order to explain my view let me start from another point where I differ from Kripke. Kripke has emphasized the difference between the *ontological* issue of what a name *as a matter of fact refers to* and the *epistemological* issue of how we *find out* what it refers to. He has focused almost exclusively on the former issue and has thereby been led to his causal view.

I tend to look upon the ontological and the epistemological issue as much more closely intertwined. This is largely because language is a *social* institution. *What our names refer to—and not only how we find out what they refer to—depends upon evidence that is publicly available in situations where people learn and use language.* I am a Fregean in holding that in the first approximation a name N refers to the object that best satisfies the sentences that contain N and that are generally regarded as true in the community.

13. Differences from Frege

There are two differences from Frege here that need emphasis.

First: I do not pick out just some of the sentences that I regard as true and that contain the name and say that they express the sense of the name, while the others express factual beliefs. Kripke, for example, in "A Puzzle about Belief" repeatedly contrasts *defining* vs. *factual* beliefs (for example on page 245) and this is one source of the trouble he finds with the Fregean theory. I see no basis for such a distinction, and I think that all these sentences contribute both to *giving* the term the reference it has and to enabling us to *find out* what this reference is. One objection Kripke has against the Fregean view is that it makes the sense, or meaning, of a name vary from one person to another, so that we each speak our own idiolect. Kripke rejects this. Since I do not draw a distinction between defining and factual beliefs, this objection does not apply to me. We would all agree that people differ in some of their beliefs about objects in the world, and on my view this affects both communication and reference. The difference between Frege and myself on this point is that while Frege distinguished language and theory, I regard the two as inseparably intertwined, and would like to speak of our language *cum* theory. (In this I have been influenced by Quine.)

Second: I call this a *first approximation*. For both what a term refers to and how we find out what it refers to depend on a complex interplay of several factors: assent to and dissent from sentences is just one; ostension is another; actions, including non-linguistic actions, are a third; and above all, our theories of how people are likely to go wrong in their perception and in their reasoning are a fourth. Here interaction within the whole speech community comes in. Some people are less likely to go wrong in certain matters, because they are better located for perception and observation, because they are better trained and perhaps specialists on these matters, etc. This "linguistic division of labor" was first observed by Putnam. However, neither he nor Kripke will probably accept my view that it actually contributes to *determining* the reference and not just to finding out what the reference is.

I have discussed this interplay in several articles and there are also many interesting observations on the relation between observation and reference in Quine's, Davidson's, and Putnam's writings.[12] I shall therefore not go into it here.

14. Change of Reference

Let us note, however, that it is in this interplay that we best can see what the *rigidity* or *genuineness,* of singular terms amounts to. Rigidity is not something that is *achieved* through the introduction of a genuine singular term in our language. Sameness of reference is never guaranteed. There is always a risk that in spite of the best of our efforts, a name comes to *change* its reference. A name does not always continue to refer to the object on which it was bestowed at the original "baptism". Change of reference is one of the problems for Kripke's view, so let us see how I account for it on my view.

Let us consider an example: I learn a name from another. I want to keep on using it with the same reference, and in order to insure this, I try to learn as much as possible about its reference, i.e. I observe what sentences containing the name the other assents to and dissents from, what he points to, etc.

Nevertheless, I may go wrong and by mistake come to apply the name to another object that is similar to but distinct from the original. When this happens I clearly go wrong. My term still refers to the object it referred to before, because of its rigidity. It does not change its reference just because my associated beliefs happen to fit another object. I may then go on and find out more about this new object, and express my findings using the old name. Later, a third person—say my student—may pick up the name from me and go on using it for the second object. This new usage may spread to the whole community.

In such cases I would say that a change of reference has taken place between the first and the third speaker. As for myself I am obviously mistaken and confused. However, I would hold that the name as used by my student and his generation refers to another object than what it referred to when my teacher used it. So a reference change has taken place without a new "baptism," i.e. without an introduction of the word with the intention of using it with a new reference.

15. Rigidity as an Ideal

Rigidity, or genuineness, as I see it, is not incompatible with such a reference shift. Instead, I look upon rigidity as an *ideal,* something like a Kantian regulative idea, that prescribes the way we use language to speak about the world. There is in our use of names and other genuine singular terms a *normative pull* towards always doing our best to keep track of the reference and keep on referring to it. Sometimes we go wrong and it is unclear both what we believe and what our beliefs are about until a new usage has been established.

All our talk about change, about causation, ethics and knowledge and belief, as well as about the other modalities, presupposes that we can keep our singular terms referring to the same objects. To the extent that we fail, these notions become incoherent.

16. Summary

To conclude this brief discussion of reference: I hold that there are genuine singular terms, or rigid designators, in our language and that they are indispensable for our talk about change, causality, modality, etc. However, my view differs from other current views on reference mainly on the following two points: (i) I do not regard preservation of reference as automatically achieved through our use of singular terms, but as something we try to achieve. This is what I mean by 'normative pull' and also by what I call a 'regulative idea'. (ii) I maintain that genuine singular terms have a *sense* in my extended sense of the word, and that they refer partly in virtue of this sense. However, while Frege held that sense determines reference, I have the opposite view. I hold that reference "determines" sense, not by itself, but in an interplay with our theories of the world and our conception of how we gain knowledge and how we are likely to go wrong in our perception and in our reasoning. Reference is *dominant* over sense in the following sense:

> *The sense of a genuine singular term is designed to insure through the vicissitudes of increased insight and changing scientific theories that the term keeps on referring to what it presently refers to.*

It is this dominance of reference over sense that in my view is the characteristic feature of genuine singular terms.

17. Postscript on Ontological Relativity

Finally a few words about the relation of all this to Quine's doctrines of ontological relativity and referential inscrutability. Quine has pointed out, in "Ontological Relativity" and in other essays, that theories can always be reinterpreted in such a way that we merely change or seem to change the *objects* referred to without disturbing either the *structure* or the *empirical support* of the theory in the slightest. There has been a revision of ontology. Yet verbal behavior proceeds undisturbed. "Nothing really has changed", to quote Quine.[13] Or as Quine said in his opening remarks at the symposium on reference at the World Congress of Philosophy in Montreal 1983: "There is no real difference between holding one ontology and holding another."

Does this mean that ontology and reference do not matter? And what happens to our genuine singular terms that are supposed to keep on referring to the *same* object when reference is so inscrutable?

Well, while many ontologies will do, many more will not do. One of the most important tasks of science, in view of the dominant role that objects play in our lives, is to find *some* ontology that will do. It is when we start comparing ontologies of different speakers with different language/theories that inscrutability sets in and there is no matter at issue to be right or wrong about. For each one of us, with our language/theory, our genuine singular terms have to keep on referring to the same object. Inscrutability does not mean that a term in my language/theory refers now to rabbits, now to rabbit stages, to use one of Quine's examples.

Therefore nothing that I have said about genuine singular terms is incompatible with Quine's views on inscrutability of reference. As you may have noticed, in my discussion of what a term refers to, I accepted Quine's view that what a term refers to depends on evidence that is publicly available.

Regardless of how inscrutable reference is, our referring expressions have the quality of rigidity or genuineness that I have discussed. It may be a deep fact of our relation to the world that we conceive of it as consisting of *objects*. Our theorizing about the world may not yield a unique ontology. All that our theorizing yields may be a *structure*. But this structure has *nodes,* and it is these nodes, that we call *objects*, that we are concerned with and try to communicate about. It is this concern, this desire to keep track of them and explore them, that is reflected in the rigidity, or genuineness, of the referring expressions of our language.

DAGFINN FØLLESDAL

STANFORD UNIVERSITY AND
THE UNIVERSITY OF OSLO
OCTOBER 1985

NOTES

1. Page 118 of the reprint in *Theories and Things;* the italics are mine.
2. *From a Logical Point of View,* page 155 of the second edition. The italics are mine.
3. "Notes on Existence and Necessity", *Journal of Philosophy* 40 (1943): 124. See also *From a Logical Point of View,* p. 148.
4. *Journal of Symbolic Logic* 8 (1943): 45–47.
5. Quine, Letter to Carnap, quoted in Carnap's *Meaning and Necessity* (Chicago: University of Chicago Press, 1947. 2nd ed., with supplements, 1956), p. 197.
6. *Word and Object,* pp. 197–198.
7. Ruth Marcus, "Essentialism in Modal Logic", *Nous* 1 (1967): 91–96; and "Essential Attribution", *Journal of Philosophy* 68 (1971): 187–202. Terence Parsons, "Grades of Essentialism in Quantified Modal Logic", *Nous* 1 (1967): 181–191; and "Essentialism and Quantified Modal Logic", *Philosophical Review* 78 (1969): 35–52, reprinted in L. Linsky (ed.), *Reference and Modality* (Oxford: Oxford University Press, 1971). See also Alvin Plantinga, *The Nature of Necessity* (New York: Oxford University Press, 1974), pp. 238–243.
8. "Three Grades of Modal Involvement", p. 80, pp. 173–174 of the reprint in *The Ways of Paradox,* my italics.
9. "Reply to Professor Marcus", p. 182 of the reprint in *The Ways of Paradox,* Quine's italics.
10. Page 174 of the reprint in *Ways of Paradox.*
11. David K. Lewis, *Counterfactuals* (Oxford: Blackwells, 1973).
12. W. V. Quine, particularly in *Ontological Relativity* and *The Roots of Reference.* Donald Davidson, *Inquiries into Truth and Interpretation* (Oxford: Clarendon Press, 1984). Hilary Putnam, *Meaning and the Moral Sciences* (London: Routledge and Kegan Paul, 1978); *Reason, Truth, and History* (New York: Cambridge University Press, 1981); *Philosophical Papers,* vol. 3: *Realism and Reason* (New York: Cambridge University Press, 1983). Dagfinn Føllesdal, "Meaning and Experience", in Samuel Guttenplan (ed.), *Mind and Language* (Oxford: Clarendon Press, 1975), pp. 25–44; "The Status of Rationality Assumptions in Interpretation and in the Explanation of Action", *Dialectica* 36 (1982): 301–316; "Intentionality and Behaviorism", in L. J. Cohen, J. Łos, H. Pfeiffer, and Klaus-Peter Podewski (eds.), *Proceedings of the 6th International Congress of Logic, Methodology and Philosophy of Science, Hannover 1979* (Amsterdam: North-Holland, 1982), pp. 553–569.
13. "Things and their Place in Theories", *Theories and Things,* p. 19.

REPLY TO DAGFINN FØLLESDAL

Føllesdal shows that the essentialism that I impute to quantified modal logic comes in two strengths. This I find instructive, but I do not see myself as having conflated two "conceptions of essentialism". Mine was a single inclusive conception of essentialism embodying just this general condition: "an object, of itself and by whatever name or none, must be seen as having some of its traits necessarily and others contingently." Which traits these might be is left open to begin with. Føllesdal grants my contention, of the early fifties and before, that some degree of essentialism thus defined is called for in quantifying into modal contexts. The necessity *de dicto* conceived by Carnap and C. I. Lewis did not suffice.

Ruth Marcus and Terence Parsons pointed out that the formalism of modal logic does not require us to reckon any trait as essential unless it is universally shared—thus existence, or self-identity. See my reply to Kaplan. This is not surprising, since they and their complements are the only traits that can be singled out in purely logical terms. A richer store of essential traits would be wanted for modal logic in use. But need it ever be so rich as to yield essential traits that are peculiar to single objects, shared by none? It was only in making sense of rigid designation and identity across possible worlds, as Føllesdal remarks, that I found need of wholly unshared essential traits. His own theory of reference offers an attractive alternative to essentialism, or should I say a congenial way of looking at essentialism, in that connection and in connection generally with quantifying in.

A word now about reparsing singular terms as general terms. When I have urged that course for certain purposes, I have suggested that any presumption of existence and uniqueness that had been regarded as intrinsic to the singular terms might be regarded thereafter as intrinsic to the corresponding general terms. Perhaps a similar line could implement a similar reparsing of Føllesdal's genuine singular terms. The resulting general terms would be interpreted as denoting their objects through thick and thin, quite after the manner of the genuine singular terms. The motivation for the reparsing would be the same as before, notably the uncluttering of quantification theory and the accommodation of singular terms to term-functor logic. In practice, as I have often stressed, the reparsing needs to be undone in any case to make way for direct substitution and interchange of complex terms.

Føllesdal celebrates reference, according it priority over predication. I have tended increasingly to depreciate reference, what with my ontological relativity and proxy functions. I have come, like Davidson, to accord primacy to sentences. Observation sentences are the entering wedge to language and the arbiters of theory, and sentences again are the vehicle of theory itself. I see reference, reification, and ontology no longer as a goal of science, but rather as a spin-off of quantification and the variables, these being in turn a mere technical aid in forging logical links between observation sentences and theoretical sentences. Their structural contribution consists, I think, in stiffening the truth functions. The looseness of conjunction and the conditional gets firmed up on occasion to '$(\exists x)(Fx . Gx . . . .)$' and '$(x)(Fx \supset Gx)$', in which the truth-functional components are bound together by joint reference to identical objects.

Despite this startling contrast, Føllesdal's orientation and mine find reconciliation in his concluding remarks. I would add that the well-argued advantages of his theory of reference matter only to intensional contexts. True, he writes that

> [p]reservation of reference is basic to our use of language even outside of modal logic, for example in connection with our talk of an object as changing over time.

But I accommodate change rather by treating bodies as extended four-dimensionally in space-time. Within extensional theories we can continue, I take it, to subordinate reference to predication in the manner of unregenerate Fregeans.

Føllesdal cites causality as a case where austere science itself has to exceed the bounds of extensionality. I am unconvinced. I am prepared to identify a particular event of walking with a particular event of gum-chewing if the agent is involved simultaneously in both, and then I am prepared to say that *that* gum-chewing, being a walking, did cause his displacement across town. We are still not committed to a general law that gum-chewings cause displacement.

Be that as it may, I do not belittle intensional discourse, nor, therewith, the scope of Føllesdal's theory of reference. Between extensional and intensional discourse there is complementarity, to invoke Niels Bohr's term, and Davidson's anomalous monism underlies their duality. But the watchword of austere science remains 'extensionality'.

W. V. Q.

4

Ulrich Gähde and Wolfgang Stegmüller

AN ARGUMENT IN FAVOR OF THE DUHEM-QUINE THESIS: FROM THE STRUCTURALIST POINT OF VIEW

I

Introduction

The following considerations aim at a detailed analysis of some essential aspects of Quine's holistic position. As summarized in the 'Duhem-Quine Thesis'[1], this holistic view is meant to relate to the totality of our knowledge. We shall not deal with this view in full generality. Instead, we will restrict ourselves to an examination of those holistic aspects which occur in single (isolated) empirical theories.

We will focus on the following theses:

(a) Theories are confronted with experience as a whole and not piecemeal.

(b) If a prediction of experience is made with the help of a theory and this prediction fails, the theory has to be revised. Normally, in cases of conflict between 'theory and experience', different possibilities for revising a theory will exist.

(c) Not all possibilities of eliminating this conflict, i.e., of revising the theory, will be regarded as equal.

(d) Instead, one attempts to immunize two kinds of statements against possible revision: 1) those statements, which describe experience directly, and 2) those which, intuitively speaking, are furthest away from these 'observational statements', i.e., the most fundamental and general laws.

(e) Necessary revisions will be made in the 'middle sectors' of the theory. If alternative ways of revising the theory again exist here, we will prefer the possibility of correction, which "disturbs the total system as little as possible".[2]

We will now analyse these theses. For this purpose, we develop and reconstruct, in a kind of thought experiment, a partly realistic, partly fictitious miniature theory within the technical framework of the structuralist concept. With the help of this theory, empirical claims can be formulated. We will simulate a conflict between one of these empirical claims and 'observational data'; different possibilities for revising the theory and their hierarchy will then be analyzed.

We shall proceed as follows: in the next section, we reconstruct the miniature theory $\hat{T}$ as an ordered pair $\hat{T} = <K, I>$, consisting of a core K (which describes the mathematical structure of the theory) and a set of intended applications I. $\hat{T}$ is realistic with respect to its mathematical structure: its core K is chosen to be identical with the core of classical particle mechanics. But $\hat{T}$ is fictitiously restricted with respect to its set I of intended applications, which consists of five elements only. In addition to core K, we will formulate an 'expanded core' E, which is obtained from K by adding a set of special laws G, a special constraint C_G, and an application relation α.

In Section III we examine the so-called 'empirical claim in the weak sense'. In the case of $\hat{T}$, this claim turns out to be mathematically true and therefore without empirical content. This result has major consequences both for the possibility of immunizing certain parts of the theory against revision and for the existence or non-existence of an *experimentum crucis:* Both the theory's most fundamental laws and the non-theoretical descriptions of its applications may be simultaneously excluded from possible revision. In addition, it further suggests a significantly modified view of what is meant by 'failure of $\hat{T}$ with regard to a set of applications Z'. The results obtained in this section are valid not only with respect to our miniature theory $\hat{T}$, which serves only as an example, but to all empirical theories for which a certain formal condition, specified in Section III, is fulfilled.

By making use of the expanded core E, an empirical claim in the strong sense (Ramsey-Sneed sentence) is formulated in Section IV. This claim turns out to be empirically non-trivial: When confronted with 'observation' it can be corroborated or fail. A conflict between this empirical claim and (kinematical) measuring data is simulated (Section V).

At this point, the advantage of making use of an artificially restricted set of applications becomes obvious: real-life empirical theories (like classical particle mechanics, Maxwell's theory of electrodynamics, etc.) have extremely extensive sets of applications. In case of a conflict with experience, the possibilities for revising an empirical claim associated with one of these theories are correspondingly numerous. Our miniature theory, in contrast, has only a very small set of applications. This makes it possible to oversee all existing possibilities to modify the central empirical claim of $\hat{T}$ with respect to E and I such that the conflict with the kinematical measuring data vanishes. In particular, we examine three alternative ways of correcting the (mathematically enriched) theory:

> weakening a special constraint
> dropping a general constraint[3]
> dropping a special law.

In Section VI the hierarchy of different ways of revising the theory will be discussed.

II

The Miniature Theory $\hat{T}$

We will now define the—partly realistic, partly fictitious—miniature theory $\hat{T}$. $\hat{T}$ makes it possible for us to examine in a new and detailed manner some of Quine's theses concerning holism. We will proceed in three steps. In a first step, the core K which characterizes the mathematical structure of $\hat{T}$ is defined. In a second step, an expanded core E is obtained from K by including a set of special laws G, an application relation α, and an additional constraint C_G.[4] In a third step, the set I of intended applications is specified. I is chosen such that the sets of objects of its elements overlap. This enables us to study not only the role of the axioms and special laws, but also the role of all constraints (general and special), which are components of K and E.[5]

The core K

With respect to core K, the miniature theory corresponds to a non-fictitious, realistic empirical theory: K is identical with the core of classical particle mechanics:

$$K = <PM, PK, CPM, r, C_m^{<\approx, =>} \cap C_m^{<o, +>}>.[6]$$

The extension of the set-theoretic predicate CPM includes all models of the theory. Each model is a quintuple $x = <P, T, s, m, f>$. Here P is a set of objects associated with some intended application of the theory. T is an (open) interval of real numbers; it is isomorphic to the time interval during which the motion of the objects of P is described. s, m and f are to be interpreted as the position, mass and force functions; they must fulfill Newton's second law. Omitting this last postulate, we obtain the predicate PM. The elements of PM are possible candidates for models of the theory; they are called 'potential models'.

As is well known, the distinction between theoretical and non-theoretical terms with respect to a certain theory constitutes one of the most fundamental concepts within the structuralist approach. For $\hat{T}$ this distinction can be made with help of the rather informal criterion proposed by Joseph D. Sneed,[7] or with help of a purely formal criterion recently developed.[8] According to both criteria, mass and force functions are theoretical, whereas the position function is non-theoretical with respect to classical particle mechanics. Because we are taking the core of the miniature theory $\hat{T}$ to be identical with the core of classical particle mechanics, this distinction must also be adopted.[9] So each (potential) model $x = <P, T, s, m, f> \in PM$ contains a non-theoretical position function s and theoretical mass and force functions m and f. Cutting off the theoretical functions m and f, we obtain what is called a 'partial potential model' $z = <P, T, s>$. Together, all partial potential models constitute the extension of the set-theoretic predicate PK. Each model of PK may be interpreted as a kinematical system.[10]

For technical purposes it is useful to introduce 'restriction functions' r, R as follows:

$$r : PM \rightarrow PK, \text{ such that}$$
$$\bigwedge x \, (x = <P, T, s, m, f> \in PM \rightarrow r \, (x) <P, T, s> \in PK);$$
$$R : Pot \, (PM) \rightarrow Pot \, (PK), \text{ such that}$$
$$\bigwedge X \, (X \in Pot \, (PM) \rightarrow R \, (X) = \{z \mid \bigvee x \, (x \in X \wedge r \, (x) = z)\}.$$

r is the fourth component of the core K.[11]

$C_m^{<\approx, =>}$ and $C_m^{<o, +>}$ are two constraints. $C_m^{<\approx, =>}$ postulates: If an object p is an element of the set of individuals of more than one application, the same mass must be assigned to this object in all of these applications. We may define $C_m^{<\approx, =>}$ extensionally as the class of all sets of potential models, in which this postulate is fulfilled:

$$C_m^{<\approx, =>} := \{X \mid X \in Pot \, (PM) \wedge \bigwedge x, y \in X \wedge p \, (p \in P_x \cap P_y$$
$$\rightarrow m_x \, (p) = m_y \, (p))\}.$$

An example: Jupiter may be regarded as part of the whole solar system or as part of the system Jupiter/Jupiter moons. Both systems can be treated as applications of classical particle mechanics; in both applications the same mass has to be assigned to this object.

Similarly, $C_m^{<o, +>}$ postulates that the mass is an extensive function: If an object has been constructed by applying a physical concatenation operation to two other objects, its mass has to equal the sum of the masses of these two single objects. Again, we may identify this constraint with the class of all subsets of PM, in which this postulate holds:

$$C_m^{<o,+>} := \{X \mid X \in \text{Pot (PM)} \wedge \bigwedge x, y, z \in X \wedge p_i, p_j, p_k$$
$$(p_i \in P_x \wedge p_j \in P_y \wedge p_k \in P_z \wedge p_k = p_i o p_j$$
$$\rightarrow m_z (p_k) = m_x (p_i) + m_y (p_j))\}.$$

The Expanded Core E

E is a septuple which is obtained from K by adding a set of special laws G, a special constraint C_G and an application relation α:

$$E = <\text{PM, PK, r, CPM, } C_m^{<\approx,=>} \cap C_m^{<0,+>}, G, C_G, \alpha>.$$

The set G contains three elements: Two restrictions of the set-theoretic predicate CPM and CPM itself. Both restrictions are gained from CPM by postulating that certain demands and special laws hold in addition to the axiom already formulated in CPM. In CPM^{IC}, it is postulated that there are only two objects which belong to the set of individuals of the application in question, that these two objects mutually exhibit only one kind of force on each other, and that this force fulfills the 'actio = reactio-principle':

$\text{CPM}^{\text{IC}} (x) \leftrightarrow \bigvee P, T, s, m, f$, such that
(1) $x = <P, T, s, m, f> \in \text{CPM}$;
(2) $|P| = 2$;
(3) $\bigwedge p \bigwedge t \bigwedge i (p \in P \wedge t \in T \wedge i \in \mathbb{N}\backslash\{1\} \rightarrow f (p, t, i) = 0)$;
(4) $\bigwedge p, q \bigwedge t (p, q \in P \wedge p \neq q \wedge t \in T \rightarrow f (p, t, 1) = - f (q, t, 1))$.

Similarly, it is postulated in CPM^{HO} that the set of individuals contains only one element, that there is only one non-vanishing kind of force exhibited on this object, and that this force obeys Hooke's law:

$\text{CPM}^{\text{HO}} (x) \leftrightarrow \bigvee P, T, s, m, f$, such that
(1) $x = <P, T, s, m, f> \in \text{CPM}$;
(2) $|P| = 1$;
(3) $\bigwedge p \bigwedge t \bigwedge i (p \in P \wedge t \in T \wedge i \in \mathbb{N}\backslash\{1\} \rightarrow f (p, t, i) = 0)$;
(4) $\bigvee s_o$ (s_o is a twice differentiable function $s_o: T \rightarrow \mathbb{R}^3$, such that

    (a) $\bigwedge t (t \in T \rightarrow \dfrac{d^2 s_o (t)}{dt^2} = 0)$;

    (b) $\bigwedge p \bigwedge t (p \in P \wedge t \in T \wedge \dfrac{\partial^2 s (p, t)}{\partial t^2} = 0 \rightarrow s (p, t) = s_o (t))$;

(5) $\bigvee k \in \mathbb{R}^+ \bigwedge p \bigwedge t (p \in P \wedge t \in T \rightarrow f (p, t, 1) = - k [s (p, t) - s_o (t)])$.

$s_o (t)$ denotes the oscillator's position of rest at time t ($t \in T$), $| s (p, t) - s_o (t) |$ the distance of the object p from this position at t. k has to be interpreted as the force constant.

We define: $G := \{\text{CPM}^{\text{IC}}, \text{CPM}^{\text{HO}}, \text{CPM}\}.$

C_G is a special constraint. It can connect only those models of the theory in which Hooke's law holds. C_G can be interpreted extensionally as follows: a set of models of the restriction CPM^{HO} of CPM is an element of C_G if and only if the force functions occuring in these models fulfill Hooke's law with identical force constants. Stated formally:

$$C_G := \{X \mid X \in \text{Pot (PM)} \,\wedge\, \bigwedge x, x' \, (x, x' \in X \cap CPM^{HO} \rightarrow k_x = k_{x'})\}.$$

Here k_x denotes the positive real number which is uniquely determined in model x by postulate (5) of the set-theoretic predicate CPM^{HO}. As we shall later see, this special constraint will play a prominent role in a simulated conflict between the 'empirical claim in the strong sense' associated with E and kinematical measuring data.

The application function α is the last component of the expanded core E. To any partial potential model $z \in PK$, this function uniquely assigns an element of G:

$$\alpha : PK \rightarrow G, \text{ such that}$$
$$\bigwedge z \, ((z \in IC \rightarrow \alpha \, (z) = CPM^{IC}) \,\wedge\, (z \in HO \rightarrow \alpha \, (z) = CPM^{HO})$$
$$\bigwedge (z \in PK \setminus (IC \cup HO) \rightarrow \alpha \, (z) = CPM)).$$

IC and HO are two restrictions of the set theoretic predicate PK, which will be explained in the next section.

The Set I of Intended Applications

Whereas K is the core of a non-fictitious empirical theory (classical particle mechanics), the class of intended applications I *is* fictitious: It consists of five elements only:

$$I = \{z_1, \ldots, z_5\}.$$

z_1 and z_2 are inelastic collisions, z_3, z_4 and z_5 harmonic oscillations. Technically, kinematical systems of a special kind may be described as models of a restriction of the set-theoretic predicate PK. For example, inelastic collisions may be described as models of a restriction IC of PK, which is obtained from PK by including additional postulates for the position function[12]: It should describe the motion of two objects which move towards each other with constant velocities, collide, and continue their motion after the collision *jointly*, i.e. with velocities identical both in value and direction.[13] Similarly, harmonic oscillations may be described as models of a restriction HO of PK, which is obtained from PK by including the following additional postulates: There is only one object which belongs to the set of individuals of this application and this object executes a sinus-oscillation with period θ.[14] By identifying these set-theoretic predicates with their extensions, we may write:

$$\{z_1, z_2\} \subset IC \qquad , \qquad \{z_3, z_4, z_5\} \subset HO.$$

In the core K of the miniature theory, two general constraints are included: $C_m^{<\approx,=>}$ and $C_m^{<o,+>}$. These constraints can be efficient only if the sets of individuals P_i of the applications z_i ($1 \leq i \leq 5$) overlap in a suitable way. Let $\widetilde{P}$ denote the set

$$\widetilde{P} := \bigcup_{i=1,\ldots,5} P_i.$$

Then $C_m^{<\approx,=>}$ and $C_m^{<o,+>}$ can be efficient only if there is an element of the set $\widetilde{P}$ which appears in more than one application and if there is at least one object from $\widetilde{P}$ which has been generated by applying a physical concatenation operation to two other elements of $\widetilde{P}$. We may now choose the sets of objects of the applications z_i as follows: Let p_1, p_2, p_3 be three concrete objects. We define:

$$P_1 = \{p_1, p_2\}, \quad P_2 = \{p_2, p_3\}, \quad P_3 = \{p_1\}, \quad P_4 = \{p_2\}, \quad P_5 = \{p_2op_3\}.$$

The first demand mentioned above is fulfilled, because object p_1 occurs in P_1 and P_3 and object p_2 occurs in P_1, P_2 and P_4. The second demand is fulfilled because of the occurrence of the 'concatenated' object p_2op_3 in P_5.

III

The Empirical Claim of $\hat{T}$ in the Weak Sense; Possibilities of Immuniz-ing the Theory

Let $\overline{R}$ be a function

$$\overline{R} : Pot^2 (PM) \rightarrow Pot^2 (PK), \text{ such that}$$

$$\bigwedge \overline{X} (\overline{X} \in Pot^2 (PM) \rightarrow \overline{R} (\overline{X}) = \{Z \mid Z \in Pot (PK) \wedge \bigvee X (X \in \overline{X} \\ \wedge R (X) = Z)\}).$$

With the help of $\overline{R}$ we may define the class $\mathbb{A} (K)$ of all sets of possible applications as follows:

$$\mathbb{A} (K) = \overline{R} (Pot(CPM) \cap C_m^{<\approx,=>} \cap C_m^{<o,+>}).$$

A set Z of partial potential models is an element of $\mathbb{A} (K)$ if and only if the following condition is fulfilled: By adding suitable mass and force functions to the elements of Z, a set X of models of CPM can be obtained in which the two general constraints $C_m^{<\approx,=>}$ and $C_m^{<o,+>}$ hold.

Theorem:

$$\bigwedge Z (Z \in Pot (PK) \rightarrow Z \in \mathbb{A} (K)).^{15}$$

Because of $I \in \text{Pot (PK)}$ the following statement (the so-called 'empirical claim in the weak sense') is also valid:

$$I \in \mathbb{A} (K).^{16}$$

These rather surprising results deserve comment. They have major consequences concerning the possibility of immunizing an empirical theory against 'rebellious observational data', the non-existence of an *experimentum crucis,* and what is meant by 'the failure of an empirical theory'. Note that the following remarks on these issues apply not only to our miniature theory $\hat{T}$, which serves as an illustrating example, but to all theories for which the following condition holds: any set of partial potential models of the theory can be extended to a set of models in such a way that the general constraints, which occur in the core of that theory, are fulfilled. They apply to classical particle mechanics in particular.[17] The theorem stated above shows that no conflict between the so-called 'empirical claim of the theory $\hat{T}$ in the weak sense' and (kinematical) measuring data can occur: this claim is mathematically true and therefore without empirical content. A conflict between an 'empirical claim' and 'observational data' can occur only if we replace the theory core K with an expanded core, which contains a richer mathematical structure (additional laws and constraints) and use this expanded core to formulate an empirical claim in the strong sense. The theorem stated above shows: In case of a conflict of this kind, two rather exposed parts of the (enriched) theory may be simultaneously immunized against possible revision: the most general and fundamental law (axiom) of the theory, Newton's second law, and those parts of the theory which contain the non-theoretical (kinematical) information about the mechanical systems in question. Necessary revisions may always be shifted to the middle sectors of the theory: to special laws and constraints.

Closely connected with this result is a surprising consequence of the theorem stated above for the much discussed question of the existence or nonexistence of an *experimentum crucis.* By an *experimentum crucis with negative outcome for $\hat{T}$* we understand a possible set of applications $Z \in \text{Pot (PK)}$, which can be carried out by experiment and which fulfills the following condition: There is no expanded core E, such that the Ramsey-Sneed sentence which is associated with E with respect to Z (or the empirical claim in the strong sense which is associated with E with respect to Z) comes out to be true.

It can be easily shown that with respect to $\hat{T}$ there can be no such *experimentum crucis.* Let Z^* be any set of partial models for $\hat{T}$. According to the theorem stated above, Z^* can be extended to at least one set X^* of models of the theory such that the two general constraints $C_m^{<\approx, =>}$ and $C_m^{<o, +>}$ are fulfilled. We do not consider here, how X^* is actually to be determined. It is sufficient to know that it exists. Given X^*, an expanded core E^*, for which the empirical claim in the strong sense with respect to Z^* is true, can be obtained in the following way: In each $x \in X^*$ there occurs a mass function m_x and a force function f_x. We now define a set of restrictions of the theory's basic predicate, which contains exactly one restriction for each $x \in X^*$. This restriction is obtained from CPM by adding the demand, that the mass and force functions are exactly the same as they are in x. In other words: which mass and force functions are to be used to extend a partial potential model $z \in Z^*$ to a model $x \in X^*$ is explicitly dictated. Furthermore, no special constraints are introduced in the extended core E^*. The theory proposition in the strong sense

$$Z^* \in \mathbb{A} \, (E^*)$$

is then trivially true.[18]

These considerations suggest a significantly modified view concerning what is meant by 'failure of an empirical theory with respect to a possible set of applications Z'. The 'failure' of $\hat{T}$ and of all empirical theories for which the 'empirical claim in the weak sense' is mathematically true—cannot consist in the fact that no expanded core can be found, so that the associated empirical claim in the strong sense with respect to Z comes to be true: an expanded core for which this condition is fulfilled can always be found. Rather, the failure consists in the fact that only those expanded cores would be accepted for which the corresponding set of laws consists of a limited number of simple special laws. The outstanding efficiency of classical particle mechanics, for example, does not consist in the fact that Newton's second law can be applied to any set of kinematical systems; this is a rather trivial mathematically true statement. Instead, the success of this theory is based on the fact that it can deal with an enormous number of sets of kinematical systems by making use of only very simple Galilei-invariant special laws, like Newton's law of universal gravitation, Hooke's law, etc., besides the axiom of the theory itself.

IV

The Empirical Claim of $\hat{T}$ in the Strong Sense Associated with E and I

We will now show that while the 'empirical claim of $\hat{T}$ in the weak sense'

$$I \in \mathbb{A} \, (K)$$

is a mathematically true statement and therefore has no empirical content, the 'empirical claim in the strong sense' associated with the expanded core E

$$I \in \mathbb{A}_e \, (E)^{16}$$

is an empirically non-trivial statement which, when confronted with measuring data, can be corroborated or fail. The Ramsey-Sneed-sentence which corresponds to this empirical claim in the strong sense can be formulated as follows:

(RS) $''$ V $x_1, \ldots, x_5$, such that

(1) $\wedge$ i (i $\in$ $\mathbb{N}$ $\wedge$ 1 $\leqq$ i $\leqq$ 5 $\rightarrow$ x_i = $< P_i, T_i, s_i, m_i, f_i > \in$ PM);
(2) $\wedge$ i (i $\in$ $\mathbb{N}$ $\wedge$ 1 $\leqq$ i $\leqq$ 2 $\rightarrow$ r (x_i) = $z_i \in$ IC $\cap$ I);
(3) $\wedge$ i (i $\in$ $\mathbb{N}$ $\wedge$ 3 $\leqq$ i $\leqq$ 5 $\rightarrow$ r (x_i) = $z_i \in$ HO $\cap$ I);
(4) $\{x_1, x_2\} \subset$ CPM^{IC};
(5) $\{x_3, x_4, x_5\} \subset$ CPM^{HO};
(6) $m_1 (p_1)$ = $m_3(p_1)$ $\wedge$ $m_1 (p_2)$ = $m_2(p_2)$ = $m_4 (p_2)$;
(7) $m_5 (p_2op_3)$ = $m_1 (p_2)$ + $m_2 (p_3)$;
(8) $\{x_3, x_4, x_5\} \in$ C$_G$.$''$

We shall now proceed to analyze conditions (1) to (8) of (RS) step by step, focussing on the question of the exact location of the empirical content of this Ramsey-Sneed sentence.

Conditions (1), (2) and (3) of (RS) postulate that the elements $z_1, \ldots, z_5 \in$ I are to be extended to potential models $x_1, \ldots, x_5$ of the theory by adding suitable mass and force functions. Limiting conditions are imposed on these potential models by the following postulates (4) to (8):

According to postulate (4), the two inelastic collisions $z_1, z_2 \in$ IC $\cap$ I are to be extended such that

(A) Newton's second law holds
(B) there is only one non-vanishing kind of force
(C) this force fulfills the 'actio = reactio-principle'.

It can be easily proven that these conditions, which are imposed on the ($\hat{T}$-theoretical) force functions, have no effect at the non-theoretical (kinematical) level. They cannot be 'translated' into limiting conditions imposed on the (non-theoretical) position functions. Instead, by making use of a force function which fulfills postulates (A) − (C), *any* kinematical description of an inelastic collision can be expanded into a dynamical description. Stated more technically: For *any* partial potential model z $\in$ IC, a model x $\in$ CPM^{IC} can be found such that r(x) = z. Precisely this is meant by the (rather informal) statement that condition (4) of (RS) is 'empirically trivial'. None the less, by conditions (1) − (4) the mass and force functions, m_i and f_i respectively, used for the theoretical extension of z_1 and z_2 are uniquely determined except for scale transformations.[19]

The information about the masses of p_1, p_2 and p_3 thus obtained is transferred to the second subset of the set of intended applications, HO $\cap$ I, with help of two general constraints. The validity requirement for these constraints is formulated in conditions (6) and (7) of (RS). (6) postulates that $C_m^{<\approx, =>}$ holds: the same mass has to be assigned to object p_1 in application z_1 and z_3 and to object p_2 in application z_1, z_2, z_4. Similarly, (7) postulates that $C_m^{<o, +>}$ holds: The mass assigned to the concatenated object p_2op_3 in application z_5 has to equal the sum of the masses assigned to object p_2 in application z_1 and to object p_3 in application z_3. Thus the mass functions m_3, m_4 and m_5 required for the theoretical extension of the three remaining applications z_3, z_4, z_5 are also uniquely determined (except for scale transformations). We define:

$$\widetilde{m} := \bigcup_{(i=1, \ldots, 5)} m_i.$$

The force functions f_i ($3 \leqq i \leqq 5$) used to extend these applications must meet the condition that there is only one non-vanishing kind of force, which fulfills both the axiom of the theory and Hooke's law (postulate (5) of (RS)). It can again be proven that this condition has no effect at the non-theoretical level.[20] It does not impose further limiting conditions on the position functions of z_3, z_4, z_5 (in addition to the limiting conditions already contained in the description of the set I of intended applications; see section 2). Instead, any $z \in HO$ can be extended to a model of CPM^{HO} by adding a force function which fulfills the conditions mentioned earlier. This statement holds even in cases where the mass function, which has to be used for the extension, is explicitly given.

Summarizing these results (together with the results already obtained in section 3), we may thus state: if condition (8) of (RS) is disregarded, (RS) is an empirically trivial statement in the sense explained earlier. In contrast, if (8) is included, (RS) is empirically non-trivial; it is falsifiable by means of kinematical measurement.

(8) postulates, that the force functions used to extend z_3, z_4 and z_5 to models of CPM^{HO} fulfill Hooke's law with identical force constants, i.e., (8) demands:

$$\text{(a)} \quad k_3 = k_4 = k_5.$$

This has to be interpreted as a condition imposed on the ($\hat{T}$-theoretical) force functions. By making use of conditions (2) and (4) of (RS) and the definitions of the set-theoretic predicates CPM^{IC} and IC^{12} it can be easily proven that masses, force constants and periods are interrelated as follows:[21]

$$k_3 = \frac{4\pi^2 \widetilde{m}\,(p_1)}{\theta_3^{\,2}}, \qquad k_4 = \frac{4\pi^2 \widetilde{m}\,(p_2)}{\theta_4^{\,2}}, \qquad k_5 = \frac{4\pi^2 \widetilde{m}\,(p_2 o p_3)}{\theta_5^{\,2}}.$$

By inserting these expressions for k_3, k_4 and k_5 into (a) we obtain the following condition:

$$\text{(b)} \quad \frac{\widetilde{m}\,(p_1)}{\theta_3^{\,2}} = \frac{\widetilde{m}\,(p_2)}{\theta_4^{\,2}} = \frac{\widetilde{m}\,(p_2 o p_3)}{\theta_5^{\,2}}$$

$\widetilde{m}\,(p_1)$, $\widetilde{m}\,(p_2)$ and $\widetilde{m}\,(p_2 o p_3)$ are uniquely determined by the postulates concerning the theoretical extension of z_1 and z_2 and by the two general constraints

$C_m^{<\approx, =>}$ and $C_m^{<o, +>}$. Thus, (b) has to be interpreted as a restrictive condition imposed on the periods θ_3, θ_4 and θ_5. This means that the limiting conditions imposed on the theoretical functions by conditions (1) to (8) of (RS) are effective on the 'non-theoretical level': from these postulates a limiting condition imposed on the position functions of z_3, z_4, z_5 can be derived. Whether or not this condition is fulfilled, can be tested by kinematical measurement.[22]

The following facts should be kept in mind: As has been stated before, conditions (1) to (7) of (RS) cannot be tested by (kinematical) measurement if separated from condition (8) (and vice versa, of course). Nevertheless, conditions (1) to (8) together constitute an empirically non-trivial statement which, when confronted with observational data, can be corroborated or fail. This may serve as an illustrating example for the thesis that empirical claims in the strong sense are to be confronted with experience as a whole, not piecemeal.

V

A Simulated Conflict with Experience

We shall now simulate a conflict between (RS) and (kinematical) measuring data. For this purpose, we will suppose that empirical measurement has revealed that the partial potential models belonging to the set I of intended applications cannot be extended to models of theory T such that all conditions of (RS) are fulfilled. Instead, we will suppose that if $z_1, \ldots, z_5$ have been extended in accordance with postulates (1) to (7) of (RS), then postulate (8) cannot be fulfilled too, but that, in contrast, the following statement holds:

$$k_3 = k_4 \neq k_5.$$

Thus (RS) is falsified and must be revised.

Although intuitive considerations would seem to uniquely localize the root of this conflict at condition (8) of (RS), we will now show, in contrast, that several alternative ways for revising (RS) exist which eliminate the conflict. These alternative ways correspond to interferences in different parts of the theory.

Alternative I: Weakening a special constraint

The preceding considerations have shown that the Ramsey-Sneed sentence (RS) becomes an empirically non-trivial statement only after condition (8) is added. The simulated conflict between (RS) and kinematical measuring data first occurred precisely at this point. These facts suggest starting the revision of (RS) at condition (8). For this purpose the following condition (8') has to be substituted for (8):

$$(8') \qquad \{x_3, x_4\} \in C_G.$$

We thus obtain a modified (and weaker) Ramsey-Sneed sentence (RS'), which is no longer in conflict with kinematical measuring data. (If, instead, we had dropped condition (8') altogether, we would have ended up with only a mathematically true and therefore empirically trivial statement.) For eliminating the conflict with observational data, no other modifications of (RS) are necessary. In particular, if we choose this alternative for revising the central empirical claim, all postulates concerning the set G of restrictions of CPM (special laws) as well as all postulates concerning the two general constraints $C_m^{\langle \approx, = \rangle}$ and $C_m^{\langle o, + \rangle}$ remain untouched.

Alternative II: Dropping a general constraint

The transition from (8) to (8') is the most obvious, but by no means the only possible way of eliminating the conflict between (RS) and the (kinematical) measuring data. A second possibility for revision is to drop condition (7) of (RS), which contains the postulate that the extensivity-constraint $C_m^{\langle o, + \rangle}$ for the mass function holds. In this case, one is not forced to assign the sum of the masses of the two single objects p_2 and p_3 to the concatenated object $p_2 o p_3$. Instead, the mass of $p_2 o p_3$ can be adapted such that condition (8) of (RS), requiring validity for the special constraint C_G, is fulfilled. For this purpose a function $\widetilde{m}'$ has to defined which differs from the mass function $\widetilde{m}$ used until now. With respect to objects p_1, p_2 and p_3, $\widetilde{m}'$ is identical with m:

$$\widetilde{m}'\big|_{\{p_1, \ldots, p_3\}} = \widetilde{m}\big|_{\{p_1, \ldots, p_3\}}.$$

To the concatenated object $p_2 o p_3$, we assign a mass $\widetilde{m}'$ ($p_2 o p_3$) as follows:

$$\widetilde{m}' \, (p_2 o p_3) := \frac{k_5' \theta_5^2}{4\pi^2},$$

where k_5' is uniquely determined by the condition

$$k_5' = \frac{4\pi^2 \widetilde{m} \, (p_1)}{\theta_3^2} = \frac{4\pi^2 \, \widetilde{m} \, (p_2)}{\theta_4^2}.$$

In this case, condition (8) of (RS) trivially holds. Now, the demand that the mass function is extensive, is violated: Because of

$$k_3 = k_4 = k_5'$$

we have

$$\text{(a)} \quad \frac{\tilde{m}'\,(p_1)}{\theta_3^{\,2}} = \frac{\tilde{m}'\,(p_2)}{\theta_4^{\,2}} = \frac{\tilde{m}'\,(p_2 o p_3)}{\theta_5^{\,2}}$$

On the other hand, the following statement holds with respect to the mass function $\breve{m}$ (see Section IV):

$$\tilde{m}\,(p_2) + \tilde{m}\,(p_3) = \tilde{m}\,(p_2 o p_3).$$

Because of

$$k_3 \neq k_5$$

we have

$$\frac{\tilde{m}\,(p_1)}{\theta_3^{\,2}} \neq \frac{\tilde{m}\,(p_2 o p_3)}{\theta_5^{\,2}}$$

By making use of

$$\tilde{m}\,(p_i) = \tilde{m}'\,(p_i) \qquad (i = 1, 2, 3)$$

we obtain

$$\text{(b)} \quad \frac{\tilde{m}'\,(p_1)}{\theta_3^{\,2}} \neq \frac{\tilde{m}'\,(p_2) + \tilde{m}'\,(p_3)}{\theta_5^{\,2}}.$$

(a) and (b) do not contradict each other if and only if the following statement holds:

$$\tilde{m}\,'\,(p_2 o p_3) \neq \tilde{m}\,'\,(p_2) + \tilde{m}\,'\,(p_3) \qquad :$$

condition (7) of (RS) (extensivity-constraint $C_m^{\langle o,\,+\,\rangle}$) is violated.

Alternative III: Giving up a special law

A third possibility for correcting (RS) will now be demonstrated. This possibility differs radically from alternatives (I) and (II). In both of these alternative ways of revising the central empirical claim, correction took place precisely at the point where the conflict between (RS) and kinematical measuring data first occurred, namely at those postulates which concern the theoretical extension of application z_5. Through use of the third (RS) correction possibility, the necessary revision is shifted to an entirely different location: Those postulates, which concern the theoretical extensions of z_1, z_3 and z_4, remain untouched. Instead, revision takes place at application z_2: We give up the postulate that the force function used to extend z_2 to x_2 must fulfill the 'actio = reactio-principle'. The following considerations show that by modifying (RS) in this way, the conflict can be eliminated. The third way of revising the central empirical claim thus illustrates the holistic thesis that in case of conflict between 'theory and experience' different alternative possibilities for revision at different parts of the theory always exist, even if intuitive considerations seem to uniquely localize the conflict.

We now define a rather weak restriction of the set-theoretic predicate CPM:

CPM$'$(x) : $\leftrightarrow$ V P, T, s, m, f, such that
(1) x = $<$P, T, s, m, f$>$ $\in$ CPM;
(2) $\wedge$ p $\wedge$ t $\wedge$ j (p $\in$ P $\wedge$ t $\in$ T $\wedge$ j $\in$ $\mathbb{N}\setminus\{1\}$ $\rightarrow$ f (p, t, j) = 0).

Intuitively, CPM$'$ is obtained from CPM by adding the postulate that there is only one non-vanishing kind of force.

Furthermore, we define a set G$'$ of restrictions of CPM:

$$G' := G \cup \{CPM'\} = \{CPM, CPM^{IC}, CPM^{HO}, CPM'\}.$$

A modified application relation α' is introduced as follows:

$$\alpha' : PK \rightarrow G', \text{ such that}$$
$$\wedge z ((z = z_1 \rightarrow \alpha' (z) = CPM^{IC}) \wedge (z = z_2 \rightarrow \alpha' (z) = CPM')$$
$$\wedge (z \in \{z_3, z_4, z_5\} \rightarrow \alpha' (z) = CPM^{HO}) \wedge (z \in PK\setminus I \rightarrow \alpha' (z) = CPM)).$$

The essential difference between α and α' with respect to I consists in the fact that we no longer postulate that z_2 has to be extended to a model of CPM^{IC} (where, in addition to Newton's second law, the 'actio = reactio-principle' holds), but only to a model of CPM$'$.

A slightly modified expanded core E$'$ takes the place of the expanded core E:

$$E' := <PM, PK, r, CPM, C_m^{<\approx, =>} \cap C_m^{<o, +>}, G', C_{G'} \alpha'>.$$

The Ramsey-Sneed sentence (RS$''$) associated with this modified expanded core E$'$ is obtained from (RS) by replacing condition (4)

$$(4) \qquad \{x_1, x_2\} \subset CPM^{IC}$$

with the following condition (4$'$):

$$(4') \text{ (a) } x_1 \in CPM^{IC};$$
$$\text{(b) } x_2 \in CPM'.$$

All other conditions of (RS) remain unchanged.

It can be easily shown that there is no conflict between the new Ramsey-Sneed sentence (RS$''$) and the kinematical measuring data: Nothing changes with respect to the theoretical extensions for z_1, z_3 and z_4. Again, by adding the mass functions

$$m_i = \tilde{m} \mid_{P_i} \qquad (i = 1, 3, 4)$$

and force functions f_i ($\tilde{m}$, f_i defined as before), these three partial potential models are extended to models x_1, x_3 and x_4. The two constants

$$k_3 = \frac{4\pi^2 m_3 (p_1)}{\theta_3^2} \quad , \quad k_4 = \frac{4\pi^2 m_4 (p_2)}{\theta_4^2}$$

are uniquely determined in x_3, x_4. In addition, the demand for validity of C_G supplies information as to which mass function must be used for the extension of z_5: Only by adding the function

$$m_5'' : P_5 \rightarrow \mathbb{R}^+, \quad m_5'' (p_2op_3) := \frac{k_3\theta_5^2}{4\pi^2} \ (= \tilde{m} \ ' (p_2op_3) \ )$$

can z_5 be extended to a model of CPM^{HO} such that C_G holds. The accompanying force function f_5'' is uniquely determined by the postulates that

(A) Newton's second law holds
(B) there is only one non-vanishing kind of force.

By inserting m_5'', f_5'', one can easily prove that Hooke's law is fulfilled.

We shall now turn to z_2. The validity requirement of the two constraints $C_m^{<\approx, =>}$ and $C_m^{<o, +>}$ supplies two conditions, which tie down the masses which are to be assigned to the two objects p_2, $p_3 \in P_2$:

(a) $m_2'' (p_2) = m_1 (p_2)$
(b) $m_2'' (p_3) = m_5'' (p_2op_3) - m_1 (p_2)$.

As was the case with z_5, the force function f_2'', which must be used to extend z_2 to x_2, is uniquely determined by two demands: (A) that Newton's second law holds and (B) that there is only one non-vanishing kind of force.

A (integral) mass function $\tilde{m}''$ may be defined as follows:

$$\tilde{m}'' := m_1 \cup m_2'' \cup m_3 \cup m_4 \cup m_5''.$$

VI

The Hierarchy of Alternative Ways of Revision

In the previous section, we simulated a conflict between the Ramsey-Sneed sentence (RS) associated with the expanded core E of $\hat{T}$ and kinematical measuring data. Different ways have been discussed of revising (RS) so as to eliminate this conflict. The aim of this section is to show that by no means can all alternative ways of correcting the central empirical claim be regarded as equal. Rather, they can be ordered hierarchically.

For this purpose, we must return to results presented in Section II. There we stated that in the case of $\hat{T}$, the 'empirical claim in the weak sense' associated with $\hat{T}$ is mathematically true. As explained, one important consequence of this fact is that no *experimentum crucis* can exist with a negative outcome for $\hat{T}$. In a very strict sense, then, this theory cannot fail. Instead, for any possible set of applications an empirical claim in the strong sense can be found which is true. Stated informally: $\hat{T}$ can always be immunized against falsification. The above mentioned theorem shows that one can not only always immunize $\hat{T}$ against rebellious observational data, but furthermore, in so doing, also exclude certain parts of the theory from possible revision: the most fundamental and general law of the theory (Newton's second law) on the one hand, and those statements which describe facts comparatively close to the observational basis (the kinematical descriptions of the physical systems in question) on the other. Instead, necessary revision can be carried through such that these rather exposed parts of the theory remain untouched. In the case of the conflict between (RS) and the kinematical measuring data, all three alternatives for revising the central empirical claim discussed above are in accordance with this demand.

Nevertheless, these three alternatives differ in the extent to which they affect the basic structure of the theory. Or, stated more informally, they differ in how far-reaching the corresponding interference in $\hat{T}$ is. According to Quine, a scientist will prefer a possibility of correction which "disturbs the total system as little as possible."[2] It can easily be shown that this principle makes a unique decision between the three alternatives possible.

Alternative II, which requires giving up a general constraint ($C_m^{<o,+>}$), can easily be excluded. The condition that mass is an extensive function is commonly regarded as a basic postulate, intimately connected with the concept of mass used in classical physics. If a physicist none the less chose this alternative for revision, he would be viewed as a scientist attempting to build up a new theory, which differs significantly from classical particle mechanics. The same statements hold with respect to attempts at giving up the general constraint $C_m^{<\approx,=>}$. Within the structuralist framework, this is expressed by the fact that both constraints are components of core K of $\hat{T}$; any revision of (RS) which touches upon the validity of one of these general constraints therefore constitutes a far-reaching interference in the basic mathematical structure of $\hat{T}$. One would hardly choose a way of revising (RS) of this kind if other, less far-reaching possibilities are at hand.

At first view, alternatives (I) and (III) both seem to touch only peripheral parts of the theory, namely the requirement for validity of a special constraint (alternative I) and of a special law (alternative III). More thorough considerations, however, reveal that both possibilities have a rather different location within the hierarchy of alternative ways of revision. The reason for this comes from the following fact:

> If the validity of Newton's second law is presupposed, the 'actio = reactio-principle' is equivalent to the law of conservation of linear momentum.[23]

Conservation laws, as well as the corresponding invariance principles, play a fundamental role within the logical structure of physical theories. Thus, though seemingly peripheral, alternative III constitutes a far-reaching interference in $\hat{T}$. Technically, the prominent role of conservation laws and invariance principles associated with an empirical theory could be adequately expressed by including these principles in the theory's core. This would make clear that any revision which affects the validity of one of these principles forces a significant modification of the basic structure of the theory.

In contrast, the revision of (RS) corresponding to alternative I has to be regarded as 'peripheral': neither the core of $\hat{T}$ nor the kinematical descriptions of the mechanical systems in question, nor general constraints or conservation laws are affected: The basic structure of the theory remains untouched. Moreover, this alternative constitutes a 'local' interference in the central empirical claim in the following sense: All postulates which concern the theoretical extensions of $z_1, \ldots, z_4$ remain the same; necessary modifications can be restricted to one application only, namely z_5. For these reasons, alternative I can be identified as the possibility for revising (RS), which, in Quine's formulation, "disturbs the total system as little as possible".[2]

The results of our thought experiment thus fit in nicely with Quine's holistic theses: In the simulated conflict between (RS) and observational data, several alternative ways for reconciling 'theory and experience' have emerged, which correspond to interferences in different parts of the theory. These different possibilities can be ordered hierarchically according to how far-reaching the corresponding interferences in $\hat{T}$ are. Our considerations further suggest that the structuralist concept might be a powerful technical tool for further investigations into the mechanism of alternative ways of revising empirical claims.

ULRICH GÄHDE

DEPARTMENT OF PHILOSOPHY
UNIVERSITY OF BIELEFELD

WOLFGANG STEGMÜLLER

DEPARTMENT OF PHILOSOPHY
UNIVERSITY OF MUNICH
MARCH 1984

NOTES

1. So called by I. Lakatos. See "Falsification and the Methodology of Scientific Research Programmes", in I. Lakatos and A. Musgrave (eds), *Criticism and the Growth of Knowledge* (Cambridge: 1970), pp. 91–195.

2. See W.V.O. Quine, *Methods of Logic,* 3rd ed. (London: 1974), pp. 2–4 and W.V.O. Quine, "Two Dogmas of Empiricism", in W.V.O. Quine, *From a Logical Point of View* (Cambridge, Mass.: 1953), pp. 20–46.

3. In accordance with common terminology we call those constraints 'general constraints' which can interrelate any models of a theory whatever. In contrast, 'special constraints' can interrelate only those models in which certain special laws hold.

4. Alternatively, we could have made use of the more modern and elegant concept of 'theory nets' (see W. Balzer and J.D. Sneed, "Generalized Net Structures of Empirical Theories", Part I, *Studia Logica* 36 (1977):195–211; Part II, *Studia Logica* 37 (1978): 167–194. However, the formulation of empirical claims associated with theory nets is still controversial. In this paper (in which empirical claims play a prominent role) we therefore make use of the concept of 'expanded cores' originally proposed by J.D. Sneed in *The Logical Structure of Mathematical Physics* (Dordrecht: 1971), pp. 179, 180.

5. See U. Gähde, *T-Theoretizität und Holismus* (Frankfurt:1983), Chapter 6; a detailed description of the miniature theory $\hat{T}$ is presented in W. Stegmüller, *Die Entwicklung des neuen Strukturalismus seit 1973* (New York/Heidelberg/Berlin/Tokyo: 1986).

6. For details see J.D. Sneed, loc. cit., pp. 110f, p. 171.

7. Ibid., p. 33.

8. See Gähde, loc. cit., chapter 5; an extensive analysis and interpretation of this formal criterion will be given in W. Stegmüller, loc. cit.

9. If the criterion proposed by J. D. Sneed is used (see note 7), for reasons of precision the core K should be provided with a time index: one can never exclude that a T-independent way of determining the values of a supposedly T-theoretical function will be discovered, which would make this function become T-non-theoretical. This would affect the restriction function r, the distinction between models and partial potential models, and thus, the core K of T altogether. In contrast, the purely formal criterion for T-theoreticity recently developed (see note 8) enables a final subdivision of all functions which occur in models of T into T-theoretical and T-non-theoretical functions. It distinguishes T-theoretical functions by means of the role they play within the logical structure of the empirical theory in question; no later modification whatever of the set of available ways of measuring this function can force a later revision of the distinction once obtained.

10. Of course, a partial potential model is not a part of the "real" world of physical objects, but a rather abstract entity—namely a triple—which contains two sets and a mathematical function.

11. See W. Stegmüller, *The Structuralist View of Theories* (New York/Heidelberg/Berlin: 1979), p. 90.

12. See Gähde, loc, cit., p. 35.

13. Furthermore, z_1 and z_2 have to fulfill the following condition: Let $[t_1, t_2]$ denote some subinterval of the observation interval of application z_i ($1 \leqq i \leqq 2$), Δv_i^p the difference of the velocities of the object p at the beginning and at the end of this interval, and Δv_i^q the corresponding velocity change of the object q (p, q $\in P_i$). It is then required

that the quotient $Y_i: = |\Delta v_i^p|/|\Delta v_i^q|$ is the same for all subintervals of the observation interval, for which it is defined. An analogous condition has to be fulfilled by all models of IC.

14. Gähde, loc. cit. p. 58.

15. For a proof see Gähde, loc. cit., pp. 82–88.

16. See W. Stegmüller, *The Structure and Dynamics of Theories* (New York/Heidelberg/Berlin: 1976), p. 120.

17. We thereby presuppose that the axiomatization of classical particle mechanics proposed by J.C.C. McKinsey, A.C. Sugar, and P.C. Suppes in "Axiomatic Foundations of Classical Particle Mechanics", *Journal of Rational Mechanics and Analysis* II (1953); 253–272 is used.

18. For details see Gähde, loc. cit., pp. 158f.

19. See Gähde, loc. cit., pp. 18f, pp. 146f.

20. Ibid., pp. 148f.

21. Ibid., pp. 48f.

22. One can easily prove that from postulates (1) to (8) of (RS) we may derive the following limiting condition imposed on the position functions of $z_1, \ldots, z_5$, which is formulated with help of $\hat{T}$-non-theoretical terms only:

$$\frac{1}{\theta_3^2} = \frac{1}{Y_1\,\theta_4^2} = \left(\frac{1}{Y_1} + \frac{1}{Y_1\,Y_2}\right)\Big/\theta_5^2.$$

For definition of Y_i (i = 1, 2) see note 13.

23. See Gähde, loc. cit., pp. 17f.

REPLY TO ULRICH GÄHDE AND WOLFGANG STEGMÜLLER

I have worked back and forth in this dense paper for glimmerings, and they have not wholly eluded me. Here is one, which may alleviate a stretch of otherwise heavy reading. Each "potential model" (PM) of classical particle mechanics (CPM) is a certain quintuple, and each "partial potential model" is a triple that is a stump, or curtailment, of such a quintuple. Where x is the quintuple, the stump is called r(x). Where X is a set of such quintuples, its image by r is called R(X). Thus R(X) is the set of the stumps of the quintuples belonging to X. In a short and familiar notation, R(X) is r"X. Next we move up to the classes of such sets X of quintuples. Where $\overline{X}$ is such a class, its image by R is called $\overline{R}(\overline{X})$. In short, $\overline{R}(\overline{X})$ is R"$\overline{X}$ and, for each X in $\overline{X}$, R(X) is r"X.

Another glimmering touches up the "Theorem" in section III, revealing that it simply identifies /A(K) with Pot (PK), the class of sets of partial potential models. The theorem as stated affirms the inclusion of Pot (PK) in A(K), and the definitions preceding it yield the converse inclusion. The authors will say *"Natürlich,"* but I am writing for others of you.

The authors have painstakingly recreated in miniature (well, somewhat in miniature) the situation where a physical theory has to be modified because of a recalcitrant observation. Their simulation nicely sets out a hierarchy of options, one more disruptive than another. At the top of the hierarchy are statements that reduce by definitions to truths of pure mathematics, purportedly devoid of empirical content.

The appeal to definitions here should be taken guardedly. In the practice of natural science there is no systematic discrimination between definitions and other equivalences, nor do I think there should be. Even when a new term is deliberately defined, the status of the equivalence as a definition is episodic and not an enduring trait. Definitions do dominate the illustrative constructions now before us, and they are indispensable; but I see them only as the authors' means of displaying their model or mock-up of a physical theory and not as part of the mock-up itself. I would regard any reorganization of definitions as leaving the depicted theory unchanged as long as the theory continued to rate all the same sentences as true.

The authors stress the contrast between the sentences in their model that reduce to mathematical truths through the definitions and those that have empirical content. I am urging that this is an artifact of the presentation. What I do regard as objective is their hierarchy of options of revision, ranged according to disruptiveness. Logic and the rest of mathematics are at the top of the hierarchy, and it is only in this sense, I hold, that we can meaningfully speak of them as necessarily true and devoid of empirical content.

A prominent feature of the Stegmüller-Gähde approach is the separation of the mathematical structure of a model from the physical terms or subject matter. The mathematical structure stands forth as a denizen of set theory, and the fleshed-out model is one of its members, a denizen of its extension. The particular organization of definitions adopted is relevant to this separation; a different lot of definitions could subtend a different mathematical structure, even when indifferent to truth of sentences in the theory. This is quite in order, provided that it is understood. Different chains of definition and different extractions of mathematical structure can constitute different but equally correct logical analyses, some tidier than others, of the same old CPM.

W.V.Q.

5

Roger F. Gibson, Jr.

TRANSLATION, PHYSICS, AND FACTS OF THE MATTER

No single doctrine of Quine's has vexed his readers more than the doctrine of indeterminacy of translation. There is little agreement among Quine's critics and commentators concerning what the correct formulation of the indeterminacy thesis is, what the thesis asserts, how the thesis is related to other of Quine's doctrines and commitments, and whether the thesis is true or false. Here I hope to shed light on some of these matters. I shall begin by considering first the arguments of some philosophers (viz., Chomsky and Rorty) who are unsympathetic to indeterminacy, thereafter turning to consider analyses of other philosophers (viz., Føllesdal and Aune) who are sympathetic to indeterminacy. I shall argue that *none* of these thinkers has securely grasped Quine's doctrine, essentially, because none has understood the central roles that Quine's naturalism and physicalism play in connection with his notion of *fact of the matter*. Next, I shall try my hand at explicating Quine's infamous doctrine, giving his naturalism and physicalism their due. In particular, my hope is to contribute something towards answering the following important question: what moves Quine to say that there is a fact of the matter to physics but not to translation?

Noam Chomsky is among the earliest critics of the indeterminacy thesis. However, his claim is *not* that the indeterminacy thesis is false. Rather, he claims "it is true and uninteresting" (Chomsky, 1980, p. 15). He thinks that Quine believes the thesis is interesting only because Quine draws an illicit distinction between analytical hypotheses and genuine hypotheses. In this regard, Chomsky writes in "Quine's Empirical Assumptions":

> To understand the thesis [of indeterminacy] clearly it is necessary to bear in mind that Quine distinguishes sharply between the construction of analytical hy-

---

Work on this essay was supported by the National Endowment for the Humanities, to whom my thanks are extended.

potheses on the basis of data and the postulation of "stimulus meanings of observation sentences" on the basis of data. The latter, he states, involves only uncertainty of the "normal inductive" kind . . . . The same is true, apparently, about
the inductive inference involved in translation (similarly, 'learning' and understanding) of sentences containing truth-functional connectives. In these cases, induction leads us to "genuine hypotheses", which are to be sharply distinguished
from the "analytical hypotheses" to which reference is made in the discussion of
indeterminacy of translation. Hence Quine has in mind a distinction between 'normal induction', which involves no serious epistemological problem, and 'hypothesis formation' or 'theory construction', which does involve such a problem. Such
a distinction can no doubt be made; its point, however, is less than obvious.
(Chomsky, 1969, p. 61)

   . . . there can surely be no doubt that Quine's statement about analytical hypotheses is true, though the question arises why it is important. It is, to be sure,
undeniable that if a system of "analytical hypotheses" goes beyond evidence then
it is possible to conceive alternatives compatible with the evidence, just as in the
case of Quine's "genuine hypotheses" about stimulus meaning and truth-functional
connectives. Thus the situation in the case of language, or "common sense knowledge", is, in this respect, no different from the case of physics. (Chomsky, 1969,
p. 61)

Putting Chomsky's point briefly, we can say that translation and physics are on
a par epistemologically and ontologically. There is, therefore, no "special indeterminacy" infecting translation. I shall argue later on that Chomsky is half
right in this claim: translation and physics are on a par epistemologically, that
is, they both go beyond their evidence. But, as we shall see, he is mistaken in
thinking that they are on a par ontologically.

A point similar to Chomsky's is made by Richard Rorty in his paper "Indeterminacy of Translation and of Truth". Rorty is, perhaps, more sympathetic
than is Chomsky to Quine's general philosophical orientation, but, like Chomsky, he believes that translation and physics are on a par.

Rorty focuses on the third of the following three theses connected with
Quine's views about indeterminacy:

    (1) A person's dispositions to accept sentences do not determine a unique interpre-
tation of those sentences.
    (2) The notions of meaning, propositional attitudes, etc., do not possess the ex-
planatory power often attributed to them by philosophers.
    (3) Though linguistics is of course a part of the theory of nature, the indeterminacy
of translation is not just inherited as a special case of under-determination of our
theory of the world; it is parallel but additional.

In effect, (3) suggests that *there is a fact of the matter* to the question of which
of two physical theories, both of which are consistent with all possible observations, is *the correct one* but that *there is no fact of the matter* to the question
of which of two translation manuals, both of which are consistent with the
speech dispositions of all parties concerned, is *the correct one*.

While Rorty accepts (1) and (2), he rejects (3). He sees no way for Quine to maintain that there is a fact of the matter to physics but no fact of the matter to linguistics (i.e., translation). Thus, he is puzzled by what he takes to be Quine's suggestion that "accepting (2) should lead to accepting (3), or *vice versa,* or both" (Rorty, p. 443). And, in order to show that one can consistently accept (2) while rejecting (3), Rorty argues that the *best* interpretation of (3), namely, "Non-inferential knowledge is always the result of the 'internalization' of some theory or other, and so we cannot appeal to the existence of such knowledge for an exemption from the usual 'underdetermination of our theory of nature' ", (Rorty, p. 450) is *not* inconsistent with (2). However, Rorty acknowledges that Quine would *not* accept this interpretation of (3). Nevertheless, he believes that Quine's reluctance in this matter is traceable to Quine's untenable distinction between 'canons' and 'laws'. Rorty wonders how Quine can "grant that the linguists' analytical hypotheses are 'not capricious' and also say that 'where indeterminacy of translation applies . . . there is no fact of the matter'? What more does it take for there to be a 'fact of the matter' than a rational procedure for reaching agreement about what to assert?" (Rorty, p. 453). In other words, how can the Quine who rejected the analytic/synthetic distinction turn around and support a 'canon'/'law' ('heuristic'/'substantive') distinction?

Rorty concludes by posing what he perceives as a dilemma for Quine: "he should either give up the notion of 'objective matter of fact' all along the line, or reinstate it in linguistics" (Rorty, p. 459). In other words, in order to be consistent, Quine should either deny that there is a fact of the matter to both physics and linguistics or he should affirm that there is a fact of the matter to both.

> On the first alternative, he can say that the notion of 'being about the world', which the positivists used to explicate both 'analytic' and 'meaningless', was as empty as these latter notions themselves, and cannot survive in their absence. On the second alternative, he can say that the linguists discover 'substantive laws' just as the chemists do, remarking merely that these discoveries are likely to hold few surprises . . . . So far in this paper I have been suggesting the second, but either alternative would make sense. (Rorty, pp. 459–460)

Thus, while both Chomsky and Rorty would have a *consistent* Quine maintaining that physics and linguistics are on an ontological par, they seem to be pointing that Quine in different directions: Chomsky wants Quine to conclude that neither physics nor linguistics has a fact of the matter, while Rorty wants Quine to conclude that both do. In short, Chomsky seems to think that there is no fact of the matter to physics, while Rorty seems to think that there is a fact of the matter to linguistics! Both thinkers are, I maintain, confused. Chomsky is confused in saying that there is no fact of the matter to physics simply on the ground that physics is under-determined by evidence, and Rorty is confused in saying there is a fact of the matter to linguistics simply on the ground that there exists a rational procedure for reaching agreement about what to assert. Neither thinker has understood Quine's notion of *fact of the matter*. I shall return to this theme below, but now let us turn to some other writers who are sympathetic to Quine's thesis of indeterminacy of translation.

One such writer is Dagfinn Føllesdal. In his paper, "Indeterminacy of Translation and Under-Determination of the Theory of Nature", Føllesdal isolates what he takes to be Quine's two arguments for indeterminacy of translation: "One that proceeds via holism and a verificationist theory of meaning, and one that is based on certain differences between a theory of nature and the analytic [sic] hypotheses used in translation" (Føllesdal, p. 290). The former argument claims that *evidence* cannot be allocated uniquely to individual sentences of theories (holism), and since evidence for the truth of a sentence is identical with the meaning of a sentence (verificationism), it follows that *meaning* cannot be allocated uniquely to individual sentences of theories (indeterminacy). In short, Duhem plus Peirce equals indeterminacy. However, Føllesdal regards this argument as "to little avail", (Føllesdal, p. 291) since he believes that the verificationist theory of meaning, upon which it turns, is "inadequate" (Føllesdal, p. 291). However, Quine's latter argument is independent of the verificationist theory of meaning, and therefore Føllesdal sees it as the more fundamental of the two. He also regards it as the "crucial" (Føllesdal, p. 291) argument for indeterminacy, since he rejects the verificationist argument.

This second argument for indeterminacy turns upon the possibility of making plausible the claim that while there is a fact of the matter to physics, there is no fact of the matter to translation. Føllesdal attempts to do just that. He claims

> that the only entities we are justified in assuming are those that are appealed to in the simplest theory that accounts for all the evidence. These entities and their properties and interrelations are all there is to the world, and all there is to be right or wrong about. All truths about these are included in our theory of nature. In translation we are not describing a further realm of reality, we are just correlating two comprehensive language/theories concerning all there is. (Føllesdal, p. 295)

But why are we not describing a further realm of reality in translation? Føllesdal's answer to this question seems to be connected with the different roles that he sees simplicity playing in physics and translation. Simplicity does not determine truth in either physics or translation. However, simplicity is a "guide to truth" (Føllesdal, p. 295) in physics, but not in semantics. In other words, "[w]hile simplicity overrides almost every other consideration in our choice between scientific theories, this is not so for translation" (Føllesdal, p. 296). At times, "the simplest translation is not always regarded as the best, simplicity is sometimes considered less crucial than, for example, agreement'' (Føllesdal, p. 296). Further, if

> in translation, simplicity were a guide to truth, then translation would be on a par with empirical theory. Translation would be underdetermined: several alternative translations would yield the required correlations of observation sentences etc. But translation would not be indeterminate, since one of the translations would be the true one. (Føllesdal, p. 295)

So, on Føllesdal's reading of Quine, the difference between under-determination and indeterminacy can be traced back to the different roles played by simplicity considerations in the two domains, physics and translation. This analysis of the difference leads Føllesdal to conclude that ''indeterminacy of translation seems to follow from empiricism alone without the need for any extra dogma [of physicalism]'' (Føllesdal, p. 296), and that ''the indeterminacy of translation seems to be with us to stay'' (Føllesdal, p. 300).

Føllesdal's paper is something of a direct response to Chomsky and Rorty. In particular, Føllesdal may be read as responding to Rorty's claim that Quine cannot consistently subscribe to a 'canon'/'law' ('heuristic'/'substantive') dichotomy. Føllesdal's answer is that a consistent Quine can do so, *if* he is willing to assign simplicity a role in physics different from the role assigned to it in translation, a notion Føllesdal seems to countenance even while admitting that ''[t]he argument is not stated in this way in any of Quine's writings, but it seems to fit in well with what Quine says on this topic'' (Føllesdal, p. 296). As we have seen, according to Føllesdal, simplicity's role in physics is that of ''a guide to truth,'' overriding almost every other consideration in our choice between specific scientific theories, while simplicity's role in translation pales by contrast, being itself overridden by such things as mere agreement. Hence, in Rorty's terms, physics discovers 'laws' while translation constructs 'canons', such is the work wrought by simplicity, according to Føllesdal.

Føllesdal's account of the difference between physics and translation with respect to facts of the matter, given in terms of simplicity considerations, is certainly clever, but it is just as certainly not Quine's view. Føllesdal shares with Rorty (and Chomsky) the mistaken notion that Quine is using the expression 'fact of the matter' in some methodological (i.e., epistemological) sense. But this is erroneous; Quine's understanding of this term is decidedly *naturalistic* and *physicalistic*. When Quine says that there is a fact of the matter to physics and no fact of the matter to translation, he is talking about physical facts, and he is talking from within an already accepted naturalistic-physicalistic theory. Thus, the error that Føllesdal and Rorty (and Chomsky) share in their debate regarding facts of the matter is the assumption that the question before them is methodological (i.e., epistemological) when, in fact ''it is ontological, a question of reality, and to be taken naturalistically within our scientific theory of the world" (Quine, 1981e, p. 23). As I shall explain further, below, physics and translation are on a par methodologically (i.e., epistemologically), but they are not on a par ontologically. And, since they are on a methodological par, one cannot therefore distinguish between them in terms of simplicity considerations as Føllesdal is wont to do.

Another writer who is somewhat sympathetic to Quine's indeterminacy thesis and who tries his hand at explaining Quine's position is Bruce Aune. In his paper, "Quine on Translation and Reference", Aune's aim "is to clarify and elaborate Quine's key arguments for translational and referential indeterminacy" (Aune, p. 221). He begins by giving an exposition of the behavioristic procedure used by Quine in Chapter 2 of *Word and Object* to explain and support his indeterminacy thesis. However, Aune centers on the question of what Quine means by his claim that there is a fact of the matter to physics but not to translation. Presumably, to say that there is a fact of the matter to physics is to claim that if we could not choose between two physical theories on such grounds as observation, simplicity, familiarity of principle, conservatism, and so on, at most, only one of them can *still* be correct. According to Aune's Quine

> [t]he fact that we might not *know* that it is correct would not show that it is in some sense incomplete. The theory would (or could) be objectively right, because there would be an objective matter to be right about—namely, the objects whose existence the theory postulates. If those objects exist and have the appropriate features, then the theory would be objectively right, whether we could ever know it or not. (Aune, p. 223)

But why should translations be treated any differently? In other words, "[w]hy does Quine think that there is no objective 'fact of the matter' about whether an expression *E* has a particular translation in some other language" (Aune, p. 223)? According to Aune, the answer to this question begins with recognizing that "Quine's thesis of translational indeterminacy seems to rest squarely on his view that language is to be viewed 'naturalistically' " (Aune, p. 224). Quine's naturalistic orientation, we are rightly told, "supports his view that a 'fact of the matter' concerning the synonymy of expressions must be found *in* observable behavior, not in a supposed reference to something nonbehavioral, such as an idea or Idea" (Aune, p. 225). And, unfortunately, observable behavior will never be able to arbitrate a conclusive settlement among competing manuals of translation:

> Since, in Quine's opinion, the most we can expect of a translation manual is that it provide . . . a systematization of native utterances and a correlation of them (or segments of them) with words of our language, there is no alternative, he thinks, to concluding that countless incompatible translation manuals are, in principle, equally good. Consequently, there can be, for him, no such thing as *the* right or

correct manual and no such thing (absolutely speaking) as *the* right or correct translation of a given utterance. Considered absolutely, translation must be regarded as
indeterminate: the totality of relevant behavioral facts does not 'determine', or single out, any *particular* form of translation. (Aune, pp. 225–226)

Aune wonders, however, if Quine does not move too hastily from his naturalistic view of language (and his rejection of Platonism and mentalism) to the
conclusion that translation is indeterminate. Is it not possible that one could
share Quine's naturalism and yet consistently maintain that translation *is* determinate? Aune suggests, and then rejects, the position of Wilfrid Sellars as just
such a naturalistic view. Aune concludes from this discussion that while
"Quine's thesis of translational indeterminacy remains subject to dispute"
(Aune, p. 230), nevertheless, "[a]t the moment, no 'naturalistic' theory clearly
supporting translational determinacy seems to be available as an alternative to
Quine's" (Aune, p. 230).

Aune's account of why Quine believes there is no fact of the matter to
translation is correct. However, Aune's account of Quine's doctrine of under-
determination (which claims that two theories may be empirically equivalent
but logically incompatible and yet one might be *the* correct one) is suspect, for
it could be construed as presupposing that there is a thing-in-itself *(Ding an
sich),* a view which Quine explicitly rejects (see Quine 1981e, p. 22). Recall
that Aune says that one of the theories "would (or could) be objectively right,
because there would be an objective matter to be right about—namely, the
objects whose existence the theory postulates. *If those objects exist and have
the appropriate features, then the theory would be objectively right, whether
we could ever know it or not"* (Aune, p. 223, my emphasis). This way of
putting the matter certainly is not Quine's way, for it at least seems to construe
'fact of the matter' transcendentally. It also suggests that a true theory is one
that "fits the facts" which is another view that Quine explicitly rejects (see
Quine 1981c, p. 39). As we shall see later, the explanation of why there is a
fact of the matter to physics lies elsewhere; it has to do with the circumstance
that facts of the matter and truth are both immanent notions.

As we have seen, Chomsky's account goes wrong because he construes
'fact of the matter' methodologically, concluding that neither physics nor translation has a fact of the matter. Rorty's account goes wrong because he construes 'fact of the matter' methodologically, concluding instead that both physics and translation have a fact of the matter because methodology is the final
arbiter of ontology (i.e., no 'canon'/'law' dichotomy is possible). Føllesdal's
account goes wrong because he construes 'fact of the matter' methodologically,
assigning simplicity dubiously different roles in physics and linguistics. Aune's
account goes wrong because he construes 'fact of the matter' transcendentally,
making the truth of physics dependent upon a thing-in-itself. None of these
accounts of Quine's position accords naturalism and physicalism the central

roles they deserve, for the proper construal of 'fact of the matter' is neither methodological (i.e., epistemological) nor transcendental; it is naturalistic and physicalistic. We have yet to eke out, however, the sense in which Quine believes there is a fact of the matter to physics and none to translation. Before we can do so, we must become clearer about just what Quine's indeterminacy thesis amounts to, and we must come to understand Quine's conception of the relationship between ontology and epistemology.

Quine's indeterminacy of translation is, one might say, of two varieties. One variety is *indeterminacy of intension* or "meaning" (taken in some intuitive sense) and can affect any expression deemed significant enough to "have meaning". The other variety is *indeterminacy of extension,* or *indeterminacy of reference* and affects terms. (Quine calls this latter variety *inscrutability of reference,* or *inscrutability of terms.*) The former variety of indeterminacy amounts to the claim:

(A) Consistent with all possible dispositions to behavior on the parts of all concerned, different systems of analytical hypotheses can be formulated which render different translations of the same use of an expression which, on intuitive grounds, differ in "meaning"; *and* there is no sense to the question of any one translation being the uniquely correct one.

Similarly, the latter variety of indeterminacy amounts to the claim:

(B) Consistent with all possible dispositions to behavior on the parts of all concerned, different systems of analytical hypotheses can be formulated which translate the same use of an expression as either a nonterm or a term, and if a term, then as either a singular term or a general term, and if either, then as either abstract singular or general term or as a concrete singular or general term; and, further, if the expression in question is translated as a term of divided reference, then there will be further alternative systems of analytical hypotheses which will settle the reference of this term differently; *and* neither in the matter of termhood nor in the matter of reference is there any sense to the question of there being a uniquely correct translation.

What (A) and (B) assert, essentially, is that "meaning" *and* reference are indeterminate on behavioral grounds and that to inquire beyond the (possible) behavioral evidence for a unique "meaning" or referent is folly.

In order to simplify our task somewhat, let us agree to stick to the version of the indeterminacy thesis that deals with "meaning", and let us simplify the thesis somewhat by regarding it as asserting the following:

(C) That translations of a foreign language can be set up in such ways that while each is consistent with the speech dispositions of everyone con-

cerned they nevertheless can have different sentence-to-sentence correlations even to the point where two translations of a foreign sentence
can be correlated with sentences having opposite truth values; *and* there
is no answer to the (pseudo-) question of which translation is the
uniquely correct one—they are *all* correct insofar as they measure up
to the speech dispositions of all concerned.

Let us take Quine's *under-determination thesis* as asserting the following:

(D) Our system of the world is bound to have empirically equivalent but
logically incompatible alternatives which, if we were to discover them,
we would see no way of reconciling by a reconstrual of predicates (cf.
Quine 1975a, p. 327).

According to Quine, the chief difference between these two theses is that there
is no fact of the matter to the question of which translation is correct, but there
is a fact of the matter to the question of which physical theory is correct. As
we have seen, some of his critics (e.g., Chomsky and Rorty) maintain that this
alleged difference is spurious. As they see it, translation and physics are on a
par ontologically: either there is a fact of the matter to *both* or to *neither*.

As I indicated above, I believe that the claim that indeterminacy and under-
determination are on a par is half right. It is true that they are on a par methodologically (i.e., epistemologically), but they are not on a par ontologically.
*It is this confusion of epistemology with ontology which stands in the way of
accepting Quine's differentiation of his two theses.* I shall now try to dispel
this confusion.

Ontology and epistemology are concerned with different issues. Ontology
focuses on the issue of what there is; and what there is is a question of *truth*.
Epistemology focuses on the issues of how we know what there is; and how
we know what there is is a question of *method* and *evidence*. And evidence is
for Quine sensory evidence, so epistemology is for Quine empiricism. It follows that empiricism is not a theory of truth but a theory of evidence (i.e., of
warranted belief—cf. Quine, 1981c, p. 39). It does not purport to tell us what
there is, but only what evidence there is for what there is. It is in this sense
that Quine suggests that empiricism is the epistemology of ontology (cf. Quine,
1983, p. 500).

Despite the fact that ontology and epistemology focus on different issues,
ontology and epistemology are, for Quine, intimately related to each other.
And, Quine's differentiation of physics from translation, indeed, Quine's entire
philosophy, cannot be properly understood without grasping the nature of this
relationship. The relationship is complex and subtle, and is best characterized
as one of reciprocal containment.

When I remark that ontology and epistemology are, for Quine, related to
each other by way of reciprocal containment, what I mean is that (A) episte-

mology (empiricism) is contained in ontology (natural science—physicalism) as a chapter of empirical psychology, and yet (B) it is epistemology (empiricism) that provides an account of the methodological and evidential bases of ontology (natural science—physicalism) including empirical psychology itself. The circularity that this reciprocal containment evidences is something which Quine fully owns up to, and while it remains something to be explained, it is not, therefore, something to be explained away.

(A) *How epistemology is contained in ontology.* Quine's epistemology—his empiricistic theory of method and evidence—is contained in his ontology (natural science—physicalism) on at least three grounds: (1) his epistemology assumes the existence of the external world; (2) the two cardinal tenets of his epistemology (to be discussed below) are implications of his ontology; and (3) epistemology's contact points with the world, sensory receptors, are physical objects—objects belonging to the ontology of physiology. Let us examine each of these three grounds, in turn.

(1) *The external world.* Traditional epistemology, rationalistic or empiricistic, attempted to deduce or to rationally reconstruct ontological claims concerning the external world from a conceptual foundation that, itself, was not to be a part of that body of ontological claims, and yet was to be absolutely indubitable. Three central assumptions of such epistemology were (i) that the external world was something whose existence needed proving, (ii) that any such proof would be viciously circular should it depend essentially on any claim about the external world, and (iii) knowledge, by its very nature, must be indubitable.

Quine rejects all three of these central assumptions of traditional epistemology. From a Quinian perspective, the three hundred years from Descartes to Carnap (Idealism aside) were dominated by a forlorn squabble revolving around the comparative foundationalist merits of innate ideas and sense data—a squabble that could only end up just where it did, namely, in a *reductio per impossibile* proof of traditional (Realist) epistemology. Both the *deduction of* and the *reconstruction of* knowledge of the external world on the basis of some epistemologically prior footing are but impossible dreams (cf. Quine, 1969a, p. 74). The moral to be drawn is, simply, that there is no such prior footing to be had: three hundred years of meditating on first philosophy have only culminated in repudiating first philosophy! But, to repudiate first philosophy is not to repudiate epistemology *in toto:* there is still *naturalized* epistemology, an epistemology that presupposes ontology—the ontology of natural science.

Such an epistemology is, of course, circular but not viciously so (cf. Quine, 1981a, p. 24). The keys to understanding this point are the following: first, scepticism about the external world presupposes the existence of the external world. The sceptic is intent to show us that the external world might be an illusion. But,

> [i]llusions are illusions only relative to a prior acceptance of genuine bodies with which to contrast them . . . . The positing of bodies is already a rudimentary physical science; and it is only after that stage that the sceptic's invidious distinctions can make sense. Bodies have to be posited before there can be a motive, however tenuous, for acquiescing in a non-commital world of the immediate given. (Quine, 1975b, p. 67)

Once this point is grasped, it is clear that the defender of the belief in the existence of the external world is also free to use scientific knowledge in his defense (cf. Quine, 1981b, p. 72; also Quine, 1974, p. 3). Second, naturalized epistemology, unlike traditional empiricistic epistemology, neither attempts to *rationally reconstruct* the ontology of natural science from some kind of pristine, unadulterated sensory experience nor does it attempt to *deduce* the ontology of natural science from sensory experience, unadulterated or otherwise. These traditional goals of empiricism must be abandoned, according to Quine, for the very notion of pristine, unadulterated sensory experience is rather dubious and, anyway, there are no unique evidential relations to be found between sensory evidence and the theories it supports. Third, and finally, this same holism opens the way for Quine's fallibilism, enabling him to reject the traditional characterization of knowledge as indubitable (cf. Quine, 1981d, p. 180). Thus Quine's program of naturalized epistemology is circular (because it presupposes ontology), but it is not viciously so (because it renounces the affectations—and afflictions—of first philosophy).

(2) *Two cardinal tenets of (empiricistic) epistemology.* We have already noted that epistemology is concerned with the theory of method and evidence, and evidence is, for Quine, sensory evidence. Thus is Quine's epistemology empiricistic. As Quine sees it, there are two cardinal tenets of such epistemology; they are: (i) "whatever evidence there *is* for science *is* sensory evidence" (Quine, 1969a, p. 75) and (ii) "all inculcation of meanings of words must rest ultimately on sensory evidence" (Quine, 1969a, p. 75).

Now, what is the *source* of these two tenets of empiricism? In a word, science. "Science itself teaches that there is no clairvoyance; that the only information that can reach our sensory surfaces from external objects must be limited to two dimensional optical projections and various impacts of air waves on the eardrums and some gaseous reactions in the nasal passages and a few kindred odds and ends" (Quine, 1974, p. 2). Nevertheless, it should be emphasized that Quine does not regard the norms of present-day science to be immutable (Quine, 1981d, p. 181). Even if unlikely, it is possible, for example, that sensory stimulation might cease to be the chief source of our expectations regarding future events in the world, being replaced, say, by prophetic dreams. "At that point we might reasonably doubt our theory of nature in even fairly broad outlines. But our doubts would still be immanent, and of a piece with scientific endeavor" (Quine, 1981e, p. 22). So, even though Quine insists that our ontology (natural science-physicalism) tells us that our epistemology is *true,* and our epistemology tells us that our ontology is *warranted,* still, both of these claims are *part of science itself* and are, therefore, mutable and fallible. I take this to be a very important point when it comes to understanding Quine's philosophy.

3. *Epistemology's contact points with the world.* We have just noted that ontology (natural science—physicalism) tells us that its only evidence is sensory evidence. But what is sensory evidence? It is the activation of (physical) nerve endings by physical objects. But the very idea of nerve endings, epistemology's contact points with the world, belongs to that part of ontology called physiology; in other words, epistemology presupposes an ontology of nerve endings. And thus it is that the two cardinal tenets of Quine's empiricistic epistemology (noted above) presuppose an ontology of nerve endings and their physical stimulators, external objects. And thus it is, too, that empiricism remains in contact with the external world, making "scientific method partly empirical rather than solely a quest for internal coherence" (Quine, 1981c, p. 39).

So much for how epistemology is contained in ontology. We now turn to a consideration of the second aspect of the reciprocal containment of ontology and epistemology, namely, of how ontology is "contained" in epistemology.

(B) *How ontology is "contained" in epistemology.*

> The old epistemology aspired to contain, in a sense, natural science; it would construct it somehow from sense data. Epistemology in its new setting, conversely, is contained in natural science, as a chapter of psychology [as we have just seen]. But the old containment remains valid too, in its way. We are studying how the human subject of our study posits bodies and projects his physics from his data, and we appreciate that our position in the world is just like his. Our very epistemological enterprise, therefore, and the psychology wherein it is a component chapter, and the whole of natural science wherein psychology is a component book—all this is our own construction or projection from stimulations like those we were meting out to our epistemological subject. There is thus reciprocal containment, though containment in different senses: epistemology in natural science and natural science in epistemology. (Quine, 1969a, p. 83)[1]

In short, ontology is "contained" in epistemology in the sense that the ontology of natural science (physicalism), which the new epistemologist relies upon in providing his account of natural science, is itself a projection from the very same kinds of stimulations attributed to the human subject of his study.

Another way of putting this same point is to say that scientific epistemologists are themselves prohibited from making appeals to any alleged *a priori* (or otherwise transcendental) sources of knowledge—after all, they deny same to the subjects of their inquiry.

Furthermore, this naturalistic account of the acquisition of science which Quine is proposing (i.e., naturalized epistemology) has both a descriptive aspect and a normative aspect but, as we have already seen, Quine thinks the normative aspect is as tentative and mutable as science itself. Contrary to the hopes of traditional epistemologists, there will be no deducing ontology from epistemology; rather:

> Our scientific epistemologist pursues this inquiry and comes out with an account that has a good deal to do with the learning of language and with the neurology of perception. He talks of how men posit bodies and hypothetical particles, but he does not mean to suggest that the things thus posited do not exist. Evolution and natural selection will doubtless figure in this account, and he will feel free to apply physics if he sees a way.
>
> The naturalistic philosopher begins his reasoning within the inherited world theory as a going concern. He tentatively believes all of it, but believes also that some unidentified portions are wrong. He tries to improve, clarify, and understand the system from within. He is the busy sailor adrift in Neurath's boat. (Quine, 1981b, p. 72)

Let us now relate this business of the mutual containment of ontology and epistemology to the topics of translation, physics, and facts of the matter.

From the point of view of *epistemology,* under-determination of physical theory and indeterminacy of translation *are* on a par: Just as alternative *ontologies* can be erected on the same observational basis, so alternative *translations* of a native expression can be erected on the same observational basis. All are equally warranted by the evidence, let us suppose. How is it supposed to follow, then, that there is a fact of the matter to physics but no fact of the matter to translation?

Facts of the matter belong to the ontological phase of inquiry, not to the epistemological phase. *Ontology* is the theory of what there is. As we have seen, epistemology's contact points with the world are, according to Quine, sensory receptors. Ontology is that theoretical structure that links past and present sensory stimulations to future ones—it is a theory of objects. Under-determination of theory is, therefore, under-determination of ontology; it is the thesis that *different* systems of objects (or systems of sentences about objects) may link past and present sensory stimulations to future ones. Nevertheless, under-determination of theory is a thesis belonging to epistemology, not to ontology; it is a statement about *evidence* for theory, not about *truth* of theory, and this despite the fact that every such theory will have its own ontology. So far so good: "But it is a confusion to suppose that we can stand aloof and recognize all the alternative ontologies as true in their several ways, all the envisaged worlds as real. It is a confusion of truth with evidential support. Truth is immanent, and there is no higher. We must speak from within a theory, albeit any of various'' (Quine, 1981e, pp. 21–22).[2] In other words, despite the fact that it is meaningful to say of alternative theories that they are *equally warranted* by the same sensory evidence, it makes no sense to say that they are *equally true*. It makes sense to say they are equally warranted, because we are speaking from *within* the same (physicalistic) theory of evidence: given all the (possible) evidence, *this* ontology is warranted, *that* ontology is warranted, and so on. However, it makes no sense to say they are equally true, because we are *not* speaking from within the same theory of objects (i.e., ontology). The trouble isn't with 'equally', it is with 'true'. Such an extra-theoretical, or transcendental, usage is without meaning, for truth is an immanent notion—à la Tarski. In order for such a transcendental usage to be meaningful, there would have to be, presumably, a first philosophy, but there isn't, according to Quine. And since there is no such cosmic vantage point from which we could survey all competing, equally warranted ontologies, we are destined to occupy the position of some historical theory of what there is, which settles for us, at that time, the facts of the matter, what there is. In just this sense, and in just the words of our historically occupied theory, then, there is a fact of the matter to physics; it is just here that we feel the force of the figure of Neurath's boat, the full weight of Quine's naturalism.

On the other hand, there is no fact of the matter to translation. Regarding this point Quine says:

> I have argued that two conflicting manuals of translation can both do justice to all dispositions to behavior, and that, in such a case, there is no fact of the matter of which manual is right. The intended notion of matter of fact is not transcendental or yet epistemological, not even a question of evidence; it is ontological, a question of reality, and to be taken *naturalistically within our scientific theory of the world*. Thus suppose, to make things vivid, that we are settling still for a physics of elementary particles and recognizing a dozen or so basic states and relations in which they may stand. Then when I say there is no fact of the matter, as regards, say, the two rival manuals of translation, what I mean is that both manuals are compatible with all the same distributions of states and relations over elementary particles. In a word, they are physically equivalent. (Quine, 1981e, p. 23, my emphasis)

The current theory of the world is physicalistic—and with good reason, Quine thinks. And this physicalistic world-view settles, for the present, the physical facts of the matter and thereby what can be said to be true or false given these facts. Any putative meanings, therefore, that fall between the cracks of the physical facts just aren't meanings at all. And, further, since there just aren't any facts for such putative semantical statements to be about, it follows that such statements are indeterminate, that is, they are neither true nor false. In this straightforward, naturalistic-physicalistic sense, then, there is no fact of the matter to the question of which of the two manuals of translation is *the* right one.

To conclude, I have claimed that under-determination and indeterminacy are on a par *epistemologically*. Under-determination of physical theory tells us that equally warranted, alternative *ontologies* can be erected on the same evidential basis; indeterminacy of translation tells us that equally warranted, alternative *translations* can be erected on the same evidential basis. However, under-determination and indeterminacy are not on a par *ontologically*. There is a fact of the matter to physics, but there is no fact of the matter to translation. Despite the epistemological fact that under-determination of physical theory occurs, we must occupy the position of one or another such theory, which settles our ontology, our facts of the matter, even if only temporarily. In short, facts of the matter, like truth, are immanent, not transcendental. And settling, at present, for a physicalistic ontology, we must conclude that while there is a physical fact of the matter to physics, there is no physical fact of the matter to translation.

ROGER F. GIBSON

DEPARTMENT OF PHILOSOPHY
WASHINGTON UNIVERSITY
JANUARY 1985

NOTES

1. In a letter to the author dated November 29, 1983, Professor Quine wrote: "It ['reciprocal containment'] is a figure that was quite explicitly guiding my thought as far back surely as 1945, though I perhaps never put it into print until . . . 'Epistemology Naturalized'."

2. The reader should be warned that while my analysis rests on this passage from *Theories and Things,* on p. 29 of the same book, but in a different essay, Quine writes: "Still, let us suppose that the two formulations are in fact empirically equivalent even though not known to be; and let us suppose further that all of the implied observation categoricals are in fact true, although, again, not known to be. Nothing more, surely, can be required for the truth of either theory formulation. Are they both true? I say yes." It would appear that Quine cannot have it both ways.

REFERENCES

Aune, Bruce. "Quine on Translation and Reference", *Philosophical Studies* 27 (April, 1975): 221–236.

Chomsky, Noam. [1980]: *Rules and Representations*. New York: Columbia University Press, 1980.

_____. . [1975]: *Reflections on Language*. New York: Pantheon Books, Random House, 1975.

_____. . [1969]: "Quine's Empirical Assumptions", In *Words and Objections, Essays on the Work of W. V. Quine*. Edited by D. Davidson and J. Hintikka. Dordrecht-Holland: D. Reidel Pub. Co., 1969.

Føllesdal, Dagfinn. "Indeterminacy of Translation and Under-Determination of the Theory of Nature", *Dialectica* 27 (1973): 289–301.

Quine, W. V. [1983]: "Ontology and Ideology Revisited", *Journal of Philosophy* 80 (September, 1983): 499–502.

_____. . [1981a]: "Empirical Content", In *Theories and Things*. Edited by W. V. Quine. Cambridge, MA: The Belknap Press of Harvard University Press.

_____. . [1981b]: "Five Milestones of Empiricism", In *Theories and Things*.

_____. . [1981c]: "On the Very Idea of a Third Dogma", In *Theories and Things*.

_____. . [1981d]: "Responses", In *Theories and Things*.

_____. . [1981e]: "Things and Their Place in Theories", In *Theories and Things*.

_____. . [1975a]: "On Empirically Equivalent Systems of the World", *Erkenntnis* 9 (1975): 313–328.

_____. . [1975b]: "On the Nature of Natural Knowledge", In *Mind and Language*. Edited by Samuel Guttenplan. Oxford: Oxford University Press, 1975.

_____. . [1974]: *The Roots of Reference*. LaSalle, IL: Open Court Pub. Co., 1974.

_____. . [1969a]: "Epistemology Naturalized", In *Ontological Relativity and Other Essays*. Edited by W. V. Quine. New York: Columbia University Press, 1969.

_____. . [1969b]: "Ontological Relativity", In *Ontological Relativity and Other Essays*.

Rorty, Richard. "Indeterminacy of Translation and of Truth", *Synthese* 23 (March, 1972): 443–462.

REPLY TO ROGER F. GIBSON, JR.

Unlike so many, Gibson fully understands the difference in status that I ascribe to the indeterminacy of translation and the under-determination of natural science. I count on the clarity of his presentation for a swelling of the ranks of those who get the point.

In reporting Rorty's interpretations of my position, however, he leaves an interpretation dangling that I must clear away: a purported distinction on my part between canons and laws. "What more does it take for there to be a 'fact of the matter', " Rorty asks, "than a rational procedure for reaching agreement . . . ?" There are indeed further virtues that we can seek and agree on, in devising a manual of translation, besides conformity to verbal dispositions. We can seek simplicity, and we can try to maximize truth in the natives' assertions. If these and kindred canons of procedure suffice to weed out all conflicting codifications of the native's verbal dispositions, which is doubtful, I would still say that they confer no fact on the matter. This is not because of any general distinction between canons and laws. It is just that the factuality is limited to the verbal dispositions themselves, however elegantly or clumsily codified.

Such, for me, are the facts of semantics. What then of physics? Føllesdal undertakes to reconcile the factuality of physics with its empirical under-determination by treating simplicity as a presumption of truth. This is not my line, as Gibson appreciates. It would fail of its purpose anyway in cases where rival physical theories are equally simple. Physics is factual in my view simply for want of a higher tribunal. As Gibson urges, naturalism is the key.

Gibson cites Føllesdal's interesting observation that the indeterminacy of translation follows from holism and the verification theory of meaning. Føllesdal mistrusts this defense because of doubts about verificationism, and I gather that Gibson agrees. But I find it attractive. The statement of verificationism relevant to this purpose is that "evidence for the truth of a sentence is identical with the meaning of the sentence"; and I submit that if sentences in general had meanings, their meanings would be just that. It is only holism itself that tells us that in general they do not have them.

Gibson points out a startling contradiction between consecutive essays in *Theories and Things*. There was an appreciable lapse of time in my writing of the two essays, and the more so in that the first one developed from still earlier lectures. I was aware of my change in attitude, but not of so abrupt a conflict. In the first passage I had held that one of two systems of the world must be deemed false even if we know them to be empirically equivalent. I shall call this the *sectarian* position. My reason for it was naturalism: my disavowal of any higher tribunal than science itself. In the later and conflicting passage, as Gibson relates, I opted for truth of both systems of the world, finding it offensive to my empiricist sensibilities to declare otherwise. This I shall call the *ecumenical* position. It raises two questions that can be satisfactorily dealt with, we shall see, and a third that seemingly cannot.

One apparent difficulty with it is that two empirically equivalent systems of the world may be *logically incompatible,* and hence incapable of being simultaneously viewed as true. This difficulty was met in *Theories and Things* (pp. 29f) by the following expedient, due to Davidson. When a sentence is affirmed in one of two empirically equivalent theories and denied in the other, the incompatibility is resoluble simply by reconstruing some theoretical term in that sentence as a pair of distinct homonyms. If the two theories have unlike ontologies, we can reconcile them by distinguishing two styles of variables.

A second apparent difficulty with the ecumenical position is the naturalistic restraint cited just now in support of the sectarian view. But this again can be accommodated. Once the two empirically equivalent systems of the world have been rendered logically compatible, they can be treated as a single big tandem theory consisting perhaps of two largely independent lobes and a shared logic. Its lobes describe the world in two equally correct ways, and we can simultaneously reckon as factual whatever is asserted in either. What can be known of the world is the common denominator of all the world systems, logically reconciled, that conform to all possible observation.

But there is a third difficulty, raised by Føllesdal in a recent conversation. To exhibit it I must distinguish cases. In the tandem theory just now contemplated, a sentence in the added lobe may or may not be couched wholly in the vocabulary of our original lobe. Those that are so couched are either already affirmed also in the original lobe or can be freely added, for they treat of the same matters without contradiction. They might even be welcome additions, as settling the truth values of some old but hitherto unadjudicated sentences.

The picture changes when we come to sentences of the added lobe that do contain alien terms, perhaps created by Davidson's expedient of forging homonyms or perhaps present in the rival theory to begin with. Can we systematically so reinterpret this deviant lexicon as to render it in our own language without distorting empirical content? If so, we are back in the benign first case and can cheerfully annex the whole lobe to our original theory. All is ecumenical still.

But the remaining case, and the sticky one, is where the alien terms of the annexed lobe are irreducible. The sentences containing them constitute a gratuitous annex to the original theory, since the whole combination is still empirically equivalent to the original. It is as if some scientifically undigested terms of metaphysics or religion, say 'essence' or 'grace' or 'Nirvana', were admitted into science along with all their pertinent doctrine, and tolerated on the ground merely that they contravened no observations. It would be an abandonment of the scientist's quest for economy and of the empiricist's standard of meaningfulness.

The sectarian position, then, is my newly recovered stance on these precarious slopes. It is called for in that last case, where no way is evident of annexing the rival system of the world without adding new terms. Our own system is true by our lights, and the other does not even make sense in our terms.

And what if, even so, we have somehow managed to persuade ourselves that the two are empirically equivalent? Then surely we must recognize the two as equally *warranted*. Having got the swing of the alien jargon without benefit of translation, we might even oscillate between the two for the sake of an enriched perspective on nature. But whichever system we are working in is the one for us to count at the time as true, there being no wider frame of reference.

W.V.Q.

6

Nelson Goodman

NOMINALISMS

In a certain village, Maria's sign reads "All clothes washed" while Anna's counters "Clothes washed in clean water." Anna always returns a wash with many articles untouched; for her spring gives clean water but not fast enough. Maria always finishes much more of a wash, but never all; for although her creek provides plenty of rather muddy water, there is always too much work to do. Whenever a traveller inquires at the inn for a laundress, he is asked whether he is a nominalist or a platonist.

Early in our association, Quine and I often discussed matters pertaining to nominalism. Nominalistic predilections had led Henry Leonard and me to develop and apply the calculus of individuals, and Quine had formulated his ontological criterion. Our common attitudes and interests soon inspired a major effort to show how nominalistic definitions could be constructed for many central concepts often cited as irredeemably platonistic.

From the beginning, our formulations of the basic principle of nominalism differed. For Quine, nominalism could countenance nothing abstract, but only concrete physical objects. For me, nominalism could countenance no classes but only individuals. This difference, noted in the second paragraph of "Steps toward a Constructive Nominalism"[1] in no way affected our interest in or the value of the constructions undertaken in that paper.

"Steps" in our view stood as something of a triumph for nominalism, since it achieved nominalistic constructions of, for instance, *proof* and *theorem,* which had always been held up as notions far beyond the nominalist's reach. But of course the platonist, unimpressed, simply pointed to other notions that had not yet been nominalized, and insisted on the inability of the nominalist to do everything, while the intransigent nominalist, observing that the platonist had not done and never can do everything either, went on working within his means.

Since "Steps", Quine has somewhat reluctantly adopted the platonist's luxuriant apparatus while I inch along in stubborn nominalistic austerity. Actually, the difference is not that marked; for Quine, given the chance, would gladly trade any platonistic construction for a nominalistic one, and I sometimes make use of platonistic constructions as temporary expedients awaiting eventual nominalization.

Roughly, as I have said, nominalism for Quine bars everything but physical objects while nominalism for me bars everything but individuals; but the matter is more complex than that. A physical object is not in and by itself, apart from all systematic construction, an individual or a class or a class of classes. A football, for example, may be construed as an individual or as a class of molecules or as a class of molecule-classes of atoms, etc. Nominalism for Quine is thus better described as barring all but physical objects and *also* barring treatment of physical objects otherwise than as individuals. By now it is clear that the two restrictions are of drastically different kinds; for while the former bars entities of certain kinds, the latter rather bars certain *means of construction*. Quine's abandonment of nominalism consisted of dropping the restriction upon means of construction while retaining the restriction to physical objects.

Nominalism for me admits only individuals, yet allows anything to be taken as an individual—that is, bars the composition of different entities out of the same elements. For instance, if a and b and $c,$ whatever they may be, are taken as individuals indivisible in a given nominalistic system, then at most four other entities may be admitted under that system: those composed of a and $b,$ of a and $c,$ of b and $c,$ and of a and b and $c.$ More generally, if the number of atomic individuals in the system is $n,$ the maximum total number of individuals in the system is $2^n - 1.$ Whether the several compositions of atomic individuals are called wholes or sums or even classes does not matter, so long as no two of them contain exactly the same atoms. But once two entities made up out of the same atoms are distinguished—for example, when a and the composition of a and b are recognized as combining to make up a different entity than do b and the composition of a and b—then nominalism is violated. platonism, using full set theory, admits a vast infinity of different entities made up out of the same atoms. Thus the restriction to individuals, even with a license to take anything as an individual, is a severe constraint.

This restriction is distinct from such other principles as finitism and particularism[2] that are perhaps no less characteristic of the nominalistic tradition. Keeping the several principles distinct matters more than deciding which deserves the name "nominalism". In my usage, the restriction to individuals is taken as the criterion of nominalism, with full recognition that nominalism seldom if ever goes by itself.

This is not the place to review the case for nominalism as set forth in "A World of Individuals",[3] but I must respond to recent questions concerning how the restrictive nominalism of that paper can be reconciled with the literal relativism of *Ways of Worldmaking*.[4] The answer should be evident in the very formulation of nominalism as free to take anything as an individual but not to take anything as other than an individual. My sort of relativism holds that there are many right world-versions, some of them conflicting with each other, but insists on the distinction between right and wrong versions. Nominalism, leaving choice of basis wide open, imposes a restriction on how a right version may be constructed from a basis. A right version must be well-made, and for nominalism that requires construing all entities as individuals.

Nominalism, often pronounced dead, still erupts every so often. Hartry Field in his new *Science without Numbers*[5] argues that a somewhat modified nominalism is adequate for physics. David Malament, in a review of that book,[6] comments that even if Field's constructions work for an absolutist physics, they do not work—or at least have not been shown to work—for a quantum physics. Ironically, one of Quine's primary reasons for deserting nominalism seems to have been that he considers it inadequate for an absolutist physics.

NELSON GOODMAN

DEPARTMENT OF PHILOSOPHY
HARVARD UNIVERSITY
DECEMBER 1981

NOTES

1. *Journal of Symbolic Logic* 12(1947): 105–122. Reprinted in my *Problems and Projects* (Indianapolis: Hackett, 1972), pp. 173–198.

2. I.e. the restriction to the concrete. See *The Structure of Appearance*, 3rd ed. (Dordrecht/Boston: Reidel, 1977), pp. 104–106.

3. In *The Problem of Universals*, a symposium with Alonzo Church and I. M. Bochenski at Notre Dame University in March 1956 (Notre Dame: Notre Dame University Press, 1956), pp. 155–172.

4. Indianapolis: Hackett, 1978.

5. Oxford: Blackwell, 1980.

6. *Journal of Philosophy* 79(1982), pp. 523–534.

REPLY TO NELSON GOODMAN

"For Quine," Goodman writes, "nominalism could countenance. . . only physical objects." No, my physicalism was additional. Nominalism as I understood the term could also countenance—unlike me—an irreducibly mental realm of sensory events. What I have called nominalism, and do not indeed see my way to maintaining, is what he calls particularism.

For Goodman, on the other hand, the distinctive trait of nominalism is that "once two entities made up out of the same atoms are distinguished, . . . nominalism is violated." My trouble with this is the metaphor 'made up out of'. He also writes 'contain', and 'composition'. It is a spatial metaphor, meant to cover the relation of properties to their instances, and of classes to their members, and how much else?

I see no way of making his intuition explicit unless in terms expressly of the negative status of classes. It is characteristic of nominalism, in what seems to be Goodman's sense, that it admits classes only casually here and there, if at all, rather than in full systematic proliferation. This is still vague, since even full-fledged set theories mount some restrictions, on pain of paradox. But let that pass. In any event Goodman is right in wanting to represent nominalism as banning *more* than classes, for there are also properties to worry about, to say nothing of novel entities that could be arbitrarily trumped up and said to be counterparts of classes, capable of all the same nefarious business. At this point the verb 'determine' comes to the rescue. It is characteristic of nominalism in Goodman's sense, we might say, that it eschews any domain that *determines* a full domain of classes. By this I mean that it eschews any domain into which a full domain of classes can be mapped by a one-many open sentence. The sense of 'full' I leave vague as before.

Regarding "Steps toward a Constructive Nominalism", finally, certain reservations want noting. We made full nominalist sense of elementary portions of applied arithmetic, but for further reaches of mathematics we retreated to a formalistic position and undertook to make nominalistic sense only of meta-mathematical discourse *about* the formulas. Even in this more modest under-taking we found the nominalistic strictures confining; nominalistic metamathe-matics is far less free than the constructivist metamathematics of the Hilbert school. The limitations thus encountered strike me as an interesting feature of our paper, and so do the strategems that we devised; for they yielded consid-erable mileage despite all.

W.V.Q.

7

Gilbert Harman

QUINE'S GRAMMAR

I

The Task of the Grammarian

According to Quine, the sole task of the grammarian of a language *L* is to provide a purely formal specification of the class of "significant sequences" of phonemes of *L*, "significant" in the sense that they are "capable of occurring in the normal stream of speech."[1] The grammarian will no doubt "follow the orthodox line . . . of listing 'morphemes' and describing constructions";[2] but he does not need to suppose that there is a uniquely right way to do this; any grammar will do as long as it yields a formal specification of the class of significant sequences. In general there will be many "extensionally equivalent" grammars, each correctly specifying this class; but Quine denies that the grammarian has to believe that only one of these grammars contains the "correct" list of morphemes and the "right" grammatical constructions. He allows that one grammar may be simpler or more elegant than another and agrees that that is at least an aesthetic reason to prefer the one to the other; however, he suggests that there will be several equally simple and elegant grammars that correctly specify the significant sequences yet yield different lists of morphemes and grammatical constructions. Quine's grammarian will not suppose that there is any reason to choose among such grammars. In particular, Quine's grammarian will not assume "that there is . . . an unarticulated system of grammatical rules which is somehow implicit in [a speaker's] mind in a way that an extensionally equivalent system is not."[3]

Now, it may seem that there is something missing in Quine's discussion, namely an account of why anyone would wish to pursue grammar in his sense. Without an account of the purpose of grammar, all we can see is that Quine's grammarian has decided, for one or another unspecified reason, to try to give a formal characterization of an arbitrarily selected empirical class of events apart from any concern with the explanation of those events, like someone who

---

Work on this paper was supported in part by NSF. I am indebted to comments Adam Morton made about an earlier version.

tries to give a formal characterization of the sounds that people make in bath-tubs apart from any concern with why they make those sounds. That is, from Quine's description of the job of the grammarian, it can seem quite puzzling why grammar in his sense should be of any more scientific interest than such a study of bathtub sounds.

Not that Quine supposes that grammar is utterly useless. On the contrary, he mentions two rather important uses of grammar. First, he indicates that grammatical analysis will play a role in the "analytical hypotheses" that are needed for manuals of translation between different languages. Second, he argues that grammatical analysis of one's own language is required for the statement of basic principles of logic. But, given Quine's views about translation and logic, neither of these uses of grammar provides a basis for taking grammar to be of any straightforward scientific interest.

II

Grammar and Translation

If a translator wishes to prepare a manual of translation between English and another language L, he will need grammars for English and L that provide lists of words and grammatical constructions. The translator will attempt to associate words of English with words of L and constructions of English with constructions of L so that sentences of English will be associated with translations in L by virtue of the grammatical analyses of these sentences together with the associations between corresponding words and constructions.

The pairings of words with words and constructions with constructions will only be approximate because of differences in usage between English and L, so additional comments and 'stage directions' will be needed if everything is to work out right. But there is no real alternative to this sort of appeal to grammatical analysis. The translator is not going to be able to give an explicit list of the pairs of sentences of English and L which translate each other. That is ruled out by the infinity of sentences that would have to be listed. And, even if he were to restrict himself, say, to sentences of twenty words or less, there are too many to list.[4]

Furthermore, if the translator has no access to bilingual speakers of English and L, he will have to appeal to grammatical analysis for another reason. There are many sentences that he will not be able to translate unless he has a grammatical analysis that enables him to relate those sentences to others that he can already translate. Quine suggests that certain observation sentences, such as *that is blue* or *this is snow* have a distinctive use that makes them relatively easy to translate when considered solely by themselves and apart from their relations to other sentences.[5] But there are many sentences for which this is not so, *clear sky is blue, water is wet, clean snow is white*. There is nothing about the way in which these sentences are used, considered in themselves and apart from the way they are used in relation to other sentences, which would indicate how they are to be translated into another language. A translator without access to bilinguals will need at the very least to make use of a grammatical analysis that allows him to relate these sentences to observation sentences, *that is the sky, this is wet, that is white, this is blue*, and so forth.

Recall that there are many extensionally equivalent but equally adequate grammars of English and similarly of *L*. It is unlikely that every pair of adequate grammars of English and *L* respectively will be useful to the translator. It is likely that certain pairs of grammars will fail to provide a way for the translator to associate words with words and constructions with constructions so as to yield an adequate manual of translation between English and *L*. Therefore, if the grammarian is pursuing his task because he is ultimately interested in providing a manual of translation, he is not solely concerned to find *any* formal characterization of the classes of significant sequences of the languages in question; he wants to find a characterization that can be used for the purposes of translation.

Would it make sense to say that *as a grammarian* he is interested in *any* formal characterization of the relevant classes while as a *translator* he is interested in something more? This would make sense if there were some independent point to grammar, apart from its usefulness to translation. But, if Quine is right about grammar, it is unclear so far that it has any further point. For we have seen no reason so far to distinguish Quine's grammarian from Quine's translator.

Quine says that the task of the translator between English and *L* is to prepare a translation manual, which in a more or less formal way associates sentences of English with sentences of *L* so that dispositions to use language are best preserved. Any such manual consists of a set of 'analytical hypotheses', i.e., a grammar of English, a grammar of *L*, an association of English words with words of *L*, and an association of grammatical constructions of English with grammatical constructions of *L*, together with exceptions and 'stage directions'. Quine argues that there will be countlessly many equally adequate but different translation manuals between English and *L* with different sets of analytical hypotheses, each manual compatible with speakers' dispositions to use English and *L*. He argues further that some of these equally adequate manuals will differ not only in the grammars ascribed to English and to *L* but also in what sentences of English are assigned as translations of sentences of *L*. Two equally adequate manuals, he says, will in countless cases assign translations that are utterly different and in no sense equivalent. Quine's translator accepts this 'indeterminacy of translation' and does not assume that one of these manuals is right to the exclusion of the others. He goes about his task without supposing that there is a 'correct' set of analytical hypotheses or that a certain sentence of English is 'really' the translation of a certain sentence of L even though different manuals provide quite different translations.[6]

But then what is the point of translation? Suppose that I were to discover that different people make different sorts of noises in bathtubs. I might then try to provide analyses of Albert's bathtub sounds and of George's bathtub sounds in such a way that I can give a general method for associating Albert's sounds with George's that preserves dispositions to make those sounds. But it is unclear what point there would be to such bathtub sound translation apart from a further interest I might have in why people make the bathtub sounds that they do. Similarly, if Quine is right about ordinary translation between languages, it is unclear what interest such translation could have for scientific theory.

Translation between English and L does have a practical point. Speakers of one language can use a translation manual in order to get along in the other language and they can have various reasons for wanting to get along in the other language. So there is a practical point to grammar; some grammar or other is needed in the preparing of a translation manual. But we have so far seen no theoretical point to grammar in Quine's sense, only this practical point.

III

Grammar and Logic

Quine sees another use of grammar in the specification of logical generalizations. Unlike ordinary nonlogical generalizations, these talk of truth and grammatical form. Given ordinary nonlogical truths like *Tom is mortal, Sue is mortal, Albert is mortal,* and so forth, it is easy to generalize without talk of language, *everyone is mortal.* Given logical truths like *Tom is mortal or Tom is not mortal, Sue is happy or Sue is not happy, Albert plays the viola or Albert does not play the viola,* and so forth, we cannot properly generalize without talk of language. According to Quine we must say something like, *any sentence of the grammatical form 'P or not-P' is true.*[7] Thus, as Quine conceives logic, it depends on a prior grammatical analysis.

Not every grammatical analysis will be useful to the logician. Many grammars will fail to contain the resources that would allow the logician to state generalizations of the sort that he wishes to state. Here, then, would seem to be an additional constraint on the grammarian who pursues his subject from an interest in logic; he seeks not just an analysis into morphemes and constructions that characterizes the 'significant sequences' but also wants an analysis that can be used in stating general principles of logic.

Still, there can be different grammatical analyses of a language with correspondingly different logics. Consider for example the status of the adverb *necessarily*, as in, *necessarily, 5 + 7 = 12.* We might treat *necessarily* as a sentential operator, like negation, and envision a modal logic, with such logical principles as that every sentence of the grammatical form *if necessarily p, p is true.* Or we might suppose that *necessarily* is a disguised quantifier, like *always,* so that our original example says, *5 + 7 = 12 in all possible worlds.* In that case we will not have a special modal logic but will make do with ordinary quantificational logic. Or, we might suppose that *necessarily* is a transformational variant of the predicate *necessary,* so that our example says *that 5 + 7 = 12 is necessary;* here we will need a logic of *that* clauses.[8]

Now, Quine's logician (which is to say Quine himself), unlike Quine's grammarian and Quine's translator, is not willing to settle for any old combination of grammar and logic that makes sense of the language. Indeed Quine has been concerned to argue for a particular one of the countless possible logics, namely, standard quantificational logic (with identity).[9]

But that is not to say that Quine would allow, as a constraint on a grammar, that a natural language must be analyzed in such a way that the resulting logic is standard quantificational logic. Quine's logician is not interested in the *analysis* of natural language; he is concerned with the *regimentation* of language for the purposes of science. Choice of logic is part of choice of one's overall theory of the world. Quine thinks that to do logic solely by analyzing ordinary language would be like doing physics by analyzing the opinions of the man in the street. Quine's attitude about *necessarily* is that, no matter how analyzed, the idea is not needed in science; so the logician can ignore it.[10]

Grammar which is useful to logic, as Quine sees it, is not concerned with the analysis of natural language but with the construction of a regimented language that will serve certain purposes of science. This connection, which Quine sees between grammar and logic, provides no scientific motivation for the grammatical study of natural language. Since the connections with translation and with logic that I have discussed in this and the previous section represent the only uses of grammar that Quine mentions, and since neither of these uses makes grammar of theoretical interest, I conclude that the study of the grammar of a natural language in Quine's sense of grammar is not part of scientific theory but represents at best one aspect of a technique for getting along with certain people (by learning to speak their language).

IV

An Alternative Conception of Grammar

Now it might be true that grammar has a practical use in helping people get along in a language, true that it is useful for science in the way that Quine describes, yet also true that grammar is a scientific subject in its own right. Noam Chomsky, for one, does treat grammar as if it were just such a scientific subject.[11] He assumes, first, that language is often used to express one's thoughts, whether in the act of communication or in simply thinking out loud. Second, he assumes that utterances in the language have meaning and the meaning which they have is often connected with the thoughts that they might express. Third, Chomsky assumes that what meaning a sentence has, what thought it can express, is a function of the morphemes and grammatical structure of the utterance. Fourth, he assumes that utterances are uttered and perceived as having a certain structure. In particular, they are uttered and perceived as a sequence of phonemes together with additional structure, words and phrases, surface structure as well as deeper structure. To speak in this way of utterances uttered and perceived as having a certain structure is to speak of mental representations. Phonemes have their reality perhaps as instructions to the voice box and diaphragm, the hearer recovering the instructions by guessing from the heard physical sounds and the linguistic and nonlinguistic context. (Phonemes apparently do not correspond to any simple physical properties of the utterance.) Similarly, the hearer guesses at divisions into words and phrases, surface and deeper structure, to form a mental representation of the sentence under analysis which the speaker uttered. We can ourselves become conscious of aspects of these structures, according to Chomsky, when we consider utterances with ambiguous structures, *they are flying planes, visiting relatives can be a nuisance*.

Grammar is here conceived as giving an account of the relevant mental structures. Universal grammar attempts to say what is common to systems of mental grammatical structures in various languages. Universal grammar is relevant to language learning and the question of how much of this system of structure is innate and built in ahead of time, how much is learned when language is learned. The study of grammar is also relevant to but different from an account of actual linguistic performance, the sorts of things speakers might say, the conditions under which they will be understood, and so forth.

From this point of view, what Quine calls grammar, namely the providing of a formal characterization of the class of sequences that could occur in the normal stream of speech, is not grammar strictly so called but is rather part of the theory of linguistic performance. The extent to which an utterance could occur in normal speech is not simply a matter of its grammaticality but also depends on ease of processing and other things. For example, *the book that the man the girl married read is interesting* is grammatical but unlikely to occur in normal speech because of processing difficulties.[12]

V

Quine's Argument

Suppose that a group of linguists develop a specific theory along the lines just indicated. They specify various 'performance factors', they suggest a set of linguistic universals, they develop grammars for particular languages, and so forth. And suppose that the specific theory that they develop accounts quite well for the linguistic behavior of speakers of various languages. We are of course quite far today from any such development, but we can suppose that it might happen. In that case, would not these linguists have excellent reasons to conclude that the linguistic universals they had proposed really were linguistic universals, that the grammars that they had written really were the grammars of the languages for which they were written, that hearers form percepts described by the relevant grammars, and so forth? Quine says that they would not.

Quine's objection is that if there is one such theory, there are certain to be others. There are certain to be similar theories that hypothesize different linguistic universals and different grammars of particular languages while accounting equally well for behavior. And, there are also going to be less similar theories with different hypotheses about performance factors which postulate grammars that are not even extensionally equivalent to the grammars of the original theory. Still, because of compensating changes in the account of performance, these theories will also account for behavior as well as the original theory. How can we say that one of these possible theories is right to the exclusion of the others? It will not help to cut open people's heads. The various states of the brain do not come conveniently labeled; they must be interpreted; and how they are interpreted will depend on the theories held by those who do the interpreting. If one group finds that it can read its theory into the brain, it is possible, even likely, that others will be able to read their own theories in. But then, Quine would say, it makes no sense to maintain that one group of linguists is right, another wrong. So it makes no sense to say that one grammar is right, another wrong. The only objective reality is speakers' dispositions to linguistic behavior; and that reality does not uniquely determine a particular set of. linguistic universals, a particular grammar for English, or even what the sentences of English are.[13]

This is an extremely powerful argument, yet it appears to conflict with common sense. Consider for example the following headline in a student newspaper, which was called to my attention by Paul Benacerraf: *UNIVERSITY SCHEDULES BENEFIT SPORTS EXHIBITIONS*. There is a grammatical ambiguity in this headline, which can be explicated in terms of phrase structure. *(UNIVERSITY SCHEDULES) BENEFIT (SPORTS EXHIBITIONS)* as against *(UNIVERSITY) SCHEDULES (BENEFIT SPORTS EXHIBITIONS)*. We can perceive this sentence in two different groupings. We can perceive *UNIVERSITY* and *SCHEDULES* as grouped together to form a unit, or we can perceive the sentence in another way in which these two words are not thus grouped together. What I have just said seems common sense. Yet Quine argues that it makes *no* sense to suppose that such remarks might be right or wrong.[14]

Common sense indicates that we perceive what is said or written as a series of words grouped into phrases. Common sense and linguistic theory indicate that we do this by forming a structured percept, indicating not only surface structure but deep structure as well. (The two ways in which we perceive *visiting relatives can be a nuisance* depend on whether we take *relatives* to be the subject or object of *visiting,* and that is a deep structure distinction not represented in surface structure.) This linguistic theory also admits of tests other than coincidence with common sense. For example, if people perceive sentences by forming structured percepts, then the structures of these percepts may have effects on other aspects of perception. Just such effects seem to have been discovered in a series of 'click' experiments done by Bever and others. Subjects who were listening to sentences through one earphone heard clicks through the other earphone; in reporting where the clicks occurred, the subjects tended to displace their location toward major phrase boundaries. This would indicate that such phrase boundaries have psychological reality, as predicted by the percept theory, and that the psychologically real boundaries manifest their presence by having an effect on perception of a sort one would expect.[15]

IV

Methodological Reflections

Since Quine's conclusion appears to conflict with common sense and with the natural interpretation of certain experimental results, we need a better understanding of his argument; and, in this connection, it is useful to consider some analogous cases, for example, the case of the inverted spectrum hypothesis. We are inclined to suppose that other people mean what we mean by color words like *red, blue,* and *green*. But other hypotheses would account for a particular person's behavior. According to one of these hypotheses, the inverted spectrum hypothesis, the other person means by *red* what we mean by *green,* he means by *blue* what we mean by *orange,* and so forth; yet because of the way in which he perceives the world, he talks just as we do (red things look green to him and so forth). There is no way to distinguish our usual hypothesis from the inverted spectrum hypothesis in behavioral terms. Yet Quine, for one, does not conclude that there is no truth of the matter as to what someone else means by *This is red.* Indeed, it is just at this point that Quine insists that there is a truth of the matter. Given that the other person applies color words as we do, he means what we mean, according to Quine.[16]

Now, the inverted spectrum hypothesis is what Chomsky and other linguists of his persuasion might call a 'notational variant' of our usual hypothesis. That is, there is a relatively simple way to translate between the two hypotheses so that the issue between them would appear to be verbal rather than substantive. So let us consider a different case which cannot be so easily treated as a merely verbal conflict.

Let us suppose that there is a particular hypothesis about a given person's beliefs, desires, and other psychological states that is compatible with that person's behavior and dispositions to behave and serves to explain that behavior and those dispositions as well as any other such hypothesis. Then it is highly likely that there are other quite bizarre assumptions about his beliefs, desires, and so forth that would be equally compatible with behavior and dispositions and equally explanatory. If so, does it follow that there is no truth to the matter as to what his beliefs and desires are?

I want to consider this question quite apart from worries about indeterminacy of translation, so let us assume that we understand that person's language. Still, even relative to that understanding of his language there are no doubt various quite different assumptions about his beliefs and desires that are compatible with and explanatory of his behavior and dispositions to behave. Instead of relatively normal assumptions about him, we might ascribe to him very strong desires to conceal his real feelings and we might ascribe quite odd beliefs about us to him, as well as odd beliefs about the world. Presumably this could be done in such a way that desires and beliefs compensate for each other so as to yield his current behavior and dispositions. However, I am not interested in proving that such bizarre hypotheses might account for behavior and dispositions as well as other less bizarre hypotheses. I want to suppose that there are such bizarre hypotheses that do account as well for behavior and dispositions. Then I want to ask whether the existence of such hypotheses would imply that there is no truth as to what beliefs and desires a person has (relative to an interpretation of his language).

The person in question is not going to think that there is no truth to the matter. He is going to suppose that he knows that he has certain beliefs and desires, anyway, so that there is a truth to the matter at least with respect to those beliefs and desires. And he will think he can tell whether or not he is being sincere when he reports that he believes certain things or has certain desires. But what does his confidence consist in? Perhaps this: that when he asks himself whether it is true that p, he is immediately inclined to answer, to himself and to others, *yes, it is true that p.* So he is confident that he believes that p. But how does he rule out the possibility that he really does not believe that p? Perhaps he wants to give the impression that he does and he has therefore developed the disposition to respond *yes* if asked whether it is true that p, even if he asks himself. Or, if it is clear that he never trained himself to respond in that way, perhaps he was born with certain dispositions to disguise his beliefs and desires.

Here we might well wonder whether it makes any sense to suppose that someone has various beliefs and desires if he is disposed to attribute to himself quite different beliefs and desires (supposing that the beliefs and desires that he does attribute to himself are compatible with his behavior). The situation here is in certain respects like the case of the inverted spectrum hypothesis, except that the various different hypotheses about a person's beliefs and desires are not in any obvious way "notational variants" of each other.

What does it mean to say that someone's sentence S means what your sentence, *That is red,* means? What does it mean to say that, relative to such and such an interpretation of someone's language, he believes that you are his enemy and he wants to conceal this from you? Quine has taught us to avoid simple reductionist answers to such questions and he has also taught us to avoid supposing that certain basic principles are true by virtue of meaning.[17] But that is not to say that certain basic principles have nothing to do with meaning. If certain principles are abandoned in the absence of any compelling scientific reason for abandoning them, then, either we will suppose that the change is merely verbal, as in the case of the inverted spectrum hypothesis, or we will wonder what meaning there can be in the novel hypothesis, as in certain bizarre hypotheses about someone's beliefs and desires. We might say that certain principles serve to anchor meaning, even though these principles are not analytically secure and are not definitive of meaning.[18]

One such principle is, roughly, that, if a person is inclined to say that he believes that p or desires that q, then it is highly likely that he does have that belief or desire. A person's talk of beliefs and desires is an anchor on hypotheses that ascribe beliefs and desires to him (relative to an interpretation of his talk). The anchor may drag; we can have reasons to suppose that he has desires or beliefs that he does not admit to; and we can have reasons to suppose that he does not have all the desires and beliefs that he says he has. We develop general psychological hypotheses. What people say about their beliefs and desires is only one anchor on such hypotheses; what people do is another; and considerations of general theory including learning theory can provide other anchors, so that we can ascribe beliefs and desires on the basis of general principles even to those who for one or another reason cannot tell us what they believe or desire. In that case, we can do without one anchor, since we have others. What we cannot intelligibly do is to cut the anchor from someone's talk of beliefs and desires to hypotheses about his beliefs and desires without some overwhelming scientific reason to do so. Various bizarre assignments of desires and beliefs to people do not make sense since they make us cut that anchor in the absence of any scientific reason for doing so.

Science is conservative. Once various substantive and methodological principles have been firmly accepted, one of them cannot be rejected unless there is a good reason to reject it, where that reason derives from the other principles that are currently accepted. These substantive and methodological principles serve to anchor meaning in the sense that, if someone simply disregards a principle by rejecting it out of hand, without any justification in terms of other principles, then his words will lack clear meaning (unless some relatively simple way can be found to translate his language into ours so that his rejection of the principle is seen to be merely verbal).[19]

VII

Quine's Argument Evaluated

Quine argues that many different linguistic theories might account for behavior, with different proposals about the relation between grammatical and performance factors, different specification of linguistic universals, different theories of language learning, and different grammars of particular languages, grammars which are not even extensionally equivalent. He concludes that there is no fact of the matter concerning the grammar of someone's language; that there is not even any fact of the matter concerning what the sentences of that language are.

We are now in a position to see that Quine's argument is simply invalid in its present form. That is the moral of our methodological reflections about inverted spectrums and bizarre hypotheses about beliefs and desires. What Quine has yet to show is that the alternative theories of language that he envisions are real alternatives. In other words, he must show that currently accepted substantive and methodological principles in linguistics (and psychology) do not sufficiently anchor the meanings of the relevant grammatical hypotheses. I do not see that he will be able to do this, given the current situation in linguistics.

It is true that linguistics is not a subject that is free from controversy. But there is, despite the controversy, a considerable amount of agreement concerning methodology and also concerning various substantive points. There is enough agreement to make Quine's attitude look methodologically unsound. I would think that linguists would be well advised to assume that there is a fact of the matter concerning the questions they are trying to answer.

I will not pretend that I could list the relevant assumed principles and then demonstrate how these fix the meanings of grammatical hypotheses. For one thing, the subject is too complex. And, anyway, I have no idea whether the principles in question do fix the relevant meanings. All I claim is that a linguist ought to assume that they fix meaning.

In order to give some content to my claim, I will try to say something about linguistic universals. Quine says, "Timely reflection on method and evidence should tend to stifle much of the talk of linguistic universals."[20] But his conclusion seems to rest on an oversimple example.

> The problem of evidence for a linguistic universal is insufficiently appreciated. Someone says, let us suppose, that the subject-predicate construction occurs in all the languages he has examined. Now of course all those languages have been translated, however forcibly, into English and *vice versa*. Point, then, in those languages to the translations of the English subject-predicate construction, and you establish the thesis; the subject-predicate construction occurs in all those languages. Or it it imposed by translation? What is the difference? Does the thesis say more than that Basic English is translatable into all those languages? And what does even this latter claim amount to, pending some standard of faithfulness and objectivity of translation?[21]

Now if this is supposed to be the sort of criticism that applies to current linguistic claims about linguistic universals, it just does not fit. Linguists believe that all natural human languages have 'transformational grammars' and that the transformations in these grammars are subject to certain surprising universal constraints, constraints that apply to transformations in any language whatsoever. There is a great deal of evidence in support of specific hypotheses about such universal constraints; yet it is quite implausible to suppose that the constraints have in any sense been imposed by translation. They were discovered only after the main transformational rules for various languages had received rough formulation; and there is, furthermore, no *a priori* reason why a language subject to such constraints should not be translated into a language that was not subject to those constraints (if there were to be such a language).

For example, there is a 'coordinate structure constraint' which prevents a transformation from moving anything out of a coordinate structure (e.g., a conjunction). Thus there is in English a transformation that has the effect of moving a relative pronoun to the front of a relative clause. So, there are sentences like, *That is the man who Bob asked Mabel to do away with—*, where the dash indicates the place from which the relative pronoun *who* has been moved. The coordinate structure constraint prevents this transformation from applying to yield this sentence, *That is the man who Bob asked Mabel to do away with*

Arthur and—. Similarly, the question transformation can be used to obtain, *Who did Bob ask Mabel to do away with—?* But it cannot be used to obtain, *Who did Bob ask Mabel to do away with Arthur and—?* Again, although topicalization of a certain sort can yield *Albert, Mabel did away with—* from *Mabel did away with Albert,* this transformation cannot apply to *Mabel did away with Arthur and Albert* to yield *Albert, Mabel did away with Arthur and—.*[22]

The coordinate structure constraint holds of all movement transformations in English. It also holds of all transformations that have been proposed for any natural human languages. The constraint has not been imposed by considerations of translation. Many of the relevant transformations were formulated before the constraint was thought of; and, anyway, failure to observe the constraint would not limit translation, since we could always make do with constructions like the *such that* construction: *Who is such that Bob asked Mabel to do away with Arthur and him?* Translations that appeal to the *such that* construction are needed anyway for languages which form questions not by moving constituents, as in English, but by some sort of pronominalization.[23]

Chomsky has argued that any constraints on transformations must be universal. His argument is that such constraints could never be learned and must therefore be built into the language learner ahead of time. Given his theory of language learning, there is a certain plausibility to his argument.[24] It is all the more relevant that there is empirical evidence that in fact constraints on transformations are always universal, for such evidence therefore then also supports his theory of grammar and his account of language learning.[25]

Now there are many disputes within linguistics as to detail. There are debates concerning the exact form grammar should take and there are controversies as to where grammar leaves off and theories of processing begin. Yet a great many interesting things have been discovered within this overall framework and they have been discovered by seeing whether or not one or another proposal could be confirmed or refuted. Participants seem to make the most progress when they assume that various apparently competing theories really are competing and they try to refute one or the other. Sometimes, if both theories survive refutation, it is suggested that they are 'notational variants' and then that is something that gets debated. Surely, the current practice of linguists is good methodological practice; it is justified by its results. But that means that Quine's assumptions about grammar should be rejected on methodological grounds.

It is of course conceivable that there are other theories of language with other suggestions about linguistic universals and grammars that account for linguistic behavior as well as current proposals yet are not ruled out by the principles that currently anchor the meanings of linguistic hypotheses. That is always conceivable. But Quine has done nothing to show that it is true; and it is surely good methodology for a linguist to suppose that there is a fact of the matter concerning the problems with which he or she is engaged.

Indeed, a linguist, or a philosopher of ordinary language, or a logician interested in the logic of ordinary language, might do well to take up Quine's suggestions concerning the connection between logic and grammar. Given an account of the way in which logic is relevant to the actual inferences people make, and given the connection Quine sees between logic and grammar, we may have here an anchor on grammar as well as a way of using grammar to investigate the logical workings of the mind.[26]

GILBERT HARMAN

DEPARTMENT OF PHILOSOPHY
PRINCETON UNIVERSITY
OCTOBER 1973

NOTES

1. W.V. Quine, "Meaning in Linguistics", *From a Logical Point of View* Second Edition, revised (New York, Harper and Row: 1963), pp. 47–64, specifically p. 52. Quine gives the same account in a number of other places. See his reply to Geach, *Synthese* 19 (1968–1969), pp. 298–302, specifically p. 298, reprinted in Donald Davidson and Jaakko Hintikka, *Words and Objections* (Dordrecht: D. Reidel, 1969), pp. 328–332, specifically p. 328. See also W.V. Quine, *Philosophy of Logic* (Englewood Cliffs, New Jersey; Prentice Hall: 1969), p. 16, and "Methodological Reflections on Current Linguistic Theory", *Synthese* 21 (1970), pp. 386–398, specifically p. 389, reprinted in Donald Davidson and Gilbert Harman, *Semantics of Natural Language* (Dordrecht: D. Reidel, 1972), pp. 442–454, specifically p. 445.

2. "Meaning in Linguistics", p. 52.

3. "Methodological Reflections", pp. 391–392 in *Synthese*, pp. 447–448, in *Semantics of Natural Language*. Quine says essentially the same thing in "Meaning and Linguistics", p. 52, and *Philosophy of Logic*, pp. 19–22.

4. George Miller estimates that there are at least 10^{20} English sentences of twenty words or less. George A. Miller, *The Psychology of Communication* (Baltimore: Penguin, 1969), pp. 79–80.

5. W.V. Quine, *Word and Object* (Cambridge, Mass.: M.I.T., 1960), pp. 42–45.

6. *Word and Object*, Chapter 2.

7. *Philosophy of Logic*, pp. 11–12. Quine deplores alternative accounts of logical generalizations which involve quantification over propositions or properties as in $(p)(p$ or not $p)$ or $(x)(F)(Fx$ or not $Fx)$, pp. 1–14, 64–68.

8. For further discussion see Gilbert Harman, "Is Modal Logic Logic?" *Philosophia* 2 (1972): 75–84; Harman, "Logical Form", *Foundations of Language* 9 (1972): 38–65; Quine, *Philosophy of Logic*, pp. 30–34, 76–79.

9. *Philosophy of Logic*, Chapters 5–6.

10. *Philosophy of Logic*, pp. 33–34, Chapter 7. *Word and Object*, Chapters 5–6. "Methodological Reflections," pp. 394–398 in *Synthese*, pp. 450–454 in *Semantics of Natural Language*.

11. Noam Chomsky, *Language and Mind* (New York: Harcourt, Brace, and Jo-vanovich, 1968; Second Enlarged Edition: 1972).

12. Noam Chomsky, *Problems of Knowledge and Freedom* (New York: Vintage, 1971), p. 46.

13. Quine nowhere states exactly this argument, but see "Methodological Reflections" and cf. W.V. Quine, "Philosophical Progress in Language Theory", *Metaphilosophy* 1 (1970): 1–19, esp. pp. 17–19. This essay also appears in Milton Munitz, *Language and Metaphysics* (Albany: State University of New York Press, 1970).

Quine *does* offer the following somewhat cryptic argument:

> The more special point is that verbal behavior is determined by what people can observe of one another's responses to what people can observe of one another's external stimulations. In learning language, all of us, from babyhood up, are amateur students of behavior, and, simultaneously, subjects of amateur studies of behavior. Thus, consider the typical learning of a word, at its simplest: you are confronted by the object of the word in the presence of your teacher. Part of the plan is that he knows that you see the object and you know that he does. This feature is equally in point on the later occasion when the teacher approves or disapproves of your use of the word. The natural consequence is that the clearest words, or anyway the words that are learned first and are used most consistently, tend to be words not for sense impressions but for conspicuous external objects . . . .
>
> But even those who have not embraced behaviorism as a philosophy are obliged to adhere to behavioristic method within certain scientific pursuits; and language theory is such a pursuit. A scientist of language is, insofar, a behaviorist ex officio. Whatever the best eventual theory regarding the inner mechanism of language may turn out to be, it is bound to conform to the behavioral character of language learning: the dependence of verbal behavior on observation of verbal behavior. A language is mastered through social emulation and social feedback, and these controls ignore any idiosyncrasy in an individual's imagery or associations that is not discovered in his behavior. Minds are indifferent to language insofar as they are behaviorally inscrutable.
>
> Thus, though a linguist may still esteem mental entities philosophically, they are pointless or pernicious in language theory. ("Philosophical Progress," pp. 4–5.)

14. "Methodological Reflections", pp. 391–392 in *Synthese*, pp. 447–448 in *Semantics of Natural Language*.

15. T.G. Bever, J.R. Lackner, and R. Kirk, "The Underlying Structures of Sentences Are the Primary Units of Immediate Speech Processing", *Perception and Psychophysics* 5 (1969): 225–234.

16. Observation sentences have the same meaning if they have the same stimulus meaning, according to Quine, *Word and Object*, p. 42.

17. "Two Dogmas of Empiricism", *From a Logical Point of View*, pp. 20–46.

18. *Word and Object*, pp. 56–57.

19. *Word and Object*, pp. 20–21. Barry Stroud, "Conventionalism and Translation", *Synthese* 19 (1968–1969): 82–96, esp. pp. 92–96, also reprinted in Davidson and Hintikka, *Words and Objections*.

20. "Methodological Reflections", p. 391 in *Synthese*, p. 447 in *Semantics of Natural Language*.

21. "Methodological Reflections", p. 390 in *Synthese,* p. 446 in *Semantics of Natural Language.*

22. See John Robert Ross, *Constraints on Variables in Syntax* (M.I.T. dissertation: 1966), Relevant excerpts appear in Gilbert Harman (ed.), *On Noam Chomsky* (Amherst: University of Massachusetts Press, 1982, second edition), pp. 165–200.

23. Edward L. Keenan, "The Logical Status of Deep Structures", in Luigi Heilmann (ed.), *Proceedings of the XIth International Congress of Linguists* (Bologna-Florence: Societa Editrice il Mulino, 1974), pp. 477–490.

24. Noam Chomsky, *Language and Mind.* For discussion see my review in *Language* 49 (1973): 453–464, in particular 461–464.

25. See also Noam Chomsky, "Conditions on Rules", in Anderson and Kiparsky, *A Festschrift for Morris Halle* (New York: Holt, 1973), pp. 232–286.

26. Harman, "Logical Form", "Is Modal Logic Logic?" and *Thought* (Princeton: 1973), pp. 155–168.

REPLY TO GILBERT HARMAN

The Task of the Grammarian

Up to a point Harman has depicted my position faithfully and effectively, as has been his wont. But at points he has over-estimated my skepticism, and at points he has under-estimated it.

The under-estimation is the least of it. It comes at the beginning, where Harman quotes me as ascribing to the grammarian the sole task of formally specifying the strings that are "capable of occurring in the normal stream of speech." The quotation is right as far as it goes. But I then proceeded to point out, in one and another of the writings cited,[1] that these vague words 'capable' and 'normal' allow the grammarian scope for shaping his task to suit his convenience. Seeking simplicity, he will round out and round off. Necessarily most of the strings that he allows as grammatical will have been individually unattested, and among these there will even be some that would provoke bizarreness reactions, being absurd in varying degrees. Some will be too absurd to be uttered unless by clowns or philosophers: perhaps Carnap's "This stone is thinking about Vienna", perhaps even Russell's "Quadruplicity drinks procrastination." Some deeply nested constructions will resist usage, as Harman notes, because of processing difficulties.

The grammarian will of course not rest content with passive observation of the native's speech. He will devise hypothetical examples and try them on the native to see if they induce bizarreness reactions or bewilderment. If the language is his own he will try them on himself. Bizarreness reactions do not suffice, though, to induce most grammarians to exclude Carnap's example as ungrammatical, or even Russell's. A grammarian could choose to exclude these, by invoking what Katz calls semantic markers. He would thus gain in economy of *Satzschatz* at some cost in economy of grammar.

Yet one feels somehow that Carnap's example and Russell's differ in kind from the examples that we unhesitatingly call grammatically incoherent. In jus-

tification of this feeling, William Haas has offered a neat and persuasive criterion:[2] the genuinely ungrammatical strings are the ones whose bizarreness can
never be relieved by embedding them in metaphorical contexts or fantastic nar-
ratives. It is a brilliant idea for separating grammar from semantics, and it puts
a gratefully fine point on the task of the grammarian. Some scope still remains
to the grammarian for tightening the grammar by distending the *Satzschatz,*
since bizarreness reactions are vague and come in degrees; but the scope is
narrow.

The foregoing considerations have to do with variation in what to regard as
"capable of occurring in the normal stream of speech": what to regard as
grammatical. Grammars that differ from one another on this point diverge extensionally: they diverge in net output. It is the scope of such divergence that
Haas shows us how to restrict. But grammars that are extensionally equivalent
may still vary freely internally, in respect of what they recognize as morphemes
and constructions and transformations. It is my acceptance of such internal
variation of grammars that Harman notes and criticizes, not broaching the
harsher matter of extensional divergence.

His objection is that by looking only to net output and allowing freedom of
internal variation I do not provide for the appreciation and control of grammatical ambiguity. The answer is to be sought in the use of grammar as an aid to
translation.

II

Grammar and Translation

This is a conspicuous use of grammar, as Harman notes. Here, conceivably, the freedom for internal variation could be exploited differentially:
one grammatical analysis of English might facilitate translation into one language, another another. There is a case of something like this in a procedure
that was developed in connection with projects of machine-aided translation.
The language to be translated would be paraphrased first into a more neutral
sort of pidgin which avoided idiosyncratic constructions and fitted more nearly
the formulated grammar of the target language. This preparatory paraphrasing
would differ for different choices of target language. If we think of this paraphrasing in analogy to Chomsky's eliciting of deep structure, which is an operation of grammatical analysis, then we have a crude example of how one
may vary one's grammatical treatment of a language to facilitate translation
into various languages.

Regarding Harman's point about grammatical ambiguity, then, I would look to the use of grammar in translation and the policy of choosing one's grammar usefully for that purpose. If the grammarian is to implement translation, the choices he makes in analyzing strings into immediate constituents or phrase structure must be such as to provide cleavages where they are needed for contrasting divergent readings of grammatically ambiguous strings. Such provision is of course wanted domestically as well as for translation; but there is no real difference here, since domestic paraphrase is just translation of the home language into itself.

Evidently I have designated the task of pure grammar as the mere settling of grammaticality, and then I have alerted the grammarian to grammatical ambiguity by asking him to pick his grammar with a view to its utility in semantics. This seems like a perverse way of sorting things out, but there was a reason, which stands forth in the cited part of *From a Logical Point of View*. I was concerned there to contrast the two basic contexts of the term 'meaning', viz., 'having meaning' and 'alike in meaning'. The former, for all its shortcomings, is in far better order than the latter. So I was concerned to set the pure linguistic theory of having meaning over against the linguistic theory of likeness of meaning; thus pure grammar over against semantics. The point was philosophical. In practice grammar and semantics need to be done together, and they regularly have been.

III

Grammar and Prehistory

Harman suggests that my views deprive grammar of theoretical interest. I shall begin my response with the story of my life. It appears elsewhere in this volume, so a brief reference will suffice: a reference to the strong and unfailing interest that linguistics in all its concrete detail has held for me for over a half century, antedating even my interest in philosophy. It would be a bitter irony if Harman could persuade me that my subsequent philosophical views deprive grammar of theoretical interest.

Grammar is of theoretical interest for the light it may throw on the prehistory of language and on the psychology of language. These prospects are not dimmed by the possibility of alternative grammars. If grammars have been formulated for two languages, with due regard for simplicity and without any devious effort to contrive a resemblance between the two, and if striking resemblances emerge, this is tentative evidence of genetic kinship of the two languages. Such resemblances are better evidence than lexical ones, because structure is less easily borrowed than lexicon. Odd coincidences are possible, but we must play the main chance. Greenberg, the leading conjecturer of linguistic superfamilies, gives greatest weight to community of structure and phonetic affinity of grammatical particles; less to affinity of lexicon.[3]

Relative clauses, discussed by Harman, are a case in point. Keenan has compared the constraints on relative clauses in English, Hebrew, and Malagasy. The mere fact that the relative-clause construction stands forth so conspicuously in these three languages could instill a hope of merging the three families that they represent, and others, into a single super-family with a common ancestry. Not much hope, granted; other shared constructions and traceably kindred lexicon would be wanted in reinforcement. And as for the constraints on relative clauses, they can contribute in two ways. If the constraints match between languages, they give added assurance that the relative-clause structure was itself a noteworthy structural resemblance rather than an insignificant reflection of translation. Second, if there is independent evidence of kinship of the languages, then differences of constraints can contribute evidence for speciation within the genus.

Some may say that the relative clause is a linguistic universal, present in all known languages. If this merely means that English sentences containing relative clauses are translatable into every language that we know well enough to translate into, it is not informative. This was my caveat about linguistic universals, to which Harman rose at points; and I think it no idle one. The ascription of relative clauses to a language has substance insofar as a construction functionally fairly similar to our relative clause tends to emerge when we construct a grammar of that language with an eye only to simplicity and general translatability, without regard to particular target languages of translation. Thus assessed, the presence of the relative-clause construction is a matter of degree; and one may wonder how well Chinese or Arunta or various languages of New Guinea stack up in this regard.

My example is fictitious, for I do not know that the relative clause has been claimed as a universal. But related considerations apply to Harman's example, which was the coordinate-structure restraint. He declares it universal in that it holds of all transformations that have been proposed for any natural language. This limits it to languages whose analysis, in the simplest way discovered, needed transformations consisting in moving a word or phrase. Moreover, what coordinate structures there are in the language will depend on the grammatical analysis adopted. Also some criterion of coordinateness is presupposed, other than in terms of English translations; for "the constraint has not been imposed by considerations of translation." No criterion as simple as commutativity will serve, for 'and' is not commutative in ordinary English.

I value the discovery of the invariability of the coordinate-structure restraint, and I want to maneuver it into the right light. I interpret the situation as follows. The grammars that seemed best to recommend themselves for various languages include phrase-shifting transformations. Some of the constructions given in these grammars are coordinate, if only in the sense of receiving so-called coordinate English constructions as their translations. And then it is found that components of those constructions are never susceptible to those transformations. This striking uniformity appeals to me not as a hint of a trait of all language, but as a hint of genetic kinship of the languages that seem most readily grammatized by appeal to phrase-shifting transformations. It is only a hint, wanting collateral evidence; but is is a nice empirical generalization to keep on the books in hope of explanation.

I believe in the genetic kinship ultimately of all languages, simply because one near-miracle is more probable than two. Therefore I do not scout linguistic universals categorically, as Harman seems to suppose. What I do urge is how sensitive such claims are to carelessness over criteria. Moreover I keep wanting light rather on the intermediate genealogy of languages.

In speculating on the bearing of grammar on the prehistory of language I have thus far treated only of common ancestry, or genetic kinship. Halle has suggested how grammar can also hint of the chronological order of development of the structural traits of a language.[4] When we have codified a language in the most economical way we can find, our transformations may be expected to fall into a partial order: some must be performed before others. Halle suggests that the ones that come earlier in this sense reflect earlier stages in the development of the language.

IV

Grammar and Psychology

Grammar bears also on the psychology of language. It affords a sketch, in a way, of a talking machine. Each grammatical construction or transformation is a working component in the machine. The structure of the machine may or may not be isomorphic to that of the speech centers of the brain; but, for a given lexical input, the sentential output is the same. Seen in this way, a grammar is a sketch not of how coherent speech is produced, but of how coherent speech is possible. It is a simulation.

But mechanical simulations may reasonably be looked to for light on psychology, and so may grammar. In fact there is a stronger case, as follows. We, for our own part, will have devised the simplest grammar we can. The native speaker, for his part, is the less to be wondered at for his ability in proportion to the simplicity of the system of component habits. Hence, despite the multiplicity of possible grammars, there is a better than random chance that our grammar will have structural counterparts in his neural hookup.

There is some room for confirmation here, not by examining the nerve net, but by studying the infant's progress in the language. We can discern his stages of competence, by noting the periods at which he overcomes various systematic errors and at which he first produces various constructions or responds appropriately to them. Such developmental studies should enable us to discover in a tentative way the child's own implicit system of grammatical rules, these being separable from one another by their different times of acquisition.

A lay native speaker cannot state his grammatical rules. He just behaves in the way that the rules describe. By this token any extensionally equivalent system of rules could be ascribed to him indifferently. Chomsky has denied this indifference, postulating rather one or more innate skeletal grammars. I cannot welcome this postulate without further light on the nature of the supposed equipment. We do see a persuasive basis on which the indifference might be challenged, however, when we think of a native speaker's linguistic competence as a system of habits that he successively acquires. One set of grammatical rules certainly has an important claim to distinction, over other extensionally equivalent sets, if its several rules correspond to temporally successive increments in the native's actual learning of language.

Bever's click technique is an ingenious way of finding out something about one's tacit rules without studying one's development. It bears out a uniformity among the speakers of a language: they do not have extensionally equivalent but radically unlike tacit grammars. We may infer that the stages of acquisition of a language, on the grammatical side, are substantially the same from speaker to speaker. This could be verified by direct studies of language learning.

Bever's click experiment is looked upon as confirming the linguist's explicit codification of grammar, by showing that the subject's tacit segmentations agree with that codification. Actually, granted the interesting uniformity already noted, this confirmation is to be expected; for the codifying linguist was himself a native speaker, sharing the uniformity.

If a linguist were to compile a grammar for an exotic and hitherto unknown language, it would be interesting to try some clicks and see whether the compiled grammar matched the native's tacit grammar or was merely extensionally equivalent. In the latter event the linguist might care to switch over. I would suggest again that the multiplicity of extensionally equivalent grammars could in theory be put to multiple uses: one grammar might best serve translation into one language, another grammar might best serve translation into another language, yet another grammar might best reflect the psychology of the native speaker, and, conceivably but implausibly, yet another grammar might be simplest. And finally, out beyond extensional equivalence, still further variants could have their uses.

V

Facts of the Matter

Harman writes that I hold "that there is no fact of the matter concerning the grammar of someone's language". I have now explained on the contrary that I can make factual sense of saying that one grammar is more faithful than another to the development of linguistic competence in the child.

Harman goes on to state that I hold "that there is not even any fact of the matter concerning what the sentences of that language are". I do hold this, but it is a more superficial point than his words "not even" suggest. Sentences, like words, are segments of speech cut by the grammarian, and this segmentation may differ even in extensionally equivalent grammars. What I call grammatical strings are not just sentences; they are any strings that can exist embedded in grammatical speech (barring quotation, of course). Example: '–ly frank. I thanked him for his cand–'. All that is required for extensional equivalence of grammars is sameness of grammatical strings, not sameness in the snipping of sentences.

Harman's methodological reflections prompt me to explain what I mean when I say regarding some pair of alternatives that there is no fact of the matter. I am not protesting, as a positivist might, that the choice would not be reflected in future experience. Nor am I protesting, as some intemperate sort of physical reductionist might, that the alternatives have not been stated in the vocabulary of physics. I am simply saying, as a physicalist, that no distribution of physical states over space-time would make one of the alternatives true and the other false. I can have reason to believe, with regard to some matter, that there is in this sense no fact of it, without dreaming of anyone's paraphrasing the matter into terms of microphysical states.

Regarding desire and belief I hold that there usually is a fact of the matter. This domain is still in a primitive state; new conceptualization is needed, and much sorting out. Some of what we say in idioms of propositional attitude would doubtless prove empty in the end, for reasons related to indeterminacy of translation. Much else would become explicated, I like to think, in terms of various dispositions, which are for me hypothetical physiological states or mechanisms. Some of these dispositions in turn would become explained in physiological terms. I would not be swerved by the possible bizarre hypotheses to which Harman alludes, because I would think them less promising as steps toward these distant goals of physiological explanation. Nor do I apply a different standard in linguistics. My standards are the same, and the merits vary from case to case.

VI

Grammar and Logic

I extolled the utility of grammar in Sections II–IV. But I do not consider grammar useful for logic. In construing this negation let us understand 'grammar' in its primary acceptation as designating a branch of empirical linguistics, and 'logic' somewhat arbitrarily as designating the logic of truth functions and quantification. (To smuggle identity in, see *Philosophy of Logic,* p. 64.)

But I do see an indirect relation between grammar and logic that sheds philosophical light on the nature of logic. Namely, there is a canonical notation into which we can paraphrase a large part of our language, including the scientifically most satisfactory part; and if now we think of this notation as if it were a language in its own right, and consider what would be its 'grammar' in analogy to the primary acceptation of that word, we find that the logical truths in the canonical notation are all and only the sentences that are instances of grammatical forms all of whose instances are true.

Logic is of course directly useful for grammar; and not only as it is useful for all science, but in a more substantive way. This is evident from the use that has been made of the canonical notation in formulating deep structures for the theory of grammatical transformations.

W. V. Q.

NOTES

1. *Words and Objections,* p. 328; *From a Logical Point of View,* p. 54.

2. William Haas, ''Meanings and Rules'', *Proceedings of the Aristotelian Society* (1973): 135–155.

3. Joseph Greenberg, ''The Measurement of Linguistic Diversity'', *Language* 32 (1956):109–115.

4. Morris Halle, ''Phonology in Generative Grammar'', *Word* 18 (1962): 54–72.

8

Geoffrey Hellman

LOGICAL TRUTH BY LINGUISTIC CONVENTION

Synopsis

After a brief résumé of their inconclusive last exchange on the subject, Quine and Carnap (superstars) are summoned to take up anew their debate on the ground of logical truth. Their dialogue falls naturally into three parts. The first (through Quine*(5)) is devoted to reformulating the linguistic doctrine so as to take account of Quinean criticisms. In the second (through Carnap*(7)), Carnap* attempts to meet Quine*'s challenge to avoid a famous infinite regress that is thought to vitiate the linguistic doctrine in its epistemological role. In their final exchanges, Carnap* points to the stipulative character of setting up logical grammar, quite apart from any general notion of "analyticity". Everything is seen to rest on our metalinguistic resources, and here it turns out to be Quine's doctrine of ontological relativity that seems most relevant, at least to Quine*. Not surprisingly, Carnap*, while perplexed, is unmoved.

In his influential paper, "Truth by Convention",[1] Quine subjected the linguistic doctrine of logical truth (LD) to a critique that, to many, has seemed devastating. Having granted the conventionalist (what Quine took to be) his

---

I owe special thanks to my colleague J. Alberto Coffa for many helpful suggestions and criticisms and for years of patient prodding. For distortions, felicitous and otherwise, in the positions of Carnap and Quine portrayed in the ensuing dialogue, I assume full responsibility.

starting points, Quine caught his opponent in a vicious regress: to proceed from the linguistic stipulations to the (full class of) logical truths requires logical rules themselves in addition to any of the stipulations. What Lewis Carroll's tortoise said to Achilles (on the need to appeal to *modus ponens* to justify any application of it) seemed an arrow in Carnap's heel.

Carnap seems never to have taken the critique very seriously. His reply to Quine's "Carnap and Logical Truth",[2] which repeated the upshot of "Truth by Convention," is couched in irony. Quine had found LD "empty" and "without experimental meaning"; moreover, he had found it "implying nothing not already implied by" the assertion—which he surely accepted—that logic is obvious. This afforded Carnap the opportunity to point out that LD implied itself and to express his wish that Quine had only *said* that he believed LD true. Further, he said that the emptiness of LD was something he had always accepted, that in Vienna that was what you expected of philosophical truths, and that in so phrasing his finding, Quine was accepting the analytic-synthetic distinction in so many words.[3]

One has the feeling that two of the century's most important thinkers were talking past each other. In order to remedy this unfortunate situation, let us see how, making occasional use of more recent developments, the debate might have continued:

Carnap*(1): In my *Logical Syntax* I was perhaps overly skeptical about using our ordinary background language to introduce logical notions.[4] As a clearer alternative, I preferred the method of implicit definition, determining meanings of logical particles by (arbitrarily) laying down postulates and transformation rules. This, I take it, was the source of the procedure you followed in "Truth by Convention", where you granted the conventionalist the "starting point" of stipulating sentences of certain forms to be true. This, however, must not obscure that it is central to LD that logical truths are true solely in virtue of the meanings of the logical words. (The logical truths (of a given sufficiently rich and well-regimented language) are, for present purposes, best specified as those truths in which only the logical words occur essentially;[5] the latter we may fix to be 'not', 'and' 'all', and ' = '. Choice of these (up to classical logical equivalence) is not arbitrary given a general notion of analyticity, but, for reasons that will emerge, I won't press that point here.) As I hinted in my reply,[6] given conventions on the interpretation of words, one is no more free to stipulate truth values for logical sentences than one is for 'the sky is blue'. And the interpretations of the logical words I regard as *capable of being given by stipulation* (as also done in the *Syntax*[7]), e.g., by truth-tables (for 'not' and 'and'), by example (for 'all', one can stipulate it to be eliminable in favor of conjunction over finite domains), and by direct specification of extension (for ' = ', one can stipulate that it holds just of each entity and itself, no matter what it may be).

Quine*(1): Since our last exchange on this topic, I have elaborated on the derivative character of word-meaning from a behavioral standpoint.[8] But those issues need not detain us here. For my procedure in "Truth by Convention" was, if anything, favorable to the conventionalist case: by construing the stipulations as rules for assigning truth to sentences of the appropriate forms, I had to do some work to develop the regress toward the end of the paper. If, instead, we regard the stipulations as governing the logical particles directly, along the lines you say you prefer, it becomes even more obvious that those stipulations alone do not suffice to generate the infinitely many logical truths, that in fact they will have to be supplemented by rules of logical inference, which was precisely the outcome of my paper.

Carnap*(2): This point is obvious. We can agree that LD in the following form is false:

> LD(I) Stipulations that particles (of a language) function as the logical words (of our special list) suffice to *generate* the class of logical truths (of that language).

Granting this, however, raises a fundamental problem I have found with your argument. If the task confronting the conventionalist were to *justify logic,* the regress you uncovered would indeed be vicious, for logical rules are indeed required to arrive at (infinitely many of) the logical truths from a finite body of stipulations. But the main thrust of conventionalism is that *logic needs no justification:* as Wittgenstein argued, logical truths are empty, they assert nothing. LD(I) is simply irrelevant to the conventionalist purpose.

Indeed the conventionalist must be able to justify, of any logical truth S, *that S is true by linguistic convention.* Given a *characterization* of the class of logical truths, e.g., as containing all sentences of certain forms (axiom schemata) and closed under certain rules (such as *modus ponens*), it can be expected that logical rules will be required in demonstrating, of complex logical truths S, that they are in the class. And if the case is made that, indeed, that class consists of stipulative, empty truths, the demonstration will have achieved its aim.

Given a sentence S (which, it is supposed, has truth-value true or false), we may indeed be uncertain of its status as a logical truth on account of its complexity. In a sense, anyone's assertion *that* S can be said to stand in need of justification. But when we succeed in deriving S from logical truths by sound rules, we show that in fact we were mistaken; we show that in fact S requires no justification precisely because it is a logical truth. The claim *that S requires no justification* is what really required justification; and in making it out we had recourse to logical rules. But that is as legitimate in this quarter as in any. What better way could there be to justify anything?

Quine*(2): The distinction you point to is clearly important. But let us see how it bears on the linguistic doctrine. We have agreed to abandon LD(I). What is to go in its place? From your reply,[9] I gather that you prefer a thesis couched in epistemic terms, such as

LD(II) Knowledge of stipulations (as in LD(I)) suffices to *ascertain* of any logical truth that it is true.

*Carnap**(3): That does seem to be a fair reconstruction of the third paragraph of my reply. I meant, of course, that, in contrast with empirical statements, no further knowledge of facts about the world is required.

*Quine**(3): As you know, I question the coherence of "facts about the world". But LD(II) well reflects the historical thrust of conventionalism, to account for *a priori* knowledge employing the (potentially) scientific terms of linguistics. Apart from my challenge to this, however, the point that needs making right now is that LD(II) is no better off than LD(I). Surely it is not in general sufficient, to ascertain of a logical truth S that it is true, simply to inspect S and "look up" the stipulations governing the logical words contained in S. To ascertain the truth of the full class of logical truths, logical rules over and above the stipulations must be invoked. This was just the predicament encountered in the last pages of "Truth by Convention". And if in reply you say "It suffices to justify the rules", you confront the familiar regress: to obtain the conclusion of any rule from its premises, a further rule will be needed, and the regress is under way.

*Carnap**(4): If I can foresee at all how this dialogue will develop, I will have another opportunity to respond to this last point. First I should treat some still more fundamental matters.

I entirely agree with what you said on the motivation behind conventionalism. But did you not ignore this when you criticized LD as "empty"?[10] There you pointed out that one attempt to assign experimental content to LD, viz., "Deductively irresoluble disagreement as to a logical truth is evidence of deviation in usage (or meanings) of words", also holds up if 'logical' is replaced with 'obvious'. Similarly, you have argued that certain other connections between logic and language could equally well be accounted for by the recognition that logic is obvious, "without help of a linguistic doctrine of logical truth".[11] Now none of this shows that LD is empty; at most it shows that LD is superfluous. But, I claim, it does not show this either. *For we need an account of **why** logic is obvious.*[12] The sort of account we can give of why "It is raining" is obvious does not work for logic. Here is a major explanatory role for the linguistic doctrine, essentially its traditional role in logical epistemology.

But how are we to frame the linguistic doctrine? Let me now propose an alternative to LD(II) which, I believe, improves upon it and earlier formulations. Roughly, instead of claiming that stipulations on logical words suffice for *ascertaining* logical truth, the conventionalist should claim that those stipulations suffice to *determine uniquely* the class of logical truths and their truth. Let us assume that we are working with a first-order language, L, containing a stock of sentence connectives, quantifier phrases, and equivalence relation signs. (These could be interpreted in various ways, not just as the usual logical particles; e.g., a connective could be read as 'because', a quantifier as 'many', etc.) Let us further assume that L is sufficiently well-regimented so that all other constructions can be worked into the form of lexicon. Next let us call a *logical structure for L* any set D together with a valuation v assigning (n-tuples of) objects in D to the lexicon of L. Now the key idea is this: once it is fixed which particles are functioning as the logical ones (of our list),[13] there is determined a unique class of sentences, the 'logical sentences', such that any two logical structures for L agree on the truth values of these, no matter how widely they may otherwise diverge. This is the intended force of

> LD(III) Stipulations (as in LD(I)) suffice to determine uniquely a class of
> sentences (of the language in question), the truth value of each of
> which is invariant over the totality of logical structures.

Thus, it follows that stipulations on words suffice to determine a class of sentences, logically valid in the usual sense. This is crucial for the conventionalist view of logic. For it is the logical validity of the logical truths that constitutes their "emptiness": no matter what entities there were, and in no matter what relations they stood, these linguistic forms would still come out true. (Thus, it is really the free version of first-order quantifier logic that is relevant, in which, to take account of the null universe, '$\forall x \varphi x \supset \varphi a$' is replaced by '$\forall x \varphi x \wedge \exists y\ y = a \supset \varphi a$'. Identity can be retained as 'logical', but we admit further imperfections in the essential-occurrence test for validity, e.g., the not-strictly-valid '$\exists x\ x = x$'.)

Notice that LD(III) does not readily generalize so as to give content to the claim that 'analytic sentences' are factually empty. For in order to obtain the analytic sentences from the logical truths, one needs to appeal, not merely to co–extensive terms, but to co–intensional terms. Fixing the intensions of lexical items would fix truth values of a class of analytic sentences (over all relevant logical structures), but how do we 'fix intensions'? Furthermore, LD(III) does presuppose that adequate interpretations of the logical particles can be *stipulated*. (So far we have both been taking that for granted, you perhaps more for the sake of argument than I. Of course, it must be defended independently.[14]) But, as you have argued, and I have been slow to realize, the sense in which meanings of words (in general) can be stipulated is far from clear. Can one stipulate "the meaning" of, say, 'positron' so as to support the LD(III) analogue for analytic truths containing it (and terms used to "define" it)? These are odd questions for *me* to be asking, but philosophy in the 1980s isn't what it used to be. (Sigh!)

Quine*(4): I have no quarrel with LD(III) itself. As you have framed it, I suppose that it is a mathematical fact about models, provided one grants the presupposition on stipulations that you mentioned. My main problem is with your interpretive claim about "factual emptiness". As I have written, it does appear natural to regard logical truths

> as the limiting case where the dependence (of the sentence) on traits of the subject matter is nil. Consider, however, the logical truth, 'everything is self-identical', or '$(x)(x = x)$'. We can say that it depends for its truth on traits of language (specifically on the usage of ' = '), and not on traits of its subject matter; but we can also say, alternatively, that it depends on an obvious trait, viz., self-identity, of its subject matter, viz., everything. The tendency of our present reflections is that there is no difference.[15]

As I see it, you are committed to there being a difference: the first description would be accepted but the second would not. And this seems to undermine the view, for what difference can there be?

Carnap*(5): I am glad that you have repeated that argument. If only I could have foreseen the effects it would have on our readers, I would have addressed myself to it in my reply. (I have turned over in my grave many times for not having done so.) First of all, I would not use the word 'obvious' at all. (This I did hint at in my reply.) Even if all logical truths are (potentially) obvious, the converse is so obviously false that it can only beg the question to suggest that there is no other way of phrasing the alternative.

Secondly, the alternative way of phrasing the alternative description is to replace the word 'obvious' with the word 'stipulated'. Self-identity is a paradigm example of what I would call a 'stipulated universal trait': we introduce ' = ' (or can: if anyone insists that the symbol ' = ' already has another use, we choose a new symbol, ' = *') by stipulating that, in any context whatever, including all modal and counterfactual contexts, ' = ' (' = *') holds just between any object and itself. In the language of models, ' = ' (' = *') is assigned the set of ordered pairs of the form (x, x) over any domain of objects whatever. Similarly, a trait such as 'being red or not red' is a stipulated (universal) trait: it is determined to hold of every object whatever in any (putative) domain of objects as a consequence of our stipulations on 'or' and 'not'. (If anyone insists that 'or' and/or 'not' already have different uses, we can introduce new symbols, 'or*' and 'not*', stipulating that they behave in accordance with the truth-tables for (classical) disjunction and negation.) All logically valid open schemata give rise to 'logically-valid traits' of this sort, and all are determined to hold of any object(s) in any domain by stipulations on the logical words (in accordance with LD(III)).[16]

Thirdly, once the irrelevant term 'obvious' is replaced by 'stipulated', understood as just described, the conventionalist has *no* objection to saying that the logical truths depend for their truth on stipulated traits of objects (and no others), with one important proviso: so long as the word 'depend' is not used to suggest that, holding the logical part of the language fixed, it could have been otherwise. In the idiom of quantified modal logic, the logically-valid traits are necessary traits, precisely because of the stipulations on the logical words. Thus, it is quite misleading to suggest (as use of 'depend' does to my ear) that we might somehow vary the trait and, after the fashion of Mill, look for a variation in the truth-value of the logical sentence in question. But if this implication of 'depend' is cancelled, the new "alternative description" is no alternative at all, but just a more longwinded version of the original: logical truths depend for their truth (solely) on stipulations governing the use of the logical words.

Thus, your argument that the conventionalist is committed to an unintelligible difference would seem to collapse, once the alternatives are properly phrased.

Quine*(5): Perhaps your notion of a stipulated (universal) trait can be invoked to give content to your claim that logical truths are "factually empty". (In provisionally granting this, I am granting at most a very limited special case of your analyticity doctrine, as you appear to have recognized already.)

If I understand you, then, the notion of word stipulation is basic to logical metatheory. Using it, but not now your general notion of analyticity, you propose a sufficient condition for "factual emptiness": a sentence S is factually empty if the truth-value of S is unaffected by arbitrary counterfactual assumptions concerning what entities there are and arbitrary such assumptions concerning their traits (including relations), save the stipulated traits. (Our stipulations dictate that we discard or declare automatically true any counterfactual with antecedent such as, 'If Caesar were not self-identical, . . . ').

I gather from your nods of approval that my paraphrase is fair. To celebrate our progress in communication, let me mention two important related points on which I believe we actually agree. First, it is no contention of mine that logic "has factual content" for presupposing, e.g., that it makes sense to speak of entities and of their satisfying predicates. (Notice that I don't say here, "having properties and standing in relations". In first order logic we never mention properties or relations; rather we use predicates, as I have said many times. In this regard, logic is ontologically neutral.) Such a contention rests on a confusion, that of a presupposition with an assertion. We agree that logic has certain *preconditions of applicability*. One of them is that any language whose reasoning is being symbolized can be represented with our paradigmatic form of predication, 'F(x)' (or 'F(x$_1$ . . . x$_n$)'). If a symbol system (language?) cannot be so represented, our logical schematism does not apply. But that schematism makes no commitment whatever that such applicability conditions actually obtain in any case. The very same can be said with regard to the true/false dichotomy. It is a precondition of applicability, not a commitment. No revision of logic is contemplated in pointing to cases (e.g., imperatives, or grunts for that matter) to which it does not apply. And debates over particular subjects, such as the classical vs. intuitionist conceptions of mathematics, are not really debates over (classical) logic at all, but over its applicability to a certain realm of discourse.[17] Logic does not proclaim its own applicability.

Second, even if I should grant the stipulative character of logic, I should not regard logical reasoning as thereby devoid of substantive purpose. For example, the demand for sound rules reflects the purpose: never to pass from truth to falsity, come what may. We agree: *Nothing in the linguistic doctrine diminishes in any way the importance or substantive character of such* **purposes of** *logic*. Questions concerning them are completely distinct from the question of the empty, assertionless character of logical truths themselves.

But now let us take stock of what has been accomplished. You have agreed to scrap both LD(I) and LD(II). In its place you have proposed a weaker "determination principle", LD(III). Two major problems remain. The first concerns the assumption, thus far unchallenged, that stipulations on the logical particles of the sort you require are really possible. The second concerns the whole epistemological thrust of the linguistic doctrine. Let us take this latter problem first.

The problem is very simple. Even if LD(III), together with your interpretive claim on factual emptiness, can be sustained, how can it be used to solve the problem of logical knowledge? Potentially at least, we know an infinite set of logical truths. Even granting your point that, since empty, they "require no justification", still—as you yourself put it at the outset—infinitely many statements of the form 'S requires no justification' do require justification. But this involves appeal to rules, and these go beyond the word *stipulations*. In the dissolution of one epistemological problem, another has taken its place. The linguistic doctrine LD(III) would seem too weak to solve it. My original regress argument still has its force.

*Carnap**(6): I said above that I believe this regress argument can be answered. As I see it, the "rules regress" arises due to a far too restrictive view of what it is to justify a (logical) rule. We can agree that what needs justification is that a given rule, let us say *modus ponens* (MP), is sound, i.e., truth-preserving.[18] Now the assertion of soundness *can be given* a conditional form: if the premises (say, A and A ⊃ B) are true, the conclusion (B) is (or must be) true. Then it is supposed that, to establish this conditional, one *must proceed* in the manner of natural deduction: assume the antecedent ('A and A ⊃ B are true') and derive the conclusion. And, of course, such a derivation requires the application of a rule, in this case (the metalanguage version of) MP itself.

But is this the *only* way in which one could come to know that MP is a sound rule? That seems to me absurd. And, before presenting any alternative story, one can see that it *is* absurd, for it would mean that *we really don't (and can't!) know* that MP is a sound rule. I submit that any epistemology committed to this is bad epistemology, for we certainly do know that MP is sound.[19]

In fact, we are not constrained to the mold (or rut) of a tortoise. We don't *have to* assert soundness in the form of a conditional; nor do we *have to* carry out a logical deduction to see that MP is sound. First, it must be emphasized that the conventionalist is content to confine his claims to idealized, formal languages. It is in these that logical truths may be rigorously expressed, and it is claimed that, so expressed, they are stipulative truths that can be known to be such by rules whose soundness can also be known, given the stipulations. Thus, by 'MP', I am referring to a particular rule governing the truth-functional conditional, which we think of as being introduced into our language. Whether particular uses of 'if . . . then' in English are properly represented by this formal operation is an entirely distinct question. And the details of an alternative justification of soundness of analogues of MP for other conditionals depend on the details of their use or introduction.

This understood, we may assert the soundness of MP in non-conditional form, as follows:

(i) There is no assignment of truth-values (T, F) that makes both A and A $\supset$ B T and B F.[20]

How can we come to know this? First by coming to know the elementary combinatorial fact that TT, TF, FT, FF are all the possible assignments of T, F to two elements, A, B. Here a story must be told, of course, that does not involve, for instance, deducing this fact in the system of *Principia Mathematica*. (Again, such a story had better be a real possibility, or else it will turn out that we *really don't know* this (or virtually any other!) mathematical fact either.) Second, by consulting our own stipulations on '$\supset$', viz., the truth-table we used in introducing it into our language. By examining each row, we see: (a) it is correctly written (the ink has the right shape, and is sufficiently stable over the time-period of the examination—or else, of course, we can do this in our imaginations as you, the reader, are doing right now), and (b) the only row assigning A T and A$\supset$B T contains T for B. Thus, all that is involved is an elementary finite search; and this need not be construed as a chain of reasoning in a logistic system.

Quine*(6): I have some misgivings about your strategy concerning the alleged status of (i) as a stipulation introducing a logical particle. But let us see now how you would treat the quantifier rules, which transcend anything so elementary as truth-tables. We can continue working with an axiomatic system of first-order logic with MP and UG as the only rules.[21]

Carnap*(7): The case of UG is quite straightforward. What must be shown is that on the basis of linguistic stipulations, we can know that UG is a sound rule. Since free variables are involved, soundness of UG takes the form:

(iii) Every valuation (over any (non-empty) domain D) making the universal closure of A true makes the universal closure of $\forall$xA true.

But what problem can there be in knowing this, since the universal closure of A and that of $\forall$xA are the same, up to some permutation of initial universal quantifiers! I suppose it is just here that one must appeal to stipulations governing the interpretation of '$\forall$': implicit in the soundness of UG is the soundness of permuting initial universal quantifiers, and knowing this does rest on conventions such as

(iv) '$\forall x\varphi(x)$' holds in a domain D (under valuation v) just in case '$\varphi(\overline{d})$' holds in D (under v) for each object d in D as value of (the dummy name) $\overline{d}$.

Given (iv), it is trivial that, for example, '$\forall x\forall y\psi(x, y)$' and '$\forall y\forall x\psi(x, y)$' are logically equivalent, for we have, for any structure (D, v):

(v) (D, v) $\models$ $\forall x\forall y\psi(x, y)$ iff   (D, v) $\models$ $\forall y\psi(\overline{d}, y)$ for all
values d of $\overline{d}$ in D   iff   (D, v) $\models$ $\psi(\overline{d}, \overline{d}')$ for all
values d of $\overline{d}$ in D and all values d of $\overline{d}'$ in D.

But also

(vi) (D, v) $\models \forall y\forall x\psi(x, y)$ iff   (D, v) $\models$ $\forall x\psi(x, \overline{d}')$ for all
values d of $\overline{d}'$ in D   iff   (D ,v) $\models$ $\psi(\overline{d}, \overline{d}')$ for all
values d of $\overline{d}'$ in D and all values d of $\overline{d}$ in D,

which is identical to (v) given commutativity of 'and', which is also true by stipulation.

More generally, one could directly stipulate satisfaction conditions for formulas with arbitrary (finite) strings of initial universal quantifiers:

(vii) (D, v) $\models$ $\forall x_1 \ldots \forall x_n\psi(x_1 \ldots x_n)$ iff
(D, v) $\models$ $\psi(\overline{d}_1 \ldots \overline{d}_n)$ for all n-sequences (with repetitions)
from D as values of $\overline{d}_1 \ldots \overline{d}_n$.

This guarantees arbitrary permuting of initial universal quantifiers since we understand that the order of dummy names doesn't matter: the same set of n-sequences (all of them) is covered in all cases.

In the present context, (vii) is to be preferred as a way of guaranteeing the permutation rule. The more usual route, via (iv), requires a proof by mathematical induction in order to obtain the general result for arbitrary strings of quantifiers. In logic texts that is perfectly in order, but here we wish to rely as little as possible on mathematical reasoning and as much as possible on direct stipulation.[22]

Quine*(7): I am glad to find you adhering to the same strategy in the case of quantifiers that you employed for sentential connectives: the (admittedly clever) strategy of working both a formulation of soundness of a logical rule and a stipulation on a logical particle into one and the same statement (nearly enough). I see no reason to question these formulations in their former capacity. It is the latter that I question. For, as comes through blatantly in (iv) – (vii), satisfaction-conditions for sentences of the form '∀xφ' are given by means of 'all'. As I have written:

> . . . one is perhaps tempted to see the satisfaction conditions as explaining negation, conjunction, and . . . quantification. However, this view is untenable; it involves a vicious circle. The given satisfaction conditions . . . presuppose an understanding of the very signs they would explain, or of others to the same effect.[23]

In short, (iv)–(vii) all presuppose familiarity with the universal quantifier (in one form or another) and are useless as means of introducing it. Similarly, (i) presupposes familiarity with 'and' and 'not' (i.e., with '⊃' in one form or another), and is useless as a means of introducing (first) truth-functional connectives.

Carnap*(8): Does this hark back to the difficulty of "self-presupposition of primitives" that you raised toward the end of "Truth by Convention"?[24] That has long puzzled me, for it seems to conflate two very distinct issues. First, there is the issue of *language learning,* the question of how we can or do acquire our first understanding of logical words. Here you quite rightly point out: not by explicit linguistic stipulations. But second, there is the issue of *language-based truth,* the question of the linguistic character of the satisfaction principles. Here what is at stake is whether knowledge of language suffices for knowledge of the soundness of logical rules. (Since the rules govern the logician's regimented language, that is the one that is relevant, of course.) It is quite irrelevant that the satisfaction conditions cannot serve the purposes of first language acquisition.

I have already argued for the connection between stipulation of satisfaction conditions (such as (i), (iv), and (vii)) and knowability of the soundness of logical rules. All that remains to be shown is that those conditions really are or can be entirely stipulative. But this is clear, since we *can* use those conditions to introduce new expressions, such as '⊃', '∀', etc., in whose terms logical sentences are to be framed. If these happen to coincide with simple expressions already in use, so much the better; but, as already noted, that is really inessential to the conventionalist case. All that is required is that *some* means be available for expressing the desired stipulations.

Quine*(8): Your new way with the linguistic doctrine, if I understand you, involves detaching it from any general analytic/synthetic dichotomy. Above, I was careful to attribute to you only a sufficient condition for "factual emptiness", one which did not rely on "meaning" or "confirmation". But now I find you invoking the distinction between knowledge of language and knowledge transcending language. But this just is the analytic/synthetic distinction in another form.

Carnap*(9): I have not invoked the distinction in anything like full generality. All that need be granted is the stipulative character of setting up "logical grammar" as you yourself have sketched it.[25]

Thus, I think we do have this general point: *one need not defend a general analytic/synthetic distinction to make the conventionalist case for logic.* One could even grant your point that any line drawn by linguistic science between knowledge of language and knowledge of extra-linguistic fact will be arbitrary in non-trivial ways. But, just as Putnam has detached from this the claim that there are some clear cases of linguistic equivalence,[26] I would insist that there are certain clear cases of linguistic stipulation, constraining any future linguistics. If the introduction of new particles by explicit rules of the sort presented above is not stipulative, what is?

Of course, metalinguistic resources for the stipulations must be available. On this score, I have been presupposing throughout that both you and I are conversant in English, and that the English expressions 'not', 'and', 'all' (or 'each', or 'every', or 'not any . . . not . . .', etc.) are available for the task, perhaps supplemented with diagrammatic devices and other "scholia as needed for precision". Do you dispute that?

Quine*(9): Much of my own logical writing seems rather to presuppose it![27] However, in a way I suppose I have disputed it in the case of quantifiers. One may read my ruminations on ontological relativity thus, as casting doubt on anyone's capacity to distinguish certain allegedly deviant interpretations of quantification over infinite sets (corresponding, e.g., to certain of their infinite subsets).[28] Just as I have found unrelativized reference behaviorally inscrutable, I would have to say the same for quantification.

Carnap*(10): This is not the place to descant upon my perplexity over inscrutability of reference.[29] I could cite some recent work that, I believe, tends to undermine its credibility,[30] but let me make these few remarks:

First, even if quantifiers are inscrutable, how does this affect the linguistic doctrine? As I see it, not at all! Its impact is simply that there is systematic ambiguity in the introduction principles (such as (iv) and (vii)). If, for example, D is the power set of the natural numbers, these stipulations would not distinguish among interpretations of $\forall$ that we would (naively?) describe as 'the standard interpretation, in which '$\forall$' ranges over all subsets' and 'deviant interpretations, in which '∀' ranges over all subsets of a proper elementary sub-model guaranteed to exist by the downward Skolem-Löwenheim theorem'. But *in any case, the soundness of UG is insured* (even) *by the* (ambiguous) *stipulations, and the rules regress is still blocked.* So long as we don't shift from one interpretation to another in midstream (in the space of a given deduction), nothing can go wrong, since by hypothesis we are dealing with *submodels* of any relevant background theory. Any such shifting that would affect soundness could, I submit, be detected and ruled out in our learning of the quantifier idioms.

Second, in your own writings, you have consistently dealt with a similar problem concerning *identity* in a way with which I am entirely sympathetic. Problems of individuation of complex objects, such as persons or mountains, are, you have maintained, misconceived as problems of identity; rather they reveal some difficulty concerning the application of the predicates ('person', 'mountain', etc.). Shouldn't any reason you have for this (very sensible) position carry over *mutatis mutandis* to quantifiers? Should we not say: "'All' is the clear notion and retains its clear truth conditions from context to context. Any problem raised by the Skolem-Löwenheim theorem (if one is raised) concerns the particular predicate whose extension is (taken to be) uncountably infinite, e.g., 'subset of integers'"?

Finally, it is perhaps an interesting question of psycholinguistics, how in detail we gain our mastery over quantifiers in discourse about the infinite. But is the problem more difficult in principle than that of acquiring dispositions to project an ordinary predicate beyond a finite sample to potentially infinitely many new cases? On the other hand, according to the inscrutability doctrine, a legitimate question has not even been posed since, on that doctrine, it is nonsense to say that we really do learn the standard interpretation of the universal quantifier.

As argued, the linguistic doctrine is in any case safe from inscrutability. As a challenge to linguistics, I find the latter intriguing; but taken literally, it seems to be a form of skepticism undermining the very intelligibility of that challenge. How would you prefer it to be understood?

Quine*(10): We have been at this long enough. Perhaps we can ask Professor Quine himself. I think he has been eavesdropping on us for some time now . . .

GEOFFREY HELLMAN

DEPARTMENT OF PHILOSOPHY
INDIANA UNIVERSITY, BLOOMINGTON
APRIL 1983

NOTES

1. W. V. Quine, "Truth by Convention", reprinted in idem, *The Ways of Paradox and Other Essays* revised edition (Cambridge, Mass.: Harvard University Press, 1976), pp. 77–106. (First published in 1936.)

2. W. V. Quine, "Carnap and Logical Truth", in P. A. Schilpp (ed), *The Philosophy of Rudolf Carnap* (La Salle IL: Open Court, 1963), pp. 385–406.

3. Rudolf Carnap, "W. V. Quine on Logical Truth", in *The Philosophy of Rudolf Carnap*, pp. 915–922.

4. Rudolf Carnap, *The Logical Syntax of Language* (London: Routledge and Kegan Paul, 1937), see the Foreword, p. xv and p. 18.

5. See the formulation in W. V. Quine, "Carnap and Logical Truth", reprinted in *The Ways of Paradox*, pp. 107–132, at p. 110 and n.2.

6. Carnap, "Quine on Logical Truth", p. 916.

7. Carnap, *Logical Syntax*, secs. 5 and 55.

8. W. V. Quine, *Word and Object* (Cambridge, Mass.: MIT Press, 1960), ch. 2.

9. Carnap, "Quine on Logical Truth", p. 916.

10. Quine, "Carnap and Logical Truth", secs. 3 and 4.

11. Ibid., p. 389; cf. W. V. Quine, *Philosophy of Logic* (Englewood Cliffs, N.J.: Prentice-Hall, 1970), ch. 7.

12. The point is hinted at by P. F. Strawson in his review of Quine's *Philosophy of Logic*, *Journal of Philosophy* 68, 6 (1971): 174–178, see p. 177.

13. Attributions of other truth-functional connectives and of existential quantification may be thought of as eliminated in favor of '$\sim$', '$\wedge$', and '$\forall$'.

14. See below, Carnap*(8).

15. Quine, "Carnap and Logical Truth", p. 390.

16. Predicates designating stipulated universal traits would be special cases of Carnap's "Allwörter", see *Logical Syntax*, sec. 76, pp. 292 ff. Note, however, two differences: the predicates of interest here are not relative to any category; and they are not introduced by means of any general notion of analyticity, but rather in terms of explicit stipulations governing logical words.

17. In *Philosophy of Logic*, p. 84, I put matters somewhat differently: I described the dissident logician as "rejecting the meaningfulness of classical negation". But this raises the puzzle: if he understands what he is rejecting, how can he reject its meaningfulness? Mere incomprehension on someone's part is of no logical interest. Perhaps the dissident is best viewed as rejecting the classicist's way of representing certain realms of discourse (for bad or better reasons, ibid., pp. 85 ff.). This comes down to questioning a precondition of applicability.

18. Note that soundness and completeness enter at different levels. It is soundness that is relevant at the "ground level" of justifying particular claims of the form,

S requires no justification,

for, typically, logical rules are used to derive S from axioms whose status (requiring no justification in virtue of emptiness) is evident. In establishing soundness of the rules, we establish in effect that *emptiness is preserved* in their application, and that is all that is required in any particular case. Completeness, on the other hand, enters at a higher level, when we ask whether the method of justification for the particular cases will always work.

It is important to recognize that establishing completeness is not required as part of the ground level justification procedure, because, in fact, proving completeness requires some relatively sophisticated mathematics whose "definitional" or "conventional" status is far from clear and would be much more difficult to secure than what is involved in soundness. But, because completeness enters only at the "metalevel", it poses no further problem for the conventionalist view of logic. (It may pose a special problem for a conventionalist view of the conventionalist view of logic. In a more traditional formulation, the question would be whether 'logic is analytic' is analytic. This would seem to turn on the status of the mathematics involved in LD(III), a problem that cannot be treated here. What is to be emphasized is that it is a separate problem about which Carnap* and Carnap need not agree.)

It should also be noted that arriving at the soundness of each rule (MP and UG, for simplicity) is, in a significant way, more elementary than arriving at the soundness of the system as a whole. The justification that the logical conventionalist is called upon to supply is, as it were, of the logical truths one by one. That is, Carnap* must be able to show of each logical truth S that it can be known solely from linguistic stipulations. This is weaker than showing that knowledge of system-soundness is a matter of linguistic convention. The difference may be brought out symbolically: writing '$\Diamond Kn$' for 'can be known', the Carnap* position requires an account of

(i) $\forall S: \Diamond Kn \ulcorner \vdash S \Rightarrow \models S \urcorner$ (S ranges over logical truths),

whereas a stronger position requires accounting for our knowledge of system-soundness, i.e., an account of

(ii) $\Diamond Kn \ulcorner \forall S: \vdash S \Rightarrow \models S \urcorner$.

Now it is true that (ii) will require appeal to mathematical induction (but see n. 22, below), but (i) does not.

19. Let 'MP_n' denote *modus ponens* for the nth level of the usual Tarski hierarchy of languages, taking L_o to be a formal language for first-order quantifier logic (as in Church, see n. 21) introduced by logicians employing L_1 as their natural language (e.g., Polish, English, etc). Carnap*'s remark here should be understood as saying that it is absurd to think that the only way of acquiring knowledge of the soundness of MP_n is to have acquired knowledge of the soundness of MP_{n+1}. At some stage it must be possible to come to know the soundness of MP_j without invoking a higher level MP. Below, Carnap* sketches a route for the soundness of MP_o that does not even appear to invoke a higher level MP. Alternatively, Carnap* might argue that, in learning 'if . . . then' of L_1, we in fact do learn the soundness of MP_1. As Wittgenstein might have put it, learning that such formal manipulations are correct (preserve acceptability—later truth— of the premises) is inseparable from mastering the 'if . . . then' idiom. In this case, MP_1 can be invoked in the course of arriving at the soundness of MP_o without the threat of regress. A similar line of argument can be developed for the few L_1 logical manipulations (involving 'not', 'and', 'there is') that might—as a matter of psychological fact—be inescapable in the hypothetical process Carnap* proceeds to sketch.

20. Formulation (i) is just a special case of a general metalinguistic stipulation on use of the terms 'sound' and 'rule of inference':

> (ii) A rule of inference with premises P_1 . . . P_n and conclusion C is sound *iff* there is no valuation making (the universal closure of) P_1 . . . P_n true and (the universal closure of) C false.

The parenthetical condition is needed for the rule of universal generalization which, together with *modus ponens,* suffices to generate all first order logically valid formulas (from standard axiom schemata). Working with this framework is particularly convenient because it reduces the problem of justification of logical rules to a very simple form.

Since (ii) *is* just a stipulation on some metalinguistic technical vocabulary, no special inference licensing passing from the right side to the left is involved: establishing the right side for a given rule *is* establishing the soundness of the rule. One possible route to regress is hereby blocked.

21. See, e.g., Alonzo Church, *Introduction to Mathematical Logic,* vol. 1 (Princeton: Princeton University Press, 1956), sec. 30, p. 172. Here UG can be stated without restrictions: from any wff A to infer $\forall xA$, where x is an individual variable. (This rule, of course, applies only to theorems, not to premisses.)

22. Even if; at some stage, it had proved necessary to invoke mathematical induction, that by itself would not have constituted a circularity or regress. We do, in fact, know that induction holds of the natural numbers. On my (Carnap*'s) view, this is guaranteed by what we mean by 'the natural numbers'. The fact that logic can be used to make this *rigorous* (as Russell showed) must not obscure the fact that we can, prior to formalization, intend 'the natural numbers' to be understood so as to insure induction. (Author's note: Although this way of phrasing the point, with its soft-pedalling of formalization, might not have appealed to Carnap, its essence emerges quite clearly in the *Logical Syntax,* sec. 34h, pp. 121–124, where mathematical induction is used in the metalanguage to establish the "analyticity" of object-language induction, and the charge of circularity is explicitly rebutted. (See p. 124.) Cf. the last paragraph of Carnap*(2), above.)

23. Quine, *Philosophy of Logic,* p. 21.

24. Quine, "Truth by Convention", p. 104.

25. Quine, *Philosophy of Logic,* pp. 22–25.

26. Hilary Putnam, "The Analytic and the Synthetic", in *Philosophical Papers,* vol. 2 (Cambridge: Cambridge University Press, 1975), pp. 33–69.

27. For example, I have written:

> . . . this logical language [of the formal logician] . . . has its roots in ordinary language, and these roots are not to be severed . . . It is enough that we show how to reduce the logical notations to a few primitive notations (say '~', '.', 'ϵ', and universal quantification) and then explain just these in ordinary language, availing ourselves of ample paraphrases and scholia as needed for precision.

W. V. Quine, "Mr. Strawson on Logical Theory", in *Ways of Paradox,* pp. 137–157, at p. 150.

28. W. V. Quine, "Ontological Relativity", in *Ontological Relativity and Other Essays* (New York: Columbia University Press, 1969), pp. 26–28; see pp. 54 ff.

29. When I think I understand it, I cannot see how it differs from my own rejection of external ontological questions. But this leaves me thoroughly confused for (a) you

have explicitly rejected the internal/external distinction on which my rejection is based (ibid., pp. 52–53), and (b) as a realist about physics (in a sense which I claim not to grasp), you would seem committed to at least the intelligibility of an "absolutist" ontological position, would you not?

30. For example, Michael Friedman, "Physicalism and the Indeterminacy of Translation", *Nous,* 9,4 (1975): 353–374, and Geoffrey Hellman, "The New Riddle of Radical Translation", *Philosophy of Science* 41,3 (1974): 227–246.

REPLY TO GEOFFREY HELLMAN

Recalling the early Quine and the late Carnap in a nostalgic dialogue, Hellman begins by coping with the regress that I propounded in 1936 in "Truth by Convention". The regress purported to show that logic could not be grounded in explicit conventions without a prior logic by means of which to instantiate the conventions. Hellman's Carnap* claims that the logical truths can be generated by stipulations—hence conventions—without the regress. He puts forward "a trait such as 'being red or not red'" as "a stipulated universal trait". But how, without prior logic, do we then infer, in particular, that the Taj Mahal has the trait? And how do we generalize the stipulation to all predicates in the role of 'red', and then infer, without prior logic, that it holds in particular for 'green'?

In "Carnap and Logical Truth" I claimed that Carnap's arguments for the linguistic doctrine of logical truth boiled down to saying no more than that they were obvious, or potentially obvious—that is, generable from obvieties by obvious steps. I had been at pains to select the word 'obvious' from the vernacular, intending it as I did in the vernacular sense. A sentence is obvious if (a) it is true and (b) any speaker of the language is prepared, for any reason or none, to assent to it without hesitation, unless put off by being asked so obvious a question. Hellman's Carnap*, like our Carnap, insisted on seeking an obscure technical meaning in my blatantly behavioral term 'obvious'. Carnap* proposes to substitute 'stipulated'. Perhaps then we are confronted here with a Pickwickian sense of 'stipulated' no less than of 'obvious'; and this may account for the puzzling talk of stipulation noted above.

However inadequate as a first cause of logical truth, stipulation in the usual sense is unproblematic as a source of truth. I recognized it in "Carnap and Logical Truth" in two forms: legislative postulation and legislative definition. I urged further in that essay that its legislative or stipulative character is episodic and confers no lasting distinction on the truths thus established.

Hellman's concern in the end is the linguistic doctrine of logical truth, and we may do better to face it directly. I proposed in *Roots of Reference* a sense in which logical truth may indeed be said to be grounded in the meanings of the logical particles. It is learned in learning the meaning, or use, of the particles.

> We learn the truth functions . . . by finding . . ., e.g., that people are disposed to assent to an alternation when disposed to assent to a component. The law that an alternation is implied by its components is thus learned . . . with the word 'or' itself; and similarly for the other laws. (P. 78)

More generally, I went on to suggest, analyticity might be construed thus in terms of the learning of words; see my reply to Bohnert. Such an approach affords no clear demarcation, since an individual's history of word learning is obscure and inconsequential when we get beyond paradigm cases such as 'bachelor'; but failure of clear demarcation suits one's intuitions of analyticity.

In "Two Dogmas of Empiricism" I remarked that analyticity and sameness of meaning are interdefinable. This pertains only to sameness of meaning of expressions in the same language; obviously analyticity in a language has no power to relate expressions between languages. Whatever success may be claimed for the explication of analyticity alluded to above therefore has no bearing on indeterminacy of translation.

Moreover I now perceive that the philosophically important question about analyticity and the linguistic doctrine of logical truth is *not* how to explicate them; it is the question rather of their relevance to epistemology. The second dogma of empiricism, to the effect that each empirically meaningful sentence has an empirical content of its own, was cited in "Two Dogmas" merely as encouraging false confidence in the notion of analyticity; but now I would say further that the second dogma creates a need for analyticity as a key notion of epistemology, and that the need lapses when we heed Duhem and set the second dogma aside.

For, given the second dogma, analyticity is needed to account for the meaningfulness of logical and mathematical truths, which are clearly devoid of empirical content. But when we drop the second dogma and see logic and mathematics rather as meshing with physics and other sciences for the joint implication of observable consequences, the question of limiting empirical content to some sentences at the expense of others no longer arises.

The air of necessity characteristic of logic and mathematics can be accounted for without help of analyticity. A year before "Two Dogmas" I made the point as follows.

> . Our system of statements has such a thick cushion of indeterminacy, in relation to experience, that vast domains of law can easily be held immune to revision in principle. We can always turn to other quarters of the system when revisions are called for by unexpected experiences. Mathematics and logic, central as they are

to the conceptual scheme, tend to be accorded such immunity, in view of the conservative preference for revisions which disturb the system least; and herein, perhaps, lies the ''necessity'' which the laws of mathematics and logic are felt to enjoy. (*Methods of Logic,* Introduction, all editions.)

The notion of analyticity then just subsides into the humbler domain where its supporting intuitions hold sway: the domain of language learning and empirical semantics.

W. V. Q.

9

Jaakko Hintikka

QUINE ON WHO'S WHO

For a while, it seemed that my dialogue with Van Quine—a dialogue partly real, partly fictional—had been carried as far as it could profitably be continued.[1] The salient points of this dialogue are worth summing up. Quine's old objections to modal logic were not all dispelled by the development of a genuine semantics (model theory) for modal logics, contrary to what the first full-fledged possible-world semanticists had hoped—and believed. The interpretational problems Quine had so vigorously made us aware of merely seemed to settle down on a new location: on the problem of cross-identification.[2] Against the superficial contrary claims of Kripke, Montague, and others, I argued that we cannot take cross-identifications for granted. It does not suffice simply to postulate a domain of individuals which would be prior to the possible worlds they inhabit and each of which then would (or would not) make its appearance in any given world.[3] There is every reason to think that Quine would approve of the purported conclusions of my arguments. Indeed, if I am not mistaken, Quine's arguments against modal logic preserve their sting even after their precise address is changed so that they now are directed against the possibility or at least the reasonableness of cross-identification.

This shift of focus admittedly means that some of Quine's old problems can be solved. In particular, Quine's problems concerning identity are independent of the cross-identification problem, and hence beyond the reach of Quine's modified criticisms.[4] But other criticisms of his, especially those directed against the possibility of mixing quantifiers and modal operators, will apply with vengeance—or so it seems.

We have to recognize, moreover, that the 'world lines' of cross-identification (notional lines each connecting the embodiments or roles of one and the same individual in different possible worlds) are not determined by God, Nature, or Logic, but are in principle drawn by ourselves. They are not drawn arbitrarily, it is true, but by means of various objective considerations, such as continuity in space and time, continuity of memory, and location in someone's visual space. Moreover, they are objectively retraceable once they have been drawn, independently of an individual language user's thoughts and doings. Nevertheless, these lines of cross-identification could in principle be drawn differently.[5]

Furthermore, the presuppositions on which the tracing of world lines rests can fail, and will fail if we consider sufficiently distant and sufficiently irregular worlds. (The reason is that these presuppositions amount to postulating various general regularities, such as the continuity of physical objects in space and time and the going together of bodily continuity and continuity of memory.) Moreover, such irregular and dissimilar worlds have to be considered in the semantics of so-called logical or alethic modalities (logical necessity and logical possibility). Hence we cannot have a set of world lines spanning all the worlds we need in alethic modal logic.[6]

Since these world lines define the individuals we quantify over when we use modal logic (more accurately, when we 'quantify into' modal contexts), we do not have well-defined individuals at our disposal in any realistically interpreted quantified modal logic. In virtue of the inseparable conceptual tie between quantifiers and individuals, which Quine has aptly emphasized, a quantified modal logic is impossible if we want to be able to interpret it in the obvious, intended way in a large scale (and not just 'locally', to wit, with respect to some previously restricted narrow class of possible worlds).[7]

Thus Quine turns out to be basically right in his criticism of quantified modal logic. A realistically interpreted quantified alethic modal logic is impossible. However, the reasons for this failure of quantifiers to mix with logical necessity and logical possibility are deeper than Quine realized. There is nothing intrinsically impossible or even awkward about cross-identification. I have argued that a great deal can be done for cross-identification by means of resources Quine himself countenances, especially by means of the continuity of objects in space and time. Whatever difficulties there may be are due to the presuppositions of these methods, which will fail in many logically possible worlds. Recently, Quine has signalled his qualified agreement with this view of the problem of cross-identification as operating essentially like re-identification.[8]

It can be argued that these presuppositions are normally satisfied for several other concepts which behave in many respects like logical modalities. Most of the so-called propositional attitudes are cases in point. Hence a quantified epistemic logic is interpretationally feasible, and so are quantified logics of belief (quantified doxastic logic), memory, perception, etc. (It is instructive to see that Quine has always been more tolerant towards propositional attitudes than towards logical modalities.)[9] But this relative success of quantified logics of propositional attitudes has no a priori guarantee, either. Success is found when people's propositional attitudes are sufficiently strong and sufficiently sweeping. For the problem is whether we can limit our attention to worlds that are sufficiently similar to each other and sufficiently orderly. Now in (say) doxastic logic the relevant possible worlds are all the worlds compatible with what someone believes. Hence these worlds are of the desired sort if and only if that person has sufficiently strong beliefs (so as to exclude enough possible worlds) and sufficiently specific beliefs (so that the remaining worlds are orderly enough). Of course there cannot be any a priori guarantee of this. Quantified logics of propositional attitudes are thus possible only in virtue of people's rationality, I am tempted to say. Of course there is nothing wrong, or even strange, in saying this; it merely amounts to saying that the applicability of logic to people's propositional attitudes presupposes that they are rational.

There exists no informed discussion in the literature of the question as to whether the worlds considered in using those modalities we employ in meaning theory are similar enough and regular enough to allow for an interplay with quantifiers. We may call these *analytic* modalities. (Once again, we are in the vicinity of Quine's ideas in that he has emphasized the parity of analyticity and modality.) There nevertheless is little hope, it seems to me, to save them from the same fate as logical modalities.

Thus my exchanges with Quine have established a much larger area of agreement than either of us probably expected. Even though a large number of smaller problems remain, it is not clear that a discussion of Quine's views is the right way of attacking them. The same goes for the big problem of our actual cross-identification methods. Esa Saarinen has cogently pointed out how some of my earlier statements on this subject rest on partial oversimplifications. But Quine's views do not seem to offer either insights or inspiration for further work in this direction.[10]

However, two interesting new avenues of further discussion have recently opened up. On the one hand, a new skeleton has been found in the cupboard of semanticists of modal logic, one which Quine obviously will relish.[11] On the other hand, Quine has sought to complement his criticism of alethic modal logic by giving reasons for being suspicious of the logic of propositional attitudes as well.[12] Dispelling these suspicions offers a natural occasion to clarify certain important issues concerning the foundation and the uses of epistemic logic, and of the logic of propositional attitudes more generally. I shall in this paper consider only the second of these two new subjects.

Epistemic logic is a particularly instructive proving ground for the issues Quine raises concerning the logic of propositional attitudes, because we have a rich supply of different grammatical constructions in terms of verbs for knowledge and a rich supply of pretheoretical linguistic and logical ideas, sometimes misleadingly labelled 'intuitions', concerning them.[13] Most of these so-called 'intuitions' can be related to what we do in epistemic logic. This is a merit which Quine acknowledges in connection with my analysis of quantified epistemic logic.[14] For instance, constructions in which one quantifies into an epistemic context are typically captured in English by interrogative constructions with verbs like 'knows'.[15] A case in point is

    (1)   Albert knows who wrote *Coningsby*

can be thought of as being (admittedly by way of first approximation only) equivalent with

    (2) (Ex) K_{Albert} (x wrote *Coningsby*).

The variable x has to be thought of here as ranging over persons. This is determined by the fact that the interrogative word in (1) is 'who'. For different who-words, we have to assign different ranges to our variables.

In particular, the interesting 'uniqueness conditions' which express the conditions on which we can quantify in (in the sense the conditions on which existential generalization is valid in a given context) often have idiomatic English counterparts. For instance, (2) can be inferred from

    (3) K_{Albert} (Beaconsfield wrote *Coningsby*),

that is,

    (3)*   Albert knows that Beaconsfield wrote *Coningsby*

only in conjunction with the further premise

    (4) (Ex) K_{Albert} (Beaconsfield $= x$).

But what (4) says is clear:

    (5)   Albert knows who Beaconsfield is.

Moreover, it is equally clear already pre-theoretically that (5) expresses the condition on which (1) is implied by (4). The corresponding uniqueness conditions for more complex cases can be expressed in a similar manner (whenever they can be expressed in the first place).

I am nevertheless afraid that Quine is praising my epistemic logic for a wrong reason. He writes on my criterion for the admissibility of quantifying in: "Unlike the criterion for a rigid designator, this brings matters gratifyingly close to home. It is very ordinary language indeed to speak of knowing who or what something is."[16]

Here Quine seems to me to turn the right heuristic priorities upside down. He seems to suggest in effect that we should employ our pre–theoretical insights concerning epistemic expressions in natural languages to elucidate what goes on in the formal language (or languages) of epistemic logic. For instance, there is a hint of a suggestion in Quine that by considering an English sentence like (1) we can see more clearly what (2) means. And even if this semantical priority of natural language and ordinary discourse were not what Quine has in mind here, it is very much the working assumption of Boër and Lycan, whose work Quine refers to with approval.[17] Even if he is not committing the mistake I am about to criticize, he is condoning it.

It is admittedly true that connections between logician's canonical notations and our familiar vernacular—connections which perhaps in some cases amount to relations of synonymy—play an extremely important role in developing the theory of formal languages, and especially their semantics. But such connections are best viewed as happy outcomes of applications of one's basic logical and semantical theory, which must first be developed. Such pleasant connections as were illustrated above are hoped-for end products of formal semantics, not its starting-points. Quine's hint exemplifies what seems to me one of the most pervasive and pernicious mistakes in contemporary philosophy of logic and philosophical logic: neglect of the fact that formal languages not only can be but ought to be, metaphorically speaking, a philosophical logician's 'mother tongue' or 'first language', first of course not genetically but systematically. Somewhat less metaphorically expressed, the first and foremost virtue of formal languages is the ease with which their semantics can be presented. For instance, Tarski-type truth-definitions for suitable formal languages constitute the clearest example of a semantical theory of the kind Davidson is looking for.[18] But the greater semantical clarity of suitable formal languages as compared with natural ones implies that formal languages can in principle be understood and mastered independently of the messy ways in which the same things are expressed in natural languages and independently of the even messier ways in which natural languages are translated into logician's standardized discourse.

Were it not for this semantical clarity of formal languages, a favorite strategy of many theorists of language would not make much sense. This is the strategy of elucidating the phenomena of natural languages by trying to translate their sentences into a formal logician's 'canonical notation'. For, if the latter were not semantically superior to our informal jargons, what would be gained by such translations?

Hence the mistake I have been criticizing is more than a little strange for Quine of all people to commit. For he has, by and large, relied on translational strategies.[19] What is more, I have surmised that Quine has been led in much of his work in ordinary extensional languages by an exceptionally clear semantical vision, even though he apparently does not think that we can theorize on a large scale about the semantics of our familiar home language.[20]

Hence it seems to me that Quine is not giving the languages of epistemic logic the same semantical credit he is giving the ordinary extensional languages, especially to the language of quantification theory.

An instructive case study of how much easier and how much more informative it is to build the bridges between natural languages and the languages of an epistemic logician from the vantage point of the latter (and especially from the vantage point of the semantics of epistemic logic) is offered by the neat solution that I have given to what may be labelled the dual ostension paradox.[21] This apparent paradox deals with the use of who-questions in ordinary discourse. For instance, somebody might walk into a meeting room and ask, pointing,

(6)   Who is the man over there?

The questioner obviously wants to be brought to a position where he or she can say, truly,

(7)   I know who the man over there is.

An appropriate response to the question might be to say, for instance, "Sir Norman Brook". This would normally bring the questioner to a point where he or she can truly say

(8)   I know that the man over there is Sir Norman Brook.

But another person might walk into the same room, for instance with a message in hand, look around, and ask

(9)   Who around here is Sir Norman Brook?

The questioner now presumably wants to be in a situation where he or she can truly say

(10)   I know who around here is Sir Norman Brook.

Now an appropriate answer might consist in pointing to someone and saying, "that man over there." Thereupon the questioner can normally say, truly, (8).

The logic underlying this perplexing double use of interrogatives has exercised philosophers and linguists.[22] How can who-questions be used in such dissimilar ways? How can the same information (the information codified by (8)) (serve as an answer to entirely different questions? What is the logic of (6)–(10), anyway? Cook Wilson used similar examples to claim that formal logicians could not cope with the allegedly different uses of 'is'.[23] Linguists and logicians alike have nevertheless failed to find a satisfactory account of the paradox. For instance, the brand-new and in many ways impressive theory of the logic and semantics of questions by Lauri Karttunen does not yield an explanation of the dual ostension paradox.[24] Even the ingenuity and patience of Steven Boër and William Lycan has not produced anything like a real theory for this paradox.[25] Furthermore, a formalization along the same lines as in (2) and (4) above does not automatically solve the problem, either.

Yet the problem is solved in one fell swoop as soon as we realize that we have here an instance of the use of two different cross-identification methods in one and the same situation. I had earlier shown the need of considering both methods quite independently of all questions about questions or their uses.[26] In (6) and (7), we are relying on the usual "descriptive" cross-identification methods. Hence (7) can be paraphrased in epistemic logician's jargon by using the same quantifiers as were employed earlier:

(11) $(Ex) K_1$ (the man over there $= x$)

But since a quantifier relies on a notion of individual and since the notion of individual is (when employed in epistemic contexts) relative to a method of cross-identification, we have to ascribe a different quantifier to (9) and (10), and to paraphrase (10) as, say,

(12) $(\exists x)\ K_1\ (\text{Sir Norman Brook} = x)$

where "$(\exists x)$" is a quantifier relying on what might be called *perceptual* methods of cross-identification. They are a special case of what I dubbed (borrowing a semi-technical term from Russell's early work) cross-identification methods by *acquaintance*.[27]

These cross-identification methods are in every serious practical sense unobtainable simply by contemplating and analyzing the ordinary-language expressions in question. Yet they are naturally and easily thought of (especially in the case of perception) at once as soon as we conceptualize that situation in terms of possible states of affairs and cross-identification between them, in effect, conceptualize it in semantical terms. For what are the relevant possible states of affairs here? They are all the states of affairs compatible with what the person in question perceives, for instance, sees. What they share most conspicuously is a matching distribution of a number of objects (those the person in question sees) in the perceiver's visual space. In brief, the perceptual alternatives to a given state of affairs share a common perceptual space, for instance a visual space. What could be more natural than to use this perceptual space as our framework of cross-identification, that is, to identify with each other objects occupying corresponding places in them?[28] (We even have informal ways of speaking of such cross-identification, albeit somewhat misleadingly. For instance, we can describe perceptual cross-identification by saying that it amounts to considering objects in the perceiver's environment merely as his *perceptual objects*.) It turns out that *this is precisely the cross-identification method that is needed for '$(\exists x)$' if the sentence (12) is to behave in the right way.*

Notice, for one thing, that this distinction between the two cross-identification methods and hence the distinction between '(Ex)' and '$(\exists x)$' cannot be made through any usual kind of restriction imposed on the range of the variable 'x'. For, in so far as we are considering the actual world only, we need precisely the same range of values for 'x' in either quantifier, viz., persons (or persons present on the occasion in question).

The perceptual cross-identification method is not any easier to recognize directly from the linguistic evidence when this evidence is extended to include some of the most striking and most satisfying consequences of my semantical observations. In order to see what they are, we need first a general observation. From examples like (6)–(8) we can see that the uniqueness conditions I mentioned earlier will do a second duty as *conditions for full (conclusive) answers*.[29] For (7) is what the questioner wanted to be brought about, while (8) is what the response "Sir Norman Brook" brought about. This response is therefore an answer if and only if (8) implies (7).

But the inferential step from (8) to (7) is one of existential generalization.

As was already mentioned, this inference is justified only in the presence of the further premise, which in this case is

(13) $(Ex)\ K_I$ (Sir Norman Brook $=\ x$),

i.e., "I know who Sir Norman Brook is."

Thus an epistemic logic yields as an extra bonus a criterion of answerhood (in the sense of a criterion of the conclusiveness of replies).

What is even more remarkable is that the same theory works for both kinds of questions and answers. Now how can we verify this claim? We are led by my theory to expect that the condition for "that man over there" to be a (conclusive) answer to (9) is

(14) $(\exists x)\ K_I$ (that man over there $=\ x$).

What does (14) say? It says that that man over there, that is, the man pointed at, is one of the questioner's acquaintance-objects. Normally, this amounts to saying that the questioner sees *that man over there*.[30] Needless to say, this is obviously the correct—and by hindsight trivial—criterion for an ostensive reply to be a satisfactory answer. (Trying to answer (9) by pointing to a man will succeed only if the questioner sees who is being pointed at.) What is far from trivial is that this condition of answerhood to ostensive questions is correctly predicted by my semantical theory.

We can also see what the colloquial renderings of many sentences with a perceptual quantifier are. For instance,

(15) $(\exists x)$ I see that (Sir Norman Brook $=\ x$)

means that Sir Norman Brook is identical with one of my visual objects; which obviously means that I *see* him. In this way we obtain more generally *an analysis of grammatical direct-object constructions* with epistemic verbs, i.e., such verbs as 'sees', 'perceives', 'remembers', 'knows', etc. . . . [31] This analysis is in terms of the that-construction with the same verb plus quantifiers relying on acquaintance. This result is full of both philosophical and linguistic consequences.

Among the philosophical consequences there is the possibility of understanding much of Russell's philosophy in 1905–1914 on the basis of the insight that he considered only quantifiers by acquaintance as being irreducible.[32] This is, I have shown, the gist of his attempted 'reduction to acquaintance'. Small wonder also that he for a while maintained that there are only three logically proper names (i.e., singular terms which always satisfy the uniqueness condition), viz., 'this', 'that', and 'I'. These, indeed, are among the few words which cannot fail to refer to a unique *perceptual* object in so far as their use is being understood.

Yet all this wealth of intralinguistic observations cannot seriously have been expected to make it evident to anyone what is really going on in the dual ostension paradox semantically, that is what real logic of the paradox is. The data could not be much simpler, and they have always been easily accessible to anyone. Yet they had not led any earlier analysts to the idea of quantifiers relying on acquaintance. The only natural way to them is semantical, and that is the way Quine seems to overlook. All the nice connections between the logical notation and various natural-language and indeed ordinary-language expressions that we just uncovered are applications of my semantical theory, not steps leading to it.

Indeed, there is more evidence of Quine's oversight. In the very act of praising my uniqueness conditions he misunderstands their role. Quine writes, after having explained what the analogues of the uniqueness conditions (13) and (14) are for belief (they look like (13)–(14) except that 'believing that' plays the role of "knowing that"; they are the conditions on which singular terms obey the usual laws of quantificational logic):

> Hintikka's criterion for this superior type of term was that Tom (i.e., the person in question) *knows* who or what the person or thing is; whom or what the term designates. The difference is accountable to the fact that Hintikka's was a logic of both belief and knowledge.[33]

This means that Quine thinks that I am using only one kind of uniqueness condition, viz., (13). Yet the first look at the *semantical* situation shows that the relation between the respective uniqueness conditions for two different propositional attitudes is one of analogy, not of identity. Uniqueness conditions formulated in terms of knowledge do not carry over to other notions. The point is very simple: a uniqueness condition like (4) says that the singular term in question ('Beaconsfield') picks out one and the same individual in all the relevant possible worlds. For knowledge, these relevant worlds are all the worlds compatible with what someone ('Albert') knows. Uniqueness of reference in all these worlds is precisely what (4) expresses. But when we are considering, say, what Albert remembers, the relevant possible worlds are those compatible with everything Albert remembers. The condition for the name 'Beaconsfield' to point out one and the same individual in all of them is not (4) but

(16) (Ex) Albert remembers that (Beaconsfield $= x$)

This need not be implied by (4). Likewise, in speaking of what Albert believes the uniqueness condition is

(17) (Ex) Albert believes that (Beaconsfield $= x$);

and analogously for other propositional attitudes. These conditions do not exhibit any regular relationship of implication one way or the other to (4).

The fact that (17) does not allow for an English paraphrase analogous to (5) (even though, e.g., (16) obviously does) admits a separate but natural explanation.[34]

The need of varying the uniqueness conditions from one propositional attitude to another is so obvious semantically that Quine's oversight on this point can only mean that he is not giving the semantical viewpoint a run for its money.

A sharper insight into the semantical situation would have saved Quine from another mistake. In criticizing my use of uniqueness conditions for quantifying in Quine writes:[35]

> Each belief world will include countless bodies that are not separately recognizable objects of the believer's beliefs at all, for the believer does believe still that there are countless such bodies. Questions of identity of these, from world to world, remain . . . devoid of sense . . . . Yet how are they to be dismissed, if one is to quantify into belief contexts? Perhaps the values of such variables should be limited to objects that the believer has pretty detailed views about. How detailed?

Here Quine is simply confused, it seems to me. Of course there is no difficulty in quantifying over individuals in some alternative doxastic world. Consider, for instance, the world which an operator for epistemic possibility invited us to consider. This operator will have the force of "in some world w_1 compatible with everything Jack believes, it is the case that—." We can quantify over the denizens of w_1 simply by using a quantifier inside that operator. Why should there be any difficulty?

Perhaps because we might want to consider the inhabitants of w_1 also *qua* neighbors of ours in our local world, i.e., in the actual world w_0. But this in itself legitimate problem has nothing to do with criteria of uniqueness or cross-reference. It is due to limitations of the notation of conventional modal logic which never allows us to return in an outside-in evaluation process to worlds considered earlier.[36] It can be cured by enriching the conceptual basis of modal logics, for instance by adjoining to their logical vocabulary Esa Saarinen's 'backwards-looking' operators.[37] It is relevant to note here that we may be able to trace an individual from w_1 back to w_0 even if it does not satisfy the appropriate uniqueness condition like (16)–(17) above. These conditions require that an individual can be cross-identified between *all* the alternative worlds. Here we are concerned only with tracing the individual back and forth between w_1 and w_0. In general, Quine is wrong in alleging that attempted cross-world identifications do not make any sense for those inhabitants of an alternative world which do not satisfy the uniqueness conditions. On the contrary, such cross-world comparisons must make sense in order for us to be able to say that they don't satisfy the relevant uniqueness condition. What the falsity of such a condition means is merely that one's search for a counterpart to the given member of a possible world does not always succeed. Once again, both the diagnosis and the cure are crystal clear once we adopt the semantical (possible-worlds) vantage point. From this vantage point, Quine's parting question in my latest quote from him is seen to be merely rhetorical.

Quine's most serious charge against my treatment of quantified epistemic logic by means of uniqueness conditions is the claim that these conditions are what he calls "indexical." After having acknowledged that "it is very ordinary language indeed to speak of knowing who or what something is" (as one has to do in the uniqueness conditions) he continues:[38]

However, ordinarity notwithstanding, I make no sense of the idiom apart from context. It is essentially indexical. You may ask who someone is, hearing his name and seeking his face; you may ask the same, seeing his face and seeking his name; you may ask the same, hearing his name and seeing his face but wondering about his claim to distinction. 'Who is he?' makes sense only in the light of the situation. Failing such light, the right answer is another question: 'What do you want to know about him?' Correspondingly the notion of knowing who someone is, or what something is, makes sense only in the light of the situation.

Quine is of course right about the variability of the truth-conditions of 'knowing who somebody is' statements (and likewise for 'knowing what something is' statements). Indeed, he acknowledges that I had pointed out that very variability fourteen years earlier.[39] But does this semantical unstability spoil the job uniqueness conditions are doing in epistemic logic and in the logic of questions? Only if their role is misunderstood, it seems to me. The weakness of Quine's argument is betrayed, at least by way of example, by his first illustration of the vagaries of 'knowing who someone is' statements. This first illustration ("hearing his name and seeking his face [or] . . . seeing his face and seeking his name") is nothing but the paradox of dual ostension analyzed above. Far from contributing evidence against my theory, this application is one of its most striking successes. One excuse for spilling as much ink as I did above on the dual ostension paradox is just that Quine in effect tries to use it as his prize specimen counter-example against quantified epistemic logic.

In more general terms, we can see the fallaciousness of Quine's conclusion by examining the role of uniqueness conditions (i.e., if the critical 'who someone is' and 'what something is' statements like (4)–(5), or (11)–(12)) in my epistemic logic. Once again, attention to the semantical situation serves us well. What happens is that the truth-values of sentences of the form[40]

(18) $(Ex) K(b = x)$

and by the same token those of sentences of the form

(19) $(\exists x) K(b = x)$

(where 'b' is an individual constant) become largely independent of the truth-values of other types of simplest sentences, including the usual atomic ones. Indeed, sentences of the form (18)–(19) can be considered a new class of atomic sentences. This reflects the fact that world lines are not determined in any simple way by the attributes of the individuals they connect. For this reason, *the variability of the truth-conditions of 'who someone is' statements is predictable on the basis of my theory,* and hence scarcely an objection to it.[41]

Moreover, my theory offers us several insights into the actual variation of the truth-conditions of sentences like (18)–(19). The contrast between cross-identification by acquaintance and by description mentioned above is a case in point.

This contrast is related to a large number of subtle philosophical and linguistic issues. My references to Bertrand Russell above will serve to indicate what some of the relevant philosophical issues are. Others are connected with Kant's notion of 'thing in itself'[42] and with Husserl's theory of perception[43] to mention only a few. These interesting relationships should have whetted a philosopher's logical appetite instead of turning him away from uniqueness conditions as being semantically unstable.

Other examples of how the issues that come up on connection with the variability of the truth-values of uniqueness conditions can be of great theoretical interest will be given below. Meanwhile, the nature of Quine's mistake is worth emphasizing. My theory, like any comparable semantical theory, gives an account of how the truth-values of complex sentences depend on those of simpler sentences, ultimately atomic ones.[44] In any particular application, the way in which the truth-values of atomic sentences are determined is taken for granted. Since the simplest uniqueness conditions (18)–(19) behave like atomic sentences, their truth-values also have to be taken as being given.

But the truth-conditions of (18)–(19) are essentially the same as criteria for drawing world lines. Hence, semantically speaking, world lines have to be assumed to be drawn before any application can get off the ground. Drawing those world lines is never itself a part of the application. The theory is essentially about the interplay of the truth-conditions of atomic and non-atomic sentences. For instance, it shows that (and how) the truth-values of all 'knows– + –a–wh–word' sentences depend on the truth-values of sentences of the form (18)–(19), that is, of the truth-values of the simplest 'knowing who someone is' and 'knowing what something is' sentences.

Quine's criticism is not even calculated to affect this central part of my theory. Quine deals entirely with what one can say of sentences of the form (18)–(19), i.e., of the new atomic-like sentences. Hence it is simply beside the point as a criticism of my semantics of epistemic logic.

An analogy may be instructive here. When Quine tries to criticize epistemic logic by pointing out the context-dependence of (17)–(18), it is just as if someone were to attempt to criticize the usual truth-table analysis of propositional connectives by claiming that some of the sentences they serve to combine are context-dependent, fuzzy, or otherwise semantically suspect. Although those shortcomings of certain atomic sentences might be highly interesting in their own right and might in fact lead to further developments in an amplified propositional logic, they scarcely constitute a viable argument for criticizing current propositional logic and its semantics. Quine's criticism of my use of uniqueness conditions is equally unconvincing, for it leaves epistemic logic proper untouched. All that this logic claims is that, no matter how the world lines are initially drawn, the structure of the rest of the semantics remains the same. This claim is both non-trivial *a priori* and highly plausible *a posteriori* in the light of evidence, as exemplified among other things by the unexpected parallelism between (11) and (12) and by the even more surprising logical parallelism between their natural-language counterparts. (This parallelism shows that uniqueness conditions operate *mutatis mutandis* in the same way no matter whether world lines are drawn by acquaintance or by description.) This claim is not affected by Quine's criticisms. An application of my epistemic logic does not presuppose that world lines are drawn once and for all by context-independent means, as Quine in effect assumes. All that is required is that throughout any one particular application the world lines do not change—or if they change, that different warps of world lines be indicated by different quantifiers.

Hence Quine's criticism is totally without any force. However, his observation concerning the vagaries of our actual criteria of knowing who is characteristically acute, and poses the further problem as to how to account for this criterial instability. Even apart from the explanations already given, there are in fact several features of my semantics which serve to make the context-dependence of uniqueness-conditions both natural and interesting.

One major source of semantical context-dependence in the general area of the logic of questions is easily pinpointed. It is the role of uniqueness conditions in question-answer relations and their precise import. There is a *prima facie* methodological reason why logicians and linguists had not reached the simple but deep analysis of the question-answer relation that was outlined above. Logicians and linguists have tried to find a criterion of answerhood that would depend only on the logical and/or grammatical properties of the given question, which are independent of the linguistic and pragmatic context of the utterance in question. (I suspect that when Quine demands of my epistemic logic semantical context-independence, he is operating in the same spirit as these earlier theorists of language.) My solution to the problem of the nature of answers does not depend on such context-independent properties alone. As shown by examples like (4) and (11) above, my *conditions of answerhood depend also on what the questioner knows in the sense of knowing that*. This knowledge of course varies from one occasion to another. If we are dealing with questions and answers, we must realize that one of the very functions of responses to a question ('answers' in a wide sense of the word) is to supply such collateral information as is needed to make true that uniqueness condition which serves on that particular occasion as the criterion of answerhood. This heavy reliance on the informational background of the different speakers makes my analysis of both direct questions and subordinate questions with 'knows' as the operative verb contextual in a sense which I have spelled out. It is probably an important part of what Quine in effect had in mind. Yet it does not justify his criticism in the least. It is true that this epistemic context-dependence goes against the aims of many linguists and logicians, apparently including Quine. However, it does not make my semantics of epistemic concepts or the corresponding logic any less objective or any less sharp. It may be considered partly

as an acknowledgement of the fact that the relationship between a question and
its answers is intrinsically a *discourse* phenomenon.[45] The epistemic backgrounds of a question and of an answer to it are typically different (otherwise
the question would most likely be pointless) and cannot therefore be 'factored
out' as similar differences are normally dealt with in sentence semantics. In
brief, this kind of context-dependence is merely a symptom of our being engaged in text semantics and not merely in sentence semantics. And this is
definitely a merit of my analysis and not a shortcoming. In general, in spite of
repeated claims to the contrary, logical analysts of language have restricted
their attention far too narrowly to sentence phenomena (e.g., sentence semantics) at the expense of text phenomena (e.g., text semantics).

This epistemic context-dependence of what counts as a conclusive answer
to a given who-question is nevertheless different from the variability of the
truth-criteria of those very uniqueness conditions themselves which define the
conclusiveness of a putative answer. It is the latter, not the former, that Quine
seems to have in mind in his specific criticisms.

It was already pointed out above that the truth-values of uniqueness conditions are largely independent of the truth-values of other types of simplest
sentences. What this means is that the world lines spanning those states of affairs or courses of events we are in effect considering can be drawn in different ways without upsetting the rest of our semantical situation. Indeed, casting
the question in the form of a problem of drawing lines of cross-world (cross-
situation) identifications is an excellent way of conceptualizing and even partly
operationalizing different criteria of knowing who and making understandable
people's choices between them. In some cases, it is possible to give systemat-
ical characterizations of the difference between different ways of drawing such
world lines. The acquaintance-description contrast is a case in point. In many
cases, it is nevertheless impossible to offer more than a pragmatic account of
what happens in ordinary discourse. Moreover, the account has to be geared to
a specific application. It is remarkable, however, that even in such cases my
framework allows for explanations which are simply impossible in competing
frameworks.

This can of course be shown only by examples. To take a trivial one,
Evelyn Waugh quotes somewhere in his diaries the old sexist saying: "Be nice
to young girls. You never know who they will be." What is the semantical
force of 'knowing who' here? It is obviously a nonstandard one, apparently
offering aid and comfort to Quine. It is indeed a safe bet that no philosophical
theories of personal identity will predict the truth-conditions of this old saw.
Yet when it is thought of in terms of world lines, the force of Waugh's *dictum*
is embarrassingly obvious. When different future courses of events are compared with each other, our male chauvinist snob is treating as identical women
married to the same gent. We don't understand Waugh without realizing that
that's how he is drawing his world lines of nubile women. His reasons for

doing so are blatant enough, but don't properly belong to the province of logical semantics.

This example is of course philosophically trivial in its own right. What is not trivial is that essentially the same kind of analysis can be given of many uses of 'identity' and 'knowing who' in psychology and psychiatry.[46] It would take us too far to examine examples of such use in detail here. It is sufficiently obvious, however, that current logical and linguistic semantics or philosophical theories of personal identity are incapable of explaining the meaning of the locutions in question. Criteria of personal identity which rely on bodily continuity or on the continuity of memory cannot account for the meaning of a psychiatrists's words when he or she is describing how a patient came to realize who he was. In contrast, an analysis which construes the patient's insight as his coming to be able to recognize himself as the same person under several different possible courses of events which may involve changes in the patient's psyche clearly has a great deal of promise here. Such an analysis is codifiable in terms of possible-worlds semantics, which once again prove to be not only a versatile tool of philosophical theorizing but also the natural framework for spelling out the meaning of our locutions.

Fuller details will have to wait for another occasion. The indications just given suffice to illustrate my point, however.

Far from being an argument against my semantics for epistemic logic, the variability of the truth-conditions of uniqueness conditions thus opens the door to a large number of highly interesting applications and hence on the contrary constitutes a strong argument for it, Quine notwithstanding. Moreover, it is precisely the semantical apparatus of possible worlds (possible states of affairs or possible courses of events) and cross-identification between them that makes these applications possible. In dismissing uniqueness conditions, those verbal counterparts of world lines, because of their context-dependence and because of their consequent variability of meaning, Quine is in effect trying to exclude from the purview of philosophical logicians some of their most promising areas of application.

JAAKKO HINTIKKA

DEPARTMENT OF PHILOSOPHY
FLORIDA STATE UNIVERSITY
JULY 1979

NOTES

1. This has of course been a part of a larger dialogue between Quine and modal logicians in general. A survey of some of its earlier stages is presented in Dagfinn Føllesdal, "Interpretation of Quantifiers", in van Rootselaar and Staal, editors, *Logic,*

Methodology, and Philosophy of Science III Amsterdam: North-Holland, 1968), pp. 271–281. I strongly feel that many modal logicians have not appreciated the force of Quine's criticisms. I have myself tried to do justice to them in my paper "Quine on Quantifying In" in Jaakko Hintikka, *The Intentions of Intentionality and Other New Models for Modalities* (Dordrecht and Boston: D. Reidel, 1975), pp. 102–136, which was originally intended as my contribution to the present volume. Some of the salient points of that paper will be summarized here.

2. Cf. W. V. Quine, review of Milton K. Munitz, *Identity and Individuation, Journal of Philosophy* 69 (1972): 488–497.

3. See the different essays collected in my *The Intentions of Intentionality* (note 1 above). Dana Scott has voiced related doubts in his unpublished paper, "Is There Life on Possible Worlds?". Many of the flaws in the views of Montague, Kripke, et al. still remain unacknowledged and partly unrecognized, however.

4. See "Quine on Quantifying In" (note 1 above), especially pp. 118–124.

5. Much of the interest of this observation lies in the further thesis of mine that these world lines are as a matter of fact drawn in at least two entirely different ways in our own conceptual practice. For this stronger claim, see below—and see also my books *The Intention of Intentionality* (note 1 above) and *Models for Modalities* (Dordrecht: D. Reidel, 1969), especially chapter 8, "On the Logic of Perception".

6. See "Quine on Quantifying In" (note 1 above), especially pp. 128–131.

7. The role of such tacit limitations has remained largely undiscussed in the literature, in spite of their tremendous importance. It is only in virtue of such 'transcendental' limitations of our attention that our analytical modalities can be hoped to be viable at all. (See below.) Moreover, such tacit presuppositions have in effect played an important role in the thoughts of several major philosophers, including Kant, who restricted the realm of possibility to what is "empirically possible", Husserl, whose notion of "motivated possibility" serves to limit our "horizon" of possible further determinations of objects, and Wittgenstein, who emphasized the role of agreement in judgements as a precondition of communication within a speech community. In connection with Kant, this point was first emphasized to me by Moshe Kroy.

8. See W. V. Quine, "Worlds Away", *Journal of Philosophy* 73, 22 (December 16, 1976) 859–863, especially first paragraph. This paper of Quine's is partly a reaction to my "Quine on Quantifying In", and my present paper can be thought of as a rejoinder to Quine's paper. An excellent independent reply to Quine is to be found in Robert Kraut, "Worlds Regained", *Philosophical Studies* 35 (1979).

9. See, e.g., W. V. Quine, "Quantifiers and Propositional Attitudes", reprinted in *The Ways of Paradox* (New York: Random House, 1966), pp. 183–194.

10. See Esa Saarinen in Merrill B. Hintikka et al., *Essays in Honor of Jaakko Hintikka* (Dordrecht and Boston: D. Reidel, 1979).

11. See my paper, "Standard vs. Nonstandard Logic" in *Modern Logic,* edited by E. Agazzi (Dordrecht and Boston: D. Reidel, 1981), pp. 283–296.

12. See "Worlds Away" (note 8 above).

13. I have offered some comments on the role of so-called intuitions in philosophical argumentation in "Intuitions and Philosophical Method", *Revue internationale de Philosophie* 35 (1981): 74–90.

14. See "Worlds Away" (note 8 above), p. 863

15. See my *Knowledge and Belief* (Ithaca, N.Y.: Cornell University Press, 1962). Important further observations concerning the treatment of natural-language locutions with "knows" are presented in my monograph *The Semantics of Questions and the Questions of Semantics,* Acta Philosophica Fennica, vol. 28, no. 4, (Amsterdam: North-Holland, 1976).

16. "Worlds Away" (note 8 above), p. 863

17. Steven E. Boër and William G. Lycan, "Knowing Who", *Philosophical Studies* 38, 5 (November 1975): 299–244.

18. See, e.g., Donald Davidson, "Truth and Meaning", *Synthese* 17 (1967): 304–333.

19. That is, by and large, Quine's strategy in the second half of *Word and Object* (Cambridge, Mass.: MIT Press, 1960).

20. Much of Quine's philosophy of language is colored by his adherence to the assumption I have called the idea of *language as the universal medium*. Cf. here my papers, "Semantics: A Revolt Against Frege", in G. Floistad, editor, *Contemporary Philosophy: A New Survey*, Volume 1 (The Hague: Martinus Nijhoff, 1981), pp. 57–82, and "Is Truth Ineffable?" (forthcoming).

21. The gist of my solution is given in my monograph *The Semantics of Questions and the Questions of Semantics* (note 15 above), section 3.6.

22. The problem was first posed to me by Barbara Hall Partee.

23. John Cook Wilson, *Statement and Inference* (Oxford: Clarendon Press, 1926), pp. 117–119. (I owe this reference to Harry Lewis.)

24. Lauri Karttunen, "Syntax and Semantics of Questions", in Henry Hiz, editor, *Questions* (Dordrecht and Boston: D. Reidel, 1978).

25. See op. cit. (note 17 above).

26. See *Models for Modalities* (note 5 above), especially chapter 8, and *The Intentions of Intentionality* (note 1 above), especially chapters 3-4.

27. See my paper "Knowledge by Acquaintance—Individuation by Acquaintance", in David Pears, editor, *Bertrand Russell: Modern Studies in Philosophy* (Garden City, N.J.: Doubleday, 1972), pp. 52–79, reprinted in Jaakko Hintikka, *Knowledge and the Known* (Dordrecht and Boston: D. Reidel, 1974), 212–233.

28. Think of the information supplied by someone's momentary visual perceptions as being summed up in a photograph. If this photograph does not enable one to tell who a certain person in the picture is, then it allows for more than one alternative state of affairs such that in some of the different states of affairs that figure is a different person. (Different person, that is to say, by our usual descriptive criteria.) But it is perfectly obvious that there is at that location in the picture one and only one person, a person about whom we can make various judgments. In doing so, we are treating him or her as a well-identified individual, and this well-definedness can only refer to what I have called perceptual criteria of cross-identification. In the different states of affairs which the picture admits of we treat those individuals as one and the same who correspond to the same character in the photograph.

29. See *The Semantics of Questions and the Questions of Semantics* (note 15 above), sections 2.6, 3.1-3.3.

30. This would be strictly true if (14) had read "$(\exists x)$ I see that (that man over there $= x$)". In so far as we are in (14) dealing with knowledge on the basis of my visual perception above, as I indicated that we are doing, the difference does not matter.

31. Cf. *The Intentions of Intentionality* (note 1 above), chapter 3; "Knowledge by Acquaintance—Individuation by Acquaintance" (note 27 above).

32. See "Knowledge by Acquaintance—Individuation by Acquaintance" (note 27 above).

33. "Worlds Away" (note 8 above).

34. The explanation is outlined in *The Semantics of Questions and the Questions of Semantics* (note 15 above), section 4.6.

35. "Worlds Away" (note 8 above), p. 863.

36. This limitation of conventional modal logic was first pointed out by David

Kaplan and his associates of UCLA. See David Kaplan. "Ted and Alice and Bob and Carol", in Jaakko Hintikka et al., *Approaches to Natural Language* (Dordrecht and Boston: D. Reidel, 1973), pp. 490–518. The intuitive idea of an outside-in evaluation procedure is vindicated by my game-theoretical semantics; see Esa Sarrinen, editor, *Game-Theoretical Semantics* Dordrecht and Boston: D. Reidel, 1978).

37. See his papers in Saarinen, editor, *Game-Theoretical Semantics* (note 36 above).

38. "Worlds Away" (note 8 above), p. 863.

39. *Knowledge and Belief* (note 15 above), p. 149n.

40. For different subscripts of *"K"* (more accurately, for different knowers), (18)-(19) are to be taken to be logically independent of each other.

41. What is directly predicted is of course only the possibility of such variability. The versatility of ordinary discourse readily turns this possibility into actuality, however.

42. See *Knowledge and the Known* (note 27 above), chapter " 'Dinge an sich' Revisited".

43. See *The Intentions of Intentionality* (note 5 above), title essay.

44. This is precisely what a semantical theory *à la* Davidson is supposed to achieve; cf. note 18 above. In this respect, Davidson's program is not affected by the criticisms I level against some of its other features in my paper, "Theories of Truth and Learnable Languages", in Jaakko Hintikka and Jack Kulas, *The Game of Language* (Dordrecht and Boston: D. Reidel, 1983), pp. 259–292.

45. Cf. "Semantics: A Revolt Against Frege" (note 20 above), last section.

46. Instructive examples of distinctions and other considerations which easily can be subjected to a possible-worlds analysis are offered by Abraham Kaplan's unpublished discussion of selfhood, which partly reproduces sections 46 and 47 of his book *In Pursuit of Wisdom* (Los Angeles: Glencoe Press, 1977).

REPLY TO JAAKKO HINTIKKA

Jaakko Hintikka has concerned himself with my remarks regarding the intensional idioms of modal logic and the propositional attitudes. In my view these idioms are semantically dependent upon the circumstances of utterance, much in the manner of the indexicals. Thus relativized, they make sense and are useful. Necessity, for instance, may typically be said of a sentence that follows logically from acceptances shared by the parties to the particular dialogue or inquiry. See my reply to Bohnert. In the case of the propositional attitudes the indexical character is instructively pinpointed, under Hintikka's approach, in the key idiom of believing or knowing who or what someone or something is; for the question who or what someone or something is depends for its force on the purposes and background information of the moment. Does Hintikka disagree with any of this?

Indexicals present no major logical or semantic problems, and furthermore they are indispensable to daily discourse. Still, for obvious reasons, they would be out of place in an enduring and impersonal formulation of a system of the world. Now in my view this last is true equally of the intensional idioms of modality and propositional attitude. They differ from the indexicals, or from other indexicals, only in not enjoying so transparent a logic and semantics.

Where I consequently disagree with many philosophers, though perhaps not Hintikka, is in scouting any notion of objective or metaphysical necessity. The logic and semantics of necessity and the propositional attitudes is of interest only as a study in linguistics and psychology, and not as a reflection of broad structures of reality.

Hintikka protests that his semantics did not purport to arrest "the variability of the truth conditions of 'who someone is' statements" or of cross-world identifications, and that it was a confusion on my part to criticize his semantics on that score. He has misidentified my target. In "Worlds Away" I was arguing that there is no objective or absolute basis for cross-world identifications, and that the analogy with temporal re–identifications in the actual world, urged by Hintikka, lends no comfort. Of his particular semantic theory I offered no criticism, though I shall, at the end, in a modest way.

Regarding the analogy of cross-world identification with temporal re–identifications, Hintikka writes, oddly, that "Quine has signalled his qualified agreement." What agreement? I cheerfully acknowledged that "identification of an object from moment to moment is indeed on a par with identifying an object from world to world." How? "Both identifications are vacuous, pending further directives." Then I went on to show how the further directives ready to hand in the one case were wanting in the other. Was this touch of irony misleading?

Apparently another one was. Hintikka quotes me thus: "This brings matters gratifyingly close to home. It is very ordinary language indeed to speak of knowing who or what something is." Who can deny it? There is indeed the overtone, ironically intended, that ordinary language is clear. It was dispelled, I hoped, by my next sentence: "However, ordinarity not withstanding, I make no sense of the idiom apart from context." No, not dispelled. Hintikka deplores at some length my inversion of the "heuristic priorities", my preference for "pretheoretical insights" over formal theory construction, and notes (rightly enough) that "the mistake. . . is more than a little strange for Quine of all people to commit." Let me stress all flat-footedly, and not for the first time, that familiarity carries no presumption of clarity. It merely breeds contentment.

Substitution of new and unfamiliar symbols for familiar and unclear expressions is not, on the other hand, of itself a step toward clarity. On the contrary, again. I think here of Hintikka's two styles of existential quantifier. Do these, between them, exhaust the senses in which we may ask who or what someone or something is? Or, again, why does he deny that they are ordinary quantifiers with differently restricted ranges? His paraphrase of his (15) suggests that the quantifier in (15) is indeed an ordinary quantifier ranging over what he calls visual objects.

W.V.Q.

10

David Kaplan

OPACITY

In 1978, as I was conducting my annual tour through the delights of "Quantifiers and Propositional Attitudes"[1] (Q&PA), I paused at a familiar transition point. It struck me, for the first time, as puzzling. What, exactly, was the argument that lay behind the transition? My investigation led me to a surprising discovery. But first, the puzzling transition.

Q&PA begins with a lesson on symbolization for the student of first order logic. Although my desire for a certain sloop is suitably expressed as:

(2) $(\exists x)(x$ is a sloop . I want $x)$

"If what I seek is mere relief from slooplessness, then (2) conveys the wrong idea." (The same lesson, though less sharply put, was offered earlier by Buridan, who noticed the difference between owing someone a particular horse and owing mere relief from horselessness.[2]) Thus, the vernacular sentence:

I want a sloop

is ambiguous between what Quine calls its *relational* reading, expressed by (2), and its likelier *notional* reading involving mere relief from slooplessness. Can we represent the ambiguity of this sentence as a mere grammatical reparsing within elementary logic? It appears so, says Quine, "with some premeditated violence to both logic and grammar."[3] The method is this: rewrite the verb as a 'propositional attitude', a form in which it becomes an operator taking, at least in part, a sentential complement. Thus *wanting* (a sloop) becomes *wishing that* one has (a sloop) in which "wishes that" takes a sentential complement.[4] The relational reading of the reformed vernacular sentence is then symbolized as a reformed version of (2):

An analytical Table of Contents for this essay can be found on page 288.

For comments, some valuable, some invaluable, I wish to thank Rogers Albritton, Joseph Almog, Tony Anderson, Paul Benacerraf, Dagfinn Føllesdal, Karel Lambert, Ruth Marcus, Nathan Salmon, and Richmond Thomason, all of whom read one draft or another of the paper; the Stanford Gang, who heard it; and W. V. Quine who did neither. I also wish to thank the National Science Foundation for patient support. Special thanks to Joseph Almog who told me what my other friends wouldn't.
                                                    © by David Kaplan 1985.

(3)   ($\exists x$)(x is a sloop . I wish that: I have x)
and the notional sense of the reformed vernacular sentence is symbolized as:
(4)   I wish that: ($\exists x$)(x is a sloop . I have x)
(The colon is used syntactically, and only temporarily, to demarcate the complement to the operator.)[5]

The remainder of the first few pages of Q&PA strengthens and develops this theme with respect to *seeking* (rewritten as "striving that: one finds . . ."), *hunting* (a variety of *seeking*), and finally, the first and foremost of the propositional attitudes, *believing* (which requires no rewriting in its primary use). In each case the contrast between relational and notional readings may be strikingly represented in terms of permutations of quantifier and verb.[6]

Beautiful! Another triumph for elementary logic! (And who would begrudge a little premeditated violence for so elegant an achievement?)

But wait; now comes the transition. "However, the suggested formulations of the relational [readings] . . . all involve quantifying into a propositional-attitude idiom from outside. This is a dubious business . . ."

What a downer! Why has Quine undercut his own logical triumph with gloomy doubts? One immediately thinks of the problems of interpreting modal logic and of the awful consequence of the third degree of modal involvement, namely, the metaphysical jungle of Aristotelian essentialism. But whereas the relational readings of sentences involving necessity lead into the jungle (and good riddance, says Quine), "we are scarcely prepared to sacrifice the relational constructions" that (3) and others like it are supposed to represent. Quine does not doubt that quantification into propositional attitudes makes *epistemological* sense. The opening pages of Q&PA, and in particular the contrast between (3) and (4), show us just what sense it makes.[7]

This point is so important that I will repeat it. The doubt which appears at the transition in Q&PA—and which generates all of the remaining maneuvers of Q&PA—is not a doubt about the plausibility of the underlying epistemology, in the way in which Quine's skepticism toward essentialism is a doubt about the plausibility of what he sees as the underlying metaphysics of quantified modal logic. In Q&PA, the epistemology is repeatedly said to be sensible, even indispensable. So there must be some other problem that drives Quine on, not epistemological but *logical*.

We need a bit of technicality. Call the position of a singular term within a sentence *open to substitution* if the result of replacing a term in that position by a co-referential one does not affect the truth value of the sentence. It can happen that a position which is open to substitution in a given sentence is no longer open to substitution when the given sentence is embedded in a larger sentential context. Quine has dubbed such larger sentential contexts *opaque*.[8] Now Quine's logical problem is this: the sensible epistemology of the symbolization lesson has the result that although positions within the propositional attitude constructions are not open to substitution (i.e. the sentential contexts produced by the propositional attitudes are opaque), these same positions appear to be open to quantification from without (as in (3)). This is thought to violate principles of logic and semantics. It is said to produce a "dilemma", for when substitution is ruled out, quantification in "goes by the board". Throughout the remainder of the paper, Quine reminds us again and again that there is a *technical* problem that must be solved. At the end of section III: "In all cases my concern is, of course, with a special technical aspect of the propositional attitudes: the problem of quantifying in." We must avoid "illicit quantification into opaque contexts" while at the same time we must "provide for those indispensable relational statements of belief." This is the task of the remainder of Q&PA.

But why is it illicit, why is there a dilemma, and how do we know we can't quantify into positions not open to substitution?[9] In Q&PA Quine only hints at an argument in eleven swift lines. We are told that the failure of substitution shows that we have ceased to affirm any property of an individual at all, that such sentences are not about an individual, and that it then becomes improper to quantify in.

> If, on the other hand, . . . we rule simultaneously that
> (12)   Ralph believes that the man in the brown hat is a spy,
> (13)   Ralph does not believe that the man seen at the beach is a spy,
> then we cease to affirm any relationship between Ralph and any man at all. Both of the component 'that'-clauses are indeed about the man Ortcutt; but the 'that' must be viewed in (12) and (13) as sealing those clauses off, thereby rendering (12) and (13) compatible because not, as wholes, about Ortcutt at all. It then becomes improper to quantify as in ["$(\exists x)$(Ralph believes that x is a spy)"]; 'believes that' becomes, in a word, referentially opaque.

Quine's theoretical speculations here are certainly plausible, but the intelligibility of the first few pages of Q&PA provides an equally plausible concrete counter–instance. That is the real dilemma. But Quine doesn't explore *that* dilemma. Instead, he takes it as an established principle of logic (in the broad sense, including semantics) that we cannot quantify into such contexts, and tries to save as much of the first few pages as possible within that constraint.

This led me to explore Quine's relevant earlier papers for a more detailed version of his argument for the putative logical principle, and that led to my surprising discovery.

Part A: The Alleged Theorem

II

I have concluded that in 1943, in his groundbreaking work "Notes on Existence and Necessity", Quine gave an invalid argument. He believed himself to have given a proof of a general theorem regarding the semantical interpretation of any language that combines quantification with opacity. The purported theorem says that in a sentence, if a given position, occupied by a singular term, is not open to substitution, then that position cannot be occupied by a variable bound to an initially placed quantifier. The proof offered assumes that quantification receives its standard interpretation. But the attempted proof is fallacious. And what is more, the theorem is false.

It is very important to separate the 'logical' problems raised by the alleged theorem from any metaphysical or epistemological problems raised by the interpretation of relational constructions. The former are independent of the specific nature of any particular opacity producing phrase, whereas the latter depend on the particular opacity producing notion such as *necessity* or *belief*. Quine has advanced both sorts of arguments against quantified modal logic. These arguments had, to some degree, run together in my mind and perhaps in the minds of others as well. I intend now to run them apart.

The structure of Q&PA makes it clear that, at least at that time, Quine himself distinguished these two sorts of arguments. In Q&PA, relational readings of sentences involving propositional attitudes are not problematical; they are indispensable. The alleged theorem is the problem. This problem is ultimately resolved by retreating from the early and elegant analysis in terms of *syntactical* ambiguity—the representation in terms of permutation of quantifier and verb—to the conclusion that there exists a *lexical* ambiguity in the propositional attitude verbs themselves. Thus, there is a relational *sense* of 'wishes that' which admits both substitution and quantification, and there is a notional sense which admits neither. The two senses differ in logical syntax and cannot be transformed into one another by moving quantifiers around. Indeed it is this syntactical difference which allows them both to conform to the requirements of the alleged theorem and, at the same time, to serve to do the work of (3) and (4).[10] If we describe the ambiguity of sentences as being resolved by *readings,* and the ambiguity of lexical items as being resolved by *senses,* we may say that there are two readings of the ambiguous vernacular sentence "I want a sloop", and that the two readings require different senses of the (concealed) propositional attitude verb. (Contrast this with the two readings of "Everyone is not hungry", which merely require grammatical reparsing and do not require one sense of 'not' for application to closed formulas and another for open formulas.)[11] This form of solution again demonstrates that it is a point of logical grammar, not the intrinsic intelligibility of particular relational readings that is here at issue for Quine.

It is evident that the same technique—propounding a lexical ambiguity between notional and relational senses—could be used to skirt the alleged theorem in the case of modalities. But there Quine is convinced that the metaphysical problems of interpreting the relational sense of necessity are so great that it is not worth the effort to avoid the logical problem.[12] I will not now argue with Quine's metaphysics, only with his logic.

But first I should state that although I believe Quine erred, I appreciate his ingenious attempts to avoid the consequences of his alleged theorem and to point out its consequences for the theories of others. In this undertaking he has provided us with a rich field of ideas, always fascinating and sometimes puzzling, ranging from the two senses of "belief" in Q&PA through the "stubborn objects" of *Word and Object* to the trans-world "physical objects" of "Worlds Away". It is my hope that a careful examination of the details of his semantical and logical arguments will help us to get a clearer perspective on the larger and more philosophically central issues in metaphysics and epistemology.

III

It is my intention to present what I take to be Quine's argument for the alleged theorem in a form more explicit than any in which it appears in his writings. To this extent, I speculate. My primary source, as noted above, is "Notes on Existence and Necessity" (Notes on E&N), though I state some parts of the argument in a way more reminiscent of "Reference and Modality" (R&M) and some later papers.

Notes on E&N opens and closes with passages that make it unmistakably clear that the work aims to establish general principles of logic and semantics which limit the logical form in which a theory of modality can be cast. Thus the opening two paragraphs:

> This paper concerns two points of philosophical controversy. One is the question of admission or exclusion of the modalities—necessity, possibility, and the rest—as operators attaching to statements. The other is the ontological question, "What is there?" *It is my purpose here to set forth certain considerations, grounded in elementary logic and semantics, which—while not answering either question—must seriously condition any tenable answers.*
>
> The logical notions that prove crucial to these considerations are the notions of identity and quantification; and the semantical ones are the notions of designation and meaning, which are insufficiently distinguished in some of the current literature. A new semantical notion that makes its appearance here and plays a conspicuous part is that of the "purely designative occurrence" of a name. (emphasis added)

The closing paragraph states four main conclusions:

(i)   A substantive word or phrase which designates an object may occur purely designatively in some contexts and not purely designatively in others.

(ii)   This second type of context, though no less "correct" than the first, is not subject to the law of substitutivity of identity nor to the laws of application and existential generalization.

(iii)   Moreover, no pronoun (or variable of quantification) within a context
          of this second type can refer back to an antecedent (or quantifier) prior
          to that context.

(iv)   This circumstance imposes serious restrictions, commonly unheeded,
          upon the significant use of modal operators, as well as challenging that
          philosophy of mathematics which assumes as basic a theory of attri-
          butes in a sense distinct from classes.

It is conclusion (iii) which I describe as the alleged theorem. Note that (iii) is
not conditioned by any metaphysical or epistemological hypotheses. The challenge, mentioned in (iv), to the theory of attributes is again an unconditional
application of the alleged theorem. "Expressions of the type that specify attributes [for example, 'the attribute of exceeding 9'] are not contexts accessible
to pronouns referring to anterior quantifiers."[13]

My reconstruction of Quine's argument that the failure of substitution implies the incoherence of quantification may now be stated as follows:

Step 1:   A purely designative occurrence of a singular term in a formula is
          one in which the singular term is used solely to designate the ob-
          ject. [This is a definition.]

Step 2:   If an occurrence of a singular term in a formula is purely designa-
          tive, then the truth value of the formula depends only on *what* the
          occurrence designates not on *how* it designates. [From 1.]

Step 3:   Variables are devices of pure reference; a bindable occurrence of a
          variable must be purely designative. [By standard semantics.][14]

Notation: Let ϕ be a formula with a single free occurrence of 'x', and let $\phi\alpha$,
          $\phi\beta$, $\phi\gamma$ be the results of proper substitution of the singular terms
          α, β, γ for "x".

Step 4:   If α and β designate the same thing, but $\phi\alpha$ and $\phi\beta$ differ in truth
          value, then the indicated occurrences of α in $\phi\alpha$ and of β in $\phi\beta$
          are not purely designative. [From 2.]

Now assume 5.1: α and β are co-designative singular terms, but $\phi\alpha$ and $\phi\beta$
                 differ in truth value,

          and 5.2: γ is a *variable* whose value is the object co-designated by
                    α and β.

Step 6:   Either $\phi\alpha$ and $\phi\gamma$ differ in truth value or $\phi\beta$ and $\phi\gamma$ differ in truth
          value. [From 5.1, since $\phi\alpha$ and $\phi\beta$ differ]

Step 7:   The indicated occurrence of γ in $\phi\gamma$ is not purely designative.
          [From 5.2, 6, and 4.]

Step 8:   It is semantically incoherent to claim that the indicated occurrence
          of γ in $\phi\gamma$ is bindable. [From 7 and 3.]

All but one of these steps seem to me to be innocuous.[15] That one is step 4 which, of course, does *not* follow from step 2. All that follows from 2 is that at least one of the two occurrences is not purely designative. When 4 is corrected in this way, 7 no longer follows.

The error of step 4 appears in later writings in a slightly different form. It is represented by a subtle shift from talk about *occurrences* to talk about *positions*. Failure of substitution does show that some *occurrence* of a term in that position is not purely referential.[16] From this it is concluded that the *context* (read 'position') is referentially opaque.[17] And thus that what the *context* expresses "is in general not a trait of the object concerned, but depends on the manner of referring to the object." Hence, "we cannot properly quantify into a referentially opaque context."[18] The shift from talk of irreferential occurrences to talk of irreferential positions links "some occurrence of a term in that position" to "all occurrences of terms in that position," and so induces the fatal step 4.

It would be easy to make the mistake in step 4 if, like Quine, one tended to see all singular terms other than variables as short for natural or contrived descriptions. There would then be no evident reason, in a concrete case of substitution failure, to discriminate between the supplanted term and the supplanting term in charging irreferentiality. There would be no reason to expect variability among terms in their disposition to go irreferential in a given position, with, say, the supplanted term purely referential but the supplanting term not.

On the other hand, it should be difficult to make the mistake of thinking that a variable cannot occupy a bindable position in which there is substitution failure for constant terms if, like Quine, one interpreted substitution failure as showing that neither the supplanted nor the supplanting occurrences were purely referential. For then, as Quine says, neither the pre-substitution sentence nor the post-substitution sentence is really *about* the referent, and hence *neither* sentence speaks to the meaningfulness of quantification in, which *is* about the referent. Far from demonstrating that quantification in is illegitimate, the diagnosis (for constant terms) of irreferential occurrence asserts the irrelevance of the test. Only if our test revealed a substitution failure in which both the supplanted and the supplanting terms had purely referential occurrences, would it show that we could not meaningfully quantify in. Given Quine's criterion, such a test result is unlikely. But the contrapositive is enlightening. It tells us that if quantification into a context:

$$. . . x . . .$$

is legitimate, then

$$(x)(y)((x = y) \supset (. . . x . . . \equiv . . . y . . .))$$

is true.

IV

In a discussion of this matter in Dubronvnik, Yugoslavia in Spring 1979, a thoughtful exponent of Quine's views (who immediately saw the fallacy in the argument as reconstructed above) put it this way: There are two kinds of variability involved. First, a given singular term can have both purely designative and non-purely designative occurrences, and second, a given position in a formula can be filled at one time by a purely designative occurrence of a term (for example, a variable) and then by a non-purely designative occurrence (for example, a definite description). In 1943, Quine saw the first kind of variability but not the second.[19]

I commented that the (tacit) assumption that there is no variability in the position was in accord with the great classical tradition of Fregean semantics. On Frege's analysis it is the *context* (that is, the position) that determines the semantics of whatever singular term occupies the position.[20]

From Frege's point of view, step 4 is correct. Alonzo Church assumes this point of view in his formalization of Frege's logic of sense and denotation. Church's formalization conforms to Quine's proscription.[21]

Church, in his review of Notes on E&N,[22] was the first to call attention to the relationship of Quine's paper to Frege's "Über Sinn und Bedeutung."[23] As will become more apparent in subsequent remarks, I see Quine, like Church, as being drawn down the same path as Frege, except that Quine travels light, without the baggage of intensional entities that is widely viewed as the hallmark of Frege's way.

In the first footnote to R&M, Quine himself identifies his notions of purely referential and non-purely referential occurrences with what he calls Frege's "*direct (gerade)* and *oblique (ungerade)* occurrences". Interestingly, Quine, typically unwilling to accept Frege's notion of indirect (oblique) *denotation* (ungerade *Bedeutung*) with its ontological commitment to senses *(Sinne)* as entities, here invents and attributes to Frege the denatured idea of an indirect (oblique) *occurrence*—definable in Fregean terms, I suppose, as one which would have indirect denotation if there were such a thing.[24]

V

So far I have not shown that the alleged theorem is false, only that my reconstruction of a proof for it is fallacious. It happens, however, that the very notions Quine uses in Q&PA to resolve the doubts caused by the alleged theorem can be used to build a counter–instance to it. This gave added poignancy to my puzzlement as to what motivated the transition in Q&PA. If the developments following the transition were correct, there was no need for them.

Quine argued from the alleged theorem to the conclusion that the propositional attitude verbs must be lexically ambiguous, concealing both a notional and—in those cases where relational readings seem to be meaningful—a relational sense (with the notional sense excluding both substitutivity and quantification in and the relational sense admitting both). His practice suggests that logic demands disambiguation. And so it does for the ambiguity between notional and relational *readings*. But once the genuine ambiguity between the readings (3) and (4) of 'I want a sloop' is resolved, what remains to do in order to 'disambiguate' the lexical item 'wish' is completely determined: (3) requires the relational sense, (4) takes the notional sense (or, what amounts to the same thing, the vacuous relational sense). Yet it was the language of (3) and (4) that was regarded as 'dubious' and as demanding reformulation. In this case, if 'disambiguation' suffices, re-ambiguation does so likewise. If we can provide meaning preserving rules which transform each logically dubious formulation into a *unique* indubitable one, then the very existence of those rules shows that the original doubts were unfounded. This does not mean that equivalent forms of language do not differ in such virtues as articulation, fluency, and user-friendliness; what it does mean is that we can quell our *logical* terrors just by viewing quantification in as the result of re-ambiguating the 'disambiguated' lexical item.

The re-ambiguated lexical item is formalized as in (3) and (4) as a single ambiguous operator phrase whose 'disambiguation' is completely determined by the presence or absence of free variables in its operand and whose interpretation *shifts*—notional where no quantification in occurs, relational where quantification in is said to require it. Substitutivity will still fail, because the test cases will be read notionally; quantification in will still be coherent because the test case will be read relationally. It is gratifying to note that the use of shifty operators has no cost in expressive power, since we could restrict the occupants of the referential positions in relational senses to variables (other cases being equivalently obtainable by quantification and identity) and since the occupants of singular term positions in the notional senses are already restricted to non-variables (unless bound internally). Shifty and shiftless formulations stand in one-one correspondance. The use of shifty operators allows us to affirm:

Ralph believes that the man in the brown hat is a spy,
to deny:

Ralph believes that the man seen at the beach is a spy,
and to find coherent:

$(\exists x)$ Ralph believes that x is a spy
wherein "believes that" has shifted to a relational sense.

Shifty operators are so called because they are introduced as a logician's trick, sobering (and deflating to the alleged theorem), but a trick nonetheless. They acquit quantification into opacity of Quine's charges, but they do so on the basis of a technicality, not by a substantive proof of innocence. In 1968 I coyly described the shifty operator as "An intriguing suggestion for notational efficiency at no loss (or gain) to Quine's theory."[25] But I meant more than that. I meant it to be recognized that if we interpret the symbolization lesson of Q&PA as containing shifty operators, then we both legitimize the syntax (from Quine's point of view) and *we retain exactly our naive understanding* of such formulas as (3) and (4), the naive understanding that originally gave the symbolization lesson its edifying punch.

At this point I must confess to a residual unease and to a sympathy for the now discredited but well-intentioned alleged theorem. Does re-ambiguation show that the combination of quantification and opacity is *coherent?* Re-ambiguation is a notational unification of what is conceptually disparate (another of those dubious but indispensable notions). It can be elegant fun to try to do this in a way that makes the stitching almost invisible, and it must be granted that what started as a task for invisible mending may end up in displaying new conceptual affinities, but we should not let delight in the handiwork blind us to the underlying question of conceptual coherence. It is possible that our original reading *was* incoherent (in the dubious but indispensable sense) and it is just dumb luck that, as it turns out, we can get away with it. On the other hand, we have not foreclosed the possibility of there being another conceptualization of the semantics of a notationally unfied treatment of the propositional attitudes which, unlike the logician's trick, is coherent. I think there must be such a conceptualization. Our naive understanding is too natural, and the logician's trick is too unnatural, for it to be just dumb luck.

At the time of my 1968 footnote I did not intend the logician's trick as proof that there was no *logical* difficulty with quantifying in because I did not then clearly recognize that it was a purported logical difficulty that drove Q&PA into the transition. But I recognize it now. And the trick *is* proof that the alleged theorem is no theorem, at least on the hypothesis that there is no further logical disability that affects all relational senses (but see Part D below). The logician's trick shows that quantification into a single undifferentiated notation for an opacity producing lexical item is just as secure as quantification into a special notation for a relational sense of such an item.[26]

I think Quine knows this. Looking backward in 1977 ("Intensions Revisited") he expounds the logician's trick in his characteristically elegant way, claiming that a unified notation (open to quantification in) is interdefinable with a notation for a relational sense.[27] What I miss in Quine's presentation is a candid evaluation of the bearing of this move on his old strictures regarding quantification and substitutivity. Instead, he launches a fresh attack on a new front by repudiating the relational senses, thus consciously cutting the ground out from under his own solution in Q&PA and from under the logician's trick as well.

Part B: Coherent Interpretations

VI

The relational senses segregate subject from predicate syntactically by setting predicate within the scope of opacity and subject beyond it. Semantically, they segregate individual from property (or predicate). We can achieve a coherent interpretation if we can semantically reunite individual and property in a way that makes the unified object at one with the unified objects of the notional senses. Quine's exposition of these matters tends to begin by invoking intensional entities (for their intuitive value in marking dramatic contrasts), and to conclude with a retreat—or is it an advance—to linguistic entities (for their certain structure and secure ontology).[28] So the task, if we are to follow his trail, is first, unification in the theory of intensional objects, and then, unification in the theory of linguistic objects. I believe both tasks can be accomplished, though both require deviations from dominant modes of thought. Let us begin with the intensional.[29]

VII

I have suggested that the alleged theorem, and its consequences in terms of disambiguation and the disquietingly smug re-ambiguation, flow from a Fregean outlook on problems of opacity and the nature of intensional entities. A quite distinct point of view was championed by Russell.[30]

Russell thought that all sentences stand for propositions. He distinguished two sorts of propositions. There are propositions (call them *singular*) that attribute properties directly to an individual, by having the individual itself occupy the subject place in the proposition. And there are propositions (call them *general*) in which individuals are only represented under descriptions, that is, the subject place in the proposition is occupied by a complex of properties which was said, in turn, to *denote* the individual.[31] Quantified forms were also regarded as general. In this way the form of the proposition was thought to mirror the form of the sentence. "Ortcutt is a spy" expresses a singular proposition with a simple subject, Ortcutt himself, and the property of being a spy as attribute. "The man in the brown hat is a spy" expresses a general proposition with a complex subject which contains the property of being a man and of wearing a hat, etc. If we were willing to accept the hypothesis that the meaning of a grammatically simple name is just the individual named, we could say that the subject of the proposition is the meaning of the grammatical subject of the sentence. But we need not accept that hypothesis in general. Russell didn't.

It is my thesis that the fundamental difference between Russell and Frege emerges in their views about singular propositions.[32] As I have noted, these entities are fundamental to Russell's intensional ontology. Frege was dumbfounded by the idea that a proposition, the objective content of thought, something capable of being apprehended by the mind, might contain a stark individual not represented by some mode of presentation.

In late 1904 Frege set out, in correspondence with Russell, to answer Russell's scepticism about the thesis that sentences (or perhaps propositions) stand for truth values in the way that complex definite descriptions stand for objects. (Russell had written, "For me there is nothing identical about two propositions that are both true or both false.") In a lengthy exposition of his theory, Frege remarks in passing:

> Truth is not a component part of a thought, just as Mont Blanc with its snowfields is not itself a component part of the thought that Mont Blanc is more than 4,000 meters high.

Russell responds:

> I believe that in spite of all its snowfields Mont Blanc itself is a component part of what is actually asserted in the proposition 'Mont Blanc is more than 4000 metres high'. We do not assert the thought, for this is a private psychological matter: we assert the object of the thought, and this is, to my mind, a certain complex (an objective proposition, one might say) in which Mont Blanc is itself a component part. . . . In the case of a simple proper name like 'Socrates', I cannot distinguish between sense and Bedeutung; I see only the idea, which is psychological, and the object.[33]

This is not the place to enter into an exact analysis of Frege's and Russell's theories of intensional entities, nor is it the place to defend Russell's theory or his understanding of Frege's theory. Let me just assert that despite Frege's incredulity,[34] current theories of reference suggest that Russell's ideas provide the more natural interpretation of what is expressed by everyday utterances involving proper names, indexicals, and demonstratives. And, most importantly for our purposes, they provide for the first step in unification, unifying subject and predicate. We can unite the property *being more than 4,000 meters high* with Mont Blanc itself (with all its snowfields) to form a single object of thought.

Once the objects of propositional attitude constructions contain individuals as components, quantification breezes in.

It seems quite clear that for Russell, the existence of singular propositions did not depend on there being sentences which expressed them. He increasingly narrowed the range of what he called *logically proper names* (names whose meaning is just the individual named) and ultimately came to regard most grammatically simple names as disguised or abbreviated complex descriptions. In this he followed Frege. But in Russell's ontology the singular propositions, even if unexpressed, retain a kind of pre-eminence. This is because his analysis of even those general propositions expressed by closed quantified sentences depends on his notion of a propositional function, which is nothing more than a function from individuals to singular propositions containing them.

As I see Russell's intensional semantics, it recapitulates extensional semantics by analyzing the intension of quantified sentences in terms of the intension of open sentences under assignments of values to free variables. An open formula expresses a singular proposition for every assignment of values to its free variables. If we hypostatize the *way* in which a given open formula associates singular propositions with values of its variable, we obtain a propositional function. The closure of an open formula expresses the attribution of a second order property to the propositional function associated with the open formula. Thus singular and general propositions are related as open to closed formulas and perhaps, given Russell's remarks about the simple proper name "Socrates", as instances to generalizations. This is the second step in unification, uniting the singular propositions with the general.

If we adopt this Russellian point of view, we can smooth the awkwardness of the logician's trick. Phrases like "believes that" and "wishes that" are thought of as standing for relations between the individuals designated by their subject and the propositions expressed by their sentential complements. Perhaps it would be more perspicuous to recut these phrases so as to capture more graphically the idea that they relate two entities, a person and a proposition. We regard "that" as an opacity-producing sentential operator. Applied to an open or closed sentence, it yields, under an assignment of values to variables, a name of the proposition expressed, under that assignment, by the sentence. We regard "wishes" as a relation between persons and arbitrary propositions. Thus (3) becomes:

(5) $(\exists x)(x$ is a sloop . Wishes (I, That [I have x])

and (4) becomes:

(6)   Wishes (I, That [$(\exists x)(x$ is a sloop . I have x)]

The two steps in unification are seen in the notation. "That", operating on open sentences, yields a name of a singular proposition, thus unifying subject and predicate; the use of the relational "Wishes", with a place for arbitrary proposition names, unifies singular and general propositions.

VIII

Quine's familiar method for moving from intensional objects to linguistic ones amounts to replacing the "That" operator with quotation marks. (6) is transformed into:

Wishes (I, "$(\exists x)(x$ is a sloop . I have x)")

which is read something like:

I wish-true "$(\exists x)(x$ is a sloop . I have $x)$"

In Q&PA and again in "Intensions Revisited" Quine raises, and replies to, various objections to this transformation.[35] Those objections are not at issue here. But Quine himself would object to the transformation of (5) into:

$(\exists x)(x$ is a sloop . Wishes (I, "I have x"))

insisting that the quantifier cannot bind the final occurrence of "x" through the opacity of quotation. That sounds like the last stand of the alleged theorem. Let's try to work around it.

There is a natural move to make. We resort, as before, to the familiar notion from extensional semantics: an assignment of values to variables. We replace

Wishes (I, "I have x")

which was read:

I wish-true "I have x"

with

(7)   Wishes (I, "I have x" , y)

(with quantifiable "y") which is read:

(8)   I wish-true "I have x", with respect to y as value of "x".

This, in effect, is exactly where Quine comes out in Q&PA. He would read (7) as:

I wish "I have x" to be satisfied by y

in which the words "wish to be satisfied by" are viewed as an irreducibly triadic predicate. (I have reason for preferring the reading (8) as will become clear below.) The last stand of the alleged theorem has forced us back to the syntax of a relational sense, segregating subject and predicate. Drat!

Can we again do the logician's trick and stitch together the dyadic "wishes-true" with the irreducibly triadic "wishes to be satisfied by"? Here, Quine has pointed the way in the very first example in Notes on E&N. He there demonstrates how two occurrences of an expression, one purely designative and one within quotes, can be consolidated into a single occurrence. He (implicitly) urges these efficiencies upon us with the encouraging remark that "it is easy, in fact, to translate"

Giorgione was called "Giorgione" because of his size

into

Giorgione was so called because of his size.

We will follow Quine's recommendation and interpret our new quotation device using his *method of consolidation*.

We introduce the new quotation device: *arc quotes,* $\ulcorner$ $\urcorner$, in a way that results in the expressions:

$\ulcorner$I have $x\urcorner$
$\ulcorner x$ has $y\urcorner$
$\ulcorner(\exists x)$ I have $x\urcorner$

being taken to abbreviate, respectively:

"I have *x*" with respect to *x* as value of "*x*"

"x has *y*" with respect to *x* as value of "*x*", *y* as value of "*y*"

"(∃*x*) I have *x*"[36]

What we have achieved is not quite shifty quotation. An open formula enclosed in arc quotes is not regarded as a well-formed part of the larger expression within which it stands. Instead it is regarded as a syncategorematic expression which in combination with an operator phrase produces a shifty operator. Using arc quotes we can now rewrite an instance of the Quine-like (7) as:

Wishes (I, ⌐I have *x*⌐)

with quantifiable "*x*". Quine would surely no longer object to the transformation of (8) into:

(∃*x*)(*x* is a sloop . Wishes (I , ⌐I have *x*⌐))

A dream realized: quantifying into quotes!

Again we have a logician's trick, a reorganization of notations to smooth the surface, but with no reorganization of the subject matter. We have been syntactically creative but ontologically conservative. We are left with a shifting relation between surface and subject. Can we replace the logician's trick with a coherent interpretation of our newly smoothed notation?

IX

The first step amounts to reparsing and slightly rephrasing (8) to bring it into the form:

I wish-true ("I have *x*" under the assignment: *y* to "*x*")

in which

("I have *x*" under the assignment: *y* to "*x*")

or, for short:

("I have *x*" under *y* to "*x*")

is brought together as a single well-formed unit. We also reinterpret arc quotes accordingly. The genius of grammar has brought us to the discovery of a new kind of sentence, the valuated formula (or, more generally, the valuated well formed expression). A valuated formula is an open formula under an assignment of values to its free variables.

It is clear that valuated formulas are a unity of individual and predicate. Furthermore, they are naturally thought of as a kind of sentence (i.e. closed formula). Open formulas cannot do the heavy truth-bearing work of sentences. They cannot even do the light sentential work of proclaiming propositions. They are incomplete, a way-station on the road to sentences and a mere artifact of one way (admittedly, a now traditional way) of doing syntax. There are two parallel ways of completing them: closure (the syntactic way) and valuation (the semantic way). Both yield results capable of sentential tasks. Valuated sentences are the linguistic (linguistic?) analogues of singular propositions.[37] Don't be bothered by the fact that Mont Blanc (with all its snowfields) can be a constituent of such a sentence; sustain yourself with the thought that all of theoretical science is subject to revision.

Before proceeding, we must settle a critical issue concerning the individuation of valuated formulas (and other valuated expressions). Let v_1 and v_2 be distinct variables, and let Γv_1 be an expression containing v_1 as its only free variable and Γv_2 be the result of replacing free occurrences of v_1 in Γv_1 by free occurrences of v_2. Does Γ satisfy the axiom:

Axiom (A) $\quad (x)((\Gamma v_1 \text{ under: } x \text{ to } v_1) = (\Gamma v_2 \text{ under: } x \text{ to } v_2))$

where Γv_1 and Γv_2 might even just be the variables v_1 and v_2?

There is a choice. Associative valuation associates a value with each free occurrence of a variable but leaves the variable in place. Valuation by substitution replaces each free occurrence of a variable with its value. (We are not practiced in substituting non-linguistic objects for expressions, so valuation by substitution must be done carefully.)[38] Associatively valuated expressions, as most naturally conceived, do not satisfy Axiom (A). Expressions valuated by substitution do. Henceforth, when I speak of valuation, I always mean valuation by substitution. One consequence of Axiom (A) is that arc-quotation is well behaved.

(B) $\quad (v_1)(v_2)((v_1 = v_2) \supset (\ulcorner \Gamma v_1 \urcorner = \ulcorner \Gamma v_2 \urcorner))$

Having finally achieved quantification into quotation, we wouldn't want it to turn out to be deviant.

The deviance we are talking about here is no minor peccadillo. It goes to one of our central issues: that all bindable occurrences of variables are purely referential. If (B) fails, (and " = " is not 'funny'), at least one of v_1, v_2 has a non-purely referential occurrence. This *is* incoherent. Variables serve only to mark places for distant quantifiers to control and to serve as a channel for the placement of values. We need no variables. We could permit gaping formulas (as Frege would have had it) and use wiring diagrams to link the quantifier to its gaps and to channel in values.[39]

$$\forall \exists (R\_\_ \_\_ \supset R\_\_ \_\_)$$

Variables are simply a way of giving the distant quantifiers wireless remote control over the gaps. Variables must not allow their idiosyncratic graphics to become ideography.

Arc-quotation is now seen not as a notational trick, a contextually defined piece of a shifty operator, but as a proper, opacity producing operator. Given an expression Γ, the result of surrounding Γ with arcs is a singular term whose free variables are the free variables of Γ and whose value, for any assignment f of values to its free variables, is the valuation of Γ under f.[40]

X

Quine saw how Frege's intensional ontology (though not so described) explained opacity and rejected quantification. He also showed us how the familiar ontology of linguistic expressions can do the same. I have aimed to describe modifications to the two ontologies which allow them to accept (and even to explain) quantification while leaving intact the prior explanation of opacity. Each modification involves two steps of unification: first, the unification of individual and property (or predicate) by enlisting, or creating, a new kind of entity containing individuals, and second, the assimilation of the new entities to the old. The success of my project—to achieve conceptual coherence—depends on the degree to which each step seems natural.

It will not have escaped notice that valuated sentences are virtually the singular propositions they express. They give us structure. They give us individuals. They bear truth (with respect to their language).[41]

I now propose to downshift from my vivid intensionalist talk to dry linguistic formulations involving valuated sentences. For most of the remainder I will stay in low gear, not only to preach to the unconverted but to manifest how much can be accomplished with one foot on the ground. Where it is worth a reminder that the class of sentences includes both the *closed* and the *valuated*, I shall refer to them as *$entences*. Note this relativity: what $entences there are depends on what values the variables can take. For the most part I ignore this relativity, assuming they can take all and only what there is.[42]

The *method of $entences*, as I shall call it, amounts to interpreting intensional operators as if they were predicates of $entences and interpreting the sentence within the scope of the operator as if it were contained in arc quotes.

XI

I pause for a methodological sermon. We interpret the sentence within the scope of the operator *as if* it were an arc-quotation name. We do not regard it syntactically as a name. Our semantical methods need not dictate syntactical form. I do not propose to reform the syntax of our imagined formal object language, treating operators as predicates and their sentential complements as names (i.e., singular terms). *Nominalization,* as I will call such a syntactical reform, would amount to more than merely calling certain expressions "names"; it would amount to regarding certain syntactical positions as open to occupation by variables and descriptions in addition to their traditional occupants.[43] It is a loosening of grammatical constraints. Nominalization would certainly increase expressibility, but it carries several hazards.

To the degree to which we regard our semantical methods as model-making (i.e., as a way of analyzing the notion of logical consequence for the object language) rather than as reality-describing (i.e., as analyzing the intended interpretation), fine-tuning the object language to bring it into conformity with our model may end up institutionalizing an artifact of the model that corresponds to no aspect of reality. I often think that my Platonizing model-making is artificial, but I see nothing objectionable in being realistic about the artifacts *qua* artifacts. We model-makers love our artifacts. Models have their own reality, and the more we acknowledge that, the less likely we are to confuse the reality of the model with the reality it models. Model-making, by helping to articulate structure, can help to make it more acceptable that there is a reality behind questioned linguistic forms. (For example, that there *is* relational belief or even that there are singular propositions.) But one can accept the linguistic forms and the logic induced by the model, without thinking that there must be 'hidden' aspects of the reality that correspond to unexpressed structural features of the model. In particular, the very ontology of the model, whether propositions, possible worlds, or $entences, need not mirror any aspect of the reality expressed in traditional formulations of modal logic or of the logic of propositional attitudes. So here is the first hazard of nominalization. With more that we can say, we may say too much.

Where the entities interpreted as values mirror the syntactical structure of the expressions, as in the case of our $entences, a further hazard attends nominalization. The change in syntax produces a change in the entities themselves. This becomes clear in the case of iteration. Tarski has taught us what profound consequences attend the shift of syntax which transforms the innocuous sentential operator "it is true that" into a predicate of sentences.[44] Montague has shown the same for the sentential operator "it is necessary that",[45] and, with Kaplan, for a version of the sentential operator "K knows that".[46] Any reform of syntax from sentential operator to predicate of sentences must be constrained by what we may think of as *Montague's Threat:* that if iteration of the operator is reformed in the natural unramified way, reflexive reference will strike.[47]

I am not advocating that we invariably avoid the shift to predicate/name form. The operator form of *truth* is a bore, and we may wish to set the interesting and important problem of analyzing such apparently nominalized idioms as "She says that whatever you say is false". But our task was to find semantical methods to interpret a *given,* putatively puzzling, syntactical form: quantification into opacity. I want to solve *that* problem before going on to the 'more interesting' problem. We certainly don't need to construct a formalism just to fully articulate the structure of the new entities we have introduced; the metalanguage already does that adequately.[48] Opacity is tough enough to deal with, even when the machinery stays behind the curtain.

XII

Here is a case of denominalization that throws light on the method of $entences. Consider the possibility of incorporating the quotes that usually accompany the predicate "says" of *direct* discourse into an operator **Says-quote,** and thus transforming:

Ralph says "Ortcutt is no spy"

into:

Ralph **Says-quote** Ortcutt is no spy

Here we have a backwards syntactical reform, from predicate to operator form, with no reform in interpretation. There is, of course, a loss in explicitness and expressibility. Most importantly, for our purposes, there is the opportunity, indeed the temptation, to create nonsense by quantifying in. This is the temptation that Quine has inveighed against. It is correct that the method of $entences never resists quantification in strictly on the grounds of ungrammaticality or 'nonsense'. But the model-theoretic intelligibility of:

$(\exists x)$ Ralph **Says-quote** x is a spy

doesn't require that any such sentence be true. Here is our fallback position. **Says-quote** is true of no valuated $entences. We take the hard line. Intelligible, yes; true, never!

Nonsense vs. falsehood is often a close call. The method of $entences opts for falsehood. What should we say about the standard direct discourse formulation:

$(\exists x)$ Ralph says "x is a spy"?

We should say that the second occurrence of "x" is not bound to the initial quantifier,[49] the initial quantifier is therefore vacuous, and unless Ralph is in a logic class the sentence is almost surely false. So the standard formulation also opts for false.

Truth or falsity in the standard formulation depends on what sentences, including open sentences, are in the extension of the predicate "says". Truth or falsity in the operator formulation depends on what $entences, including valuated $entences, are in the extension of the operator **Says-quote.** We have not included open sentences among the non-valuated $entences, but we could have by using a different style of variable for quantifying into arc-quotation. So we can imagine that the $entences include all the sentences and more. If we interpret **Says-quote** as having the same extension as "says", we have denominalized the syntax with no shift in interpretation.[50] No shift in interpretation implies no valuated $entences in the extension of the operator.

operator. This is what I call taking the hard line. In the case of **Says-quote** it seems reasonable, since it is reasonable to think that we cannot say (in the direct discourse sense) valuated $entences.[51] In the case of operators not arising from denominalization, it may be less reasonable to take the hard line. But there is nothing in the method of $entences to rule it out.

Having brought direct discourse into the operator form, **Says-quote,** we may compare it with the indirect discourse operator, **Says-that,** which arose in this form. I think it reasonable to count as true some quantifications into **Says-that.** Thus, I take no hard line on *indirect* discourse. Still one would expect the extension of **Says-that** to be dependent on the extension of **Says-quote,** exactly how, depends in part on the resolution of the problem of *exportation*[52] and in part on how literal indirect discourse is required to be.[53] One expects these two operators to differ independently of the hard line.

XIII

The method of $entences provides generally for quantification into opaque contexts but says nothing specific about which $entences are in the extension of any particular opacity producing operator. That is a matter for the interpretation of the particular operator.

The method of $entences imposes no 'closure' conditions of any kind on the extension of an operator, not even that if "$(\exists x)(x$ is a spy)" is in the extension, then so must "$(\exists y)(y$ is a spy)" be. Closure conditions would likely make it impossible to represent direct discourse as an operator, since even the simplest equivalence transformations may fail.[54] Closure conditions have also been thought to be a burden on the attempt to represent certain epistemic notions in operator form, since we may lack the acumen to close our beliefs.[55] I think there should be no closure conditions for arbitrary intensional (i.e., opacity producing) operators, although some intensional operators, like the modal operators, may have closure conditions of their own.

Consider the language formed by adding intensional operators to the language of first order logic. We can construct models for this language by adjoining to a model M for first order logic an appropriate extension for each operator **O.** If the operator has no special laws of its own, any set of $entences of M (i.e., $entences whose 'objects' are drawn from the domain of M) is appropriate. An assignment f satisfies $\ulcorner O\Gamma \urcorner$ in a model, if and only if the valuation of Γ by f is a member of the extension of **O** in the model. If no valuated $entences are in the extension of **O** in a particular model, then no quantifications in will be true in that model.

Let us call the logic of this language *first order intensional logic.* In the absence of closure conditions, we would expect an intensional operator to behave as if it were no more than a new non-logical non-truth-functional sentential connective. (Which is what it is.)[56] We would still expect the basic laws of first order extensional logic to hold (but without any 'anomolous adjuncts' such as primitive rules permitting instantiation to terms other than variables). If we assume no closure conditions, these laws wouldn't hold *within* opaque contexts, but then application of the basic laws of logic to subformulas has always been, at best, a derived rule whose derivation depended on the laws governing the possible contexts of subformulas. Both quantifier and identity laws would, of course, reach *into* the opaque contexts.

You can see where I am headed. I conclude that there is a general logic for the addition of opacity producing operators to first order logic, and it turns out to be: first order logic. This, I think, was the viewpoint of Barcan and Marcus when they invented axiomatic quantified modal logic. They aimed just to add the modal operators to good old first order logic, along with some laws specific to modality.[57] There are subtleties in the way in which good old first order logic is to be formulated, but that doesn't vitiate the point (if I am correct) that the logic should be traditional.[58]

The situation, it seems to me, is analogous to that of quantification theory. If the rules of monadic quantification theory are properly formulated, no changes are required for full quantification theory. All that is required is an enrichment of the language. The logic, in this sense, remains the same. This does not prevent the metalogical situation from being quite different. The enriched language requires an enriched semantics, and yields new and changed metalogical results. The enriched language of first order intensional logic also requires an enriched semantics, and will certainly affect metalogical results (for example, derived rules involving definite descriptions). Thus, my thesis: first order intensional language is an enrichment of first order extensional language, but first order intensional logic *is* first order extensional logic.

Part C: ESSENTIALISM

XIV

In 1953, in "Three Grades of Modal Involvement",[59] a new theme appears in Quine's writing. He appears to retract the alleged theorem, the *logical* problem. He remarks that quantification into modal contexts "is not *prima facie* absurd if we accept some interference in the contextual definition of singular terms. The effect of this interference is that constant singular terms cannot be manipulated with the customary freedom, even when their objects exist."[60] A new charge is leveled. "There is yet a further consequence, and a particularly striking one: Aristotelian essentialism.'' Those who would quantify into modal contexts must be prepared to adopt an invidious attitude toward certain ways of specifying an individual, counting some attributes of a thing as essential, and others accidental. The ground has shifted from the logical legitimacy of quantifying into opaque contexts to its philosophical consequences.

What truth is there in the charge that essentialism is a consequence of quantified modal logic?

To apply our methods to quantified modal logic we must provide an interpretation for the necessity operator. This amounts to finding a plausible classification of the $sentences into those which are necessary and those which are not. As noted above we *could* view all modal operators as being false of any valuated $sentence. (We would lose the usual interdefinability of ''☐'' and ''◇'' when either governs an open sentence.) It would be a hard line. It wouldn't be plausible. So let us proceed.

Let me make two simplifying assumptions. First that our quantified modal language is, as is usual, the language of first order logic with identity and descriptions and with the addition of the necessity operator ''☐''. Second, that there are no iterations of necessity. Hence, that which occurs in the scope of ''☐'' is a purely first order formula without occurrences of ''☐''. This is an unusual assumption made to avoid technical complications; iteration has not been the focus of Quine's concerns.[61] Given these two assumptions, we can take the problem to be to classify the $sentences of the language of first order logic.

There is a simple and natural way to do this: classify by *logical truth*. A $sentence is logically true if it is true in every model. The valuation of Γ under f is logically true, if f satisfies Γ in every model. There is a technical detail here I do not wish to scant. In the case of valuated formulas, logical truth requires truth even in domains which do not contain the values assigned to free variables. Assigning me to ''x'' yields a valuation of:

$\qquad$ [(y) y is unmarried $\supset$ x is unmarried]

which is not true in the domain of bachelors.[62] So formulas like:

$\qquad$ [(y) Fy $\supset$ Fx]

whose universal closures are logically true may have valuations that are not logically true. In fact, no valuation of this formula will be logically true. This calls for some adjustment in our usual semantical ways, but nothing difficult.

$\qquad$ (($\exists y)(y = x$) $\supset$ [(y) Fy $\supset$ Fx])

$\qquad$ (Fx $\supset$ Fx)

$\qquad$ ($x = x$)

are all logically true under all assignments.

$\qquad$ (Fx $\supset$ Fy)

$\qquad$ ($x = y$)

are logically true under just those assignments that assign the same value to "x" and "y".

For the model-wary we can express logical truth for valuated formulas in terms of first order provability. We can also thereby gain some insights into the notion. Let ϕ be a formula containing the distinct free variables $v_1,\ldots,v_n$, and let f be an assignment of values to these variables. We can capture the valuation of ϕ under f in different domains by relativizing all variable binding operators in ϕ to a new monadic predicate π not already occuring in ϕ. For the familiar operators of first order logic, the quantifiers and the descriptions operator, this is done in familiar ways.[63] Let the result be ϕ^π.

One way in which logic is not invidious is in *the fungability of individuals*. Thus if the valuation of ϕ by f is logically true, any valuation of ϕ by an isomorphic assignment g (which maintains the same relative identities and diversities among the values of $v_1,\ldots,v_n$) will be logically true also. We can capture the isomorphism class by means of a conjunction of identity and non-identity formulas for the variables. Let I^f be the conjunction (in some fixed order) which contains, for every pair i, j (i, j $\leq$ n) such that $f(v_i) = f(v_j)$, the conjunct $\ulcorner(v_i = v_j)\urcorner$, and which contains for every i, j such that $f(v_i) \neq f(v_j)$, the conjunct $\ulcorner(v_i \neq v_j)\urcorner$. Now form the universal closure of the conditional with I^f as antecedent and ϕ^π as consequent. If we wish to exclude the empty domain, we can add $\ulcorner(\exists x)\pi x\urcorner$ to the antecedent.[64] The result, a closed sentence, will be a logical truth in the ordinary sense, if and only if the valuation of ϕ by f is true in every model.

Let's try it. The valuation of the formula:

(9) $(\exists z)(z = x \equiv z \neq y)$

by any assignment f such that

(10) $f(``x") \neq f(``y")$

has as its corresponding closure:

$(x)(y)[((x \neq y) . (\exists x) Fx) \supset (\exists z)(Fz . (z = x \equiv z \neq y))]$

which is not a logical truth. Hence, no valuation of (9) by an assignment satisfying (10) will be a logical truth. Intuitively, any valuation of (9) by such an assignment f, will be false in every model in which neither $f(``x")$ nor $f(``y")$ is an element of the domain. In that case every element of the domain will be different from $f(``y")$, but none will be identical with $f(``x")$.

We have characterized a class of $entences, the class of logical truths. By the method of $entences, we can interpret "$\Box$" as true of exactly the members of this class. We might call this weak form of necessity *logical necessity*.

Quine should be relatively happy with this interpretation of necessity. He was relatively happy to call the logically true *closed* sentences necessary; he just didn't see how to extend the notion of logical truth to valuated formulas. So far, so good. Now, where's the essentialism?

XV

Curiously enough, essentialism is to be found in our notion of logical necessity. Not the Invidious Aristotelian kind (you will recall the fungability of individuals), but the Benign Quinean kind.

Note first that the acceptance of *singular properties*, i.e. those which have an individual as a component, follows unto the acceptance of singular propositions as two follows unto one. In a similar way the acceptance of *valuated predicates* follows on the acceptance of valuated formulas. For any individual *a*, we have the singular property of *being a* which uniquely characterizes it, and we even have the valuated predicate:

$$(``(x = y)"\text{ under the assignment: } a \text{ to } ``y").[65]$$

According to our theory of logical necessity, such uniquely characterizing properties are essential to their bearers.[66] Thus they confirm the presence of essentialism in our system.

It is Marcus's law[67] for modal logic:

$$(x)(y)((x = y) \supset \Box \ (x = y))$$

(a validity of the logic of logical necessity) that demands the presence of this form of essentialism. Benign Quinean Essentialism is Quinean because of Quine's unswerving insistence on Marcus's law (which is said, in "Reply to Professor Marcus", to follow from "$\Box \ (x = x)$" by 'substitutivity').[68] He admonishes us that even if we were to ignore his strictures against quantifying into positions that resist substitutivity of identity for descriptions, "this does not mean violating substitutivity of identity for variables, which would simply be a wanton misuse of the identity sign."

Benign Quinean Essentialism is benign because it makes a specification of an individual essential only if it is logically true of that individual. It is not that benign essentialism fails to discriminate among the attributes of a thing. Every modal logic will discriminate between the attribute of *self-identity* and the attribute of *self-identity while P* (*P* being any contingent truth). But discrimination in favor of logical truth hardly seems invidious. *You can't be harmed by logical truth.*[69]

XVI

Quine seems not to have noticed our modest logical necessity. He may have thought that logical truth couldn't be extended to valuated formulas directly; that it was only by way of a closed surrogate that a valuated formula could be counted logically true. The use of surrogates is a general method for the interpretation of quantification into opaque contexts. It was my method in "Quantifying In".

The simplest way of forming a surrogate, though by no means the only way, is to associate with each value of the variables (or as many as possible) a *proxy name* (i.e., a closed singular term), and then to substitute for each free occurrence of a variable in the open formula the proxy name of its value. Because of opacity (i.e., the fact that different names of the individual will result in different answers to questions of logical truth for the surrogate), we must discriminate among the names of a thing and cannot indifferently rely on any name to serve as proxy. Thus rears essentialism of the invidious kind. Something like the intuitive idea of a tag (Marcus)[70] or a rigid designator (Kripke)[71] may guide our choice of proxy names. But however we choose, the resulting proxy name could hardly fail to *appear* essential, since if α is any name, the truth of the sentence

$$(x)((x = \alpha) \supset \square \, (x = \alpha)$$

which seems to express the fact that α is an essential name, reduces to the truth of:

$$\square \, (x = \alpha)$$

under an assignment to "x" of the individual for which α is name. And if α is a proxy name, the truth of this formula under that assignment is *defined* by the truth of:

$$\square \, (\alpha = \alpha).$$

Another way to form a surrogate is to associate with each value of the variables (or as many as possible) a proxy predicate, possibly compound, expressing a condition which specifies the individual, and then to relativize each free variable in the open formula to the predicate which is proxy for its value. There are actually two ways of doing this, with universal and with existential quantifiers, but because the existential form would lead to the obviously unacceptable result that no valuated formulas are logically true, it is natural to choose the universal form. If "Gx" were the open formula valuated by the assignment of an individual a to "x", and "F" were the proxy predicate expressing a condition which specifies a, then the valuated formula

("Gx" under the assignment: a to "x")

has as its surrogate

$$(x)(Fx \supset Gx)^{72}$$

Again we cannot indifferently rely on any arbitrary specifying conditions to serve as proxy since some may make the relativized surrogate logically true and others not.[73] Essentialism again appears inevitable, since if "F" is any proxy predicate, the truth of the sentence

$$(x)(Fx \supset \square \, Fx)$$

which seems to say that the property expressed by "F" is essential to whatever has it, is ultimately *defined* by the truth of

$$\square \, (x)(Fx \supset Fx).$$

Quine hasn't spelled out his argument in exactly this way, in terms of surrogates for valuated formulas, but I think it may well be what he thought. At any rate, in connection with logical necessity it's wrong. There is no need for surrogates. We can classify the logical truths among valuated formulas directly, as we have. And for this we needed no *essence of Ortcutt* other than Ortcutt.

A final point on the method of surrogates: I have been careful to hedge by saying that the method 'appears' to make essentialism inevitable. It doesn't really. We can choose surrogates on any basis we like. Once we explain honestly how we are interpreting quantification, a kind of semi-substitutional interpretation, the question is no longer "Why do you think of that specification as essential to that individual?", but is rather "What made you choose that specification as proxy for that individual?". To which the answer *may* be, "Because I think it essential to her." There's the essentialism.

XVII

Perhaps the reason no Invidious Aristotelian Essentialism has shown up is that our weak logical necessity yields too anemic a modal theory to concern Quine. Quine expects the champion of modal logic to insist of nine that it is necessarily greater than seven.[74] So let us consider a case where I.A.E. appears by invitation. I suggest that, far from being foisted upon us by a desperate semantics, I.A.E. is entirely within our control and has its uses as a means to express widely shared, and justifiable, convictions about the natures of things.

Quine would not agree. Despite his careful advice to the modalist: to insist of nine, *independently of mode of designation,* that *it* is necessarily greater than seven, he continues to believe, in Marcus's memorable phrase, "that modal logic was conceived in sin, the sin of confusing use and mention", and he hints that the confusion, though not *required* of modal logicians, still sustains them. Moreover, he is confident that I.A.E. is wrong. He describes talk of a difference between necessary and contingent attributes of an object as "baffling—more so even than the modalities themselves" (the 'objects' he has been discussing are nine and Ortcutt). He says that one attributes this distinction to Aristotle. "But, however venerable the distinction, it is surely indefensible."[75] He seems highly sceptical that there could be reasonable arguments, even in limited cases, for I.A.E. It is such arguments that I now wish to take up.

Consider modalized set theory and the intuitively plausible I.A.E. claim that singleton Quine would not exist if Quine did not:
$$(x)(y)[(x = \text{Quine} . (z)(z \in y \equiv z = x)) \supset$$
$$\Box(\sim (\exists w)(w = x) \supset \sim (\exists w)(w = y))]^{76}$$
We can argue for this claim by asking whether there are plausible alternatives, alternatives that allow singleton Quine to exist where Quine does not? One immediately thinks that if singleton Quine were to exist and Quine not, then

singleton Quine would have no members. But there already is a set which has no members, the null set. Would singleton Quine then be identical with the null set? (*Was* singleton Quine identical with the null set on June 25, 1808?) Wouldn't this violate:

$$(x)(y)((x \neq y) \supset \Box \, (x \neq y)) \, ?$$

If singleton Quine could be identical with a null set, could our own null set conceal distinct fused possibilia, say, the singletons of Quine's merely possible seventh and eighth sons? Wouldn't this violate

$$(x)((x = y) \supset \Box \, (x = y)) \, ?$$

Maybe Quine's singleton could be empty without becoming identical with any other thing. (It may appear empty because we count only 'existing' members.) Then there would be at least two (apparently) empty sets. This has the consequence that the axiom of extensionality is, at best, only contingently true, and probably not even that. Unacceptable!

So far, this little bit of reasoning—admittedly not definitive—has used only modest methods: some benign essentialism plus the necessity of the axiom of extensionality.[77] It favors the conclusion that sets have their members essentially, at least in the weak sense:

(11) $(x)(y)[x \in y \supset \Box \, ((\exists z)(z = y) \supset ((\exists z)(z = x) \, . \, x \in y))]$

It wasn't a proof, of course, but it should be responsive to the claim that (11) is 'baffling'.[78]

I think that (11) is true, but I am willing to listen to argument. The arguments may not be compelling, but I am convinced such arguments are legitimate. They turn on our understanding of the nature sets. The issues are metaphysical, not mere points of logic and certainly not mere confusions of use and mention. I studied section 4 of *Mathematical Logic* as a freshman, and taught it as a graduate student. Confuse use and mention? Me? Never!

My acquiescence in (11) and even my connivance at argument for it do not imply that I regard every I.A.E claim that can be expressed in the language of quantified modal logic as accessible to reasoning of a similar kind. Could Richard Nixon have been a turnip? This matter does not seem ripe for debate. It seems to call more for decision than for argument. Either decsion will have consequences. This is a matter of (modal) logic. But I see little present reason to call one or the other decision correct.

XVIII

The logic of logical necessity is exhaustive, in the sense that for every sentence of the form $\ulcorner \Box \, \phi \urcorner$, either it or its negation is true in every model when "$\Box$" is interpreted as logical necessity (for the $entences of that model). (And incidentally, this logic is not axiomatizable, for if it were, the non-theorems of first order logic could be axiomatizable and thus the theorems decidable.) By its exhaustiveness, the logic of logical necessity excludes I.A.E. No matter how sympathetic to this goal, we can perhaps agree that rulings on I.A.E. should be a matter of metaphysics, not logic. What this shows is that I.A.E. makes its claim under an interpretation of "$\square$" other than logical necessity. (This we knew already, since logical necessity is benign.) Let us call this interpretation *metaphysical necessity*. I would not attempt to characterize the truths of meta-physical necessity, but I will try to characterize its logic. I think that the logical features of metaphysical necessity are just these: truth and closure under logical consequence.[79] This leaves it open that some metaphysican may assert that all truths are metaphysically necessary. It wouldn't be the first time. And it wouldn't be an abandonment of modality, just a peculiar doctrine about it, an extremely pervasive sort of metaphysical determinism. Logical closure and truth also leave it open that some metaphysician may assert that there are no metaphysically necessary truths beyond the logical truths. So be it.

If we use "$\boxed{L}$" to signify the logical necessity whose truth theory was given in section XIV, we can adopt "$\boxed{M}$" to signify the metaphysical necessity whose truths we debate. In a model, an appropriate extension for "$\boxed{M}$" is any set of first order $entences of the model that is closed under logical conse-quence and all of which are true in the model. $\boxed{M}$ is bounded on the bottom by $\boxed{L}$ and at the top by falsehood. It is not unreasonable, and it may be Quine's position, to argue that there are no properly metaphysically necessary truths, briefly, that

$$\boxed{M} = \boxed{L}.^{80}$$

XIX

Quine's first argument, involving the alleged theorem, was an argument against the intelligibility of the language of quantified modal logic. His argument charging invidious essentialism is not an argument against the intelligibility of the language; it is an argument against the truth of certain modal statements. In the "Discussion on the paper of Ruth B. Marcus"[81] he says, "I'm not talking about theorems, I'm talking about truth, I'm talking about true interpre-tation. . . . [I]n order to get a coherent interpretation one has got to adopt essentialism . . ."

The earliest appearance of Quine's essentialism argument seems to be at the end of "Three Grades of Modal Involvement" (1953).[82] There, Aristotelian essentialism is first bruited in terms of essential rationality and accidental two-leggedness. We could formalize thus:

$(\exists x)(\square\ x$ is rational . x is two legged . $\sim \square\ x$ is two legged)

Heady stuff. Insofar as this *form:*

$$(\exists x)(\Box\, Fx\, .\, Gx\, .\, \sim \Box\, Gx)$$

is all there is to Aristotelian essentialism, quantified modal logic is infested. Since, as Quine quickly shows, if "P" stands for any contingent truth, it will be true that

(E) $(\exists x)(\Box\, (x = x)\, .\, ((x = x)\, .\, P)\, .\, \sim \Box\, ((x = x)\, .\, P))$

Clever, but hardly likely to quicken the pulse or, for that matter, to 'baffle' anyone. If this is a metaphysical jungle, then so is every logic classroom in Harvard University.

I cannot believe that benign essentialism of the kind exhibited in (E) could have been Quine's target. His concern must have been that (E) opens the door to the heady stuff, to real I.A.E., not just to the 'form' of I.A.E. The argument charging essentialism must come down to this: (i) Adoption of a relational sense of necessity (or acceptance of quantification in) permits one to formulate I.A.E. claims. (ii) Those who adopt such a sense must wish to assert such claims. (iii) Such claims are unjustifiable. Viewed in this way the argument shows itself to be an *ad hominem: those who would foist this logic upon us are just the kind to foist some notorious falsehoods.* This may well be true, but like other *ad hominem* arguments it diverts attention from the details of the arguments at hand.

One aspect of Quine's methodology has been used by some of his opponents. They too have based their investigations on attempts to syntactically characterize the 'form' of I.A.E. Model theoretic or proof theoretic methods are then used to demonstrate the presence or absence of theorems of this form in quantified modal logic.[83]

My methodology goes the other way around. I develop what I take to be the intuitive notion of logical necessity *qua* logical necessity, first from a model theoretic perspective and then independently by means of a reduction to nonmodal first order logic. I then *define* as benign any essentialist sentence, however invidious its 'form', that is true in this theory.[84]

I contend that in order to convince us that there is a metaphysical jungle in quantified modal logic, Quine would have to derive, from plausible premises (for example, that there are contingent truths), an essentialist statement that is incompatible with our theory of logical necessity. And since quantified modal logic, as ordinarily practiced, is compatible with our theory of logical necessity, that cannot be done.

The morals of our essentialist studies so far are these. The language of quantified modal logic can be interpreted without appeal to surrogates of any kind; thus, without appeal to essential names, whether tags or descriptions, other than variables. One fundamental theory of necessity, the theory of logical necessity, asserts no essentialism other than the benign Quinean kind. Even taken as a characterization of the logic of metaphysical necessity, quantified modal logic is not committed to invidious essentialism, which is a question of truth not logic. Some may take the view that there is no metaphysical necessity beyond logical necessity. Others will find it justifiable, in particlar cases, to accede to essentialist claims of the invidious Aristotelian kind. Quantified modal logic allows us to explore the consequences of such claims. It must be recognized, however, that insofar as we regard any invidious Aristotelian claims as true, we move beyond the theory of strictly *logical* necessity, into the realm of metaphysics proper.[85]

Part D: CONTEXTUALITY

Because of their importance in the development of Quine's thought about opacity, we must now digress to review some of his more recent views.

XX

In "Intensions Revisited", Quine recognizes that relational senses of psychological verbs suffice to interpret quantification in. This leads not to reconsideration of the tenability of quantification in but to reconsideration of the tenability of the relational senses of psychological verbs. He had already charged that essentialism is required to interpret the relational sense of necessity.[86] Now a seemingly parallel methodology leads to a seemingly parallel challenge to the relational sense of belief. This time the charge is *utter dependence on context*. Quine now thinks necessity and belief are quite parallel with regard to their relational senses. He asserts that even the notion of essence makes sense in context. I sense here the gathering forces of a new attack on quantification into opacity.

The discussion of contextuality begins by considering certain special, and what are to be taken to be central, cases of formulations involving relational senses. Cases we can represent with quantification in as:

(12) $(\exists x) \ \square \ (x = \alpha)$

and

(13) $(\exists x)(\text{Ralph knows that } x = \alpha)$

where α is a singular term. Quine lays great importance on those singular terms α which satisfy (12) and (13). He reads (12) as asserting that α expresses an 'essence'. He reads (13), following Hintikka,[87] as asserting that Ralph knows who α is. He then goes on to remark:

> The notion of knowing or believing who or what something is, is utterly dependent on context. Sometimes, when we ask who someone is, we see the face and want the name; sometimes the reverse. Sometimes we want to know his role in the

community. Of itself, the notion is empty . . . this leaves us with no distinction between the admissible and inadmissible cases of exportation . . . Thus it virtually annuls the seemingly vital contrast . . . between believing there are spies and suspecting a specific person. At first this seems intolerable, but it grows on one. I now think the distinction is every bit as empty, apart from context, as . . . that of knowing or believing who someone is. In context it can still be important. In one case we can be of service by pointing out the suspect; in another, by naming him; in others, by giving his address or specifying his ostensible employment . . . We end up rejecting *de re* or quantified propositional attitudes generally, on a par with *de re* or quantified modal logic. Rejecting, that is, except as idioms relativized to the context or situation at hand.

There is a sub-theme, almost a presupposition, in "Intensions Revisited" (reappearing in "Worlds Away") that the availability of terms α for which (12) and (13) are true is critical to our understanding of quantification in, and in particular to our understanding of the distinction between (3) and (4). With regard to the role of (12) in modal logic, he remarks ". . . the whole quantified modal logic of necessity . . . collapses if essence is withdrawn." The suspicion that Quine is surrogate-minded grows.

Quine's new thrust against quantification in develops as follows: We begin with the sub-theme of surrogatism. Sentences of the form (13) are then seen as indicating the surrogates, and thus as crucial. Next, by reading (13) in terms of the knowing-who idiom, it is made plausible that the choice of surrogates is utterly contextual. (And thus that contextuality infects all quantification in.) And finally, contextual relativity is assumed to imply the (ambivalent) rejection of "quantified propositional attitudes generally, on a par with quantified modal logic". (More on ambivalence later.) I think each of the four steps is incorrect.

First let us clear the ground of surrogatism. It is clear that our methods do not require the use of surrogates, and indeed we used no surrogates to interpret quantified modal logic. Our classification of the logically necessary valuated $ sentences was in no way reductive, in no way dependent on a prior classification of the closed sentences.[88] Second, even given the surrogate interpretation, not every name that satisfies (13) need be a proxy name. (In footnote 56 it was shown that if the attitudes are not closed under logical consequence, then contrary to Quine's claim, (13) may not play the role for the attitudes that (12) plays for modality, namely to justify treating α as an instantial term for quantification.) Third, although I have been convinced that knowing-who, in its most natural sense, is utterly dependent on context, this could not be the proper reading for (13). This takes a brief argument:

Quine acknowledges that quantified propositional attitudes do make sense relative to context. So pick a context to which to relativize. The following is a theorem of logic (no matter *how* we have relativized to context):

(y)[Ralph knows that $(y = y) \supset (\exists x)$ Ralph knows that $(x = y)$]

According to the proposed reading, logic tells us that if Ralph has noticed of a certain man in a brown hat that he is self-identical, then Ralph knows who he is. Or, to put it in the contrapositive, if Ralph doesn't know who you are, then he doesn't know anything about you. (Note that if he knows anything about you, he knows that you are self-identical.) This could not be correct. We went wrong in thinking that the benign

$(\exists x)$ Ralph knows that $(x = y)$

says, in the natural sense, that Ralph knows who y is.

XXI

I believe there is a significant use of the idioms symbolized by quantification into propositional attitudes which is not dependent on context. When Ralph saw Ortcutt in his brown hat behaving suspiciously, I think Ralph came to believe of Ortcutt that he was a spy, and this despite the fact that he didn't know, in any helpful way, who Ortcutt was. However, I will not argue that point. Instead, I will address as the main issue, the *consequences* of dependence on context, assuming it exists. Should we reject, at least for purposes of constructing a logic, a form of language in which truth is dependent on context?

I want to discuss dependence on context within a framework of critical notions which, I rush to acknowledge, I do not understand well. I aim for a useful, rough cut.

We need a better understanding of the different ways in which the 'meaning' (in a very loose sense) of a linguistic form may seem to vary from utterance to utterance and of the liabilities of each of these styles of inconstancy. For example, we are told that what counts as *knowing who* the man in the brown hat is, will vary from context to context. Does this show that the idiom $\ulcorner$knows who α is$\urcorner$ is ambiguous (like "bank"), vague (like "bald"), indexical (like "today"), a theoretical term (like "intelligent"), or what? Whatever the ultimate analysis, such variance in 'meaning' must raise the possibility of *equivocation,* the assignment of different 'meanings' to the same linguistic form within the same discourse. Let us assume that the linguistic forms with which we are concerned are *contextually determinate,* in the sense that their 'meaning' is determined by the context of their utterance. And let us suppose that the sentences in which these forms occur are otherwise sufficiently well behaved that there is a *relativized* notion of *truth with respect to a context of utterance* for them.[89]

There is an important methodological point to be made. A relativized notion of truth is no impediment to the construction of a logic. Logic aims to preserve truth. If truth varies with context, logic must preserve truth for each context. It goes without saying that premises and conclusion must be relativized to the same context. To do otherwise would be to commit the fallacy of equivocation. Logic abhors equivocation; it does not abhor a relativized notion of truth.

I earlier mentioned Quine's "ambivalent rejection" of quantified propositional attitudes. On my reading of "Intensions Revisited", Quine accepts a relativized notion of truth for these idioms. Each denunciation of the absolute emptiness of the idioms is balanced by acknowledgment of their relativized seemliness. This is the ambivalence I saw. If this is the correct account of Quine's views, then there is no argument against a modal logic.

Quine is certainly aware of the methodological point. But he doesn't seem to come to grips with the way in which it conflicts with his idealization of eternal sentences.[90] For example, in section III of "The Scope and Language of Science"[91] he argues that deductive logic is simplified and facilitated if we rid our language of indexicals. The reason given seems to be that a sentence containing indexicals could change truth values between its appearance in a premise and its appearance in the conclusion. (Does this reflect a strangely concrete conception of the constituents of a logical argument? Is logic about tokens?) However, in the very next paragraph there is a tentative turnabout. He points out that "In practice one merely *supposes* all such points of variation fixed for the space of one's logical argument. . . ." (Why only in practice; why not in theory?) And again in *Word and Object* page 227 he clearly states, "We do apply logic to sentences whose truth values vary with time and speaker", and he warns of the fallacy of equivocation. (This time he is right on the money.)

Let us suppose that it was never the *logic* of contextually determined expressions that exercised Quine, it was always their theory of *truth* (as he says in the passage quoted at the beginning of section XIX). Here, I think he is simply too undiscriminating in rejecting the contextually determined.

The most straightforward way in which the contribution of a linguistic form may be determined by context is for the linguistic form to make explicit reference to, or other explicit use of, features of context. This is the way in which the indexicals: "I", "today", "here", etc. are contextually determinate. The indexicals are *explicitly contextual*. A pronoun whose antecedent lies within the context of the discourse, but beyond the sentence in which the pronoun occurs, is also explicitly contextual. It is not entirely trivial to develop the logic for a language containing indexicals, but it is clear that there is one.[92] The same holds for the theory of truth for such a language. I have no trouble with explicit contextuality. It is at worst benign, at best indispensable.

Is the same true of the *implicitly* contextual? In order to see how implicit contextuality affects logic, consider two cases of implicit contextuality involving ambiguity. Suppose that the ambiguity of "checks" were always completely resolved by context. (Perhaps by the discourse context, whether we are discussing haberdashery or finance; perhaps by the speaker's intentions, if that is a legitimate part of context.) And suppose that the referential ambiguity of "President John Adams" were always completely resolved by context. (Not necessarily by the intentions of the speaker but perhaps by his connections.) Oddly enough, it is trivial to develop the logic of a language containing this kind of ambiguity. The injunction not to equivocate in the course of an argument makes the ambiguities disappear for logical purposes. Logic is unaffected by this kind of ambiguity.

Still, implicit contextuality is troubling from the point of view of truth. Implicit contextuality seems misleading in a way that explicit contextuality is not. One wants to say, mimicking Frege, "So long as there is contextual determination such variations in sense may be tolerated, although they are to be avoided in the theoretical structure of a demonstrative science and ought not to occur in a perfect language."

I think that Quine and I share discomfort with what I have called implicit contextuality, and would not like to see it appear in austere scientific language. (Though I think it is probably unavoidable.) However, Quine's conception of proper scientific language seems to lead him to want to avoid even explicit contextuality.[93]

What is the nature of the contextuality that Quine finds in the quantified propositional attitudes (and in quantified modality as well)? Let me try to formulate a *Thesis of Contextuality* I see in "Intensions Revisited":

> When we attribute a relational attitude to someone, the truth of our attribution may depend not only on the person's circumstances but on ours, in particular, on the purpose and context of the discourse in which we make the attribution.

This sounds like a thesis of implicit contextuality. And if so, and if true, it is unfortunate. (I am undecided whether it is true.[94]) But there is so much of that sort of thing going around nowadays, that it shouldn't provoke an agony of self-doubt. (Remember, even Quine was ambivalent.) As we have already seen, contextuality is no bar to our studying the notions involved with the tools of logic. I believe that with the possible exception of a few bridge laws, the logic will turn out to be the same for all contexts anyway. These studies should proceed.

Part E: Technology and Intuition

We now return to the main line of argument.

XXII

There are historical reasons that help to account for Quine's attitude toward opacity. The contexts he first investigated were quotation contexts and modal contexts. He reports early arguments with C. I. Lewis and E. V. Huntington over the interpretation of modal logic, arguments in which "I found it necessary to harp continually on the theme of use versus mention."[95] The quotation context was seen as the paradigm of opacity. This makes the alleged theorem plausible. Quine's outlook from the early period when he began his long and fruitful studies of opacity is summed up in R&M:

> It would be tidy but unnecessary to force all referentially opaque contexts into the quotational mold; alternatively we can recognize quotation as one referentially opaque context among many.

At least since the time of "Intensions Revisited", Quine has known that *if* there is any opacity producing phrase with a legitimate relational sense, the alleged theorem is false. But he remains suspicious. His old essentialism challenge to the relational sense of necessity has been joined by a new contextuality challenge to the once secure relational senses of propositional attitude idioms.

What is the bearing of our results on Quine's doubts?

We have outlined some technological innovations (arc-quotation, valuated $entences, etc.) that promise to remove technical obstacles to quantification into arbitrary opaque contexts (arbitrary, in not requiring closure conditions).[96] The alleged theorem, which provoked the technological research, posed a *technical* objection to quantification in. So we have shown that quantification in is technically feasible.

We have done a bit more than that. We have contrasted two conceptions of the objects of intensional operators, and thus two conceptions of opacity. We have attempted to link our technology to a grand, historical, philosophical tradition, and to contrast that tradition with another grand, historical, philosophical tradition, one with which we associate Quine's doubts.[97] In this way I hoped to bring a larger philosophical perspective to bear, or, more accurately, to open the door to bringing such a perspective to bear. I know from my own case how powerful the arguments showing the inadequacies of Frege's outlook can be in dispelling a certain simple and intuitively appealing conception of opacity. Quine's doubts are not exactly Frege's. Quine is so much less theory bound, so much more 'experimental' in philosophical temperament. But his paradigm of opacity, quotation, is structurally similar to Frege's. And a paradigm may be all the difference there is between the natural and the artificial.

And we have done one thing more in a positive direction. We have argued for the intuitive reasonableness of one theory of quantified modality and the not unreasonableness of some others. But how much intuition and reasonableness can be brought to bear on a topic like modality?[98]

Beyond that we have played the traditional defense: drawing of distinctions, counter–instances, blocking moves, etc. I question the efficacy of these moves. They may defeat arguments; they rarely exorcise doubt.

What more is there to say to someone who still feels that there is something wrong with all those operators that are blithely said to be true of valuated $entences, something that is hard to put your finger on, but having to do with a promiscuous extension of the basic notional intuitions associated with the operator, the kind of promiscuous nonsense that would appear if we slipped the interpretive constraints of our direct discourse operator **Says-quote** and began regarding some quantifications in as true?

Our technology is neutral. It cannot insure against that sort of nonsense (or that sort of *falsehood,* as we earlier termed it). On the other hand, it also cannot insure against arbitrary constraints that limit all operators to a notional core; it cannot force surrender of the hard line.[99] Technology cannot insure against bad philosophical judgment. Nothing can.

What then remains to be said to instinctive hard-liners? We can try to exhibit an easy, highly intuitive case of quantification into opacity about which there are no legitimate doubts. In this way we aim to show that even beyond technology, there can be no general *philosophical* argument in favor of the hard line. With the hope that intuition will be more compelling than sophisticated technology, we also aim to nudge the intuition of the hard-liners away from the paradigm of quotation toward a new paradigm of opacity.

XXIII

Suppose Quine had begun his studies of opacity not with quotation and modality but by studying temporal operators. Consider, for example, "It will soon be the case that", which we abbreviate "**S**". Temporality involves non-purely referential occurrences of names just as surely as do necessity and belief. We may assume it true that

(14)   S(the President of the United States is a woman)

It is also true that

(15)   The President of the United States = Nancy Reagan's spouse

But it is highly unlikely that

(16)   S(Nancy Reagan's spouse is a woman)

Thus, substitutivity fails. Contexts of **S** are opaque. Now what about quantification? Let us consider:

(17) $(\exists x)(x$ is a child . $\mathbf{S}(x$ is a woman$))$

Typically, Quine would ask, who is this child who will soon be a woman? Is it, as (14) suggests, the President of the United States, that is, Nancy Reagan's spouse? But to suppose this conflicts with the fact that (16) is false.

Does the apparent intelligibility of (17) therefore commit us to a jungle of temporal essentialism or utter dependence on context? Certainly not. *Being the President of the United States* need not currently characterize the individual whom it will characterize when, according to (14), she is President, and *being a woman* is also a fugitive property. The intelligibility of (17) is quite independent of any surrogates including the singular terms of (14) and (16).

As to temporal essentialism, there are those who say that there are eternal properties (that is, properties which are temporally essential), and they might offer: *being human* (here, some Aristotelian-like essentialism), *being Nancy Reagan* (a not purely-qualitative property), or *being President of the United States in 1984* (a 'time indexed' property). There is much to say about the metaphysical views according to which *being human* is temporally essential and *being Nancy Reagan* or *being Nancy Reagan's spouse in 1984* are properties at all. I have said some of it. The important point is that such sophisticated matters, including the existence of not purely-qualitative properties, let alone their expressibility in the language of temporality, are quite irrelevant to our ability to understand (17). Indeed, if we could not already understand sentences such as (17), how could we even formulate the claims of these temporal essentialists? The intelligibility of quantification in is *prior* to the acceptance (or rejection) of essentialism, not tantamount to it.

Let me sum up the case of quantified temporal logic. Substitutivity fails, thus opacity reigns; quantification receives its standard interpretation; quantification in offers no problems of intelligibility (neither logico-semantical nor metaphysical); the interpretation of quantification in requires no surrogates, no invidious distinctions among ways of characterizing an object; the interpretation is not dependent on context; and finally, for you stubborn object fans, the objects can be characterized in inequivalent and fugitive ways. We do, of course, accord a special place to the purely referential role of variables, but we need not have any other way of specifying an object which is especially 'germane' to the question whether the object satisfies a formula containing a free variable within a temporal context. Thus we see, in a single case: counter–instances to the alleged theorem as well as to many 'philosophical' sorrows that have been thought to result from quantification into opacity.

Here is just a bit of sophisticated analysis as to what makes quantification into temporal operators work. You may think it depends on a doctrine of enduring objects. It doesn't. It depends on the doctrine that it is meaningful to ask of our objects, enduring or not, what properties *they* will or did have at other times. And we must, of course, ask this of the object itself, independent of any particular form of specification. To see this, think of the rich realm of temporal truths regarding long enduring heirlooms like Maytag washing machines and Mercedes Benzes. Now imagine that the lives of these individuals grow progressively shorter, perhaps due to a declining standard of workmanship. The temporal truths become more boring. Suppose that ultimately, like some elementary particles, they come to last for only a moment. There would then be little reason to want to discuss their future and past (they have none, in a certain sense), but it would still be meaningful to do so. There would no longer be those interesting invidious temporal *truths,* but the language and its logic would still be impeccable (though useless, as is so much that is impeccable).

There may be sophisticated disagreement about what makes quantification into opaque temporal contexts work, but it does work. And that's a fact. I cannot help but think that had Quine turned his attention in 1942 first to reference and temporality (before modality and before quotation), the recent history of semantics would have been quite different. I hope we soon learn what Quine now thinks about the bearing of temporality and opacity on the problem of quantification into opacity. How I wish we could know what Frege would say about it.

The purpose of this volume is not to praise Quine, but to query him. Still, having said so much in dispute, and so much that he will want to dispute, I wish to add what is indisputable, that tracking his thought is constantly enlightening and a continual delight.

DAVID KAPLAN

DEPARTMENT OF PHILOSOPHY
UCLA
JANUARY 1985

Appendix A: PARAPHRASING INTO PROPOSITIONAL ATTITUDES

The tenability of the transformations which carry intensional verbs that do *not* take sentential complements—like the notional sense of "*wants* (a sloop)" and "*seeks* (the author of Waverly)"—into compounds in which the main verb *does* take a sentential (or 'propositional') complement—(like "*wishes that* one has (a sloop)" and "*strives that* one finds (the author of Waverly)"—is critical not only for Quine's analysis but also for the tradition of analyzing such constructions in accordance with Russell's theory of descriptions. Without an inner *sentential* context, Russell's distinctions of scope disappear, as do Quine's. And with them goes the thesis, so dear to Quine, of the first order eliminability of singular terms other than variables.

But it is not obvious that such transformations can always be made with preservation of meaning, not even if we take preservation of meaning to be so weak a thing as necessary equivalence.[100]

If, as Quine claims in the opening sentence of Q&PA, the incorrectness of rendering "Ctesias is hunting unicorns" in the fashion

$$(\exists x)(x \text{ is a unicorn . Ctesias is hunting } x)$$

is conveniently attested by the non-existence of unicorns, then similar considerations may attest to the incorrectness of rendering "The Greeks worshiped many gods" as

(There are many x)(x is a god . the Greeks worshiped x)

or "The Greeks worshiped Zeus" as

($\exists x$)(x is-Zeus . the Greeks worshiped x)

But how shall "worships" be transformed into a propositional attitude? (The point—that such examples pose a problem for analyses by Russell's theory of descriptions—is originally due to Alonzo Church.[101] The example is from Kamp, one of four cited by Montague.[102])

And when a hunting accident so traumatizes Ctesias that he comes to fear unicorns[103] (not, to fear *that there are unicorns* or *that he will encounter a unicorn,* but to have a true unicorn phobia—one that has begun to 'generalize' to take in horses and antelopes), what propositional attitude will capture his psychological state? "What is it that you fear will happen?", we ask Ctesias. "Nothing", he replies. "I just don't like unicorns." Now it may be that even in this case there is some expression of Ctesias' fear in terms of his propositional attitudes (perhaps from a behaviorist perspective). But it would certainly be surprising if on the basis of an *a priori* linguistic analysis, it were possible to establish such a far-reaching conclusion about the grammatical form of the primitive predicates of cognitive psychology.

There is also the complication (noted in footnote 7) that hidden *relational* senses of psychological verbs may appear when *notional* senses of psychological verbs are paraphrased into the propositional attitude idiom. In some of these cases, a theory of indexicals or quasi-indexicals will not suffice. For example, the notional sense of "I seek a lion" seems to be more adequately rendered by:

I strive that ($\exists x$)(x is a lion . I find x while recognizing that x is a lion) than by Quine's formulation which omits the relational use of "recognizes" and adopts an extensional use of "find". If a lion seeker does not recognize the object he perceives close at hand (i.e., 'finds' in the extensional sense) to be a lion, he will not have satisfied his striving.[104] Here again it may be possible to find a remedy (perhaps by moving "I recognize that" to the front of the quantifier), but the matter is delicate.

There is another course. We could give up the attempt to paraphrase all the psychological opaque constructions in terms of propositional attitudes. We would lose the striking contrast between (3) and (4). We would lose the utility of elementary logic in representing internal structure for all the notional senses (for example, to represent the difference between wanting a sloop and wanting all the sloops). And, of course, the adherents of Russell's theory of descriptions would lose their confidence that their theory could solve all of the logical problems of opacity. What would we gain? First, surcease from what I believe to be a vain attempt, and the marginal benefits that sometimes accrue from facing reality. Second, an appreciation for some of the subtlety and utility of higher order intensional logics in providing entities for "at least one sloop" and "every sloop" to mean.

Montague took exactly this course in "The Proper Treatment of Quantifiers".[105] Russell insisted, in "On Denoting", that such phrases had no meaning in isolation, but in the higher order intensional logic of *Principia Mathematica* he developed the means of providing that meaning. In Church's "Outline of a Revised Formalization of the Logic of Sense and Denotation" such meanings would be the senses of the expressions:

"λf ($\exists x$)(x is a sloop . fx)" and "λf (x)(x is a sloop $\supset$ fx)".

Appendix B: THE SYNTACTICALLY *DE RE*

In English we have negation in a pedantic *de dicto* form: "It is not the case that Ortcutt is a spy", as well as in the more colloquial *de re* form: "Ortcutt is not a spy". Corresponding to the *de dicto* modality: "It is possible that Ortcutt is a spy", we have the adverbial *de re* "Ortcutt possibly is a spy". And corresponding to the *de dicto* attitude: "Ralph believes that Ortcutt is a spy", we have the passive + infinitive *de re:* "Ortcutt is believed by Ralph to be a spy". I speak here of unproblematical matters of English syntax. I acknowledge that the semantics of these English forms is problematical. Still, the syntactically *de re* has long been used (at least since 1358) to explain the semantically *de re*. In formal systems the semantically *de re* has usually been represented by quantification into the syntactically *de dicto*. Driven by the alleged theorem, Quine introduced a formal version of the syntactically *de re* in Q&PA (where he calls it a 'relational sense'). I think it interesting and important to study these forms in their own right, their misconception notwithstanding.

Let **O** be a syntactically *de dicto* sentential operator. Then, if Γ is a formula (open or closed), $\ulcorner O\Gamma \urcorner$ is a formula (open or closed, according as Γ is).[106] Quantification into the syntactically *de dicto* is permitted. ("$\square$" is a typical syntactically *de dicto* sentential operator.) The syntactically *de re* operator also takes a formula as its operand, but rather than forming a formula it forms a compound predicate. It does this, in the manner of the λ operator, by binding variables to produce new argument places. The *degree* of the compound predicate (monadic, dyadic, etc.) is determined by the number of variables bound by the *de re* operator. If $v_1,\ldots,v_n$ are distinct variables, Γ is a formula, and $\alpha_1,\ldots,\alpha_n$ are terms, then O is the *de re* variable binding operator corresponding to **O**, $\ulcorner (Ov_1\ldots v_n) \urcorner$ is an n-place *de re* variable binding operator phrase, $\ulcorner [(Ov_1\ldots v_n)\Gamma] \urcorner$ is an n-place predicate expression, and $\ulcorner [(Ov_1\ldots v_n) \; \Gamma \;] \; \alpha_1\ldots\alpha_n \urcorner$ is a formula. Free occurrences of $v_1,\ldots,v_n$ in Γ are bound by the operator, whose scope extends just to the end of Γ. We need not require that $v_1,\ldots,v_n$ include all of the free variables of Γ.[107]

Quine's original motive for introducing the syntactically *de re* was to use it to express, in a less 'dubious' form, quantification into the syntactically *de dicto*. However, in suggesting how to translate from the syntactically *de dicto* into the syntactically *de re* he committed a subtle error. Recall Ralph's situation. He has seen Ortcutt twice, under different circumstances, and not recognized him as the same person. Thus Ralph may have *de re* beliefs relating Ortcutt (seen in a brown hat) to Ortcutt (seen at the beach). For example, he may believe that the former is taller than the latter. Now this presents a problem for the syntactically *de dicto*, since there is no way, without additional logical resources, to distinguish a report of this *de re* belief from a report of the absurd *de re* belief about Ortcutt that he has the monadic, reflexive property of being taller than himself. The problem is that:

(18) $(\exists y)(\exists z)(y = z$. **Bel** (y is taller than z))

is logically equivalent to:

(19) $(\exists y)$ **Bel** (y is taller than y)

(where "**Bel**" abbreviates "Ralph believes that").

If, however, we use the syntactically *de re*, we can easily distinguish these beliefs. Ralph's situation is this:

(20) $(\exists x)([(\textbf{\textit{Bel}}\ yz)\ y$ is taller than $z]\ xx)$

not this:

(21) $(\exists x)([(\textbf{\textit{Bel}}\ y)\ y$ is taller than $y]\ x)$

and these two are not logically equivalent. Quine's proposal translates (18) into a formula equivalent to (20), and (19) into (21). One of these translations must be incorrect, since equivalent formulas could not translate into inequivalent ones.

Here is the heart of the matter. How do we understand

(22)   **Bel** (y is taller than z)

when "y" and "z" have the same value? Do we understand it as:

(23) $[(\textbf{\textit{Bel}}\ yz)\ y$ is taller than $z]\ yz$

or as:

(24) $[(\textbf{\textit{Bel}}\ y)\ y$ is taller than $y]\ y$?

(Note that since the scope of the operators ends at the right bracket, the final occurrences of "y" and "z" in (23) and (24) are free.) Since we do not, in general, know when distinct variables have the same value, it seems that an understanding of (22) which would be uniform for all values of "y" and "z" should favor (23) over (24). If we do translate (22) into (23), then in view of the equivalence between (18) and (19),

(25)   **Bel** (y is taller than y)

should translate into

(26) $[(\textbf{\textit{Bel}}\ yz)\ y$ is taller than $z]\ yy$

rather than into (24). (18) and (19) would then translate into equivalent formulas, as they should. The subtlety in translating the syntactically *de dicto* into the syntactically *de re* lies in the translation of (25) into (26). When a free variable has more than one occurrence in the operand of the syntactically *de dicto* form we must first *articulate* the operand by eliminating repetitive free occurrences of variables.

Let the free variables of Γ be $w_1,\ldots,w_j$ (some of which may have more than one free occurrence in Γ). We replace each free recurrence (after the first free occurrence) of a variable with a free occurrence of the alphabetically first new variable. Let the free variables of the result, Γ^*, be $v_1,\ldots,v_n$, each of which will have exactly one free occurrence in Γ^*. Let the replacement be such that replacing free occurrences of $v_1,\ldots,v_n$ in Γ^* with $u_1,\ldots,u_n$ respectively restores Γ^* to Γ. (Example: let Γ be "$Rxyx$". Then $w_1,\ldots,w_j$ are "x", "y"; Γ^* is "$Rxyz$"; $v_1,\ldots,v_n$ are "x", "y", "z"; and $u_1,\ldots,u_n$ are "x", "y", "x".) In the second step we translate as follows:

$$\mathbf{O}\Gamma \iff [(\mathbf{O}v_1\ldots v_n)\Gamma^*]u_1\ldots u_n$$

(In our example, $\mathbf{O}Rxyx \iff [(\mathbf{O}xyz)Rxyz]\,xyx$) Note that the *de dicto* form and its translation have the same free variables. If Γ has no free variables, Γ^* is Γ, and we have a degenerate case of the syntactically *de re:* $\ulcorner[(\mathbf{O})\,\Gamma]\urcorner$.

The question of adequacy for a translation depends upon the operator involved. When $\mathbf{O}$ is "$\boldsymbol{Bel}$", the inequivalence of (24) and (25) shows that:

(27) $(x)([(\mathbf{O}xy)Rxy]\,xx \equiv [(\mathbf{O}x)Rxx]\,x)$

fails.[108] Hence articulation is required when translating the syntactically *de dicto* form of **Bel** into the syntactically *de re*. (And similarly for the other attitudes.) Although they translate no syntactically *de dicto* formula, syntactically *de re* formulas like the right hand side of (27) (or like (21)) are grammatically correct. This suggests that the syntactically *de re* has more expressive power than the syntactically *de dicto*. But suppose that $\mathbf{O}$ were the syntactically *de re* form of $\square$ or of the **S** of temporality. One would then expect (27) to hold. (Since Ortcutt and Ortcutt could not stand in the relation R unless Ortcutt were to have R to himself.) Hence one need not be so fastidious about articulation for $\square$ and **S**. (Though I would still regard the two sides of (27) as differing in meaning.)

Do not think that the recalcitrance of (27) for *Bel* is due to any logical deficiency on Ralph's part. Even if Ralph were logically omniscient, (27) would still fail from left to right; though in my view it would hold from right to left.[109] This difference between the *de re* forms of what I am wont to call 'metaphysical' operators (modality, temporality) and what I call 'epistemological' operators (psychological attitudes, etc.) *even as applied to the logically omniscient,* marks an important distinction between the form of logical consequence under which, say, the modalities are closed and the form of logical consequences under which, say, logically-omniscient-belief is closed. If Ortcutt were correctly introduced to Ralph as "the Mayor", and later, not recognizing him to be the same person, Ralph were to observe him behaving suspiciously, it could well be the case that:

(28) $(\exists x)(x = $ the Mayor) . **Bel** $((x = $ the Mayor) . x is a spy))

But no amount of *reasoning* on Ralph's part, though he be logically omniscient, could bring him to:

(29)   **Bel** (the Mayor is a spy)

The failure of this inference reinforces the point made in footnote 56 that $\ulcorner(\exists x)$ **Bel** $(x = $ the Mayor)$\urcorner$ does not suffice to make "the Mayor" an instantial term.[110] Note that if **Bel** were replaced by one of the metaphysical operators the inference from (28) to (29) would go through.

We can sum up the logical situation by isolating three pairs of principles (in each case the second is simply the converse of the first):

Abstraction:	$O\Gamma \supset [(Ow_1...w_j)\ \Gamma]\ w_1...w_j$
(Example:	$ORxx \supset [(Ox)Rxx]\ x\ )$
Concretion:	The converse of Abstraction

Articulated Abstraction:	$O\Gamma \supset [(Ov_1...v_n)\ \Gamma^*]\ u_1...u_n$
(Example:	$ORxx \supset [(Oxy)Rxy]\ xx\ )$
Articulated Concretion:	The converse of Articulated Abstraction

Reflexivization:	$[(Ov_1...v_n)\ \Gamma^*]\ u_1...u_n \supset [(Ow_1...w_j)\ \Gamma]\ w_1...w_j$
(Example:	$[(Oxy)Rxy]xx \supset [(Ox)Rxx]\ x\ )$
Reflexive Elimination:	The converse of Reflexivization

The first pair (Abs/Con) is equivalent to the conjunction of the second pair (Articulated Abs/Con) and the third pair (Reflexive Intro/Elem). I proposed Articulated Abs/Con for translating the syntactically *de dicto* into the syntactically *de re*. I believe that Reflexive Elimination holds for modal and temporal operators as well as most of the familiar propositional attitudes (though the case of the attitudes is a bit complicated). This puts the focus of attention on Reflexivization. The inadequacy of Abs/Con as a translation of the propositional attitudes from the syntactically *de dicto* into the syntactically *de re* can be localized in Reflexivization. Similarly, the satisfaction of Reflexivization by modal and temporal operators implies that Abs/Con is an adequate translation scheme for them, and thus that the syntactically *de re* offers no greater expressive power than the syntactically *de dicto* for such operators.

Even in the case of the attitudes, the question of relative expressive power is somewhat delicate.[111] It is natural to consider translating the syntactically *de re* back into the syntactically *de dicto* thus:

$$[(Ow_1...w_j)\ \Gamma]\ z_1...z_j \Longleftrightarrow O\ (\exists w_1)...(\exists w_j)(\Sigma\ (w_i = z_i)\ .\ \Gamma)$$

where "$\Sigma\ (w_i = z_i)$" stands for the conjunction of all $\ulcorner(w_i = z_i)\urcorner$ for $i \leq j$.

(Example: $[(Ox)\ Rxx]\ z \Longleftrightarrow O(\exists x)((x = z)\ .\ Rxx)\ )$

The difficulty with such a scheme lies in the implied inner existential import. I may wish of you that you didn't exist, without wishing that you were an existing thing that didn't exist. Or, mistakenly thinking you to be an apparition, I may believe of you that you don't exist, without believing that you are an existing thing that doesn't exist.[112]

I see no way to interpret (i.e. translate) the syntactically *de re* attitudes within the syntactically *de dicto* (without increasing the expressive power of the syntactically *de dicto*).[113]

There are still further reasons for liking the syntactically *de re*. As Richard has shown, we can use a variant of it to express what Lewis has called belief *de se*—roughly, the beliefs one expresses about oneself through the use of the first person.[114] We write "[(Bel^s xy) $\sim$ x spied on y] Ralph y" to report the belief voiced by Ralph's indignant denial to y: "I did not spy on you."[115] This suggests a more perspicuous notation, "($Bel^{I'}$ xy)", in which we exhibit the pronoun. We might generalize to "($Bel^{you'}$ xy)" and even to "($Bel^{Hesperus'}$ xy)", thus allowing a bit of direct discourse to mix with the indirect.

There is so much more of logical interest to say about the syntactically *de re*, that I will say no more. Except to ask where our seeming inability to translate the syntactically *de re* into the syntactically *de dicto* and our difficulties (involving articulation) in translating the syntactically *de dicto* into the syntactically *de re* leaves 'the logician', with his casual trick of re-ambiguation? He hedged. ("*If* we can . . . transform each logically dubious formulation into a *unique* indubitable one . . .") And he was vague. (He didn't say how the transformation went for the difficult cases, which involve multiple occurrences of the same externally bound variable.) His concern was the same as Quine's: Is it legitimate to quantify into the syntactically *de dicto*, or must a new syntactical form be created to express what was attempted by quantification in? The expressive power of the new syntactical form was not at issue for him. He's O.K.

In 1968 I made the vague claim that the syntactically *de dicto* could represent the syntactically *de re* with "no loss to Quine's theory." (I, also, didn't say how.) Did this mean with no loss to the expressive power of the syntactically *de re?* Alas, it probably did. Not good.

In 1977, Quine, abjuring vagueness, proposed to show precisely how to represent the syntactically *de re* within the syntactically *de dicto*, and succumbed to the risk of falsifiability.[116] Dangerous business!

Appendix C: ARCS VERSUS CORNERS

Arc-quotation names turn out to name exactly what they should name: a concatenation of the "closed" part of the quoted material with the individuals that are the values of the bindable occurrences of variables. If variables occurring within a form of quotation marks are to be regarded as bindable, this seems the inevitable result. Using $\frown$ to indicate concatenation:

(30)　　$(y)[\ ^{\ulcorner}(\exists x)\ y$ exceeds $x^{\urcorner} = ($ "$(\exists x)$" $^{\frown}y^{\frown}$ "exceeds x" $)]$

Quine also has introduced a device, corner-quotes, for quantifying into quotation.

(31)　　$(\alpha)[\ ^{\ulcorner}(\exists x)\ \alpha$ exceeds $x^{\urcorner} = ($ "$(\exists x)$" $^{\frown}\alpha^{\frown}$ "exceeds x" $)]$

Quine restricts the values of his variables to traditional expressions; I have removed this artificial restriction. Quine syntactically distinguishes his bindable occurrences of variables by font, using Greek letters; I use the italic Latin letters of the object language and syntactically distinguish my bindable occurrences of variables in the traditional way, by freedom.[117] When α is "Quine", $^{\ulcorner}(\exists x)\ \alpha$ exceeds $x^{\urcorner}$ is a traditional true sentence. When y is Quine, $^{\ulcorner}(\exists x)\ y$ exceeds $x^{\urcorner}$ is an untraditional true sentence. As I have argued above, for the purposes at hand—semantical purposes—the untraditional sentences serve shoulder to shoulder with the traditional.

Scientific candor compels me to acknowledge that there may be disanalogies between closed and valuated sentences. Both are, of course, types, but do valuated sentences have tokens?[118]

Thought of in terms of (30) and (31), it would seem that if the value of the variable "y" were an expression (in the traditional sense), then my arcs would amount to Quine's corners.

$$(y = \alpha) \supset (\ ^{\ulcorner}(\exists x)\ y \text{ exceeds } x^{\urcorner} = \ ^{\ulcorner}(\exists x)\ \alpha \text{ exceeds } x^{\urcorner})$$

This is not correct. When the value of "y" is "Quine", $^{\ulcorner}(\exists x)\ y$ exceeds $x^{\urcorner}$ is not the traditional true sentence. It is the untraditional true sentence which asserts of the *object* "Quine" (with all its vowels) that it exceeds something. Otherwise there would be an ambiguity in our notation whenever the value of the variable is an expression. This shows that we must revise our formulation of (30). Our metaphorical use of "concatenation" to describe the relation between object and predicate in a valuated sentence cannot be expressed by an extension of the ordinary concatenation notion, $\frown$, since when the object is an expression we must distinguish the traditional concatenation of it (*qua* expression) with the predicate, from our new form of 'concatenation' of it *qua object* with the predicate. For that matter, we must also distinguish treatment of the predicate *qua* predicate from its treatment *qua* object. (A reason for focusing on the subject is that if the predicate is treated as an object, the resulting valuated expression will not be well formed.) Let us, therefore, adopt bracketed concatenation, $\zeta\ \zeta$, to mark the object places.

$$(y)[\ ^{\ulcorner}(\exists x)\ y \text{ exceeds } x^{\urcorner} = (\text{"}(\exists x)\text{"} \ \zeta y\zeta \text{ "exceeds } x\text{"})]$$

The primary difficulty, of course, was not with our notation, it was with our intuitive representation of valuated sentences as sequences of expressions and objects. *This representation is inadequate* in that it does not distinguish those of its component expressions that are to be regarded as expressions from those that are to be regarded as objects. We thus have a kind of logical imperfection in our syntactical representations.[119] The new notation suggests a way out. Instead of embedding the 'objects' differently from the 'expressions', mark the entities which are to be regarded as objects in such a way that even if they were expressions before marking, after marking they no longer will be.

Here is the moral: my arcs are a complement to Quine's corners, not a replacement for them.

Appendix D: The Second Law of Identity

Several authors, seemingly emboldened by their awareness that substitutivity does not hold in general in opaque contexts, have announced formalisms in which they casually reject instances of the second law of identity, especially those instances of the form:

ID2 $(x)(y)((x = y) \supset (\Gamma xx \equiv \Gamma xy))$

with the variables occurring within an opaque context in Γ. (Their thought seems to be that distinct variables can carry the same individual off in different directions.) It is they whom Quine justly accuses of wantonness. However, it is possible to reformulate the second law of identity so that it is no longer a principle of substitutivity. By this I mean that *the second law need not involve any replacements of one variable by another within the context* Γ. Let v_1 and v_2 be any distinct variables, and let Γ be any formula having free occurrences of at least v_1. (Γ may also have free occurrences of v_2 and other variables as well.) The following, along with the first law of identity: "$(x)(x = x)$" (reflexivity), suffices to axiomatize identity theory.

ID2* $(v_2)[(\exists v_1)((v_1 = v_2) . \Gamma) \supset (v_1)((v_1 = v_2) \supset \Gamma)]$

I call ID2* the "why not take all of me" principle.

It has been my experience that even systems that proclaim their defiance of ID2 tend to satisfy ID2*. Unless "$=$" is made manifestly deviant, it is not easy to design a semantics that counts ID2* as well-formed and does not satisfy it. The recursive definition of truth would have to keep track not merely of the value of a variable, not merely of the typographical identity of a variable, but of the quantifier, long since passed over in the recursion, which originally governed the variable. I don't say it couldn't be done, but it's hard. And, practically speaking, unheard of.

If ID2 is derivable from reflexivity and ID2*, what does it mean for a system to defy ID2 but satisfy reflexivity and ID2*? It means that something entirely independent of identity has gone wrong in the sentential or quantificational part of the system.[120] Wantonness with identity has its roots in baser sins.

ID2* is also usefully applied backwards to test whether an identity sign signs identity. I wonder whether Carnap, who was already cautious enough not to use the normal identity sign, would have been quicker to concede Quine's point about his 'neutral variables' (see footnote 18) had he applied the ID2* test.

Appendix E: SCHEMATIC VALIDITY AND MODAL LOGIC

I have argued that there are (at least) two distinct notions of necessity: logical necessity and metaphysical necessity, the first benign, the second invidious.[121] I concluded therefore that there are (at least) two modal logics: the logic of $\boxed{L}$ and the logic of $\boxed{M}$. But the situation is complicated by the fact that there are two notions of what a logic should attempt to capture.

Consider the sentence:

$(x) \sim (x$ is a spy $. \sim x$ is a spy$)$

with the variables understood to range over persons. We call this sentence *logically valid*. Do we call it logically valid because it would be true no matter what the non-logical facts were (i.e., no matter what persons there were and no matter which of them were spies)? If so, we have in mind what I, with some hesitation, call *modal validity*. (Set theoretically represented by the technical notion of truth in every model.) Do we call the sentence logically valid because, given the facts as they are, it would be true no matter how we were to reinterpret its non-logical signs (i.e., no matter what grammatically appropriate expressions are substituted for the non-logical signs and no matter what domain of discourse the variable is taken to range over)? If so, we have in mind what I unhesitatingly call *schematic validity*. The notions are different, but for classical first order extensional logic they pick out the same validities. This is a wonder, and wonderful.[122]

I will not duplicate Quine's excellent technical discussion of the classical case.[123] What is important for our purposes is that the two notions do not pick out the same class of validities for the logic of "$\boxed{L}$". It is the modal validities of $\boxed{L}$ that we earlier called the *logic* of logical necessity. But although "$\sim \boxed{L}$ Ortcutt is a spy" is modally valid, it has the counterinstance (i.e., false reinterpretation): "$\sim \boxed{L}$ (Ortcutt = Ortcutt)". Hence, it is not schematically valid.

The two approaches to validity interact with the two notions of necessity in a somewhat surprising way that makes it difficult to determine whether certain modal logicians are studying logical necessity or metaphysical necessity. For the sentential modal logic S5, the theorems can be regarded *either* as the modally valid laws governing $\boxed{M}$ *or* as the schematically valid laws governing $\boxed{L}$. The laws are the same.[124] When quantification is added, the laws are still largely the same. Whatever is modally valid for $\boxed{M}$ is still schematically valid for $\boxed{L}$. But there are schematic validities for $\boxed{L}$ (for example, "$\sim \boxed{L}\ (\exists x)(\exists y)(x \neq y)$") that are not modal validities for $\boxed{M}$.

Carnap and C.I. Lewis seem rather clearly to have $\boxed{L}$ in mind as their modality.[125] Whereas Kripke, and perhaps Church, seem to have $\boxed{M}$ in mind.[126] I have sometimes wondered whether the self-righteous rejection of the essentialism charge by certain modal logicians (despite their leaving various negative $\boxed{L}$ validities undecided) did not stem from the unarticulated thought that schematic validity was their project.

NOTES

1. *Journal of Philosophy* 53 (1956); reprinted in slightly revised form in W.V. Quine's *The Ways of Paradox and Other Essays* (Random House, 1966) and in L. Linsky (ed.) *Reference and Modality* (Oxford, 1971).

2. *John Buridan: Sophisms on Meaning and Truth*. Translated and with an introduction by Theodore Kermit Scott (Appleton-Century-Crofts, 1966) pp. 137ff.

3. I note that in reprinting the paper, the editor of *The Ways of Paradox* has acquitted Quine of premeditation.

4. This move—to express the verb as what Russell called a *propositional attitude*—is an important one. Russell's term reflects his semantical view that the objects of the attitudes are 'propositions'. Our use is only to indicate a syntactical feature of the verb phrase. The move is not without difficulties. See Appendix A: Paraphrasing into Propositional Attitudes.

5. There is a subtle difficulty here that is obscured by the first person formulation. Although "I want a sloop" may be revised as "I wish that I have a sloop", it is incorrect to rephrase "Ernest wants a sloop" as "Ernest wishes that Ernest has a sloop". Ernest may not know that he is Ernest, and thus his benevolent wish that Ernest have a sloop may be irrelevant to his own wanting a sloop. We must somehow capture the idea that what Ernest wishes has the first person form "I have a sloop". What is required is a version of Casteñada's "Ernest wishes that *he-himself* has a sloop" [H.N. Casteñeda, "Indicators and Quasi-indicators", *American Philosophical Quarterly* 4 (1967) or a variation on the formulations of belief *de se* by Lewis or by Richard [D. Lewis, "Attitudes *De Dicto* and *De Se*", *Philosophical Review* 88 (1979), Mark Richard, "Direct Reference and Ascriptions of Belief", *Journal of Philosophical Logic* 12 (1983)].

6. When I echo Quine's words, sometimes I quote, sometimes I don't.

7. I properly should say that *in 1956* Quine did not doubt, since 21 years later in "Intensions Revisited" [in P. French et al. (eds.), *Midwest Studies in Philosophy* II (University of Minnesota Press, 1977); reprinted in Quine's *Theories and Things* (Harvard, 1981)] he champions a more severe epistemological stance and renounces this position. His renunciation has the strange and seemingly unnoticed consequence that his own ultimate formulation ((27) of Q&PA) of the *notional* sense of "Someone wants a sloop":

$$(\exists x)\ (x \text{ wishes that: } (\exists y)\ (y \text{ is a sloop } . \ x \text{ has } y))$$

also ceases to make sense.

8. Page 142 in "Reference and Modality", *From a Logical Point of View* (Harvard, 1953); the paper is somewhat revised in the second edition, 1961.

9. One obvious reason would be that in their usual formulations the logical inference rules of universal instantiation and existential generalization fail. But that is not Quine's reason. Already in "Notes on Existence and Necessity" [*Journal of Philosophy* 40 (1943); reprinted in L. Linsky (ed.) *Semantics and the Philosophy of Language* (University of Illinois Press, 1952)] and again in "Reference and Modality", Quine anticipates one version of what is now called "free logic" by remarking that these inference rules are "anomalous as an adjunct" to the purely logical theory of quantification. See, for example, "Notes on Existence and Necessity", paragraph 9 of section 2, refined in "Reference and Modality", paragraph 4 of section 2. Also, see Church's comments on this matter in his review of "Notes on Existence and Necessity" [*Journal of Symbolic Logic* VIII: 45].

10. There is much of interest in the relation between the two syntactical forms independently of the use Quine makes of them. See Appendix B: The Syntactically *De Re*.

11. The original purpose of reforming (2) into the propositional attitude form (3) was to exhibit the two readings of "I want a sloop" as a *grammatical* ambiguity. The analysis in terms of a *lexical* ambiguity makes this goal unachievable. There remains no obvious reason not to leave (2) unregenerate. Quine seems not to have considered this course, which is considered at the end of Appendix A.

12. See, for example, the third to last paragraph of his reply "To Kaplan" [in D. Davidson and J. Hintikka (eds.), *Words and Objections* (D. Reidel, 1969)].

13. Although Quine is not explicit about it, this argument is almost surely aimed at the intensional logic of *Principia Mathematica* in which expressions like "the proposition that *x* is bald" are said to signify propositional functions and to be accessible to quantification. More about this later on.

14. Nathan Salmon pointed out the possibility that the occurrence be within quotation marks and suggested the use of "bindable" to forestall this possibility.

15. The interested reader can easily find the citations which verify Quine's commitment to each of steps 1–4. It may be objected that although the argument is one whose premises Quine probably believed and which he might have given, there is no direct evidence in any of the papers from 1943 on that he ever actually did give exactly this argument. I agree. Had he filled in the details of steps 5 through 8 he would have immediately seen the fallacy in 4. But Quine clearly believes himself to have given an argument in establishing conclusion (iii) of Notes on E&N, and I still find this the best detailed reconstruction of that argument. I have already called it "speculation".

16. Although it is not necessarily the occurrence to be supplanted, as is claimed in paragraph 2 of R&M: "Failure of substitutivity reveals merely that the occurrence to be supplanted is not purely referential. . . ". Note also that I have shifted from the "purely designative" language of Notes on E&N to the "purely referential" language of R&M.

17. R&M, last half of paragraph 8.

18. Ibid., paragraphs 8 and 9 of section 2.

19. The thoughtful exponent also speculated that perhaps it was Quine's 1943 use of "designate" rather than "refer" that led him to assume tacitly that the semantics was determined by the position rather than the occupant. "Designation", he said, brings only closed terms to mind; variables don't 'designate', they refer.

20. Such at least seems to be the Fregean tradition. There is little that I have been able to find in Frege's writings that goes directly to this point although his examples all

suggest that it is the context which determines whether the constituents have direct or indirect denotation. He does not explicitly discuss the question of a variable—which presumably has no indirect denotation—occurring in such a context, though he does indicate, in the letter to Russell quoted below, that he is flabbergasted by Russell's idea that the proposition expressed by a sentence might have an object as one of its components.

Frege, of course, gives the matter an added twist. By using his notion of indirect denotation, he restores the occurrences of singular terms to purely designative status, though with an altered designatum. He thus validates quantification into such positions provided that the values of the variables are of the kind *indirectly* denoted by the singular terms. Church follows Frege in this.

An alternative, adopted by Carnap, is to accept the Fregean injunction against variability in position *without* using a notion of indirect denotation, and thus be driven by Quine's argument to the conclusion that quantification in must receive a non-standard interpretation. Carnap uses what he calls "neutral variables" with both "value-extensions" and "value-intentions". He appears to acknowledge Quine's criticism that this usage is non-standard but argues that the deviance is benign. See especially section 44 of *Meaning and Necessity* (University of Chicago Press, 1947; enlarged edition, 1956) and footnote 11, page 892, of *The Philosophy of Rudolf Carnap* edited by P. A. Schilpp (Open Court, 1963).

21. Church's formalization appeared in abstract in 1946 and full-blown in 1951 "A Formulation of the Logic of Sense and Denotation" [in P. Henle et al. (eds.), *Structure Method and Meaning* (Liberal Arts Press, 1951)]. His "Outline of a Revised Formulation of the Logic of Sense and Denotation" appears (in two parts) in *Nous* 7 (1973): 24–33 and *Nous* 8 (1974): 135–156, wherein see further references. Within Church's rather complex system it is, in fact, possible for an occurrence of an individual variable within the scope of a modal operator to be bound by an initially placed quantifier. Therefore a somewhat more sophisticated formulation of Quine's proscription is required in order to show that Church's system conforms to it. But it does. The critical point is that despite the multitude of syntactical forms, Church's version of quantified modal logic, like Carnap's in *Meaning and Necessity,* does not permit expression of the characteristic statement of the familiar version—that an individual, *independently of how it is conceptualized,* has some property necessarily.

Quine should recognize and applaud the fact that Church and Carnap share his intuition that it is only an *individual-under-a-concept* that can be said to have a property necessarily. Church is careful to point out that even the statement that an individual has only contingent existence must be "corrected in form in accordance with a Fregean analysis." We can say, regarding various concepts of an individual, that they are possibly vacuous, but it would not be meaningful to say of the individual itself that it might not have existed ["Outline of a Revised . . ." 147, 148].

As an historical sidelight I note that the characteristic statement *is* expressible in the system of Carnap's path-breaking "Modalities and Quantification" [*Journal of Symbolic Logic* 11 (June, 1946)], which preceded *Meaning and Necessity.*

22. Cited in footnote 9.

23. *Zeitschrift für Philosophie und philosophische Kritik* 100 (1892). Translated as "On Sense and Nominatum" in I.M. Copi and J. A. Gould (eds.), *Contemporary Readings in Logical Theory* (Macmillan, 1967); and elsewhere.

24. A further result of Quine's unwillingness to make use of indirect *denotation* is this. Quine claims the identification of his notions with Frege's on the basis of a common criterion: substitutivity of identity. But I think that Frege regards failure of

substitutivity more as a *consequence* of an indirect 'occurrence'—that is, as a consequence of the fact that the occurrence manifestly (to Frege) has indirect denotation—than as a *criterion* for it. Were substitutivity to fail in a case in which no entity plausibly presented itself as the object of indirect denotation, I think Frege would not call the occurrence "oblique". 'Accidental' occurrences like that of the term "cat" in the context "cattle" may be of this kind.

25. Footnote 3 of "Quantifying In", *Synthese* 19 (1968–69); reprinted in *Words and Objections* and in Linsky's *Reference and Modality*.

26. Thus, there is no threat of logical inconsistency from quantification into an undifferentiated notation, nor, as has been suggested, is there an imminent logical threat of modal collapse. See, for example, pp. 197–198 of *Word and Object* (The Technology Press of M.I.T., 1960). D. Føllesdal ["Quine on Modality", in *Words and Objections*] sees this threat as among Quine's primary challenges to modal logic. However, if worse comes to worst, we can always fall back on the logician's trick.

27. The interdefinability claim, however, seems too strong, and stronger than needed for mere re-ambiguation. Especially in the case of *belief*, the bilateral definition seems incorrect and doesn't square with intuitions of Q&PA. See Appendix B.

28. In such expositions, Quine provisionally adopts a strategy like that of Frege, assigning an indirect denotation to explain failure of substitutivity. Even Quine's choices of indirect values: intensions and expressions, mirror Frege's.

29. Intensional entities are those of a kind capable of being the intension of an expression, thus propositions, properties, etc. I use "intension" (of an expression) in a loose but traditional way to contrast with "extension". (Tradition speaks more precisely of extension than of intension.) My use of "intension" connotes neither Carnap's technical use (according to which logically equivalent expressions have the same 'intension') nor a use designed specifically for the propositional attitudes.

30. In 1903 Russell claimed that the points of disagreement between Frege's theory and his own were "very few and slight". [*The Principles of Mathematics* (George Allen & Unwin, 1903), pages 501–502.] But two years later, "On Denoting" includes a lengthy argument purporting "to prove that the whole distinction of meaning and denotation has been wrongly conceived. . . . Thus the point of view [to which this distinction belongs] must be abandoned." [*Mind* 14 (1905); reprinted in *Contemporary Readings in Logical Theory* and in many other places.] The unintelligibility of the argument supporting this claim has caused many to ignore its secessionist implications.

Quine tells us that his metaphor of *opacity* (roughly, Frege's *oblique* de-ontologized) is intended to contrast with Russell's use of *transparency*. The contrast in notions chosen for highlighting reflects an important difference in paradigms between Frege-Quine and Russell. Whereas Frege-Quine regard *opaque* contexts as deviant and what Russell called *transparent* contexts as the norm, Russell regards *transparent* contexts as deviant and *opaque* contexts as the norm. As one pursues these differences one comes to see why Russell did not regard descriptions as 'denoting'. Their *normal* semantic value for Russell is closer to Frege's *sense* than to Frege's *denotation*. This point must be kept in mind when reading the work of contemporary Russellians like R. Marcus' "Modalities and Intensional Languages" [*Synthese* 13 (1961); reprinted in *Contemporary Readings in Logical Theory* and elsewhere].

In connection with what is 'normal', I should note explicitly that I do not understand Quine's claim that the elimination of singular terms other than variables does not make opacity less problematic. It seems normal to regard descriptions as Frege did, as denoting, and thus to find failure of substitutivity to be *prima facie* puzzling. But who, other than Frege and his followers, ever thought that it was normal *(gewöhnlich)* to regard predicate expressions as standing for their extensions. As we all know, extensional contexts are simpler, but are they the norm? (Can you remember how odd it seemed that all those sentential connectives were truth functional?) I'm with Russell on this one. I don't see failure of predicate extensionality as *prima facie* puzzling.

31. This was the view of *Principles of Mathematics*. In the later, better known, "On Denoting" stage of Russell's views the properties in these complexes were no longer held together in subject position but were distributed throughout the proposition. The only explicitly subject-predicate propositions remaining were the singular propositions.

32. The thesis is argued in my "How to Russell a Frege-Church" [*Journal of Philosophy* 72 (1975); reprinted in M. Loux (ed.), *The Possible and the Actual* (Cornell, 1979)]. Therein I cited two ways of formulating a view I called "Haecceitism", the first in terms of possible worlds, the second in terms of singular propositions. As will emerge below, I now regard the second formulation (or a descendant of it) as having wider applicability and being more closely connected to our understanding of opacity, as well as being more ontologically congenial.

33. The correspondence is translated in G. Gabriel et al. (eds.), *GOTTLOB FREGE: Philosophical and Mathematical Correspondence* (Basil Blackwell, 1980). See especially pages 159, 163, 169. I have used the original "Bedeutung" where the translator wrote "meaning". I wish to thank Joseph Almog for bringing these apt quotations to my attention.

34. Frege's incredulity surely stems from the point that for an 'object of thought' to be an object of *thought,* all of its parts have to be thinkable. According to Frege, material objects are not, in this sense, thinkable. They are presented to us only indirectly, being represented by some concept. It is these representations that are to be the parts of an object of thought. There is an asymmetry in intelligibility here; one which I have observed in myself and others. From Russell's point of view, Frege's theory looks rather like a subtheory of his own in which the singular propositions are excluded, and thus proper names that do not abbreviate descriptions are excluded. From Frege's point of view, Russell's way of 'extending' his (Frege's) ideas is utterly baffling because it seems to miss the point (as well as the method) of the whole enterprise.

35. Quine is aware that the Conservation of Intensionality governs the analysis of psychological verbs. The move (be it retreat or advance) to replace intensional entities with linguistic ones shifts the intensionality from the objects of a theory to its relations, from what Quine calls *ontology* to what he calls *ideology*. This shift is one that Quine has ever been happy to make. An interesting earlier discussion of these matters was set off by section 13 of *Meaning and Necessity* and trails through Carnap's "On Belief-Sentences: Reply to Alonzo Church" [reprinted in the second edition of *Meaning and Necessity*] which contains further references.

36. The result of surrounding an expression with arc quotes is here taken to abbreviate the expression formed by: quoting the contained expression, followed (for the alphabetically first variable α free in the contained expression) by $\ulcorner$ with respect to α as value of $\urcorner$, followed by α in quotes, followed (in alphabetical order for all other variables β which occur free in the contained expression) by $\ulcorner$, β as value of$\urcorner$, followed by β in quotes.

37. We *close* formulas, resulting in a *closed formula*. We *valuate* formulas, resulting in a *valuated formula*. Both are kinds of sentences. A sentence achieved entirely by closure is a *closed sentence;* one achieved partially by valuation is a *valuated sentence*.

38. It is easy to represent both kinds of valuated expressions, if traditional expres-

sions are represented as sequences of primitive symbols. But it is not quite as easy as it seems. See Appendix C: Arcs Versus Corners.

39. Quine made the point with a different metaphor in §12 of *Mathematical Logic* (Norton, 1940; Revised Edition published by Harvard, 1951, 1981).

40. More on the technology of arc-quotation in Appendix C.

41. Church has given reasons to think that sentences will never perfectly mimic propositions. ["On Carnap's Analysis of Statements of Assertion and Belief", *Analysis* 10 (1950); reprinted in Linsky's *Reference and Modality*.]

42. If the variable takes on an infinite number of values, there will be exactly as many $entences as values. Thus, in doing model theoretic semantics, if the domain of a model forms a set (as is usual), the collection of $entences of the model will also form a set.

43. Quine's well known dictum: to be is to be the value of a variable, draws the line at the point of introduction of the bound variable. This is already *within* nominalization as I conceive it. The reason for this discrepancy between Quine and me is that Quine is concerned to show how far we can go with *virtual* nominalization, such as contextually defined notations whose nominal syntax vanishes in primitive notation, before reaching the absolute barrier of variables bound to 'referential' quantifiers.

The importance he attaches to this barrier may have contributed to his downplaying other uses of variable binding operators such as substitutional quantification (a legitimate form of virtual nominalization) and the use of variables bound to non-referential purely grammatical operators. It is mildly ironic that in the elegant transition from the logic of terms to quantification theory in the fourth edition of *Methods of Logic* (Harvard, 1982) (sections 21 and 22, newly written for this edition; see also the first half of "Predicates, Terms, and Classes" in *Theories and Things*), the section entitled "The Bound Variable" involves a non-referential variable binding operator used to mimic relative clause constructions in English, a kind of lambda-operator less reference. These bound variables, "mere devices for pronominal cross-reference", have no values. The two sections reinforce one's view that on Quine's conception, ontological commitment should be seen as flowing fundamentally from domains of quantifiers and only derivatively from 'values' of variables.

44. A. Tarski, "Der Wahrheitsbegriff in den formalisierten Sprachen", *Studia Philosophica* 1 (1935); translated as "The Concept of Truth in Formalized Languages" in A. Tarski, *Logic, Semantics, Metamathematics* (Oxford, 1956).

45. R. Montague, "Syntactical Treatments of Modality with Corollaries on Reflection Principles and Finite Axiomatizability", *Acta Philosophica Fennica* Fasc. XVI (1963); reprinted in R. Thomason (ed.), *Formal Philosophy: Selected Papers of Richard Montague* (Yale University Press, 1974).

46. D. Kaplan and R. Montague, "A Paradox Regained", *Notre Dame Journal of Formal Logic* 1 (1960); reprinted in *Formal Philosophy: Selected Papers of Richard Montague*.

47. The damage it will do depends on the nature of the operator and whether avoidance maneuvers, such as those due to Martin and Woodruff ["On Representing 'true-in-L' in L," *Philosophia* 5 (1975)] and to Kripke ["Outline of a Theory of Truth", *Journal of Philosophy* 72 (1975)], are taken.

48. Dana Scott offered similar advice on modal logic.

49. There are two possible explanations, depending on how we conceptualize occurrences of variables within (standard) quotation marks. If we regard the 'quotation name' as a single, simple symbol, and the occurrence of *"x"* as accidental, like the *"x"* in *"ex post facto"*, we might say that the variable does not occur *as a variable.*

This would be to regard quotation names as not really forming *contexts* at all. Alternatively, if we regard quotation marks as a non-extensional functor, and the occurrence of *"x"* as part of the argument expression to the functor, we might say that free occurrences of variables within the argument expression are no longer free after application of the functor. (I hesitate to say that the quotes 'bind' the free occurrences of variables.) Nathan Salmon has urged that both conceptualizations be taken seriously.

50. Why then, you ask suspiciously, denominalize at all? In part for the reasons of the preceding section; in part to explore a model of a 'quotation context' along the lines of the second alternative of the preceding footnote; in part for future use; in part for fun.

51. Possible doubt is raised in the autobiographical footnote to Appendix C.

52. Raised in Q&PA, discussed in "Reply to Kaplan".

53. I cannot resist pointing out that if indexicals appear in the direct discourse, we cannot be *too* literal. "Ralph **Says-quote** I am a spy" does not imply "Ralph **Says-that** I am a spy". (Do not allow reactionary sentiments to make you uncomfortable with the naked "I" in the **Says-quote** context. Remember the phantom arc quotes.)

54. It is an oddity that $\ulcorner$**Says-quote** (ϕ and ψ)$\urcorner$ implies $\ulcorner$**Says-quote** $\phi\urcorner$ and $\ulcorner$**Says-quote** $\psi\urcorner$. The converse, of course, fails.

55. It is what we may call the *direct discourse,* or *literal,* epistemic notions that are subject to this liability, like the notion of belief according to which to believe ϕ is, roughly, to be disposed to assent to ϕ. (As we have seen, the direct discourse structure of the intuitive notions does not prevent its being brought into operator form.) We can construct *indirect discourse* versions of belief that allow any degree of latitude in our reports, thus building in closure conditions.

56. Consider an arbitrary operator **O** and the sentence:

(P) $(\exists x)\mathbf{O}(x = \alpha)$

where α is not a variable. Does (P) confer the special privilege of acting as an instantial term upon α (as Quine claims in "Intensions Revisited," page 120)? (P) is true in a model just in case a valuation of $\ulcorner(x = \alpha)\urcorner$ is in the extension of **O** in that model. Now suppose $\ulcorner\alpha$ is a spy$\urcorner$ is also in the extension of **O**. What requires any valuation of "*x* is a spy" to be in the extension? Nothing, unless the extension were closed under a certain form of logical consequence, but it need not be. Thus (P) alone does not imply that α can serve as instantial term for application of quantifier rules.

57. More strictly, they added good old first order logic to modal logic. They did not, like Carnap, Church, and others, rethink the nature of quantification theory as it interacts with modality. See R.C. Barcan and R.B. Marcus, "A Functional Calculus of First Order Based on Strict Implication", *Journal of Symbolic Logic* 11 (1946).

58. Regarding the subtleties, see, for example, S. Kripke's interesting discussion in "Semantical Considerations on Modal Logic", especially pp. 88ff. [*Acta Philosophica Fennica* Fasc. XVI (1963); reprinted in Linsky's *Reference and Modality*]. The subtleties may give us a clearer view of how first order logic *should* be formulated.

59. *Proceedings of the XIth International Congress of Philosophy* 14 (1953); reprinted in *The Ways of Paradox.*

60. He even goes so far—too far, in my view—as to propose a new criterion for opacity. "Fundamentally the proper criterion of referential opacity turns on quantification rather than naming, and is this: a referentially opaque context is one that cannot properly be *quantified into* . . ." All of this leaves me profoundly puzzled regarding Quine's thinking between 1953 and 1956 (Q&PA) when, as is shown in the passages quoted in section I above, he reverts to the old criterion for referential opacity and to the alleged theorem.

Note also that the very possibility of contextually defining constant singular terms is challenged in Appendix A.

61. Quine discusses iteration briefly in "Three Grades of Modal Involvement".

62. There is room here for decision. I here treat "unmarried" as an atomic predicate, and treat atomic predicates as true, in a model, only of the members of the domain of the model. Other approaches are possible.

63. For the familiar operators, the relativized forms are expressible in terms of the unrelativized. This is a happy accident, not an inevitability. For example, we cannot express the relativized majority operator, $\ulcorner$Most x such that ϕ are such that $\psi\urcorner$, in terms of the absolute operator $\ulcorner$Most x are such that $\Gamma\urcorner$. In this case relativization might require introducing a new operator.

64. I have assumed that the language contains no singular terms other than variables and descriptions. If individual constants and operation symbols are present, there are choices as to how relativization should proceed. If we wish to require that operations be closed within the domain, additional clauses would be added to the antecedent.

65. In a richer notation, the valuated predicate would be: ("$\lambda x (x = y)$" under the assignment: a to "y")

66. In a sense, the essentiality to its unique bearer of a singular property like *being a* flows from the essentiality to all individuals of the general property *being self-identical*. But mark well the difference between the two properties. The uniquely characterizing properties, which we all see as imminent in the *general* property, could never be extracted without singularity. It is singular properties that make the identity of indiscernibles look like a *principle*.

67. More properly attributed to R.C. Barcan ["The Identity of Individuals in a Strict Functional Calculus of First Order", *Journal of Symbolic Logic* 12 (1947)].

68. There is a way other than by 'substitutivity' to derive Marcus's law from "$(x) \square (x = x)$". See Appendix D: The Second Law of Identity.

69. A speculation: it may be that what distinguishes logical truth from the invidious forms of necessary truth is simply the fungability of individuals.

70. "Modalities and Intensional Languages".

71. "Naming and Necessity", in G. Harman and D. Davidson (eds.), *Semantics of Natural Language* (D. Reidel, 1972); revised edition published as a separate monograph, *Naming and Necessity* (Basil Blackwell, 1980).

72. The same result is obtained if the method of proxy names is used, the names are Quinized into descriptions, the descriptions are Russelled away, and the existence condition is dropped for the reason stated above.

73. An argument of Quine may be regarded as pressing this point in the opposite direction. If we were to regard arbitrary uniquely specifying predicates as proxies, there would be a 'modal collapse' of necessity into truth. See, for example, *Word and Object*, page 198.

74. See, for example, page 155 second edition of *From A Logical Point of View*, and elsewhere.

75. *Word and Object*, page 199.

76. I have purposely chosen a formulation that avoids complex singular terms such as "{Quine}" in favor of predicates and quantifiers. I could have avoided even "Quine" if he is right.

77. Another alternative, not ruled out by modest methods, is that singleton Quine would be empty, while our null set would have singleton Quine (an empty set) as its only member. This seems bizarre.

78. For references to further reasoning about these matters and for an enlightening

discussion, see the long footnote 10 on page 89 of N. Salmon's *Reference and Essence* (Princeton University Press, 1981). The point of the footnote, like the overall point of this valuable book, is that I.A.E. is not derivable, as some may have thought, from generally accepted non-essentialist premises. On this, Quine, Salmon, and I stand together.

79. Recall that it is just uniterated necessity that is at issue. A $entence of the language of first order logic is a logical consequence of a set of $entences if it is true in every model they are.

80. For further reflections on the relation between $\boxed{M}$ and $\boxed{L}$ see Appendix E: Schematic Validity and Modal Logic.

81. *Synthese* 14 (1962), p. 140.

82. Found with the help of Dagfinn Føllesdal. I note that the argument does not appear in the approximately coeval first edition of *From A Logical Point of View*.

83. Terence Parsons, in his elegant little paper ''Essentialism and Quantified Modal Logic'' [*Philosophical Review* 78 (1969); reprinted in L. Linsky's *Reference and Modality*] follows the methodology of Quine and Marcus [''Essentialism in Modal Logic'', *Nous* 1 (1967)] but gives a different syntactical characterization of the 'form' of I.A.E. Parsons starts from a paradigm like:

$(\exists x) \ \Box \ x$ is rational $\cdot \ (\exists x) \sim \Box \ x$ is rational

and generalizes it, in a subtle way, to account for other than monadic formulas. His result is opposite to Quine's. Using what amounts to logical necessity—but under the description ''maximal Kripke model''—he shows that no sentence of the invidious form is a theorem or even true at any 'world' of the model. The paper also contains interesting remarks regarding I.A.E. in modalized number theory.

84. Parsons and Marcus must also have this idea in the back of their minds, for whenever they came up with a syntactical characterization of invidious essentialism that *was* satisfied by what I call 'logical necessity', they rejected it as too weak.

85. Unless we could make out a case that, like the distinction between individuals that are identical and those that are not, the seemingly invidious distinctions were logical distinctions.

86. *Word and Object*, pp. 198–199.

87. *Knowledge and Belief* (Cornell, 1962).

88. Of course, the fact that there is no methodological requirement to use surrogates does not mean that their use is always inappropriate. In the case of the propositional attitudes, in contrast to the case of modality, it would not be unnatural to expect the classification of valuated $entences to be dependent on a prior classification of the closed sentences, and it would not be unnatural to think of this dependence in terms of surrogates. At least I did not think it unnatural when I proceeded this way in ''Quantifying In''. I now have some doubts.

89. What we count as part of context will affect what linguistic forms are contextually determinate (as will the way in which we individuate 'meanings'). But one can imagine cases in whch even a wide notion of context does not fix the 'meaning' narrowly enough for the relativized notion of truth. Vague terms may be of this sort.

90. Quine does seem to acknowledge that relativity to context need not unfit a language for completely precise use when he tells us how 'eternal' expressions are introduced on the basis of demonstratives. See for example section 21 of *Word and Object*.

91. In *The Ways of Paradox*.

92. See my ''On the Logic of Demonstratives'', *Journal of Philosophical Logic* 8

(1979); reprinted in P. French et al. (eds.), *Contemporary Perspectives in the Philosophy of Language* (University of Minnesota Press, 1979).

93. I have two highly amorphous worries regarding Quine's conception of scientific language. My first worry is that he too much divorces the resources appropriate to the pronouncement of scientific results (eternal sentences) from the resources required to do science collaboratively in the laboratory. I emphasize ''required'' rather than ''used'', because Quine sometimes writes as if the language of the laboratory (with all its fugitive features: tense, demonstratives, indexicals, perceptual reports, vagueness, etc.) has only practical advantages over the 'eternal' language of the lectern. My second, and related, worry is that the conceptual and linguistic resources of indexicals may be essential to us because of our subjective perspective on the world (roughly, the way perceptual information flows in and action flows out). Our subjective perspective requires special, non-eternal, resources for internal processing. It is a perspective which science can study but cannot, and should not, take. For relevant views I largely share, see T. Burge, ''Belief *De Re*'', *Journal of Philosophy* 74 (1977), and J. Perry's ''The Problem of the Essential Indexical'', *Nous* 13 (1979).

94. There is a question, in purported cases of implicit contextuality, whether what is at issue is truth or conversational propriety. Quine would probably reject this dichotomy in the critical cases.

95. ''Reply to Professor Marcus''.

96. The new technology is not yet fully developed and is untested in the marketplace, but let us assume it pans out.

97. Again, much more detail is required to solidify the two pictures and to make plausible the links to current theories.

98. Joseph Almog even wonders whether logical necessity, as I characterize it, should be considered a modality at all, or should it be thought of merely as a matter of 'combinatorics'.

99. Explicit, stipulative surrogatism could make it appear that one had been forced out of the hard line. But it could also make it appear that one had been forced into it.

100. It should be noted that the Fregean analysis of intensional verbs, as developed by Church, does not require this transformation. See section I of ''How to Russell a Frege-Church''.

101. Alonzo Church, ''The Need for Abstract Entities in Semantic Analysis'', in *Proceedings of the American Academy of Arts and Sciences* 80 (1951): footnote 14. Church's examples are: ''I am thinking of Pegasus'', ''Ponce de Leon searched for the fountain of youth'', and ''Barbara Villiers was less chaste than Diana''.

102. In ''On the Nature of Certain Philosophical Entities'', *The Monist* 53 (1960); reprinted in *Formal Philosophy: Selected Papers of Richard Montague*. The other three verbs cited are: ''conceives'', ''is about'', and ''thinks of''.

103. Or, in a less common sense of ''fear'', to *revere* them.

104. There are the makings here of an *ad hominem* against Quine's rejection of relational attitudes. First we provoke him to seek something notionally. (''Quick, get a policeman, any policeman'' we shout.) Though he may have no relational attitudes, his own analysis (with our amendment) requires that he strive to have one. How long will he be able to maintain this ambivalent state of rejection mingled with desire. (I predict that he will soon be driven to utter contextuality.)

105. In J. Hintikka, et al. (eds.), *Approaches to Natural Language* (D. Reidel, 1973); reprinted in *Formal Philosophy: Selected Papers of Richard Montague*.

106. By treating only *sentence-forming* sentential operators, I swallow up the sub-

ject (e.g. "Ralph") of a propositional attitude verb (e.g. "believes that") into the verb (e.g. "Ralph-believes-that"). It is natural to want to break-out the subject, perhaps for quantification, and this is easily done. Nothing of theoretical importance would change, though the description of the syntax would be more tedious.

107. The only compound predicate expressions I permit are those formed by syntactically *de re* operators. Quine takes a different approach to the syntax of the syntactically *de re*, introducing compound predicate expressions in their own right, in a way suggesting that they might well appear within the operand of the syntactically *de dicto*. If so, Quine's syntax provides more expressive power to the syntactically *de dicto*, and thereby affects some of the metalogical issues discussed below, in particular, those involving the 'translation' of the syntactically *de re* back into the syntactically *de dicto*. D. Wiggins and C. Peacocke both follow Quine's syntax in their treatment of the syntactically *de re*. ["The *De Re* 'Must': A Note on the Logical Form of Essentialist Claims" and "An Appendix to David Wiggins' 'Note'", both in G. Evans and J. McDowell (eds.) *Truth and Meaning* (Oxford, 1976)]. I do not think my syntax superior to Quine's, but it is simpler and steers clear of some intriguing issues that are best held in abeyance for now.

Note that I italicize the variable binding *de re* operators. I would use negation as an example if I could figure out how to italicize a tilde.

108. Quine appears to share this view. In Q&PA, Quine denies:

$$[(\textbf{\textit{Bel}}\ x)\ (x \text{ is a spy} . \sim x \text{ is a spy})]\ \text{Ortcutt}$$

(see (23) of Q&PA), while affirming what is virtually:

$$[(\textbf{\textit{Bel}}\ xy)(x \text{ is a spy} . \sim y \text{ is a spy})]\ \text{Ortcutt Ortcutt}$$

What Quine actually affirms (in (15) and (22) of Q&PA) is equivalent to:

(i) $([\textbf{\textit{Bel}}\ y)\ y \text{ is a spy}]\ x . [(\textbf{\textit{Bel}}\ y) \sim y \text{ is a spy}]\ x).$

Because Ralph might fail to 'put two and two together' (i.e. to believe the conjunction of whatever he believes separately), we cannot immediately conclude:

$$[(\textbf{\textit{Bel}}\ xy)(x \text{ is a spy} . \sim y \text{ is a spy})]\ xx$$

But I think Quine would not object to counting it as true. We could easily modify the story to make it as plausible as (i).

109. I believe that we can capture the form of closure that we would attribute to *Bel* if Ralph were logically omniscient by using the methods of section XIV.

110. I assume that **Bel** distributes over conjunction. Then (28) yields $\ulcorner(x)((x = \text{the Mayor}) \supset \textbf{Bel}\ (x \text{ is a spy}))\urcorner$ and $\ulcorner(\exists x)\ \textbf{Bel}\ (x = \text{the Mayor})\urcorner$. Hence if the latter sufficed to make "the Mayor" an instantial term, the former would yield (29). This result is not dependent on the use of *belief* rather than *knowledge*. The story could easily be amplified in a way that would justify a knowledge claim in (28). Still (29) would not follow.

111. Even putting aside the special delicacies introduced by iteration of propositional attitudes.

112. An analogous difficulty appears if the translation is attempted using universal quantifiers.

113. I speak intuitively. For the matter to be a well defined logical problem would require model theoretic or axiomatic formulations of the two forms of a particular operator.

114. These matters arose in connection with footnote 5.

115. The operator $\ulcorner\textbf{\textit{Bel}}^s\ v_1...v_n)\urcorner$ might also be taken to form an n-1 place predicate, omitting the redundant argument expression "Ralph". I prefer it as it is.

116. In Q&PA Quine doesn't say how, in general, to translate quantified *de dicto* forms into the *de re* form. In "Intensions Revisited" the specific form of a bilateral

interpretation between the syntactically *de dicto* and the syntactically *de re* is proposed, first for necessity and then for belief. There Quine omits to articulate.

117. The idea of arc-quotes stems from my analysis in "Quantifying In" of Quine's corners.

118. Autobiographical note: When I first set out to try to construct a non-Fregean semantics (in "Dthat" [in P. Cole (ed.), *Pragmatics: Syntax and Semantics* 9 (Academic Press, 1978); reprinted in *Contemporary Perspectives in the Philosophy of Language*], written during the summer of 1970) I worked from the idea that the use of a demonstrative could be thought of as a device for putting an object into the very syntax of the sentence, as if we were to display the object and then utter a predicate, like the caption "wants to party" worn on a T-shirt. From this point of view, a closed sentence containing a demonstrative is, as it were, syntactically incomplete. "The mere wording, as it is given in writing, is not a complete expression. . . . It must be supplemented by certain accompanying conditions of utterance . . . . The pointing of fingers, hand movements, glances may belong here too." (Who said that in 1918?) Thus a *use* of a closed sentence containing a demonstrative becomes a token of a valuated sentence. (I here contrast a *use* with an arbitrary token such as this one: It is blue.) When the linguistic tokens are not sounds, but material objects: piles of ink or twisted neon tubes, it seems easy to set another material object among them. There remains the singular result that the object is a token of itself.

119. It has long been my view that this 'ambiguity', when translated back into the intensional framework of singular and general propositions, is one of the keys to understanding Russell's lengthy 'unintelligible' argument against Frege in "On Denoting", an argument which I see as prefiguring Carnap's worries about oblique senses. But that's a story that also requires a lengthy argument.

120. It was Saul Kripke who first pointed out that one of the wanton systems failed to satisfy a quantifier law. See footnote 13 of *Naming and Necessity*. D. Lewis does not agree. See his *Philosophical Papers*, Vol. 1 (Oxford, 1983), pp. 45–46.

121. I have taken the easy way by treating logical necessity as preordained by classical logic. A more probing, less prejudiced, investigation of logical necessity, of what is the domain of logic proper, would blur the dividing line between logical and metaphysical necessity.

122. There is, of course, a third equivalent notion, the notion of *derivational validity*, based on the idea of a truth preserving syntactical transformation.

123. See Chapter 4 of *Philosophy of Logic* (Prentice Hall, 1970). I should note, however, that although he professes tolerance, "The theorems establishing equivalence among very unlike formulations of a notion—logical truth or whatever—are of course the important part. Which of the formulations we choose as the somehow official definition is less important.", he stacks the deck in two ways: by taking as his official explicandum, "a sentence is logically true if all sentences are true that share its logical structure", and by introducing what I call *modal validity* directly by a set theoretical representation, with no mention of the idea that the sets could be thought of as representing possible extensions of the predicates.

124. This result was first obtained by Steven K. Thomason ["A New Representation of S5", *Notre Dame Journal of Formal Logic* XIV (1973)] based on the completeness theorem of Saul Kripke ["A Completeness Theorem in Modal Logic", *Journal of Symbolic Logic* 24 (1959)].

125. Carnap develops almost exactly the modal validities of logical necessity in "Modalities and Quantification".

126. Church doubts that it should be a principle of logic that there are true propo-

sitions that are not necessary ["A Formulation of the Logic of Sense and Denotation", page 22], and his heuristic models do indeed make all true propositions necessary when there is only one 'possible world' ("Outline of a Revised Formulation of the Logic of Sense and Denotation"). This suggests to me that he has metaphysical necessity in mind, despite the fact that he calls his notion "logical necessity". In my understanding of Church's system both logical necessity and metaphysical necessity are used. The first to formalize the principle of individuation for senses: that expressions express the same sense if and only if they are equivalent by logical necessity. The second to capture the notion of necessity associated with the heuristic of 'possible worlds'. I should caution that if my understanding is correct, Church erred in the way he used the heuristic models to individuate senses. Hence, I have probably misunderstood him.

TABLE OF CONTENTS

REPLY TO DAVID KAPLAN

It is providential that such a long essay should be fun to read. It was also rather a workout. Fun the way squash or handball is said to be fun.

In 1943, Kaplan recalls, I took the failure of substitutivity as my criterion of opacity and then proclaimed the incoherence of quantifying in. This he calls my "alleged theorem". In 1953 he finds me taking the incoherence of quantifying in as my criterion of opacity, and thus bypassing the alleged theorem. In 1955, when I wrote "Quantifiers and Propositional Attitudes", he finds me reverting to the stance of 1943. What happened, he wonders, in between?

His puzzlement comes of his over-formal representation of these matters in terms of criterion and alleged theorem. In 1943 I did argue from failure of substitutivity to incoherence of quantifying in, and thenceforward both traits served me indifferently as marking opacity. My reason for treating the quantificational aspect as primary in my 1953 paper, "Three Grades of Modal Involvement", was explained earlier that year in *From a Logical Point of View,* p. 145. My reason was that the substitutivity consideration hinges on constant singular terms, which are mere frills that can be "Quinized into descriptions," as Kaplan puts it, "and Russelled away." But I continued to regard opacity as describable either way, and when I was writing "Quantifiers and Propositional Attitudes" in 1955 it was convenient to focus on substitutivity.

My actual use of the term 'opacity' dates only from *From a Logical Point of View;* in the 1943 paper I spoke rather of not purely designative occurrences of terms. By 1953, along with the emergence of 'opacity', my term 'designative occurrence' had evolved to 'referential occurrence'; and in 1955, in "Quantifiers and Propositional Attitudes", I oscillated between 'occurrence' and 'position'. I did not see myself as proving an alleged theorem *more geometrico,* early or late; my business was clarification and persuasion in an informal medium.

Kaplan conjectures an eight-step reconstruction *more geometrico* of my proof of the alleged theorem, and rightly impugns his Step 4 as not following from Step 2. This is just where my last-mentioned terminological reform is wanted: 'position' for 'occurrence'. Kaplan remarks on this change of terminology, but makes inadequate use of it. If we rephrase *both* Steps 2 and 4 to refer to positions, then Step 4 does follow from Step 2. They come to read as follows.

Step 2.   If a position in a formula is purely referential, then the truth value of the formula depends only on what the term in that position designates and not on how it designates.

Step 4.   If α and β designate the same thing, but $\phi\alpha$ and $\phi\beta$ differ in truth value, then the position of α in $\phi\alpha$ (and of β in $\phi\beta$) is not purely referential.

To whatever extent Kaplan's original versions of Steps 2 and 4 reflect my earlier tacit reasoning, they reflect that I was position-minded all along and that the changed terminology was overdue.

There is a further reason for speaking primarily of position rather than occurrence if my old adjective 'designative' is retained instead of 'referential'; namely, as I said in Dubrovnik (cf. Kaplan's note 19), we want those positions to admit variables, and variables cannot be said to designate.

Purported proofs aside, is the alleged theorem true? It says, in a word, that a position that resists substitutivity of identity cannot meaningfully be quantified. Does this mean that no meaning can be assigned to such quantification? Surely not; meaningless expressions are precisely the ones that stand unencumbered and receptive to the assignment of any meanings we like. What I was pointing out was the muddle that besets our original conception of quantification in such cases. Such quantifications do commonly serve good purposes and seem to make good sense until scrutinized in the light of what the quantifier is literally taken to mean. So, in ''Quantifiers and Propositional Attitudes'', I explored paraphrases that might serve those same good purposes while not straining our conception of quantification.

In 1968, then, there emerged footnote 3 of Kaplan's ''Quantifying In'': if the quantifyings in are meaningless, why not *assign* them meanings—the very meanings offered in those paraphrases? Splendid! When I read, admired, and responded to ''Quantifying In'' in 1968 I somehow missed or failed to appreciate that footnote, but nine years later I hit upon the same idea myself. By a fluke I discovered or rediscovered Kaplan's footnote before returning the printer's proofs of ''Intensions Revisited'', so I managed to acknowledge it.

Should we say that the alleged theorem was true of naive quantification but that we now have a sophisticated version of quantification to which it does not apply? Or should we say that the alleged theorem was false and the quantifying in made good sense all along, namely, the same sense that was expressed in such paraphrases as I offered in "Quantifiers and Propositional Attitudes"? Either account seems all right.

But today the analysis of quantifying in that is afforded by Kaplan's footnote and "Intensions Revisited" is in Kaplan's eyes disconcertingly artificial— "a logician's trick". In the essay now before us he strives for a more natural and illuminating analysis. He revives Russell's idea, which has seemed so bizarre, of letting all manner of objects figure as components of propositions— thus "Mont Blanc (with all its snowfields), . . . the object 'Quine' (with all its vowels)," the object Quine (with all its bowels). His resulting propositions are what he calls valuated sentences, or $entences. They are amalgams of expressions and other things. Such an amalgam presents no ontological problem; I think of it as a sequence, in the mathematical sense, whose elements are atomic signs and other things. In an appendix Kaplan incorporates some pointy brackets *(spitze Klammern)* into his $entences at certain points to avert, I gather, a subtle confusion of use and mention. Where they bracket a non-expression, such as Mont Blanc, perhaps the pointy brackets can be seen as quotation marks to form a name of the object—as if we were to plant an open-quote in France and a close-quote in Italy in such a way as to bracket Mont Blanc and all its snowfields. The interpretation of $entences as sequences can take the pointy brackets in its stride. However, the resulting analysis does not strike me as more natural than what was afforded by Kaplan's old footnote and "Intensions Revisited." Perhaps its added virtue lies rather in accommodating unspecifiable objects.

We turn then to essentialism. I accept the notion of logical truth, as Kaplan observes. I accept it in an epistemologically innocent way, on a par with chemical truth, economic truth, and ornithological truth; it is merely a question in each case of what expressions occur essentially rather than vacuously. When we modalize logical truth into logical necessity by shifting from a predicate of sentences to an operator on sentences, essentialism supervenes. It is a benign essentialism, Kaplan urges, in that whatever is essential to one object is essential to all. There is no gainsaying its benignity, as essentialism goes. The same could be said of a modal logic based not on logical necessity but on its chemical, economic, or ornithological analogue. Most of the interest that modal logic has commanded, however, hinges rather on a notion of metaphysical necessity that invokes rigid designators and a semantics of possible worlds; and this course is committed to an invidious essentialism, as Kaplan calls it, in which an essential trait of one object can be an accident of another. Moreover it is this pattern, rather than the benign one, that I see as useful and customary in daily discourse, though only meaningful in context. See my reply to Bohnert.

A striking divergence between Kaplan's intuitions and mine is keynoted midway in his section XVIII, where he writes that "some metaphysician may assert that all truths are metaphysically necessary. . . . And it wouldn't be an abandonment of modality." I would not see what point the metaphysician was trying to make, for want of invidious distinctions.

Kaplan wonders, in section XXIII, whether my attitude toward opacity and quantifying in would have been different if I had taken tense rather than quotation as my paradigm of opacity. Possibly so. At any rate it should be clear that I now recognize quantifying in, if only in the for Kaplan perhaps obsolescent sense of his old footnote and my "Intensions Revisited".

I have appreciated parallels between tense and modality, but one readily sees why I have not dwelt on tense and pursued its logic. In *Methods of Logic* (§ 31), *Word and Object* (§ 36), and elsewhere I have stressed the importance, rather, for logic and metaphysics alike, of thinking tenselessly in four dimensions. Kaplan's puzzles in section XVII about the unit class to which I now belong indicate the sort of thing that a tenseless quadridimensionalism dissolves, especially when such quadridimensionalism is coupled with a wholesome insensitivity to metaphysical modalities.

I do indeed prize quotation as paradigm, especially for the propositional attitudes. Kaplan's amusing operator **'says-quote'** is the ultimate attitudinative.

Kaplan raises in section XX an interesting point about

(1) $\ulcorner(\exists x) \ \square \ (x = \alpha)\urcorner$

and its epistemic analogue

(2) $\ulcorner(\exists x)($Ralph knows that $x = \alpha)\urcorner$

where α is a singular term. I had taken these to be the conditions for rigidity of α—that is, legitimacy of α in instantiating quantifications. Kaplan points out that since (y) (Ralph knows that $y = y$), it follows that

(3) $(y) \ (\exists x)$ (Ralph knowns that $x = y$).

We may note similarly that since $(y) \ \square \ (y = y)$, it follows that

(4) $(y) \ (\exists x) \ \square \ (x = y)$.

However, this does not vitiate the criteria (1) and (2), for we cannot legitimately put α for 'y' in (4) and (3) to infer (1) and (2) unless α is rigid. But it does leave one uncomfortable with the reading of (2) in which I followed Hintikka, namely, as $\ulcorner$Ralph knows who α is$\urcorner$; for (3) then says that Ralph knows who everyone is.

Kaplan's footnote 43 reflects an alarming misconception of my views. I never regarded my bound variables of term abstraction as ontologically innocent. They are objectual and quite on a par with my variables of quantification. I claimed ontological innocence only for the term abstracts themselves, taken as relative clauses and contrasted with the ontologically committed class abstracts of set theory.

The utility of variables and pronouns is indeed combinatory, but that is not an alternative to reification. According to my metaphysics it is a major utility of reification itself.

Whether a variable is objectual or substitutional is a separate question, hinging partly on exhaustiveness of designation. But even substitutional quantification is not ontologically innocent. It is just ontologically inscrutable, pending a choice of objectual translation. To be is, as always, to be the value of an objectual variable.

Finally let me call attention to Kaplan's keen detection and ingenious correction, in his footnote 27 and toward the end of his Appendix B, of a subtle error in my "Intensions Revisited" (*Theories and Things,* middle of page 116).

W.V.Q.

11

Harold N. Lee

DISCOURSE AND EVENT: THE LOGICIAN AND REALITY

I

S ymbols are the stock in trade of the logician, whether they be the words of a natural language or the more abstruse ideograms of an artificial language. What the logician in his proper vocation deals with is not grasped by perception. Logical relations are general and abstract in that they apply indiscriminately to prescinded aspects of different concrete instances of perception. Hence, they must be expressed in symbolism. Human rationality depends on the ability to make and use, to respond and react to symbols. Verbal symbols are articulated into languages, and elaborate rules of syntax are set up to facilitate clarity and precision of communication. Both the symbols of language and the rules of syntax contain enough arbitrary features to ensure that multitudes of different languages can be constructed.

Considerations such as these are sufficient to account for Quine's emphasis on words and translation. An investigation of the problems of translating one language into another, especially where there is no initial common basis, can shed light both on the relation of language to experience and on the structure of language itself. Symbols, in the simplest cases, refer to aspects of direct conscious experience, and the articulation of discourse can be surrogate for the connectedness of experience. Grammar and syntax study the structure of specific languages, but it is within the province of logic to study the structure of language in general and the articulation of symbol systems so that they can become the vehicles of conceptual schemes whereby the connectedness of experience can be grasped and understood.

Experience is made up of events; discourse is made up of language. Men communicate by discoursing about events, and it is assumed, at first naively and then more critically, that the events are the same for all those who communicate successfully. The evolutionary survival of man has depended upon successful communication. As discourse can be broken down into words and the way they go together, so it would seem that events can be broken down into objects and the relations between them. Quine's ontology is an ontology of existent objects though he is not dogmatic about it. A person who would be satisfied with phenomenalism could have an ontology of events, but Quine is not so inclined.[1] He holds that commitment to objects is implicit in the conceptual scheme that makes sense out of raw experience (LPV 16 and 44): the existence of objects is bound up with the structure of logic. Quine holds that to be an entity is to be the value of a bound variable (LPV 13).

In circumstances such as these, if a person is concerned with the problems inherent in the relation between the symbol system of logic on the one hand and the fields of ontology and epistemology on the other, it would seem incumbent upon him to undertake a thoroughgoing analysis of symbols and their use. This Quine does not undertake. He takes symbolism for granted, and as a result he is able by a flourish of Occam's razor to keep meanings out of his ontological menagerie. He holds that since meanings are not entities they do not belong to the ontological realm. He recognizes a difference between meaningful and unmeaningful sentences, but nevertheless he dispenses with meanings. Later, I shall point out, following C. S. Peirce's theory of signs, that a semiotic theory of meaning can define meanings satisfactorily without hypostatization, and thus can avoid the strange appearance of Quine's doctrine of meaningful sentences without meanings.

In this essay I shall confine my attention to Quine's epistemology and ontology. I shall not treat of his logic proper; in particular, I shall not challenge the extensionality of his logic. I am convinced that in a system of pure logic the notation must be used and interpreted according to the principle of extension, and that when intensions are introduced they are applications. My acceptance of extensionality in logic does not carry over into epistemology, however, or to the way that logic impinges on epistemology or ontology.

I am sympathetic with many of Quine's conclusions in the general fields, and would be willing to state some of them more emphatically than he does— for example that there are no absolutes, and that the conditions of knowledge warrant a doctrine of underdetermination. On the major point of ontology, however, I maintain that Quine has not altogether freed himself of that objectionable but almost ubiquitous trait of logicians to constrain reality to fit within the confines of their logic.[2]

William James, in his *Principles of Psychology,* directed attention to what he called "the psychologist's fallacy";[3] namely, the confusion of *what* the psychologist thinks about with the *way* in which he thinks about it. In a somewhat parallel fashion I shall call the tendency of many logicians to constrain reality to fit within the way they symbolize it "the logician's fallacy". Quine's doctrine of ontological commitment, though not so blatant a commission of this fallacy as may be found in the writings of many logicians, is, I maintain, not free from it.

The particular considerations upon which my adverse criticism will center are Quine's ontology of objects and his dismissal of meanings. In both doctrines he commits the logician's fallacy; and the doctrines are related to each other insofar as the ontology of objects demands that what is not an entity does not have ontological status. Since meanings are not entities according to Quine they cannot be allowed. On the other hand, I hold that meanings are essential as part of the subject matter of epistemology, but that they can and ought to be defined and used without hypostatization. Quine rejects the sort of analyticity and synonymy and entailment that involves meanings. He often expresses a pragmatic point of view (LPV 20, 46, 79), and is held by many of his contemporaries to be a pragmatist. I hope to show, however, that the only analyticity and synonymy and entailment needed by a pragmatic philosophy can be introduced and justified without the hypostatization of meaning.

II

Objects comprise the ontological realm for Quine. These objects are discrete entities; that is, they are separate, discriminable, have self-identity, and are independent of the mind knowing them. "The familiar material objects may not be all that is real, but they are admirable examples."[4] Objects of this sort can be perceived, but there may also be abstract objects that cannot be perceived. Numbers in arithmetic, classes, attributes, propositions, meanings among others claim to be entities, but their claims must be critically assessed and may be granted, Quine holds, only if established by logical procedures.

Among abstracts, the claim to be entities must be granted to first order classes and to numbers whether or not they be defined as classes (WO 243n). Quine suggests that levels of abstractness, modeled on Russell's Theory of Types, might be established: "In the beginning there are only concrete objects" (LPV 123). These constitute type zero and are the values of bound individual variables. "To be is to be a value of a variable."[5] Next come first order classes and relations: they constitute entities of type 1 and are the values of bound predicate variables. Classes of classes, and relations constitute entities of type 2; and so on. Always the criterion is the same: "entities of a given sort are assumed by a theory if and only if some of them must be counted among the values of the variables in order that the statements affirmed in the theory be true" (LPV 103).

This is Quine's highly controversial doctrine of ontological commitment (or ontic commitment, WO 120n); and it depends on his theory of the variable, which in turn depends on his view of the nature of logic. The three are a package, and later I shall find occasion adversely to criticize the package, but first the contents must be examined. The word 'variable' is used in it in a special way. Not everything that many mathematicians and logicians would call a variable is a genuine variable in Quine's technical terminology. A variable is "rather like a pronoun; it is used in the quantifier to key the quantifier for subsequent cross reference, and then it is used in the ensuing text to refer back to the appropriate quantifier" (LPV 102–103). Letters or any symbols not bound, thus, are not genuine variables but are only so-called place holders: dummy predicates or dummy sentences (LPV 108). Thus, Quine's theory of the variable is part of the theory of quantification.

This theory of the variable appears early in Quine's writings,[6] but he argues it most explicitly in *The Roots of Reference,*[7] where he distinguishes between two kinds of so-called variables, the substitutional and the objectual (RR 98).[8] Only the objectual is a genuine variable, he holds; the substitutional is merely a place holder. According to the *substitutional* view, the value of a variable is whatever can be substituted for it, including any notation or construct of the system in which it is used that can be legitimately put in its place in accordance with the rules of the system.[9] Thus, values of substitutional variables often are other symbols or formulas. "*Objectually* construed, on the other hand, the variable refers to objects of some sort as its values" (RR 98, Quine's italics). The values of a variable refer "to the objects in the universe of discourse over which a quantifier ranges" (WOP 154).

It is the values of the variables in a quantified formula that make the formula materially true or false (LPV 110). To use Quine's illustration, take the formula '$x + 3 > 7$'. If a person substitutes any one of the numbers 1, 2, 3 or 4 for x, the ensuing sentence is false, but the substitution of any number larger than 4 makes it true. Note that it is not the substitution of the numeral '2' that makes it false or the numeral '5' that makes it true. It is the substitution of the number itself, of which the numeral is the name, that determines truth or falsity. Thus, there must *be* numbers in order that the sentence '$5 + 3 > 7$' can be true.

Quine is concerned with the material truth of sentences because "Logic, like any science, has as its business the pursuit of truth" and "truth ordinarily attaches to statements[10] by virtue of the nature of the world."[11] Twenty years later he says "logic is the systematic study of the logical truths" and "a sentence is logically true if all sentences with its grammatical structure are true" (PL xi), but it is clear that the truth of each sentence of the same grammatical structure goes back to the nature of the world.[12]

Although Quine holds an ontology of objects, he is not dogmatic about it. Other points of view are possible, in particular one in which events instead of objects are fundamental. Quine does not establish his objectual ontology from an analysis of raw experience. If one started from raw experience, one might come to the conclusion that events are ontically prior to objects. This would yield a phenomenalism, Quine thinks (LPV 17); but if more than one ontological view is possible, it becomes essential to ask "How are we to adjudicate among rival ontologies?" (LPV 15). He answers that we adopt, "at least insofar as we are reasonable, the simplest conceptual scheme into which the disordered fragments of raw experience can be fitted and arranged" (LPV 16). Every conceptual scheme is, from the points of view of rival schemes, a myth, and "The myth of physical objects is epistemologically superior to most in that it has proved more efficacious than other myths as a device for working a manageable structure into the flux of experience" (LPV 44). So Quine posits the existence of objects to make true quantified sentences possible.

The passages quoted in the preceding paragraph could have been uttered by a pragmatic process philosopher; and J. J. C. Smart assumes that they express the pragmatic or instrumentalist point of view. He says that Quine, in *Word and Object,* abandoned the pragmatism and instrumentalism of his earlier writings in favor of a clear-cut realism.[13] Quine's reply to Smart is somewhat cryptic, but he says that Smart's contention is based on a misunderstanding, and denies that he (Quine) vacillates between pragmatism and realism. My own interpretation is that Quine, throughout his writings, consistently maintains a realistic point of view[14] but that he is fully aware that he has no warrant to be dogmatic about it. There are other points of view and there are other considerations in favor of them (LPV 17). As a final choice, a person has to adopt the point of view that seems most adequate to him and argue from it; so Quine posits the existence of concrete objects, the values of bound individual variables, and of classes and relations that must be interpreted as the values of bound variables. I take it that Quine adopts a pragmatic position only methodologically in order to get started without dogmatism, but does not espouse pragmatism or instrumentalism except methodologically;[15] and I also take it that he did not abandon this position in the interval between the writing of "Two Dogmas of Empiricism" and the writing of *Word and Object.* His position is neither equivocal nor vacillating although it allows the possibility of other points of view.

Quine's undogmatic attitude is further evidenced by his insistence that "We look to bound variables in connection with ontology not in order to know what there is, but in order to know what a given remark or doctrine, ours or someone else's, *says* there is" (LPV 15, Quine's italics). And again, "What is under consideration is not the ontological state of affairs, but the ontological commitments of a discourse" (LPV 103).

The dogmatic goal of classical empiricism (and the Vienna Circle as well) to base positive knowledge on observation supplemented only by logico-mathematical principles must be given up according to Quine because alternative bodies of theory are always possible (OR 74-80). Although his ontology is an ontology of objects, Quine holds that we cannot know with certainty what those objects are. Ostension to what is perceived helps, but the inscrutability of reference qualifies the knowledge. It is further qualified in relation to language and communication by the indeterminacy of translation. "It makes no sense to say what the objects of a theory are, beyond saying how to interpret or reinterpret that theory in another" (OR 50); and again, "Reference *is* nonsense except relative to a coordinate system" (OR 48, Quine's italics). Some of Quine's critics have held that these doctrines display skepticism on his part. I do not think they do, because they are clearly expressed as parts of a more inclusive positive doctrine, and reasons for holding them are clearly given. I suppose their import to be similar to Peirce's doctrine of fallibilism, though Quine does not draw on that doctrine for support.

Neither language nor the structure of language determines what is real for Quine, but although reality does not depend on language, knowledge, in part, does. Knowledge, in his doctrine, arises from the application of language to sense stimulation (WO 26). Accordingly, if the quantified language that deals successfully with the stimuli can yield truth only in case the language refers to entities, it is justified to say that the entities are known. The convergence of truth, knowledge, and the structure of language warrants the posit of objectual ontology.[16]

Quine rejects the doctrine that meanings are entities: there are no meanings in his ontology. He says "I have protested more than once that no empirical meaning has been given to the notion of meaning" (RR 78). He cannot consistently have meanings because, as ordinarily conceived, they are intensions, and his ontology and epistemology follow his logic in being extensional. He says "I feel no reluctance toward refusing to admit meanings, for I do not thereby deny that words and statements are meaningful" (LPV 11), and this provides him with an extensional substitute for meaning. Although there is no abstract entity to be called a meaning, 'meaningful' is a meaningful predicate, but apparently one that does not allow of quantification.[17] Neither is meaning an attribute of propositions, for attributes and propositions are rejected along with meanings.

The meaningfulness of sentences, according to Quine, is based not on their possessing meanings but ultimately on their reference to things in the world. This reference depends on setting up a connection between sense stimulation ("nerve-hits" or "surface irritations", WO 23) and spoken language. Quine has two accounts of this connection, one in *Word and Object* and another in *The Roots of Reference,* but they differ only in explanatory concepts, not essentially. The account in *Word and Object* bases the meaningfulness of sentences on stimulus meanings, which do not come under the ban since they are not entities, are identified ostensively, and are defined in extension (insofar as definitions can be extensional). A brief definition of stimulus meaning for a given speaker at a given time is "the class of all the stimulations . . . that would prompt his assent" when confronted with a suitable sentence in the interrogatory mood.[18] It is important to note that stimulus meaning is always for a particular person at a particular time; otherwise it could not be ostended and could not be only extensional. The class of stimulus meanings is a subclass of physical events, but this does not make events fundamental in Quine's view, for the stimulus meanings are caused (physical causation) by objects (RR 6).

In *The Roots of Reference* Quine does not speak of stimulus meanings, but distinguishes between reception, which corresponds to his earlier nerve-hits, and perception, which is accompanied by awareness and yields *Gestalts* (RR 4). The perception of *Gestalts* is behaviorally identified, and this leads to a behavioral definition of perception and perceptual similarity. Dispositions to react to perceptual similarities take the place of the earlier stimulus meanings and avoid the use of the undesirable word 'meaning', although at the expense of introducing dispositions, but Quine insists that dispositions are behavioral factors (RR 10). Psychological conditioning attaches sentences to perceptual similarities, and these are observation sentences. (They may be one word sentences, WO 5–6.) Observation sentences play the part in Quine's theory that protocol sentences played in early logical positivism, but they are reached in a much less dogmatic and positivistic fashion, and are more clearly defined; and as Quine points out, in contrast with protocol sentences they do not stand alone (OR 85).

The difference in the accounts in *Word and Object* and *The Roots of Reference* of the setting up of observation sentences is unimportant because both start from sense stimulation, both get stimulation connected with language by psychological conditioning, and both emerge with observation sentences. "A sentence is observational insofar as its truth value, on any occasion, would be agreed to by just about any member of the speech community witnessing the occasion" (RR 39). Quine calls to attention that this offers a behavioral criterion of an observation sentence. The important thing is to provide a way of treating observation sentences in extension, thus avoiding an appeal to hypostatized entities called meanings or to "sense data or other epistemological preconceptions" (RR 39). In this manner the truth value of an observation sentence can be determined by reference to nerve stimulation together with language usage.

Quine points out that his doctrine of observation sentences yields a verification theory of meaning (OR 89), as did that of the logical positivists. "The meaning of a sentence lies in the observations that would support or refute it" (RR 38, see also OR 80). Nevertheless, the logical positivists were wrong in supposing that the stimulus meanings of individual sentences can stand alone.

"Most sentences do not admit separately of observational evidence. Sentences interlock" (RR 38, see also LPV 41). Earlier he had called this interlocking "the interanimation of sentences" (WO 9). He does not subject it to a rigorous analysis but indicates that it follows from the conditioning of words to other words which themselves are conditioned, finally, to sense stimulation.

Thus, inasmuch as meaning is the extension of the class of meaningful sentences, Quine reduces all meaning to reference. He had been early influenced by Frege's essay *Ueber Sinn und Bedeutung*. The Vienna Circle, emphasizing Frege's *Bedeutung,* held that denotation is the only significant kind of meaning, and Quine's theory accomplishes a closely similar result.[19] Although he adversely criticizes the positivists for not introducing the principle of interlocking sentences, he does not hold that the principle qualifies his extensionalism. I shall later argue that it does: if it were developed, it would be an entering wedge for the introduction of intensional meanings, and intensional meanings depend on more than stimulation and language. As a result of Frege's separation of intensions from extensions in deductive reasoning, many logicians have denied the validity of allowing intensions in the theory of deduction. Some have denied such validity in ontological and epistemological reasoning as well. Chief among these is Quine. Denotation and extension are based on sense stimulation. Since to him sense stimulation is occasioned by material objects, and since the meaningfulness of observation sentences is to be traced to the use of language in connection with sense stimulation, and since the meanings of theoretic knowledge and knowledge in general are to be traced finally to the verification of observation sentences, Quine adopts an ontology of objects. Let us turn now to a criticism of the adequacy of his views concerning objects and meanings.

III

The principle of extensionality works very well for the logician, but he should not on that account apply it to epistemology, and even constrain the whole of reality to be subject to it: to do so is to commit what I am calling the logician's fallacy. There is no warrant for the logician to assume that because his symbols operate only in extension there *are* only extensions. Terms or concepts have intension as well as extension, and although Quine seldom uses the word 'concept',[20] he often speaks of conceptual schemes, his own and others. He not only needs concepts when he ventures into epistemology, he uses them (and quite explicitly in the essay "Epistemology Naturalized"; OR 67-90). 'Term' belongs to the language of logic; 'concept' is its parallel in the language of epistemology. Even as sentences can be broken down into terms and their connections, so discourse can be broken down into concepts and their connections.

I shall talk of concepts and use the word as part of the ordinary idiom, laying aside for the moment the question of the ontological status of concepts, whether they be entities, mental events, functions of organic activity, relations or abstract terms. Concepts, though carried in words, are more than words: they are words with articulate meanings;[21] that is, words involved in certain relationships. *Articulate* meanings, however one defines 'meaning', are joined together, and the connections are neither fortuitous nor independent of the behavior of organisms. I am not persuaded that reference to sense stimulation (nerve-hits) is a sufficient source of meaningfulness. It never is a source by itself. Meaningfulness arises from a symbolic relationship involving habits of organic response: a presently experienced object or gesture or word becomes a sign of a possible action or response, and therewith the object, gesture or word acquires meaning.

All concepts have intension as well as extension (although either may be null) regardless of whether the intension may be used as a factor in constructing a formal theory of deduction. Extension designates actual existence, as Quine holds, but he is not explicit about intension since he does not use the notion technically although he recognizes it (OR 118). He must acknowledge, however, that concepts may be defined in terms of other concepts. As ordinarily used, intension is the expression of the articulation of concepts: the intension of a concept is a limitation or qualification by other concepts of its use. Technically, the intension of a given concept is the *conjunct* of the intensions of all the other concepts that would be applicable to *whatever* the given concept may be applied. Extension depends on the relation of a concept to existence, but intension depends on its relation to other concepts, and these relations may be specified whether or not the logician uses them. They are primarily relations of relevance, subsumption, consistency or inconsistency. The intension, that is, the limitation of the use of a given concept, may be verbally summed up in the dictionary definition of the word designating the concept.[22] Thus, intension is the most characteristic uncritical meaning of 'meaning', and it is that meaning which Quine would like to avoid because it *is* uncritical and does not lend itself to a precise algorithm.

Intensions are systematically interrelated. What is important is that the intension must be such that the use of the concept of which it is the intension will be consistent with the use of all other concepts to which the given concept may be related either directly or indirectly. The intensions and extensions of the concepts of natural language are developed in relation to each other, and by means of mutual step by step clarification. In ordinary discourse where language is intended to apply to experience we seek to relate intensions to each other in such a way that the concepts of which they are the intensions will have an extension that is not null; that is, so that the intensions will allow of consistent application to actualities.

For example, if as a matter of empirical knowledge the extension of 'mammal' is included in the extension of 'vertebrate', the intension of 'vertebrate' is taken to be one of the limiting conditions of the application of 'mammal' as another expression of the same empirical knowledge. What is not a vertebrate is not to be called a mammal. Thus, the intension of 'vertebrate' is included within the intension of 'mammal', while the extension of 'mammal' is included within the extension of 'vertebrate'. If the intension of 'viviparous' had ever been included in the intension of 'mammal', a lexical crisis would have arisen upon the discovery of the platypus: the taxonimists would have had to decide whether to alter the intension of 'mammal' or to classify the platypus as other than a mammal.

I have been talking about concepts whereas Quine talks about sentences, but the difference is unessential here because the distinction between intension and extension is the same whether applied to concepts or sentences. I do not hold, however, that any concept has meaning by itself; concepts are parts of discourse, the grammatical unit of which is a sentence. Thus, as a first approximation toward the status of a concept, it may be said that a concept is a collapsed sentence.[23] Sentences are meaningful partly because sentences depend on each other in symbolic usage. As Quine says, sentences interlock. I maintain that this is because all intensions are articulate and go beyond the confines even of simple sentences to wider, more inclusive discourse such as the content of at least incipient theories.

Concepts are generalizations: they signify more than a particular nerve-hit. They involve reference to past and to future possible instances. No words in natural language except proper names and demonstratives signify a particular (or unique) instance, and sentences cannot be constructed from proper names and demonstratives alone. As Abelard pointed out in the Middle Ages, all sentences involve a universal or universals. A generalization responds to organic memory of past stimulations and anticipation of future stimulations as well as to the stimulus actually present. Generality is an abstract term whose meaning is primarily intensional since it depends on its relation to all the concepts involved in the act of generalization. We *construct* generalities in the act of making generalizations. No one ever *observed* a generality, but all meanings except those of proper names are general, so there is something in the composition of meaning that goes beyond observation. My contention is that this something depends on selective human behavior.

If the notion of the interlocking of sentences is unpacked, it is seen to involve a recognition not only of intensional meanings, but of the indispensability of intensional meanings. A statement both precise and complete of the intension of an empirically applicable concept would be impossible in practice, however, because the *complete* intension would stretch indefinitely, and any *actual* statement of it would fail to exhaust it, and so be at least somewhat vague. This undoubtedly is why Quine wants to avoid intensional meanings and why intensions resist algorithmic treatment. Being a logician, Quine shuns vague expressions. It may be, however, that human experience inescapably trails off into vagueness. Beginnings and ends and boundaries are ideal limits in a continuum, and cannot be exactly located in experience because experience is a continuum. No point in a continuum has an immediate predecessor or an immediate successor. Thus, although vagueness is to be avoided in logic it cannot be altogether avoided in epistemology without omitting some considerations relevant to knowledge.

By avoiding or denying status to intensions, Quine succeeds in omitting relevance itself. Relevance depends on intensional meanings. Two concepts are relevant insofar as they share intensional content; and two sentences are relevant insofar as they share conceptual content. The connectedness of intension depends on organic response. Without an organic response a nerve-hit would not be even an effective stimulus. Stimuli are selected (though not consciously) by the organism from the infinite continuity of process in relation to possible responses.[24] Except in relation to the response, each nerve-hit would be just a different occurrence, but insofar as two nerve-hits elicit the same sort of response, they are connected through the shared response and become meaningful.

Intensional meaning takes its rise because something can be done to and with stimuli. The object means what it means because of the way that it can enter into action and response. Mead points out that "Man lives in a world of meaning. What he sees and hears means what he will or might handle."[25] Varied responses take place as a result of varied nerve-hits, and in the light of the possibility of the responses, the nerve-hits become meaningful stimuli. This is the heart of the pragmatic insight, and Quine's failure to recognize it makes it incorrect to characterize him as a pragmatist, notwithstanding his excursions into pragmatic methodology from time to time.

Quine, throughout his essay "Epistemology Naturalized", maintains that sense stimulation yields both the source and the verification of *meaningfulness* (OR 75–81), and in his exposition he appeals to a doctrine which he attributes to C. S. Peirce (OR 78).[26] Peirce, however, had emphasized, in the article in which he introduced what came later to be called pragmatism, that meaning is due to action and habit formation. He says "what a thing means is simply what habits it produces" and again "there is no distinction of meaning so fine as to consist in anything but a possible difference in practice."[27] Peirce later developed this pragmatic theory of meaning in the context of his theory of signs.

The semiotic-pragmatic theory of meaning is an empirical theory[28] in which meanings are not entities but are relations. I shall briefly sketch a semiotic-pragmatic theory, though I do not present it as an exposition of Peirce and will not be concerned with the historical connection with Peirce's philosophy but only with its relevance to the present context.[29]

Meaning is a triadic relationship between a symbol, what it symbolizes (the referent), and what Peirce called an interpretant. The interpretant is the effect the symbol produces on response or behavior; that is, it is the resultant in behavior of the use of the symbol. The interpretant may itself be another sign-act such as the production of another symbol (word or gesture), but in this case it entails another meaning and so requires another interpretant.[30] An infinite regress of interpretants is to be avoided, however. The final logical interpretant of a sign is a habit or a change in habit in the behavior of the interpreting organism. Thus, meaning arises in the situation where the use of a symbol affects or can affect action or habit.

Meaning does not lie in any one part of the relationship alone although the word is often used elliptically to designate sometimes the referent and sometimes the interpretant–the habit or the indicated response. Such elliptical usage is harmless so long as it is recognized, but the accurate and literal designation of 'meaning' is only to the whole situation. If there is no symbol or no referent (direct or indirect), there is no meaning; but also if the act of symbolization has no effect on response or possible response, there is no meaning. Meaning is not an entity on this view: the only entities are symbol tokens and referents, as in Quine's theory; but Quine does not recognize Peirce's interpretant.

Quine sometimes speaks as if relations were entities, and his principle of ontic commitment seems to demand that they be regarded as entities when they can be quantified. But if relations are entities, the application of 'entity' to existences becomes confusing. Only what is relatively stable and fundamental in the scheme of things should be called an entity.[31] Entities do not pop into and out of existence as do relations when their conditions change. The transitory nature of relations is so apparent that some philosophers have challenged their claim to existence. Relations, instead of being entities, are connections between entities. We must have both terms and connectives in building a logical system and also in explaining experience. If we do not, we are involved in the Lewis Carroll paradox of "What the Tortoise Said to Achilles".[32] Entities are *in* relations to each other.[33]

Reference alone does not constitute meaningfulness, and hence, observation alone is not a sufficient basis for knowledge. Reference is necessary to meaning, but equally necessary are organic responses and the selections determined by these responses. Quine holds that the referent of the symbol must be ultimately identifiable in terms of sense perception, and I agree. In this sense, both Quine's theory and the semiotic-pragmatic theory are naturalistic; but in the semiotic-pragmatic, organic behavior and response as well as observation are necessary constituents of meaning and of knowledge.

The semiotic-pragmatic theory affords an explanation of intensional meaning. It has been pointed out above that often the interpretant in a meaning relation is the production of another sign, and this other sign may be a word or gesture or other means of communication. A clear-cut case of such a situation is when the meaning of an unfamiliar word is given in more familiar words as in a dictionary definition. Another case would be the interpretant of a highly abstract term, such as 'number'. If I say that the number of chairs in a room is six, the effect of my locution is not necessarily to produce the actual process of counting as its interpretant: it may produce some other symbol of the number; but if there were no ability to count, there could be no symbol signifying number. Since signs can be interpretants of other signs, the meanings of one sign-operation are bound up with the meanings of others. Such interrelationships of meanings comprise intensions.

Thus, meaning requires 1) symbol, 2) referent, 3) interpretant. The extensional logic in terms of which Quine constructs his theory of meaning recognizes only 1) and 2); organic responses and habits of behavior are not topics of formal logic. In the semiotic relation, however, the symbol signifies a referent, and this referential relation further signifies an habitual response. A full theory of meaning embraces this complex semiotic relationship.

The semiotic-pragmatic theory of meaning does not *commit* one to a world of ready-made objects with a ready-made structure as does Quine's extensional theory. Nevertheless, the semiotic theory can have objects for symbols and referents even though the world is a continuum, because pragmatism can provide a way of having *discreteness within a continuum*. Quine's theory, on the other hand, has no such provision; it is not clear that it even recognizes any fundamental continuity. There must *be* a world of discrete objects disposed in a ready-made structure according to it. Quine's logic purports to be the representation of such a structure. This is a doctrine of logical realism, and it is bound up with a realistic theory of truth. Because logic can deal successfully with reality, it is assumed that the structure and delineation of logic somehow captures and represents the structure and delineation of reality. I suggest, however, that the logician's realism is due to the confusion engendered by the logician's fallacy. An unconfused logician, instead of assuming that logic represents the structure of reality, might realize that he is constraining reality to fit within his logic; and that instead of a realistic theory of truth there might be substituted a pragmatic theory—a true sentence is one which fits within the context of a long-range successful response and adaptation to the environment.[34] Quine's doctrine of ontic commitment should come as no surprise: it is a detailed formal elaboration of what is involved in his initial view of the nature of logic as a vehicle of truth.

I find no objection to the sort of position that derives its conclusions from its initial assumptions so long as these assumptions are explicit and plausible and involve no fallacies. In this case, however, the logician's fallacy is involved. The logician should not confuse the way that he deals with reality and the nature of reality itself. Without the assumption of the logician's fallacy, I could accept much of Quine's argument and doctrine. I hold all theoretic knowledge to be interdependent and in the last analysis circular in the way that what is systematic is circular. Quine's philosophy seems to point in the direction of this sort of circularity of knowledge, but his actual argument never gets far away from the haunting conviction that ready-made objects and structure account for the truth of meaningful sentences.

A pragmatic process philosophy, although it has no ready-made objects, can provide for obtaining objects from the continuum as the result of the selective responses of an organism.[35] Logic, in this view, instead of reflecting a ready-made structure is the elaboration of a pragmatic structure—one which enables us to put an inchoate experience into an order whereby we can handle it. Logic is an essential ingredient in the process of achieving a world of objects instead of being the formal aspect of such a world conceived as ready-made. Quine's assumptions of objects and structure are unnecessary and gratuitous. His own essay entitled "Natural Kinds" (OR 114-138) seems sometimes to indicate as much. There he argues that his notion of natural kinds is based on the naive (he calls it "intuitive") notion of similarity, but he can find no satisfactory logical definition of similarity, and in the final outcome "it is the mark of maturity of a branch of science that the notion of similarity or kind finally dissolves, as far as it is relevant to that branch of science" (OR 121). Yet later in the same essay he says that if a sense of comparative similarity "fits in with the regularities of nature . . . it is presumably an evolutionary product of natural selection" (OR 134); and he speaks of "similarity itself, what the man's judgments purport to be judgments of" (OR 135). Accordingly, to Quine, there *are* regularities in nature, and similarity *is* really there.

To the contrary, there cannot be either absolute identities, regularities or common elements in a concrete continuum because there are no absolute parts in a continuum. Pragmatic accounts of generality and similarity can nevertheless be given.[36] Conceptual similarity is to be accounted for by a lack of discrimination between differences in stimuli for the purposes of action. Although there are unlimited differences in stimulation, the possibilities of response are limited by the conditions of the organism. For example, the stimuli that humans accept as the signs of food are immensely varied, but there is no such universal as food except as whatever may be ingested and digested. There is an economy of response: the same response answers to many different stimuli. Fish, apples, and ice-cream look, taste, smell, and feel different, but the sameness of response gives rise to what is called similarity in the stimuli; they are all food. By "sameness of response" I indicate a lack of discrimination in the response. Discrimination is always selective and always behavioral.

Quine clinches his argument for reference to objects by his theory of the variable. He holds that a genuine variable is objectual; the so-called substitutional variable is only a place-holder. This position, however, depends on his theory of the nature of logic as yielding truth. On the other hand, if pure logic is the structure of uninterpreted systems, the distinction between the objectual and the substitutional variable is extra-logical. What bothers Quine on pages 99 and 110 of *The Roots of Reference* is not the systematic validity of a formula, but the suitability of interpreting the x of the formula as an apple or a rabbit or some such individuated existent. The formula must yield truth when so interpreted. This, I should say, is clearly a question not of structure but of interpretation. Since all truth cannot be assimilated to formal truth (validity), truth should be considered not a topic of logic but of semantics.

Opposed to Quine's doctrine of the nature of logic, it may be held that logic is the science of pure form, or order, abstracted from considerations of truth or of actual existence, and is displayed in uninterpreted systems which are independent of any locus in experience or any application to the empirical world that may be given them.[37] The human organism has learned to construct such systems by manipulating according to strict procedural rules notation completely abstracted from content. In the construction the empirical meanings that have given rise to successful action can be used heuristically, but the principles of the construction are governed only by considerations of rigorous internal consistency.[38] Quine's view, on the other hand, entails that when a system does not yield truth when applied to apples and rabbits (and numbers, too, both rational and real), it is not to be called logic. Thus, formal systems which have no application, invented by logicians as exercises in ingenuity, are not within this view logic; but if an application is later found, they are, as at the magic stroke of midnight, transformed into logic.

If all variables in pure logic are substitutional, the so-called existence of existential quantification is only notational: the only concrete actualities indicated are the notation itself. This does *not* entail the view, however, that logic *is* notation or that numbers *are* numerals. Quine rejects the view that numbers are numerals (RR 118) and holds that numbers are entities that numerals name (LPV 110), but this, according to the semiotic-pragmatic theory of meaning, is an unnecessary hypostatization. If intensions are allowed, numbers can be interpreted as the intensional meanings generated by the systematic use of symbolism which, when so used, are called numerals. Meanings ontologically are not entities but are relationships. Logic, on this interpretation, would be not notation but the system of purely internal intensional meanings generated by the rigorously consistent use of notation. Such internal intensional meanings would accrue to the so-called logical constants involved, and are simply the relationships that are established by the manipulation of the notation according to procedural rules.[39] These are thoroughly abstract relationships, but because of their conditions, are behavioral. They have no extensional content until given such by interpretation.

IV

Quine is quite correct in protesting that meanings are not entities. Nevertheless, knowledge requires intensional meanings, but these are symbolic relationships developed in minds as the result of response to the environment. They are not subjective in the sense of that word opposed to objective since they arise from and are answerable to behavioral conditions. Neither are minds entities; they are functions of the organism. The organism is what has developed and survived in the course of evolution, but evolution is a continuous process, and in this process intelligence has emerged as the major survival mechanism of humans. Intelligence depends on the ability to construct and use symbolism in responding to the environment, and the result of symbolism is the rise of the meaning relation. Insofar as the organism's responses are successful, man lives in a world of meanings. Meanings are interpretations of stimuli, and stimuli are selections from the continuity of process in which the organism is immersed. The selections are due to the reactions and responses of the organism, and are infused with meanings in the light of these reactions and responses.

Intelligence is more than linguistic conditioning to sense stimulation; it relates sense stimulation to action through the mediation of symbols. The linguistic response is a necessary condition of intelligence since it supplies the symbolic factor, but it is not a sufficient condition. Intelligence involves learning in a wider sense than the learning of language. We see with our habits, and this applies not only to vision but to all sense perception. Habits are set up by the coordination of sense stimuli with bodily activity, and this coordination in humans is a learned factor and is basic to all other learning processes—even to the process of language conditioning; the infant has achieved a high degree of sensory and muscular coordination before he is capable of learning language.

Intelligence involves the formation of habits, foresight, and voluntary choice of responses. These activities are consciously performed, but consciousness is neither an entity nor a state, it is a way of doing things; that is, the status of consciousness is primarily adverbial—activities may be *consciously* performed, and this means performed in response to stimuli with which the organism is *not* confronted at the time of the response. Conscious response always includes response to stimuli that are not present—only surrogates are present in the form of symbolism or imagery (imagery may also function as symbol). Foresight and deliberation comprise the ways in which past responses and the anticipation of future responses influence present action. All this is involved in the theory of meaning according to the semiotic-pragmatic view, and that view is primarily a theory of intensional meaning. Quine's extensional theory is only a truncated account of meaning—an account that is inadequate for a theory of meaning and intelligence.

As Quine says, sentences interlock, but I add that the interlocking is through intensional meanings. Intension is the interconnectedness of concepts. Concepts are the mental grasp of meaning, and thus are intensional, but there is no such *thing* as a concept; being a grasp, it is a functional activity. Two concepts of *exactly* the same intension would not be two but one, and thus it appears that Quine's demand that synonymy ought to allow of unqualified substitution is a chimera. All the synonymy needed by a pragmatic philosophy is sufficient overlap of intensions to allow for substitution within a given context *for purposes relevant to that context*. Of course Quine himself uses this kind of synonym. The same sort of criticism holds concerning Quine's strictures against analyticity: if the intension of one concept includes that of another, the second may be said to be the analytic result of the first. It would be difficult if not impossible to establish in the case of an empirical concept that there was absolutely *nothing* in the intension of the second not included in the intension of the first, but again, *within the context of action,* an adequate approximation can be achieved. If a high degree of abstraction is allowed, the intensions of the two concepts can be adjusted to each other by definition until a close approximation toward precision is achieved. It is true that such synonymy and analyticity would not be of the absolute precision required for use in an algorithm, but they would allow of the degree of approximation necessary for purposes of action, and knowledge, within a pragmatic philosophy, is a function of action and the habits produced by action.

Knowledge is not founded wholly or even primarily on observation sentences. Observation is necessary, but in addition knowledge requires intensions—the way that meanings are interconnected because of the interconnection of successful responses, and 'successful' here means having positive survival value in the evolutionary process. The evolutionary process is a continuum, and the world of a naturalistic philosophy such as Quine's should be a world of continuity, not of discrete objects or entities. There can be no ready-made structure in a continuum. The structure applying to a continuum is formulated by reaction and response to the continuum. No theory of meaning is adequate that omits the importance of human response in formulating the world in which the human being survives. If he does not survive, we have nothing to talk about.

Harold N. Lee

Newcomb College
Tulane University
July 1975

NOTES

1. W. V. Quine, *From A Logical Point Of View*, second edition, revised (Cambridge, Mass.: Harvard University Press, 1961), p. 17. Hereafter cited in the text as LPV with page number.

2. Quine's attitude is far more relaxed and good humored than is that of many logicians. In contrast, compare the following: "When the logical forms cope with reality more successfully than any others could do, then there is no reason to question the ontological significance of logic." A. P. Ushenko, *The Logic Of Events* (Berkeley: University of California Press, 1929), p. vii.

3. Op. cit. (New York: Dover Publications, Inc., 1950), vol. 1, p. 196; see also p. 353 and vol. 2, p. 281.

4. W. V. Quine, *Word And Object* (Cambridge, Mass.: The Technology Press, 1960), p. 3. Hereafter cited in the text WO with page number.

5. W. V. Quine, *The Ways Of Paradox* (New York: Random House, 1966), p. 66, Quine's italics. Hereafter cited WOP with page number.

6. In a paper of 1939 Quine says "Variables are pronouns, and make sense only in positions that are available to names" (WOP 65).

7. W. V. Quine, *The Roots Of Reference* (La Salle, Ill.: Open Court Publishing Co., 1973). Hereafter cited RR with page number.

8. In *Ontological Relativity* (New York: Columbia University Press, 1969), p. 64ff he had called the objectual 'referential quantification'. Hereafter cited OR with page number.

9. See C. I. Lewis and C. H. Langford, *Symbolic Logic* (New York: Dover Publications, Inc., 1959), p. 182n.

10. Later he changed his terminology and would have said "sentences" at this point. See his *Philosophy of Logic* (Englewood Cliffs, N.J.: Prentice-Hall, Inc., 1970), p. 2. Hereafter cited PL with page number. I have adhered to the revised terminology except in direct quotations.

11. W. V. Quine, *Methods of Logic* (New York: Holt, Rinehart and Winston, 1962), p. xi. See also WO 26.

12. The more technically accurate explanation of logical truths in terms of the pattern of sentences where only logical particles occur essentially does not alter the situation since the logical particles must occur as they do in discourse about the world. See W. V. Quine, *Mathematical Logic* (New York: W. W. Norton & Company, Inc., 1940), p. 2.

13. *Words And Objections*, edited by Davidson and Hintikka (Dordrecht, Holland: Reidel Publishing Company, 1969), pp. 8–9. For Quine's reply see p. 293.

14. Realistic both in the senses of physical realism and a stringently qualified scholastic realism.

15. I shall later argue that his doctrine of truth is not pragmatic but is realistic. It requires a fully structured state of affairs independent of the mind.

16. The argument above is Quine's except at one point where it goes beyond what Quine explicitly says. It assumes that what is genuinely known must be true. I have not found any place in Quine's writing where he discusses the question "Can we have genuine knowledge that turns out to be false?". It seems to me that Quine assumes that all sentences of genuine knowledge must be true. I reject such an assumption because it makes the definitions of truth and knowledge narrowly circular. I hold that knowledge depends on evidence, not truth.

17. In the example from round pebbles on WOP 64–65, 'pebbles have roundness', substitute from meaningful sentences, 'sentences have meaningfulness'.

18. For the conditions of the test confrontation, see WO 32–33. For a detailed adverse criticism, see Paul Ziff, *Understanding Understanding* (Ithaca, N.Y.: Cornell University Press, 1972), pp. 90–106.

19. The result differs in that one cannot denote a class; but the extension of the class is given in the denotation of its members.

20. He never uses it in a technical sense, presumably for the reason given in the essay "On Frege's Way Out" (see W. V. Quine, *Selected Logic Papers* (New York: Random House, 1966), pp. 146–158). In formal logic I would avoid the use of the word 'concept' very much for the same reason as does Quine, but it is part of the vocabulary of epistemology.

21. I use 'articulate' in the sense "to unite by a joint or joints" (Webster's New Collegiate Dictionary), not in the sense "clearly enunciated speech".

22. See C. I. Lewis, *An Analysis of Knowledge and Valuation* (La Salle: Open Court Publishing Co., 1946), pp. 43–44.

23. I would rather say "a collapsed proposition" since a sentence is primarily a grammatical unit, but I do not here wish to enter into the controversy over the ontological status of a proposition.

24. Compare the following quotation from G. H. Mead: "In the end what we see, hear, feel, taste, and smell depends upon what we are doing, and not the reverse. In our purposively organized life we inevitably come back upon previous conduct as the determining condition of what we sense at any one moment, and the so-called external stimulus is the occasion for this and not its cause."; *Selected Writings of George Herbert Mead*, edited by Andrew J. Reck (Indianapolis: the Bobbs-Merrill Company, Inc., 1964), p. 37.

25. *Selected Writings . . . .* , p. 294.

26. I am more disposed to attribute it to James's interpretation of Peirce. See W. James, *Pragmatism* (New York: Longmans Green and Co., 1943), p. 45.

27. "How To Make Our Ideas Clear", *Popular Science Monthly* 12 (1878). See *Collected Papers of Charles Sanders Peirce* (Cambridge, Mass.: Harvard University Press, 1960), vols. 1–6 edited by Hartshorne and Weiss; vols. 7–8 edited by A. W. Burks. The present quotations may be found at 5.400.

28. In contrast to that in Chapter III of Lewis's *Analysis of Knowledge and Valuation*, which is analytical; i.e., it analyzes the concept of meaning.

29. For a discussion of the interpretation of Peirce, see John J. Fitzgerald, *Peirce's Theory of Signs as Foundation for Pragmatism* (The Hague: Mouton & Co., 1966), especially Chapter IV. See also William Alston, "Pragmatism and the Theory of Signs in Peirce", *Philosophy and Phenomenological Research* 17 (1956–57); and George Gentry, "Habit and the Logical Interpretant", in *Studies in the Philosophy of Charles Sanders Peirce*, edited by Wiener and Young (Cambridge, Mass.: Harvard University Press, 1952).

30. The entailment of other meanings is the ground of the articulation of intensions.

31. Although Quine does not analyze the concept 'entity', he uses it freely, and apparently with the assumption that the world is composed of entities.

32. Lewis Carroll, "What the Tortoise Said to Achilles", *Mind* N. S. 4 (1895): 278ff. Reprinted in R. M. Eaton, *General Logic* (New York: Charles Scribner's Sons, 1931), pp. 43–46.

33. I prefer to hold, however, that both entities and relations are terms of analysis.

We can dispense with them as building blocks of reality. If reality is process, passage, it is not constituted of building blocks. See H. N. Lee, "Are There Any Entities?", *Philosophy and Phenomenological Research* 40 (1979): 123–129

34. I have sketched such a doctrine in "A Fitting Theory of Truth", *Tulane Studies in Philosophy* 14 (1965).

35. I have elaborated this position in "Process and Pragmatism", *Tulane Studies in Philosophy* 23 (1974): 87–97.

36. See David L. Miller, "Mead's Theory of Universals", in *The Philosophy of George Herbert Mead,* edited by W. R. Corti (Amriswiler Bücherei, 1973) pp. 89–106. For a citation to Mead, see *Mind, Self, and Society* (Chicago: the University of Chicago Press, 1934), p. 125.

37. I am here showing the influence of H. M. Sheffer on my view of the nature of logic, though I did not originally get it from him. Several years before I met Professor Sheffer I made a careful study of Royce's "Principles of Logic" in Windelband and Ruge's *Encyclopaedia of the Philosophical Sciences* (London: Macmillan and Co., Ltd., 1913), vol. 1 (there were no other volumes). For a clear-cut statement of Sheffer's influence, see my *Symbolic Logic* (New York: Random House, 1961; London: Routledge and Kegan Paul, 1962), Ch. 20.

38. It would be out of place to go into detail here concerning the construction of an abstract conceptual scheme. I have presented greater detail in "Conceptual Models in Knowledge", *Tulane Studies in Philosophy* 17 (1968): 101–113.

39. It is instructive to note that the logical particles (constants) in Quine's view expressed in *Mathematical Logic,* p. 2, have the meanings that they have in natural language.

REPLY TO HAROLD N. LEE

Lee begins with a sympathetic sketch of my position that is faithful in large part, but needs adjustment at points.

My ontology, according to Lee, is an ontology of existent objects. If by this he means spatiotemporal particulars, he is wrong; my ontology admits also the full complement of extensional universals, mathematical and otherwise. If on the other hand he is using 'exist' in the broader way, as mathematicians do, then I agree; but I would expect anyone to say the same of his own ontology. At later points he speaks of my ontology as limited to objects, but here I would counter with the same dilemma: spatiotemporal objects, no; objects in an unrestricted sense, yes, of course. At still other points he speaks of my ontology, most discouragingly, as limited to entities. I am not fond of this word, and have resorted to it only to forestall the narrower interpretation that plagues 'exist' and 'object'. I understand 'entity' as a neutral term for whatever there is. Lee may disagree with me as to what there is, but I would have expected him to apply the word 'entity' to whatever he takes there to be. However, he understands the word differently; he admits relations, minds, and meanings, but denies that they are entities. "Only what is relatively stable and fundamental in the scheme of things," he writes, "should be called an entity." What I need is a general term for what there is. I thought I had it.

It emerges at later points that what he objects to in my ontology is that my objects are discrete and ready-made. But I admit the real numbers. If these are discrete, what are continuous? Are my objects discrete merely in that I hold with Bishop Butler that "everything is what it is and not another thing"? If so, I own the soft impeachment.

And I miss the force of his "ready-made", for I do believe in a future full of novelty. Maybe his point is that I regard man as discovering scientific truth rather than partly inventing it; for Lee suggests this elsewhere. This impeachment, however, I disown. Scientific theory outruns all possible data; hence the indeterminacy of translation, and hence the latitude of alternative scientific theories compatible with all possible evidence. The difference between two such alternative theories is a measure of man's contribution to scientific truth. Even our ontology, the range of values of our variables, is far from determined by experience. When Lee wrote in ostensible opposition that

> logic is an essential ingredient in the process of achieving a world of objects instead of being the description of the formal aspect of such a world conceived as ready-made

he was not far from my own position.

Perhaps he was misled by my realism, not appreciating that it is consistent with recognizing man's creative role in science. The reconciliation lies in my naturalism. Disavowing as I do a first philosophy outside science, I can attribute reality and truth only within the terms and standards of the scientific system of the world that I now accept; only immanently. But also, within this system, I can study man at work and appreciate how his theory—mine—is underdetermined.

Note that this immanent standard of truth is what Tarski's construction gives us. I think Lee would do well to use Dewey's phrase 'warranted assertibility'[1] for what he is calling truth, and reserve the word 'truth' for Tarski's.

Now I return to Lee's criticisms of my ontology, for there is more to say. He represents me as not admitting events, and not admitting relations; and he suggests that events can be broken down into objects and the relations between them. In fact I do admit relations, as classes of pairs. So his way of construing events is available to me. Also I have suggested a way of construing events as physical objects.[2]

He further describes me as holding "that since meanings are not entities, they do not belong to the ontological realm". For me this would be a circular argument of unit circumference. Actually my strictures against the notion of meaning are not ontological. They are of a piece rather with my criticism of the notion of analyticity, and they are developed in my doctrine of the indeterminacy of translation. I object to the lack of a reasonably intelligible explication of synonymy, as distinct from extensional equivalence. See my reply to Alston.

He writes that I take "symbolism for granted, and as a result [am] able to keep meanings out of [my] ontological realm." Matters are rather the reverse. My effort in the philosophy of language has been to understand the relation of language to mind and nature, and my objection to mentalistic semanticists is that they shirk this task by their facile appeal to an unexplicated notion of meaning. I am not complaining of vagueness, as Lee supposes; in *Word and Object* I wrote in praise of vagueness. But I find the notion of meaning an obstacle to the very study, semantics, to which it gives its name. I have tried to devise more suitable notions to implement that study: thus stimulus meaning, analytical hypothesis, receptual and perceptual similarity.

When Lee wrote that I reduce all meaning to reference, he may have supposed that I mean my observation sentences to refer to their stimulus meanings; but I do not. When he wrote of "symbolic relationships developed in minds as the result of response to the environment", on the other hand, he was unwittingly stating my real semantic concerns. When he wrote that "conceptual similarity is to be accounted for by a lack of discrimination between differences in stimuli for the purposes of action", he was unwittingly describing what I called perceptual similarity, and describing it in terms of which I approve. We are closer than he thinks.

But our agreement, however covert, stops short of intensions. Just barely. I can still agree when he writes that "there is no warrant for [Quine] to assume that because his symbols operate only in extension there *are* only extensions." This would evidently be a case of what he calls the logician's fallacy, and I can agree that it would be a fallacy. However, it is not mine. My reasons for not accepting intensions are different, and they are very much in print. The main one was just now mentioned in connection with synonymy.

In denying intensions I am not denying that classes are normally specified intensionally, if this merely means stating a membership condition. Classes are seldom specified by enumeration, and anyway that is a kind of membership condition. Even extrapolable ostension of members is a kind of membership condition. There would be no debate over intensionality if this were the point.

"Technically," he writes,

> the intension of a given concept is the *conjunct* of the intensions of all the other concepts that would be applicable to *whatever* the given concept may be applied.

The words "of the intensions" here are perhaps inadvertent and should be deleted; they seem to create a circularity, as well as a rather bewildering piling up. Since furthermore he allows at one point that concepts may be construed as verbal, it may appear that his formulation can be paraphrased thus: The intension of a given open sentence is the set of all the other open sentences that are satisfied by everything that satisfies the given one. Certainly I have no quarrel with intensions in this sense, except that they serve no purpose. The intension, in this sense, of an open sentence is uniquely determined by the extension of that open sentence, and consequently anything that could be said in terms of intensions could be paraphrased in terms of extensions, or classes.

If intensions are to make a difference, we must take the words "would be" seriously in Lee's formulation. We must take the intension as comprising just the open sentences that not only *are* satisfied by everything that *does* satisfy the given one, but also *would* be satisfied by anything else if it *were* to satisfy the given one. These modal auxiliaries are what break extensionality, and their acceptance is equivalent to accepting analyticity and synonymy.

Lee holds that logic is "the science of pure form, . . . displayed in uninterpreted systems." Certainly logic, in what I consider the properly narrow sense of the term, is displayed in quantificational schemata containing uninterpreted sentence letters and predicate letters and having an unspecified range of values for the bound variables. But the logical connectives and quantifiers retain the interpretations that render them useful in extra-logical discourse. Also, beyond the bounds of logic proper, there is a higher "science of pure form" in abstract algebra. See an early page of my reply to Parsons where I consider the place of this subject in set theory.

Use and mention are mixed up in Lee's account of objectual and substitutional quantification. "According to the *substitutional* view, the value of a variable is whatever can be substituted for it." Better: the variable admits substitutes but no values. "The values of a variable refer 'to the objects . . .'." No; the values *are* the objects. "It is the substitution of the number itself, of which the numeral is the name, that determines truth or falsity." No; it is the substitution of the numeral.

"The class of stimulus meanings", Lee writes, "is a class of physical objects." No, it is a class of pairs of classes of classes of receptors. "Quine insists that dispositions are behavioral factors." Well, I wrote that they were hypothetical physical states or mechanisms.

W.V.Q.

NOTES

1. John Dewey, *Logic: The Theory of Inquiry.*
2. "Whither Physical Objects?" *Boston Studies in Philosophy of Science* 39 (1976): third paragraph, 497–504.

12

Arnold B. Levison

TRANSLATIONAL INDETERMINACY AND
THE MIND-BODY PROBLEM

I

In this paper I attempt to explain the bearing of Quine's thesis of translational indeterminacy on the mind-body problem. I am concerned with two main issues: the status of "phenomenal objects" such as sense data, and the place of "introspective reports" in scientific psychology and epistemology. In particular, I want to consider whether Quine's thesis of translational indeterminacy, if true, would tend to undermine the Cartesian view that the deliverances of introspection, or "knowledge by acquaintance," are foundational for scientific knowledge in general or as a whole. I believe that Quine intends the thesis of translational indeterminacy to have this consequence, and I hope to show that it does not. If my remarks are cogent, they may provoke a response from Quine which will clarify his epistemological views and deepen our understanding of them.

II

What philosophers generally discuss under the heading of "the mind-body problem" is a curious mixture of scientific, epistemological, metaphysical, semantical, and psychological issues. Consider, for example, the following attempt by Herbert Feigl to set the stage for introducing the problem in a contemporary setting:[1]

> If I report moods, feelings, emotions, sentiments, thoughts, images, dreams, etc., that I experience, I am *not referring* to my *behavior*, be it actually occurring or

I have benefited from comments by John L. King, Irving Thalberg, Jr., and William G. Lycan on earlier versions of this paper.

likely to occur under specified conditions. I am referring to those states or processes of my direct experience which I live through (enjoy or suffer), to the "raw feels" of my awareness. These "raw feels" are accessible to other persons only indirectly by inference—but it is *myself* who *has* them.

The following is a partial list of some of the more important problems or questions raised by this passage:

1. What is it to "report" one's own moods, sentiments, thoughts, images, dreams, etc.?
2. Do such "reports" contain referring terms? If so, do they refer to objects of a peculiar kind, such as "raw feels" of one's direct experience or awareness?
3. How do we distinguish between behavior (and physical processes generally), on the one hand, and the "raw feels" of our direct awareness on the other?
4. What is the nature of the relation between "behavior" and "raw feels"? Is it, e.g., empirical (causal) or logical (conceptual)?
5. Are "raw feels" particular concrete events or are they repeatable patterns (universals)?
6. Are my "raw feels" bodily states or processes, or are they states of something altogether distinct from my body or any part of it?
7. Are there at least three distinct and independent kinds of knowledge: (a) the knowledge each of us has of his own "raw feels" (introspective knowledge or knowledge by acquaintance); (b) the knowledge one may have of the "raw feels" of other minds, and (c) the knowledge we may have of "behavior" and physical objects and events generally?
8. What is a "self" or "subject of experience," and what is it for such a "self" to *have* "raw feels" (i.e., moods, sentiments, emotions, sensations, thoughts, etc.)? (Can the "self," for example, be identified with the body it is said to "occupy" uniquely at a given time?)

An interesting feature of this list is that answers to the later questions depend on how we answer earlier ones. For example, if my "reports" of my "raw feels" are not genuine descriptions containing referring terms, but have some other linguistic function, then questions (3) through (7) simply do not arise. In other words, no "mind-body" problem arises. To get the mind-body problem off the ground, then, we need to assume that when we "report" our moods, thoughts, etc., we are referring to *something,* be it "raw feels" or mere behavior.

It is important to understand that this assumption may be unjustified. The bearing of Quine's thesis of translational indeterminacy on the mind-body problem may be found precisely here, if I am not mistaken. So we might begin by considering whether the "reports" in question are genuine descriptions containing referring terms.

From Quine's standpoint, of course, no sentence, first-person or other, wears its reporting function on its sleeve. Whether any of the grammatical components of a sentence are properly construed as referring terms is a question whose answer depends on how we choose to analyze the sentence into semantical and syntactical elements. There is no satisfactory criterion, no matter of fact or logic, to which we can appeal for guidance in making this choice. Thus any decision is more or less arbitrary. This is the essence of the indeterminacy of translation. On the other hand, once these choices and decisions have been made, however arbitrary, we can proceed with our scientific theorizing. For purposes of theory, we can appeal to the degree of utility involved in positing objects of a certain kind or refraining from such positing. Any question concerning the existence of objects of a certain kind should be decided in this fashion. Introspection plays no role whatever in determining relative or comparative utility, and neither introspection nor sensory observation "reveals" objects either of a mental or a physical kind. Thus Quine writes:[2]

> We are virtually bound . . . to hold to an ontology of external objects; but it is moot indeed whether the positing of additional objects of a mental kind is a help or a hindrance to science. Or perhaps not so moot. At any rate, it is moot or else it is clear that they are a hindrance.

But if we have a free choice whether or not to posit objects of a mental kind, and such positing would lead to the mind-body problem, then the rational procedure would be to *refrain* from such positing. By not indulging ourselves in this way we are rewarded by having no mind-body problem to solve. The assumption of the existence of a "sensory component" of our experience (e.g., Feigl's "raw feels"), distinct from any behavior including the physical stimulations of sensory organs, neural responses, etc., is strictly speaking an ontological or metaphysical one. But the only non-circular basis we have for making the assumption is *epistemological*. We contrast the way in which we know behavior and the way in which we know our own inner states. According to the traditional Cartesian account, each of us is supposed to have direct, non-inferential or immediate knowledge of his own psychological states, while external objects are known only indirectly or by inference from the data of immediate experience. But it is a non sequitur to conclude from this sort of epistemological dualism that "the raw feels of our direct awareness" are not "behavior," unless we are using the term "behavior" in an unduly restricted and narrow sense.

Quine's theory of posits as applied to objects of a mental kind might strike many philosophers, materialists and immaterialists alike, as plainly false. According to J. J. C. Smart, for example:[3]

> . . . we do report something, in a perfectly full-blooded sense of "report", when we tell the dentist that we have a pain or the psychologist that we are having an after-image.

For Smart there is a "problem about the mysterious nature of the putative objects of these 'reports'. . . ." Thus Smart, like Feigl, evidently takes the objects as *given,* and not as something we have a choice about. For Quine, on the other hand, the alleged problem of the "mysterious nature" of the "putative objects" apparently referred to in first-person psychological sentences does not arise.

Many recent philosophers—so called philosophical behaviorists—have questioned whether first-person psychological sentences (e.g., 'I feel depressed', 'I'm experiencing pain', 'I'm thinking of the Taj Mahal') are indeed "reports", in the sense of being logically true-or-false sentences. They have suggested that these sentences, when uttered, are mere behavior, comparable to wincing, crying aloud, gesticulating, and so on. If the philosophical behaviorists are right, first-person psychological sentences would not have any descriptive or reporting function, so no question could arise regarding the nature of the objects referred to by their imbedded terms. As Smart describes this view,[4]

> When I say that it looks to me that there is a roundish yellowish-orange patch on the wall I am expressing some sort of temptation to say that there *is* a roundish yellowish-orange patch on the wall. Similarly, when I "report" a pain I am really not reporting anything at all but am doing a sort of wince. As Wittgenstein says, "The verbal expression of pain replaces crying and does not describe it." (Nor, as I interpret Wittgenstein, does it describe anything else.)

Quine does not propose the theory that all first-person psychological sentences are mere avowals. Nor does he deny that any of the terms in such sentences *refer.* What he questions is the utility of the assumption that if such terms do refer, they must refer to objects of a non-physical kind. He also rejects the idea that first-person psychological sentences express a form of direct or immediate knowledge, which is the foundation of our knowledge of the external world.[5] Thus suppose that Quine is right in saying that we posit mental objects just as we do other kinds of objects, and that this positing is under-determined by considerations of observation and logic. It follows that we have considerable latitude of free choice in making decisions about what sorts of objects to posit and what sorts to refrain from positing. In this way Quine's theory and the "avowal theory" may be said to aim at the same goal: deflating the significance traditionally claimed for first-person psychological reports by epistemologists since Descartes. This result in turn would undermine the epistemological basis for believing that the mind-body problem is a genuine and not a pseudo-problem.

I shall attempt to document these claims by reviewing Quine's treatment of the problem of "sense data," i.e., whether relevant scientific theorizing requires that we posit sense data (or a sensory component of experience) in addition to physical objects and events (including of course neural ones) in order to explain human behavior, experience, and knowledge. Next, I shall consider whether Quine's doctrines successfully undermine the Cartesian view of the primacy of first-person knowledge. I shall argue that the mind-body problem, at least in its epistemological form, is not wholly laid to rest by Quine's arguments.

III

Let us begin by considering certain passages that occur in Quine's *magnum opus, Word & Object,* especially in the first and seventh chapters, concerning sense data. A curious feature of Quine's discussion of this topic is that he allows approximately 230 largely unrelated pages to intervene between the beginning and the end of a connected line of argument. One may easily misinterpret the earlier portion as a commitment to orthodox sense datum theory, if one fails to connect it to the later portion.

In the following passages from Chapter One, for example, Quine seems to presuppose the traditional empiricist dualism of subjective experience, on the one hand, and object experienced on the other.[6] (In fact, however, Quine intends to reject this subject-object dualism from the very beginning.)

> . . . Physical things generally, however remote, become known to us only through the effects which they help to induce at our sensory surfaces. . . . Entification begins at arm's length; the points of condensation in the primordial conceptual scheme are things glimpsed, not glimpses. . . .
> Talk of subjective sense qualities comes mainly as a derivative idiom. When one tries to describe a particular sensory quality, he typically resorts to reference to public things—describing a color as orange or heliotrope, a smell as like that of rotten eggs . . . he best identifies his sense data by reflecting them in external objects. . . .

In this passage, Quine speaks of "glimpses" as opposed to "things glimpsed", of "subjective sense qualities" as opposed to "physical things". He also speaks of describing "a particular sensory quality", and of *identifying* "sense data". Surely a reader of this passage would be justified in assuming that Quine is a sense datum theorist of some sort, in the tradition of Locke, Berkeley, Hume, J. S. Mill, Russell, G. E. Moore, etc. Nor is there much in the immediately succeeding pages to disabuse him of this impression.[7]

> Impressed with the fact that we know external things only mediately through our senses, philosophers from Berkeley onward have undertaken to strip away the

physicalistic conjectures and lay bare the sense data. Yet even as we try to recapture the data, in all their innocence of interpretation, we find ourselves depending upon sidelong glances into natural science. . . . (pp. 1–2)

A "natural" way of interpreting this passage is this. Quine is concerned with the following question: how we are led to believe that *there are* sense data? The answer he suggests is that scientific theory, not introspection, is responsible. Since scientific theory depends on observational evidence, it follows that observational evidence is presupposed by the sense datum theory, rather than conversely, as is usually thought. But Quine seems to take for granted that *there are* sense data, however limited their value as primordial evidence for the existence of physical objects, as things we know directly and immediately, in the way traditional empiricists imagined. Lampooning the latter idea, Quine writes:

. . . our philosopher may . . . try . . . to abstract out a pure stream of sense experience and then depict physical doctrine as a means of systematizing the regularities discernible in the stream. He may imagine an ideal "protocol language" which, even if in fact learned after commonsense talk of physical things or not at all, is evidentially prior: a fancifully fancyless medium of unvarnished news. Talk of physical things he would then see as, in principle, a device for simplifying that disorderly account of the passing show. . . . (p. 2)

But this parody of "phenomenalism", or "reductive sense-data theories" leaves the main ontological question of the existence of sense data untouched. The "trouble" with phenomenalism, Quine says, "is that immediate experience simply will not, of itself, cohere as an autonomous domain. Reference to physical objects is what keeps it together." (p. 2) Here Quine seems to beg the question. A sceptic might ask how he knows that we succeed in referring to physical objects. But even if we waive this question, Quine's point is epistemological, not ontological. He is arguing for the epistemic primacy, or at least equal priority, of the observable behavior of physical objects for providing basic evidence for theory and language acquisition, over and above immediate experience and sense data. But his argument up to this point does not close the door to dualism, whether epistemological or ontological; on the contrary, it appears to be a particular variant of both those forms of dualism. Quine seems to be denying that sense data are epistemically prior to the behavior of physical objects and language acquisition. He has said nothing which implies that *there are no* sense data or that sense data may not play an important role in our understanding of the world. The impression that Quine himself is committed to sense data is reinforced when Quine writes that references to physical things

. . . give us our main continuing access to past sense data themselves; for past sense data are mostly gone for good except as commemorated in physical posits. All we would have apart from posits and speculation are present sense data and present memories of past ones; and a memory trace of a sense datum is too meager an affair to do much good. Actual memories mostly are traces of past conceptualization or verbalization. . . . (pp. 2–3)

In this passage, Quine appears to refer to sense data. He speaks of our having "continuing access" to them, and of "a memory trace of a sense datum". Thus, once again, he appears to have taken the existence of sense data for granted. However, as we shall see, this conclusion is not strictly warranted, since there is no real inconsistency in Quine's *appearing* to mention sense data, in the first chapter, and later denying that we need to "posit" them, given his general view that it makes no sense to ask for the reference of individual terms in a sentence except in the context of a system of sentences comprising a theory. There is no real inconsistency because, for Quine, it is only a theory as a whole which determines whether a term in a sentence has a referring function, and we have a choice among possible theories. Evidently, Quine feels justified in using expressions such as "sense data", since for him this use does not necessarily constitute reference. The following quotations from his essay, "On Mental Entities", make this clear:[7]

> The crucial insight of empiricism is that any evidence for science has its end points in the senses. This insight remains valid, but it is an insight which comes after physics, physiology, and psychology, not before. Epistemologists have wanted to posit a realm of sense data, situated somehow just me-ward of the physical stimulus, for fear of circularity: to view the physical stimulation rather than the sense datum as the end point of scientific evidence would be to make physical science rest for its evidence on physical science.

Quine embraces this conclusion:

> . . . if with Neurath we accept this circularity . . . then we dispose of the epistemological motive for assuming a realm of sense data . . . .

Quine writes further:

> . . . we decide what things there are, or what things to treat as there being, by considerations of simplicity of the overall system and its utility in connection with experience. . . .

But, he immediately adds:

> . . . I do not want to force the issue of recognizing experience as an entity or composite of entities. I have talked up to now as if there were such entities; I had to talk some language, and I uncritically talked this one. But the history of the mind-body problem bears witness to the awkwardness of the practice.

Thus, describing the role of sense data in the history of philosophy does not constitute reference to sense data as objects of scientific theory. Quine has not been talking about *sense data,* but about the *term* "sense data"; the role this term (or notion) has played in conceptualizing the world. His view is that while physical objects are needed in order that our conceptual scheme, theories of language learning, physical theories, etc., cohere or "hold together," so called "mental entities" are not. Thus in Chapter Seven of *Word & Object,* he remarks:

> . . . our terms for physical objects are commonly learned through fairly direct conditioning to stimulatory effects of the denoted objects. The empirical evidence for such physical objects, if not immediate, is at any rate less far-fetched and so less suspect than that for objects whose terms are learned only in deep context. (p. 234)

For Quine, the language of sense data is a derivative idiom, and its terms are learned only in deep context. In this respect sense data can be compared to the theoretical entities of physics. But this consideration does not affect the claim made by sense-datum philosophers that our knowledge of sense data can be *shown* to be "immediate" by reflective analysis on the logic of justification. Quine is aware of this, as he goes on to remark that although the above consideration counts as a "defensible reason" for "relative confidence in physical objects", it is still "contestable on two counts", the first of which is this:

> . . . it makes no case for physical objects of highly inferential sorts, and . . . it makes yet more of a case for sense data or sense qualities than for physical objects. (p. 234)

And the second "count":

> . . . insofar as it champions sense data in the sense of concrete sensory events (as against recurrent qualities), [it] is an objection . . . to physicalism. . . . [But] the likely rejoinder to the objection is independent of whether the subjective sensory objects envisaged are events or qualities. It is that *no sufficient purpose is served by positing subjective sensory objects.* (p. 234; my italics)

Quine then considers "three real or fancied purposes of positing such objects". The first is already familiar to us: it is the phenomenalist's project: to make "such objects suffice to the exclusion of physical objects". As Quine says: it "seems pretty widely acknowledged nowadays" that we cannot "hope" to accomplish this. Since arguments to refute phenomenalism are readily available in current literature, I shall not consider this issue any further.

The second ostensible purpose to be served by "positing" subjective sensory objects or sense data is that we "need them in addition to physical objects, as means e.g. of reporting illusions . . ." and, one might add, pains, twinges, tickles, itches, and other sensations, as well as phenomena like dreams and after-images, etc. But:

> . . . one might claim that such purposes are adequately met by a propositional-attitude construction in which 'seems that' or the like is made to govern a subsidiary sentence about physical objects. One might claim that special objects of illusion are then no more called for than peculiar non-physical objects of quest or desire. . . . (p. 235)

Two problems arise in connection with this suggestion. The first is that "propositional-attitude constructions" are typically non-extensional contexts, while for Quine the ideal language of scientific theory is restricted to extensional contexts and constructions. Insofar as the language of psychological science needs to employ propositional-attitude constructions, it would fall short of Quine's standards for a scientific language. The second problem is that even if the apparent need for non-physical objects of psychological attitudes is eliminated by the method of paraphrase, we are still left with the psychological attitudes themselves, and thus apparently left with "states of mind" as opposed to physical states of bodies. This consideration brings up the third ostensible purpose for "positing" subjective sensory objects in addition to physical objects. In Quine's words, the question is whether we "need sensory objects to account for our knowledge or discourse of physical objects themselves". Quine's reply is as follows:

> . . . the relevance of sensory stimulation to sentences about physical objects can as well (and better) be explored and explained in terms directly of the conditioning of such sentences or their parts to physical irritations of the subject's surfaces. Intervening neural activity goes on, but the claim is that nothing is clarified, nothing but excess baggage is added, by positing intermediary subjective objects of apprehension anterior to the physical objects overtly alleged in the spoken sentences themselves. (p. 235)

Moreover, Quine argues:

> The supposed function of sense datum reports, in contributing something like certainty to the formulations of empirical knowledge, may more realistically be assigned to observation sentences. . . . These enjoy a privileged evidential position in the directness of their correlation with non-verbal stimulation; yet they are not, typically, about sense data. (p. 235)

Here Quine seems to be suggesting that "directness of correlation with nonverbal stimulation" is a criterion for determining epistemic priority, or "basic" evidence. Since "observation sentences", in Quine's sense, are about "physical objects" and since they provide basic "data" for scientific theorizing about the world, this criterion also helps to justify the "posit" of physical objects. However, a difficulty arises here:

> What had been confronting us was the plea in behalf of sense data that if some physical objects are to be preferred to abstract ones on the score of comparative directness of association with sensory stimulation, then sense data are to be preferred *a fortiori*. The answer proposed was predicated on utility for theory: that sense data neither suffice to the exclusion of physical objects nor are needed in addition. Now here we begin to witness the collision of two standards. Comparative directness of association with sensory stimulation was counted in favor of physical objects, but then we raised against the sense data themselves a second standard: utility for theory. Does one then have simply to weigh opposing consideration? (pp. 235–6)

In other words, Quine seems to be working with two criteria for positing objects, which conflict in the present context. The first criterion is "comparative directness of association with sensory stimulation". By this criterion, we are led to posit subjective sensory objects, as being more directly associated with stimulation of sensory organs than physical objects, which exist only "at arm's length". The second criterion is "utility for theory". By this criterion it seems to follow that while physical objects are indispensable, subjective sensory objects are not, and may even be a "hindrance". Obviously, the hindrance is that their admission creates the mind-body problem with its concomitant obstacles for unifying physical and psychological knowledge.

We are now in a position to understand the relevance of Quine's thesis of translational indeterminacy for the mind-body problem. For in Quine's view, translational indeterminacy establishes pretty conclusively that there is really only one adequate criterion for "positing" objects. It is not "comparative directness of association with sensory stimulation", which is Quine's version of the criterion of traditional empiricism. It is simply and solely the criterion of "utility for theory".

> . . . let us recall the predicament in radical translation, which showed that a full knowledge of the stimulus meaning of an observation sentence is not sufficient for translating or even spotting a term. (p. 236)

The empiricist criterion, in other words, is not a criterion of *reference to objects,* since it is of no help in identifying putative referring words or "terms".

> In our own language, by the same token, the stimulus meaning of an observation sentence in no way settles whether any part of the sentence should be distinguished as a term for sense data, or as a term for physical objects, or as a term at all. How directly the sentence and its words are associated with sensory stimulation, or how confidently the sentence may be affirmed on the strength of a given sensory stimulation, does not settle whether to posit objects of one sort or another for words of the sentence to denote in the capacity of terms. (p. 236)

Thus introspective sentences such as "I have a pain", or "I seem to see an after-image" have no privileged status. Whether we regard them as "reports" depends on how we analyze them into terms, syncategorematic words, connectives, quantifiers, and so on. And how we do this depends in turn on a single criterion: utility for theory.

> We may be perceived to have posited the objects only when we have brought the contemplated terms into suitable interplay with the whole distinctively objectificatory apparatus of our language: articles and pronouns and the idioms of identity, plurality, and predication, or, in canonical notation, quantification. Even a superficially termlike occurrence is no proof of termhood, failing systematic interplay with key idioms generally. (p. 236)

Furthermore, according to Quine:

> Let a word . . . have occurred as a fragment of ever so many empirically well-attested sentential wholes; even as a rather termlike fragment, by superficial appearances. Still, the question whether to treat it as a term is the question whether to give it general access to positions appropriate to general terms, or perhaps to singular terms, subject to the usual laws of such contexts. Whether to do so may reasonably be decided by considerations of systematic efficacy, utility for theory. (pp. 236–7)

To take an example, recall our earlier discussion of the problem that concerned Smart "about the mysterious nature of the putative objects" of first-person psychological "reports". So long as considerations of utility for theory do not lead us to posit such objects, no problem about them can arise. According to Quine, ordinary physical objects, including bodily and neural processes, will suffice for purposes of theory.

What basically distinguishes Quine's epistemic stance, then, from the attitude of sense-datum philosophers and other proponents of traditional empiricism, is that the latter assume that evidential sentences can be cognized in isolation, independently of scientific theory of a whole, by the closeness of their association with experience. If the mind-body problem depends on this assumption, then from Quine's point of view the mind-body problem rests on a mistake. This mistake is the belief that we can know which terms are to be treated as referential in first-person psychological sentences just by being able to understand the sentence or utter it on an appropriate occasion. If Quine is right, such sentences have no privileged status; like every other sentence, they are meaningful only in the context of theory, and theory is governed by the single criterion of utility. Thus Quine writes:

> . . . any subjective talk of mental events proceeds necessarily in terms that are acquired and understood through their associations, direct or indirect, with the socially observable behavior of physical objects. If there is a case for mental events and mental states, it must be just that the positing of them, like the positing of molecules, has some indirect systematic efficacy in the development of theory. (p. 264)

This passage is misleading so far as it suggests that in Quine's view, mental events and states are "theoretical entities" like molecules. His point is rather that mental events and states are "posited", just like any other objects. Perhaps Quine would say that it is easier to see this in the case of molecules than in the case of headaches, twinges, and the like, because the former are introduced in the first place only in scientific theory, while the latter occur as putative objects of reference in ordinary language. But that consideration does not affect their ontic status; it only means that considered as putative objects, they are more familiar to us than molecules and the like. Hence Quine can say:

> . . . if a certain organization of theory is achieved by thus positing distinctive mental states and events behind physical behavior, surely as much organization could be achieved by positing merely certain correlative physiological states and events instead. Lack of a detailed physiological explanation of the states is scarcely an objection to acknowledging them as states of human bodies, when we reflect that those who posit the mental states and events have no details of appropriate mechanisms to offer nor, what with their mind-body problem, prospects of any. The bodily states exist anyway; why add the others? Thus introspection may be seen as a witnessing to one's own bodily condition. . . . (p. 265)

In other words, introspective reports may be treated as observation sentences, distinguished not by their having a privileged epistemic status, but by the location of the observed object inside the outer surface of the body of the observer. In this way, Quine thinks, we may deny that introspective reports are more "basic" to our empirical knowledge than other kinds of observation sentences.

IV

In the preceding section we considered some important advantages of Quine's method for by-passing traditional riddles usually lumped together as "the mind-body problem". We saw that Quine answers the question whether or not to posit "phenomenal objects" in the negative, by considering their utility for theory in a pragmatic spirit. In every case, according to Quine, refraining from such postulation promises greater theoretical gain than indulging in it, since bodily states, neural processes and the like suffice for purposes of theory. We saw, in addition, that Quine's thesis of translational indeterminacy plays an essential role in defending his methodological views, especially his view that "utility for theory," and not introspection or closeness of association with sensory experience, is the appropriate criterion for deciding whether or not to "posit" objects of various kinds. Finally we saw the bearing of these considerations on the question of the epistemic status of first-person psychological sentences, a question which lies at the heart of the mind-body problem. We must now shift our perspective a little, and consider whether Quine's doubts about the utility of introspective "data" for scientific psychology are justified. For this purpose, we must briefly reconsider the import of Quine's views for the problem of determining the epistemic status of first-person psychological sentences.

To employ one of Smart's examples, suppose I say "It looks to me that there is a roundish yellowish-orange patch on the wall" in the following circumstances: (1) the sentence is true, (2) there is no patch on the wall, and (3) I do not believe that there is a patch on the wall. In these circumstances my sentence is "a report of an after-image". According to Quine, describing my sentence as a "report of an after-image" does not imply that something *is* an after-image; i.e., that there exists a certain object, namely a phenomenal roundish yellowish-orange patch, which appears to me to be on the wall. Whether we ought to "posit" phenomenal patches in addition to ordinary colored surfaces is a question that can only be answered by considerations of utility for theory. Similarly for a sentence such as "I am in pain." This sentence does not imply "Something is a pain". What, then, if anything, do such sentences "report"?

What is reported is not that there exists a phenomenal object ("a pain", "an after-image"), but that some person or organism is having a certain experience ("I am having a painful experience", "I am having an after-image experience"). In other words, the following would be incorrect analyses of these reports:

(1) (Ex) (x is a pain and I have x),
(2) (Ex) (x is an after-image and x appears to me to be on the wall).

A step toward a correct analysis would be the following:

(3) (Ex) (x is having a painful experience),
(4) (Ex) (x is having an after-image experience).

Thus interpreting first-person psychological sentences as "reports" does not commit us to the existence of phenomenal objects. However, it does seem to commit us to individuals who have certain experiences or are in certain states. What I am reporting in the above sentences, then, if I am reporting anything, is minimally a fact about my own state (which, for all I or anyone knows, may be a state of my body).

So far, then, no "mind-body problem" arises from interpreting first-person sentences as "reports". However, the following questions do arise: (a) when a person makes such a report, does he know a fact about himself, e.g., the fact that it does look to him that there is a roundish yellowish-orange patch on the wall, or the fact that he is having a painful experience, etc.; and (b) given that he does know such a fact about himself, does his *belief* that he is in such-and-such a state or is having such-and-such experience depend in any way on the semantical structure of the sentence he uses to make his report, or on the semantical relations of this sentence to other sentences of his language?

An "introspectionist" who has reviewed Quine's arguments for translational indeterminacy might answer this question in the following way. To say that a person may have knowledge of his own state in such circumstances implies nothing whatever about language. For his having such knowledge depends only on his *being* in that state and believing of himself that he *is* in that state. Thus, in order for me to know, e.g., that I am in pain, nothing more is required than that I be in pain and believe that I am; in order for me to know that it looks to me that such-and-such (e.g., that there is a roundish yellowish-orange patch on the wall), nothing more is required than that it does look to me that such-and-such, and I believe this. Similarly for other first-person psychological states. It is for this reason, the "introspectionist" might claim, that Smart is correct in saying that first person psychological sentences are "full-blooded reports" and not mere "avowals". For what such sentences report are facts about ourselves.

So far as I can see, nothing in Quine's arguments for translational indeterminacy establishes the conclusion that the possibility of first-person knowledge depends on a person having any beliefs about language. Therefore, nothing in this thesis is inconsistent with the "introspectionist's" answers to the above questions. The epistemic significance of translational indeterminacy is that in order to determine which terms in a sentence (if any) refer to objects, we must place the sentence in the context of a theory or a system of interrelated sentences. Talk of objects, according to Quine, is meaningless apart from such a system. Since the system is forever under-determined by experience, a multiplicity of such systems is possible. Several of them might be consistent with all our experience but inconsistent with one another. Therefore, experience alone cannot provide a criterion for selecting among such systems. Nor can anything else.

Since this is a thesis about language, about talk of objects and not about objects, an "introspectionist" could consistently accept it while denying that it has any logical bearing on *his* thesis that in first-person knowledge we are acquainted with ourselves and our own states. If a person may have knowledge of his own states independently of having any beliefs about sentences or the conditions of reference of terms occurring in them, then the existence of first-person knowledge does not depend on the existence of any beliefs about first-person sentences. Imagine, then a person who knows of himself or is aware that he is in pain, and who has the ability to speak a language. *He might succeed in expressing his knowledge in a first-person sentence, although he were forever unable to determine which terms in his sentence referred to himself or his state.* Therefore introspection might acquaint us with objects such as our own states and attitudes, and ourselves, despite translational indeterminacy. And this acquaintance might supply each of us with concrete "data" which is not "theory-laden", so that we need not construe "data" as consisting merely in sentences of the observational kind, as Quine suggests.

If Quine should attempt to counter this argument by claiming that the beliefs in question must be beliefs about language, then an even greater difficulty arises. For if the beliefs in question must be about language, then translational indeterminacy would *conflict* with the thesis that a person may be aware or know of himself that he is in pain, when he *is* in pain and believes that he is.

If such a conflict arises, the introspectionist would ask which thesis is better founded, which we are justified in believing: translational indeterminacy or the doctrine of acquaintance. And surely, he would say, the answer is obvious. For if someone asks him how he knows, e.g., that he is having a painful experience, when he *is* having such an experience and believes this of himself, then he need only reply that he knows it because he is having that experience. But if he is asked how he knows that translational indeterminacy is true, then he must reply, if he is reasonable or honest, that neither he nor anyone else *knows* that this thesis is true, and that one's reasons for believing it, if one does believe it, are highly theoretical and complex. Thus if translational indeterminacy really does conflict with his belief that he knows his own experiences when he is having them, then he must give up the thesis of translational indeterminacy. In fact, he has what appears to be a conclusive reason for rejecting it.

Thus Quine seems to be confronted with a serious dilemma. If he accepts the conclusion that a person may be acquainted with himself and his own states, then "utility for theory" is not the sole criterion for "positing" entities. Ourselves, and our own states and attitudes would be "given". Acquaintance would provide an alternative criterion for admitting entities. But if Quine appeals to the thesis of translational indeterminacy in order to reject the conclusion that a person may be acquainted with himself and his own states, then translational indeterminacy is jeopardized.

In his comments on "the mind-body problem", Quine concentrates almost exclusively on the question whether introspection discloses phenomenal *objects* such as "sense data" or "raw feels". This is understandable, given the importance that philosophers traditionally have attached to this claim. But in berating this view he fails to notice that to dispose of phenomenal objects is not to dispose of introspection. Thus while Quine may be said to avoid the problems that arise from the ontological version of the mind-body problem, he is not equally successful in undermining the epistemological aspect of the problem. There is one passage, however, where Quine seems to notice this. When he suggests that we view introspection as a "witnessing to one's own bodily condition", he does not deny that it is a "witnessing" but only that it is a witnessing of something nonphysical. But when Quine goes on to suggest that we don't have privileged knowledge of our own *witnessings,* he goes beyond anything that translational indeterminacy, simplicity, utility, and similar criteria can justify.

While it is probably true, therefore, that scientific psychology need not "posit" sense data or other phenomenal objects, it does not follow that it can avoid the use of propositional attitude constructions, for example, constructions such as "it looks to me that . . .", at least if it includes human cognition within its scope. But the use of such constructions apparently implies that there is knowledge by acquaintance, and hence that "introspection" must continue to play a significant role in scientific psychology and epistemology. Evidently, then, Quine has not shown that epistemology can be "naturalized" in the way that he would like, if only because he has not shown that psychology can be "naturalized" in this way.

ARNOLD B. LEVISON

DEPARTMENT OF PHILOSOPHY
UNIVERSITY OF NORTH CAROLINA AT GREENSBORO
MARCH 1977

NOTES

1. Herbert Feigl, "Mind-Body, *Not* a Pseudoproblem", in *Dimensions of Mind,* edited by Sidney Hook (New York, 1961), p. 34. See also Herbert Feigl, "The 'Mental' and the 'Physical' ", in Herbert Feigl, Michael Scriven, and Grover Maxwell (eds), *Concepts, Theories, and the Mind-Body Problem,* vol. 2 of *Minnesota Studies in the Philosophy of Science* (Minneapolis, 1958), pp. 370–498.

2. "On Mental Entities", in W. V. Quine, *The Ways of Paradox and Other Essays* (New York, 1966), p. 213.

3. J. J. C. Smart, *Philosophy and Scientific Realism* (London, 1963), esp. Ch. V, and Smart's references on p. 92.

4. Ibid.

5. Op. cit., pp. 236–237. See esp. "Epistemology Naturalized", in W. V. Quine, *Ontological Relativity and Other Essays* (New York, 1969), pp. 69–91; and "On Mental Entities", in *The Ways of Paradox and Other Essays* (New York, 1966), pp. 208–215.

6. Willard Van Orman Quine, *Word and Object* (Cambridge, Massachusetts, 1960), p. 1. See also "Grades of Theoreticity", in Lawrence Foster and J. W. Swanson (eds), *Experience & Theory* (University of Massachusetts Press, 1970), pp. 1–17. Subsequent references to *Word and Object* will be indicated by page numbers in parentheses after quoted material.

7. Pp. 212–13.

REPLY TO ARNOLD LEVISON

I am prepared to believe that the positing of a more or less appropriate sort of denotata for the controversial term 'raw feel' or 'sense datum' could be useful for theoretical psychology, but I would not identify them with behavior. I would identify them with hypothetical neural processes, ones not necessarily understood in respect of physiological mechanism. Behavior would figure only as a symptom, helping us to detect the occurrence of these processes in people other than ourselves. In one's own case the handiest symptom is afforded by introspection, to which I am more receptive than Levison thinks. The intro-spective testimony would qualify as a genuine report of a neural event, not-withstanding the reporter's ignorance of its actual mechanism. But it would not qualify as an observation sentence in my sense of the term, for the requirement of agreement of witnesses would not in general be met. It is just here that the behaviorist discipline obtrudes, in its modest way: introspective reports do not qualify as observation sentences.

Levison asks whether the man making the introspective report is reporting something about himself which he knows to be true. From the point of view indicated above my answer is affirmative, except that I bridle at the absolute-ness of the verb 'know'. There are degrees of certainty, and this one is high. If with the progress of neuropsychology we were actually to isolate a neural process that lent itself pretty neatly to identification with the sense datum in question, we might thereafter impute occasional errors of introspection rather than give up the neat identification.

It must be borne in mind in general that such identifications are not abso-lutely right or wrong. Identification of sense data with the corresponding neural processes, and repudiation of sense data in favor of the corresponding neural processes, are two ways of saying the same thing.

Must we talk of sense data in reporting illusions? In *Word and Object* I suggested resorting instead to a propositional-attitude construction, 'seems that'. Levison cites this and protests that propositional attitudes have no place in my ideal language. *Touché!* I can only applaud his point. Instead of "It seems that the stick is bent" let me say something like: "I am in a neural state commonly induced by the sight of a bent stick." This dodge amounts to reinstating sense data and then construing them neurally as suggested above.

Levison represents me as

> arguing for the epistemic primacy, or at least equal priority, of the observable behavior of physical objects . . . over . . . immediate experience and sense data.

A better picture presents a bifurcation. Observation sentences, typically about physical objects, are indeed the social embodiment of the evidence for science. But at the same time the subjective role of sense data in epistemology is taken over, in my naturalism, by neural stimulation. What joins the two branches of the bifurcation is the conditionability of the observation sentences to stimulations.

Surely, then, Levison has the wrong slant in this passage:

> What basically distinguishes Quine's epistemic stance, then, from the attitude of sense-datum philosophers and other proponents of traditional empiricism, is that the latter assume that evidential sentences can be cognized in isolation, independently of scientific theory as a whole, by the closeness of their association with experience.

In my view observation sentences can indeed "be cognized in isolation, independently of scientific theory as a whole, by the closeness of their association with"—stimulation.

These occasion sentences qualify holophrastically as observational, but their parts recur as terms in theoretical science. That is how observation sentences link up with scientific theory, bearing evidence. If a recorded observation wildly at odds with theory is ultimately repudiated, as may happen, still what is repudiated is a dated statement of history, itself theoretical, and not the occasion sentence at its occurrence.

A "curious feature" of *Word and Object*, Levison notes, is that

> 230 largely unrelated pages intervene between the beginning and the end of a connected line of argument. One may easily misinterpret the earlier portion as a commitment to orthodox sense-datum theory.

I am glad he saw through it. Traditional epistemology was my point of departure, and it was only after presenting a theory of meaning, reference, and ontology that I was in a position fully to explain and defend my departures. Levison betrays a related perplexity thus:

> Evidently, Quine feels justified in using expressions such as "sense data," since for him this use does not necessarily constitute reference.

No, that is not the justification. The passages in question should be read rather as boring from within: as setting up a traditional doctrine for attack.

He observes, tentatively, that I have two criteria for positing objects, and that they can conflict. One is "comparative directness of association with sensory stimulation". The other is "utility for theory". Presently he decides, rightly, that only the second applies to the positing of objects. But let me say that they both do apply to the acceptance of predicates, and that they can indeed compete.

W. V. Q.

13

Robert Nozick

EXPERIENCE, THEORY AND LANGUAGE

For the past twenty-five years Quine's powerful and deep philosophical views have been, deservedly, the focus of more attention, discussion, and controversy than those of any other philosopher in the English-speaking world. His powerful reductionist philosophy attracts those who wish to fit things into a sleek, limited, tight framework (quantification theory, loved by Quine and central to his philosophizing, also exemplifies the virtues he seeks in his philosophy as a whole), while it repels those who think it excludes much that is important about our intellectual lives or ourselves. I myself, strongly subject to *both* the attraction and the repulsion, am ambivalent about his view, and about such reductionist views. The basis of these contrasting pulls and pushes is itself an interesting and different topic, but to metaphilosophize on the sources of our (my?) philosophical ambivalence would be inappropriate on this occasion. Instead, I shall discuss some of Quine's themes, sometimes critically assessing his positions, and sometimes sympathetically defending or extending them. This will result in a clouding of rhetorical force, as perhaps befits an essay written out of ambivalence.

Quine is the theorist of slack.* Data underdetermine theory, there is leeway about which component to modify when data conflict with a theory, and translation is indeterminate. Also, theory underdetermines the world (the doctrine of ontological relativity).

These particular theses ramify throughout philosophy, and the fact of slack itself is of great philosophical interest.

> We cannot strip away the conceptual trappings sentence by sentence and leave a description of the objective world, but we can investigate the world, and man as a part of it, and thus find out what cues he could have of what goes on around him.

---

*Quine's view countenances slack galore; how then can some have held it to be rigid? It excludes what on other views fixes things in determinate place. (Apparently, there is not enough slack to admit, as compatible with the data, a theory of fixed meanings.)

Subtracting his cues from his world view, we get man's net contribution as the difference. This difference marks the extent of man's net conceptual sovereignty—the domain within which he can revise theory while saving the data.[1]

I

Experience and Language

Duhem and Experiential Meaning

What explains why, vide Duhem, our statements don't face the tribunal of experience singly? (Is it cowardice?) Would a language whose statements did this, a non-Duhemian language, be impossible for us? If not, in what ways would such a language be inferior? I do not ask these questions from the standpoint of what Quine calls first philosophy. *Within* our current theory, what explains Duhem's facts?

Our experiences are dependent upon the state and condition of our sensory apparatus, on our orientations in the world, and on what the world is like, including those aspects of the world which are distinguished as conditions of observation. Furthermore (one is tempted to continue), our experiences of the world depend upon many interconnected facts about the world. Since experiences are dependent upon so many things, which may vary independently, a being would have to know enormous amounts to have any hope of formulating statements with individual experiential content.

But this purported explanation dissolves when we notice that we have no clear language-independent notion of number of facts. We count facts in our language. Our view that our experiences depend upon many facts derives from our not having single statements with individual experiential content. We cannot explain why our statements do not singly connect with experience by the multiplicity of facts upon which experiences depend. Nor can we appeal to how complicated the facts are. For if we measure the degree of complicatedness of a sentence, language-independently, by the nature of its connection to experience, then long conjunctions which uniquely map onto experience will come out as quite *un*complicated.

The statements (in English, complicated conjunctions) which (arguably) singly have experiential content run athwart those which are important to us, and have been in the course of evolution. The precise experiential content of "there is an unrestrained tiger in front of me" is less important than avoiding knowledge of the experiential content of "I am being eaten by a tiger", a content which once known is unlikely, in any event, to be conveyed to others. About such dangers as there being a tiger present, type two errors (accepting an hypothesis when it is false) were preferred to type one errors (rejecting an hypothesis when it is true) and were selected for. Better to flee unnecessarily than to stand and refine the experiential content of one's statement!

The interest of many other statements stems from the diverse ways they fit into people's plans. Trees before you can be walked around, hid behind, climbed up, and cut down. What one wants to know is whether there is a tree there. That multi-purpose statement does not have the separable experiential content had by conjunctions about trees and lighting conditions and the state of one's eyes and lack of non-transparent obstruction between you and it, and so forth. What it has is utility.

The facts that evolution selects for attentiveness to, facts which have multi-purpose utility in our lives, lie athwart those with specific experiential content. If language is geared to the former facts, and its component sentences state them, then these sentences will not have (be exhausted in) separate experiential content. Relative to the grid set by our evolutionary past and activities, sentences with separate experiential content will be very complex, and our experiences will depend upon the conjunction of many (language identified) facts.

Since language is geared, for evolutionary reasons and reasons of practical activity, to facts which lie athwart (those facts which correlate with) experiences (as represented perhaps by firings of nerve endings), it would be surprising if some significant unit of language was marked off via experiential content. In particular, it would be very surprising if the *unit of meaning* of the language were those entities (whatever they might be) with separate experiential content. Why should something have evolved or been formulated or come to be, whose units were *that?* If we were designing a language to be taught to organisms who had not developed their own, in order to aid them in surviving and acting in the world, would it be organized around units of distinguishable experiential content? Would distinguishable experiential content be a theoretically significant notion for a language with that purpose?

The claim that something with separate meaning must have separate experiential content, is a philosophical imposition which rests on considerations about learning a language, to which I turn below, and on the question "how else *can* something have meaning?", which I take to be a symptom of being trapped by a picture. The explanation of why Duhem's thesis holds, makes implausible the view that the units of meaning are the units with separate experiential content. That the facts that language is geared to state lie athwart those with separate experiential content is understandable and explicable; that the sentences stating those facts which language is geared to state should lie athwart the language's units of meaning, is not to be believed.

Not only are our individual sentences without separate experiential content;[2] there is no reason to think our total scientific theory has it either. Given the range of factors (as counted by our current partitioning of the world) upon which our experiences depend, including the facts of sensory psychology, one would have to know all of these (and that they were all), as well as the theory which connected them to our experiences, in order to know that one's total theory had experiential content. (And would there be open *ceteris paribus* clauses in one's body of theory?)[3] In the history of mankind, when did we reach the point of having theories extensive enough to have separate experiential content? Before then were all sentences without meaning? Through assuming separate experiential content must be *somewhere* in the language if language is to be meaningful, and not finding it in individual sentences, one might think it *must* lurk in the total set of sentences we would assert. Not there either.

If our total theory *did* have separate experiential content, we might think to assign experiential content to its *individual* sentences as follows. Consider the set of sentences of the language of length $\leq$ n (setting n high enough so that we don't exclude as too long any sentences we are interested in), and take the power set of this set. Within each set in the power set order the sentences alphabetically, and then order these sets alphabetically. For any sentence S and any set X within the ordered power set, we may consider the experiential content (observational consequences) of $\{S\} \cup X$. (S may already be contained in X, or its denial may be, or there may be no observational consequences of this particular union.) Against the structure provided by the ordered power set, we may now specify the experiential content (observational consequences) of any sentence S as $O_S = \langle \{T_1\}, \{T_2\}, \ldots \ldots, \{Tn\} \rangle$, where Ti the observational consequences of $\{S\} \cup$ the ith member of the ordered power set. The observational consequences of S would be specified as its observational consequences relative to all other sentences, and translation between languages would depend upon isomorphism between the components of such structures.

Is this then a way to formulate separately the experiential content of individual sentences? Actually not all (or even many) possible sets of sentences are conditioned to experience; instead only one evolving set is (that is, a sequence of sets). Since it is this actual process of conditioning to experience which, on Quine's view, gives the tie to experience, we *cannot* assume that *other* large conjunctions do have this tie to experience. For this assumes the conjuncts come already with their own individual (relative) observational content and that the content of the conjunction results from fitting together the individual contents. (How else would a conjunction, itself unconditioned to experience, have experiential content?) Quine, therefore, would reject this method whereby the individual observational content of the sentences we accept is to be specified relative to an ordering of all other sets of sentences, I conjecture. For these total sets (all but one) will not, on his view, have observational content since they will not have been actually conditioned to observation.

Duhem and Determinate Content

Since those facts we are interested in, for evolutionary reasons, lie athwart facts with specific experiential consequences, a language limited to stating these latter facts would fail to serve our purposes. But what would such a language be like? Would this be a non-Duhemian language: the applied lower functional calculus with one atomic predicate 'n fires at t', where n ranges over nerve endings and t over instants (or intervals) of time? Label all nerve endings and specify the person. This language is suggested by Quine's remarks about information (*Philosophy of Logic*, p. 5), directed to showing that we cannot specify the meanings of our English sentences individually in this language. All sentences in this language have determinate informational content (*Philosophy of Logic*, pp. 4–5). But, whether in the first or the third person, these are highly theoretical statements of sensory psychology which are themselves subject to Duhem's thesis. (Is this very sophisticated language of psychological theory also the observation language? With community wide agreement about its sentences?) These sentences may perform for the "naturalistically inclined" epistemologist *some* of the functions of introspectible sense data, in that their obtaining underlies a person's observation sentences; but they are unlike sense data statements in not being incorrigible, being theoretical, and being subject to Duhem's thesis. Being subject to Duhem's thesis does not, apparently, insure lack of determinate informational content or failure to state a separate fact of the matter. Therefore, Duhemian considerations do not show that sentences do not have separate meaning. (Such considerations would do so only along with a verification theory of separate meaning, but that theory would be difficult to square with Quine's remarks on the objective information of sentences.)

Quine also considers the possibility of specifying the content of sentences by specifying which distributions of elementary particles they are true in, and notes that we cannot do this. (*Philosophy of Logic*, pp. 4–5). But there *are* sentences which are already, without analysis, sentences about the distribution of elementary particles. These sentences of physics would have determinate informational (factual) content surely, for if it were possible to translate other sentences into these, this (Quine says) would show that *the others* had determinate content. Yet still these sentences are subject to Duhem's thesis. For the statement that a certain distribution of particles obtained could be tested only in conjunction with many other sentences.

Let us say that a language's sentences have *uniform determinate content* if and only if there is some matrix of alternatives into which all the sentences are uniquely translatable. (The *one* matrix provides the uniformity, the uniqueness provides the determinateness.) Failing this, will the sentences of a language lack individual meaning? That would be too stringent a criterion. For even if two languages each satisfy the criterion (relative to two different matrices which do not 'interfere'), it would exclude their union as containing individually meaningful sentences. Yet to admit any language which was the sum of languages which did satisfy the condition would exclude no language, without some constraint upon admissible matrices to prevent every atomic fragment of the language from providing its own matrix.

It might be objected that when Quine says that some statement S about distributions of elementary particles or firings of nerve endings does have separate content, he is speaking from within a theory which contains and utilizes a sub–theory about particles, nerve ending firings, etc; the sentences of this theory, when viewed from the outside, however, have no separate content and are subject to Duhem's thesis. But from *within* a theory *each* of its statements (excluding the ambiguous) has a determinate content. Yet Quine does not merely say (leaving us to realize he's speaking from within a theory) that *every* sentence has a determinate content.

"We can never hope to arrive at a technique for so analyzing out ordinary sentences as to reveal their implications in respect of the distribution of particles." (*Philosophy of Logic,* pp. 4–5) Our ordinary sentences are not geared to talk of what may micro–reduce what actually is their subject matter. Our interests lie elsewhere. (Would we know what someone who spoke such analyses of ordinary sentences *meant?*) The distributions of particles does not constitute a privileged matrix into which we must translate our ordinary sentences. It is notable, though, that Quine thinks that sentences would have determinate meaning ("objective information") if we *could* analyze their implications in respect of the distribution of particles. One might think that determinateness is the crucial criterion of separate meaning, rather than separate experiential content, which the particle statements lack. But Quine, I think, is concerned with and favors two distinguishable things, determinate content and experiential content. So he would view with some favor a particle language whose individual sentences separately have the first though not the second. Since separate experiential content is *one* way of providing uniform determinate meaning, his concerns converge in his treatment of determinate experiential content. But he has not yet given us a rationale or motivation for being concerned with uniform determinate content.

We have no argument for a sharp criterion connecting meaning with experiences. (Why is Quine so sanguine about holistic verificationism? "Epistemology Naturalized", p. 81.) Quine grants, moreover, that some sentences have separate informational content even though they are subject to Duhem's thesis and are not separately testable, and we would expect the unit of meaning not to be connected with experiential content anyway. Hence, it seems unlikely that any interesting conclusion about the theory of meaning will emerge from Duhemian considerations.[4] But something interesting *might* emerge from asking how we would expect a language to be organized, given the considerations adduced above to explain why Duhem's thesis holds.

Language Learning and Indeterminacy

One might think that considerations about language learning *do* show that the matrix of nerve-ending firings constitutes a privileged matrix into which our ordinary sentences must be translated. For it is through such firings that we learn language; how can what we learn transcend how we learn? And if meanings are artifacts shaped by us, will they not be fired in the kiln of our nerve endings?

Comfort for viewing meanings as going beyond stimuli might seem to come from a much studied phenomenon: on the basis of a few firings we generalize along pre-existing lines in quality space, thereby transcending the stimuli from which we learn. (Psychologists speak of generalization gradients; these vary from species to species.) However, we do not thereby transcend that type of stimulus, which can be used to check that we do generalize along the same paths. It is striking that we do generalize alike past particular data in those cases we can check with other data. One might speculate that we move similarly beyond the data in other uncheckable cases, but unlike the former case, direct evolutionary selective pressure would not explain the latter.

Another way to detach (partially) meaning from stimuli offers more promise. Consider specifying (not *defining*) X as that thing or mechanism which actually explains data D.[5] Here the reference of X is fixed by D and by the world. D may have separate experiential content, or it may have been originally explained, as X here is, but in terms of data with separate experiential content, and so on. Let us suppose that X stands in the ancestral of the explains-relation to something with separate experiential content. Cannot the meaning of X be fixed in this way, has it not been given separate meaning, even though clearly it itself does not have separate experiential content?

It might be said that if we fix the reference of X in this way, we can't *know* what X means or refers to. And it might seem as if the whole truth about the meaning or mechanism of reference of our terms must be exhausted by psychological truths about us. How can there be more to what *I* mean, to the meaning of the term as I use it, than is contained in my intentions, beliefs, etc.? There are numerous counterexamples to this apparently compelling view, e.g., Wittgenstein's on how what the person means by chess is fixed outside of *his* intentions and beliefs, Kripke's causal story about proper names, Quine on dispositions; and recently Putnam, in his illuminating talk about division of linguistic labor, has shown how unintuitive it is, how inefficient it would be, if we each had to carry around with us the complete meaning of what we say.[6]

One might think to use the way in which external facts fix meaning to resolve Quinean indeterminacies. But before looking at details, note how such views *undermine* one objection to Quine on indeterminacy. Many who object to Quine think it's perfectly certain what *they* mean, treating this as some incorrigible psychological fact about themselves. On the external determination view, of course, they *can* be wrong. (Add to this Wittgenstein's erosion of viewing meanings and intentions as internal psychological pellets, thereby undercutting a platform on which one might think to stand in confidently attacking Quine.) So how can they be so certain about what their fixed meaning is?

A tale will be useful here, which also will serve to combat the view that within neurology lies determinacy of translation. Suppose we send two ships off in opposite directions, containing infant children and teachers. One group of teachers will teach the children English, speaking it to them. The other group of teachers on the other ship will speak stage-English, which is the stage-language of English. (This is the language, described by Quine, whose terms denote temporal stages of enduring objects. It has nothing special to do with the theater!) The words of stage-English are some trivial phonetic transformation of the corresponding English words, "Blegg" instead of "egg", etc. Locked in a safe in the captain's cabin is a dictionary which states the meaning of stage-English words and sentences in English. Now suppose almost exactly the same things happen on the two ships; for each sentence heard on an occasion on the English speaking ship, a corresponding sentence will be heard on the stage-English ship on the parallel occasion. (They are almost parallel worlds). The children on the first ship will learn to speak English, and the children on the second will learn to speak a language which, let us suppose, is stage-English. The only neurological differences between a child on one ship and a corresponding child on the other ship, will be due to the trivial phonetic differences; otherwise they are neurologically identical.

Indeed, it was not necessary that the children on the stage-English ship be taught a phonetically different language. If the phonetically different stage-language was somewhat longer, couldn't they be taught an abbreviation of it (recorded also in the captain's cabin), and mightn't this abbreviation be phonetically identical to English? So their neurology would be *identical* to that of English speakers, though of course there would remain the separate dictionaries in the different captain's cabins (and perhaps interested social scientists telemonitoring from afar).

Whatever neurological configuration realizes one of the languages will also realize the other; any neurological model of English will also be a neurological model of stage-English. Given the formal relations between the two languages, how could it be otherwise? Perhaps we can reduce the psychology of a speaker of English to neurology, identifying his believing there is a table before him (believing that semantic content) with a particular neurological state N. But there can be a parallel identification of his believing this corresponding stage-

English sentence with the very *same* neurological state N. We can parallel one reduction by another; no determinacy lurks in neurological reduction.

But did the children on the second ship learn, as we supposed, stage-English? Though an attempt was made to teach them that language (perhaps their teachers even silently translated into English whenever they spoke, or silently said "that was stage-English; in English it means. . . . ."), perhaps the children really learned English, for perhaps a stage language is unlearnable as a first language. But we have seen that the grounds for saying this cannot lie in neurology; what then can they be?

The view that the children on the second ship learn stage-English fits in very well with theories of the fixing of meaning by external facts. Here, the central external facts are the setting up of the experiment and the book in the captain's safe. Suppose these children are taken to an island, settle, have children, etc., and two hundred years later the misplaced captain's safe is discovered and opened. Would what the descendants learn then be important? What would they have to do to change their language to a non-stage-language? Suppose instead that the children on the two ships were settled on the same island. Would the differences between them, as they fluently spoke together, be linguistically or semantically important? The children grow up, intermarry with those from the other ship, and raise their children who learn language from their parents and from others around them in the normal way. These latter children have learned language equally from persons from each of the ships who themselves were unaware of any linguistic differences among them. Do these children speak English or stage-English? *Is* there a fact of the matter about which *they* speak?

The mingling together of two distinct external sources produces an example of "no fact of the matter" about which language they speak. They just. . . . .speak. Someone who thought there *couldn't* be a case of "no fact of the matter" can, via the external fixing view, be brought to accept the possibility as making sense. Now, how *important* are our differences from those people for whom there is no fact of the matter? (And are you *sure* that we *are* different, that our language wasn't such a commingling of different streams?) How important a fact is it about us that we are in our group and not the one in which there is no determinate propositional content? Should we stop our children from intermarrying with theirs, so that our descendants will speak determinately, so that there will be a fact of the matter about which they mean? Whatever differences there are seem trivial, hardly worth making central to a philosophical position.

We have supposed, until now, that the fixing of meaning by external facts would fix determinate meaning. (Even on that supposition, we were led to conclude that the differences between determinate meaning and no determinate meaning were trivial.) But how will the intentions of people in the initial fixing situation have gained determinacy? And for any factual relation R between y (data, things, use of a word, etc.) and the x which is "fixed" by standing in that relation R to y, there will be an x' and R' such that x'R'y, or a y' such that x'R'y', and there will be no apparent way to resolve the indeterminancy between terms denoting R and those denoting R' (or between those denoting y and those denoting y').

The topic of the relationship of language acquisition to meaning has led us to discuss introducing a term X to denote what explains data D. This mode of term introduction clearly does not attach the meaning of X to firings of nerve endings. (On the other hand, we have argued, it also does not fix X so as to narrow Quinean indeterminacies.) We *cannot* get a cogent argument for experiential content being what fixes the unit of meaning from considerations about language learning. The example of introducing terms via the explanation-relation which shows this, also provides a special explanation of why Duhem's thesis holds for some sentences. Introduced via the notion of 'explanation', the term X will live for us upon the notion of 'best explanation', which is a non-local notion, looking at large portions of theory.

Stimulus Meaning

Quine's own positive account of the relationship of meaning and experiential content centers on the notion of stimulus meaning; "stimulus meaning . . . may be properly looked upon still as the objective reality that the linguist has to probe" *(Word and Object,* p. 39). The stimulus meaning is the ordered pair of affirmative and negative stimulus meanings, and these meanings "of a sentence (for a given speaker at a given time) are mutually exclusive". (p. 33)

> A stimulation σ belongs to the affirmative stimulus meaning of a sentence S for a given speaker if and only if there is a stimulation σ' such that if the speaker were given σ', then were asked S, then were given σ and then were asked S again, he would dissent the first time and assent the second. *(Word and Object,* p. 32)
>   A stimulation σ belongs to the negative stimulus meaning of a sentence S for a given speaker if and only if there is a stimulation σ' such that if the speaker were given σ', then were asked S, then were given σ, and then were asked S again, he would assent the first time and dissent the second.

The immediate difficulty is that since each of these definitions uses an existential quantifier ("there is a stimulation σ' "), it is left open that for the same σ and S, there are two different stimulations σ' and σ'' which serve to place σ both in the affirmative and in the negative stimulus meaning of S. To have these be disjoint, we would need the truth of (∃σ')(if the speaker were given σ' then were asked S, then were given σ and then were asked S again, he would dissent the first time and assent the second) ⊃ ~ (∃σ'')(if the speaker were given σ'' then were asked S, then were given σ and then were asked S again, he would assent the first time and dissent the second), and also of the statement which is gotten from this by interchanging "assent" and "dissent". We have been given no argument for these very strong statements, and they appear to be false. First, an intuitive case. Let σ' be the auditory stimulation "Please say 'no' to the first question and 'yes' to the second". If this is an admissible stimulation, then (σ) (S) (σ belongs to the affirmative stimulus meaning of S); and we can proceed similarly with negative stimulus meaning. Excluding such stimulations[7] would make it difficult to ascertain (or define) the stimulus meanings of sentences like "He has just spoken well" or "He has just spoken loudly".

For any σ which would appear to fit S, let σ' be a stimulation which fits S and which leads the person to believe that though σ occurs, not-S; e.g., the evolving occular radiation which occurs when he sees people construct and place a brown paper maché rabbit alongside a white rabbit. σ is the ocular radiation of seeing a brown rabbit with no white rabbit around. He assents to "gavagai" the first time and dissents the second (because he thinks he's still looking at the paper maché rabbit), so that, according to Quine's criterion, σ is in the *negative* stimulus meaning of "gavagai". And so on. Intuitively, what one will assent to on the basis of stimulation depends upon one's other beliefs, and even though Quine means to include this by speaking of stimulus meaning for a particular person at a particular time, different preliminary stimulations σ' can change the person's beliefs in different ways.

Can the tasks Quine sees for the (as we have seen, defective) notion of stimulus meaning be accomplished without its use? Quine adduces two areas of use: for the philosophy of science, to demarcate the intersubjective tribunal of evidence for science (See "Epistemology Naturalized," pp. 86–89) and for linguistics, within the theory of a child's (or scientists's) language learning and within the theory of translation. (We shall consider linguistics in the next section, after taking up here the use in the philosophy of science.)

The widespread agreement among scientists, Quine holds, stems from there being sentences (the observation sentences) "on which all members of the community will agree under uniform stimulation." ("Epistemology Naturalized," p. 87) This notion gets Quine into problems about intersubjectively uniform stimulation, the homology of nerve endings, etc. Why not focus instead upon those sentences for which each person can arrange (or have arranged) circumstances (or stimulations, if you wish) to prompt him to assent? There is no need that the circumstances or the stimulations be intersubjectively *the same*. There is agreement enough for science to proceed if everyone can be brought to assent; there is no need for them to follow exactly the same path to this agreement. The explanation of why each assents in some arrangeable situation, for Quine, will speak of each individual's history of conditioning of language to situations. To be sure, there must be enough perceived similarity in the circumstances so that they all think they're *agreeing* (rather than merely using homonyms) and hence supporting each other. Such would be the case if each sees the circumstance in which another assents as one in which, with some slight modifications, he also would be led to assent to the sentence. Each need only see the situations of the others as (modifiable into) ones which present a discriminative stimulus for himself to utter S.

It is fortunate that the concept of stimulus meaning is not necessary for the philosophy of science, for, in addition to the difficulties with Quine's definition, there is further trouble. What a linguist treats as assent and dissent (and a query also?) is underdetermined, not merely inductively but "on a par with the analytical hypotheses of translation that he adopts at later stages of his enterprise." ("Replies [to Critics], in *Words and Objections,* edited by Donald Davidson and Jaakko Hintikka, p. 312. Does *this* indeterminacy about assent and dissent also begin at each of our homes?) Even if the "on a par" puts it too strongly, it would seem there is strictly speaking no fact of the matter about whether something is assent (or dissent) or something else, and hence, strictly speaking, no fact of the matter even about stimulus meanings.[8]

II

Language and Theory

Why Linguists?

If "stimulus meaning by whatever name may be properly looked upon still as the objective reality that the linguist has to probe,"[9] and stimulus meaning crumbles, why do we need linguists? What is it that linguists are trying to do, and what is their subject matter? Let us consider some possible answers, and criticisms of these answers of a sort that would appear to be congenial to Quine. Later we shall face the question of whether similar criticisms don't apply to Quine's own answer.

   a) the job of the linguist is to produce a theory that explains the linguistic facts
      about the sentences of the language: grammatical facts, and semantic facts,[10]
      e.g., that some phrases and sentences are synonymous, that some words are
      semantically similar to each other in a respect in which other words aren't, that
      some words are antonyms (have incompatible meanings), that some expressions
      are meaningful and others are semantically anomalous, that words or sentences
      have multiple senses, that some phrases have senses that contain superfluous
      information, that some sentences are true by virtue of the fact that the meaning
      of the subject contains the property expressed by the predicate, that some sen-
      tences are false just by virtue of the fact that the meaning of the subject contains
      information incompatible with what is attributed to it in the predicate, that some
      sentences are neither true nor false on the basis of meaning alone, that some
      pairs of sentences are inconsistent, that a sentence sometimes follows necessar-

ily from another one by virtue of a certain semantic relation between them, that some interrogatives presuppose the truth of some declaratives, that some sentences are possible answers to a question whereas others are not, that some questions answer themselves.

The 'facts' in this list are heavily *theoretical;* they are not what, in the first place, a linguist has to explain, though in explaining what he must he might be led (or forced) to a theory which countenances such facts, and so have to explain them also. But what is it that the linguist must explain in the first place, what sets him his original task?

> b) the job of the linguist is to explain how we communicate to each other via language, how one person transmits his inner thoughts to another by encoding them in the form of external observable acoustic events which the other decodes thereby obtaining for himself his own inner representation of the speaker's thoughts.[11]

Once again, this can hardly be the data which the linguist starts out to explain, though he might be led to such a theoretical picture in the course of explaining, e.g., people's talking to each other.

> c) the job of the linguist is to explain linguistic performance, that is, how someone utilizes his linguistic competence to communicate with his fellow speakers in actual speech situations, that is, how someone utilizes what an ideal speaker knows about the grammatical structure of his language, stated as the system of rules that formally represents the ideal linguistic structure of natural speech, abstracting from memory limitations, noise, what situation the person is (interested) in, etc., to communicate with his fellow speakers in actual speech situations.

Again we have a heavily theoretical description of the linguist's task. Linguistic performance is what is to be explained. The *hypothesis* is that a theory explaining this performance will incorporate and attribute to the speaker-hearer linguistic competence in the form of (tacit knowledge of) an internalized system of rules which describe (or perhaps constitute) the language. "In general, it seems that the study of performance models incorporating generative grammars may be a fruitful study; furthermore, it is difficult to imagine any other basis on which a theory of performance might develop". (Noam Chomsky, *Aspects of the Theory of Syntax*, p. 15.) Can it turn out that the power of this internalized set of rules is beyond the power of the organism who internalizes it? "A model of the speaker's knowledge of his language may generate a set so complex that no finite device [models which represent actual performance, Chomsky holds, must necessarily be strictly finite] could identify or produce all of its members. In other words, we cannot conclude, on the basis of the fact that the .rules of the grammar represented in the brain are finite, that the set of grammatical structures generated must be of the special type that can be handled by a strictly finite device."[12] Thus, it is mistaken to think (as is often done) that the results of formal linguistics are supposed to apply directly to psychology, by showing how powerful a psychological model of us must be, on the assumption that we must be at least as powerful as the language we speak. We should be wary of concluding that our language (*our* language) is more powerful than we are, solely because such a more powerful language is most elegantly described. ("In general, the assumption that languages are infinite is made to simplify the description of these languages." Noam Chomsky, *Syntactic Structures*, p. 23). Since we have no need to attribute to the organism itself, knowledge of the description of its linguistic output (and so need not worry about *its* handling such complexities), we may choose the less elegant but psychologically more realistic description, striving for theoretical elegance in our psychological theory of what produces its speakings (and other behavior).[13] In any case, it is puzzling to encounter the confidence that a psychological theory of our speaking and acting on heard speech will incorporate the *more powerful* abstract structures (admitted to be beyond our power) that linguists present.

> (d) the job of the linguist is to (help) explain linguistic performance, which is "the actual use of language in concrete situations."[14]

Do we now, at last, have a sufficiently theoretically low-key statement of the initial task of the linguist? What could be more down to earth than trying to explain the actual use of language in concrete situations? The use of *what?* If on this view language *is* the internalized rules, physically realized, or (to avoid having the language transformed when its speakers die) an abstract entity of some sort,[15] then we are back to case c) above. We do not want to interpret 'the actual use of language in concrete situations' as committing us to '($\exists$x) ($\exists$y) ($\exists$z) (x is a person, y is a language, and z is a situation, and x used y in z)'. In particular, we don't want to be committed to quantifying over entities which are languages in explaining the *task* of the linguist, in explaining why there's a job for him to do. Instead, we want the task to be something like helping to explain those events in the world which are people's talkings and their behavior before and after producing or hearing talkings. I am indebted to conversations with Burton Dreben for suggesting that Quine would criticize these specifications of the linguist's task which are offered by Katz and Chomsky in the above ways, as being heavily laden with philosophical assumptions and theories, and would favor instead descriptions of the task and data of linguistics which were less theoretically committed.

Quine on the Linguist's Task

However, cannot this line of criticism be turned against Quine's own description? Even if there can be no wholly neutral description of the data, isn't Quine's description also more laden with theory and assumptions than need be, especially as assessed from a more minimalist standpoint Quine should find congenial, that of Skinnerian psychology? Quine offers the following:

(e) the job of the grammarian is to demarcate the class of all the strings of phonemes that get uttered or could get uttered within the community as normal speech without a bizarreness reaction.[16]

Why does the grammarian try to demarcate the class of all strings of phonemes that *could* get uttered?[17] Perhaps the picture is as follows: the grammarian wants to (help) explain what *does* get uttered. The meta-hypothesis is that the explanation of a particular utterance will have two parts or components: first, a component which specifies everything that could be uttered (by anyone, anytime, under any conditions), and secondly a selective component which operates on the specification of the set of all possible sentences (on the first component) to select the one which actually gets uttered. This meta-hypothesis that the explanation of the actual utterance of a particular sentence will refer to the set of all possible utterances, is a very strong hypothesis. Will the explanation of a particular home run by Hank Aaron (that particular swing, trajectory, landing place, and number of RBI's) involve a specification of all possible home runs by him, and some further bit of theory which explains why he hit a (that) particular one *of those?* Nor is there any reason to think that the explanation of any particular home run will *refer to* the set of all *actual* home runs he hits during his baseball career. The explanation of a particular knockout by Joe Louis does not incorporate reference to the set of all knockouts he could have made or did make, or to the set of all punches he could have thrown or did throw. It is certainly *not* generally true that the explanation of a particular activity will refer to and utilize a specification of all possible (or actual) activities of that sort. An explanation of a particular activity may, however, *yield* (as opposed to utilize) a specification of all actual or possible activities of that sort. From the story of how a particular one was (or all the actual ones were) produced we may be able to see which ones *could be* produced; a specification of that set might drop out of the theory. But the explanatory task would not be to produce that specification, and the specification need play no explanatory role in the explanations one does give.[18]

Thinking the primary task of the linguist is to demarcate and study the set of sentences of the language, the set of sentences that *could* be uttered, fits in nicely with the unQuinean conception of language as an existent entity to be studied, knowledge of the totality of which plays a role in the production of individual sentences. But there is also another route to thinking the linguist must specify the set of all sentences which could be produced, that on the face of it might be more congenial to Quine. This route runs as follows.

Each sentence S a person does utter, it might be said, evidences a disposition to utter it in some circumstances C and perhaps in other circumstances as well. This disposition will be an internal (neurological) condition of the organism, in virtue of which the person utters S in C. Had the person not been in circumstances C he still would have had the disposition to utter S in C. There is something about him which makes him an S-utterer-in-C. The set of sentences a person is disposed to utter under some circumstances or other will be the sentences he *could* utter, and will correspond to facts about his internal neurological condition. The job of the grammarian, on this conception, is to specify this set of sentences, as an aid to specifying these occurrent neurological facts. However, this view encounters difficulties.[19]

The set of all circumstances a person could be under is ill-specified. Does it include someone's saying "repeat after me", in which case the set of sentences will include all sound combinations the person can (be taught to) produce?[20] Does it include the application of instruments of torture? The meeting of extra-galactic visitors and all they might tell us? Does it include thinking for years and coining new terminology to deal with theoretical problems, e.g., "category", "muon", "stimulus meaning"? A child of ten will not be disposed to utter "I am twenty years old" until approximately ten more years have passed. Shall we count it as disposed at ten to utter "I am twenty years old" under the circumstance of ten years passing. For at age ten, it seems there is something about the child which, when ten years pass, eventuates in its saying "I am twenty years old". But then an infant would be disposed to utter all the sentences of English which it can learn. For isn't its internal state such that under certain circumstances it will utter those sentences of English? Also, which language you speak depends on how you were raised; did you as an infant have the disposition to utter all sentences of *every* language? Would the grammarian aid the student of your behavior by specifying the set of sentences of every actual, and possible, language?[21]

Consider a uniform homogeneous pinball about to be launched on a stationary pinball machine without flippers. The path the ball will follow will depend on the force applied and the surface of the machine, its frictional forces, placement of obstacles, their elasticity, its placement of holes, etc. Of course, even given all this, the path also will depend upon the nature (mass, shape, elasticity) of the ball. In virtue of these facts about the ball, it will follow the path it does in those circumstances. It has the disposition, we might say, to follow that path in those circumstances. Similarly it has another disposition to follow another path in other circumstances (on another machine, say); this disposition (as internal structure and properties of the ball) though distinct from the first disposition is not discrete from it,[22] for it is the same physical state as the first.

Suppose now it were suggested that since the ball does behave as it does, and lawfully, and could behave differently under other circumstances and lawfully, the theorist of the ball has the job of listing its possible paths, the different ones it is disposed to follow under different circumstances. After all, these all correspond to facts about the ball, being (internal) states of it. Yet it does not follow that this is the theorist's task. Listing of dispositions would be a central task for the theorist only if it were thought that (usually or often) distinct dispositions are discrete. Otherwise, the theorist should give a statement of the one or few states of the entity, and the laws governing its behavior.

Linguists and Psychologists

An alternative conception of the linguist's task is that of aiding the psychologist in the construction of a theory of verbal behavior,[23] with no initial commitment to the theoretical centrality of language as an entity or even to sentences as entities. It is not obvious that to say "there is not language, there are not sentences" is to be entwined in pragmatic contradiction. Quine has already rejected one traditional explanation of talking behavior and the changes in behavior it leads to, viz, the explanation that uses the idea idea, the myth of the mental museum, etc. The *language story* is another theoretical story, also open to scrutiny. If it is an old story, so is the museum myth; if the theorists who treat language as a structural entity trace elaborate patterns among its parts, so do the theorists of relations among ideas or semantic markers. Why then does Quine not begin with the Skinner of *Verbal Behavior,* what leads him to a more traditionally oriented *language*-position? My aim here is *not* to endorse Skinner's view, but to show how close it is to Quine's views, and so to press the question of whether it isn't really his view.

The explanation of each individual's behavior would be an individual explanation; other persons and their actions would occupy the position of external conditions.[24] This is compatible with everything that Quine says about language being a "social art." If we view the linguist as aiding in the explanation of an individual's behavior, treating other individuals merely as sources of input for the individual in question, we avoid problems about the homology of nerve endings, and worries about being "unable even to negotiate the A-B-Cs of behavioristic psychology".[25]

What explanatory task is the "intersubjective equating of stimulations" needed for? (Defining some (surrogates for) notions of traditional semantics; but what explanatory function do these latter notions have?) Compare the situation in economics, where no notion of interpersonal comparisons of utility is needed for the explanatory tasks of positive economics. Each individual's behavior is explained by his own utility function, joint behavior as the aggregate of individual behavior, perhaps coordinated, but the explanation of this needs no interpersonal comparisons. Sometimes a person may act on a belief about interpersonal comparisons (e.g. he might make a threat only if he believes its realization will hurt another person more than it will hurt himself), but to explain his actions we only need a theory about how *he* makes such comparisons.

The situation of psychology would seem to be the same, with interpersonal comparisons of stimulations serving no useful function.

"But how can we make translations without interpersonal comparisons of stimulations or of something?" And Quine tells us that he is in favor of translation.[26] But what are translations *for?* Will translations aid in the task of psychological explanation of another's behavior including verbal behavior? To the extent that we explain people's actions and speech by attributing to them (in indirect discourse) beliefs and intentions, and we take what they say as indicating and sometimes stating their beliefs and intentions, then psychological explanation will involve translating. Our everyday psychological explanations do proceed by such attributions.[27] But such explanations are not offered or endorsed by Quine. Presumably he hopes they can be dispensed with. If they can, then insofar as translation rides on their back, it can be dispensed with also. The fundamental story of behavior and speech, for Quine, talks of conditioning, innate distances, and stimulation of nerve endings. Sentences attributing beliefs and intentions are rough and ready *summaries* of these more fundamental facts. A translation of S tells us that S stands to stimulations of its believer or to discriminative stimuli for him *roughly* as that which translates it does to our stimulations or discriminative stimuli. A translation *abbreviates* fact, and is only roughly accurate. It serves the purposes of psychological explanation when its inaccuracies or distortions do not matter, when the relevant portions of our theory of behavior do not cut so finely as to be perturbed by the roughness. Explaining by using translations is like navigating a ship on the geocentric theory; the distortions due to placing ourselves at the center don't matter for our purposes, but the simplifications do.

Within psychology, translations are convenient summaries; not only do they feed into a theory, the grain of the theory determines what is convenient and will not mislead. So a summary of facts about discriminative stimuli or stimulation of nerve endings, as presented in translations, need be only as fine, and accurate, as the theory connecting behavior to stimuli can make use of. Furthermore, we should expect that in using our everyday theory of belief, intention, and action, our psychological theory would, given its latitude, allow a great range to attributions of propositional attitudes.

Psychology remains a theory of individuals' behavior. It need not provide a notion of same or similar stimulation so as to provide the foundation for linguistics or the theory of translation. Instead, translating is the handmaiden of psychology, helping it conveniently to describe facts about discriminative stimuli and stimulations. Whatever rough and ready similarity translating brings will help the psychologist describe how it is with that particular person ("it's like. . . . . "); no fact of stimulation-similarity is used as an explanation, there is nothing for *it* to explain.

Other more practical purposes of translation, e.g., to enable us to have fluent interchange, social relations, economic relations with others, raise no new issues of principle that need concern us, especially since "going native" will be the best route and need involve no translating at all. The fact that we read literary and scientific works in translation and learn much from them raises no new problems of explanation special to translation; it presumably will be explained by judiciously combining our existing theories of learning from speech in your own language, and responding to writing in your own language, with our theories about the author's behavior. We may learn differently from different translations of the same text, and the question "which did the author mean?" will either be rejected or be transformed into the question of the psychological explanation of the author's behavior. Still, translations *are* made, read, and enjoyed. The theory of translators' behavior will be a part of psychology. Translators themselves will lean on learned aids, maxims, traditional equatings, etc. to carry out their task to the satisfaction, instruction, and delight of their readers, but in all this there is no *subject matter*.

Why might one think that the concept of stimulus meanings aids the psychologist (even when it is limited to intrapersonal use, thus avoiding problems of homology)? Perhaps one hypothesizes that a theory of linguistic performance, a theory of speakings (and changes in behavior from hearings?), will be based upon stimulus meanings, in that:

(a) some speakings just are assentings after σ which itself is after σ'' and dissenting; that is, just are the speakings in Quine's 'judicious experiment' ("Replies "[to Critics"], p. 308)

(b) some speakings are sayings of S after σ which is in the affirmative stimulus meaning of S. Though it does not logically follow that a person will say S when σ stimulated if he will assent if stimulated (σ',S? and then) σ,S?, it may be assumed that a small bit of psychological theory will fill in here.

However, if S is a standing sentence which the person believes, it will have a null affirmative stimulus meaning, as Quine defines this, for there will be no sequence of σ',S? to which the person will dissent. If we drop the initial setting σ',S?, altering Quine's notion to let σ into the affirmative stimulus meaning of S if the person merely assents to S? after σ, then every stimulation (which doesn't get him to give up believing S) will be in the affirmative stimulus meaning of a standing sentence he accepts. In either case, as Quine is well aware, the notion of stimulus meaning would seem to have little use in explaining utterances of a standing sentence, except perhaps in the situation of being asked S?.

Just as for the hypothesis that a theory of linguistic performance is to be based upon one of linguistic competence, we might interpret the concern with stimulus meanings as based upon the particular hypothesis that a theory of speaking is to be based upon stimulus meanings (centrally utilize the notion of 'stimulus meaning'). (Note the partial parallels to the mold of Chomskian theorizing.) The merits of this hypothesis are unclear; however, Quine does not present stimulus meanings within this framework of *explaining* speakings. Instead, I think, he introduces stimulus meaning to see how much of traditional philosophers' talk of meaning he can save. Quine is not, on this view, the revolutionary exciser of meaning he is reputed to be; rather he tries to conserve some of the tradition with his 'strictly vegetarian imitations'. (*Word and Object*, p. 67.) Why bother? Isn't this a case where considerations of simplicity of theory outweigh conservatism? (*Roots of Reference*, p. 137)

Of Quine's tasks for the concept of stimulus meanings, we have discussed translation, and its use in the philosophy of science to demarcate the observation sentences. We should mention its possible use in our theory of a child's (or scientist's) language learning. But if language learning is learning *meanings*, we don't need a theory for this; if it is coming to use words so that others reinforce and don't penalize, we have Skinner's story of shaping and reinforcing in three-term contingencies. Is stimulus meaning "a device, as far as it goes, for explaining the fabric of interlocking sentences, a sentence at a time" (*Word and Object*, p. 35)? What is it we hope for from such reconstruction? Not meaning; "net empirical import of each of various single sentences" then. (*Word and Object*, pp. 34–35) Is this notion of *import* a notion useful to explanatory psychology? If not, what philosophical theory is it that Quine wishes to rescue it for? And what would that philosophical theory explain? Whatever it would, we presumably should find it writ large in the philosophical theory of science, the philosophical use Quine mentions, but we have seen it to be unnecessary there.

Even if it is granted that we can explain agreement among scientists without introducing the concept of stimulus meanings, can a radical "no language" view explain the historical success of science, its predictions and its technological achievements? To do this we seem to need the notions of *reference* and *truth*, yet how can we engage in such metalinguistic talk if language itself vanishes as an *entity* to be studied. It might appear that only a realist philosophy of science (which says the scientific theory has a model, namely, the world) can explain the success of science.[28] Quine, standing within his theory, can say what the realist says, (e.g., " 'electron' refers to electrons, which we have discovered to have properties . . . .") even though reference is a notion within the indeterminacy of translation. (*Roots of Reference*, pp. 81–82)[29]

The theorist I am imagining would first try to show how the scientists' speech was shaped,[30] second (using the first) to show what explained the scientists' and technologists' actions, and then, *speaking himself*, would say why those actions led in the world to the results they did. He would have no more difficulty in saying why those results ensued, than why any event, not having to do with language, has its results. "Yes, he could *say* those things, but when he does, does he also think he's talking *about* the world, *referring to* the world?" He thinks his talk has been shaped in various ways in (by) the world. ("But when he says *that,* does he think he's talking *about* the world?" Loop back.) And he will offer to tell you how his, and your, use of "refers" and "about" was shaped.[31]

My aim in this last section has been to draw out Quine's response to a hard-line Skinnerian view of language, that is, verbal behavior. There is reason to think Quine should embrace this view, yet he continually uses notions from traditional theories of language, e.g., "reference", which have no place or explanatory purpose within the Skinnerian picture. What scientific explanatory purpose *does* Quine see these notions as necessary for? Or is there some non-explanatory and more traditionally philosophical role they play? *Is* there a baby, or is it *all* bathwater?

Does the thesis of the underdetermination of theories undercut even Quine's notion of truth? If no theory is superior except as judged by canons whose connection with truth is unclear, and all theories would explain the data, then is there a fact of the matter about which one is true? Quine reassures us (*Word and Object*, pp. 24–25) that we can apply 'true' to a sentence which we see from within the theory which embeds that sentence, and which we take seriously as our own theory. But why doesn't a full appreciation of the under-determination of theories undermine the seriousness and earnestness with which we take our own theories?

A theory of the truth of sentences of an object language, one might have thought, would have to describe and segment the world and show how the sentences of the object language connect with the world. Tarski saw that one could avoid independently describing and segmenting the world by using the object language's view of it. Translate the object language (perhaps homophon-ically) into the metalanguage, and speak about the world through the object language translated. But if underdetermination of theory raises the worry that there's no fact of the matter about which of alternative theories is true, one will similarly worry about the factual status of their metalinguistic translations. Nor are things helped by additional worries about the determinacy of the trans-lating! Let *S* and *T* be alternative theories underdetermined by, yet admissible for, the data, and let S and T be particular sentences in them respectively. To explain what it means to say S and T are true we translate them into the me-talanguage as s and t respectively, and proceed à la Tarski. But what makes s a correct translation of S rather than of T? If there's no fact of the matter about *this,* then in what sense are we, by using s, affirming the truth of S as opposed to that of T? It does not help to say that the translation into the metalanguage takes place *within* a theory which includes analytical hypotheses which translate its object language subcomponent. For similarly, we would have the notion of *unique translation,* to be sure within a theory which includes fixed analytical hypotheses. Hence, this route would give us a notion of truth which is no more secure than the notions of 'unique translation' or 'unique meaning'! In what way does Quine see "truth" as better off than these other notions he has done so much to undermine?

Is the problem solved "by acquiescing in our mother tongue and taking its words at face value"? (*Ontological Relativity,* pg. 49) What is it to take the words at face value? To translate them homophonically? And why don't we have to iterate that translation, to ensure that we're taking it at face value? To use the same words in the translation in the meta-metalanguage for the truth definition of the metalanguage? (Can't all this be done without understanding the words at all?) To take s at face value is not to translate it in a certain way, for what it is translated into will raise the same problem. Quine offers one picture of understanding: one understands a language if one can translate it into some language. (Those monolinguals among us, less linguistically agile than Quine, may find themselves reduced to only the homophonic translation.) Clearly one must translate it into a language *one understands*—we can homophonically translate languages we don't understand—and *this* notion of understanding will have to come down to something which is *not* translation; presumably, it will be fluent use and application, uncorrected by other fluent users and appliers. But all such use tests will be *within* the indeterminacy of translation, and will not distinguish s from t, and so cannot fix s for the purposes of a truth definition.[32]

ROBERT NOZICK

DEPARTMENT OF PHILOSOPHY
HARVARD UNIVERSITY
AUGUST 1975

NOTES

1. *Word and Object,* p. 5.

2. We need not worry here whether some scattered sentences might have it, e.g., "red here now".

3. Could a person deductively connect his body of beliefs B with experience E by adding to B the belief: if B then E will occur? He couldn't formulate his total body of beliefs so as to place it in the antecedent of this conditional; anything he could state in the antecedent would be only a tiny fragment of his beliefs, yielding something much smaller than a total theory as having experiential consequences.

4. Does Duhem's thesis have even the consequence that sentences don't have some experiential content of their own, even if this does not exhaust them? To derive this consequence one would have to add to Duhem's thesis that individual statements

are not disconfirmed by experience, the additional claim that they also are not confirmed by experience.

This is an appropriate place to note that Quine's notion of stimulus meaning does not delineate separate content, in the sense of Duhem. For due to a person's assumptions and other current beliefs, much will be in the negative (or affirmative) stimulus meaning of a sentence for him at a time, which Duhem would hold is not part of the sentence's isolated content. (And wouldn't Quine follow Duhem here?)

5. Compare Quine on dispositions as underlying mechanisms, in *The Roots of Reference,* pp. 10–12; "Natural Kinds", 130–138.

6. Hilary Putnam, "The Meaning of 'Meaning' ", in K. Gunderson (ed) *Minnesota Studies in the Philosophy of Science,* vol. 7 (MN: University of Minnesota Press, 1975)

7. As remarks on pp. 37, 48 of *Word and Object* hint Quine might do.

8. Yet the facts of scientific agreement to be explained can be specified, I believe, so as not to run afoul of this. Note also that within a psychological theory of spoken utterances of the sort to be discussed below (in terms of past conditioning and three term contingencies), nothing special would ride on the question of whether a particular sound was a "sign of assent" or not.

Quine uses the notions of assent and dissent to develop the notion of a *verdict function,* and notes that conjunction and disjunction are, though truth functional, not (completely) verdict-functional. (*Roots of Reference,* pp. 77–78) We can further delimit conjunction and disjunction by special verdict tables which use negation, which *is* verdict functional as well as truth functional. In Quine's verdict tables (p. 77), let q be not-p; we get six cases which don't arise, but we also get dissent as the center entry for conjunction and assent as the center entry for disjunction. *If* to learn *and* and *or* is also to learn these special verdict tables, we have the law of non-contradiction and excluded middle centrally bound up with the very learning of these notions. (Contrast Quine's remarks on p. 80 of *Roots of Reference.*)

9. *Word and Object,* p. 39. A more limited view of stimulus meaning as individuating what can be learned in ostension, is taken by Quine in "Replies", p. 313.

10. I take the following listing of 'facts' to be explained by semantic theory from Jerrold Katz, *Semantic Theory,* pp. 5–6, who goes on to say (p. 7), "that the phenomena cited . . . are semantic in nature and that together they provide us with a reasonable conception of what phenomena the subject of semantics is concerned with seems to me beyond serious doubt."

11. See Katz, p. 24, for this description of communication.

12. Noam Chomsky, "Formal Properties of Grammars", in Luce, Bush, and Galanter (eds) *Handbook of Mathematical Psychology,* vol. 2 (N.Y.: John Wiley and Sons, 1963), p. 330.

13. The standard position within the philosophy of science would have it be the simplest linguistics plus psychology that is desired, just as it is the simplest geometry plus physics. A partial focus on the simplest linguistics corresponds to Poincaré's commitment to the simplest geometry. On the view to be described below, in which linguistics disappears within psychology, what would be desired is the simplest total psychology.

14. Chomsky, *Aspects,* p. 4.

15. Katz, *Semantic Theory,* pp. 16–17, in a section entitled "Theories about the objective reality of language", takes this view of language. See also de Saussure, *Course in General Linguistics* (McGraw Hill, 1959), p. 9; and Louis Hjelmslev, *Prolegomena to a Theory of Language* (University of Wisconsin Press, 1963), pp. 5–6.

16. Quine, *Philosophy of Logic,* pp. 15–16; "The Problem of Meaning in Linguistics", in *From a Logical Point of View,* pp. 49, 51–54.

17. Quine asks, "What is the rationale behind that infinite additional membership of K, over and above the finite part J?", and answers that the linguist rounds off. ("Problem of Meaning in Linguistics", p. 54). But wouldn't this Quinean linguist reject a rounding off which failed to fit a complicated utterance he could produce yet hadn't (with none like it being in J already)? "Without this notion (of significant sequence or possible normal utterance) or something to somewhat the same effect, we cannot say what the grammarian is trying to do." (p. 52) This should not be too worrisome if, even with the notion, we can't say why he's trying to do it.

18. There is no objection to describing patterns among the actual products of a process when this serves to explain some further facts identifiable *apart* from the theory which describes the patterns, viz., biologists doing taxonomy or describing the functions of organs or the physiology of organisms.

Shall the set of sentences of the language be delineated in order to specify the output the psychological theory must have, thus serving as an eternal condition of adequacy on the psychological theory rather than as a component of it? But for that purpose, one would not (contra linguistics) offer a specification which goes far beyond anything we know an actual person can do.

19. As Quine, I think, would agree. I discuss it briefly here only because it would provide a rationale for the grammarian's task as Quine states that task; and I see no other rationale.

20. "Problem of Meaning in Linguistics", *From a Logical Point of View,* pp. 55–56.

21. We cannot distinguish circumstances which trigger an existing dispostion to utter a sentence from those which teach the language and create such a disposition by the duration of circumstances C; consider sentences such as "I have been ___ing for n years", where presently you have been ___ing for a far shorter time. And any acquisition of a disposition to say will itself be based upon pre-existing disposition (neurological condition) to acquire the first disposition. In what way is this pre-existing disposition ruled out as the requisite disposition to utter S?

22. *The Roots of Reference,* p. 15.

23. B. F. Skinner, *Verbal Behavior.*

24. "The behaviors of speaker and listener together compose what may be called a total verbal episode. There is nothing in such an episode which is more than the combined behavior of two or more individuals. Nothing 'emerges' in the social unit. The speaker can be studied while assuming a listener, and the listener while assuming a speaker. The separate accounts which result exhaust the episode in which both participate." Skinner, p. 2.

25. "Propositional Objects", in *Ontological Relativity,* p. 158; See also *Roots of Reference,* p. 41.

26. *Words and Objections,* p. 284.

27. "The idioms of propositional attitudes have uses in which they are not easily supplanted." *Philosophy of Logic,* p. 34.

28. A view of realist philosophy of science as an explanatory theory is presented by Richard Boyd in an unpublished manuscript.

29. Within his theory, Quine thinks "we give content to the ontological issue when we regiment the language of science strictly within the framework of the logic of truth functions and objectual quantification." Otherwise, saying constructions are innocent of referential intent "would be meaningless for want of a standard of referental intent."

(*Roots of Reference,* p. 136) But what *content* does the ontological issue have when given content? What we quantify over; but what is that standard a standard of? What (we think) there is; what our speech commits us to there being. But then Quine's remarks about why we shouldn't assess our referential intent via seeing what we quantify over with *branched quantifiers* are puzzling. For why should the fact that ordinary quantification theory "determines an integrated domain of logical theory with bold and significant boundaries", "enjoys an extraordinary combination of depth and simplicity, beauty and utility" and admits of complete proof procedures for validity and inconsistency, whereas branched quantification theory doesn't (See *Philosophy of Logic,* pp. 89–91, "Existence and Quantification", pp. 111–113) recommend it over branched quantifiers as our criterion of ontological commitment? If these virtues are relevant to "referential intent", then either we need a sharper discussion to show why, or "referential intent" doesn't mean what we thought it did. When the choice of criterion is so delicate, what is the value or purpose of the ontologist's (standing on the best current theory and) telling us what exists?

30. See Skinner, *Verbal Behavior,* Epilogue 1, "The Validity of the Author's Verbal Behavior", pp. 453–456.

31. See Skinner, pp. 114–115.

32. In the long interim between the writing of this essay in 1975 and its publication now, a piece was detached and published elsewhere instead. See "Simplicity as Fallout", in Leigh Cauman, et al. (eds) *How Many Questions?; Essays in Honor of Sidney Morgenbesser* (Hackett Publishing Company, 1983).

REPLY TO ROBERT NOZICK

Nozick's ascription to me of a "powerful reductionist philosophy" strikes me as odd. If the oddity is terminological, well and good. Clearly I espouse no translation of natural science into terms of sense data or sensory stimulation. I do emphasize that our data regarding the external world reach us only through sensory stimulation, but surely we are agreed on this. I accord a central role to quantification theory in order to clarify ontology, but I gain no reduction of ontology thereby. I eschew intensional objects for their want of satisfactory individuation, but I acquiesce in the far from cozy universe of general set theory.

He goes on to characterize me as "the theorist of slack", and this is reassuring; for slack is the antithesis of what I would think of as reductionism. He asks if "there is not enough slack to admit, as compatible with the data, a theory of fixed meanings". My point is rather that the slack deprives fixed meanings of a foundation. We could posit them out of hand, but they would be nomological danglers.

Turning to holism, he asks whether a non-Duhemian language would be impossible for us. Let me say that the observation sentences, in my behaviorally defined sense, constitute already a rudimentary language of the kind. It admits of non-Duhemian enlargement, moreover, without clear limits. The tight-fitting sort of science that I speculated on at one point in my paper "On Empirically Equivalent Systems of the World" would be non-Duhemian. But I see no hope of a science comparable in power to our own that would not be subject to holism, at least of my moderate sort. Holism sets in when simple induction develops into the full hypothetico-deductive method.

"Our view that our experiences depend on many facts derives", he writes, "from our not having single statements with individual experiential content." May not the observation sentences, in my behaviorally defined sense, be said to have individual experiential content? Anyway he proposes an artificial construction whereby an experiential content for each sentence, not just each observation sentence, might be derived from the assumed experiential content of the whole theory, and he suggests why I would not accept the derivation. As I see it the method is obstructed by slack.

Nozick adduces statements about activation of nerve endings, statements also about distributions of particles, as examples of statements that have "determinate informational (factual) content", though still subject to Duhem's thesis. But then he rightly points out that this informational content is relative to a pre-assigned theoretical matrix of alternatives. Information theory always requires a preassigned matrix.

He ponders a causal approach to meaning. The suggestion seems to be that the meaning of a term is the thing or mechanism that causes the stimulatory data that lead us to apply the term. I have three problems here: how much causal backgound should we include? how does the suggestion work for terms for whose application there are no separable data? and when there are such separable data, why not just take them as the meaning instead of the causes? Evidently I have not grasped the idea.

I am pleased by Nozick's parable of the two brands of English. It brings out what I have found very difficult to make clear to my students and critics; namely, why it is that even a full understanding of neurology would in no way resolve the indeterminacy of translation.

Nozick takes up stimulus meaning. He observes that my exclusion of verbal stimuli has the undesirable effect of crippling the stimulus meaning of certain sentences in an arbitrary way. I was aware of this, but felt that I had to accept it. Stimulus meanings do not carry us far in any event.

He conjures up situations in which the sentence 'Gavagai' or 'Rabbit' would fail to meet my intersubjective standard of observationality. My answer is that these circumstances, if realized, simply show that the sentence is not observational, or not *as* observational as some. Strictly, observationality comes in degrees. According to my *intra*subjective version of observationality, moreover, in *Theories and Things* and elsewhere, one man's observation sentence need not be another's.

He rightly notes the indeterminacy of the signs of assent and dissent themselves, at the very root of stimulus meaning. I would caution only against overestimating it. See my reply to Thompson.

Moving to my verdict tables, he points out that if the learning of 'or' involves learning, among others, the table for 'p or $\bar{p}$', then, contrary to *Roots of Reference,* the law of excluded middle is indeed clinched in the learning. It is an interesting point, but I think it unlikely that cases of 'p or $\bar{p}$' would figure among the samples from which the child learns 'or'.

Nozick launches a skeptical inquiry into the *raison d'être* of linguistics. The question is salutary. Let us look to the practical side for the beginnings of an answer. The linguist's ultimate technological concern, if any, is to help people to influence others and to be influenced by them, in their actions, insofar as language contributes. To this end the major task is inculcation of foreign languages. This has to be done systematically, because of the boundless multitude of possibly useful strings of phonemes. Recursive generation is thus called for, in which a finite lot of so-called morphemes is specified, along with a finite lot of constructions by which to generate longer strings from shorter ones. Such is the lexicon and grammar. Whether semantics is dealt with concurrently or subsequently is as may be; see end of section II of my reply to Harman.

Nozick rightly doubts the utility of specifying an infinite class of purportedly permissible or grammatical strings. That specification is a mere by-product, determined, unavoidably, by the recursion itself. What is useful, to the point of indispensability, is the recursion.

Even this need would perhaps lapse, so far as the practical purpose is concerned of helping people to influence others and to be influenced by them, if there were no question of foreign languages. There would be practical reasons still for coaching people in their own language, with a view to enhancing persuasiveness, perspicuity, or aesthetic quality; but this work might or might not require recourse to recursion. If not, the infinite class of purportedly grammatical strings would no longer obtrude even as a by-product.

There is room also for theoretical interest in language. It can be interesting to speculate on mechanisms of language learning; also on ultimate origins. Here again we must resort, surely, to recursions. The learning of language consists necessarily in an internalizing of recursive procedures, and the genesis of language was necessarily a genesis of recursive procedures. Given the recursions, we are regaled willy nilly with the potential infinitude of so-called grammatical strings. Has Nozick supposed that the recursions are inspired by a prior concern to demarcate such a class? I submit that the shoe is on the other foot.

Nozick raises a problem about dispositions that I first heard from Stephen Stich. How are we to distinguish between an early and perhaps innate disposition to behave in a given way at some particular later stage of development, and a newly acquired disposition so to behave, acquired only at the stage in question? This quandary is one of my reasons for regarding the general dispositional idiom as an inseparable affix, devoid of independent scientific content. Each particular disposition to behavior is to be recognized on its own as a present mechanism or state of nerves on a par with any other, and worth positing insofar as it promises to contribute to an explanatory physiological theory. The dispositional affix—'-ile', '-ble', or 'disposition to'—imputes no distinctively dispositional character to the mechanism or neural state in question, but serves merely as a signal that the mechanism or state is being tagged by reference to its conspicuous symptom. (*Roots of Reference,* pp. 10–11).

He speculates on how we might manage to dispense with the "intersubjective equating of stimulations". I agree in wanting to dispense with it, and in *Theories and Things* I moved in that direction by defining observationality intrasubjectively.

In some later pages Nozick wonders why I should be preoccupied with translation and with reference and even with seeking a "vegetarian" simulation of meaning, however partial, in stimulus meaning. Why not "a hard-line Skinnerian view of language, that is, verbal behavior"? Evidently he under-estimates my negativity in these matters. My thesis of indeterminacy of translation was meant to undermine the traditional uncritical notion of sameness of meaning and hence of meaning. My development of stimulus meaning was an exploration of the limits of an empirically defensible and scientifically indispensable core idea of meaning. Reference, finally, gets cut down to size in *Ontological Relativity* and the opening essay of *Theories and Things*.

I conclude with a response to Nozick's closing paragraphs. Gibson has plausibly surmised that the major obstacle to understanding my position is a failure to take my commitment to naturalism seriously. Truth, for me, is immanent. Factuality, or matterhood of the fact, is likewise immanent. We do not adjudicate between our aggregate system of the world and a rival system by appeal to a transcendent standard of truth or factuality.

Quite within our going system of the world, still, we can study other systems, much as we study mathematics and foreign languages. We may even persuade ourselves that a rival system is as well warranted by observation as ours, and we may oscillate between the two systems for the sake of a broader perspective on nature. But truth, as Tarski appreciated, is meaningfully predicated, rightly or wrongly, only within the theory that is operative at the time. Similarly for factuality. See the last page or two of my reply to Gibson; also *Theories and Things*, foot of page 21 and after.

Ontological relativity, which puzzles Nozick and others unduly, is just an adjunct of translation. To say what objects someone is talking about is to say how we propose to translate his terms: such is the relativity. At home—i.e., homophonically—reference is captured by trivial paradigms in Tarski's style: 'Caesar' designates Caesar and 'rabbit' denotes rabbits, whatever *they* are. Such is face value, and in my naturalism I ask no better. See *Theories and Things*, top half of page 20.

W. V. Q.

14

Charles Parsons

QUINE ON THE PHILOSOPHY OF MATHEMATICS

T he 'philosophy of mathematics', where it has not concentrated on specific methodological issues in mathematics, has chiefly sought to explain a single impressive gross feature of mathematics: its combination of clarity and certainty with enormous generality. Mathematics shares this feature with logic, but for some reason in the past it was in the case of logic found less impressive. Presumably in earlier times this was due to the much more restricted scope of formal logic and its being combined into a body of knowledge with much reflection on language, inference, and knowledge that is neither so clear nor so certain. More recently, logic has simply been treated together with mathematics; of course they have been considered to be one subject.

Quine's discussion of these matters is in the tradition of considering logic and mathematics together, although in his later writings the distinction between elementary logic and mathematics proper assumes some importance.[1] With respect to clarity and certainty, another distinction has arisen in the last century with the development of set theory: the higher or more abstract parts of set theory have not been found to be so clear and certain as the more elementary parts of mathematics, particularly the arithmetic of natural numbers. On the other hand, the advent of set theory led mathematics to be seen as even more

Though written for the present volume, this paper has appeared in my *Mathematics in Philosophy* (copyright © 1983 by Cornell University Press), and is included here by permission of that publisher.

Sections I-V of the paper, in almost their present form, were presented in October 1975 to the Chapel Hill Philosophy Colloquim, with Professor Quine as commentator. Quine's reply prompted some local revisions. However, although Quine convinced me that his attitude toward the concept of "physical or natural" necessity was more negative than I had thought, I have let my interpretation stand, because of the issues to which it gives rise.

Other revisions have been made in response to comments by Saul Kripke, the late Gareth Evans, and an anonymous referee.

general than before. In earlier times, mathematics was often thought to be applicable only to spatio-temporal entities.

Quine's approach to these features is influenced, though largely negatively,
by two characterizations of mathematics of a more technical philosophical nature: the theses that mathematical truths are *necessary* and that mathematical
knowledge is *a priori*. He has of course carried out an elaborate criticism of
the whole notion of a priori knowledge, particularly where it was to be explained by the analyticity of the propositions known a priori. I do not want to
concentrate on this criticism in this essay, since it has been so much discussed.
Most of the essay will be devoted to Quine's views on the *necessity* of mathematics and logic. In this connection I shall discuss the notion of "mathematical
possibility", which Quine has hardly discussed directly. This will lead to a
discussion of Quine's interpretaion of *existence* in mathematics. I shall discuss
the bearing of set theory on Quine's views on these matters. In a final section,
I shall take up some other aspects of Quine's conception of set theory.

I

In common sense and science, many attributions of necessity are made, and it
is clear that a variety of types or concepts of necessity are at stake. Philosophers have held, however, that there is a single "highest" type of necessity,
which is often called logical necessity, but "logic" here would have to include
more than formal logic. What is necessary in this sense would be necessary in
any other sense. For this reason, perhaps the best term for it would be *absolute*
necessity. According to tradition, whatever can be known a priori would be
absolutely necessary. On the other hand, the tradition would hold that even
quite fundamental laws of empirical science are *not* absolutely necessary.

The truths of logic and pure mathematics have been held to be absolutely
necessary by those who have used this notion. There is also a weaker claim
that logic and mathematics are necessary in a sense that is more stringent than
that in which scientific laws are necessary (at least for the most part). It is this
claim that I shall discuss.

Historically at least, the alleged apriority of mathematics has been linked
with its alleged strict necessity, although it is not so easy to state the connection
precisely. We can express the traditional (e.g., Kantian) view of the connection
of necessity and apriority by the following two principles:

(1)   If a knows that $\Box$p, then a knows a priori that p.
(2)   If a knows a priori that p, then $\Box$p.

The truth of these principles is not at all evident if one supposes that necessity of the relevant type is not an epistemic notion.

(1)   certainly presupposes a standard of knowledge that knowledge resting on testimony does not meet. But given the strong claim of mathematics to certainty, that seems appropriate enough to the case that concerns us. Quine can be interpreted as denying the apriority of mathematics. If (1) holds, it would follow that mathematics does not possess necessity of the relevant type.

A Quinian argument against the necessity of mathematics would assume (1) and then apply his critique of the a priori: if mathematics is not known a priori, then (1) implies that mathematical statements are not known as necessary, and it is then very implausible that they *are* necessary. In fact, this seems to be Quine's principal argument. He seems to adhere to (1), though perhaps only as an explication of notions that he does not accept. The place where he most explicitly discusses the necessity of mathematics is in the popular lecture "Necessary Truth".[2] There he introduces considerations bearing on analyticity and apriority. Moreover, when he discusses the problems of modal logic, he sometimes assumes that absolute necessity means something like analyticity. His unfriendliness to *de re* modalities derives partly from that source.[3]

Both (1) and (2) have been questioned, notably by Saul Kripke,[4] and in the absence of a positive defense of (1) this Quinian argument against the necessity of mathematics has a major gap. The discussion below indicates the difficulty I see in filling it. If the necessity of mathematics can be defended, then Quine's critique of the a priori is a powerful argument against (1); it would leave (2) vacuous, though not false, for mathematical statements. I shall not consider the interesting question whether the direct consideration of the necessity of mathematics yields an argument for its apriority, thus rehabilitating (1) in the mathematical case.

Quine apparently does regard as usable a notion of necessity according to which the laws of science are necessary, although that would be an extension of the specific explication of necessity he sketches in "Necessary Truth".[5] There it is *instances* of laws, not the laws themselves, that are necessary. At any rate, he describes the necessity involved as "physical or natural" necessity and says there is no "higher or more austere" necessity.[6] The latter would be a necessity which logic and mathematics would possess but empirical natural science would not.

II

It might seem that Quine should find a specifically logical necessity quite clear. A statement should be logically necessary if and only if it is logically true in the sense of first-order quantificational logic with identity. Then for a statement in canonical notation it would be quite sharply defined whether it was logically necessary or not, and moreover it would be easy to show that at least some of the basic laws of physics are not logically necessary; indeed even so simple a statement as (∃x) (∃y) (x ≠ y) would not be logically necessary.

Such a notion would of course not agree with the intuitive conception of absolute necessity, since on that conception statements can be absolutely necessary even though they contain nonlogical predicates essentially.[7] But it does seem perfectly clear. Moreover, if one reads the '☐p' of modal logic as 'it is logically true that p', the theorems without nested modalities of the usual modal propositional logic are true.[8]

It seems that from Quine's point of view this notion is not unclear or incoherent, but perhaps he would not see any need for it: the purposes that talk of logical necessity in this sense would serve are already adequately served by talking of logical truth.

The concept turns out in any case to be a somewhat anomalous notion of necessity, and not quite so clear as it seems at first sight. We have: if 'p' is a first-order sentence,

(3)   'It is logically necessary that p' is true if and only if 'p' is logically true.

But our necessity statement is not itself in the Quinian canonical form of a first-order sentence. Here there are two main alternatives.

The first is to hold to Quine's notion of canonical form and take the right-hand side of (3) as the canonical paraphrase of 'it is logically necessary that p'. Since for a given sentence 'p', ' ''p'' is logically true' is not a logical truth (however the details of the characterization of logical truth go), it follows that 'it is logically necessary that it is logically necessary that p' is always *false*. The rule of necessitation of ordinary modal logic will fail.[9] Moreover 'it is logically possible that p' will also not be a truth of logic. Logical possibility proves to be a concept of a different character from logical necessity.

Consider the more informal notion of necessity of Quine's "Necessary Truth". According to this, a statement should be logically necessary if it is an instance of a (specifically envisaged) law of logic. But what is a law of logic? A logical truth (other than a pure identity statement) will contain non-logical predicates and is rather an instance of a law than the law itself. Quine in fact says that the laws of logic cannot be stated without semantic ascent. Then the law of which

(4)   It is raining or it is not raining
is an instance would be something like

(5)   Any sentence of the form 'p or not-p' is true
which is not a logical truth. Thus on this conception, the laws of logic are not logically necessary.

The second alternative is to depart from Quine's notion of first-order logic with identity as the canonical framework. Then we might treat '☐', interpreted as logical necessity, as itself a logical operator. So far it has been explicated only when applied to non-modal sentences, and the extension of the interpretation is not unique. Evidently for 'p' a non-modal sentence, '$\Diamond$p' will be true if and only if '$\sim$ p' is *not* logically true in the original sense. If our extended interpretation is to make all theorems of S5 true, then '$\Diamond$ p' will be logically necessary, but then, since such 'p' are not recursively enumerable, there will be no proof procedure for logical truth. For Quine that would be a strong reason to reject such an alternative. But an interpretation with these properties can be given. Another definition in the spirit of Quine's definition of the logical truths as the truths containing only logical expressions essentially will yield the result that all theorems of S4, but not all theorems of S5, are logically necessary in the extended sense.[10] For if 'p' is a consistent first-order sentence with an inconsistent substitution-case, '$\Diamond$ p' will be true and '$\Box \Diamond$ p' false on this interpretation. But this means statements of logical *possibility* are not truths of logic.

Another possible expansion of the canonical notation would be to allow, as Quine does not, quantification of sentence and predicate places. The law of which (4) is an instance would be not (5) but

(6) (p)(p v $\sim$ p),

which is a theorem of second-order logic.[11] Similarly, a truth which is an instance of a valid first-order schema, say:

(x) $\sim$ Fxx & (x) (y) (z) (Fxy & Fyz . $\supset$ Fxz) . $\supset$ (x) (y) (Fxy $\supset$ $\sim$ Fyx),

call it A(F), would be an instance of the law (F)A(F), which is again a theorem of second-order logic.

This proposal again has the consequence that statements of logical possibility are not truths of logic. For example, let B(F) be a non-valid first-order schema whose negation is satisfiable only in an infinite universe. (F)B(F) would on the above conception express a false "law" of logic. But $\sim$ (F)B(F) is not a logical truth: it can be true only if the universe of individuals is infinite.

The obstacle all these attempts face is the following: We assumed that if 'p' is a first-order statement, 'p' is logically necessary if and only if it is logically true in the usual sense. We sought to extend the notion of logical necessity to a wider class of logical forms. But our initial condition implies that the first-order statements that are logically possible are just the negations of *non-valid* ones. It follows that either logical possibility is not certifiable by logic alone, or there is no complete proof procedure for logic in the extended sense. The second-order alternative, if validity is taken in the usual way, has *both* these consequences.

The former conclusion derives plausibility from some simple reflections on the relation of logic and mathematics. The completeness theorem tells us that if a sentence is not logically true (in the first-order sense) then a *mathematical* construction of restricted complexity, but which must in some cases involve an infinite universe, yields a counterinstance. Logical truths, since they are true regardless of the size of the universe, seem to have no ontological commitment. But its *absence* requires countermodels which may be infinite.

In terms of *mathematical* modalities, we could say that the *logical* possibility of the truth of a statement of the form B(F) is the *mathematical* possibility of a model of the schema. In this sense, the logical modalities are not really more general than the mathematical modalities.

III

Let us now focus on the latter. Quine seems not to challenge the assertion that the axioms and theorems of mathematics have the character of laws, rather than accidental generalizations. As we saw above, his objection is rather to the distinction between mathematics and natural science, and thus between mathematical and natural necessity. In large part this objection rests on the claim, which I do not want to discuss at the moment, that there is no interesting sense in which mathematics is a priori and theoretical science not. Where he discusses directly the existence of a distinctive notion of logico-mathematical necessity[12] and in another place where he introduces similar considerations about the difference between mathematics and science,[13] it is not clear that Quine is really trying to give a case against a notion of logico-mathematical necessity independent of his case against apriority.

There is, however, a reason for wanting distinctly mathematical modalities that Quine does not really consider. This is that modality is naturally appealed to in explicating *existence* in mathematics and related notions. To make this clear, we need to concentrate not on the necessity of mathematical truths, but on *possibility*.

Corresponding to stringency of necessity is, of course, liberality of possibility. The notion of absolute possibility would allow that states of affairs are possible that are not countenanced by the laws of nature and that must therefore be counted "naturally" impossible. If the mathematical modalities are to be interesting, the same should be the case where absolute possibility is replaced by mathematical possibility.

A simple example from constructive mathematics already indicates why mathematical possibilities might be thought to go beyond the "naturally" possible. Whatever the process is by which the natural numbers might be constructed, it is one that *can* be continued to infinity. One implication of this is that at any stage of this construction (at which representatives of a certain initial segment have been constructed) it is always possible to continue. Moreover one assumes a transitivity rule (i.e. '$\Diamond \Diamond p$' implies '$\Diamond p$') from which it follows that at any stage, for any n it is possible to continue for n more steps.[14]

Traditionally, such a construction is thought of as an activity of the human mind. However, it seems we cannot represent this in terms of the actual natural capacities of the human organism: for then there will be a definite bound to the number of possible steps, since certainly there is a limit to the speed with which the construction could proceed and a definite outer limit (certainly less than 175 years) to the possible life-span of a man.

The traditional recourse in this situation is to conceive the capabilities of the *mind* in abstraction from those of man as an organism. This course is not at all in accord with Quine's naturalism. One can ask whether it does not amount to defining the capacities of the mind in terms of certain theories about the mind's objects—mathematics in particular.[15] If so, then using it in an argument against Quine's view on the necessity of mathematics would require that mathematical possibility be to some degree antecedently clear.

An alternative apparently more congenial to Quine would be to think of the construction of the natural numbers as a physical process. Then what the "potential infinity" of the natural numbers would amount to is the physical possibility of the generation of representatives of any initial segment of the natural numbers.

This should remind us of a version of "nominalism" related to that of Nelson Goodman, which at one time attracted Quine.[16] Such nominalism is essentially the above suggestion with the modal element removed. Rather than assume the natural numbers or other mathematical objects directly, one assumes that the physical world has enough structure to represent the system of mathematical objects that one wants. The difference with the physical interpretation of constructivism alluded to above is the rejection of the modal interpretation of mathematical existence and the distinction of "potential" and "actual" infinity.

Such nominalism has the advantage of avoiding the conceptual complication of modality. Still it may seem that the modalist account is on stronger ground because its hypotheses are weaker. The nominalist has to assume that there actually are infinitely many individuals: that is, he must have, say, a two-place predicate which, in Platonist terms, describes a one-one mapping of a certain collection of individuals properly into itself. This assumption could hardly be justified by direct empirical evidence. As an hypothesis, its plausibility surely rests on the idea of space and time as infinitely divisible or infinite in extent. But then the existence of such an abstract structure (however "existence" in this case might come to be explained) is more certain than any hypothesis of the existence of a realization of it by actual physical entities such as bodies or particles. This additional assumption seems gratuitous, at least from a purely mathematical point of view. It seems to seek to undo an abstraction already carried out by the Greeks—distinguishing between space and time as abstract forms—one might say of *possible* objects—and the actual physical objects and events, and giving a sophisticated, rigorous theory of the former.

On the modalist view, this assumption of the *existence* of infinitely many physical individuals is dropped. The concrete existence of infinitely many individuals, as opposed to that of any arbitrary finite number, does not even have to be *possible*.[17] But one might ask whether the assumption that the existence of arbitrary finite sequences is *physically* possible is not also gratuitous. Is it any more necessary to mathematics that the laws of the physical universe should permit some *potential* infinity than that some sort of infinity should *obtain* in the actual world?

I shall not inquire further into this question, because one immediately meets an obstacle. To inquire in a serious way about physical possibility, one would have to appeal to physical theory. Then the difficulty is that physical theory as it stands is founded on mathematics. One could not inquire into anything by physical theory while treating as genuinely open the question of the possibilities that constitute the existence of the natural numbers.

IV

At this point we should rejoin the views of Quine. For one is inclined to conclude from the above difficulty that mathematics is prior to physics. If we think of mathematical existence in modal terms, the possibility involved must be more general than physical possibility, either absolute or distinctively mathematical possibility. However, it seems clear that Quine would not accept this conclusion. Mathematics and physics constitute a single body of theory. While it may be relevant to mathematics to consider the possibility of physical realizations of certain structures, this is part of the process of rebuilding the ship of science while it is afloat.

Quine goes further in that he does not demand any specific relation at all between the existence of natural or real numbers and the possibilities or the facts of physical existence. This does not mean that facts about concrete objects have no relevance to mathematics or mathematical existence. But the relevance is that mathematics belongs to a body of theory that includes empirical science and that relates as a whole to experience. But in order to see how the relation of mathematical existence, possibility, and necessity look from Quine's point of view, we have to consider Quine's view of mathematical existence. I maintain that Quine's view here is somewhat awkward for his view that there is no higher necessity than "physical or natural" necessity. Namely Quine's view is more "Platonist" than the constructivist views alluded to above, not only in the generally conceded sense that mathematical existence and truth are treated as independent of the possibilities of construction and verification, but in the additional sense that it is treated as independent of the possibilities of representation in the concrete.

Quine does not separate mathematical existence from existence in general. The classical objectual existential quantifier is for Quine in effect a primitive.[18] It is "defined" by the theories in which it occurs, the general framework for which is classical first-order quantificational logic. Although Quine makes some use of very general divisions among objects, such as between "abstract" and "concrete", these divisions do not amount to any division of *senses* either of the quantifier or the word "object"; the latter sort of division would indeed call for a many-sorted quantificational logic rather than the standard one. Moreover, Quine does not distinguish between objects and any more general or different category of "entities" (such as Frege's *functions*).[19] There is no difference between saying there is *something* satisfying some condition and saying there are *objects* satisfying the condition.

The effect of this way of proceeding is that what can be said about existence and objecthood in general is common to the most abstract and the most concrete, the most theoretical and the most immediately perceived objects. Moreover, no particular kind of existence has a central or paradigmatic role in a canonically formulated theory, although it might from a genetic point of view.

From some phrases where Quine gives what he considers "intuitive" and "picturesque" characterizations of the difference between singular and general terms, P.F. Strawson derives the view that identifying reference to spatio-temporal particulars is the central, basic form of reference to objects, and that spatio-temporal particulars are "the very pattern" of objects.[20] He goes on to say, "Insofar, then, as things other than spatio-temporal particulars qualify as objects, they do so simply because our thought, our talk, confers upon them the limited and purely logical analogy with spatio-temporal particulars which I have just described."[21]

In his reply to Strawson, Quine does not discuss this point. Rather, he rejects the demand for an explanation of the distinction between singular and general terms that goes beyond giving such formal criteria as accessibility to quantification and relating the logical apparatus of quantification theory to our own language. His reason is the indeterminacy of translation and the "parochial" character of the apparatus of objective reference. He does not say why that *is* a reason. Moreover, some of the elements of Strawson's account occur in Quine's own genetic speculation.[22]

Existence thus takes on not only a theoretical but also a formal character. It is emancipated not only from perception but also from spatio-temporality and other marks of concreteness. In the case of abstract entities, certain protests against Platonism become irrelevant. There is no mysterious "realm" of, say, sets in the sense that they need to have anything akin to location, and our knowledge of them is not based on any mysterious kind of "seeing" into such a realm. This "demythologizing" of the existence of abstract entities is one of

Quine's important contributions to philosophy, although it has its antecedent in Frege and Carnap.[23]

It is noteworthy that for Quine this "emancipation" is achieved for existence as such, so that abstract entities are accommodated without the kind of sharp separation of abstract and concrete existence that would be implied by the view that "exists" has a different *sense* or *meaning* in the two cases. This view Quine firmly repudiates,[24] but given his general account of meaning, the question cannot be a fundamental one. What he seems to do is to characterize the notions of "object" and "existence" in minimal terms so as to apply to all cases of "being", "existence", or "subsistence". Any alleged distinction of senses of "exist" is to be replaced by a suitable distinction of kinds of objects. Since Quine assesses ontology in terms of the *classical* logic of quantification, his conception of existence is not only incompatible with constructivism but can make sense of constructivist theories only by classical models. Although I find that attitude unduly restrictive, I do not wish to pursue the point here. More could be said than I have said elsewhere,[25] but now I am more interested in the consequences of accepting set theory.

Some writings on existence in mathematics have given prominence to what, following Leibniz, can be called the "incompleteness" of mathematical objects. The only properties and relations of such objects that play a role in mathematical reasoning are those determined by the basic relations of some system or structure to which all the objects involved belong. This may be the natural numbers, some other number system, Euclidean or some other space, a given group, ring, field, or other such structure, or the universe of some model of set theory. A further natural step would be to say that the objects just do not *have* properties and relations other than those derived from the basic relations of some comprehensive structure. However, it seems that to accommodate applied mathematics we need to consider also certain "external" relations (see below).

If we think of "structures" in the usual algebraic way, then this view implies that all the "real" properties and relations of mathematical objects will be invariant under any isomorphism of the comprehensive structure with another. Suppose we are concerned only with natural numbers. Then we can see them as a structure consisting of a set N and a binary relation S (the successor relation), such that the Dedekind-Peano postulates hold.[26] Now of course a structure so conceived can have different *realizations:* sets N_0 and relations S_0 satisfying the Peano postulates. If such realizations consist of mathematical objects, the above thesis implies that the properties and relations of these objects—including the elements of N_0 and S_0—derive from the basic relations of some other structure. Notorious examples are the different construals of natural numbers as sets, such as the Zermelo and von Neumann numbers, where the underlying structure is the universe of set theory with the ϵ-relation.

By "external relation" I mean the sort of relations that arise in application between the elements of a structure and other objects, such as the relation between a city x and a natural number n when x has n inhabitants. Such relations are in general definable in terms of the basic relations of the structure and others which do not depend on any choice of realization of the structure. Thus 'x has n inhabitants' is true if there is a one-one mapping of the inhabitants of x onto the natural numbers less than n, where "less than" is definable in terms of N and S. Particular numbers are also given by notations definable in these terms, e.g.,

$$0 = (\imath \, x) \, (x \in N \, \& \sim (\exists \, y) \, Sxy),$$
$$1 = (\imath \, x) \, Sx0, \text{ etc.}$$

Thus these relations can be "construed" in terms of any realization of the structure and they are invariant under isomorphism.

Different ontological morals have been drawn from these facts. The traditional view, most explicit perhaps in Leibniz with the contrast of incomplete objects and individual substances, is that these features are characteristic of mathematical objects or at least abstract objects.[27] The above quotation from Strawson goes a step further in suggesting that such objects are objects only in a derivative or extended sense. Benacerraf goes another step in denying for this sort of reason that numbers are genuine objects at all.[28]

The wide net that Quine's notion of object casts is shown by the fact that he never suggests that the "incompleteness" of mathematical objects is an ontological deficiency or even peculiarity. There are hints that it is characteristic of objects generally. Harman tentatively suggested that the possibility of construing numbers as sets in different ways was an instance of the indeterminacy of translation.[29] Quine has used natural numbers and other mathematical examples to illustrate his thesis of the relativity of reference.[30] In recent writings he has some tantalizing comments about identity which point to the conclusion that identity is just indiscernibility with respect to the predicates of a language and is therefore relative to the richness of its vocabulary. This would imply that the "incompleteness" of mathematical objects does not contrast with anything, or rather that in the case of mathematical objects (and perhaps also some theoretical objects in science) a definite system of relations is given, whereas with ordinary objects the "structure" is much vaguer and more open-ended.[31]

I am not sure how far Quine is ultimately willing to go in this direction. I also shall not criticize these hints. I do not myself have a theory of "concrete objects" or "individual substances" to oppose to them. I do want to say that the general ideas Quine expresses about objecthood are somewhat awkward for his view of necessity and possibility. To see this, let us consider set theory and Quine's views on it.

V

It is only when the higher infinities of Cantorian set theory are introduced that mathematical objects must violate the conditions of representability in the concrete discussed above. Space-time is always construed as a set of $2^{\aleph_0}$ points or at least not of essentially higher cardinality. This puts a definite bound on the number of possible "spatio-temporal" objects, say $2^{2^{\aleph_0}}$. If the "physically possible" is what can in some sense be realized in space and time, then structures of sufficiently high cardinality whose acceptance is uncontroversial among set theorists (e.g., whose existence is provable in ZF) are not physically possible. Although we may think of the existence of sets in modal terms, as the *possible* existence of objects satisfying certain conditions, it hardly makes sense to take such possibilities as possibilities of *physical* objects, where high cardinalities are involved, or even as possibilities of *concrete* objects, whatever the decisive marks of concreteness are taken to be. Whatever convinces us, for example, that "there is" a cardinal number $\beth_\omega$[32] surely does not convince us that a structure of that cardinality having any but the most bloodless reality is possible: if concreteness demands causal efficacy, or perceivability in some strong sense, or temporality, or even some genuine individuality, we have no reason whatsoever to believe that $\beth_\omega$ can be concretely represented.

This is a sense in which set theory is "Platonist" in which even the impredicative theory of real numbers is not. The preceding remarks are meant to indicate that in this case a modal conception of mathematical existence has little force in overcoming nominalist scruples about the objects postulated in higher set theory, although perhaps it does for the objects of pre-Cantorian mathematics. For even modally construed set theory requires a conception of "object" and "existence" so general that objects can exist which have none of the marks of concreteness.[33] What the modal construal does accomplish is to bring out the fact that for pure set theory as for arithmetic the usual distinction of actual and merely possible existence does not apply.

Philosophers have sought to avoid admitting such inclusive conceptions of object and possibility either by rejecting set theory or by not admitting that set theory means what it says—usually by adopting some form of formalism. Quine, we have seen, grasps the nettle by admitting a conception of object with the requisite generality. But his view has some affinity with formalism. Neither the meaningfulness nor the truth of set theory as it stands has a trustworthy intuitive foundation. Both the axioms and the logic have a certain conventional character. However, in this respect set theory does not differ in principle from other theories, particularly scientific theories. For the latter, a non-conventional factor in determining belief is of course the relation to sense-experience. Because according to Quine mathematics and science constitute a single body of theory, the same connection exists even for set theory. Quine differs from other theorists of mathematics such as Kant, Brouwer, and Gödel in denying that there is any fundamental intrinsically mathematical or logical form of evidence. He also does not place much emphasis on the derivative types of evidence employed in plausible reasoning in mathematics, such as the analogies appealed to in arguing for large cardinal axioms or the consideration of consequences by which Gödel argues for the falsity of the continuum hypothesis.[34] However, there is no systematic reason why Quine should not regard such considerations as relevant; he would no doubt insist that they are not compelling, but that is generally agreed upon. However, the logical and "class-theoretic" orientation of Quine toward set theory (discussed below) is probably at least a psychological barrier.

Quine seems to be in the following awkward position: Both epistemologically, in terms of the evidential basis it rests on, and ontologically, in terms of the nature of its necessity, set theory is on a par with physics. However, the notion of object in set theory, and the structures whose possibility it postulates, are much more general than the notion of physical object or spatio-temporally or physically representable structure. How can he still maintain that these possibilities are "natural" possibilities and that the necessity of logic and mathematics is not "higher"?

Quine would no doubt reply that by "natural" possibility and necessity he means possibility and necessity as it would be assessed in terms of the laws of a theory that includes *both* set theory and physics; the idea that there is no "higher" necessity than natural necessity in effect rests on the claim that there is no definite line between mathematics and empirical science. All possibilities are "natural"; some of these are possibilities of spatio-temporal structures; others are only of sets of perhaps very high rank.

The claim that there is not a clear line between mathematics and empirical science seems to me implausible, at least if it is made independently of Quine's epistemological arguments. In a canonical formulation of scientific theory, the distinction between mathematics and the rest is quite as clear as that between first-order logic and the rest. Quine prefers here formulations in terms of first-order set theory: then the truths of mathematics would be those that contain only 'ϵ', '$=$', and the operators of first-order quantificational logic essentially.[35] Moreover, the step from delineating a class of mathematical *truths* to using purely mathematical *modalities* is more useful than the corresponding step in terms of first-order logic that I discussed above, and it does not have the formally awkward features I mentioned.

In unregimented science, the distinction between pure mathematics and individual sciences seems quite clear, although in applied mathematics it may not always be sharp. Quine compares the relation of mathematics to physics to that between theoretical and experimental physics.[36] I find this analogy unpersuasive. Theoretical and experimental physics are both about the same subject-matter—space-time, energy, physical particles, physical bodies. Experiments are carried out to verify or falsify the theories of theoretical physics; theories are concocted to explain the data yielded by experiments. There is no similar unity of subject-matter or interrelation of purposes between mathematics and physics. Quine mentions the applicability of mathematics to other sciences; this is to me an indication of the greater generality of mathematics.

However, it is clear that Quine is ultimately thinking of the epistemological situation: it is perhaps less important for him to deny the existence of a clear and in some way important *distinction* between mathematics and physics, or even to deny that mathematics has a *content* which is more general, than to challenge the idea that mathematics is disconnected from *observation* in a fundamental sense in which physics is not. This raises a whole range of issues which I have not wished to take up in this paper: My discussion of the necessity of logic and mathematics has tried to proceed independently of their alleged apriority. But it does seem to me that the considerations developed here reflect back on Quine's epistemological position at a few points.

To begin with, from the fact that the statements of set theory contain quantifiers such that only a very restricted part of their range is relevant to observation it seems clear that the role of purely theoretical reasoning in our judgment of the truth or falsity of set theories must be much more central than that of observation, although it is conceivable that the latter could play a role. More specifically, if ability to explain observational data in the ordinary sense were the reason for accepting set theories, then weaker theories (perhaps only some form of second-order number theory) would be preferred to full set theory on grounds of simplicity and perhaps lesser risk of inconsistency. Quine's actual accounts of set theory proceed in a much more abstract fashion (cf. below).

The following point seems relevant to some of the examples that have been used to argue that logic and mathematics are empirical. A mathematical theory of an aspect of the empirical world takes the form of supposing that there is a system of actual objects and relations that is an instance of a structure that can be characterized mathematically. The implications of this supposition will vary greatly and may not be altogether clear: an outstanding case is the attribution of a certain geometrical structure to space-time, and this is not necessarily taken to imply the physical reality of the *points* which on the most usual mathematical formulation are the elements of the structure. The point I wish to make is that what confronts the tribunal of experience is not the pure theory of this type of structure but its being supposedly represented by a definite aspect of the actual world. If the resulting theory is abandoned or modified, the form is likely to be that of replacing this structure by a different structure from the mathematician's inventory, even if it was developed only for the purpose.

In one sense mathematics may change as a result: the theory of one type of structure may become more salient, that of another type less so. But no proposition of pure mathematics has been *falsified*. If we view mathematics in this light, no proposition of Euclidean geometry is falsified by the discovery that physical space is not Euclidean. One could object that this claim rests on a conception of pure geometry that did not prevail when it was almost universally believed that actual space *is* Euclidean; then the axioms of Euclidean geometry were thought of as at the same time truths of mathematics and statements about real space. However, from the fact that the differentiation of mathematics from physics that I am defending has developed historically, it surely does not follow that it is unsound. I do not even have to assume that it is complete at the present time: there may be aspects of physics or other sciences today of which the mathematical content is not so neatly separable. I do not know of any example, still less an example where such a separation seems impossible in principle.[37] The prevailing methodology of mathematicians, with its emphasis on rigor and abstraction, works for carrying through such a separation in any given case. The point is, however, that on the *general* conception of mathematics I am presenting, the known or easily conceivable examples of empirical falsification of mathematical theories in *science* do not yield any instance or model of empirical falsification of pure mathematics.

VI

In practice, Quine assimilates set theory to physics rather less than some of his general epistemological remarks might suggest. He has always related set theory closely to *logic*. Logic has, in turn, been connected particularly closely to *grammar* and to certain grammatical constructions, most explicitly in *Philosphy of Logic*. He is tempted by the characterization of logical truths as "true by grammatical structure" but stops short of adopting it because of its suggestion that logical truth is linguistic in a sense that can be meaningfully opposed to factual truth.[38] Nonetheless, the connection with specific grammatical constructions also extends to set theory, as *The Roots of Reference* shows. Set theory for Quine has always been a theory of extensions of predicates, in that the paradigm of a set is the extension of a predicate, and the axioms of set theory are taken as attributing extensions to certain predicates (to be sure with parameters). I want to close this essay by some comments on this.

By the extension of a predicate 'Fx', I mean an object $\hat{x}Fx$ associated with 'Fx', such that *coextensive* predicates have the same extension; that is, '(x) (Fx $\equiv$ Gx)' implies '$\hat{x}Fx = \hat{x}Gx$'. Moreover, anything is a *member* of $\hat{x}Fx$ just in case 'Fx' is true of it. Hence we have the principle

(7) $(z)(z \in \hat{x}Fx \cdot \equiv Fz)$.[39]

The category of objects that are extensions of predicates I shall call *classes*, as Quine himself does when he is talking about the elements of the subject.

One can think of the conception of classes as arrived at by steps of three types; nominalization of predicates to yield the noun phrases of which class abstracts are a regimentation, taking such noun phrases as standing for objects, and adopting (for classes as opposed to, say, attributes), co–extensiveness of the predicates as the criterion of identity.

In the genetic account of *The Roots of Reference,* these steps are regarded as natural steps to take, and they form the central elements in the genesis of set theory. However, the second step divides into two: first nominalized predicates are quantified *substitutionally,* and then this quantification "goes objectual".[40]

The manner in which I introduced the notion of extension recalls Frege. I want to claim that Quine's conception of a class or set is Fregean, in that for him the origin of the concept of class lies in predication, and the only requirements on a set theory which is not to a certain degree artificial are that with certain predicates 'F' be associated objects $\hat{x}Fx$ satisfying (7), and that classes obey extensionality: two classes having the same members are identical. This hypothesis about Quine's underlying conception of the subject-matter of set theory serves to explain some of the features of Quine's views on set theory that are "deviant" from the point of view of most contemporary thought on the subject.

Quine seems to express this conception in the Introduction to *Set Theory and Its Logic.* "Set theory is the mathematics of classes. Sets are classes." He then introduces the notion of extension, and although he goes on to mention the ideas of "aggregate" and "collection", he seems to understand these as classes and classes as extensions.[41]

It is characteristic of contemporary thought on the foundations of set theory to explain the idea of set in such a way that the universe of sets is taken to have a *hierarchical* structure. The simplest model for this is the simple theory of types: the objects of the theory are divided into ground-level objects (individuals), classes, classes of classes, and so on. Russell's procedure was to have different styles of variables for different levels of the hierarchy, but the formal theories used by set theorists today are first-order (or sometimes second-order, where the second-order variables range over classes rather than sets; see below), derived historically less from Russell than from Zermelo. But according to the "standard" theories, every object can be assigned an ordinal number as its *rank,* in such a way that a set has higher rank than any of its elements.[42]

The simple idea that the elements of a set are *prior* to the set already rules out the applications of the comprehension schema (7) (assuming '$\hat{x}Fx$' to denote) that lead to paradoxes such as Russell's. For example, no set can be an element of itself, and hence there can be no universal set and no set of all non-self-members.

The explanation given above of the notion of *extension* does not obviously give rise to the priority of the members of the extension to the extension itself, in a sense that would exclude self-membership. Even if we have granted, in the wake of Russell's paradox, that not all predicates have extensions, for a contradictory pair, say 'x is a woodchuck' and 'x is not a woodchuck', there is no obvious reason why one should have an extension and the other not. But the natural assumption that extensions are not woodchucks implies that the class of non-woodchucks, if such there be, is a member of itself. Moverover, consider any ordering of some totality of entities according to some notion of priority. Suppose further that the class of non-woodchucks is among the entities so ordered. Then the only way all its members could be prior to it would be if all the objects that are *not* prior to it are woodchucks. Then if the class of non-woodchucks is posterior to all its members, we can expect other classes (probably including the class of woodchucks) to violate this condition.

This reasoning will of course be unpersuasive if one thinks of extensions from the beginning as *sets* and of sets in terms of standard axiomatic set theory. Then 'x is not a woodchuck' will have no extension, at least not in the strict sense of a set containing absolutely everything except the woodchucks. For if there were such a set it would have a certain ordinal α as its rank, but then there are objects, such as the ordinal $\alpha + 1$, which could not belong to it and yet which are not woodchucks.[43]

Quine has long been identified with the position that the hierarchical aspect of ordinary set theory is not essential to it. His own theories NF and ML, although derived in a way from the theory of types, are incompatible with the hierarchical conception of the universe of sets.[44] The reservations that Quine expresses in "New Foundations" about the theory of types apply in part to Zermelo-type theories as well, though they are mitigated when proper classes are added.[45]

In his more recent writings, Quine emphasizes set theories closer to the standard. Thus most of *Set Theory and Its Logic* is devoted to developing what is *de facto* a subsystem of ZF, and the genetic process of *The Roots of Reference* eventuates in the simple theory of types.

However, characteristic of all these writings is the conception of extensions as the objects of set theory, and reserve toward what I have called the "standard" conception. Quine seems (at least before *The Roots of Reference*) to be motivated by the idea that the most intuitively natural set theory would be based on the idea that every predicate has an extension; since the obvious formalization of that is inconsistent, one restricts the comprehension schema in some way that will avoid paradoxes but still preserve certain desirable features—mainly the derivation of ordinary mathematics. However, it seems even now to be Quine's view that such restrictions have an unavoidably artificial character.[46]

Quine is also somewhat cool to the axiom of foundation, which expresses in first-order set theories the idea that sets form a well-founded hierarchy.[47]

It seems to me that what often comes out as a formalistic approach to set theory in Quine's writings derives as much from his Fregean conception of what a set *is* as from his epistemology. The extent to which the set theorist's intuitive concept of set is a development of Frege's, or rather derives from different sources, is a difficult question that would deserve a paper for itself. That *some* new conceptual element is needed seems pretty clear. If one sticks as closely to the Fregean explication of extensions as Quine most of the time seems to, then it seems that intuition will indeed carry us no further than Quine admits.[48] Viewing the matter from the other side, the idea that the elements of a set are prior to it is in recent literature justified by the quite un-Fregean idea that a set is in some way formed from its elements.[49]

However, Russell's theory of types would suggest that the conception of extension can be developed in a natural way so that extensions form the sort of hierarchy that the standard conception calls for. I do not here want to enter into how Russell's own development of the theory of types bears on this question. In the genesis described by Quine in *The Roots of Reference,* class quantifiers are first introduced as substitutional quantifiers either of predicates or of nominalized predicates, so that the strictures of the theory of types are obeyed: the syntactical difference between predicates and singular terms induces a syntactical difference between (objectual) individual variables and (substitutional) class variables. But then one encounters obstacles with respect to impredicative definitions, just what led Russell to assume the axiom of reducibility. It is then another "leap" to take class quantification as objectual, and Quine interprets this as licensing impredicative classes. However, the simple type hierarchy is preserved if one remembers the substitutional origin of the class quantifiers, for at that stage one was operating with two different types of quantification.[50]

Still, Quine does not quite "see Russell's theory of types as dormant common sense awakened".[51] The reason is that mixing the levels of the type hierarchy is also a possible leap in the extension of the conceptual apparatus. It seems to Quine unnatural to forbid that and to permit, say, impredicativity. Thus, in spite of the fact that types have a certain genetic centrality, Quine maintains his earlier position that the theory of types is at least in part an "artifice" for blocking the paradoxes.[52]

I shall assume that Quine means here by the theory of types a theory of sets or classes according to which they form a well-founded hierarchy, and not more specifically a formal theory in which different levels of the hierarchy are indicated by different syntactical styles of variables. To discuss adequately whether Quine would be right on this interpretation, one would have to examine more deeply the intuitive basis of the hierarchical conception.

However, without such an examination one can at least observe that the assumption of the priority to a set of its elements blocks the paradoxes in a simple and natural way, and that no non-hierarchical theory has been developed that is remotely comparable to standard set theory. Then one could reply to

Quine's contention that "mixing the levels" of the type or rank hierarchy is no more impermissible than impredicativity by observing that accepting the latter and not the former has led to a powerful theory that has shown its workability through rather long experience.

In the sense that standard set theory should be regarded as an established theory, I would accept this argument. However, quite apart from the general fact that established theories can, by later turns in the history of science, be modified or abandoned,[53] it is not the last word. For there is still a temptation toward a non-hierarchical theory of extensions, not as a substitute for standard set theory but as a supplement to it. Even in the development of set theory, one is not content to rest with the view that all extensions are sets in the sense of the usual conception. For this reason, set theorists talk of "proper classes", classes that are not sets. Among such proper classes are the complements of sets, such as our class of all non-woodchucks.

It is not clear that the set theorist's talk of classes really commits him to *extensions* as a kind of object different from sets, not obeying the general restrictions the concept of set imposes. The actual use of classes by set theorists is predicative or at least in accord with the simple theory of types (with sets as individuals), so that it does not violate the basic idea of hierarchy. Moreover, there are ways of viewing the classes of set theory so that they are either not new objects at all or "really" or "ultimately" sets.[54]

Nonetheless, the interpretation of the concept of class in set theory is disputed, and there are those to whom a hierarchical theory of classes has seemed unsatisfying and incomplete.[55] Why this should be so can be brought out by recalling the connection between the notion of extension and the notion of *truth*. Briefly, the notions of class and attribute serve to generalize predicate places in a language, while the notions of truth and proposition serve to generalize sentence places. Since a predicate is just a sentence with an argument place, the notion of truth *of* (satisfaction) does the jobs of generalizing both for sentences and for predicates. Thus there is an elementary parallelism between predicative theories of classes and Tarski-style satisfaction theories.[56]

In the use of the notions of truth and truth of, what corresponds to the principle of hierarchy is, roughly, Tarski's hierarchy of language levels; truth at a given level is predicable only of statements at lower levels. Indeed, the theories of truth that arise directly from Tarski's ideas are predicative. But many intuitions concerning the possibilities of thought and expression, particularly in relation to natural language, suggest to some that the notion of truth is not essentially predicative or even hierarchical. Thus what one says using the word "true" seems to be true or false. More generally, talk in a natural language involves much that is of a "metalinguistic" character; in particular, it seems just an evident fact that the word "true" is applicable to statements made in English, including those that contain the word "true" itself. Even the sentences that express the Liar and other semantical paradoxes cannot just be ruled out of the language on any obviously convincing grounds, even if in some stricter sense they fail to express propositions.

For this reason, the program of a "non-Tarskian" account of the concepts of truth in natural languages has seemed attractive to some.[57] A similarly non-Tarskian account of *satisfaction* would give rise to a theory of classes of a non-hierarchical sort. Paradoxes would have to be avoided by some other device. The one most often suggested would not be congenial to Quine, since it involves a deviation from standard logic: allowing truth-value gaps.[58] I do not myself have anything to contribute to such a program; indeed, elsewhere I have criticized it.[59] It does seem to be in the spirit of the point of view about *classes* that I have attributed to Quine. It may be that some of Quine's earlier ideas have relevance to it.

The motivations from natural language for a non-hierarchical semantics carry over to set theory, all the more since satisfaction and truth for formalized mathematical theories are themselves mathematical notions. Thus the carrying out of the program indicated above would have a tangible advantage for set theory: one would then have a strong, though still incomplete, theory of truth for set theory within set theory. However, there may be more specific advantages; for example, the concept of proper class plays a role in motivating some strong axioms of infinity. I would say that no non-Tarskian account of satisfaction and truth, or non-hierarchical theory of classes, has up to now been put forth which is intuitively satisfying enough for it to compete with hierarchical accounts.[60] But in this area, where we try to deal with the outer limits of thought and expression, the last word has surely not been said.

CHARLES PARSONS

DEPARTMENT OF PHILOSOPHY
COLUMBIA UNIVERSITY
APRIL 1975

NOTES

1. *Philosophy of Logic* (Englewood Cliffs, N.J.: Prentice-Hall, 1970), pp. 64–70; also *The Roots of Reference.*

2. *The Ways of Paradox* (2d ed., Cambridge, Mass.: Harvard University Press, 1976), pp. 68–76. The lecture dates from 1963.

3. *From a Logical Point of View* (2d ed. Cambridge, Mass.: Harvard University Press, 1961), pp. 134, 149–53; "Three Grades of Modal Involvement", in *The Ways of Paradox,* passim; cf. *Word and Object* (Cambridge, Mass.: Technology Press; New York: Wiley, 1960), p. 199.

4. In *Naming and Necessity* (2d ed., Cambridge, Mass.: Harvard University Press, 1980). Kripke is probably the most influential recent defender of absolute necessity. He prefers the term "metaphysical necessity". A number of Kripkean examples, such as identities between names, would offer direct counterexamples to (1). However, his principal examples are not mathematical. He does give (p. 159) the example of a mathematical statement that someone has come to know by carrying out computations with a computer. Of such examples, one might reply that although an individual may know them and not know them a priori, they *can* be known a priori; one may even hold that one does not really know them unless a priori, i.e., by a proof or computation that one has carried out oneself. Where computations of sufficient complexity are involved, the sense in which the statements in question can be known a priori becomes more and more attenuated; it involves applying to the possibility of *knowledge* modes of inference going with the conception of mathematical possibility discussed in the text. Cases in which, in practice, our knowledge of some mathematical theorem depends on computers in such a way that it is not a priori by any reckoning have recently assumed more importance with the proof by Appel and Haken of the four-color theorem. See Thomas Tymoczko, "The Four-Color Problem and its Philosophical Significance", *Journal of Philosophy* 76 (1979): 57–83.

Kripke's examples of "contingent a priori" statements might be offered against (2). They seem unlikely to bear on mathematics and are perhaps more problematic in themselves.

5. *The Ways of Paradox,* pp. 70–71.

6. Ibid., p. 76.

7. Since it follows that some truths are absolutely necessary but not logically necessary, there is an apparent conflict with the claim of absolute necessity to be the "highest" type of necessity. The conflict could be resolved by assuming a distinction between "real" and formal, logical, or verbal modalities; absolute necessity is the most general *real* necessity. Thus if it is not logically necessary that p, it may not be *really* possible that ~p (for example if 'p' is 'Cicero = Tully', Michael Jubien's example in "Ontological Commitment to Particulars", *Synthese* 28 (1974): 513–532, p. 524), but if it is not absolutely (metaphysically) necessary that p, then it is really possible that ~p. I am not here claiming either that these notions make genuine sense or that they do not.

8. It is usually maintained that the logic of logical necessity is S5, but the modal logics as strong as T and no stronger than S5 agree with respect to the validity of propositional schemata without nesting of modalities. In the Kripke-type semantics, it is easy to see that any such schema either is T-valid or has an S5 countermodel.

9. This notion of necessity is one of those considered by Quine in "Three Grades of Modal Involvement"; he makes essentially the above criticism of it (*The Ways of Paradox,* pp. 169–71).

10. I owe this observation to Saul Kripke, who pointed out confusion in an earlier version of this paragraph.

11. As Henry Hiz reminded me, (6) is already a theorem of truth-functional logic with quantification merely of sentence places. In general, logic with quantification only of sentence places is much simpler than second-order logic in the genuine sense (with quantification of predicate places). Extensionally, the former is naturally interpreted with the bound variables ranging over the two truth-values.

12. *The Ways of Paradox,* pp. 74–6.

13. *Philosophy of Logic,* pp. 98–100.

14. Cf. my "Ontology and Mathematics", *Philosophical Review* 80 (1971): 151–176, pp. 160–3.

15. Cf. my "Infinity and Kant's Conception of the 'Possibility of Experience'",
Philosophical Review 73 (1964): 182–197; reprinted in *Mathematics in Philosophy* (Ithaca, NY: Cornell University Press, 1983).

16. Nelson Goodman and W. V. Quine, "Steps toward a Constructive Nominalism", *Journal of Symbolic Logic* 12 (1947): 105–122; also in Goodman, *Problems and Projects* (Indianapolis and New York: Bobbs-Merrill, 1972).

17. In the mathematical sense in which, on this view, arbitrary finite sequences are possible. The existence of infinitely many individuals can be shown to be in a sense *logically* possible: Certain theories which intuitively (or in terms of set-theoretic semantics) must have an infinite domain for their bound variables can be shown by constructive (finitary) means to be formally consistent. See for example D. Hilbert and P. Bernays, *Grundlagen der Mathematik* I (Berlin: Springer, 1934, 2d ed. 1968), §6. This case illustrates the remark made above about the relation of logical and mathematical modalities.

18. "Existence is what the existential quantifier expresses. There are things of kind F if and only if $(\exists x)Fx$. This is as unhelpful as it is undebatable, since it is how one explains the symbolic notation of quantification to begin with. The fact is that it is unreasonable to ask for an explanation of existence in simpler terms." "Existence and Quantification", in *Ontological Relativity and Other Essays* (New York: Columbia University Press, 1969), p. 97.

19. Quine nowhere comments explicitly on Frege's theory of functions, but that he disapproves of it is made clear by his comments on second-order logic (*Philosophy of Logic*, pp. 66–8).

20. "Singular Terms and Predication", *Journal of Philosophy* 58 (1961): 393–412, reprinted in Donald Davidson and Jaakko Hintikka (eds.), *Words and Objections* (Dordrecht: Reidel, 1969). Quotation from *Words and Objections*, p. 115.

21. *Words and Objections*, p. 115.

22. Reply to Smart, *Words and Objections*, pp. 292–3; also *The Roots of Reference*, passim, e.g., p. 88.

23. Frege insisted on distinguishing between existence and actuality *(Wirklichkeit)*, and his principle that "it is only in the context of a proposition that words have any meaning" (*The Foundations of Arithmetic*, tr. J. L. Austin (Oxford: Blackwell, 2d ed. 1953), p. 73) was applied especially to the case of numbers. This might, however, have suggested the *eliminability* of locutions talking of such objects. The principle is not emphasized in Frege's later writings. Cf. Michael Dummett, *Frege: Philosophy of Language* (New York: Harper and Row, 1973), pp. 7, 195–6, 495.

Carnap's views about abstract entities are too closely tied to conventionalism about the *truth* of claims about such entities for Quine's and my own taste.

24. *Word and Object*, pp. 131, 242; *Ontological Relativity and other Essays*, p. 100.

25. "Ontology and Mathematics", esp. pp. 152–4; cf. "On Translating Logic", *Synthese* 27 (1974): 405–411. I should emphasize that on my view constructivist and Platonist theories of mathematical existence are neither totally reducible to the other and that it is not necessary to make a final choice between them. Set theory is certainly more powerful and comprehensive than any constructive theory developed up to now, and if one *had* to choose between set theory and constructivism, it would be folly to give up set theory.

Quine's arguments for preferring classical logic are partly pragmatic. Pragmatism would allow accepting different theories for different purposes. Why not different logics and "theories of being"?

On Quine's attitude toward "deviant logic", see *Philosophy of Logic,* pp. 80–94; also Adam Morton, "Denying the Doctrine and Changing the Subject", *Journal of Philosophy* 70 (1973): 503–510, and my "On Translating Logic".

26. Of course I here assume the "background theory" is set theory. First-order number theory requires additional relations, at least addition and multiplication.

27. Thus Paul Bernays, "Mathematische Existenz und Widerspruchsfreiheit", in *Études de philosophie des sciences, en hommage à F. Gonseth à l'occasion de son soixantième anniversaire* (Neuchâtel: Griffon, 1950), pp. 11–25, and my "Frege's Theory of Number", in Max Black (ed.), *Philosophy in America* (London: Allen and Unwin, 1965), pp. 180–203, reprinted in *Mathematics in Philosophy.*

28. "What Numbers Could Not Be", *Philosophical Review* 74 (1965): 47–73.

29. "Quine on Meaning and Existence", *Review of Metaphysics* 21 (1967): 124–151, 343–367; "An Introduction to Translation and Meaning: Chapter Two of *Word and Object*", *Words and Objections,* pp. 14–26. Cf. "Ontology and Mathematics", pp. 156–7.

30. *Ontological Relativity and other Essays,* pp. 44–5.

31. *Philosophy of Logic,* p. 64; "Identity", unpublished.

32. $\beth_\omega$ is the smallest cardinal of a standard model of the simple theory of types with an infinite number of individuals; it is the least cardinal greater than $\aleph_0$, $2^{\aleph_0}$, $2^{2^{\aleph_0}}$, etc.

33. Cf. Hilary Putnam, "Mathematics without Foundations", *Journal of Philosophy* 64 (1967): 5–22, reprinted in *Mathematics, Matter and Method* (Cambridge University Press, 1975); "What is Mathematical Truth?" in *Mathematics, Matter and Method.* In the former paper, Putnam speaks of the possibility of "concrete models" of set theory. He explicitly assumes (p. 57 of the reprint) that there is nothing inconceivable in the idea of a *physical space* of arbitrarily high cardinality. I would certainly agree that there is nothing inconceivable in the idea of a *space* of arbitrarily high cardinality, if what is meant is a structure of the general sort considered in geometry. But what makes such a space "physical"? Putnam seems to require here a distinction between a "necessary" and a "factual" aspect of fundamental physics, such that the cardinality of space-time falls on the factual side. This raises a host of questions. But a prior question is what is gained for the plausibility of the axioms of set theory by the assumption that models of it are possible which are in some way "concrete" or "physical", particularly if one considers that the ideas of set and function are quite central to the specific conceptions we have of cardinalities higher than the denumerable, even that of the continuum.

In the discussion at a symposium (in December 1965) at which Putnam presented this paper, he qualified his position by expressing doubt whether the structures required by large cardinal axioms really were possible.

In the latter paper, the conception of a concrete model does not occur; perhaps Putnam no longer maintains that the structures whose possibility is in question in the modal interpretation of set theory are concrete.

34. "What is Cantor's Continuum Problem?" expanded version in Paul Benacerraf and Hilary Putnam (eds.), *Philosophy of Mathematics: Selected Readings* (Englewood Cliffs, N.J.: Prentice-Hall, 1964), p. 267.

35. However, a complication arises from the fact that the set-theoretic framework of a scientific theory would normally allow individuals *(Urelemente).* Then if we add a name '$\wedge$' for the null set, which clearly should belong to the mathematical vocabulary, we can define 'x is an individual' ('Ix') as

$$x \neq \wedge \;\&\; (y)(y \notin x)$$

and then state in the mathematical vocabulary that there is a certain number of individuals. Such a statement we would not want to count as a mathematical truth.

Clearly, in this setting a mathematical truth must satisfy the additional condition of being indifferent to what individuals there are. If we assume ZF (with Foundation), we can meet the difficulty as follows: Let 'F' be a new one-place predicate. Given a sentence 'p', let 'p^F' be the result of restricting its quantifiers to 'F'. Then we say that 'p' is a mathematical truth if and only if

$$(x)[\sim Ix \supset ((y)(y \in x \supset Fy) \equiv Fx)] \supset p^F$$

is true and contains only '$\in$', '$=$', '$\wedge$', and logic essentially. This amounts to saying that a sentence is a mathematical truth if it is *valid* in the following sense: it is true under any interpretation standard with respect to '$\in$', '$=$', '$\wedge$' and with the universe a transitive *class* U such that $(x)(x \subseteq U \supset x \in U)$, i.e. closed under set formation. Of course this formulation presupposes that the intended range of the variables does not contain proper classes.

The difficulty here is analogous to a simpler one that arises for logical truth: Such statements as '$(\exists x)(\exists y)(x \neq y)$' are true and, if identity is counted as logical, they contain only logical vocabulary essentially. This is resolved by the observation that logical truth must be indifferent to the range of the quantifiers.

Note that on the above proposal, '$(\exists x)(\exists y)(x \neq y)$' is a mathematical truth, but '$(\exists x)(\exists y)(Ix \& Iy \& x \neq y)$' is not. This is the right result if, as the formulation envisages, all mathematical objects are construed as sets.

One might still object that I am counting as mathematical truths some statements whose truth depends on the structure of the class of individuals, where this might have been otherwise. For a given U, the individuals in U are a subclass of the actual individuals. Hence if P is a property of a class that can be expressed in the language of set theory, such that for any class V, P(V) implies P(V′) for any subclass V′ of V, if the class of *all* individuals in fact possesses P, it will be a mathematical truth that P ({x: Ix}).

It is certainly not clear that this *is* an objectionable consequence, but perhaps it is not evident that it is not. A particular case of some interest arises from the axiom of choice. Let P(V) be 'Every subset of V can be well-ordered'. Then P has the above subclass property. If the axiom of choice is stated in the simplest way, that *every* set of nonempty sets has a choice function, then it follows that every set of individuals can be well-ordered; i.e., P({x: Ix}). Thus on our criterion, this is a mathematical truth.

Given that set theorists usually leave individuals out of consideration, it is not quite so clear as it should be that the often expressed intuition that the axiom of choice is "evident" is meant to exclude the possibility of a non-well-orderable set of *individuals,* as opposed to a non-well-orderable pure set. (A set is pure if no individual is a member of it, or a member of a member, or . . . .). To my intuition the axiom of choice does cover the situation with individuals, but it is perhaps not quite inconceivable that the world should have been like a Fraenkel-Mostowski model in which the axiom of choice obtains for all pure sets but not for sets involving individuals. The above view implies that this is logically possible, but not mathematically possible.

It seems to me doubtful that a convincing characterization of mathematical truth could be given which does not have consequences like this, unless mathematical modality or some functional equivalent is allowed in the metalanguage. Quine might object that then the criterion would be circular. It seems to me that this is small comfort for him, because I do not see that the objection to my non-modal formulation has any force unless we have an intuitive grasp of mathematical possibility to begin with.

I have carried out the above discussion in a metalanguage with class variables, although I assumed that the object language did not have them. However, since the metalanguage will surely contain predicates of satisfaction and truth for the object language, the required class variables can be *defined*, since the classes needed are all definable in the object language. See for example my "Sets and Classes", *Noûs* 8 (1974): 1–12, p. 5.

36. *The Ways of Paradox*, p. 75.

37. Quantum mechanics may seem to be a case where the development of physics leads to a revision of *logic*. See Hilary Putnam, "Is Logic Empirical?" *Boston Studies in the Philosophy of Science* V (Dordrecht: Reidel, 1969), pp. 216–241, reprinted as "The Logic of Quantum Mechanics" in *Mathematics, Matter, and Method*.

This is a matter about which I am not competent technically. But I am not convinced that the case is basically different from that of geometry. Quantum mechanics is still a theory formulated with classical mathematics in which the underlying logic is classical. The "propositions" and "connectives" that obey a nonstandard logic are constructions within this classical framework, as in the case of a classical model of intuitionism.

However, I have to admit that this is an extremely superficial comment about a complex and highly disputed question.

38. *Philosophy of Logic*, p. 95.

39. Of course I have here simply adapted Frege's characterization of the notion of extension to the situation where we do not assume Frege's theory of *concepts*, entities of a predicative character that are not objects. Frege allows himself second-order logic, so that for him membership is definable: 'x ∈ y' can abbreviate '(∃F)(y = x̂Fz & Fx)'. (7) follows from his axiom V, which I here state in two parts. I disregard the fact that Frege talks more generally of functions and value-ranges rather than merely of concepts and extensions.

(Va) $(x)(Fx \equiv Gx) \supset \cdot \hat{x}Fx = \hat{x}Gx$
(Vb) $\hat{x}Fx = \hat{x}Gx \cdot \supset (x)(Fx \equiv Gx)$.

Given (7), (Vb) follows by substitutivity of identity, at least if the extensions exist. (Va) follows from extensionality.

For Frege, (Va) is an instance of the extensionality of concept places in his formal language. He makes it clear in his discussion of Russell's paradox that it is (Vb) that gives rise to the paradox. See *Grundgesetze der Arithmetik*, vol. II (Jena: 1903), p. 257.

40. *The Roots of Reference*, §§27–29, 31.

41. *Set Theory and Its Logic*, pp. 1–2. I say "seems to" because although I believe this interpretation of the passage to be correct, my colleague Mark Steiner does not find it so clear. Peter Geach, in discussion of an earlier version of this paper at the University of Pennsylvania, mentioned a remark in a letter to him from Quine which would be more unequivocal in identifying classes with Fregean extensions.

I am indebted to George Boolos and especially to Steiner for their criticisms of earlier versions of this section.

42. The rank of a set is the least ordinal greater than the ranks of all its elements. Of course to show that such a rank always exists, one needs the axiom of foundation.

43. This reasoning requires the axiom of foundation. If we assume that there is a set of all *woodchucks*, then it follows trivially in Zermelo-type set theories, without foundation, that there is no set of all non-woodchucks.

44. "New Foundations for Mathematical Logic", in *From a Logical Point of View* (the paper first appeared in 1937); *Mathematical Logic*, revised ed. (Cambridge, Mass.: Harvard University Press, 1951). Quine discusses these systems in the light of recent

research on them in chapter XIII of *Set Theory and Its Logic* and in his reply to R. B. Jensen in *Words and Objections*.

45. *From a Logical Point of View*, pp. 91–92. Donald A. Martin, in his review of the revised edition of *Set Theory and Its Logic*, (*Journal of Philosophy* 67 (1970): 111–114) seems a little unfair in saying that NF is "the result of a purely formal trick intended to block the paradoxes" (113). Quine's own remarks (*From a Logical Point of View*, pp. 90–91) indicate that stratification was motivated by Whitehead and Russell's idea of *typical ambiguity:* of leaving the types of variables in formulae of the simple theory of types indefinite, provided that the arguments of 'ϵ' are of consecutive ascending types. However, Quine may have neglected to consider that in applying this idea to a first-order theory, the variables had to range over the whole domain of a model, which is not the case for variables on the "typical ambiguity" reading of a formula of the simple theory of types.

46. *The Roots of Reference*, pp. 102–3, 122.

47. *Set Theory and Its Logic*, pp. 285–6; cf. "Reply to D. A. Martin", (i.e., the review cited in note 44 above), *Journal of Philosophy* 67 (1970): 247–248.

A little further comment on the axiom of foundation is in order. Set theorists characteristically motivate the axioms of the subject by conceiving of sets as "generated" by transfinite iteration of formation of sets from their elements, beginning either with nothing (yielding the theory of pure sets) or with individuals. On this interpretation, the axiom of foundation (suitably formulated) is evident. The axiom is integral to an account of the structure of the universe of sets that is generally accepted. On the other hand, it is not necessary for the derivation of "ordinary mathematics" in set theory. But the defenders of what is called the "iterative conception" (e.g. Martin) can reply that the reason for this is that the objects constructed for arithmetic (finite and transfinite) and analysis can be generated in this iterative way without the assumption that such a generation yields *all* sets. More technically, the sets yielded by iterating the power set operation, beginning with the empty set, yield an inner model of, say, ZF, which satisfies the axiom of foundation and contains the usual representatives of ordinals, cardinals, real numbers, etc.

A highly illuminating and clear discussion of the universe of sets is George Boolos, "The Iterative Concept of Set", *Journal of Philosophy* 68 (1971): 215–231.

A small technical point is relevant to Quine's comments on the axiom of foundation (*Set Theory and Its Logic*, p. 285). The standard formulation of the axiom rules out self-membership and hence rules out identifying individuals with their own unit classes, as Quine did in *Mathematical Logic*. However, it seems to me to bend the general idea that motivates the axiom at most very slightly to see the question whether an individual is to be distinguished from its unit class as one of convention. Quine's idea can be accommodated by reformulating the axiom to exempt sets that have themselves as sole members. If all such objects are assigned the rank 0, then the hierarchy of ranks is still obtained. One does have some slightly unattractive phenomena, such as that a set consisting of two individuals has rank 1, although every proper subset of it has rank 0.

48. This is admitted by Martin (review of *Set Theory and Its Logic*, p. 112), though he criticizes Quine severely for his neglect of the intuitive basis of hierarchical conceptions of set.

49. Boolos, "The Iterative Conception"; J. R. Shoenfield, "Axioms of Set Theory", in Jon Barwise (ed.), *Handbook of Mathematical Logic* (Amsterdam: North-Holland, 1977), § 2; Hao Wang, *From Mathematics to Philosophy* (London: Routledge and Kegan Paul, 1974), pp. 181–2.

On Frege's relation to these ideas, cf. my "Some Remarks on Frege's Conception of Extension'', in M. Schirn (ed.), *Studien zu Frege* (Stuttgart: Fromann, 1976), I, pp. 265–277. Frege differs from the now dominant tradition on the elements of set theory in his unequivocal claim that classes are constituted by predicative entities (concepts) and in his firm rejection of any constructive or genetic conception of objects. In *The Roots of Reference*, Quine holds to the first at the very least in that talk of classes originates by nominalization of predicates. The genetic psychological framework, and in particular the derivation in it of the theory of types, represents a move on Quine's part away from his previous agreement with Frege on the second point.

50. *The Roots of Reference,* pp. 120–121.

51. Ibid., p. 121.

52. Ibid., p. 122.

53. In order to avoid the imputation of inconsistency with what I have said above (pp. 30–32), I should say that in the case of pure mathematics, theories might be modified or abandoned on *mathematical* grounds—contradictions, unclarity in the conceptual foundations, or perhaps counter–intuitive consequences of abstract axioms.

54. See pp. 39–47 of my "Informal Axiomatization, Formalization, and the Concept of Truth'', *Synthese* 27 (1974): 27–47; also "Sets and Classes'', pp. 10–12.

55. For example, Donald A. Martin, "Sets versus Classes'', unpublished comment on "Sets and Classes''.

56. Sets and Classes'', pp. 4–6.

57. For discussion of several such views, see Robert L. Martin (ed.), *The Paradox of the Liar* (New Haven: Yale University Press, 1970); cf. also Hans G. Herzberger, "Dimensions of Truth'', *Journal of Philosophical Logic* 2 (1973): 535–556.

58. Thus van Fraassen and Skyrms (in *The Paradox of the Liar* and articles referred to there), also D. A. Martin (note 54 above).

59. "The Liar Paradox'', *Journal of Philosophical Logic* 3 (1974): 381–412.

60. I learned of Saul Kripke's very elegant work on the concept of truth when this paper was substantially complete. (See "Outline of a Theory of Truth'', *Journal of Philosophy* 72 (1975): 690–716). Kripke combines a hierarchical approach with truth-value gaps. It seems clear that theories of proper classes could be constructed on the basis of his ideas. The most obvious way of doing so would lead to a theory with a certain predicative character, which would apparently not realize the ideas of Martin (note 55 above). Cf. also Solomon Feferman, "Toward Useful Type-Free Theories, I'', in R. L. Martin (ed.), *Recent Essays on Truth and the Liar Paradox* (Oxford: Oxford University Press, 1984).

REPLY TO CHARLES PARSONS

Parsons has been much concerned with necessity: with types of necessity and how to distinguish them: logical necessity, mathematical necessity, physical necessity. Necessity is a theme that has exercised philosophers for a long time, and it is much in vogue at the present day, largely because of the strange fascination of modal logic. A necessity predicate can also be entertained without modal logic, simply as a predicate predicable of sentences. But the notion of necessity encourages modal logic, and quantified modal logic requires a really deep notion of necessity, necessity not *de dicto* but *de re*. It invites an essentialist metaphysics, a metaphysics of possible worlds. Formal systems of modal logic of course admit of innocent models, trivial reinterpretations; but I am speaking of modal logic modally interpreted.

We are spared the worst of this by shunning quantified modal logic and settling for a predicate of *de dicto* necessity predicable of sentences. Parsons has discussed necessity mostly at this level. But in my own philosophy there is no place for necessity even of this restrained sort. Truths are classifiable into truths of logic, truths of mathematics, truths of chemistry, truths of economics, and so on; but I find the notion of logical or mathematical *necessity* unclear insofar as it is intended to convey more than such mere classification of subjects. As for the notion of physical necessity, it suffers from all the familiar troubles of the general notion of a law or lawlike sentence.

Ordinary language abounds in seeming references to necessity and possibility, but I think we can accommodate these usages without building such categories into our philosophy. Ordinarily when we attribute physical necessity or possibility we are speaking elliptically: we have some physical truths in mind from which the sentence in question is logically deducible or with which it is logically consistent. Similarly, when in ordinary discourse we use the adverbs 'necessarily' and 'possibly' without qualifying them as logical or mathematical or physical, the usage may again be conceived as elliptical, in the way suggested at the beginning of my reply to Hintikka.

Parsons argues for the utility of a notion of mathematical necessity or, more directly, of mathematical possibility. One example: he would like to be able to say that the construction of natural numbers "can" be continued without limit. I have no desire to say this. I can say instead that the successor function has every number in its domain, and when successively applied yields a new number every time as value.

Another example is afforded by the decidability of monadic logic. Any monadic schema "can" be tested for validity. This again is mathematical rather than human possibility, since many schemata are too long to be tested by mortal man. However, we are spared this modal idiom by the theory of recursion; we can simply say that the set of valid monadic schemata is recursive. In my view the philosophical achievement of recursion theory is two-fold: besides explicating the hitherto vague idea of an effective procedure, it spares us this recourse to modality.

I recognize that we are spared such recourse to modality only by recourse to an extensional Platonism of sets. This is involved in my appeal to the successor function and again in my appeal to recursiveness. Putnam argued, conversely, that modality could be useful in avoiding or minimizing such recourse to mathematical objects; and Parsons has been critically scanning this prospect. My own scale of values, however, is the reverse; my extensionalist scruples decidedly outweigh my nominalistic ones. Avoidance of modalities is as strong a reason for an abstract ontology as I can well imagine.

In "Steps toward a Constructive Nominalism," long ago, Goodman and I got what we could in the way of mathematics, or more directly metamathematics, on the basis of a nominalist ontology and without assuming an infinite universe. We could not get enough to satisfy us. But we would not for a moment have considered enlisting the aid of modalities. The cure would in our view have been far worse than the disease.

Actually I am not even clear on what to count as existence in a modal framework. When I construe the objects of a theory as the values of its bound variables, I am supposing the theory to be regimented in standard fashion as a first-order extensional predicate logic with interpreted predicates. Other devices, whether modal operators or ancestral functions or intuitionistic connectives or substitutional quantifiers, simply obstruct ontological comparisons: they raise a problem of foreign exchange, the question how much additional ontology would have brought equivalent strength to a standard theory. I make sense of the ontology of a non-standard theory, e.g., a modal theory, only relative to the choice of some translation into the standard form. For such a theory as it stands, the ontological question in my sense simply does not arise. [See my reply to Strawson.]

Parsons assumed that I would distinguish between laws and accidental generalizations. But from what I have now been saying it becomes clear that along with the notion of logical or mathematical necessity I reject also the notion of physical or natural necessity, and thus also the distinction between law and accidental generalization.

Differing though we do in how emphatically we contrast pure mathematics with natural science, Parsons and I seem to agree in our conception of how pure mathematics applies to natural science. Let me make this conception more explicit with help of examples.

Take groups. In the redundant style of current model theory, a group would be said to be an ordered pair (K, f) of a set K and a binary function f over K fulfilling the familiar group axioms. More economically, let us identify the group simply with f, since K is specifiable as the range of f. Each group, then, is a function f fulfilling the axioms. Each group is a class f of ordered triples, perhaps a set or perhaps an ultimate class.

Note that f could not be ultimate if we kept (K, f). Furthermore f need not be a pure class, for some of its ordered triples may contain individuals or impure sets. This happens when the group axioms are said to be *applied* somewhere in natural science. Such application consists in specifying some particular function f, in natural science, that fulfills the group axioms and consists of ordered triples of bodies or other objects of natural science.

The actual formula 'f is a group', with variable 'f', does belong to pure mathematics; grouphood is a mathematical property of various mathematical and non-mathematical functions. Various mathematical truths about groups are derivable from the definition, and they remain in force even when some particular function in natural science that was thought to be a group turns out to be otherwise. Here I think we have a paradigm case of the application of mathematics as Parsons was picturing it, and it is one I accept. A mathematically specified property is ascribed to a physically specified object or relation.

Another example of applied mathematics is the use of number in measurement. In terms of physical testing procedures we describe a Fahrenheit temperature function whose arguments are place times and whose values are real numbers. Fahrenheit temperature is a class of pairs of pure real numbers and concrete place times. Similarly distance in meters is a class of triples, each comprising one pure real number and two concrete localities.

Mathematical objects and concrete objects are thus in perpetual interplay, participating in the same triples and pairs. Mathematical vocabulary and empirical vocabulary are in perpetual interplay, participating in the same sentences. We see this already at the most primitive level of applied mathematics, when we say there are fifty people in this room: the pure abstract number, fifty, is how many concrete people there are in the concrete room. I see pure mathematics as an integral part of our system of the world.

I am belittling the difference between mathematics and natural science, but

I am not denying all distinction between them. Parsons seems at points to think I do, but this would be wrong. I even recognize boundaries between one natural science and another. For instance chemistry, in the classical acceptation of the term, is demarcated from other sciences by its distinctive business: that of distinguishing the elements and studying their ways of combining. A more widely applicable method of demarcating a branch of science is the one I used in "Truth by Convention": the method of listing the vocabulary. Then the logical truths, or mathematical truths, or chemical truths, are the truths in which only the logical or mathematical or chemical vocabulary occurs essentially, and all further vocabulary occurs only vacuously; that is, only subject to free substitution *salva veritate*.

Parsons remarks that this criterion does not quite square with our intuitions in the case of logical truth, inasmuch as we can make some statements about the size of the universe in purely logical terms. But he notes further that this defect is easily corrected by requiring further of logical truths that they stay true under relativization of quantifiers. Indeed there is no lack of extensionally equivalent ways of demarcating the class of logical truths when these are regimented in canonical notation. The class is specifiable by reference to substitutions, or to models, or to specifically numerical models, or to proof procedures. It is a nicely segregated class of truths; but to say this is not to say that these truths enjoy some special necessity. I do not know what that would add.

Parsons notes that the mathematical truths cannot quite be defined as the truths in which all non-mathematical vocabulary occurs only vacuously; we must again adjust the definition to exclude information about the size of the universe. The point is similar to what was noted in the case of the logical truths, except that what now wants excluding is information, more specifically, about the number of individuals. Parsons has pondered how to make such an adjustment compatible with various forms of set theory. Some such adjustment is imperative if we want to be able to say that the number of individuals in the world is mathematically contingent rather than mathematically necessary. But the adjustment holds little interest for anyone who, like me, will settle for truth and let necessity go.

I have said that I am belittling the difference between mathematics and natural science, but not denying it. And I am belittling it only to some degree. At the end of *Philosophy of Logic* I contrasted mathematics and logic with the rest of science on the score of their versatility: their vocabulary pervades all branches of science, and consequently their truths and techniques are consequential in all branches of science. This is what has led people to emphasize the boundary that marks pure logic and mathematics off from the rest of science. This also is why we are disinclined to tamper with logic or mathematics when a failure of prediction shows there is something wrong with our system of the world. We prefer to seek an adequate revision of some more secluded corner of science, where the change would not reverberate so widely through the system.

This is how I explain what Parsons points to as the inaccessibility of mathematical truth to experiment, and it is how I explain its aura of a priori necessity. In what sense, after all, is a statement even of theoretical physics accessible to experiment? Let S be such a statement. The physicist proceeds to test it, as he says, by arranging certain observable conditions and then seeing whether a predicted observation ensues. But the prediction is not a logical consequence simply of S and the arranged experimental conditions. A substantial body of associated physical and mathematical premises is needed, not just S, in order to clinch the implication. Failure of the prediction will show only that this substantial body of physical and mathematical theory is not tenable intact. What is special about the particular statement S is just that the physicist has chosen to finger it. Because perhaps of considerations of simplicity or symmetry or analogy or confinement of reverberations, S happens to be the one component statement of his theory that the physicist would be happiest to revoke if the experiment shows that the theory is not tenable intact. And I have said why he may be counted on not to choose S from the purely mathematical part of his inclusive theory.

Pure mathematics, in my view, is firmly imbedded as an integral part of our system of the world. Thus my view of pure mathematics is oriented strictly to application in empirical science. Parsons has remarked, against this attitude, that pure mathematics extravagantly exceeds the needs of application. It does indeed, but I see these excesses as a simplistic matter of rounding out. We have a modest example of the process already in the irrational numbers: no measurement could be too accurate to be accommodated by a rational number, but we admit the extras to simplify our computations and generalizations. Higher set theory is more of the same. I recognize indenumerable infinites only because they are forced on me by the simplest known systematizations of more welcome matters. Magnitudes in excess of such demands, e.g., $\beth_\omega$ or inaccessible numbers, I look upon only as mathematical recreation and without ontological rights. Sets that are compatible with 'V = L' in the sense of Gödel's monograph afford a convenient cut-off.

Parsons spoke of the ontological contrast between pure mathematics and nature. Citing Leibniz, Strawson, and Benacerraf, he suggested that mathematical objects be viewed as incomplete or unreal in one or another way. Natural numbers afforded the paradigm case: they do all their useful work on the strength of forming a progression, and no matter what set-theoretic explication we may adopt for them. May we then view them as incomplete objects, endowed with only enough properties to make them a progression? This doctrine would badly complicate the underlying logic, by requiring truth-value gaps; and nothing is gained by it. I prefer to say with Benacerraf simply that there are no natural numbers, and there is no need of them, since whatever purposes we might have used them for can be served by any progression,[1] and set theory affords progressions in generous supply. In practice, of course, when we use some progression of sets for counting or for other purposes commonly served by numbers, we are apt to call these sets numbers and refer to them by numerals; but this is a mere notational convenience, conveniently dropped when philosophical questions arise. Or, on the strength of this notational convention, we could come full circle and say that natural numbers are incomplete objects after all, in a manner of speaking: there are really no such things, but only a role, which can be played by any progression of real sets. Mostly in numerical work we do not even bother to settle which progression of sets we are using, but we can do so whenever the question arises. This way of making sense of a doctrine of numbers as incomplete objects is quite all right, but notice that it is purely a verbal accommodation. Ontologically what we have are real sets of all sorts, some or others of which may be called up now and again for numerical duty.

What then of applying a doctrine of incomplete existence to the sets themselves? Here my earlier objection recurs: the doctrine would complicate the underlying logic by requiring truth-value gaps. Still, because of the intangibility of sets, and the essential incompleteness of set theory, and the latitude of choice regarding even the basic structure of set theory, one is reluctant to accord sets full existence. Is there perhaps hope of demoting them to a sort of incomplete existence without incurring the penalty of truth-value gaps?

A theory of incomplete existence has been proposed elsewhere[2] by Parsons. He intends it not for sets but for what he calls linguistic abstract entities—including classes, which he opposes to sets. His incomplete existents are the values of the variables of *relatively substitutional* quantification, as he now calls it.[3] (I meanwhile called it semi-substitutional.) What I remarked of substitutional quantification is true of the relatively substitutional: it is not directly accessible to ontological assessment. However, because it so closely parallels objectual quantification, it affords an attractive explication of incomplete existence. It is ill suited to impredicative classes, as Parsons notes; and this would explain his not applying it to sets.

I have been dwelling on the ontological contrast between mathematics and nature, and on whether to accommodate it in terms of two grades of existence, and, if so, how. But I would now suggest an opposite line of thought: that the ontological contrast between mathematics and nature has been overdrawn. Granted that sets are by no means robust, what better can we say for the hypothetical particles of physics? Imagine two neighboring electrons, and consider the question whether some given point event and some later one belong together as moments in the career of the same electron or belong rather to different electrons. Quantum mechanics teaches, I think, that this question will sometimes lack physical meaning. One hears also of cyclic resolution of particles, as if they could be proper parts of themselves. These and other odd findings suggest that the notion of a particle was only a rough conceptual aid, and that nature is better conceived as a distribution of local states over space-time.

The points of space-time may be taken as quadruples of numbers, relative to some system of coordinates. The regions will be sets of such quadruples. The states will be quantitative, typically, and the language will contain various functors, one for each state; thus '$f\alpha = x$' will mean that region α is in state f to degree x. The schematic letter 'f' here represents some functor in a finite lexicon; 'x' and 'α' are the variables, and their values are a number and a set of quadruples of numbers. We are down to an ontology of pure sets. The state functors remain as irreducibly physical vocabulary, but their arguments and values are pure sets. The ontological contrast between mathematics and nature lapses.

Where I see a major discontinuity is not between mathematical theory and physical theory, but between terms that can be taught strictly by ostension and terms that cannot. A proper name for an individual visible object can be taught by persistent ostensions. Each pointing conveys that some part of the intended object is in line with the pointing finger. Extrapolating by subjective similarity considerations, the learner guesses at the bounds of the intended object, and does some pointing of his own for possible correction. He eventually gets it right, thanks to a general conformity of his similarity standards to those of the society that named the object. A mass term for visible stuff can be taught in the same way, by successive pointing at samples. To teach a general term such as 'horse', finally, for visibly individuated objects, we need to teach not only what stuff counts as horse, but how much counts as one horse. This can be managed by flurries of ostension; each flurry points out several sample places on one sample horse.

Terms that can be taught in these ways may be called observation terms, in contrast to theoretical terms. An observation term may happen to be acquired rather through definition or description or context, but it need never be; a theoretical term must be. Statements of scientific theory contain both kinds of terms, and it is only by occurring in such statements along with observation terms that theoretical terms imbibe a dilute empirical meaning. There is nothing to know about the intended denotata of the theoretical terms, except that they eke out the observable objects to complete the structure that the theory imputes. On this score, the objects of pure mathematics and theoretical physics are epistemologically on a par, even apart from any reduction to the mathematical ontology. Epistemologically the primary cleavage is between these on the one hand and observables on the other. Being epistemological, however, this is properly a cleavage not between kinds of objects but between kinds of terms.

The objects denoted by observation terms are physical objects still, on a par ontologically with the theoretical ones, and theoretical physics describes their inner nature.

Parsons's paper concluded with a discussion of set theory on which I need comment only briefly. What he calls the standard conception of set theory is compatible with my psychological speculations if that standard conception is recognized as a matter of hindsight: of wisdom after paradox. I do not agree with him that Martin was unfair in saying that the system of "New Foundations" is "the result of a purely formal trick intended to block the paradoxes," but I hold that Martin was mistaken in not saying the same of the "standard" hierarchical conception. The psychogenesis of sets was indeed hierarchical, on my theory, but the levels of the hierarchy merged as they emerged, and impredicativity prevailed. See the beginning of my reply to Ullian. The eventual separating of levels, all the while condoning impredicativity, is again a "formal trick intended to block the paradoxes." On the whole therefore Parsons may be right in calling my view of sets Fregean.

Parsons mentions in a footnote the important difference between the range of variables in the theory of types and in "New Foundations." The role of stratification is radically different in the two cases. But he is wrong in thinking that I may have neglected to consider this. When the theory of types is translated into a notation using unrestricted variables, a system results that is akin not to "New Foundations" but to Zermelo's. See the last part of *Set Theory and Its Logic* as well as my 1942 paper "On Existence Conditions".

In another footnote Parsons discusses my device, in "New Foundations" and *Mathematical Logic,* of identifying individuals with their unit sets. The virtue of the device is that it enables us to admit individuals as Parsons does, and without having to complicate the axiom of extensionality. The bizarreness of my device may be minimized by viewing it as the banishing of all unit sets of individuals and the reinterpretation of epsilon as 'is either a member of or an individual identical with'. The banishing of unit sets of individuals is itself simply a step toward pure set theory. The plan is compatible, of course, with the commonly adopted one of banishing all individuals and impure sets, but it does not require it. See further my reply to Ullian.

W. V. Q.

NOTES

1. Strictly, as Benacerraf has urged, any *effective* progression.
2. "A Plea for Substitutional Quantification", *Journal of Philosophy* 68 (1971): 231–237. See also the end of my *Roots of Reference.*
3. "Sets and Classes", *Nous* 8 (1974), p. 6.

15

Hilary Putnam

MEANING HOLISM

The Holism of Belief Fixation

Quine's argument for meaning holism in "Two Dogmas of Empiricism" is set out against the meaning theories of the positivists. Sentences, he insisted, do not have their own "range of confirming experiences". Assertibility depends upon trade-offs between such *desiderata* as preserving the observation reports to which we are prompted to assent, preserving past doctrine, and securing or preserving simplicity of theory. The idea that the meanings of individual sentences are mental or Platonic entities must be abandoned. Instead, we must recognize that it is a body of sentences, and ultimately our whole system of evolving doctrine, which faces the "tribunal of experience as a corporate body".

A literal minded philosopher might object that even on Quine's account a sentence *does* have a "range of confirming experiences"; it is confirmed by each experience which confirms at least one total body of theory which contains the sentence. But this reply is pure legalism. It concedes the point that is really at issue: that it is *not by reflecting on some object, say a rule, associated with the individual sentence*, that the scientist or the man of common sense is able to determine (in an arbitrary situation) what does and what does not confirm or "infirm" that sentence. Frege taught us that words have meaning only in the sense of making a systematic contribution to the truth-conditions of whole sentences. Quine argues that to the extent that there are "procedures" for deciding what is and what is not assertible, such procedures are associated with the entire language, not with any single sentence. Individual sentences are meaningful in the sense of making a systematic contribution to the functioning of the whole language; they don't have "meanings", in the form of isolable objects, properties, or processes, which are associated with them individually and which determine individual assertibility conditions.

This is, perhaps, clear in the case of theoretical sentences. But non-observation sentences in ordinary language, and even observation sentences, exhibit similar features. For Quine, an observation sentence is not one which is formed from a privileged set of non-logical names and predicates (''observation terms''), as for Carnap—Quine knows no ''observational/theoretical dichotomy'' of that sort—but, rather, one which is intersubjectively conditioned to certain ''sensory stimulations''. These sensory stimulations—the ones that ''prompt assent'' to the sentence and the ones that prompt dissent from it (or the ordered pair of these two sets)—constitute the ''stimulus meaning'' of the observation sentence in the relevant community. This—the ''stimulus meaning''—*is* something associated with the individual sentence. But it cannot be called the *meaning* of the individual sentence, Quine argues, for at least two reasons. One, the more technical reason, is that even in the case of the simplest sentences (''Lo, a P'') the ''meaning''of the sentence is supposed to determine the extensions of the predicates out of which the sentence is built, and sentences built out of predicates which are not even coextensive can have the same stimulus meaning (''Lo, a rabbit'' and ''Lo, an undetached rabbit-part''). The other is that an observation sentence is sometimes assertible when it does not *appear* (to theoretically uncorrected sense experience) to be true. The stimulus meaning determines the *normal* confirmatory situation and the normal disconfirmatory situation; but in abnormal situations the decision to accept or reject the sentence is based on holistic considerations (on care for the value of overall theory). To take stimulus meaning to be meaning *simpliciter* would be to oversimplify our account of the functioning of even the observation sentences.

Meaning and Change of Meaning

I have described Quine's argument in the form which I myself find most convincing. In the sequel, I shall make use of a distinction Quine did not himself introduce: the distinction between holism with respect to meaning and holism with respect to belief fixation. In this essay, I shall not attempt to say when my arguments reproduce Quine's, when they merely parallel Quine's, and when they are completely my own; one of the things I hope to learn from this exchange is to what extent the considerations that lead *me* to embrace the doctrine of meaning holism are acceptable to Quine.

My intention in describing Quine's arguments in this particular way is to focus on two ways in which philosophers are tempted to counter it. One way is obvious: to deny holism even with respect to belief fixation. The other way is to concede that Quine's holistic account of belief fixation is correct, while maintaining that an ontology of ''meanings'' is still scientifically or philosophically necessary and useful. In the present section, I shall consider only the first way; the remainder of the essay will concern the second.

Those philosophers who have taken the first way (for example, Carnap in his debate with Quine on these issues) generally concede that Quine's account, or one like it, is correct in theoretical science. They are thus led to draw a more or less sharp boundary between theoretical science and observational statements (or, in the case of some philosophers, "ordinary language").

Rather than concede that the notion of a "meaning" is not helpful (at least not in the case of theoretical sentences and/or "theoretical terms"), these philosophers typically take the meaning of such sentences and terms to be in one way or another a function of the *theory* in which those sentences and terms occur. (Various devices from set theory, for example the Ramsey sentence and the Hilbert epsilon operator have been used to formalize this approach.) The theory, for this purpose, is not the mere formal system, but the system *together* with the interpretation of the observation terms and the interpretation of the logical terms. Theories, on this view, are "partially interpreted calculi".[1]

The most serious problem with such a theory of meaning is the number of *meaning changes* it makes it necessary to postulate.[2] Suppose someone asks, "Were electrons flowing through such-and-such a crystal at such-and-such a time?" It may easily happen that, by the time the question is answered, the theory in which the term "electron" occurs has been modified as a result of ordinary inductive and abductive inference. If so, the sentence "Electrons were flowing through the crystal at that time" that the scientist utters today does not have the *meaning* that it had at the time of the original question. Evidently a distinction central to the traditional theory of meaning, the distinction between *discovering the answer to a question* (by employing the appropriate method of belief fixation) and *changing the meaning of the question* has been abandoned (or altered beyond recognition).

Not only is it the case that this proposal (to take the meaning of the theoretical term or statement to be the theory or a suitable function of the theory) involves an unmotivated departure from our pre-analytic use of the notion of *meaning;* it has the effect of robbing that notion of all epistemological interest. If I want to know whether electrons are flowing through a certain crystal, I want the best scientific answer that can be discovered; I do not care whether discovering that answer requires modifying the current theory of electrons. Whether an answer is rationally supportable is epistemologically important; whether it "changes the meaning of the question" is no longer of any epistemological interest, if *any* change in the theory is going to count as a "change in the meaning of the question". If meanings are not invariant under normal processes of belief fixation, then concern with meanings loses its *raison d'être*.

In the case of observation terms, anti-holists have usually taken the meaning to be given by the "ordinary" criteria for the application of the terms. The word "water", for example, would be governed by some such rule as this: *apply "water" to anything which is liquid, colorless, tasteless, odorless, quenches thirst, does not poison the drinker, etc.* Carnap is not completely consistent here: he speaks of "P-Postulates" (Physical Postulates) such as "Water is H_2O" as (indirectly and incompletely) *fixing the interpretation* of "H_2O", but he could not have been unaware that they *also* have the effect of making the assertibility conditions for "this is water" dependent on physical theory. Be this as it may, he often writes as if they did *not* have this effect; as if the assertibility conditions associated with "observation terms" were in no way *altered* by the incorporation of those terms into a scientific theory.

Ordinary language philosophers who have taken a similar line (I am thinking of Norman Malcolm, and, with less confidence, Michael Dummett) tend to compartmentalize the language; the presence of water in a physical theory ("Water is H_2O") is held to involve a different use (i.e., a different *sense*) from the "ordinary use". (This compartmentalization is often ascribed to Wittgenstein; incorrectly, in my opinion.)

This compartmentalization theory seems to me to be simply wrong. Our language is a cooperative venture; and it would be a foolish layman who would be unwilling to *ever* accept correction from an expert on what was or was not water, or gold, or a mosquito, or whatever. Even if I drink a glass of "water" with no ill effects, I am prepared to learn that it was not really water (as I am prepared to learn that a ring that seems to be gold is really counterfeit); we do not and should not treat scientists' criteria as governing a word which has different application-conditions from the "ordinary" word *water,* in the sense of having *unrelated* (or only weakly related) application-conditions.

There are, to be sure, respects in which the ordinary use of the word "water" differs from the use in, say, physics. In physics "water" means chemically pure water; in ordinary language, things are more complicated. On the one hand, "water", in the ordinary sense, may have impurities; on the other, tea and coffee are *not* "water". What sort of or degree of departure from ideally "pure" taste, color, or odor disqualifies H_2O-cum-impurities from being "water" in an ordinary context is interest relative and context sensitive. But this is not to say that "water", in ordinary language, is an *operationally defined* word, pure and simple.

A thought-experiment may be of assistance here. Let us suppose there exists a liquid which is colorless, tasteless, odorless, harmless, but does *not* satisfy the need for water. (For all I know, there may actually be such liquids.) Call this liquid "grook". Let us suppose that a mixture of 50% grook and 50% water will pass all the lay tests for being water, *excluding* "sophisticated" tests (such as distilling the liquid, or measuring its exact boiling point or freezing point with a thermometer). On the theory that "water" means "odorless, transparent, tasteless, liquid which quenches thirst and is not harmful to drink", grook plus water just *is* water, "in the ordinary sense". But this is plainly wrong; even a layman, on being told by a scientist that what he is drinking is a mixture of a liquid which is indistinguishable in composition from paradigm examples of "water" and a liquid which does *not* occur as a part of typical water, will say that what he is drinking is *not* water (although it *is* 50% water). Ordinary language and scientific language are different but *interdependent*.

Why "Sophisticated Mentalism" Appears to be an Option

If denying the holistic character of rational belief fixation (or restricting it to "science") is a hopeless move, there is another option available to the philosopher who wishes to defend the psychological reality and philosophical importance of meanings (as independent entities), and that is to challenge the step from that holistic character to what I have called "meaning holism". The general idea which defines this option is easy to describe: *postulate "meanings" as psychological entities* (*not*, at most times, available to consciousness—this is the difference between contemporary mentalism and the "naive mentalism" of the older empiricists). Let these entities be, in some way, *associated with individual words, morphemes, and sentences* (so that meanings will be *non*-holistic). Account for the holistic character of *belief fixation*, by *postulating that the step from the meaning of a sentence to its assertibility conditions involves "top down processing"*—that is, the use of general intelligence and available information.

This option appears to be open simply because the identification of "meanings" with assertibility conditions (or with rules which determine assertibility conditions) is only evident to a philosopher who wishes to retain the verifiability theory of meaning in some form. Quine himself does, and he is willing to pay the price: to the extent that there are processes (he is leery of talk of "rules", "inductive logic", "confirmation theory"), or vague notions of "justification", "coherence" and the like, which guide us in deciding when to accept and when to reject sentences; these processes and notions are *associated with the whole language,* in his view, and not associated with individual sentences in a piecemeal fashion. That is why I call him a "meaning holist": because in *his* view the acceptance of his doctrine is just a further step in the direction of seeing the "unit of empirical significance" as something larger than the *word*. Prior to Quine we had already been forced to see the sentence and not the word as the primary unit; since Quine we are (he holds) forced to see the *whole language* as "the unit of empirical significance".

If the verifiability theory is wrong, even in its holistic version (and I myself cannot accept it in *any* version), then there would appear to be a serious gap in Quine's argument. Why should the meaning of a sentence be *directly* tied to its conditions of assertibility, to the experiences which confirm it and the experiences which "infirm" it? Perhaps the holistic character of all "top down" processing infects the step *from* meanings (whatever they are) *to* the knowledge that certain experiences confirm a sentence (in a particular context) and others "infirm" it. Or so one might suppose.

Quine himself dismisses the idea that "meanings" can have explanatory value as out-of-date and "obscure". But since he wrote "Two Dogmas" and "On What There Is" there has been a New Wave in psychology, a wave of talk about concepts, "contents", and "mental representation", and even if this talk has not resulted in a single *theory* of these entities, it has had the effect of making them no longer seem "obscure". What we countenance in present-day intellectual life is (as perhaps it always was) a matter of what is in vogue and not of what is intelligible. Quine (and Wittgenstein) were hostile to mentalism, it is said, because they knew only the mentalism of the eighteenth century empiricists (and because they are "behaviorists", it is sometimes said). Even those who do not make the error of reading Quine or Wittgenstein as simple behaviorists often suppose that their arguments have weight only against naive mentalism; *sophisticated* mentalism is thought to be at a higher level in the evolution of thought than the reflections of even the greatest giants of the century's philosophy could reach. If, as I have argued, there *is* a gap in Quine's argument, then there is certainly room for "sophisticated mentalism" as a *program:* our question must be, whether there is reason to hold out any hope for the success of such a program.

Three Constraints on any Theory of "Meanings"

If *all* that was wanted to carry out the "sophisticated mentalist" program were any entities at all which are (1) "psychologically real", (2) associated with individual sentences, and (3) involved in the "processing" of those sentences, then things would be easy. There would be a great many possible choices of entities to play the role of "meanings". For example, the *sentences themselves* have all three properties listed: so one could simply take each sentence as its own "meaning"! But this clearly will not do.

Why it will not do is obvious: it is part of our pre-analytic use of the notion of "meaning" that different sentences can have the *same* meaning and that the same sentence can have different meanings. A theory which gave up beliefs about meaning as central as these could not be regarded as having anything to do with our pre-analytic notion of "meaning" at all. A proposal which conceded that our pre-analytic notion has to be scrapped, and which simply recommitted the *noise* "meaning" to a new use, would, in effect, grant Quine's point.

It is, then, a constraint on any theory of "meanings" that different meanings should, in general, be assigned to sentences which we pre-analytically *suppose* to differ in meaning and that the same or closely similar meanings should be assigned to sentences which we pre-analytically suppose to be alike in meaning. In short, "meanings", whatever they may be, must have the right powers of *disambiguation*.

This constraint operates in Quine's own argument against a proposal he himself raises only to reject: the proposal to take the *stimulus meaning* to be the *meaning,* in the case of observation sentences.

Quine points out that "gavagai" (a word in a "jungle language") could mean "undetached rabbit part" or could mean "rabbit"—assuming there were a "fact of the matter" as to what *gavagai* means—without altering in stimulus meaning. Indeed, if talk of "undetached rabbit parts" became common in English, then "Lo, an undetached rabbit part" might become an English observation sentence with exactly the same stimulus meaning as "Lo, a rabbit"— but we want a theory of meaning or of meanings to disambiguate these two sentences, if only because we accept "rabbits are not the same things as undetached rabbit-parts" as a *true* sentence.

Here is another example to the same effect: as we actually use the word "tiger" it is not *analytic* that tigers have stripes. (Many people incorrectly suppose that albino tigers have no stripes: actually the stripes are still visible, though fainter; but the mistake shows that we understand "tiger" so that a stripeless tiger is not *ruled out*). Assume that a totally stripeless tiger would, however, cause one to hesitate and ask an expert (if only because the non-experts couldn't be sure that it wasn't a stripeless *leopard*). Then the stimulus meaning of "Lo, a tiger" could be exactly the same as the stimulus meaning of "Lo, a striped tiger"; but again there is (speaking intuitively) a "difference in meaning". In fact, it is quite easy to see that stimulus meaning is highly insensitive to exactly what we take to be the "meaning" of the terms in an observation sentence, provided only that the various alternative "meanings" that are offered are *known* to pick out the same classes by all the members of the speech-community.

Again, if all the members of the speech-community become adept at recognizing tigers without relying on the presence or absence of *stripes,* then the stimulus meaning of "Lo, a tiger" will change: but this is not what we think of as the word "tiger" *changing its meaning.* What this illustrates is that stimulus meanings are not *invariant under normal processes of belief fixation.* And, as I argued above, a notion of "meaning" according to which normal processes of belief fixation (including inductive inference) change the "meanings" of the questions we are trying to answer is not only a poor explication of the pre-analytic notion, but one which robs the notion being "explicated" of all epistemological significance.

The constraint just mentioned—*invariance of meanings under normal processes of belief fixation*—rules out another proposal I have occasionally encountered: the proposal to take the meaning of a sentence to be its "canonical" method of verification. In the case of observation sentences this would seem closely related to, if not the same as, the proposal to take the stimulus meaning as the meaning; but let us consider a different kind of sentence, a sentence about the past, say, "A couple with six children lived here two hundred years ago". If this has a "canonical" method of verification today, it involves the consultation of certain kinds of written records. Prior to the invention of writing, one would have had to rely on oral traditions passed down and preserved by the elders of the tribe. So "canonical method of verification" is not even invariant under technological change, let alone normal process of belief fixation.

The last constraint I shall impose has been implicit rather than explicit in the discussion so far: it is simply that "meanings" should be implicitly known (or "associated" with the relevant words and sentences) by *every* speaker who *counts as fully competent in the use of the language*. This might be called the constraint of *publicity*: it requires that meanings should be public. Alternatively, one might think of this as a constraint of *psychological reality;* a theory in which "meanings" are known only to experts could not be a *mentalistic* theory, since the guiding idea of mentalism is that "meanings" are psychological entities which play an explanatory role in accounting for the competence of the native speaker. If we took the "meaning" of *electron* to be the theory of electromagnetism, for example, then we might be able to account for the competence of experts (ignoring the problem with invariance under belief fixation, which has already been discussed), but we could not account for the competence of the average speaker, since the average speaker does not know this theory. So whatever the meaning of "electron" may be for an average speaker, it can't be the sophisticated physical theory.

We can now make the question we are investigating more precise: has "sophisticated mentalism", in its various forms, been able to come up with entities which have psychological significance and which could be taken to be "meanings" without violating at least one of the three constraints just listed?

The question is not whether we are *allowed to talk* of words and sentences "having meaning" or "not having meaning", "having the same meaning" or "not having the same meaning", etc., in normal contexts (in which it is clear why the question arises and what one is going to do with the answer); of course we are. The question is whether the idea that meanings are *objects,* isolable events, states, processes, or what have you, with some sort of explanatory role in a theory, has the slightest foundation.

"Twin Earth Cases" and the Linguistic Division of Labor.

Readers familiar with my essay "The Meaning of 'Meaning' "[3] will notice that there is one very famous constraint on the notion of meaning which I have *omitted*. That is the traditional requirement that the "meaning" of a term (its Fregean sense) should fix its extension. In "The Meaning of 'Meaning' " I argued that, in fact, *no* theory can make it the case that "meanings" are "in the head'' and simultaneously make it the case that ''meanings'' determine external-world reference.

To establish this point, the point that while ''concepts'', as we have thought of them ever since the seventeenth century, are supposed to be ''individualistic'' entities, entities that one isolated individual (or a brain in a vat) can ''have'', and simultaneously supposed to fix external-world reference, in fact this is impossible, I employed two different sorts of cases. On the one hand, I described cases in which two groups of speakers are in the same mental states, in all respects one might think relevant to a mentalistic theory of meaning, although the reference of some term changes upon going from one community to the other. For example, imagine that ''water'' (the liquid so-called) is actually a mixture of 50% H_2O and 50% grook on Twin Earth. Let the year be 1750 on both earth and Twin Earth (so that earth textbooks do not yet contain the statement that ''water is H_2O'' and Twin Earth textbooks do not yet contain the statement that ''water is 50% H_2O and 50% $C_{22}H_{74}$§ . . . (the chemical formula for grook). Although there will be differences between earth and Twin Earth ''water'' (Twin Earth people will need twice as much ''water'' a day, on the average as earth people, unless we modify their bodies so that they need less H_2O), we may suppose that these differences are noticed only by a few experts; or let both societies be pre-scientific village societies. Then the things that Twin Earth speakers will tell you about ''water'' will be exactly the things earth speakers will tell you about ''water'', what they have noticed about ''water'' will be just what earth speakers have noticed about water, etc. In short, the conceptual content of the word ''water'', for an average speaker, will be the same on earth and on Twin Earth.

What such ''Twin Earth cases'' show is that what we intend to refer to when we use such a word as ''water'' is whatever liquid has the same composition as . . . (here one can substitute almost any of the local paradigms without affecting what we call the ''meaning''). In short, the reference is partly fixed by the substance itself (through the use of examples). The word ''water'' has a different extension on earth and on Twin Earth because the *stuff* is different, not because the brains or minds of Twin Earth speakers are in a different state than the brains or minds of earth English speakers in any psychologically significant respect.

The second kind of case I used is the case of words such as ''elm'', ''beech''. Here the average speaker knows that the species are distinct, but cannot tell you *how*. The conceptual content associated with the words ''elm'' and ''beech'' is practically the same; but the extensions are determined by criteria known to experts with whom the average speaker is in a cooperative relation. In short, extensions cannot be determined by (individualistic) ''concepts'' because extensions depend upon other people. Because of both of these sorts of cases, if we are going to be mentalistic, then we have to omit the traditional requirement that "'sense fixes reference''. However, this weakens the constraint that "'meanings'' can do what we pre-analytically suppose they can do in the way of disambiguating words and sentences. Jerry Fodor has recently proposed the name "'contents'' for "'meanings'' which *are* (according to sophisticated mentalism as practiced at M.I.T.) "'in the head''. Fodor concedes that "'elm'' and "'beech'' have the same "'content'' (for a speaker like *me*, at any rate), and abandons the traditional idea that the content is what fixes the reference. But notice; it was *also* a traditional idea that "'elm'' and "'beech'' differ in *meaning*. Even at this early stage in our discussion, the danger appears on the horizon that we shall find ourselves rescuing the noise "'meaning'' by merely recommitting it to something there is no good reason to call by that name.

The Analytic and the Synthetic

One philosophically central strand in the complex network of traditional assumptions about meaning is the idea that there are some sentences which are *true* in virtue of what they mean, and *simply* in virtue of what they mean—the analytic sentences. If we are to see why it is impossible to fulfill the desire to have a notion of meaning which obeys our three constraints, it is well to begin by unravelling this strand (as Quine did, in "'Truth by Convention'' and "'Two Dogmas of Empiricism'').

If S is true simply by virtue of what S means, and meanings are invariant under scientific and common-sensical belief fixation, then the status of S must likewise be so invariant. S must be an *unrevisable* truth (Quine tends to assume the converse—that any unrevisable truth would have to be analytic, but this is a hangover from empiricism).[4] If the technical notion of meaning obeys our first constraint—if the lines it draws correspond, at least in general, to pre-analytic uses of the notion of "'meaning''—then the analytic sentences must be ones which it is not counterintuitive to classify as such, at least in the majority of cases. In particular, then, such traditional examples as "'A bachelor is an unmarried man'', "'A vixen is a female fox'', and (perhaps) "'force is mass times acceleration'', must turn out to be analytic, and hence to be unrevisable under normal processes of induction, theory construction, etc. But these sentences are *not* so invariant.

Consider first "'Force is mass times acceleration''. Many physicists say this is "'true by definition'', i.e., analytic. But I am sure they would also say "'The force on a body is the vector sum of all the individual forces acting on the body'' is "'true by definition''. Together, however, these two "'definition'' imply that "'The vector sum of the individual forces acting on a body is equal to the acceleration vector of the body multiplied by the mass''. This last principle hardly *looks* analytic. Kant might have considered it a "'synthetic *a priori* truth''—it justifies the rule that, if the known individual forces are not sufficient to account for a body's state of acceleration, one should always postulate unknown individual forces, and one might regard this as a "regulative principle" in physics—but is there any reason to regard it as correct by virtue of *meaning?* (In fact, it is *given up* in quantum mechanics—the effect on a body of the sum of the individual forces is, in general, *statistical* and not deterministic.)

The argument I have just used against calling either of these "force is . . ." statements analytic resembles an argument Reichenbach used against the Kantian notion of a synthetic *a priori* truth. In *Theory of Relativity and A Priori Knowledge* (1922) Reichenbach listed a number of statements (the general reliability of induction, normal causation, Euclidean geometry, etc.) each of which Kant would have regarded as synthetic *a priori,* and each of which can be held immune from revision (the Duhem thesis!), but which *collectively imply statements that are empirically testable,* and that Kant would, therefore, have had to regard as *a posteriori.*

In short, given that it is part of Kant's theory that the *a priori* truths are a *deductively closed class,* Kant's intuitions about what is *"a priori"* are in deep trouble. Similarly, given that the *analytic* truths are supposed to be a deductively closed class, or at least not to imply any *testable* statements (otherwise the conjunction of analytic *truths* could imply something *false,*) some phsyicists' intuitions about what is "true by definition" are incoherent.

In general, if we call *any* truth which contains law-cluster concepts[5]—terms which are implicated in a number of scientific laws—"analytic", we are in trouble. "Momentum is mass times velocity" may have originally entered physics as a "definition" and the law of the conservation of momentum may have originally entered as a "law", but in the actual history of later physics they functioned on a par, and when it was discovered that (in the presence of Special Relativity) one could not have both, it was the former statement that was the revised and not the latter. The attempt to draw an analytic/synthetic distinction not only does not assist us in understanding belief fixation in the exact sciences; it positively distorts the picture.

What of less scientific examples? As long as being an unmarried (or never-been-married) male adult person is the only known and generally employed criterion for being a bachelor, then the word "bachelor" will continue to function (in purely referential contexts) as virtually an abbreviation of the longer phrase "male adult person who has never been married". And similarly, unless "vixen" becomes an important notion in scientific theory, and various important laws about vixens are discovered, that word will continue to be used virtually as an abbreviation for "female fox". But either or both of these situations may change *as a result of empirical discovery,* with no stipulative redefinition of these words, and no unmotivated linguistic drift, being involved.[6]

In any case, the fact is that very few one-criterion words exist. It is not only such "theoretical" terms as *force* and *momentum* that lack "analytic" definitions; natural kind words such as "tiger" and "leopard" and "water" lack them as well. We are left with no standards, except pragmatic and context-sensitive ones, for deciding which of our beliefs about tigers, or leopards, or water, are to count as somehow connected with the "meaning" of these terms. Even the belief that tigers are animals is not immune from revision (they might turn out to be robots remotely controlled from Mars). We can make the decision I once recommended[7] in the case of the one-criterion words, to look for beliefs which are *relatively* central, relatively immune from revision (barring revolutionary discoveries), thereby very much weakening the constraint that meanings should be invariant under belief-fixation (we shall have to in any case); but then the whole problem of what to count as "sameness of meaning" rearises as the problem of what to count as *sufficient similarity* in such central beliefs. The impossibility of a notion of "meaning" which agrees at all with our pre-analytic intuitions about sameness and difference of meaning *and* which is invariant under belief-fixation dooms the notion to be exactly what it is; a vague but useful way of speaking when (by intuition and by experience) we correlate words and phrases in different languages and discourses.

A Little Bit of Indeterminacy

Quine is famous for the thesis of the "indeterminacy of translation". This is an immense thesis, connected with views on the rootlessness of reference and the notion of a "fact of the matter". I shall confine myself for the moment to just a little bit of indeterminacy, the little bit that follows more or less directly from the considerations just reviewed. In particular, I will for the most part not consider the indeterminacy of *reference* as opposed to *meaning*.

Let us consider an actual case in which translators disagree. *Eudaemonia* is standardly translated as "happiness". John Cooper, however, proposes that it would be more faithful to the meaning of the word in Aristotle's *oeuvre* to render *Eudaemonia* as "human flourishing". What shall we say about this?

The difficulty is that there seems nothing to be right or wrong about. One can ask whether Cooper's translation of any reasonably long chunk of Aristotle's text, or even of a key paragraph, "brings out the sense of the whole"; but (assuming that "happiness" and "human flourishing" *are* coextensive in Aristotle's *theory*) a translation might undeniably bring out the sense of the whole *either* by translating *eudaemonia* as "happiness" (with appropriate glosses, footnotes, compensatory adjustments in the translation of other words) *or* by translating *eudaemonia* as "human flourishing".

To see the relevance of our discussion of the analytic/synthetic distinction to this case, observe that the difference between the two translations is that one makes it in effect "analytic" that "eudaemonia is happiness" and "synthetic" (perhaps synthetic *a priori*) that "eudaemonia is human flourishing", while the second has it the other way around. But "eudaemonia" is not the sort of word that has an analytic definition, least of all in a philosopher's writing.

The case may seem highfalutin', but it does not really differ from the question: is it or is it not *part of the meaning* of "leopard" that leopards are typically spotted? We have an enormous number of "central" beliefs about almost anything; there is no general rule which decides in each case which of these to take as part of the meaning of a word or a given context and which to take as "collateral information" that will, given what speaker and hearer know, surely be conveyed by the use of the word. (Grice's distinction between what a word "literally means" and what is a "conversational implicature" is just what we *can't* draw in any systematic way.)

Let me move to a different example: I imagine (perhaps wrongly, but if so let this be more "science fiction") that all the cats in Thailand (formerly "Siam") are of the breed we call "Siamese". A person growing up in Thailand has a quite different stereotype of a cat from the one we have! In fact, the idea *he* normally associates with the Thai word *meew* (the Thai word dictionaries translate as "cat") is just the stereotypical idea of a "Siamese cat".

If sophisticated adult speakers of Thai *know* that there *are* other breeds of "meew", then that is, perhaps, a good reason in this case for assigning the set of cats as extension to "meew"; it's certainly sufficient justification for *not* assigning the set of just *Siamese* cats as the extension the word standardly has in the Thai language.

I am myself the son of a translator, and I learned at my father's knee the elementary fact that no translator worth his salt would stick to the "dictionary translation" in all contexts. Undoubtedly, a good translator would sometimes render "meew" as "Siamese cat", sometimes as "cat", sometimes as "puss", sometimes as "tom cat", sometimes as "tabby", . . . depending on the situation; and there is no general rule determining when one translation is better and when another is better.

Let us, however, "stipulate" that "meew" has as its extension *the set of all cats* in *all* contexts in which we are interested. It is (we have just stipulated) coextensive with "cat" and not coextensive with "Siamese cat". Even so, does it have the same *meaning* as "cat"? Why or why not?

If such facts as the fact (or putative fact) that "leopards are typically spotted" and "tigers are typically striped" count as part of the *meaning* of the natural kind words "leopard" and "tiger", then the fact that "cats typically look thus and so . . ." must, by parity of reasoning, be counted as part of the meaning of "cat". And if the Siamese stereotype is different from the European stereotype, should that, then, not count as a meaning difference . . . ? But things are not so simple.

Stereotypes are not just images (or "perceptual prototypes", in psychological jargon) but beliefs stated in words ("aluminum is a metal"). Thus, knowing what someone's stereotype of something is *presupposes* we understand his language; a theory which takes the notion of a "stereotype" as basic cannot *explain* interpretation.

But we are going to ignore that for the time being; we "stipulate" that we have some kind of holistic understanding of what the Thai speaker believes (as in the case of Aristotle). We may even suppose that some psychologist has come up with a reasonable and operationally meaningful criterion for determining whether a feature of something is "stereotypical" for a given subject, at least in the case of features that can be *pictured* (stripes on a tiger, spots on a leopard, whiskers on a cat . . .).

To count *every* difference in "stereotype" (in such a sense) as a difference in *meaning* would depart totally from actual practice in disambiguation. Not only would it turn out that "meew" does *not* have the same meaning as "cat" (even when it has the same extension), and that "gorbeh" in Persian does not have the same meaning as "cat", but worse, if Tom next door does not (by the psychological criterion) use the whiskers of a cat (or the milk-drinking) as part of his *stereotype* and Dick does, then the meaning of the word is different for Tom and for Dick. Of course, many "folk philosophers" *say* just this: "no word has quite the same meaning for two different people"; but that's *not* how we actually *use* the notion of "meaning" when we *aren't* being folk philosophers. In fact, all the sophisticated mentalists I know *attack* the idea that meanings simply *are* stereotypes (and rightly so; can we even make sense of the notion of a "stereotype" in the case of such words as "mind", "esprit", "Geist"?); but if someone were so ill-advised as to hold this view, we should just advise him to *drop* the word "meaning" and to talk about the role of stereotypes in communication. (Of course, they aren't invariant under belief fixation, even barring scientific revolutions; they don't determine paraphrase relations, ...)

Suppose, on the other hand, we go to the opposite extreme and decide that stereotypes have *nothing to do* with the meaning of natural kind words. Then the stereotypical stripes have nothing to do with the meaning of "tiger", the stereotypical spots have nothing to do with the meaning of "leopard", and so on. What about the knowledge that "tigers are *animals*"? It is not more *analytic* that tigers are animals than that tigers are striped (although it is more permanent; tigers could *in fact* evolve to the point of losing their stripes, though not to the point of ceasing to be animals). Should we count *some* very *central* stereotypical features ("animal, vegetable and mineral", perhaps?) as part of the meaning, and not the less central ones? Even if we could decide on what counts as a sufficiently "central" feature, it seems that on such a theory there would be no difference in the "content" (the meaning, apart from the actual *extension*) of the words "leopard" and "tiger". It seems to me that a theory of "meanings in the head" that gives up the idea that "tiger" and "leopard" have different "content" has, in effect, conceded Quine's point that no psychologically useful notion of meaning exists (at least not in the case of natural kind words). This has, in fact, been proposed by Dretske, who would treat "tiger" and "leopard" as names with an extension but no "content". But what goes for natural kind words goes for many verbs as well (consider the verb "breathe"). If so many words have no "meaning" (content), then the notion of meaning cannot play the fundamental explanatory role that mentalists want it to play.

The course we actually follow in disambiguation is a middle one between the extremes just described. In the first place, when the two short words have exactly the same *extension* we will tend to treat them as synonyms *regardless* of what's "in the head". This is why mentalistic theories of an M.I.T type are in trouble from the start: they try to *factor out* extensions; but extensions are what most strongly guide us in interpretation, especially when there is no specific context to guide us. (Yes, I know all about "creature with a heart" and "creature with a kidney" having a different meaning but the same extension; but the *parts* of these phrases don't even have the same *extensions*.)

In the second place, when we consider factors beyond the extension, we *do* consider stereotypes (those stripes *are* somehow connected with the meaning of "tiger"), but what we are concerned with is not *identity* of stereotype (however that might be defined) but *sufficient similarity*. And there is no general rule for deciding when two stereotypes are sufficiently similar; it depends on the particular context, including the reasons why someone wants to know what a word means and what he is going to do with the answer.

To sum up: I have not argued that meaning is indeterminate even in typical contexts (although Quine would so argue, and in cases such as the highfalutin' one I described it *is* indeterminate). What I have argued is that *when* meaning is determinate it is *no one thing* that makes it so. The "standard meaning" of *meew* in Thai and of *gorbeh* in Farsi is *cat;* not because the *same* entity is in the heads of Thai, Persian, and English speakers, but notwithstanding the fact that there are psychological differences. The sameness of meaning is the reasonableness of ignoring the difference in the psychological processes.

Mentalism: Sophisticated and Naive

The form of mentalism associated with Noam Chomsky and Jerry Fodor depends on the notion of a "mental representation". As developed by Fodor,[8] the theory postulates an internal code, a "language of thought"—call it *Mentalese*. It further postulates that "all concepts are innate", i.e., that Mentalese has the resources to express all the "contents" a human mind could understand. While I much admire Fodor's articulate and scientifically informed writing and his philosophical ingenuity, I have to say (as John Haugeland once put it) that "one philosopher's *modus ponens* is another philosopher's *modus tollens*"; the very fact that *artichoke* and *carburetor* have to be innate notions if Fodor's theory is right, shows (me) that some of his premises must be wrong. It also seems to me that the empirical fact is that our "concepts" are *not* "universal" in the way that I am told syntactic categories are: the fact that French, English, and German have the very different concepts "esprit", "mind", and "Geist" (at least sensitive translators judge them to be quite different) rather than some one "universal concept" is evidence *against* the Innateness Hypothesis at the level of semantics. But let us assume that Harvard is wrong and M.I.T. is right, and the mind does, as it were, express things twice: once in the public language (when a verbalized thought occurs either in my speaking or in interior monologue), and again in Mentalese. How does this help the notion of meaning?

The answer is that it does not help at all. Mentalese, if it exists, must have much the same character as any other language (apart from having an unthinkably huge vocabulary). Belief fixation must be just as *holistic* in Mentalese as it is in public language. For the holistic character of belief fixation is no *accident:* it is required by rationality. Mentalese cannot, any more than scientific language, obey the two Dogmas of empiricism: individual "words" in Mentalese cannot, in general, have operational definitions if Mentalese is to be an adequate vehicle for *general intelligence*. Here I am not disagreeing with Fodor; in his writings Fodor visualizes reasoning in Mentalese as generally abductive and holistic. But then, what reason is there to think that there is a precise, context-independent, more-than-merely-pragmatic notion of "sameness of meaning" that we possess or could construct *for Mentalese?*

Even if Mentalese existed, and we could "eavesdrop" on a person's Mentalese, how would that help with the problem, whether "meew" in Thai has the same meaning as "cat" in English? Dictionaries will still give "cat" as the translation of "meew" whether the corresponding "mental representation" (the hypothetical Mentalese word-analogue-in-the-brain) is the same or different. Again, let us suppose that most adult English speakers know that *brass* and *gold* are both shiny yellow metals, and that gold is precious and does not tarnish. An immature speaker may well not learn all these facts at once. Suppose a child knows that gold is a shiny yellow metal, but has not yet learned any more about it. Suppose a second child has the same information about *brass.* If at *that* stage the Mentalese representations are *different,* then (since the total "content" must be the same on any theory, if there is nothing the one child believes about *gold* that the other does not believe about *brass*), *difference* in "mental representation" has no relation to difference in "content".

Now suppose the contrary, that when the beliefs are not yet different, the representations are the *same* (or belong to some computationally defined equivalence class). What happens as the first child learns that gold is precious and does not tarnish?

If the Mentalese word correlated to *gold* does not change, then *it* will become associated with different "collateral information" and with a different "stereotype" as a result of normal belief fixation just as English words will. In that case, we are no better off with respect to having a scientifically useful and explanatory notion of meaning (or even "content") for Mentalese than we are for English.

If, on the other hand, the "mental representation" *does* change as the stereotype changes (and learning that gold is precious and does not tarnish is run-of-the-mill stereotype change), then it would be extremely odd if the "mental representations" associated with "meew", "gorbeh", and "cat", were not all different. In *that* case, sameness-or-difference-of-mental-representation would be a useful neurophysiological criterion for stereotype-sameness-or-difference, but, as we have already seen, stereotypes aren't *meanings*.

I don't have the impression that Fodor now disagrees with this. He has recently denied ever holding the view that sameness-of-content is a computational relation in the case of Mentalese (i.e., that one can effectively decide when Mentalese "words" have the same "content") and, in a recent article,[9] he expresses doubt that there are type-type identities between *propositional* "contents" and syntactically defined types of sentences in Mentalese. "Contents" are not the *same* as "mental representations", and are, indeed, in a rather mysterious relation to them. So what is left of the claim that we can *now* see how "contents" could be scientifically well-defined explanatory entities?

It is instructive to see how analogous (what I view as) the collapse of M.I.T. mentalism into total obscurity is to the collapse of the naive mentalism of Locke and Hume.

If Locke's "ideas" are *not* taken to be *images* (they weren't taken to be images by Locke himself, of course), then (in the context of Associationist Psychology) it is totally unclear *what* they are. So Hume took them to be images. But (as, for example, Frege pointed out—and Kant had already seen) to think a thought just *isn't* the same thing as running a sequence of pictures through one's mind. So the theory can't explain what we want explained; what one informally explains in terms of "thinking thoughts" can't be scientifically explained in terms of "having a vivid sequence of images", because the casual powers of images are all wrong.

But now it turns out that even if we accept Fodor's *modus ponens,* even if we *buy* Mentalese and all that, we are in the same boat. There is simply no reason to believe that what we informally explain by saying, "'meew' means *cat* in Thai", can be explained by R*(meew)* = R*(cat)*, where R is the function that carries a word onto its hypothetical "underlying" Mentalese counterpart. The similarity relations between psychological objects (perceptual prototypes, "mental representations", "canonical methods of verification", etc.) just don't correspond in any way to *semantic* relations. Nor can they, given that psychological objects are so extremely changeable under belief fixation, while the principles underlying interpretation (e.g., the "principle of charity") have as their *raison d'etre* precisely keeping "meanings" *invariant* under a *lot* of belief fixation. To say, "Well, perhaps *sentences in Mentalese* aren't invariant under belief fixation to the extent that intuitive 'meanings' are, but their *contents* are", is to talk about the we-know-not-whats of we-know-not-what. After Quine, one can no longer get away with this sort of talk.

Other Folks, Other Strokes

The M.I.T. attempt to revive mentalism has the virtues of scientific sophistication (Chomsky's work in syntax is world famous; Fodor has done extremely interesting experimental work in psycholinguistics) and serious scientific ambition. The aim is to sketch a way in which rehabilitated meanings (or "contents") could play a serious explanatory role. Even the willingness to entertain extravagant hypotheses and to accept the counterintuitive consequences is a virtue as well as a vice. The other well known brand of modern mentalism, associated with the names of Grice and Schiffer, has (up to now) less of a scientific flavor, but also less extravagant claims to make.

In a given situation, what I mean to convey by an utterance of a sentence may deviate widely from what anyone would regard as a standard reading of the sentence. If I am asked about the intelligence of a student, and I reply "He knows how to spell his name correctly" with the intention of conveying the belief that the student is stupid, then "The student is stupid" is what *I* mean (or part of what I mean) by the sentence on that occasion, but it certainly isn't what the sentence means in English. In the terminology applied by advocates of "intention based semantics", "The student is stupid" is (part of) the *speaker's meaning* on that occasion, as opposed to the *sentence meaning*.

This distinction is certainly an important one. The program of Grice and Schiffer is to develop a theory of speaker's meaning, and then later (they hope) to use that theory as the basis of a theory of what sentences mean in a language or in a speech community.

I cannot elaborate further here: as is well known, Grice has an elaborate theory of what might be called *dialogic intentions* (intentions in a situation in which there is a complex mutual recognition of intentions) and an elaborate theory of maxims governing conversation which aid in the mutual recognition of those intentions. When I say that speakers' meaning is a function of intentions, it is to these mutually recognizable dialogic intentions that I refer.

That Grice has a great deal to teach us about communication, I do not doubt. It is the idea that any of this rehabilitates mentalism that seems misguided to me.

If I say "That chair is comfortable" to someone, then my intention is usually to get that someone to believe that some contextually definite chair is comfortable. In such a situation, I can say something of the form, "My intention in uttering that particular utterance of P was to get so-and-so to have the belief that P". In short, I can use the sentence P again to say what the speaker's meaning of P was on that occasion. If this were the *only* way of doing this, then Grice's theory would be of no interest.

I can, however, answer other questions about the beliefs I would like my hearer to acquire (by recognizing my dialogic intentions), and so can any sophisticated speaker. If Mrs. Shayegan (a Farsi speaker) says that there is a "gorbeh" on the chair, I can ask her whether she intends to convey the belief that there is a generic cat on the chair or the belief that there is a Persian cat on the chair; in the later case, the speaker's meaning is (in part), *there is a Persian cat on the chair* even though the standard sentence meaning (relying on dictionaries) might be *there is a cat on the chair.*

To say what the "speaker's meaning" is (assume Mrs. Shayegan speaks *only* Farsi) I have to *translate* her answers, however. Without a notion of sentence meaning, all I have is her dispositions to assent and dissent from various questions put to her in Farsi. Such Rylean dispositions (complex dispositions to speech behavior) cannot be regarded as expressing the same "intentions" and the same "beliefs" unless we *already* have a practice of translation in place. To regard such intentions and beliefs as well-defined entities underlying (and ultimately explaining) translation is to reify meanings under another name.

My old friend Paul Grice will now tell me, with some exasperation, that he is not now, never has been, and does not intend to be Gilbert Ryle. His "beliefs" and "intentions" are *not* "multi-tracked dispositions" in Ryle's sense. But that is precisely the problem! *What* they are is not one bit clearer than what "meanings" are.[10]

Michael Dummett, whose attacks on metaphysical realism have had a profound influence on my own thinking, would revive mentalism by restricting the holism of belief-fixation to *science*. Ordinary language sentences he supposes to have definite verification conditions associated with them by a systematic and "surveyable" procedure. I have already discussed this approach, which seems to me radically misguided.

John Searle supposes that there are mental states which are, on the one hand, constituted or, as he says, "internally caused", by the chemistry and physics of the brain and which *intrinsically refer to external things* . . .

And Quine is *wrong* in thinking that "meanings" are *obscure?*

Quine, Wittgenstein, Davidson

I have taken Quine not to be rejecting our ordinary talk about what words mean, but as insisting upon the informal (and unformalizable) character of our decisions of "synonymy". It is not saying that "cat" and "gorbeh" are "synonyms" that Quine attacks, but the idea that our account of such statements can be an informative one if it posits independent objects called "meanings".

This reading of Quine is based not only upon many conversations with Quine, but also upon many conversations with Burton Dreben, who has long insisted on the deep similarities between central parts of the philosophies of Quine and Wittgenstein. As far as Wittgenstein is concerned, the relevant reading is well expressed in a recent paper[11] by Warren Goldfarb. Commenting on Section 20b in the *Investigations* (in which Wittgenstein tells his interlocutor not to think of the meaning as if it were a shadow sentence, and remarks curtly that what it comes to for two expressions to have the same meaning is that they have the same use), Goldfarb writes:

> It might be objected that this is false, and that, indeed, no two sentences have (exactly) the same use, since there will inevitably be some occasions where one would be employed but not the other. I take Wittgenstein to be aware of this (although it does not come out in section 20); the reply is not simply that he means "more-or-less the same use". To ascribe sameness of sense to two sentences is to say that they have features of their application in common. What features might be essential to the ascription is not given beforehand; for that depends on our aims in the classification, on the reasons we are talking—in the particular context—of sense at all. I would argue that there is no general notion of use; and I would claim that Wittgenstein agrees. For these sorts of reasons, I read his notorious "definition" of meaning as use (section 43) not as a definition, not as explanatory, and certainly not as suggesting a "use-based theory of meaning". (My reading is closely connected to my taking Wittgenstein not to be a behaviorist. It should be clear that if he is not, then little can be made of talk of use simpliciter.) Given that invoking use by itself carries little information, I take his remark in section 43 to be, by and large, a denial of the possibility and the appropriateness of theorizing about meaning.

If this reading is correct, as I believe it to be, then it is striking that two of the very greatest analytic philosophers of the 20th century have so powerfully argued against the same error (and even more striking how persistent the error is, in spite of the criticism directed against it).

If I have not discussed Donald Davidson in connection with mentalism, it is because the theories of meaning that he speaks of presuppose translation-practice. This is the reason that Quine is not hostile to Davidson's enterprise. (But this point seems not to have been grasped at Oxford.)

Does Quine go too far?

Where I do *not* follow Quine is in his doctrine of the almost total indeterminacy of *reference* (and of *meaning* even when the context is specified). Quine's argument is long and subtle, and I will not attempt to sketch it. Suffice it to say that it moves from such premisses as "No change without a physical change'' (which I accept, as I think Quine intends it) and "All facts are phys-ical facts'' (which I do *not* accept—the relation between these two premises is obscure to me), to the conclusion that there is "no fact of the matter" about meaning or reference.

Quine's argument is so abstract that it applies to all of mentalistic talk (talk about beliefs and desires) as well as to meaning talk, whether scientific or informal. The idea is that if the negation of a statement could be incorporated into a theory which is compatible with the same *trajectories of bodies* as the theory which contained the original statement, then the statement has only a theory-relative truth-value. *"Gorbeh* means *cat"* may be true relative to our present mentalistic linguistic "theory", but there is an empirically equivalent theory relative to which that statement is *not* true, and there is no "fact of the matter" as to which of these empirically equivalent theories is correct.

This is another case in which "another philosopher's *modus ponens* is my *modus tollens"*. Even if the extreme counter-intuitiveness of the conclusion did not force me to reject one of the premises, the fact is that Quine's argument for the indeterminacy of mentalistic talk applies equally well to *philosophy*. A philosophy based on St. Thomas might well be compatible with every "trajec-tory of bodies" that Quine's philosophy accommodates, and imply that there is a fact of the matter about translation, that meanings exist, that Quine's use of "fact of the matter" is incoherent, and so on. Can Quine consistently hold that there is no *fact of the matter* about any of *these* things? But my purpose in this paper is not to discuss Quine's scientism, but his meaning holism. And the latter, though not the former, seems to me to be a revolutionary contribu-tion to thinking about talking and thinking

HILARY PUTNAM

HARVARD UNIVERSITY
CAMBRIDGE, MASSACHUSETTS
FEBRUARY 1982

NOTES

1. Cf. *The Structure of Scientific Theories,* edited by Frederick Suppe, Univ. of Illinois Press, 1974, for a good description of the rise and fall of the "partially inter-preted calculus" account of scientific theories.

2. Cf. Jane English's excellent paper, "Partial Interpretation and Meaning Change", reprinted in *The Philosopher's Annual,* vol. 2, 1979, edited by Boyer, Grim, and Sanders (Rowman and Littlefield, publisher).

3. "The Meaning of 'Meaning'" is reprinted in my *Mind, Language and Reality* vol. 2 of my *Philosophical Papers* (Cambridge: Cambridge University Press, 1978).

4. Cf. my "Two Dogmas Revisited", in Gilbert Ryle, ed., *Contemporary Aspects of Philosophy,* (Oriel Press, 1976) for elaboration of this point. This paper was reprinted in *Realism and Reason* vol. 3 of my *Philosophical Papers* (Cambridge: Cambridge University Press, 1982).

5. This is a good opportunity to refute the suggestion (made by Saul Kripke in *Naming and Necessity*) that I once thought it was *analytic* that most (or even *some*) of the laws connected with a law–cluster word must be true for the word to have an extension. I wrote in 1960 that

> I mean not only that *each* criterion can be regarded as synthetic, but also that the cluster is *collectively* synthetic, in the sense that we are free in certain cases to say (for reason of inductive simplicity and theoretical economy) that the term applies although the whole cluster is missing. This is completely compatible with saying that the cluster serves to fix the meaning of the word. The point is that when we specify something by a cluster of indicators we assume that people will *use their brains*. That criteria may be over-ridden when good sense demands is the sort of thing we may regard as a "convention associated with discourse' (Grice) rather than as something to be stipulated in connection with the individual words.

(See p. 328 of my *Mind, Language and Reality*. That the cluster which "fixes the meaning" may change without our saying the "meaning" has changed was pointed out in my 1957 "The Analytic and the Synthetic"—Chapter 2 of *Mind, Language, and Reality*.)

6. Suppose, for example, we discovered that vixens are telepathic. If we thought that they were the only telepathic animals, then "vixens are telepathic animals" might come to be even more "central" than "vixens are female foxes". And if we then discovered a male telepathic fox, we might very well say "a few male foxes are vixens".

7. In "The Analytic and the Synthetic", loc. cit.

8. See Jerry Fodor's *The Language of Thought* (Crowell, 1975). Noam Chomsky has never committed himself to the possibility of finding "psychologically real" entities which have enough of the properties we pre-theoretically assign to "meanings" to warrant an identification. The "representations" and "innate ideas" of which Chomsky writes are deep *syntactic* structures and *syntactic* universals; Fodor's program is thus not identical with Chomsky's, but is rather a daring extension of it.

9. "Cognitive Science and the Twin-Earth Problem", *Notre Dame Journal of Formal Logic* 23 (1982): 98–118

10. To say, as Schiffer does in a forthcoming article ("Intention Based Semantics") that Gricean beliefs and intentions are functional states of the organism-cum-environment is no help at all. Given the informal and context-sensitive nature of our interpretative practice, we have no reason to think even *one* such state could be defined in finitely many words, that it would not be infinitely disjunctive, that the disjunction would not fail to be effectively specifiable (as in the phenomenalism case), etc.

11. "I Want You to Bring Me a Slab", *Synthese*, LVI, 3 (September 1983): 265–282.

REPLY TO HILARY PUTNAM

Much to my satisfaction, Putnam has written understandingly, approvingly, and persuasively of my strictures on the notion of meaning and of the holism that underlies them. Conversely, I applaud his contributions to the analyticity issue: his doctrine of cluster concepts and one-criterion words. These last generate sentences that are analytic in the sense suggested in *The Roots of Reference* (p. 79); see my reply to Bohnert.

Still I must caution against over-stating my holism. Observation sentences do have their empirical content individually, and other sentences are biased individually to particular empirical content in varying degrees. I was urging this already in "Two Dogmas," as witness the brick houses in Elm Street. Moreover, even the diffuse content of a whole theory is the content also of a single long sentence in which the theory can be encapsulated.[1]

Ironically, even so, the objection to extreme holism that Putnam cites will not stand. He cites the objection himself as "pure legalism", but it is worse. What it says is that any sentence "is confirmed by each experience which confirms at least one total body of theory which contains the sentence." An extreme holist could reply that in this sense every sentence is confirmed by every experience, since any one sentence can be safeguarded by changing others. For my own part, however, as appears from the preceding paragraph, I see extreme holism itself as "pure legalism".

What Putnam calls "top down" confirmation goes with a coherence theory—a more extreme holism than mine. He seems to underestimate my observation sentences, the channel through which empirical content is imbibed.

He writes that

> the "stimulus meaning" of the observation sentence . . . cannot be called the *meaning* of the individual sentence, Quine argues, for at least two reasons.

On the contrary, I did intend the stimulus meaning to capture the notion of meaning—for the linguistic community in the case of an observation sentence, and for the individual speaker in the case of many other occasion sentences. It was the meanings of standing sentences that were elusive.

What then of my supposed two reasons to the contrary? One, he writes, was that the stimulus meaning of a sentence does not determine the extensions of the component predicates. I agree that it does not; doubly not. It determines neither the meanings nor the extensions of the predicates (and, contrary to widespread opinion, the meanings of predicates do not determine the extensions either, as we shall see). But what Putnam misses is my distinction between taking an occasion sentence holophrastically and taking it analytically, i.e., analyzed. When the infant or the field linguist learns one of his early observation sentences by ostension, he learns it holophrastically. It is holophrastically that these sentences are conditioned to ranges of stimulation, and it is holophrastically that their stimulus meanings are their meanings. Even when they are one-word sentences, it is anachronistic at first to reckon them as terms referring to things. A one-word observation sentence or a component word of a longer observation sentence will eventually make its way into standing sentences of increasingly theoretical character, and the child is then on his way to acquiring the word as a term and as referential. I have speculated on this development in *Roots of Reference*. In the case of the field linguist, the corresponding development proceeds rather through his devising of what in *Word and Object* I called analytical hypotheses. At that stage a semantic wedge is indeed driven between the stimulus-synonymous sentences 'Lo, a rabbit', 'Lo, rabbithood', 'Lo, undetached rabbit parts', and the rest. Analytical meaning then supervenes upon holophrastic meaning, and resists satisfactory general explication.

I have not wanted in these past two paragraphs to be pedantic about terminology. But I have wanted to clarify and stress the contrast between taking sentences holophrastically and taking account of the purported references within them, for it is crucial to ontological relativity.

In a parenthesis above I denied that meaning determines extension. Putnam has here given two arguments to show that it does not, and I gave a third one elsewhere when I argued ontological relativity on the strength of proxy functions. He feels that my argument, "long and subtle", went too far. It is not so long and subtle any more; see the opening essay of *Theories and Things*.

At several points Putnam inveighs in my behalf against the reification of meanings as objects. His emphasis on reification is wrong; see my reply to Alston.

In his concluding paragraphs Putnam objects to my notion of a fact of the matter. Though he makes light of his remarks as lying aside from the theme of his paper, I eagerly rise to them.

First, a dull point of detail. The version in terms of trajectories, cited by Putnam, belongs only in the fictitious context of an atomic physics in the ancient style. My serious version appeals rather to the distribution of microphysical states over space-time.

Next let us turn to my notion of a fact of the matter in what was for me its primary application, namely, to translation. Speech is an activity of a physical body, and dispositions to speech are for me actual enduring states of nerves, however ill understood. My thesis of the indeterminacy of translation is that mutually incompatible manuals of translation can conform to all the same distributions of speech dispositions. But the only facts of nature that bear on the correctness of translation are speech dispositions. Thus mutually incompatible manuals of translation can conform to all the same overall states of nature, hence all the same distributions of microphysical states. Yet, being incompatible, both manuals can scarcely be right. Which one is, if either? I say there is no fact of the matter. This illustrates my identification of facts of the matter with distribution of microphysical states.

Contemplating the application of my standard of fact of the matter to beliefs and desires, Putnam feels impelled to *modus tollens*. Is it because he supposes that in beliefs and desires I recognize no fact of the matter? Then he misconstrues me. Some beliefs, perhaps belief in the essential nobility of man *quâ* man, are indeed not readily distinguishable from mere lip service, and in such cases there is no fact of the matter by any reasonable standard. But most attributions or confessions of belief do make sense, within varying limits of vagueness. The states of belief, where real, are dispositions to behavior, and so, again, states of nerves. Similar remarks apply to desires, except that desire has less tendency than belief to grade off into meaninglessness.

Putnam has me concluding "that there is no 'fact of the matter' about meaning and reference". Yes and no; let me sort out. We have been seeing that I challenge the notion of meaning, in anything like its traditional guise, and that what the challenge comes down to is a challenge of synonymy. This is not a general rejection of "meaning talk, whether scientific or informal". Semantics remains important; it has wanted cleaning up. Analyses and comparisons of the use of words are significant, and so is translation. See my reply to Roth.

As for reference, what my argument from proxy functions shows is that there is no fact of the matter except relative to a target language and a manual of translation. Domestically, translation being homophonic, reference resolves into trivial paradigms; see again my reply to Roth. But let us remember that even apart from parameters there is a fact of the matter that 'Gavagai' is stimulus–synonymous with 'Rabbit', 'There's a rabbit', 'Lo, rabbithood', and the rest.

Putnam ends on a Thomistic note *(soll mir nicht schuldigen)* to which it is not easy to respond. If I am to judge whether the Thomistic philosophy in question is compatible with every distribution of microphysical states, I am going to have to understand it. I am going to have to judge it relative to some translation into my language. One bit that I am going to have to understand, for purposes of Putnam's example, is the bit that he renders as "Meanings exist." As already remarked, the existence of meanings poses no problem beyond synonymy; they can be taken as equivalence classes. Since I have despaired of making general sense of synonymy, perhaps Putnam is right in supposing that I make no fact of this matter and I am right in not doing so.

Dreben once put me a related but more challenging question: is there no fact of mathematical matters? For me, unlike Carnap, mathematics is integral to our system of the world. Its empirical support is real but remote, mediated by the empirically supported natural science that the mathematics serves to implement. On this score I ought to grant mathematics a fact of the matter. But how, asks Dreben, does this involve the distribution of microphysical states? What would there being a largest prime number have to do with the distribution of microphysical states?

Carnap would have said that we have here a contrary-to-fact conditional with an L-false antecedent, 'There is a largest prime number', from which anything and everything follows vacuously as consequent. That avenue is closed to me, but I can still protest that there is no coping with intensional conditionals with wildly implausible antecedents. My suggested standard for facts of the matter is directed rather at concrete situations, and pales progressively as we move upward and outward. Evidently then the upshot is that the factual and the mathematical stand apart, for me as for Carnap; but for me, unlike Carnap, the separation is a matter not of principle but of degree.

All this belaboring of the notion of a fact of the matter has brought us regrettably far from translation, which was what brought the notion up. I hope at any rate to have clarified my claim that there are no linguistic differences without physical differences, and that between the two imagined manuals of translation there is no fact of the matter.

Finally I should like to clarify what Putnam and others have called my scientism. I admit to naturalism, and even glory in it. This means banishing the dream of a first philosophy and pursuing philosophy rather as part of one's system of the world, continuous with the rest of science. And why, of all natural sciences, do I keep stressing physics? Simply because it is the business of theoretical physics, and of no other branch of science,

> to say what . . . minimum catalogue of states would be sufficient to justify us in saying that there is no change without a change in positions or states. ("Facts of the Matter").

If telepathic effects were established beyond peradventure and they were clearly inexplicable on the basis of the present catalogue of microphysical states, it would still not devolve upon the psychologist to supplement physics with an irreducibly psychological annex. It would devolve upon the physicist to go back to the drawing board and have another try at full coverage, which is his business.

W.V.Q.

NOTE

1. See my reply to Vuillemin; also "Posits and Reality", last two pages, and *Theories and Things*, p. 71.

16

Paul A. Roth

SEMANTICS WITHOUT FOUNDATIONS

Quine has frequently asserted that the notion of meaning which he is opposing by arguing for the "indeterminacy of translation" is the "myth of a museum" ([26]: 27; [11]: 495). The myth (which is akin to the view of language disparaged from the outset by Wittgenstein in the *Philosophical Investigations*) ([31]: 77) has a protean quality, appearing here as logically proper names and there as Platonic ideas. In its various forms, this myth asserts the existence of a "fact" of some type which, in turn, fixes or determines the meanings of words. At issue in the *attack* on the myth and related confusions about semantics is not only the rejection of a cluster of distinctions thought (in the not too distant past, anyway) to be important—analytic-synthetic, language-fact, conceptual-empirical (the list is Rorty's)—but also, as Richard Rorty has urged, the displacement of epistemology from a central place in the philosophic enterprise (or, at least, a rejection of the purpose of epistemology as one of providing or uncovering the foundation—the determinate basis of—knowledge) ([33]: 169). Yet even those philosophers, such as Rorty, who feel that Quine has done as much as needs to be (possibly: as much as can be) to dispel the myth are, paradoxically, apt to assert that Quine's arguments for "indeterminacy", i.e., his justification for his doubts about meaning, are either intentionally circular ([36]) or unsound because inconsistent with other theses he asserts ([33]: 181ff.). Quine's doubts about meaning are matched by a skepticism on the part of his critics concerning his justification of his doubts. My initial concern in this paper is to establish a sound Quinean argument for his indeterminacy thesis. A further concern is to correct what I take to be a pervasive misunderstanding of the force and nature of Quine's attack on the museum myth.

These considerations serve, in turn, to support a still more general claim.

My thanks to Larry Davis, Robert Feleppa, Roger Gibson, Jr., Barry Gottfried, Dick Ketchum, David Phillips, Dennis Rohatyn, and Manley Thompson for their comments on earlier drafts of this paper.

There is a conventional wisdom about how to read Quine, viz., as an updating and refurbishing of certain positivist doctrines.[1] This wisdom perceives Quine's empiricism as enriched by a sophisticated holism but, in addition, impoverished by a recalcitrant commitment to a verificationist view of meaning ([13]; [33]: 195–209; [3]: 757). The problem is most visible in Quine's commitment to the "indeterminacy of translation of theoretical sentences". My claim is that this conventional wisdom is wrong on both counts. On the one hand, Quine is not offering yet another variant of a traditional answer to certain traditional epistemological questions. On the other hand, the supposed tarnish perceived in Quine's "new empiricism" becomes, when viewed aright, an inextricable part of the Quinean position. By way of providing a corrective to the conventional wisdom, I offer, first, a reconstruction of Quine's epistemology which details the interconnections of his characteristic themes. Second, I argue that my reconstruction allows for a superior assessment of the significance of the "holist turn" in epistemology which, I suggest, is both Quine's most significant philosophic contribution and the one which has yet to be properly appreciated.

I will be concerned with five Quinean theses:

(DT) *The Duhem thesis:* The claim that sentences (within either natural language or formal languages) have their evidence only as a related set (I refer to this as Quine's holism).

(UT) *Under-determination of theories:* The claim that it is possible to formulate empirically equivalent but logically incompatible scientific theories.

(IT) *The indeterminacy of translation of theoretical sentences:* The claim that theories wherein we formulate hypotheses about what words or sentences mean lack a fact of the matter, i.e., fail to be objective in the way in which theories in natural science are. Despite acknowledging fundamental methodological parallels between theories of "translation" and theories in the natural sciences, Quine insists that the former are *not* objective in the way the latter are. There are no "facts of meaning" parallel to the "facts of nature." This failing distinguishes translation *in kind* from proper scientific inquiry.

(IR) *Inscrutability of reference:* Whereas (IT) asserts that there is no fact of the matter concerning the intension of terms, (IR) asserts that there is likewise no one right answer concerning the extension of a term. "The only difference between rabbits, undetached rabbit parts, and rabbit stages is in their individuation . . . . The only difference is in how you slice it. And how you slice it is what ostension, or simple conditioning, however persistently repeated, cannot teach" ([27]: 32). "Reference, extension, has been the firm thing; meaning, intension, the infirm. The indeterminacy of translation . . . cuts across extension and intension alike" ([27] 35). Reference, too, is related to a museum myth, i.e., the view that there is one fixed or correct connection between words and "ideas" or words and the world.

(OR) *Ontological relativity:* "The relativistic thesis to which we have come is this, to repeat: it makes no sense to say what the objects of a theory are, beyond saying how to interpret or reinterpret that theory in another" ([27]: 50).

Quine holds or has held that the following relationships obtain among these theses.

(a) DT + "Peirce premise" → IT ([27]: 80–81)

(b) UT or IR → IT ([26]: 182–183)

(c) UT ↛ IT ([18]: 66–67)

(d) UT ≠ IT ([26]: 180; [29]: 303–304)

(e) DT → UT ([20]: 42–43)

(f) DT ↛ UT ([25]: 220; [24]: 314)

(g) IR → OR ([26]: 182–183)

Clearly the claims on the list, as they stand, are inconsistent; what is needed, at a minimum, then is to determine which of the claims in (a)–(g) are sufficient for Quine's attack on the museum myth. To make matters worse, critics have insisted:

(h) IT is untenable ([33]: 192–212)

(i) IT is just an empirical hypothesis ([17])

(j) IR is false ([9]; [10]); or, Quine's argument (g): IR → OR constitutes a *reductio* for his own views on reference ([5]; [38])

(k) IR and OR are inconsistent and OR is false ([7]; [8])

The above critics, by and large, adhere to the conventional wisdom in that they take b: (UT or IR) → IT to be Quine's central argument. My strategy is to maintain that (a): DT + Peirce → IT is the critical argument in Quine's attack on the myth of the museum; more generally, my concern is to establish that (a), (d): UT ≠ IT, (f): DT ↛ UT and (g): IR → OR are correct and sufficient for Quine's purpose (of discrediting the museum myth). The misinterpretations of Quine's position, in turn, I see as developing from two basic sources. One source is that those critics with whom I am concerned accept (e): DT → UT; the problem here is that if one accepts (e), then (b): (UT or IR) → IT and not (a): DT + Peirce → IT appears as the primary argument for (IT). But (b) is, as critics insist, untenable. The other source of confusion is that Quine often fails to distinguish the two distinct epistemological views present in his writings; the result is a failure to keep separate the particular consequences of each view. ([34]) I argue that (IT) develops from Quine's *critical remarks* on the museum myth; (IR) and (OR), however, are consequences of adopting Quine's account of the form of proper scientific theories.

In Part I, I develop and defend argument (a). (See also [35].) Part II presents an argument for (g): IR → OR which is immune to the criticisms raised by Davidson, Field, et al. One consequence of the reading proposed in Parts I and II is a repudiation of Quine's own, much discussed, suggestion that (IT) can be argued for by "pressing from above" (from UT) or by "pressing from below" (from IR), i.e., I disavow (b): (UT or IR) → IT entirely. Part III reverts to a concern, noted at the outset of this paper, with regard to the philosophic import of Quine's skepticism about semantic theory.

I

Before attempting to defend argument (a)—a derivation of the indeterminacy of translation of theoretical sentences which proceeds from Quine's holism—I will briefly consider three popular construals of the argument for (IT). Putnam offers two of these (although rejecting one and accepting the other); Rorty offers the third. Both of Putnam's arguments are noteworthy because they explicitly take (UT) to be the key premise; Rorty offers an interpretation which does not make explicit appeal to (UT). My central concern in this section is to show that (IT) can be derived without appeal to (UT), and also without invoking the sort of crypto-positivist considerations which Rorty perceives as an illicit premiss in Quine's argument.

Putnam offers a twin Quine hypothesis: Quine$_1$ is a figment of the professional philosopher's imagination, while Quine$_2$ happens to be the person who authored, among other works, *Word and Object*. Each Quine has his own argument for the indeterminacy of translation of theoretical sentences. Paraphrasing Putnam ([17]: 160), the argument of Quine$_1$ runs as follows:

(A) A manual of translation, formed as described in Ch. 2 of [31], provides a general recursive function whose domain is the set of all terms and sentences of an alien language and whose range is some subset of all terms and sentences of the home language. The function yields, for each argument (an alien term or sentence), a value which is observationally and/or truth functionally equivalent to the argument.

(B) It is possible to have more than one such function, and the functions need not be compatible, i.e., they may be empirically equivalent to one another and yet yield different (and incompatible) values for the same argument.

(C) Relative to a particular function, a translation is correct; however, there is no empirical basis for deciding between conflicting functions.

(D) Since correctness is defined relative to choice of function, there is no fact of the matter to the question "Which translation (of the different ones provided by different functions) is correct?"

> "Quine₁ might well have summed this up by saying that *the
> choice of* [a function] . . . *is a matter of convention.*" ([17]: 161)

This interpretation has its supporters; (e.g., [14]: 94; [16]: 131; [12]) however, Putnam's criticism of Quine₁ seems decisive. For the argument depends on the stipulation that the functions be constituted according to certain conventions (specifically, the conventions discussed in Chapter 2 of *Word and Object*). The problem is that premiss A, so interpreted, embodies what Putnam calls the "conventionalist fallacy". The fallacy lies in a decision to *limit* the number of canons which may be used in translation. "The negative essentialist, the conventionalist, intuits not that a great many strong properties are part of a concept, but that only a few *could be* part of a concept" ([17]: 164). Quine₁ guarantees the existence of competing translations by circumscribing the constraints on translation. But why accept *only* those constraints Quine₁ suggests? There is, in other words, no good reason to assume that Ch. 2 of [31], unsupported by arguments, delimits either the possible or the proper constraints on translation. The inference from the fact that certain constraints fail to restrict the number of functions to the claim that, in effect, there are no additional constraints which will, commits what Putnam calls the conventionalist fallacy.

Quine₂, on Putnam's view, avoids the conventionalist fallacy although he (Quine₂) otherwise subscribes to the argument A-D (amending A by deleting "formed as described in Ch. 2 of [31]"). On the revised reading, "Quine's view of the indeterminacy of translation is a hypothesis, not something of which Quine claims to have a logical or mathematical proof" ([17]: 178). The hypothesis is that, even after all the methodological constraints are in place, conflicting translations will still occur. Whether this is true, of course, remains to be seen.

What I wish to note here is that Putnam's formulation, in both cases, assumes (B), which is just UT applied to translation manuals. More generally, Putnam's discussion of Quine proceeds from the assumption that (b): (UT or IR) → IT is correct. This reading, with its emphasis on under-determination (premiss B above), is abetted by Quine's remarks in some places. For while Quine will insist ([26]: 180) that indeterminacy is "additional" to under-determination, Quine then, in the passage just noted, phrases the problem of (IT) as follows: "Where physical theories A and B are both compatible with all the possible data, we might adopt A for ourselves and still remain free to translate the foreigner as believing A or as believing B." But, then, this is no different in some philosophically interesting way from any other instance of having to choose between under-determined theories. Quine's reader is left wondering whether indeterminacy is genuinely additional to (UT).

One reason for being reluctant to accept the derivation of (IT) from (UT) is that (IT), so interpreted, is perfectly compatible with tolerating propositions as posits. (IT) would just be the claim, on this account, that the correct translation is unknowable. ([2]) But, Quine insists, (IT) is to rule out the belief that such posits are scientifically acceptable ([31]: 205–208). Even worse, (IT), understood as Putnam, et al., suggest, does nothing to undercut a museum myth, i.e., to refute the claim that there really is *one* right "translation", one correct interpretation of another's utterances (or our own). On this interpretation, Quine would have inferred (IT) from methodological considerations, which cannot be done. It is precisely Quine's opposition to museum myths, his animus toward determinacy of meaning, which motivates him, in the first place, to formulate his argument for (IT). This is why (b) ought not to be considered Quine's primary argument.

(IT) does *not* depend on some supposed difference in the methodology of translation as opposed to that of natural science. Quine is explicit in stating that physical theory and semantic theory are alike—parallel—with regard to *methodological* resources and rigor ([31]: 75–76). The cause of the asymmetric relation between truth in science and meaning in semantic theory—the "failure of the parallel" in Quine's phrase—must be sought in reasons *other* than those of the specific canons involved.

With regard to IT, Quine asserts that "the problem is not one of hidden facts" ([26]: 180). Thus, the issue is not an empirical one, for the indeterminacy thesis is to put in disrepute the *very question* of whether "the foreigner *really* believes A or believes rather B" ([26]: 181). (IT) obtains "in principle", i.e., it is not contingent on what further empirical inquiry might reveal. This "in principle" formulation is needed if (IT) is to undercut the museum myth, for, if successful, the argument for (IT) should show that questions concerning what someone, or ourselves, really means—either by appeal to absolute meaning (e.g., a Platonic Form) *or* even by appeal to meaning relativized to a manual of translation (and so viewing an explanation which cites the meaning of terms as no worse off than an explanation which cites current physical theory)—are misguided. The effort is one of philosophic therapy, of trying to break the hold certain questions, bad questions, have on us ([29]: 304).

If the foregoing is correct, then a derivation of (IT) from (UT), understood in the sense of the arguments Putnam attributes to Quine$_1$ and Quine$_2$, will not do for the purposes for which (IT) is wanted. And while there is text enough to support Putnam's view, I have suggested that an alternate formulation of the argument is offered by Quine, viz., (a): DT and Peirce $\rightarrow$ IT, and that only an argument which sustains the "in principle" sense of (IT) will have the desired therapeutic effect.

While Rorty endorses Putnam's criticism of Quine$_1$, he also suggests an interpretation of the argument for (IT) which does not appeal to (UT). Rorty's reading suggests that it is primarily a stubborn streak of residual positivism which engenders Quine's animosity to semantic theory.[2] Briefly stated, what

Rorty does is to suggest Quine's statement that there is "no fact of the matter" to translation is untenable in view of the following argument.

(A) Either there are "facts" of nature or there are not.

(B) If there are, then (DT) is wrong (for (DT) entails that there are no *special* "statements of fact").

(C) If there are not, then semantic theory is no more lacking in objectivity or internal coherence than, e.g., chemistry ([33]: 194). That is, (IT) is false.

(D) But the Duhem thesis is not wrong (or, alternatively, Quine presents much better arguments in support of (DT) than he does in support of "observation sentences"—the putative "facts of nature").

(E) There are no priviledged "facts of nature" (from D, B).

(F) (IT) is false (from C, E).

Rorty's strategy, in short, is to insist that (DT) and (IT) are inconsistent.

The above argument explicates Rorty's claim that there is "a genuine contradiction in Quine's view" ([33]: 207). The problem arises because, we are told, Quine stubbornly insists on taking "contemporary physics as paradigmatically matter-of-factual" ([33]: 203). However, Rorty argues, "This tactic makes his preference for physics over psychology, and thus his concern about 'irresponsible reification,' purely aesthetic" ([33]: 203).

Rorty's argument to the falsehood of (IT), taken in conjunction with Putnam's interpretation, indicates the course which any defense of (IT) must steer. A defense must, on the one hand, be stronger than Putnam's, i.e. strong enough to undo the hold of the museum myth. But, on the other hand, the interpretation must avoid a reading of Quine's notion of "a fact of the matter" which distinguishes science from semantics at the cost of running afoul of (DT) in the way in which Rorty details. We must, in short, show that (IT) is not a variant of (UT) and that (IT) is not inconsistent with (DT).

The argument which I defend—(a): DT + Peirce → IT—together with a concise statement of the view to be debunked by means of this argument, receives clear expression at ([27]: 80–81). However, before I explicitly defend this formulation of the argument, the Quinean claim needs to be more precisely stated. That is, just what is at issue when Quine insists that manuals of translations lack the sort of objectivity possessed by theories in the natural sciences?

Quine maintains that the notions of meaning and of truth can be understood only as relativized to a particular theory: a manual of translation in the case of meaning and a theory in natural science in the case of truth. Yet the "analytical hypotheses"—hypotheses concerning, e.g., equivalences of meaning—which are products of our manuals are *not* on a par with the "genuine hypotheses" of scientific theory: "The point is not that we cannot be sure whether the analytical hypothesis is right, but that there is not even, as there was in the case of 'Gavagai', an objective matter to be right or wrong about'' ([31]: 73, 68–72). If we stick with just this way of formulating the differences between truth and meaning (which, I readily admit, Quine himself does not), we see the alleged distinction between truth and meaning can be made *without appeal* to the existence of any multiplicity of theories, i.e., without invoking the under-determination of theories by evidence. *The problematic notion, on this formulation, is that of there being a "fact of the matter" in one case but not the other.* And it is unpacking this last mentioned notion which, I contend, reveals the defensible distinction between the two types of theories, i.e., an argument for (IT) which makes no use of under-determination, and which circumvents the criticisms noted above. *Quine's claim that there are facts of nature and not facts of meaning is derived from social/behavioral considerations.* It is precisely the need to have a *socially* grounded concept of evidence which Quine stresses ([31]: 75); given that there is a need for a ''social checkpoint'' in order to make sense of how it is possible to teach language, and given that the natural sciences are our means for probing, for better or worse, the nature of this social check, what is warranted is the assumption that there are facts of nature, i.e., a world to which we respond and which science investigates.[3]

If we consider the case of translation, however, we find that there is no warrant for assuming facts of meaning akin to the warrant for facts of nature. Semantic theory is indeterminate, I argue, because what is necessary to provide, even in principle, a translation with the requisite fact of the matter would be a warrant for positing the existence of a meaning for a term or sentence *prior* to translation. The indeterminacy of translation obtains because Quine's argument establishes that there is no basis on which to assume a prior standard of meaning. That is, if one could contrast the imposed translation/semantic theory with some prior—theory–independent—fact of the matter (some ''meaning'' the utterance has *per se*), then there would be something about which translation can be right or wrong. This contrasts with Quine's argument which establishes that we do have a basis for believing in a fact of the matter in natural science. *The inability to warrant the assumption that there exists a meaning-in-itself is the key to Quine's arguments with regard both to the inscrutability thesis and the indeterminacy of translation of theoretical sentences.* (For details, see [35].)

The argument for (IT), then, is as follows:

(A) Given Quine's holism, there is no making sense of the notion of truth or of the notion of meaning as applied to individual theoretical terms or sentences *apart* from one or another theory.

(B) From within our ''web of belief'', we need to posit an intersubjectively available stimmulus to which speakers or potential speakers of a language are jointly capable of responding as a necessary condition of language learning. That is, in order to explain the social and public character of language, and the fact that it is teachable, we assume that there is a fact of the matter to which we respond and around which our use of language is initially co-ordinated. (The argument for this claim involves what I call the "paradox of language learning". See [35]: 355–363.)

(C) Given that we must assume there is an intersubjectively available fact of the matter as a necessary condition of language learning, there is a warrant for a belief in objective evidence which arises from considerations *within* our language/theory.

(D) Natural science is the best means for exploring the intersubjective/public domain. Hence, theories in natural science are about (have) a fact of the matter.

(E) A belief in a fact of the matter for semantic theories is *not* warranted by appeal to any absolute standards (given (A)); moreover, such a belief is *not* warranted *within* the Quinean web as a necessary condition for there being a public and teachable language. (See [35]: 363–367.) We "misjudge the parallel" ([31]: 75) between the relativized notions of truth and of meaning if we think that the *internal* considerations which mandate attributing a fact of the matter to scientific theories also extend to semantic theories.

(F) Since there is no warrant, either internal to theories or external to them, for attributing a fact of the matter to semantic theories, such theories are indeterminate, i.e., not ultimately about "facts" in the way we are entitled to assume that scientific theories are.

This argument proceeds without appeal to (UT), thus avoiding the pitfalls encountered in Putnam's (and Quine's other) formulation. In addition, it avoids Rorty's criticism because the argument is consistent with (DT). My analysis indicates how the requisite Quinean conception of evidence develops naturally from *within* a holistic view of language and knowledge. Rorty treats (DT) as if it were simply descriptive, as if it were the case that language and culture form a hermetic web. He does not consider the problems posed to those, e.g., infants, who have to break into this web of belief via something like "radical translation." (One problem with the Quinean image of the field linguist faced with an unknown language is that the problem is not radical enough, for both the intrepid linguist and his quarry have, *ex hypothesi,* fully developed languages. If we think instead of an infant faced with the task of making sense of utterances which themselves make sense only in the context of large, related blocks of a language, some of the philosophic consequences of (DT) become more plausible.)

Indeterminacy obtains due to an *inability* to warrant an assumption which is warrantable for the natural sciences. This (the warranting in the one case and not the other) is the explanation for the asymmetric relation between truth relative to natural science and meaning relative to semantic theory. We "misjudge the parallel" when we think that methodological similarities are all important, when we believe, like Rorty, that from within the web of belief, i.e., given (DT), all posits look alike, be they mental or physical, extensional or intensional.[4]

A confusion between Quine's Duhemian holism and (UT) is abetted by Quine's tendency to stress the methodological parallels between underdetermination in natural science and the indeterminacy of manuals of translation.[5] The parallels *can* be illuminating if one attends to the reason why they *fail* at the critical point, viz., the point where we have a warrant for assuming that science appeals to (is about) facts despite its being underdetermined, but mistaken in extending this assumption to the case of translation. The explanation of this failure requires that we recognize that the very possibility of language as a social institution presupposes a public, non-verbal fact of the matter. *The objectivity of the natural sciences arises from the a priori need of there being some such non-verbal matter which gives language its all-important social dimension.* However, there *is no parallel guarantee for the case of semantic theory—because arguments for a semantic theory as a necessary condition of there being a language cannot be adduced, consistent with the Duhem premises.*

The parallel between science and semantics fails, then, for reasons related to (DT); we have reason to posit the existence of a subject matter of physical theory but not so for semantic theory. This is *not* to claim that science interprets, in Rorty's words, "nature's very own vocabulary". Nor is it assumed that Nature but not Man has its own determinate mode of being. All that is claimed, i.e., the basis for believing that there are facts of nature and not facts of meaning, is that such an assumption is necessary in order to explain the social (teachable) dimension of language. It is not illicit invoking of positivist dogma, but, rather, a sober thinking through of what is involved in a Duhemian view of language which leads Quine to conclude that there is no fact of the matter to semantic theory.

II

In turning to consider (IR) and (OR)—inscrutability of reference and ontological relativity—I shall argue that (IR) is to be derived from (DT) plus certain assumptions borrowed from Quine's account of scientific theories. Once I have outlined the main lines of argument for (IR), I defend the inference (g): IR → OR.

Quine classifies both (IT) and (OR) as types of "indeterminacy"; the former applies to theoretical sentences, the latter applies to the "apparatus of identity and individuation". ([27]: 45) Jointly, (IT) and (OR) complete Quine's attack on the museum myth. (IT) constitutes a rejection of the museum myth for intentional and intensional accounts of meaning because the argument shows that there is no warrant for positing meanings, unlike the considerations which warrant positing a fact of the matter to natural science. (IR), on the other hand, is meant to dispel any confidence in the belief that a determinate word-world relation can be established by appeal to a better scientific understanding of the world.

Even though (IR) is termed by Quine a form of indeterminacy, he also notes that (IR) and (IT) are *not* equivalent. For one, terms in observation sentences, should there be any, are held to be subject to complete inscrutability but to be only tangentially affected by sentence indeterminacy ([26]: 182). Second, the inscrutability of reference does, while sentence indeterminacy does not, function in the argument for (OR). These differences, I shall argue, are explained by the differing *scope* of (IT) and (IR). Inscrutability of reference has in its purview specific scientific theories, while sentence indeterminacy concerns our "theory of theorizing," concerns, that is, the nature and limits of all theoretical knowledge (given the Duhem premise, of course) ([34]). This is *not* to claim that the theses are restricted, (IT) to natural languages and (IR) to scientific discourse. For failure to find determinacy of reference in science implies a corresponding lack of determinacy for natural language. Parallel considerations hold for (IT) as applied to theoretical sentences in scientific theories. The non-equivalence is a function of the fact that (IR) concerns indeterminacy of the *extension* of terms while (IT) asserts the indeterminacy of their *intension*.

The argument for (IR) shares with the argument for (IT) the Duhem thesis.

Premiss 1: Given (DT), there are no indubitable standards by which to settle questions about what a theory says there is.

Premiss 2: Relative to the best standards available at the present time—the sentences of scientific theory expressed in first–order logic—there is still no determinacy of reference, i.e., no restricting the models of a theory so expressed to some one domain.

Premiss 3: The determinacy of reference, i.e., a specification of the denotata of the terms of a language, is not made possible by extra-theoretic considerations (given 1) or by intratheoretic ones (given 2).

∴ Reference is indeterminate

In important respects, the problems with regard to the notion of reference parallel the problems which affect the notions of truth and of meaning. Each is said by Quine to make sense only relative to some given theory. Quine argues that it is an error to think that a non-relativistic understanding is possible. Specifically, he argues that given the Duhem premise, one must foresake the very intelligibility of the belief that there is some one "ideal" explication of these notions. Reasons given from *within* any theory beg the question (the question being just the adequacy of current theoretical discourse to talk of some correspondence between the theoretical picture and things-in-themselves). And if the Duhemian is right, *there are no other sorts of reasons to be offered*, i.e, there are no other standards to avail ourselves.

Any claim to knowledge of some necessary word-world correspondence is contravened by our failure, given (DT), to have non-contingent standards by which to arbitrate such claims ([24]: 327). Theories can remain "tied for first place" because ultimately there is no way to break the tie, no standard from which to judge knowledge claims *sub specie aeternitatis*. *Even if the problem is narrowed to the case where there is only one theory*, and it is confirmed by all possible evidence, the standards are those which the theory offers, and so the best available canons remain those contingently affirmed by that theory ([23]: 80–81). Thus, the philosophical puzzle concerning reference, given the Quinean view, is *not* to be understood in terms of our inability to construct an ideal scheme, for of no theory can we ascertain that it corresponds uniquely to the way The World (as Putnam has put it) is.

Quine's claim is that reference lacks determinacy—a fact of the matter—even when spoken of from *within* the framework of an accepted theory ([27]: 54). The claim that reference is inscrutable is *not* based on the possibility that there is some currently unknown on unknowable multiplicity of objects: "the inscrutability of reference is not the inscrutability of a fact; there is no fact of the matter" ([27]: 47). The inscrutability thesis has the "in principle" character of (IT), not the empirical-hypothetical character of the underdetermination thesis.

I claimed that (IR) proceeds from two premises: (DT) plus certain aspects of Quine's concept of what constitutes a theory in natural science. Characteristically, for Quine, we find in the argument for (IR) an interplay of two senses of the term "theory" ([34]). The sense of "theory" relevant to (DT) is "theory" in Quine's most general sense of that term, where a person's "theory" includes "everything he accepts as true". It is the nature of theories, whether the "theory" in question be a natural language or a specialized scientific theory, to conform to (DT). However, Quine also speaks of theories in a narrower sense, one which includes only those theories which are properly part of Quine's conception of the natural sciences. For Quine, scientific theory will be expressed in first-order predicate logic—Quine calls this the "canonical idiom" for science ([31]: 158). Theories expressed in the canonical idiom are not free of the characteristics cited with regard to (DT). Rather, "the doctrine is only that such a canonical idiom can be abstracted and then adhered to in the statement of one's scientific theory. The doctrine is that all traits of reality worthy of the name can be set down in an idiom of this austere form if in any idiom" ([31]: 228, and see generally Quine's remarks in [31]: 226–232).

The point, then, is that while (DT)—the first premiss of the argument we are considering—applies to theories in the extended sense, the second premiss—which includes as a constraint on theories that they be in canonical form—applies only to theories in a narrower sense, viz., those theories which Quine counts as a proper part of natural science. The argument, then, between the first premiss and the second, shifts the scope of the term "theory". That is *not* to suggest that the argument is fallacious; quite the contrary, I shall maintain the argument is sound. However, in order to understand why Quine claims there is no "fact of the matter" to reference, it must be understood that he is looking at theories in two senses, one general and the other more specific. At issue is the question of what standards a theory, *in either sense,* has to offer for the purpose of determining meaning, truth-value, or reference.

Having already argued, with regard to (DT), that there is no making sense of a theory-independent fact of the matter, premiss two must address the question: from within a narrowly scientific conception of reality, is reference determinate? Quine is not primarily concerned with the analysis of "ordinary language" because questions about reference are more precisely posed for scientific theories. However, in Quine's conception of a proper scientific theory, the ontological commitments will be expressed via the bound variables, i.e., within the theory in canonical form. *The question "Is reference determinate?" is then equivalent, for Quine, to the question "Will only one domain of objects satisfy our scientific account of reality?"*

Quine's approach to this question is illustrated by his discussion of the "thoughtful protosyntactian" ([27]: 41ff.). Let us ask, in particular, what are the well-formed formulas (wffs)? Given a specification of atomic formulae, a recursive definition of a wff can be specified in one of the usual ways. But it certainly does *not* make sense, *prior* to some specification of the atomic wffs and the recursive clauses, to ask which strings of symbols are wffs and which are not. More generally, Quine's point is that the intended interpretation of the laws is not the only interpretation of them. Quine applies this point to a discussion of number theory. "The subtle point is that any progression will serve as a version of number so long and only so long as we stick to one and the same progression . . . . Arithmetic is, in this sense, all there is to number: there is no saying absolutely what the numbers are; there is only arithmetic" ([27]: 45).

How is the ontology of a theory in science ascertained? For Quine, a scientific theory, when turning seriously ontological, will be expressed in first order predicate logic. "To paraphrase a sentence into the canonical notation of quantification is, first and foremost, to make its ontic content explicit, quantification being a device for talking in general of objects'' ([31]: 242). A theory so regimented, i.e., translated into the notation of formal logic, is in canonical form. But there is an important, if ironic, philosophical consequence of so turning. We look to scientific theories thus expressed in order to clarify our ontological commitments. Lacking the regimented discourse, we cannot specify what our sayings commit us to. It is the sense in which the laws of our currently accepted scientific theory are constitutive of objects which provides the important link between the case of the protosyntactician or number theorist and more mundane discourse about the world. The irony is that the theory, once in canonical form, is *not* restricted to just those objects, which, when left unexplicated, ordinary discourse includes. There are, in short, other models, other interpretations, which the theory allows ([27]: 53).

Because the theory permits alternative models, there is no saying, *from the perspective of the canonical form of the theory*, that there exist only the objects of the ''intended'' interpretation. Yet from the perspective of noncanonical (ordinary) discourse, we cannot state what objects there *need* be, for arbitrating disputes about reality is a task for the scientist. The notion of ontological commitment is well defined for theories in canonical form; but given the corresponding theory form, this theory is indistinguishable from a theory with the same form but a different model. As we make precise the canonical form, we cut our tie to the ''loosely referential'' idiom of the ordinary language model ([19]: 195). *Reference is inscrutable—objectively indeterminate—because determinate judgements are possible only at the level of theory form and at this level many domains will do* (will provide a model for the theory form). Science begins with our everyday talk of objects; science refines this talk to the point, however, where the assumption that there are *just those* objects about which we initially talk itself becomes untenable ([27]: 54).

Note that the objective indeterminacy of choice of model is *not* due to (UT), for we are talking about some *one* theory, canonically expressed. *Although we look to natural science to clarify our notion of what an object is, what we learn is that we have no scientific sanctions for talking of just as we presently do.* This is not to say, of course, that current talk is ''wrong,'' but, rather, the point is that such talk enjoys no privileged status. For not only is ontology open to future revision, but, here and now, there are various choices of universes by which to satisfy the bound variables of a regimented theory. We cannot, given arguments for (IT), assume that there is one correct translation (the intension is not fixed); *now we find that we cannot assume that there need be a reference relation as ordinarily understood in order to have a language.*

> Growing up in a community of believers in stones and rabbits, we first learn 'there is' in connection with stony and rabbity sorts of stimulation. Eventually, after mastering the logic of quantifiers and identity or their vernacular equivalents, we invest

'there is' with a theoretical quality and are prepared, in an extremity, to warp it away from its paradigm cases. *This is why I have urged the inscrutability of reference; existence in its final estate is theoretical.* ([29]: 293)

The "final estate" of our explication of what there is is within science, canonically expressed. And it is here, where ontic commitments are explicit, that the notion of there being just one particular set of objects which makes our theory true ceases to have any support. To the extent that reference can be made sense of at all for ordinary language, the argument for the indeterminacy of reference within scientific theory then applies, *a fortiori*, to natural languages as well. Yet this relativising of ontologies to choice of models does not threaten us with incoherence in communication; one's choice will be governed by the usual pragmatic reflections and constraints.[6] (Note Quine's distinction cited above between how we *first learn* to use "there is" and our later analysis of existence claims.)

In summary, then, we see that by accepting (DT), we forego appeal to any extra-theoretic standard. What then is the best intra-theoretic sense that can be made of reference? Here we turn to what Quine says about determinacy of reference from *within* scientific theories, canonically expressed. Quine argues that there is no fact of the matter because given a theory in canonical form, different models—and so different universes of discourses—are possible. A theory may be understood as quantifying over rabbits, undetached rabbit parts, and natural numbers with equal facility ([27]: 96). The conclusion, then, from these two premises is (IR)—there is no fact of the matter to reference. There is no reason to assume that there is some fixed and determinate relation either between natural language terms and the world (given DT) or between scientific terms and the world (given model theory). The mythic character of a belief in determinacy is made clear; the therapy, if successful, frees us from the compulsion to seek determinate links between words and the world. (For a related account of Quine's views here, see also [1].)

The argument for (IR), as outlined above, makes no appeal to (UT). Yet Davidson, for one, in his discussions of (IR) and (OR), assumes that (UT) is central to Quine's argument: "the argument for the inscrutability of reference has two steps. In the first step we recognize the empirical equivalence of alternative reference schemes" ([7]: 14). Field, for his part, better understands the import of the indeterminacy thesis ([9]: 202). I examine below Field's claim that Quine's account of reference cannot be "relativized" to a background language without committing Quine to the very "museum view" of meaning that Quine is otherwise concerned to reject ([9]: 207).

By way of approaching what Field has to say, let us consider an implication of the model-theoretic account of reference with which Quine leaves us. This model-theoretic account accepts as an ontology of a theory any universe which provides a model for the theory. But this theoretical tolerance contrasts with my interpretation of my neighbor's remarks about what he sees scamper across his lawn, or for that matter, my interpretation of my own remarks. Quine's theory of reference does not seem to explain the practice of using language to make (seemingly) determinate remarks that are (often, it appears) well understood as determinate. In other words, how is reference, as a matter of fact, ever settled in the social (inter-subjective) realm ([27]: 47)? That is, one implication of Quine's position is that we should converse interchangeably about rabbits and, e.g., Gödel numbers. But we do not.

Quine's proposal for alleviating this strain within his account is found in his comparison of reference to relativity theory. What we need, and, fortunately, what we have, is a coordinate system by which to refer. There is no absolute scheme of reference, no absolute fact of the matter. But there does exist an *accepted* format for talking about the world ([27]: 48). How is the quandary, the tension between theory and practice, resolved by the principle of relativity, i.e., the assertion that our usual stock of terms and predicates constitutes a coordinate system by which to talk about the world? Quine's apparent answer is that we explain reference by "regress into" a background language— a metalanguage. And how do we come to determine the reference of terms in this metalanguage? An infinite regress seems to threaten. Quine responds to the threat by stating that "in practice of course we end the regress of coordinate systems by something like pointing. And in practice we end the regress of background languages, in discussions of reference, by acquiescing in our mother tongue and taking its words at face value" ([27]: 49–51). There is no saying, independently of one or another coordinate system, what it is we are referring to. We explain terms such as "refers to" by use of a background language; if the theories we are dealing with are formalized, this background language is the meta-language. Having "explained" the object language terms in this background language, the background language, can, in turn, itself be interpreted by appeal to another background language.

Ontology will, on Quine's account, be a function of our *chosen* universe of discourse, but there is more than one choice that can be made. "Which of these models is meant in a given actual theory cannot, of course, be guessed from the theory form . . . . *Paraphrase in some antecedently familiar vocabulary, then, is our only recourse; and such is ontological relativity"* ([27]: 53–54, emphasis mine). The substance of ontological relativity is a formal point concerning scientific theories which are canonically expressed. We accepted the move to theories, so formulated, given the two premises of Quine's argument for (IR). In response to the question regarding how we ever, in the first place, learn to refer to rabbits and not Gödel numbers, i.e., in answer to the question why the problems which arise at the level of the theory form do *not* ordinarily arise in our use of language, Quine states, as noted above, that we acquiesce in our mother tongue and take the words at "face value." (See also [29]: 293.) *We can take words at face value precisely because we learned to talk that way.* Reference becomes a word-word relation, a matter of how we were taught to use language. The reluctance of science to remain confined to the domain of objects of the natural language/theory first learned—to isolate one model as the intended one—is no obstacle to discourse normally under-stood, but only to the *naturalized* explication of language and the world. If all there is to reference is a translation which makes the best empirical sense pos-sible of a person's utterances, then, indeed, "reference *is* nonsense except rel-ative to a coordinate system" ([27]: 48). An infinite regress of coordinate sys-tems is avoided by the fact that one of these "coordinate systems"—modes of translating referential terms etc.—is just the first language which we learn—our mother tongue. At the level of scientific theory, canonically expressed, no one model is privileged; *but we can always stop doing model theory when we want to.* If we distinguish the scientific study of reference from our initial use of language, then Quine's suggestion that we "acquiesce" in other mother tongues reflects what we, in fact, do. "Such talk of subordinate theories and their ontologies is meaningful, but only relative to the background theory with its own *primitively adopted* and ultimately inscrutable ontology" (27: 50–51, emphasis mine). We can fit new schemes to our present "background theory", but if we ask for a corresponding specification of our background theory, we can do no more, ultimately, than revert to our native tongue. Our native tongue does *not* possess some special determinacy other languages lack. What it does have is an accepted public use, and this "loosely referential" idiom is suffi-cient for ordinary communication.

Yet Quine's reliance on a background language is precisely what provokes Field's criticism. Field argues that Quine cannot resolve the tension between reference relative to a theory and reference in ordinary use by simply suggest-ing that we ignore the problem ([9]: 207). (IR) precludes making sense of the word-world relationship; relativizing the notion of reference will not, Field ar-gues, solve the problem either. "It is clear, then, that Quine's indeterminacy thesis forces us to give up not only the absolute notions of denotation and signification, but even the relativized notions which Quine has proposed as surrogates for them" ([9]: 208–209). Thus there is no sense to be made of Quine's relativized account because, Field insists, we never arrive, on Quinean relativized account, at a connection between words and the world. The general complaint with regard to (IR), then, is this: "The suggestion that one's own language be accepted at face value is puzzling . . . . Conspiring to ignore the fact of referential inscrutability will not make reference any clearer" ([38]: 55). Field sharpens this objection by suggesting an important disanalogy between the relational account of position and velocity and Quine's proposed relational account of reference. The disanalogy, at the critical point, is that while we make relational sense of objects in space by appeal to the physical objects, we cannot make relational sense of reference by any analogous appeal, for Quine offers only accounts of translational relations between one or another *language*. ("[N]o one holds that physical objects are constituted, by the relations of words" ([9]: 208). The problem is, in other words, that Quine appears to provide a hierarchy of translation schemes, but no account as to how these schemes connect in some important way with the world ([9]: 208fn). The dilemma facing Quine, then, is as follows. If the unrelativized account of reference obtains in the home language, then Quine is wrong to claim that nowhere is there determinacy of reference; on the other hand, if reference is indeterminate even in the home language, then it seems as if the understanding of reference for any language, in including our mother tongue, is going to engender the threatened infinite regress.

However, if we return to consider the two premises of Quine's argument for (IR), the resolution to this apparent dilemma is forthcoming. Quine's appeal to an unrelativized notion of reference comes when Quine is talking about theories—here including natural language—*prior to* any formal analysis of these theories. In English, or whatever one's native language happens to be, "we can say in so many words that this is a formula and that a number, this a rabbit and that a rabbit part, this and that the same rabbit, and this and that different parts. *In just those words*" ([27]: 48). Of course, when we talk casually, no problems of the type imagined above ordinarily arise. And this is the way which people learn to talk, i.e., the initial sense of "there is". However, when we begin to ask what there really is, more serious methods for taking stock of the world than ordinary discourse offers are developed. The more serious criteria—for Quine, first-order logic and physics—are not bound by or limited to "just those words" which constitute our initial and usual way of conversing about the world. What is confusing about Quine's account, i.e, the point overlooked by his critics, is the fact that the Quinean epistemologist begins *in medias res;* we begin with a language which we do, as a matter of fact, use to communicate. What actually divides Field's view and Quine's is the question of how loosely tied to the world a language can be ([10]: 399ff.). For Quine, the world impinges only at the periphery of a language/theory, via observation sentences. The need to incorporate such sentences is a basic constraint on theory-building. The constitutive process—the theory-building—is constrained by experience. One result is an (initially) unrelativized way of talking about the world. Given (DT), it follows that this way of talking is not determinate. However, it takes further reflection on the implications of the more refined referential idiom (the canonical idiom) to make apparent (IR) and, finally, (OR). Hence, Field is mistaken when he insists that Quine's appeal to the home language commits him to some form of semantic determinacy. What it *does* commit Quine to is the claim that we develop our notions of reference and truth based on epistemic relations which are weaker even than Field's notion of "partial signification" ([9]: 204ff).

The foregoing discussion holds the answer, I suggest, to Davidson's difficulty about the inference from (IR) to (OR). Davidson believes that (IR) is true, but, he admits, "it is ontological relativity that I do not understand" ([8]: 11). His problem is that he, like Field, does not see how the relativizing of ontology ever allows us to make sense of reference. "The fixing of reference and ontology for the object language has been done on the basis of an arbitrary choice; but the arbitrary choice succeeds in doing this only if the relativized 'refers' of the metalanguage has somehow been nailed down. And this is what we argued cannot be done for any language" ([8]: 11). However, by keeping in mind Quine's two uses of the term "theory" then Davidson's difficulty disappears. For acknowledging the fact that our usual terms and predicates allow for communication does *not* beg the issues raised when we take the measure of this discourse by other, more scientific and formal, standards.

Quine has elaborated on the respects in which the very notion of a physical object may vanish once we take science seriously (e.g., [27]: 91–113; [30]: 303–310). Our initial theory of the world, our mother tongue—the language we first learn to use—embodies whatever connection with shared experience makes this language learnable and teachable in the first place. Given that we accept the Duhemian account of language and of science, we can never make better sense of this language than its internal resources allow. Ontology becomes relativized because as the construction of models is not, in the end, constrained by any commitment to the objects of ordinary discourse.

The inscrutability of reference, I have argued, arises when we look to *within* the theory to find a basis—a foundation—for semantic determinacy. (DT) functions to preclude our establishing some determinate relation between the way we naturally talk about the world and the way the world is. Science, canonically construed, fails to support the assumption that reference can be understood by appeal to the "concrete denoted object", because there is no license for beliefs in such unique objects. Ironically the multiplicity of interpretations countenanced by science so construed is broken by abandoning science for our mother tongue. Reference here, in turn, obtains by whatever factors allow the language to be taught *in the first place*. What is discovered is that when we try to make scientific sense of what there was "in the first place" (and there is, of course, an intimate relation between the stimulus conditions which make language teachable and the belief that science does have access to a fact of the matter), no unique origin is locatable. For, as a matter of fact, the stimuli to which we are individually exposed differ, in some respect, from those which another receives. We have only the general guarantee that there must be non-verbal stimulations to which speakers are jointly exposed because otherwise, given the Duhemian view of language, there would seem to be no teaching of language possible at all. In light of this apparent "condition for the possibility" of language, we can, perhaps, understand Quine's remark that "both truth and ontology may in a rather clear and even tolerant sense be said to belong to transcendental metaphysics" ([27]: 68). They belong, that is, to the study of the characteristic forms of human judgement. But what determines the form our judgments take are not the stimulations-in-themselves.

III

While the arguments for (IT) and for (IR) share a common premiss, viz., (DT), each argument requires different subsidiary premises. In the case of the argument for (IT), the subsidiary premises construe the notion of "evidence" pragmatically and behavioristically (what Rorty has called "epistemological behaviorism"). And in light of the paradox of language learning, we assume a fact of the matter to scientific inquiry. There exists no warrant for any such assumption in the case of semantic theory. Hence, there is indeterminacy of translation of theoretical sentences. The argument for (IR) involves Quine's view of the proper form of scientific theory; the conclusion—(IR)—states, in effect, that no matter how we understand the term "theory", i.e., either generally so as to include natural language or formally so as to include only canonically expressed theories, the available standards fail to guarantee any determinate word-world relationship. Appeal to natural languages is circular; appeal to formal languages encounters the possibility of alternate models. There is no saying from within, as Quine insists, that only one of these universes is the "right" one. (OR), then, is just a *formal* consequence of the view of theories taken in arguing for (IR). Together, the arguments for (IT) and (IR) count against believing in the determinacy of a term's intension or extension. The mythic quality of the museum view of meaning is that there are neither facts which support the museum view nor any fact which only the museum view is needed to support.

What I have urged here is a general reading of Quine's epistemological position which orders his theses in terms of their philosophical importance—in particular, shows the central importance of Quine's Duhemian views to his general notion of indeterminacy—and traces their various interrelations. Second, and more generally, however, I have tried to show that Quine has presented a very powerful set of arguments for an extremely constricted conception of philosophy.

If successful, I take the arguments of this paper to establish that the central thrust of Quine's epistemology is to determine the *inherent* limits of such theorizing. Quine has delineated the bounds of possible knowledge; this is, I suggest, the prime and fundamental import of his discussions of indeterminacy in its various forms. Even when Quine cautiously, and rather late in his philosophical writings, turns to the question of the possible details of a naturalized epistemology, he cautions his reader to remember that "I have asked how our ontological notions are *possible, not* why they are *right*. Even in the case of bodies, these prototypical objects of reference, I offered no hope of justification" ([28]: 136 emphasis mine). (DT) imposes severe restraints on what can be said to be prior to, or as necessary for, there being a language. The "transcendental condition" comes to no more, on Quine's analysis, than the claim that if language is to be socially transmitted, then some sentences must function as observation sentences.

Most of what we would like to ask with regard to the semantics of natural language becomes a type of transcendent inquiry. My use of the terms "transcendent" and "transcendental" alludes to a Kantian strain in Quine's writings which others have noted ([6]; [15]; [39]; [40]). However, insofar as there are parallels to be noted between Kant and Quine, the Kantian aspects of Quine's thought are, I suggest, most akin to those which prompted Kant's contemporary Moses Mendelssohn to call Kant "the All-destroyer" ([37]: 58). For Quine has not articulated a metaphysics of experience, but, in essence, a counsel of despair. The more appropriate historical analogue, as Quine himself believes, is Hume. For what Hume argued with regard to knowledge of causal relations, Quine maintains concerning knowledge of semantic notions.

The expositors of the conventional wisdom on Quine err not just in the particulars of their analysis, but also in construing Quine as providing yet another version of the answers offered by a particular tradition ("empiricism") to a traditional set of problems about the origins of knowledge and the verification of statements. Quine's holism engenders a rather different problematic for philosophic inquiry, i.e., a problematic not defined by disputes between realists and idealists, by controversies over correspondence theories of truth and coherence-theoretic accounts. Quine, in his Herculean effort to cleanse empiricism of its dogmas, has transformed it. His *immanent* account of truth, meaning, and reference offers no special insight into any word-world relationship. His empiricism results from considering the necessary conditions for having a language like ours. The analysis of knowledge which Quine offers, on my reading, is therapeutic, for properly understood, it undoes the compulsion to ask about how language "corresponds to" or "pictures" the world.

Quine, as his essay "Epistemology Naturalized" [27] makes plain, strongly identifies himself with the empiricist tradition in philosophy. And, by and large, others have been content to read him in this way. What has been missed, and what I have in this essay attempted to show, is just how radical a reformulation of philosophy is implied by Quine's holism. Quine, in seeking to preserve the Humean heritage, leaves us unable to make sense of any descendants of "unvarnished" evidence. It is left to us to assess the dimensions and the implications of this transformation. I would suggest that Quine, like Hegel or Aristotle, stands at the culmination of a particular tradition; put more prosaically, I do not see that "empiricism" has anywhere left to go.

The problematic which Quine bequeaths us is to determine how knowledge is to be analyzed given (DT). Having spiked the museum myth, to what sort of explanation of human knowledge are we to turn? An answer, urged on us by Rorty (who has pondered the significance of (DT) more than any other serious student of Quine's thought), is that the "unit of empirical significance" be larger than Quine allows, viz., be taken to the whole of culture (see, e.g., [33]: 201). But Rorty is so impressed by the holist side of Quine's thought that Rorty's therapy calls for the destruction of the science/non-science distinction. "In the view that I am recommending, we might . . . view morality, physics, and psychology as equally 'objective'" ([33]: 335). This is in explicit contrast, of course, to Quine's own adamant repudiation of the *Geisteswissenschaften* (see, for example, [31]: 219–221). Whether truth (and whatever else we deem important) is to be found in edifying conversation, or in the laboratory, or somewhere else again, and the role of philosophy in all of this, remains a matter of debate. Quine's legacy is at least this: that he has forced a fundamental discussion of method upon us.

PAUL A. ROTH

DEPARTMENT OF PHILOSOPHY
UNIVERSITY OF MISSOURI - ST. LOUIS
MARCH 1982

REFERENCES

[1] Bruce Aune, "Quine on Translation and Reference", *Philosophical Studies* 27 (April 1975)
[2] William Bechtel, "Indeterminacy and Intentionality", *Journal of Philosophy* 75 (November 1978): 649–661
[3] Richard Bernstein, "Philosophy in the Conversation of Mankind", *Review of Metaphysics* (June 1980)
[4] Christopher Boorse, "The Origins of the Indeterminacy Thesis", *Journal of Philosophy* 72 (1975): 369–387
[5] M. C. Bradley, "How Never to Know What You Mean", *Journal of Philosophy* (March 13, 1969)
[6] Rudiger Bubner, "Kant, Transcendental Argument and the Problem of Deduction", *Review of Metaphysics* (March 1975): 453–467
[7] Donald Davidson, "The Inscrutability of Reference", *Southwestern Journal of Philosophy* 10 (Summer 1979)
[8]———, "Reality Without Reference", *Dialectica* (1977)

[9] Hartry Field, "Quine and the Correspondence Theory", *Philosophical Review* (April 1974)

[10]_____, "Conventionalism and Instrumentalism in Semantics", *Nous* 9 (November 1975)

[11] "First General Discussion Session", *Synthese* 27 (1974)

[12] Gilbert Harman, "Quine on Meaning and Existence", Part I *Review of Metaphysics* (Sept 21, 1967): 124–151, Part II *Review of Metaphysics* (Dec. 21, 1967): 343–367

[13] Mary Hesse, "Duhem, Quine, and a New Empiricism", in *Challenges to Empiricism* (Belmont, Ca.: Wadsworth): 208–228

[14] Charles Landesman, *Discourse and Its Presuppositions* (New Haven: Yale University Press, 1972)

[15] Kenton Machina, "Kant, Quine, and Human Experience", *Philosophical Review* 81 (October 1972): 484–497

[16] Alex Orenstein, *Willard Van Orman Quine* (Boston: Twayne, 1977)

[17] Hilary Putnam, "The Refutation of Conventionalism", in *Mind, Language and Reality* (London: Cambridge University Press, 1975)

[18] Willard Van Orman Quine, "Comment on Newton-Smith", *Analysis* (June 1979)

[19]_____. , "Facts of the Matter", in Shahan and Merrill (eds.), *American Philosophy from Edwards to Quine* (Norman, Okla.: Univ. of Oklahoma Press, 1977)

[20]_____. , *From a Logical Point of View* (New York: Harper & Row, 1961)

[21]_____. , "Grades of Theoreticity", in Foster and Swanson (eds), (Amherst, Mass.: University of Massachussetts Press: 1970)

[22]_____, "Mind and Verbal Dispositions", in Guttenplan (ed.), *Mind and Language* (Oxford: Clarendon Press, 1975)

[23]_____, "Nature of Natural Knowledge", in Guttenplan, op. cit.

[24]_____, "On Empirically Equivalent Systems of the World", *Erkenntnis* 9 (1975)

[25]_____, "On Popper's Negative Methodology", in P. A. Schilpp (ed.), *The Philosophy of Karl Popper* (La Salle, IL: Open Court, 1974)

[26]_____, "On the Reasons for the Indeterminacy of Translation", *Journal of Philosophy* 67 (1970)

[27]_____, *Ontological Relativity and Other Essays* (New York: Columbia University Press 1969)

[28]_____, *Roots of Reference* (La Salle, IL: Open Court, 1973)

[29]_____, "Replies", in Davidson and Hintikka (eds.), *Words and Objections* (Dordrecht: Reidel, 1969)

[30]_____, "Whither Physical Objects?", *Boston Studies in the Philosophy of Science* 39: 303–310

[31]_____, *Word and Object* (Cambridge, Mass.: MIT Press, 1960)

[32]Richard Rorty, "Indeterminacy of Translation and of Truth", *Synthese* 23 (March 1972): 443–462

[33]_____, *Philosophy and the Mirror of Nature* (Princeton: Princeton University Press, 1979)

[34]Paul Roth, "Theories of Nature and the Nature of Theories", *Mind* (July 1980): 431–438

[35]_____, "Paradox and Indeterminacy", *Journal of Philosophy* 75 (July 1978): 347–367

[36] Richard Schuldenfrei, "Quine in Perspective", *Journal of Philosophy* (Jan. 13, 1972): 5–16

[37] Norman Kemp Smith, *A Commentary to Kant's "Critique of Pure Reason"* 2nd ed. (New York: Humanities Press, 1962)

[38] Jacqueline Thomason, "Ontological Relativity and the Inscrutability of Reference", *Philosophical Studies* 22 (June 1971)

[39] Manley Thompson, "Quine and the Inscrutability of Reference", *Revue Internationale de Philosophie* 26 (1972)

[40] Henry Veatch, "Is Quine a Metaphysician?", *Review of Metaphysics,* (March 1978): 406–430

NOTES

1. The locus classicus is Harman [12].

2. Rorty's admiration for Quine is based on Quine's espousal of (DT) and Quine's critique of traditional epistemology (or, at least, certain dogmas thereof). Rorty's own position is that the museum myth is just part of the baggage of a certain philosophic tradition, and that once we abandon the foundationalist aspirations of this tradition, the myth will die from neglect. Consequently, Rorty sees no need to assert (IT) since his strategy for spiking the myth relies on a different therapeutic approach than Quine's. However, Rorty cannot be neutral with regard to (IT), for (IT), as Rorty understands it, requires us to distinguish between the *Geisteswissenschaften* and the *Naturwissenschaften*. But, Rorty argues, this distinction is untenable given (DT) [33]. "Edifying" philosophy grants no privileged place to any one voice in the conversation of humanity. While I do not argue the issue here, I would maintain, against Rorty, that (IT) entails only what Rorty terms "epistemological behaviorism" ([33], p. 174). The real issue, I suggest, is whether epistemological behaviorism, which Rorty endorses, is consistent with his casual attitude toward the notion of objectivity.

3. The primacy of the social/public criterion for determining what counts as objective evidence is a central, but, I suggest, much neglected aspect of Quine's epistemology. See [31]: ix; [19]: 177, 179; [23]: 74; [22]: 88–89.

4. Quine's concern to repudiate Berkeleyian-style skepticism and so to assert that the existence of the external world is a warranted assumption is evident throughout his writings. E.g., [31]: 1–2; [21]: 2; [28]: 1–4.

5. Since the question of how to derive (IT) from (UT) has been a focus of discussion for so long, some explanation is owed with regard to how this came to be. Of course, Quine endorses just the inference I claim we ought to reject. But this fact does not explain how Quine came to offer *two different* arguments for (IT), one proceeding from (DT) and the other from (UT). My suggestion as to why there are two different arguments and why one works and the other does not is as follows: Quine early on confused the relation of (DT) and (UT), a confusion expressed in his asserting both (e): DT → UT and (f): DT ↛ UT. Ultimately, Quine endorses only (f). However, I suggest, Quine never perceived that he entangled in his writings a thesis—(IT)—which is properly only a consequence of (DT) with what is implied by (UT).

There is no denying that Quine sometimes states that (UT) is a reason for concluding (IT) (e.g., [26]: 181, 183). Yet to accept what Quine says here is to overlook the fact that it is inconsistent with the distinction between (UT) and (IT). For Quine asserts that if we ignore (UT), indeterminacy persists ([29]: 303). If (UT) is critical for the argument for sentence indeterminacy, then settling underdetermination, even if only by fiat, should have some consequence for (IT); but it does not.

How do I account for the alleged confusion? Confusion arises because Quine deploys (DT) as a key premise in support of both (UT) and (IT). My suggestion, in short, is that since Quine does not clearly distinguish in his early writings between (DT) and (UT), he assumes that whatever (DT) implies, (UT) does also. And while he later concludes that (DT) and (UT) are not equivalent, Quine does not notice that (IT) is properly a consequence only of (DT).

How Quine's views change, and the import of this change for the issue at hand, is seen by comparing an argument first formulated in "Two Dogmas of Empiricism" and later repeated, to a different effect, in "Epistemology Naturalized" (Compare [20]: 37–42 and [27]: 81). In each case the argument takes as a premiss a version of the verificationist theory of meaning which Quine imputes to Peirce, i.e., the view that the meaning of a sentence is the difference its truth would make to experience ([27]: 80; [20]: 37). In developing his counter-suggestion to the dogma of verification, Quine conjoins the "Peirce premiss" with a position he attributes to Duhem: "our statements about the external world face the tribunal of sense experience not individually but only as a corporate body" ([20]: 41). Yet a version of (DT) is stated as follows: "But the total field is so *underdetermined* by its boundary conditions, experience, that there is much latitude of choice as to what statements to reevaluate in light of any single contrary experience" ([20]: 42–43, emphasis mine). The Duhemian view of theories is, in this key early passage, *identified with* underdetermination.

When Quine returns to the explicit premises in question almost two decades later, however, it is the relation of (DT) to (IT) which he stresses ([27]: 80–81). The identical reasons—(DT) plus the Peirce premiss—which earlier formed his account of underdetermination are now adduced as the grounds for sentence indeterminacy. This would account for the apparent parallels in Quine's discussion of (UT) and (IT). However, it is important to note, (DT) and (UT) are, subsequent to "Two Dogmas," shown by Quine to be importantly different. Quine now believes that (DT) and (UT) are not equivalent and that (DT) does not entail (UT). Thus, in those cases where Quine cites (UT) in support of (IT), I suggest that he does so only because he has confused the logical consequences of (DT) and (UT).

What, then, is the relation of (DT) and (UT)? Quine, in recent writings, warns against identifying them ([24]: 313). As Quine now sees the matter, underdetermination does *not* concern the intra-theoretic dependence of terms and sentences, as does (DT), but emphasizes the methodological/logical problem of the possible compatibility of a set of observations with theories which are, in turn, not compatible with one another. (DT) emphasizes that it is laws taken in conjunction which imply observable consequences; (UT) asserts that the evidence implies theories in alternation ([25]: 220). (DT) is concerned with the internal relation of theoretical terms and sentences; (UT) is concerned with the relation of distinct theories compatible with the same body of evidence.

What is philosophically significant about (DT) on the foregoing interpretation is that it is true of each and every theory; even if there is only one theory, the sentences of that theory would, on Quine's view, have their meaning and their evidence only as a related group. In order for there to be a "genuine" case of (UT), however, two conditions must obtain: a) there be at least two empirically equivalent theories, and b) these theories be logically incompatible and cannot be made compatible by any reconstrual of their predicates ([24]: 323).

The Duhem thesis is consistent with either the truth or the falsity of (UT). (DT) is a thesis about the truth conditions for individual theoretical statements. (UT) fails if it is the case that theories which are equivalent empirically are not, as a matter of fact, logically incompatible ([24]: 322–23). But the failure of (UT) does not affect the point about the truth conditions for individual theoretical statements. For in the absence of a "first philosophy", the only standard of truth for a single theoretical sentence is that which its containing theory offers, and that is, of course, just what a Duhemian claims. Since (DT) can be true and (UT) false, the theses are obviously not equivalent and (DT) does not entail (UT).

At best, Quine believes, (DT) makes plausible the claim that (UT) is true ([24], 313). Indeed, Quine now seems quite uncertain about whether or not there are any compelling reasons for believing (UT) to be true ([22]: 80). (UT) is best understood, perhaps, as "a thesis about the world" ([24]: 324), i.e., a statement about the nature of our most current explanation of the world.

6. On the role of pragmatic considerations in Quine's account of reference, see Thompson [39].

REPLY TO PAUL A. ROTH

Early in his essay Roth methodically sets forth seven relations (a)–(g) of implication, non-implication, or inequivalence that I have purportedly affirmed between various theses. He gets some right and some wrong.

(a) Holism and verificationism together imply the indeterminacy of translation. Right.

(b) Under-determination of science and inscrutability of reference each imply indeterminacy of translation. Partly right. Inscrutability of reference implies
indeterminacy of translation of terms, obviously, but not of sentences, as remarked in the very place that he cites in support of (b).

(c) Under-determination of science does not imply indeterminacy of translation. This one startles me, for, as he notes, it contradicts (b). Evidently it did
not startle him, or he might have looked twice at his purported source, my
"Comment on Newton-Smith". I wrote there that the implication in question
does not hold by virtue of simple instantiation but does hold by virtue of a
more devious argument, which I there cited—an argument that Roth himself
cited in support of (b).

(d)–(e) Under-determination of science is not equivalent to indeterminacy
of translation but is implied by holism. Right.

(f) Under-determination of science is not implied by holism. Another
shock, contradicting (e). He cites two places in my writings to support this
startling ascription, and I cannot see why he thinks either reference supports it.
So much for the contradictions.

(g) The inscrutability of reference implies ontological relativity. I have no
quarrel here, but I do not see what difference there is between the two.

Farther along he seems to ascribe to me a thesis (F) to the effect that "there
is no warrant . . . for attributing a fact of the matter to semantic theories."
On the contrary, the conformity of a translation manual to speech dispositions

is decidedly a matter of fact. It is only the choice between certain rival manuals that lacks factuality.

A major thesis of Roth's essay is that the indeterminacy of translation is best argued from a somewhat Duhemian holism and a somewhat Peircean verificationism—hence (a) above—rather than from the under-determination of physical theories. I quite agree. I took line (a) in *Ontological Relativity and Other Essays*, page 80, as Roth observes, and I remarked the inferiority of the other approach in my "Comment on Newton-Smith".

The last half of Roth's essay is concerned mostly with the inscrutability of reference. We must remember that the present volume languished for well over a dozen years; the essays are thus not uniformly recent, and Roth's evidently antedated *Theories and Things*. He had to cope with the murkiness of my original "Ontological Relativity". In that essay I indeed allotted six pages to proxy functions, but it was only later that I appreciated how fully they of themselves support the thesis of inscrutability of reference and how much clearer that thesis becomes when propounded independently of the indeterminacy of translation. The brain-cudgeling that Roth records in the last half of his essay could have been largely spared him if history had vouchsafed him a look at the opening essay in *Theories and Things*.

One murky matter that this later rendering clears up is the status of the background language. Another is the status of reference in the home language. Another is the nature of the relativity: What is ontology relative to? Within the home language, reference is best seen (I now hold) as unproblematic but trivial, on a par with Tarski's truth paradigm. Thus 'London' designates London (whatever *that* is) and 'rabbit' denotes the rabbits (whatever *they* are). Inscrutability of reference emerges only in translation. When we say that 'Londres' designates London and that 'lapin' denotes the rabbits, this simply means that we are translating 'Londres' as 'London' and 'lapin' as 'rabbit'. Ontological relativity is the relativity of ontological ascriptions to a translation manual. What I once called the background language is just the language into which we are translating.

Clarity this supervenes, but triviality does not. Proxy functions retain their punch. Ontology can be recast by reinterpretation of predicates without prejudice to truth values or observational support.

Finally some comments on scattered points. Roth's remarks on recursion, after the middle of his essay, suggest that he thinks the inscrutability of reference in number theory and protosyntax issues from an inadequacy on the part of recursive definition. On the contrary, there is no slippage there; any indefiniteness must lurk in the base term of the recursion or in the step relation.

In an ensuing discussion he represents inscrutability of reference as arising from the regimentation of language in predicate logic and the consequent identification of ontology with the values of the variables. On the contrary, ordinary language with its relative clauses and pronouns presents the same situation; the regimentation serves only to clarify and simplify and to bring reference explicitly to the forefront. Proxy functions have full access to ordinary language. Roth's sense of the referential scrutability and ontological absoluteness of our naive and unregimented language is due, I suspect, to his thinking of terms rather than one-word sentences at the observational level. In my recent "Ontology and Ideology Revisited" I have suggested an accommodation of such intuitions.

"The Quinean epistemologist," he writes at a later point, "begins *in medias res*." Here he is very nearly right. The Quinean epistemologist plunges *in medias res;* he begins *in mediis rebus*.

W. V. Q.

17

Henryk Skolimowski

QUINE, AJDUKIEWICZ, AND THE PREDICAMENT OF 20TH CENTURY PHILOSOPHY

I

The Mythos of Science As Shaping Analytical Philosophy

Philosophy of every epoch is *sui generis*. It cannot be reduced to the underlying context of a culture, be it science or religion; nor can it be rendered as a mere shadow of past philosophy, as mere footnotes to Plato or Descartes. The original minds of each epoch express the predicaments of their times in quite a unique way as each mind has been moulded by the particular experiences of the epoch. This is true of Willard Van Orman Quine. To the extent that he is an original mind, his philosophy is *sui generis*.

Yet another proposition must be entertained, namely that philosophy is a part of culture which begot it. And so is analytical philosophy in the 20th century. It conveys and expresses the unique achievements of 20th century rational mind; and it also reflects—in an indirect way—the hidden myths of the culture: its aspirations, its ambitions, its conception of the world. We shall argue throughout this essay that the *ethos of science,* specifically of physical science and of logic, has been the chief inspiration and the guiding force that has motivated and moved analytical philosophy.

From what we have said it follows that to understand a given philosopher completely, we have to understand the subtle but pervasive dialectic between the voices of the culture expressed through him, and his particular unique voice. And we should not be surprised that the voices of culture camouflage themselves so well that that which is considered to be a unique expression of

---

My thanks and gratitude to Professors Morris Engel and J. O. Wisdom for reading an earlier draft of this paper and helping me with their comments.

the individual vision is but a melody within a larger fugue which a given culture plays through individuals. This metaphoric way of putting things may be viewed with suspicion by the rational mind which praises itself for being on its own, independent of aesthetic ornaments and cultural crutches. Yet the very rationality of this mind is a cultural crutch. In the apparent independence which the analytical mind assumes we can hear the echos of distant rumblings of the underlying thunder of the whole rational/objective/secular culture. To make my point explicit, although couched in his unique, succinct, and almost aphoristic language, Quine's philosophy is much more an echo of scientific culture than most are aware of, including perhaps Professor Quine himself. And this I shall endeavor to demonstrate.

Human understanding is one of continuous comparison. In this essay I shall compare some of Quine's views with the views of the Polish philosopher Kazimierz Ajdukiewicz (1890–1963). As a prelude to this comparison, I shall attempt to locate Quine, and the whole analytical tradition, on a larger canvas of 20th century scientific culture. In so far as Quine is a part of a larger body of 20th century philosophy, called for the sake of brevity analytical philosophy, it will be important to assess the place of this philosophy in the entire western culture of 20th century.

We are now at the end of an epoch. The feeling is growing among philosophers that the philosophical idiom which has been used during the last 50 years (perhaps we should say the last 70 to 80 years) has exhausted its strength and its potential. We simply repeat over and again the same kind of results with only slight modification of the form of expression. The time has arrived for an appraisal and for asking where we can go from here. For as long as the human mind is alive, philosophy cannot be dead; it may only atrophy for a while.

The significance of philosophy derives from its place in the larger context of culture. Even if one insists (idiosyncratically) that analytical philosophy should be considered to be a part of the corpus of the sciences (exact disciplines, that is), one cannot escape the ultimate criterion of significance: the sciences are significant in so far as they contribute to human culture. To reflect on the relation of philosophy to culture while examining the philosophy of Willard Quine is as good a place as any, for he represents a supreme achievement of 20th century rational philosophy, linguistically and logically oriented. He also embodies the grand vision of analytical philosophy that we can save the world through logic and (properly refined) language.

Every philosophy is based on some myth; another expression for the term 'myth' is: a general outlook on the world in a period. The myth of analytical philosophy is that of exactness; or logic and language combined. It is believed that through powerful means of the new logic and properly refined language we can formulate our questions properly and then resolve our problems satisfactorily; so that ultimately we should be able to arrive at the rational world in which the clarity of our understanding would be a sure guide to all our cognitive journeys, as well as the journeys into the land of morals and social problems.

Such, it seems, have been deeply held assumptions of the founding fathers of analytical philosophy: Russell, Wittgenstein, Carnap, Austin (in Poland: Łukasiewicz, Lesniewski, Kotarbinski, Ajdukiewicz—see H. Skolimowski, *Polish Analytical Philosophy, 1967*). This, almost messianic, role envisaged for philosophy inspired the minds and generated the conviction that philosophy, for the first time in history, will talk sense and create assertions and systems which are responsible and exact, in fact on a par with the exact sciences. Such was Russell's idea of scientific philosophy of 1910, and such was Łukasiewicz's program of the scientific system of philosophy of 1927; as well as Carnap's pronouncements of the late 1920's and early 1930's; as well as Austin's more subtle disquisitions of the 1950's according to which a 'clean' language will cleanse the field of morals.

The dilemma of analytical philosophy, conceived in cultural terms, could be expressed as follows: while we have developed a great capacity for analyzing particular leaves, we have somehow lost the corresponding capacity to see the trees and forests behind these particular leaves. Analytical philosophy has deliberately chosen to be piecemeal. As the result it now has become completely bogged down with small unrelated issues. The deeper we analyze and the more virtuosity we acquire in the act of analysis, the more detached we become from the original purpose of analysis. We have analyzed all 'ifs' and 'cans' and 'buts'. For J. L. Austin this analysis was meant to be a vehicle for arriving at the right understanding of morals. With our monumental mountain of analyses of moral concepts we have not brought a new understanding of morality. On the contrary (though quite inadvertently), this stupendous analytical scrutiny of moral propositions has brought about, as its consequence, moral relativism and, subtly following it, moral nihilism. On logical grounds it does not follow that a meticulous analysis of any sort or kind should be instrumental in bringing about nihilism. Moral life is not lived by logic alone. Preoccupation with semantic and logical scrutiny has caused a moral vacuum into which relativism and nihilism have crept quite naturally. Nature abhors vacuum; and so does morality. Analytical philosophers praise themselves for being tough-minded and rational. Tough-minded perhaps they are, to the point of being narrow minded. But their rationality seems to be of a rather limited kind. It is more an adulation of abstract features of classical physics and of formal logic than rationality *per se*. Sometimes this rationality is simply limted to logicality. Thus, it is not rationality in the comprehensive sense, conceived as the use of reason to arrive at enlightened conclusions, but rather a narrow quest dictated by the criteria of the ideology of science.

By uncritically accepting the predilections of the epoch, as formulated by the protagonists of science and material progress, analytical philosophy at-

tempted to re-make all philosophy in the image of science. Hence it has shared
with scientific culture an aversion for so-called unscientific prejudices and for
metaphysical humbug (which often simply meant non-empirical speculations);
it has insisted on being secular to the core and not infrequently it has been
aggressively atheistic; it has been much taken with the idea of exactness of
results to the point of making a fetish of it. Thus analytical philosophy's minimalist bias, its distrust of synthesis, of speculation, its hard rationalism, its
obsessive preoccupation with method, are all part and parcel of the ethos of
science and of scientific culture.

It is surprising indeed that those tough, *rational* minds could not see critically and reflect rationally on the prejudices of the epoch and swallowed whole-
sale the myths of the scientific *Weltanschauung*. But there it is. Let us clearly
see that not all analytical philosophers have been science-obsessed. Some
were—as for example many philosophers of the Vienna Circle. Some obviously were not—as for example many Oxford linguistic philosophers. But
nearly all were in the grip of the *ethos* of science. This can be best brought out
by the fact that philosophers from other schools who 'dared' to criticize the
whole formation were called 'irrational', 'antediluvian', 'remnants of the past'.
Obsessed with its peculiar kind of vision which shuns imagination, analytical
philosophers could not *see* that one cannot be a genuine philosopher without
speculation. Speculation means imagination. All philosophy is based on imagination.

The Myth of Exactness

Yet what distinguishes analytical philosophy and gives it strength, undreamt of
by previous philosophies, is the exactness of its results. So goes the argument.
Let us look at this argument more carefully. For it claims a great deal for
analytical philosophy, while subtly disparaging not only past philosophies but
also other realms of human thought. Can it be reasonably claimed that the
results of analytical philosophy—and its language—are uniformly exact while
the languages of other realms of human discourse are uniformly vague and
ambiguous? I wish to submit that this is not so. Poetry, even metaphysical
poetry, can be exact. Consider the line:

> "To see a world in a grain of sand."

This is quite an exact idea; while some notions and functions of analytical
philosophy are inherently ambiguous. Consider the notion of the existential
quantifier, so crucial to Quine's ontology; it has been a notion ridden with
ambiguity and endless difficulty.

All genuinely new philosophy is groping. Such was the case, among others,
with Wittgenstein's *Tractatus Logico-Philosophicus,* which has set the standards of exactness for generations. The philosophy of logical atomism pro-

pounded in the *Tractatus* has been an implicit inspiration for most analytical philosophers. For what can be more endearing to the rational mind than the idea that our entire ontology can be mapped on the matrix of a propositional calculus? Yet the doctrine of logical atomism, and the entire *Tractatus,* are full of riddles and exquisite ambiguities. This must be granted to Wittgenstein: he did not commit ordinary ambiguities. Consider the last statement of the *Tractatus;* "What we cannot speak about we must consign to silence." Or take the opening line of the *Tractatus:* "The world is all that is the case." Are those not highly evocative and delightfully ambiguous propositions?

The issue has far-reaching cultural consequences. *The mistaken pursuit of exactness has damaged the creative potential of the whole society.*

Let me try to defuse a possible misunderstanding at the outset. By attempting to examine critically the myth of exactness, we are not furnishing a license for vagueness; far from it. The Norwegian philosopher, Arne Naess while commenting on an earlier draft of this paper, and some of my other writings, has suggested that my style of writing seems to show *"self-imposed* vagueness as a war against 'positivism'." To which I replied, "Vagueness be damned. No one who has any respect for creative and intellectual faculties of the human mind would ever dream of indulging in deliberate vagueness. I also wonder what is so great about precision that so many people are still hung up on it, including you and me . . . . No, I do not try to cultivate vagueness. But with Aristotle I remember that every subject matter should be treated with the degree of precision that is proper for it. The mythical quest for precision is nothing but a mythical quest."

Yet chasing the chimera of exactness seems to have an irresistible attraction for us. Even now when we know that the field which was once providing the yardstick of precision is presently in shambles. I have in mind the present state of physics, that is, particle physics at its cutting edge. " 'Tis all in pieces, all coherence gone." The mathematical formulations of quantum physics cannot mask the fact that there is a pervasive ambiguity and a deep uncertainty as to what we are talking about. It is unreasonable to think that we can attain higher standards of precision in philosophy than those attained in hard sciences.

Indirectly we have touched on one of the perennial problems: what is philosophy? Philosophy has always been in this unenviable position that it has had to define its scope and substance continuously. At present, as many times before, we are not certain how to define the field. The notion is no longer held with any conviction that through 'clean' language we can cleanse all of the messy stables of the present tottering world.

Analytical philosophy was once called *the* revolution in philosophy. As with so many revolutions, this one was also an abortive attempt to start a new millenium. After the revolution there inevitably comes the period of stability, and then one of stagnation. The second and third generations are short-changed. They only hear the tales of the revolution. They participate in none.

The present generation of analytical philosophers (to use Kuhn's language) is doing 'normal science' within philosophy; they are merely technicians, elaborating studiously and meticulously various forms of propositions—which has become an art for its own sake—and quite oblivious of the fact that the whole venture was meant to be a great adventure; was meant to bring about new forms of understanding; and following it new forms of rational governance of society. Professor Quine was fortunate enough to be a part of a revolution. His formative years were lived in the period of excitement when the belief in the 'messianic' role of analytical philosophy was strongly held.

Rudolf Carnap epitomized the 'revolutionary' positivist position in its purest form. He may have been the only one, among the great ones, to adhere to the pristine version of logical empiricism to the end of his days. Nearly all founding fathers of logical empiricism (and indirectly of analytical philosophy) renounced it, one by one, as too narrow and too constraining; really betraying the great tradition of philosophy.

That philosophy must be seen as a larger enterprise is now accepted by most analytical philosophers themselves. But so often they cannot do justice to this conviction because the confining rigour of their training pushes them back to analytical scrutiny of propositions. And here is a real dilemma: a certain form of tyranny seems to be killing their philosophical imagination. Although analytical philosophy has cast its perilous shadow over a large part of our century, particularly in the Anglo-Saxon countries, it is not entirely true to say that it has been pre-eminent. The most important philosophical series of the 20th century, the *Library of Living Philosophers,* is eloquent evidence that the traditional conception of philosophy has persisted throughout: no philosopher has been honored in the series who did not struggle with perennial philosophical problems.

Yet exactitude is an appealing concept. Its defenses can be numerous. One of the strong arguments in its favor is that exactitude is not a goal but a means. We want to be responsible for what we maintain and how we express ourselves. Exactitude is a safeguard and an expression of this responsibility. So much can be granted. But the argument must not stop here. We must further ask: responsiblity for what and with regard to whom? Is it not the case that Plato, Aristotle, Kant (even the derided Hegel and Heidegger) wanted to be responsible as well? Furthermore, is it really responsible to produce hundreds over hundreds of articles, aspiring to 'exact' results, which are simply repetitions of each other, which (it is sad to say) remain largely unread and which (again apologies to many) are such boring stuff anyway? I am of course not talking of Quine himself here but of his numerous followers. No doubt we are touching a sensitive spot here. *Rational* philosophers should not get too easily offended for this would only indicate their emotional vulnerability not their supreme rationality. If philosophy is a critical enterprise, then we should not be afraid of criticism by others, for criticism is a vehicle of enlightment as it often points out the path of improvement. I venture to suggest that little will remain of 20th century analytical philosophy in centuries to come. By the 25th century those thousands upon thousands of 'exact' articles will be swept to oblivion. What will remain? Not much. Perhaps half a dozen pieces from the entire analytical tradition.

The Crisis of Atomistic Understanding

Analytical philosophers are no dummies; often indeed sharp and brilliant minds. What is therefore the reason for their submission to forms of thought which cannot possibly survive? At the heart of the problem lies not the plethora of detailed specialized studies which are so repetitious. The problem has its roots in our culture which, as it were, compels us to accept a certain kind of vision. Expressed more simply: the problem is that the *ethos of science* has been imposed on philosophy. As we said before, analytical philosophy shares with science the conviction that the way to ultimate understanding is via smaller and smaller units, until we arrive at ultimately small units. Whether we call these atomic facts or by some other name; whether we are more inclined toward empiricism or to language analysis, the overall thrust is the same—a truly Cartesian imperative—divide and rule, until you arrive at the indivisible; when you have reached rock bottom, start reconstructing out of the ultimate units.

This whole strategy has now visibly failed. It has demonstrably failed in science. The search for the ultimate elementary particles has not led us to the final bricks of the universe, but to the proliferation of entities beyond necessity. The discovery (some say invention) of the staggering number of subatomic particles has led to the view that perhaps these are not particles in the physical sense at all. If so, then the entire quest of anchoring matter in indissoluble hard bricks is ending up in elusive quanta of energy. The whole model of explanation has dissolved under our very eyes. Physicists nowadays talk about *quarks,* (a 'particle' which can never be seen or experienced in any human way) as the underlying substratum of all the physical world. Other strange notions and entities are proposed which are not only boggling our imagination but, more importantly, have no empirical attributes whatsoever. In short, physicists no longer believe that there are ultimate particles or that there is any rock bottom. Rather they talk about the universe as the eternal dance of Shiva. This is a startingly new notion as compared with the Newtonian, mechanistic metaphor. The overall philosophical conclusion is that the atomistic structure of comprehension has collapsed.

In so far as the whole strategy of Newtonian (atomistic) science has failed, in so far as the atomistic structure of comprehension has collapsed, analytical philosophy, participating in the dream of ultimate *analytical* understanding, is a relative failure, too; not by itself, but in virtue of sharing, with Cartesian-Newtonian science, a specific model of comprehension. The consequences of this are enormous and so far not fully grasped either by science or by philosophy. These consequences, however, are grasped by a new breed of (non-academic) philosophers, who cut across all traditional boundaries and try to comprehend in a new way this new chapter of human history. They are occasionally called pop-physicists and pop-philosophers and subtly derided by the Establishment for not being rational enough, while the rationality of the Establishment has become an instrument of incomprehension.

Let us underscore some main points. The relentless drive of modern physics to find the ultimate constituents of matter has resulted in something else—in undermining the very idea of elementary particles, and indirectly in undermining the whole program. True enough, the real search nowadays is for a unified theory which would overcome the present conceptual and ontological crisis. But this search is still guided by the models of particle physics (or quantum physics). The newest experimental results (showing that protons do not decay) seem to suggest that the entire quest for a unified theory—within the existing parameters—may be misguided. From the epistemological point of view this is devastating.

The present crisis of particle physics is at the same time the crisis of atomistic comprehension: not only in physics, but also in all other branches of knowledge in which this form of comprehension has become dominant, including analytical philosophy. Indirectly, this is the crisis of modern Western rationality as based on science; consequently, this is also the crisis of the rational philosophy of the 20th century.

This crisis spells out an eclipse of scientific culture. The rational reconstruction of the world, according to the tenets of classical science, has simply failed. Even less viable appears the logical reconstruction of the world along the lines of Carnap's *Der Logische Aufbau der Welt*. One should qualify these assertions and add that the rational reconstruction along the mechanistic-deterministic-empiricist view of the world of the Laplacian, Lockean, Carnapian kind did not work. Every new reconstruction will be rational, although undoubtedly within new boundaries of rationality; (see H. Skolimowski, "Evolutionary Rationality," *PSA 1974*, edited by R. S. Cohen et al.). The 'rational' grid imposed on the whole culture has created depersonalized, objective, sterile institutions which reify human beings and markedly contribute to the malaise of the century. Institutions of learning, including universities, have become factories for producing morally desensitized technicians who go to the world with the technical know-how and no moral sense, and who in turn further contribute to the atomization and reification of society and nature. Individual human beings caught in the iron grid of this 'rationality' rebel against it and go to the other extreme—*ir*rationality. The flourishing of cults and a blatant rejection of rationality in our times is but a backlash against 'rationality' which mutilates us and diminishes us as human beings. Hence lies the tragedy of our 'rational age'.

In so far as analytical philosophy has contributed to the *climate* of scientific culture and to the preponderance of narrow rationality, analytical philosophers must be prepared to bear a part of the responsibility.

When seen from the perspective of the last two millennia, the contribution of analytical philosophy appears unimpressive, mainly because the whole program of atomistic comprehension is in a quandary. And also because scientific culture, instead of creating—as it had promised—the epoch of universal peace, prosperity, and enlightment, has produced alienated and atomized consumers, living in continuous anxiety; a people not blessed by the Lord but rather cursed by a Demon. The two failures combined, epistemological and cultural, make the achievement of our century, and the role of analytical philosophy in it, very dubious indeed. The failure of scientific culture automatically transfers to analytical philosophy as it has been its guardian and expositor. As we suggested before, there is no valid appraisal of philosophy in itself. Philosophy is a par excellence part of human culture and must be judged accordingly. While emphasizing that analytical philosophy has been an integral part of scientific culture, I will try to show that Willard Quine has been a magnificent repository and also an unwitting victim of this scientific culture in precisely allowing his philosophy to be guided and determined by the criteria of scientific validity.

Quine and Scientific Culture

Willard Quine has been hailed as a supreme practitioner of exact philosophy. Yet Quine can be tantalizingly evasive about the ultimate positions he holds. We are therefore forced to reconstruct them from various clues. In *Word and Object,* as well as in his other writings, Quine emphasizes over and again— which is in keeping with his conventionalism—that we are at liberty to choose among various conceptual frameworks that are available to us. But when one reads him very carefully his bias beomes apparent: he forces on us one particular framework within which truth and meaning must be determined. It is science, according to Quine, that determines our conceptual and philosophical destinies. Let us illustrate this by a quote from *Word and Object:*

> What reality is like is the business of scientists, in the broadest sense, painstakingly summarized; and what there is, what is real is part of that question. The question how we know what there is is simply part of the question . . . of the evidence for truth about the world. The last arbiter is so called scientific method, however amorphous. (Chapter 1, "Language and Truth," pp. 22f.)

This formulation is surprisingly weak and really totally unsatisfactory: scientific method should be our final arbiter, although Quine admits that it is an amorphous entity! Can we talk sensibly about the arbiter of truth, when this arbiter is amorphous? In other contexts, Quine takes considerable pains to salvage scientific method without once defining it precisely. What kind of science does he have in mind? Science has in our day become as amorphous an entity as scientific method itself (see especially Paul Feyerabend, *Against Method,* and his other writings.) On the surface we are encouraged to entertain a variety of conceptual schemes. This epistemological pluralism is part of our ontological freedom. But what is the use of this freedom if finally we must reduce ourselves to one scheme? On the ultimate level we are to be guided by the criteria of science. The whole strategy appears to be another exercise in crude reductionism after which scientism triumphant rules supreme.

For all Quine's novelty, originality, and independence of mind, his thinking seems to be forever moulded by logical empiricism. Perhaps Carnap's influence on him has been too lasting. It seems that ultimately, though not explicitly, Quine endorses a form of traditional empiricist *Weltanschauung* with observational entities to be grasped and established by science—all of this in spite of his own trenchant criticism of the dogmas of empiricism.

Let me illustrate this point by another formulation from *Word and Object,* which again strikes me as surprisingly weak in spite of the verbal virtuosity with which it is stated. After having asserted that truth attributions are made from the point of view of the surrounding body of theory, Quine asks whether this irrevocably dooms us to relativism. "Not so", he responds. "The saving consideration is that we continue to take seriously our own particular aggregate science, our own particular world-theory or loose total fabric of quasi-theories, whatever it may be. Unlike Descartes, we own and use our beliefs of the moment, even in the midst of philosophizing, until by what is vaguely called scientific method we change them here and there for the better" (p. 25).

So it is science again "and what is vaguely called scientific method" that are the arbiters. When I reread these statements lately, I could hardly believe that such a fine mind as Quine's would put himself at the mercy of such weak formulations. This is particularly striking as Quine knows that frameworks of science—and the observational entities postulated by them—may be circular, although he euphemistically calls them "reciprocal" (p. 16).

Actually Quine's idea that we use our beliefs of the moment—even in the midst of our philosophizing and attempt to change them here and there as we go along (by what is vaguely called scientific method)—is reminiscent of Popper's program. Karl Popper contended (*The Logic of Scientific Discovery,* 1934, 1959) that our foundations are piles driven into a swamp. From time to time these foundations begin to totter. At such times we drive new piles into the swamp. While in Popper this metaphor is beautifully supported by a whole epistemology, based on the idea of conjectures and refutations, I do not see any such support system in Quine's philosophy. In more recent times Popper himself seem to have moved away from his science inspired epistemology, partly as the result of the debate over T. S. Kuhn's *The Structure of Scientific Revolutions*. This debate seems to have undermined every tenet held about the nature of science, including its rationality and, of course, including the alleged invariance of scientific method.

The human mind is a continuous enigma, including the rational mind. Why should the best philosophical minds of the 20th century so deliberately imprison themselves in a sort of cage? Equally fascinating is the question: Why were philosophers of the Middle Ages so obsessed with religion? The answer to both questions is similar: their culture made it so. The conditioning effects of culture, its mythos, aspirations and visions, hypnotize, as it were, not only laymen and ordinary TV watchers but also philosophers. In our times the scientific *Weltanschauung* and the mythos of science became embedded in our thinking. Professor Quine is a case in point. Hypnotized by scientific culture, he reiterates, in his elegant way, that we must look to science for the ultimate criteria of validity of our conceptual schemes; while nowadays science is tottering and in fact full of metaphysical speculations.

I remember the excitement with which Quine's *From a Logical Point of View* was greeted in Warsaw in 1956. Quine was read and extensively discussed in Poland in the mid-1950s and was hailed as one of the world's leading philosophers. Each of the essays was thoroughly analyzed in Kotarbinski's seminars and much praise was awarded to Quine. He was clearly an inspiration and a pathmaker. Even more was expected of Quine's next book. When it came out in 1960 *(Word and Object)*, it was felt to be a disappointment. And people did not exactly know why. Somehow the promise of his earlier work was not fulfilled. Radical conventionalism did not translate itself into a new philosophical proposition of some lasting value.

Word and Object strikes me now as somewhat labored, as if Quine did not enjoy writing it, as if the passion that inspired *From a Logical Point of View* was no longer there. Also, the main thesis of the book, concerning the indeterminacy of translations, is not that world-shattering. *Word and Object,* and Quine's subsequent writings, seem to represent a retreat from commitment. There is no new development. Indeed one finds a retreat from earlier bold pluralism of radical conventionalism and a retrenchment into monistic physicalism which verges on 19th century scientism.

One could speculate why Quine's philosophy has consolidated itself in such a conservative mould. Perhaps the reason is that those whom the Establishment enshrines are elevated at a price to be paid later. What Daniel Bell has been in sociology, Willard Quine has been in philosophy—a pillar of the Establishment. The subtlety of the game is subtle indeed. Once you join the Establishment, you adjust your views subconsciously to the unwritten demands of the status quo. Might this be the reason why Professor Quine's once exciting phi-

losophy has become a rendering—in sophisticated philosophical terms—of the
ideology of science, which, after all, is the pervading ideology of the status
quo? Therefore, God save us from being too successful while alive, for then
we are pitted against impossible odds.

Has Philosophy Lost Contact with People?

We may wonder how Quine's ideas on the nature of philosophy are expressed
in most recent years. His latest opus *Theories and Things* (1981) tellingly reiterates his bias in favor of scientific philosophy. One essay (of the 1981 opus)
deserves our special attention. Its title is the same as the heading of this section:
"Has Philosophy Lost Contact with People?" One of my philosopher friends,
when he read the question, said emphatically "Does this have to be asked?"
Yet in the first part of his essay Quine seems to suggest that philosophy has
not lost contact with people; at least that present scientific philosophy is continuous with the best of traditional philosophy. In the act Quine says such strange
things as "Plato was among other things a physicist." In the latter part of the
essay Quine seems to ascertain that this contact is not important anyway, that
the question may be of little significance. He explicitly states: "I think of organic chemistry; I recognize its importance, but I am not curious about it, nor
do I see why the layman should care about much of what concerns me in
philosophy. If instead of having been called upon to perform in the British
television series 'Men of Ideas' I had been consulted on its feasibility, I should
have expressed doubt." (p. 193)

This is very curious. And curious indeed is Quine's language. It would
seem that Willard Quine was called upon to perform at the BBC without being
properly consulted. I was not aware that one is forced to perform at the BBC
even if one has grievous doubts about the value of the exercise. Whom is Mr.
Quine kidding? Are we supposed to be so obtuse that we do not see the soph-
istry of his statements?

Finally, towards the end of this essay, Quine does say explicitly what he
thinks of philosophy and, so to speak, spills the beans. I shall quote the whole
passage, in order to preserve the integrity of the context and to demonstrate the
incredible narrowness of his views:

> What I have been discussing under the head of philosophy is what I call scientific
> philosophy, old and new, for it is the discipline whose latter-day trend Adler crit-
> icized. By this vague heading I do not exclude philosophical studies of moral and
> aesthetic values. Some such studies, of an analytical cast, can be scientific in spirit.
> They are apt, however, to offer little in the way of inspiration or consolation. The
> student who majors in philosophy primarily for spiritual comfort is misguided and
> is probably not a very good student anyway, since intellectual curiosity is not what
> moves him.
> Inspirational and edifying writing is admirable, but the place for it is the novel,

the poem, the sermon, or the literary essay. Philosophers in the professional sense have no peculiar fitness for it. Neither have they any peculiar fitness for helping to get society on an even keel, though we should all do what we can. What just might fill these perpetually crying needs is wisdom: *sophia* yes, *philosophia* not necessarily. (p. 193)

What a one sided and cripplingly narrow statement it is! In the domain of philosophy, as Quine conceives it, there is no room for moral insight, or aesthetic insight, or metaphysical insight; indeed all metaphysical speculation is barred. What is allowed and what matters is analytical scrutiny. By Quine's criterion, the major philosophers of the past, Socrates, Plato, Kant (to say nothing of Pascal, Nietzsche, and Marx), do not amount to much; indeed, are almost dismissed as philosophers; an attitude typical of the early logical empiricists.

Let us reflect on the middle part of Quine's peroration. It seems to me highly irresponsible to say that the student who seeks spiritual nourishment in philosophy "is probably not a very good student anyway, since intellectual curiosity is not what moves him." Plato had quite a different conception of "intellectual curiosity"; for him the search for enlightenment and for spiritual nourishment were aspects of each other. To ever suggest that a student who is on a spiritual quest is not a very good student anyway is to divert the best students from the path of wisdom to the path of technicism.

Our students are vulnerable and suceptible to influence, as Professor Quine was as a young man. Being brought up in a morally desensitized environment, being simply brainwashed by the ideology of technicism, they suppress their moral impulses and spiritual aspects of their being, and pretend that these aspects have disappeared altogether. But the history of human cultures is abundant in evidence demonstrating the spiritual nature of man. One neatly contrived philosophical system of an excessive logical purity does not change that history nor does it change the nature of man. Yet, when the process of analytical purging is carried out to the point of spiritual castration, a great deal of damage is done to human beings. We are so often victims of the tyranny of language.

I must question Quine's wisdom on yet another issue, namely, when he insists that philosophers do not have any peculiar fitness for helping to get society on an even keel. The reverse seems to be true. Philosophers are peculiarly fit for this task. After all, they got society into the variety of present predicaments. We are now reaping the bitter harvest of those great philosophical visions that were enunciated in the 17th century: "Knowledge is power" (Bacon); "Nature is there to be quantified" (Galileo, Newton); "Divide everything into smaller and smaller components" (Descartes). Philosophers can help society to seek alternative visions within the scope of which our problems can be addressed at their root causes and not at the level of symptoms. What is presently at stake is the whole intellectual formation, perhaps the future of the whole society being *systematically misguided* by the lack of any guidance, or a wrong kind of guidance. Analytical guidance is an inadequate one (in an important sense, a wrong guidance) for our social, moral, existential, and ecological problems, which require a *normative* approach in some kind of global framework. Great traditional philosophers knew this truth very well.

Professor Quine drastically separates *sophia,* from *philosophia* and in this way does violence to both. In so doing he almost seems to be oblivious of the origin of *philosophia.* At his point Quine's interpretations are really amputations. The result is belittling and downcasting of traditional philosophical wisdom and a perversion of the traditional philosophical vision.

Present scientific philosophy is in a dire predicament. What is so often presented as its forte, namely its exactness, under close scrutiny turns out to be sterility. Willard Van Orman Quine may be considered the archbishop of present analytical philosophers. Through his authority and uncompromising technicism, which excludes important metaphysical, moral, and social problems of our times, he is partly responsible for the climate that holds so many philosophers in the analytical cul-de-sac and prevents them from seeking radical alternatives.

While reflecting on some of my pronouncements about Professor Quine, I notice that I seem to be harsh and uncompromisingly critical. Criticism for nihilistic purposes is not my aim. As a young man I had a great deal of admiration of Quine's lucid mind and his new philosophical ideas; I still do. Yet, when writing about him I cannot confine myself to analytical niceties "while the forest is burning", while society is being abandoned, (in a sense systematically misguided) by philosophers' retreat from commitment. I happen to be one of those philosophers who believe in a larger social mission of philosophy. Hence, reluctantly, I have had to throw the gauntlet at Professor Quine's great authority. In so doing, I do not mean to insinuate that Professor Quine is exerting an ideological party control and keeping philosophers in line. No single philosopher has the power to do that. The ethos of the whole scientific culture, through its numerous institutions, in a subtle but pervasive way, does it.

Jan Łukasiewicz, one of the earliest advocates of the *system* of scientific philosophy (1927), labored for many years to construct such a system. In 1946 he finally gave up, and he said:

> I cannot provide such a system. I do not believe that it is possible today to construct a philosophical system which would fulfill the requirements of scientific method. (J. Łukasiewicz, *Selected Papers,* p. 114)

One should be entitled to cherish one's dream—even if reality does not conform to it. We cannot blame Professor Quine for having his dream of a scientific philosophy. But there is a time for all things, and a time to recognize that a dream was but a dream, as Łukasiewicz did; otherwise the dream may become a delusion. If this delusion has the power to influence others and make their lives into its image, this then becomes a dangerous delusion.

Now a major objection to my entire discourse may be stated as follows: "You have missed the whole point. The locus of analytical philosophy, its genius and its peculiarity lie not in its 'scientific' character but in its special ways of handling *language;* and in the results obtained through the new linguistic sensitivity."

I shall examine this claim in the next part of this paper. During the course of my arguments, I will try to show that even if we examine analytical philosophy through the locus of language, we shall still find this philosophy to be profoundly influenced by the ethos of scientific culture. For our language has been moulded in the image of science and is pervaded by the ethos of science.

II

The Vicissitudes of Language Within Analytical Philosophy

Aldous Huxley reminds us that language is a cultural force par excellence; a living substance of culture; detached from it and mummified in abstract logical categories, it atrophies and degenerates as an instrument of human understanding. Here is Huxley on language (in the Foreword to *Mystics as a Force for Social Change,* by S. Ghose):

> Every culture is rooted in a language. No speech, no culture. Without an instrument of symbolic expression and communication, we should be Yahoos, lacking the rudiments of civilization. It is because he starts by being *Homo loquax* that man is capable of becoming *Homo sapiens.* But this is a world in which everything has to be paid for. Language makes it possible for us to be more intelligent and better behaved than dumb brutes. But whereas the dumb brutes are merely bestial, we loquacious humans, who can talk ouselves into pure reason and almost angelic virtue, can also talk ourselves down into being devils, imbeciles and lunatics.

Language is the universe. If this claim is slightly exaggerated, it only means to highlight the extreme versatility and power of language. Yet there are limits to language, particularly in determining our ontology and the structure of reality, both outside and inside. Though uniquely tied to language, analytical philosophy is ridden with paradoxes in attempting to demonstrate its prowess as *sui generis* language philosophy.

In the second part of this essay I shall attempt to show that by assuming language to be all important and by pushing the inquiry into language to its limits, analytical philosophy ended with a paradox, as it has inadvertently proven that language is not of paramount importance—by language alone we cannot solve any major problem, philosophical or otherwise.

Secondly, I will attempt to argue that specific achievements of analytical philosophy—as uniquely rooted in language—cannot be specified.

Thirdly, I attempt to show that the early promise of (Quine's) conventionalism remains largely unfulfilled.

We have deified language, and then found that it is a deity of a rather limited power. Since this aspect of analytical philosophy is not sufficiently recognized, let me underscore the paradox, which applies to all three constituents of analytical philosophy—rationality, logic, and language. By pushing each to its limits and beyond, by assuming that they are all important, we have discovered the limits, and most importantly, the fact that they are not that important. If they were, we should have resolved our philosophical problems; philosophy would have been in a flourishing, not a stagnant state; we should have been excited with philosophy and not bored with it; we should have earned the appreciation of society, not its disdain.

Thus, the overall achievement of analytical philosophy is both positive and negative: it has shown the power of language (and of logic) and inadvertently it exhibited the limits of both. Analytical philosophy has made us strikingly aware how elusive the relationship between language and reality is; how elusive the reality of language itself is. We witness here what I call the paradox of achievement. We have attempted to establish a kind of linguistic monism: we attempted to ground all in language. Instead, we have proved that this is not possible. By going to the extremes, we have shown the program to be untenable.

As I already have mentioned, we witness a similar situation in subatomic physics. The program was to establish a firm foundation for the existence of matter as based on *ultimate* particles. In the process, we have shown that the very idea of *ultimate particles* is a fiction. The program was shown to be untenable, but only *after* we have gone to the extreme and accomplished (in a sense) more than we had desired. Hence the paradox of achievement. The last word on the nature of language and its role and function in philosophy, and in particular its role in conveying the variety of realities, has not yet been spoken. It seems to me, however, that the new knowledge of language will come with new philosophical insights, with new bursts of consciousness, not through the grinding scrutiny of present analytical models.

I have said that specific achievements of analytical philosophy (as rooted in language) are difficult to enumerate. My question is: what kind of singular achievements were accomplished through new elucidations of language performed by analytical philosophy? Which of these results may be viewed as a permanent contribution of analytical philosophy to the history of philosophy? Quine writes in *Theories and Things* (1981):

> Now philosophy, where it was continuous with science, progressed too. There as elsewhere in science, progress exposed relevant distinctions and connections that have been passed over in former times. There as elsewhere, problems and propo-

stions were analyzed into constituents which, viewed in isolation, must seem uninteresting or worse. (p. 191)

Yet nothing is said of what has been accomplished through these distinctions.

When Einstein articulated his famous equation $E = mc^2$, this led to a profound conceptual change in our outlook on the world (it also made a profound difference on the level of our practical lives, as we live now in anxiety of the possiblity of a nuclear holocaust). When Bohr and others came up with the planetary conception of the atom, this again led to far-reaching consequences, which resulted in our new understanding of physical reality and perhaps also in our understanding of the nature of all reality. When Einstein pointed out that there was an incoherence built into the notion of "simultaneity", this again led to important conceptual and philosophical consequences. Now, what comparable achievements are there in analytical philosophy?

Yes, Tarski's formulation of the classical concept of truth in his famous essay *Pojecie prawdy w jezykach nauk dedukcyjnych (The Concept of Truth in Formalized Languages)*, 1933, may be such an achievement. Gödel's undecidability theory belongs to the realm of mathematics. Let us look closer at Tarski's achievement, which was formulated in 1933, in the heyday of analytical philosophy, when prospects seemed boundless and further achievements leading to scientific philosophy were expected, indeed taken for granted.

What of Tarski's achievement fifty years later? His concept of truth, which beautifully and semi-formally articulated the paradigm of classical physics, based on the correspondence notion of truth, is now seriously challenged by the New Physics. The whole empiricist scheme that there is the world "out there" as stable as a rock, and that we are "in here" with our scientific apparatus and concepts, which uniquely, objectively, and adequately grasp, isomorphise, and express what is out there; and the contention that our theories and statements correspond to reality, as they faithfully describe it—this whole scheme has collapsed, or at least is seriously undermined and in doubt.

What we have experienced during the last two decades, as the result of new insights of the New Physics is a partial collapse of the classical or correspondence theory of truth. If so, then Tarski's achievement represents a beautiful formalization of a concept that no longer holds. If we take science seriously, especially if we take the cutting edge of present science seriously, then we must realize that we are in another universe, and another kind of correspondence must be conceived of, different from that of classical physics. In the words of the astrophysicist J. A. Wheeler:

> The universe does not exist "out there" independent of us. We are inescapably involved in bringing about that which appears to be happening. We are not only observers. We are participators. In some strange sense this is a *participatory universe*. (From: "The Participatory Universe", Gordon Mills Lecture on Science and the Humanities, University of Texas at Austin, March 24, 1982)

If we fail to take notice of this changed universe and continue our researches and analyses, as if the old empiricist paradigm were still holding, we betray the very scientific spirit of analytical philosophy and make a mockery of its pride in being "exact" and *au courant* with science. In the process, we engage in merely scholastic activities whose universe of discourse may very well be empty.

Will it be sacrilegious to suggest that a great deal of analytical philosophy consists of elucidations and articulations of various tenets and assumptions of classical empiricism, which upon close inspection reveal themselves as a merely scholastic process in the sense mentioned above? If such is the case, then the suspicion may arise that analytical philosophy has been a pursuit of refined tools to bolster a bad, outdated metaphysics—empiricism.

Quine, alas, is not free from this charge. The bulk of his analysis—in spite of his trenchant criticism of empiricism in earlier days—is steeped in the empiricist world view. At times his position seems to be very curious indeed, almost unbelievable, as he goes on (in recent publications) refining and justifying his empiricist predilections, and then innocently notices that, after all, New Physics seems to invalidate those empiricist tenets. And he leaves it at that. A striking example is his essay on "Facts of the Matter" (1979), which is a virtuoso performance, a tremendous intellectual feat—in the name of what? Of the primacy of bodies, a kind of somatic monism. (Incidentally, T. Kotarbinski proposed and articulated this kind of monism in great detail in the late 1920s, and then abandoned it later as untenable; see, H. Skolimowski, *Polish Analytical Philosophy*). Quine writes:

> What are posited as objects for the terms to refer to will be, primarily, objects that are counted indentical under changes of perspective. *This explains the primacy of bodies* [italics mine, H.S.]. If clarity can be ascribed to things as well as to words, then bodies are things at their clearest. If enquiry is to begin with what is clear, then let us begin as physicalists. (In: *Essays on the Philosophy of W. V. Quine*, Shahan, Swoyer, eds., p. 159)

But the era of pure faith in pansomatism (Kotarbinski) or any other materialist or linguistic monism is gone. Curiously and significantly, in the course of his essay Quine undermines his earlier somatic monism by saying that,

> When bodies came first into my story, I warned that they, even they, were theoretical. All theoretical entities are here strictly on sufferance; and all entities are theoretical. What were observational were not terms but observation sentences. Sentences, in their truth or falsity, are what run deep; ontology is by the way. (Ibid., p. 165)

These sentences are riddled with ambiguity. What does it mean that "ontology is by the way", or that "all theoretical entities are here strictly on sufferance"? Quine never explains. Instead, in a soft way, he continues to push the doctrine of physicalism. Quine on physicalism:

What now of physicalism? To profess materialism, after all this, would seem grotesquely inappropriate; but physicalism, reasonably reformulated, retains its vigor and validity. Our last previous formulation came to this: there is no difference in the world without a difference in the number or arrangement of trajectories of atoms. But if we make the drastic ontological move last contemplated, all physical objects go by the board—atoms, particles, all—leaving only pure sets. The principle of physicalism must thereupon be formulated by reference not to physical objects but to physical vocabulary. Let us take stock of the vocabulary. (Ibid., p. 165)

This is Quine at his conceptual best and at his most agonizing. Does he mean to equate physicalism with pure sets? What kind of physicalism is that? A curious entity it is—physicalism reduced to pure sets. "All physical objects go by the board . . . ." In the full maturity of his mind, Quine owes us more than this kind of explanation.

The somersaults that I find in the passage just quoted are—as far as I can judge—quite characteristic of the last decade of Quine's writings: always brilliant, crisp, fascinating to read. But there is a sense of ad hocism in the whole enterprise; to which I shall return in the summary of this essay.

I do not share the view of some (Roger F. Gibson in *The Philosophy of W. V. Quine,* for example) who profess to have found a systematic unity in Quine's philosophy, as well as an expression of a post-positivist empiricism. My reading of Quine, on the contrary, shows ad hocism (performed with a great bravado) and an adherence to logical positivist tenets with its tendency toward somatic physicalism; all of which is at times reduced to pure sets; which would suggest a new kind of logical atomism.

In "Facts of the Matter" Quine also asserts that his physicalism admits "no minds as additional entities". This is at least sharply and unequivocally stated. "No minds as additional entities". In so far as the idea is clear, let us see whether it is valid. In the light of the New Physics, it is demonstrably not valid. To put the matter otherwise, there is no such thing as knowledge without minds. There is no such thing as language without minds. Mind is an evolutionary phenomenon which we must accept, if we are to understand anything of the human condition, of human knowledge, and of "pure sets". Mind can look at matter, but matter cannot look at matter without mind. Quine says that ontology is not what mainly matters, "ontology is by the way". But what does finally matter? Something must matter. In my opinion the existence of the mind matters, for without minds there is no knowledge, no language, no argument; and according to the New Physics (and Wheeler's conception of the participatory universe)—no reality. Quine does not seem to have any *evolutionary* dimension to his philosophy. Logicians usually don't.

Quine is aware of some of the important consequences of New Physics, *and* he seems to know that it vitally undermines his ontological schemes, as he writes:

Atoms have since given way to a bewildering variety of elementary particles. Latter-day physicists have been finding even that the very notion of particle is inappropriate at points; paradoxes of identification and individuation arise. There are indications that the utility of the particle model, the extrapolation of the primordial body into the very small, is now marginal at best. A field theory may be more to the point: a theory in which various states are directly ascribed in varying degrees to various regions of space-time. Thus at last bodies themselves go by the board—bodies that were the primordial posits, the paradigmatic objects most clearly and perspicuously beheld. *Sic transit gloria mundi.* (Ibid., p. 164)

When one reads carefully these statements, one is astonished by the conceptual jumble—which, admittedly, is expressed with finesse and adroitness.

Perhaps we should take the clue from *Sic transit gloria mundi* and move to an altogether new philosophy. For the conceptual epicycles Quine offers do not seem to lead us anywhere.

I have selected two important issues (physicalism and the alleged nonexistence of minds) from a recent article of Quine, in order to show that his pervasive brilliance is accompanied by disturbing ambiguity; not the ambiguity of particular expressions, but of the philosophical conclusions. This I also find in Quine's latest book *Theories and Things* (1981), particularly in the leading essay "Things and Their Place in Theories". I shall not test the reader's patience by quoting lengthy passages. But I must notice that I find this recent exposition of Quine's philosophy equally unsatisfactory. Toward the end of the essay Quine finally comes with some clear assertions, which reaffirm ontological realism: "my unswerving belief in external things—people, nerve endings, sticks, stones. This I reaffirm." This unswerving belief of his, Quine calls "robust realism". But how is it to be reconciled with the barren scene that I have just been depicting? [—the inability of empiricism to resolve the various epistemological and ontological problems, i.e., providing the rational reconstruction of the world from sense data]. The answer, Quine says, "is naturalism: the recognition that it is within science itself, and not in some prior philosophy, that reality is to be identified and described." (Ibid., p. 21)

We just have a new label "robust realism". However, the *legitimacy* of this realism is to be derived from science. "It is within science itself . . . that reality is to be identified and described." To say this in 1980 is for me a sad abdication of the philosophical responsibility to re-think *de novo* the whole predicament of science. It is again the case of asserting an almost blind faith in science, at the time when science is experiencing one of its deepest crises ever. We are all hypnotized by our culture, and as I argued in Part I, analytical philosophers are no exception.

The Unfulfilled Promise of Conventionalism

Quine's radical conventionalism was an exciting doctrine when it was first formulated. Yet the early promise of conventionalism has remained unfulfilled.

Let me explore this point. The original doctrine of conventionalism was formulated by Le Roy and Poincaré, as the result of the emergence of non-Euclidean geometries and new unexplained phenomena—such as radiation—which classical physics could not cope with. The thesis of the early conventionalism was modest, namely, that scientific problems cannot be solved by reference to empirical reality alone. With regard to some problems, we must introduce certain conventions first, which, together with empirical data, will lead us to a solution. The solutions obtained, therefore, derive partly from data of empirical reality and partly from linguistic or conceptual conventions, which we accept prior to our gathering of empirical data. The role of language, and particularly of axioms of formal systems, began to be emphasized and started to assume a position of importance.

The 19th-century conventionalists did not go the whole way, did not claim that language uniquely determines the nature and structure of reality; and that by adopting different languages, we create different pictures of reality. This radicalized form of conventionalism was to emerge in the 20th century. It actually emerged from three independent sources: from Benjamin Lee Whorf, Kazimierz Ajdukiewicz in Poland, and Willard Van Orman Quine. Whorf's major book, *Language, Truth, and Reality,* is a collection of essays, which were originally published between the years 1933 and 1941. Perhaps the most significant of these essays was "Science and Linguistics" of 1939, in which the so-called linguistic relativity principle was formulated and proclaimed. This principle holds that "All observers are not led by the same physical evidence to the same picture of the universe, unless their linguistic backgrounds are similar, or can be in some way calibrated." (Op. cit., p. 214) Some of the consequences of this linguistic relativity principle were: "We dissect nature along lines laid down by our native languages." (p. 213) "Every language contains its own metaphysics . . . each language performs this artificial chopping up of the continuous spread and flow of existence in a different way." (p. 253)

Whorf's hypothesis evoked a great deal of interest and discussion in the 1960s. It was tested in various ways, and it was pronounced by many professional linguists as "unproved". However, it has not been disproved, either: if only because we had to handle it by means of a language, which itself would be a biassed interpreter, not an impartial judge.

Now, in 1934 Kazimierz Ajdukiewicz proclaimed his conception of radical conventionalism in the paper "Das Weltbild und die Begriffsapparatur" (The Picture of the World and the Conceptual Apparatus), originally published in *Erkenntnis,* the mouthpiece of the Vienna Circle. Ordinary conventionalism distinguished these empirical statements which state facts from those statements which *interpret* facts. The main difference between report statements and interpreting ones is that the assertion of the latter is conditioned by some conventions of arbitrary choice. For Poincaré the choice of a set of axioms, which either leads to Euclidean geometry or a non-Euclidean one, was a matter of arbitrary choice.

Ajdukiewicz's radical approach maintained that the difference between reporting statements and interpreting statements is somewhat fictitious. The data of experience alone do not force us to accept either interpreting or reporting statements. The very concept of "data of experience" is an ambigous one; it is always interpreted within a language, or more precisely, within a specific conceptual apparatus. When confronted with empirical data, we can deny either of the two kinds of statements, that is to say, if we choose a different conceptual apparatus, in which neither reporting nor interpreting statements can be formulated.

Expressed in general terms, Ajdukiewicz's position maintains that not only *some,* but in fact *all* the statements, which make up our picture of reality depend, at least partially, on a choice of a conceptual apparatus, which is to a large degree arbitrary. When this is spelled out, it simply means that empirical data, out of which we construct a picture of reality, can lead to different pictures of the world, if fitted into different conceptual apparatuses. Empirical data alone do not force us to accept one picture of reality or another; decisive in the process is the choice of the conceptual apparatus which "frames" the data appropriately. Such, in brief, is Ajdukiewicz's position. For further discussion see: H. Skolimowski: *Polish Analytical Philosophy.*

The connoisseurs will readily recognize that this position anticipates Quine on many points. Whether and to what extent Quine was directly influenced by Ajdukiewicz, is difficult to ascertain. My first guess is that he wasn't much influenced, as the doctrine of radical conventionalism was in the air, so to speak. Yet the possibility should not be excluded that there may have been such influence of Ajdukiewicz on Quine through writing and personal contacts. Quine did visit Poland and specifically Warsaw and spent some time there in the mid-1930s. At this time, Warsaw was a most vigorous and highly charged center of analytic philosophy where new logical and semantic doctrines were springing like mushrooms after a rain. At this time, Lesniewski, Łukasiewicz, Kotarbinski, Ajdukiewicz, and Tarski (among others) were housed virtually under one roof, teaching in the same department of philosophy.

Quine went on to develop his own version of radical conventionalism, which to my knowledge has never been stated in a comprehensive way in a book or a lengthy article, but given to us in fragments. The clearest formulation of Quine's conventionalism can be perhaps found in the introduction to *Methods of Logic* of 1950.

> The system of statements as a whole has its experiential implications; but the individual statements, apart from the peripheral few which directly describe experience as such, are relevant to experience only indirectly through their participation in the system. It is only by way of the relations of one statement to another that

the statements in the interior of the system can figure at all in the prediction of experience, and can be found deserving of revision when prediction fails. Now of these relations of statements to statements, one of conspicuous importance is the relation of logical implication: the relation of any statement to any that follows logically from it. If one statement is to be held as true, each statement implied by it must also be held as true; and thus it is that statements internal to the system have their effects on statements at the periphery.

Or, take this famous pronouncement:

Mathematical and logical laws themselves are not immune to revision, if it is found that essential simplifications of our whole conceptual scheme will ensue. (p. xiv)

Quine's statements on the subject are too well known to bear repeating. Let me, however, present one more quote from the same text, which I shall break into three parts, in order to bring to the reader's attention that the second part is very close to Ajdukiewicz both in spirit and wording.

a) As far as knowledge is concerned, no more can be claimed for the whole body of affirmations than that it is a devious, but convenient system for relating experiences to experiences. The system as a whole is underdetermined by experience, but implies, given certain experiences, that certain others should be forthcoming . . . .

b) We retain a wide latitude of choice as to what statements of the system to preserve and what ones to revise; any one of many revisions will be sufficient to unmake the particular implication which brought the system to grief.

Now comes the conclusion of the passage, which is Quine par excellence and perhaps the very essence of his radical conventionalism.

c) Our statements about external reality face the tribunal of sense experience not individually, but as a corporate body. (p. xii)

Quine has reiterated the ideas quoted above many times since the publication of *Methods of Logic:* that the choice of a given conceptual scheme is to a large degree arbitrary; that it is the whole context, our entire frame of reference, our world view that is the arbiter of the validity of our statements. And yet, the strange thing is that Quine has done very little with the idea of radical conventionalism since its formulation. The whole program of radical conventionalism seems to have been left unexplored and in a sense the whole venture abandoned. True enough, Quine periodically repeats that the context of one's conceptual scheme determines the nature of one's reality, but this did not lead to any new interesting philosophical results. Whether it was because of Chomsky's linguistic universalism, or because of some other reasons that so little was made of his gradualist epistemology in more recent years—we are in no position to know. But there is a gap, a glaring open space, between what appeared as a new exciting conceptual possibility in the 1950s and the result of Quine's philosophy during the last three decades.

It seems to me that in the 1940s and 50s, Quine was quite successful in liberating himself from the empiricist straitjacket. Yet, in the 60s and 70s, he seems to have returned to the straitjacket, which in turn has inhibited and almost paralyzed his earlier epistemological and conceptual departures. In my view, we have a choice, either conventionalism, and all the consequences it entails—including those concerning the active role of language and the active role of the mind; or empiricism which, if allied with logic, becomes logical empiricism—the doctrine so remorselessly pushed on to the scene in the 1930s and which Quine has criticized with such a gusto in his "Two Dogmas of Empiricism."

If we accept the dictum of empiricism, whether of the traditional or the logical variety, then we are forced to prefer one specific conceptual scheme; they are all reduced to one: to the empiricist conceptual scheme as dictated by science. Karl Popper has shown that this is a sterile and unpromising approach to knowledge. The preference for empiricism also undermines the very premise of conventionalism—the freedom of a variety; for empiricism reduces all options to one.

If conventionalism is upheld and language is acknowledged as active (and not only as a mirror, in which reality is faithfully reflected), and as co-contributing to our knowledge and to our picture of the world—as was the premise of original conventionalism—then this implies also the *recognition* of the active role of the mind in the knowledge process. I find it strange indeed that Quine would maintain: "no minds as additional entities", while not renouncing in any way his early conventionalism. In view of the results of the New Physics, the mind *must* be recognized as active par excellence, and co-contributing to our picture of reality.

Radical conventionalism could have become a new exciting and far reaching proposition, had it realized that in the post-Newtonian era the role of the mind becomes of paramount importance. The physicists of the new persuasion are prepared to go as far as to maintain: "no mind, no world." Thus the theory of (active) mind becomes the key to our epistemology, which, in its turn, becomes the key to our ontology. At a certain point of analysis the theory of mind and the theory of knowledge (within the universe of the New Physics) merge and become aspects of each other; that is when we realize that we *are* in a participatory universe, in which "we are inescapably involved in bringing about that which appears to be happening." (J. A. Wheeler)

Radical conventionalism could have become a vehicle of this new understanding, a new platform on which the creative aspects of language and the creative dimensions of mind meet to map out new shapes of the changing reality of physics. *Sic transit gloria mundi.* Unfortunately, radical conventionalism has not become such a vehicle. In the next section I shall outline, in a most rudimentary manner, the position of *the new conceptualism* which is an epistemological proposition attempting to meet the challenge of the New Physics.

The New Conceptualism

Karl Popper has met the challenge of Einsteinian physics. In the process he created his unique 'conjectural' epistemology (no knowledge can ever be absolute), which separates itself clearly from traditional empiricism and also from 20th century logical empiricism. Yet the challenge of quantum physics and the crisis of particle physics is even greater—in epistemological terms—than that of Einsteinian physics. Analytical philosophers, instead of meeting this challenge and going beyond Popper, seem to be turning backward the clock of history: by accepting the tenets of empiricism (of whatever variety), they almost invariably *assume* the Newtonian world-view. This is a very strange situation indeed. They do not reject the New Physics, and in particular the new findings of particle physics, yet they embrace the world-view which totally ignores these findings, and in many ways contradicts them. Such a situation is rationally almost incomprehensible. But there is a deeper reason. Most of the tools of logic and semantics, as well as many concepts which analytical philosophers use, were worked out by empiricists who believed in sense data, in rock bottom of knowledge, in protocol statements as depicting the ultimate facts (Carnap et al.). While accepting this methodological equipment, analytical philosophers are unwittingly endorsing their ontological underpinnings. They seem not to understand that the New Physics calls for radical departures in epistemology; otherwise our rationality is but a fossilized form reflecting the state of knowledge of the yesteryear. Even Popper seems to be unable to face the new epistemological challenge. After John Archibald Wheeler ("We are living in a participatory universe") gave his brilliant presentation on quantum physics and its philosophical consequences, in Schloss Kronberg near Frankfurt, Popper is purported to have replied: "What you say is contradicted by biology and fact."[1] Which was a question-begging strategy indeed. No old form of explanation and no 'facts' as established by the old form can 'contradict' a new form of explanation which transcends the old form. We need to work out a new epistemology, relevant to the new findings of the New Physics. The new conceptualism I am proposing is a step in this direction.

Let us imagine the cosmos (our reality, ontology) to be contained within the walls of an open cone, opening upward. (see diagram—broken lines.) In every culture there is a notion that the boundaries of the cosmos are firm and well established. We know what is out there and what is not out there. Hence it makes sense to talk about the 'walls' of the cosmos. These walls delineate reality as we know it; or as a given culture knows it; or as a given mind knows

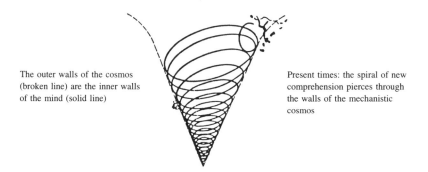

The outer walls of the cosmos (broken line) are the inner walls of the mind (solid line)

Present times: the spiral of new comprehension pierces through the walls of the mechanistic cosmos

it. Every culture conditions its people to accept these 'walls' as something given. Our understanding is conditioned by these 'walls' and corresponds to them. There is a close fit between the two. The walls of the cosmos are filled with the spiral of understanding (see diagram—solid lines) which accepts the cosmos and articulates it.[2]

The spiral of understanding includes our language and the variety of conceptual schemes we use to explain the universe. This spiral—which in a sense constitutes our cosmos—is a radicalized version of the 19th century conventionalism. This is the road which radical conventionalism *could* have taken.

Let me comment, if ever so briefly, on the relationship of the spiral of understanding to what we call the confines of our universe or our cosmos. At those points at which the spiral of understanding (solid line) pierces through the walls of the cosmos (as we envisage it), some extraordinary things happen: our understanding—at least the understanding of some individuals—has outgrown the confines of the cosmos as defined in our knowledge. We do not know what to do with our new insights—acts of comprehension that spill over the cone of the cosmos. These new insights are "beyond our world"; until they are incorporated in our enlarged cosmos, they do not make sense. They begin to make sense if and when the walls of the cosmos are loosened and enlarged to incorporate these insights.

This is the situation which we witness at present: the new insights (of New Physics and other disciplines representing the new paradigm) signify those parts of the spiral of understanding which visibly go beyond the wall of the cosmos as established for us by Western science. We do not know how to handle these insights—until we enlarge our cosmos and *see* that these new insights are perfectly compatible with the enlarged cosmos. Enlarging one's cosmos is not child's play. Hence we resist it and resent it, for among other things it requires updating our own spiral of understanding and loosening up and rearranging our own walls of the cosmos—an exercise always difficult, sometimes impossible. This is why new breakthroughs so often come from younger people not totally imprisoned by the walls of the bequeathed cosmos.

The history of human knowledge is a magnificent story of the human mind breaking through the confining walls of the cosmos, in spite of the seeming impossibility of doing so—as it is maintained in a given culture. Every major discovery, every major conceptual breakthrough—take Einstein's theory of relativity, for example—is an instance of the mind (part of the spiral of understanding) piercing through the walls of the cosmos (reality) as defined by present knowledge. In one sense we all know it. Yet it is most surprising that nobody has articulated this insight.

The basic idea of the new conceptualism is that the dimensions of the universe correspond to the spiral of understanding; and indeed are constituted by the spiral of understanding, with its immensely complex tributaries. This is the beginning of a new epistemology which attempts to meet the challenge of the New Physics.[3]

I can anticipate Professor Quine's response to my proprosals. He is likely to say that he doesn't know what I mean by my assertions about the spiral of understanding as corresponding to the walls of our cosmos. It has been an unfortunate strategy of many analytical philosophers to say to their critics, particularly those who propose larger schemes and more embracing frameworks: "I don't know what you mean." One suspects that at times this is an indirect way of saying: "I don't want to understand what you are saying." At other times, it may very well be true. But then it is a terrible indictment of the narrowness of analytical philosophers, for many indeed bar themselves from understanding larger schemes.

We are living in most exciting times, when so many new vistas are opening up; new horizons are examined and tested. We are experiencing a paradigm shift in many important realms of knowledge and of human experience. Philosophy, to be worthy of its name, should register and analyze in depth these epochal changes. Under the dust of change, there is hidden a new road, which philosophy is in a unique position to reveal. All great philosophy has been an attempt to reveal deeper structures hidden behind the welter of immediate experience. Our times call for in-depth philosophical reflections on the problems we have generated, on the vistas of the cosmos we have unveiled, on the new discoveries and inventions we have made. Analytical philosophers could be of great help in this process if only they choose to. But this choice must be accompanied by broadening their vision and enlarging their tolerance to views and ideas which so far they do not consider their own.

Conclusions

Willard Van Orman Quine has supremely exemplified the epoch of 20th century rational philosophy. He expressed in a most elegant form what the scientific culture in the middle of the twentieth century could create and offer in the.

realm of exact philosophy. Although exactness has been much praised, it is not an unmitigated virtue, as we have shown. For the other side of exactness is rigidity not infrequently accompanied by the sterility of imagination. Originality and exactness can be obtained simultaneously but only in mathematics and logic, not in philosophy. Thus we expect exactness from logic, while from philosophy we expect illumination. Genuinely new philosophy is always groping. When Professor Quine expresses his new philosophical ideas, whether regarding conventionalism, or physicalism, or robust realism, the precision of his language is not on a par with his discourses on mathematical logic.

Quine's philosophy was very exciting and challenging through the 1950s. Then he seems to have lost himself in his conceptual epicycles—as I have tried to show in the second part of this essay. The early promise of radical conventionalism, including the gradualist conception of knowledge, which provoked so many discussions and provided so much inspiration has been left unfulfilled. The whole early program seems to have withered away, as Quine embarked on a series of conceptual ventures which seem to be ad hoc in character. The reassertion of empiricism in later years seems to me an evolution going backward. Extensive analyses of language did not lead to new illuminations and lasting philosophical results, except for rather technical distinctions within the field of semantics, and these distinctions do not seem to have much bearing on our understanding of reality and of philosophy itself.

Without any question Willard Quine is one of the most brilliant minds of our times; and one of the most inventive for that matter. No one would want to begrudge the fact that he is now the most prominent analytical philosopher in the world. His accomplishment within the analytical tradition is formidable. One can only congratulate him for a life of achievement. It is not his achievement that I question, but the achievement of the culture that he has served. In a sense we do not choose the gods we serve; they are usually imposed upon us. To the extent that the ethos of science has been imposed on Quine's mind, he has been an unfortunate victim, who in turn victimized others with all his convictions and brilliance. I do not mean to be paternalistic, but it is a terrible indictment of a culture which has had so many powerful minds at its disposal and has produced so little in positive terms. This is not limited to philosophy and humanities. Technology is a still more glaring example. While older cultures with very frugal means created spectacular monuments which sustain us unceasingly, we, with our spectacular means, create very insignificant things which future generations will not find so sustaining. *We are at the mercy of the culture of means.* Our individual achievement is short-changed because of the insignificance of the culture.

Of course, the final debate is not about empiricism or conventionalism; not even about philosophy; it is about the shape of life. The consequences of Quine's philosophy, and of nearly all analytical philosophy, are belittling the phenomenon of man, also are degrading and belittling life as it can be lived. For these reasons, analytical philosophy, when it pretends to be the arbiter of our destinies, must be opposed. So often mechanistic philosophies, while heralding the dawn of rationality and the liberation of man from the constraints of the dogma, end up as worst oppressors, attempting to bind us with their own dogmas, and in the process mutilating the variety of life by trying to squeeze it into antiseptic logical boxes; in the process these philosophies also undermine the creative *élan* of the mind and the very rationality they pretend to champion. Rudolf Carnap is a case in point. W. V. Quine is a case in point. The agonizing paradox is that the more accomplished you become as a master of analytical techniques, the more surely you leave behind the larger interests of the human family and life itself. This is not a necessary proposition but a contingent one; its truth is not to be revealed by analytical tools, but only by a deeper reflection into the nature of things. That tools alienate themselves from the original purpose for which they were conceived, is an old story. The tale of the sorcerer's apprentice brings home the point most vividly. But modern technology brings the point equally vividly—the arsenal of tools beyond our control.

Beware of powerful tools. After a while they acquire a life of their own and have a tendency to dominate their inventors. Philosophy was originally conceived as a reflection upon ends; it atrophies when it is reduced to mere means and techniques. As technicians philosophers do not command any special respect nor do they serve any useful purpose in society. We don't want to be a joke, for philosophy is not a joke but one of the most ambitious and glorious enterprises which man has conceived in order to see the universe more clearly and in order to live in it more meaningfully.

HENRYK SKOLIMOWSKI

UNIVERSITY OF MICHIGAN
ANN ARBOR, MICHIGAN
APRIL 1983

NOTES

1. As reported in *Structure of Science and Art* (Amsterdam-Oxford-Princeton: Excerpta Medica, 1980), Peter Medawar and Julian Shelley, eds.

2. For further discussion of these points see H. Skolimowski, "A Model of Reality as Mind", in Alwyn Van Der Merwe (ed.) *Old and New Questions in Physics, Cosmology, Philosophy and Theoretical Biology: Essays in Honor of Wolfgang Yourgrau* (Plenum Publishing Corporation, 1983). See also, H. Skolimowski, *Eco-philosophy* (1981), and *The Theatre of the Mind* (1984).

3. Of late, I have called this New Conceptualism—the Participatory Theory of Mind; see especially my "The Interactive Mind in the Participatory Universe", *The World and I*, No. 1, Vol. 1, Feb. 1986, pp. 453-470.

REPLY TO HENRYK SKOLIMOWSKI

Skolimowski holds that the analytic philosophers, nebulously so called, and I among them, have been led irrevocably into atomism and a correspondence theory of truth by following what they took to be the lead of theoretical physics. He notes further that elementary particles are themselves now a matter of grave doubt, and he cites my friend John Wheeler to the effect that the duality between theory and its object is doubtful as well. Analytic philosophy is left high and dry.

I find myself in unrecognizable company as thus described, and myself unrecognizable as well. In "Whither Physical Objects?", "Facts of the Matter", and elsewhere I have made quite a point of the plight of elementary particles. In *Ontological Relativity* and more emphatically in *Theories and Things* I have argued further that ontology itself is an arbitrary point of theory, open to revision without doing violence to any evidence. The basis for this rather Kantian thesis was already visible in "Ontological Reduction and the World of Numbers", 1964.

Skolimowski deplores my loss of the sweep and clarity of vision that he was kind enough to detect in my writings of thirty-odd years ago. I have descended, he feels, to scattered technical details. The view of ontology sketched above does not strike me in that light; my sweep has broadened, for better or worse. His characterization of *Word and Object* as a miscellany of grubbing detail suggests that he missed the main thrust of that book, its challenge to semantic absolutism.

He deplores my failure to persist in and develop the conventionalism, as he calls it, of "Two Dogmas." Surely the point about ontology mentioned above, as well as the central idea of *Word and Object,* carry this so-called conventionalism far beyond "Two Dogmas." Readers as well as writers can fail to see the woods for the trees.

He misunderstands his compatriot Tarski, despite citing the Polish edition.

He thinks that the bankruptcy of a correspondence theory refutes Tarski's definition of truth. Tarski casually noted a subtle kinship between his account of truth and the correspondence theory, and he has been criticized for this by philosophers who read too much into it. Let us look beyond the word. Tarski's paradigm and his technical construction are epistemologically neutral. They are neutral even as between the cognitive and the emotive.

Skolimowski complains that for all my approval of the scientific method, I never analyze it. In a way it is cheering that so stern a critic of the grubbing analysts should complain of this. It would have been more cautious, however, to say that I never analyze it in anything he has read; more cautious still to say that I never analyze it in anything that he has read and understood. Actually this last caution is superfluous in the present instance, for the principal locus is *The Web of Belief,* which Ullian and I wrote for courses in freshman English. I have treated the matter mainly at that level because I have known little to say of it that was not pretty common knowledge.

Skolimowski predicts that I will pretend not to understand what he means by his "assertions about the spiral of understanding as corresponding to the walls of our cosmos." I am tempted, perversely, to pretend that I do understand. But let us be fair: if he claimed not to understand me, I would not for a moment suspect him of pretending.

He misunderstands my suggestion that philosophers as a class have no distinctive gift for moral edification, if he interprets me as undervaluing moral edification. On the contrary, I applaud it; nor do I hold that philosophers as a class have any distinctive disability at it. If Skolimowski in particular has an aptitude for it, by all means let him get on with it. We can all agree that the world is in a bad way.

W. V. Q.

18

J. J. C. Smart

QUINE ON SPACE-TIME

I

Introduction

For the philosophy of space-time[1] Quine's work is important in three main ways. (1) Quine's criterion of ontic commitment[2] and his criteria for the reducibility of theories[3] can be used to sharpen the issue between absolute and relational theories of space-time. (2) Quine's critique of the notion of analyticity is relevant to discussions of the conventionality or otherwise of geometry. (3) Quine's rejection of indexical expressions, so far as canonical notation is concerned, and his claim that the modern theory of the space-time manifold and the tenseless notation appropriate to quantification theory are mutually consilient,[4] both raise questions about the relation of his austere canonical notation to the homely but untidy conceptual scheme implicit in common language. These three topics are related to one another. The first two are connected because a defender of analyticity might hold that in so far as geometrical statements are analytic they are devoid of ontic commitment. The first and third are connected because some philosophers might hold that something is left out in Quine's canonical notation, namely a reference to the supposed flow, passage, or transience of time; there are also problems about the relation between the concept of a thing as a four-dimensional space-time solid and the (possibly different and Aristotelian) concept of a thing as substance, the permanent in change.

II

The Ontic Commitments of Geometry

It is usual to distinguish between pure geometry on the one hand and physical geometry on the other hand. Quine deals with the ontic commitments of theories of the former sort by taking points as n-tuples of real numbers, as in coordinate geometry, so that geometrical theories become part of analysis. In the extreme case of topology the geometrical theories become part of the general theory of relations.[5] Quine also considers the possibility (canvassed by Poincaré and others) of considering geometries as "a family . . . of uninterpreted theory-forms".[6] In this light a pure geometry becomes in effect a substructure of quantification theory, and its sentences are mere schemata, not capable of truth or falsehood.

The theoretical interest of a system of pure geometry normally lies in its application as part of physics. If the sentences of the system are mere schemata, then we must turn them into physical statements by appropriately interpreting the relevant symbols. If, on the other hand, the system is already interpreted as part of analysis and about n-tuples of real numbers, then these n-tuples have to be correlated in some way with points of physical space or else the relations between the n-tuples have to be correlated with relations of distance and the like between physical objects or events. The question of the truth of the geometrical sentences now becomes part of the question of the truth of the physical theory in which they are embedded.

We now have a physical geometry. The geometry of modern physics is a geometry of space-time, and so it is quite natural to take physical geometry as ontically committed to a special sort of entity: space-time points. Such points would be theoretical entities of physics just as electrons and neutrinos are. This would give us an absolute theory of space-time, as opposed to a relational one. However in *Word and Object* Quine sketches the beginning of a relational theory of space-time.[7] In a later publication he hints that he leans towards an absolute theory.[8] According to this line of thought, space-time points are part of our ontology just as much as elementary particles are. Indeed should science develop in the direction indicated by J. A. Wheeler's geometrodynamics[9] then space-time points would turn out to be the *only* ultimate entities (apart from abstract objects such as sets) there are. For example in Wheeler's theory electrons and protons are "wormholes" in a multiply connected space-time. I gather that Wheeler is no longer so hopeful for such a theory,[10] but from a philosophical point of view his geometrodynamics is interesting because it is a modern version of the Cartesian theory of matter as extension. Wheeler's theory avoids some of the difficulties which arose for Descartes who knew only of Euclidean space. Because of the homogeneity and isotropy of such a space Descartes was not able to distinguish between matter and empty space in a way which was consistent with his own theory.

It is sometimes erroneously thought that the theory of relativity supports the relational (or Leibnizean) position against the absolute (or Cartesian) one. Perhaps this impression may in part have arisen on account of the misleadingly operationist form in which Einstein put his original paper on special relativity.[11] An operationist philosophy and a relational theory of space and time often go together, though not in the case of Leibniz himself, who was an extreme rationalist.[12] In part also the confusion may have arisen from little more than a pun on the words "relative" and "relativity". For this reason it is best to call Leibniz's theory a "relational" rather than a "relative" one. If this usage had been generally adopted it would not have been necessary to contrast Leibniz's relativity with Einstein's, as Quine does in one place.[13] Quine himself is quite clear about the distinction in question, and rightly asserts that the theory of relativity is quite independent of a relational theory of space-time. He points out that though the partition of space-time into space and time is dependent on the state of motion of the coordinate system, we can restore the absolute by "speaking of positions not in space but in space-time".[14]

A necessary (though not sufficient) condition for a relational theory of space-time is that the inertia of bodies should be explicable in terms of the general distribution of matter in the universe. (This would give backing to Ernst Mach's conclusions in his criticism of Newton's well known discussion of the rotating bucket of water.[15])

I gather that within the context of the general theory of relativity it is still an open question as to whether this can be done. In its present form the general theory of relativity cannot account for inertia except on the basis of an independently existing space-time. Hence in the context of the general theory of relativity to confuse a relativistic theory with a relational one is even more objectionable than it is in the context of the special theory.

Nor must we assume too readily that Mach's principle (that inertia is explicable in terms of the general distribution of matter in the universe) would by itself ensure the viability of a relational theory of space-time. To ensure this we should need to show that a Machian physics could be paraphrased in a canonical notation which does not quantify over space-time entities, such as points. In *Word and Object*[16] Quine shows how to paraphrase some rather simple statements of physical geometry so that they are about physical objects or events alone. He chooses five particle-events not quite at random, and then the position of any arbitrary particle-event can be given as a quintuple of real numbers, each real number being a distance in centimetres (say) between two particle-events. However it is questionable whether all the geometrical statements which are needed in physics could be so paraphrased. In physics we find differential equations, and this would seem to imply that coordinates have to be given to non-denumerably many points. A lot depends on what counts as a particle-event. If the value of a field at a point is a particle-event, then there are perhaps non-denumerably many of them, but this is cold comfort for the relationist unless he can show that such particle-events do not have to be understood in terms of points of space-time. To avoid this sort of difficulty relationists commonly use contrary to fact conditionals in order to define points of space-time at which no particle-events in fact exist. This expedient would rightly be rejected by Quine because the semantics for such contrary to fact conditionals is highly obscure. It would probably have to refer to such dubious metaphysical entities as real but not actual possible worlds.[17] It is true that a less objectionable theory of contrary to fact conditionals is perhaps possible in terms of deducibility from agreed background assumptions.[18] But apart from the imprecision of such a theory, there is the objection that a construal of contrary to fact conditionals in terms of background assumptions would lead to our quantification over unoccupied points being substitutional quantification only, and this does not enable us to deal with the non-denumerable infinity of space-time points. (I also think that similar difficulties would arise from other theories of possibility, such as in Kripke's more recent writings.[19]) Of course if we have *already* got space-time points in our ontology we can construe possibilities of position in a harmless metalinguistic sense, that of it not being inconsistent with the laws of nature that particle-events should be at these positions.

Let us go back to Quine's quintuple of particle-events. Let the particle-events be A, B, C, D, E. Then the position of some other particle-event P is given by the quintuple of real numbers $(P_A, P_B, P_C, P_D, P_E)$ where P_A, etc., are the distances in centimetres between P and A, etc. Suppose now that we resurrect points of space-time but identify them with such quintuples of real numbers. We would now have a non-denumerable infinity of points, including, of course, points at which no particle-event exists. Quine proposes a theory of this sort in his "Propositional Objects".[20] Such a theory is in the spirit of the relational theory in that it allows us to do away with unreduced geometrical points. The theory is also in the spirit of the absolute theory in that it asserts the existence of points (quintuples of real numbers) in a way which does not allow a complete paraphrase in terms of the distances between particle-events. Moreover it allows (without recourse to contrary to fact conditionals) points at which no particle-event exists. Let us call such a theory a "quasi-absolute" theory.

In the light of his discussion in "Ontological Reduction and the World of Numbers"[21] one would expect Quine to be happy with such a quasi-relational theory. He is already committed to the set-theoretic apparatus which assures him of quintuples of real numbers, and there is certainly a specifiable "proxy function" from space-time points to quintuples of real numbers. This function would of course be specified in a theory whose ontology comprised both the entities to be reduced (points) and the entities to which they are to be reduced (quintuples of real numbers). As Quine explains, this does not matter because the reductionist argument is of the form of *reductio ad absurdum:* it shows that if the original entities (unreduced space-time points) were needed then they would not be needed, and hence that they are not needed.[22] (I have some worries about this. Here ". . . is needed" is a referentially opaque context.) However there are considerations which possibly suggest that such a quasi-relational theory of space-time would not have the explanatory power of an absolute theory. If so this would suggest that something extra is needed to be added to Quine's criteria for ontological reduction.[23]

One problem arises from the referential opacity of the context ". . . is explained by . . ." when we take what is to be explained to be events (as opposed to sentences).[24] Will quintuples of real numbers have the explanatory power which space-time points have, even though it is the case that the observation sentences which are deduced from sentences about quintuples of real numbers are the same as those which are deduced from sentences about unreduced space-time points? Perhaps some of my worry comes from naïve intuitions which ought to be discounted. One has a tendency to think of space-time as rather like a sea in which physical things swim. Can a particle-event be *at* a quintuple of real numbers? Can a physical object be *in* a set of quintuples of real numbers? The reply will presumably be that the old predicates of "at" or "in" which relate physical events or objects to points or sets of points are replaced in the paraphrase by new predicates which relate physical events or objects to quintuples of real numbers or sets of these, and that it is mere pictorial thinking which makes us tend to feel that the new predicates are not as good as the old ones.

A more substantial worry perhaps arises from the need to relate our quintuples of real numbers to a coordinate system, the five reference particle-events. If we chose a different coordinate system we should have different quintuples of real numbers to deal with in our theory. If we believe in space-time points as the real explanatory entities this will not worry us: in different coordinate systems a given space-time point is merely *represented* by different quintuples of real numbers. There is an undesirable particularity, therefore, about quasi-relational theories from which absolute theories are free.

In his "Propositional Objects"[25] Quine is concerned with overcoming this sort of difficulty. To define a world state he needs points of space (or, finally, of space-time). For expository purposes he is concerned only with a Newtonian universe in Euclidean space, and an instantaneous world state is specified by a function which assigns "occupied" or "unoccupied" to every point of this space. He identifies points of space with triples of real numbers. To get rid of the arbitrariness implied by a particular coordinate system he takes a world state as a class of classes of number triples: the class of classes into which a particular class of triples can be converted by translation and rotation of coordinate axes and by similarity transformations.

If this sort of thing can not be done generally (e.g. for spaces of variable curvature) then we are left with an undesirable particularity in the quasi-relational theory, since the number triple with which we identify a point will depend on the particular particle-events with which we define the coordinate system. One feels that the ultimate laws of physics should make no implicit reference to particulars. On the absolute theory the trouble does not arise: the number quintuples are used merely accidentally to single out points of space-time, and it is the points of space-time which function in an explanatory way.

Independence of a particular coordinate system is achieved in physics by writing the laws of nature in the form of tensor equations. Does this allow us to get unscathed between Scylla and Charybdis (the particularity of a coordinate system on the one hand and the postulation of absolute geometrical entities on the other hand)? A tensor is a multilinear functional from the Cartesian product of vectors over a sequence of vector spaces to the real number continuum. Vectors such as electric field vectors can be defined easily enough if we already have geometrical vectors. Let us concern ourselves with these latter vectors. In physics they are defined in terms of certain basis vectors, which are usually singled out by means of a coordinate system. So here we have particularity. Suppose that to avoid this we define the vectors simply as elements of a model of the vector algebra axioms. This would mean that in effect we *postulate* the existence of vectors, and we might just as well have postulated points of space-time in the first place. (If the vector algebra axioms are part of a mathematics for physics they must be regarded as physical postulates, not just as abstract algebra. Abstract algebra in pure mathematics of course provides no ontological worries for Quine.[26]) Perhaps we might define a vector as the class of ordered pairs of sequences of basis vectors and coordinate systems. This would be a generalization of Quine's procedure in ''Propositional Objects'', but the trouble seems to lie in giving a clear account (without begging the relevant questions) of ''all coordinate systems''.

There therefore seems to be a difficulty for the quasi-relational theory of space-time: it is liable either to collapse into the absolute theory or else to retain an undesirable particularity. In any case in the quasi-relational theory of space-time there would seem to be a blurring of the distinction between a real physical space and an abstract mathematical space such as the Hilbert spaces of quantum theory. Both sorts of space would enjoy a rather shadowy set theoretic existence. Hilbert spaces are pretty clearly reducible to Quine's set theoretic universe, but their operation can look mysterious and incline us towards instrumentalism.[27] Once more the absolute theory of physical space seems to me to be superior in explanatory power, but this may be due only to the naïveté of my intuitions.

III

Conventionality and Physical Geometry

So far I have been concerned with Quine's philosophy in so far as it bears on the question of the ontic commitments of physical geometry. Another cluster of questions in the philosophy of space-time is concerned with whether there is, and if so how much there is, a conventional element in geometry. In particular, Adolf Grünbaum has argued for the conventionality of the metric.[28] As he has put it, space-time has no "intrinsic metric". On the other hand Grünbaum is of the opinion that the *topology* of physical space-time is *not* conventional. In an interesting paper Roman U. Sexl has defended Grünbaum's thesis of the conventionality of the metric and has argued in addition for the conventionality of the topology and dimensionality.[29] It is of interest to examine these theses in the light of Quine's denial of a clear analytic-synthetic distinction. If physical geometry depends on congruence conventions, for example, then it would seem that there are sentences which are analytic in virtue of these conventions. Thus suppose that a space-time interval PP' at a place P is measured by the period between successive wave crests of a certain sort of radiation which exists at P. Then it might be a convention that a space-time interval QQ' at some other place Q is to be counted equal to PP' if it too corresponds to the period between successive wave crests of the same sort of radiation. In this case it might be argued that the statement that $PP' = QQ'$ is analytic.

When a physicist says that something is "conventional" he often means to say something which has no particular connection with analyticity. He means something like "arbitrary". Thus it may be said to be conventional that the coordinates of position are such and such, but the conventionality here is the mere arbitrariness of specifying a position of a particle-event in a certain way. If we use Quine's method of quintuples, the coordinates are the distances of the particle-event in question from the five chosen particle events. It has to be ascertained by observation that the distances in question are what they are. A similar sort of arbitrariness would exist if we decided to give the heights of men by saying "so many centimetres shorter or taller than the Duke of Edinburgh". Someone of even more royalist persuasion might prefer to say "so many centimetres shorter or taller than the Queen". Which of these two impracticable systems to adopt might well be said to be a matter of convention. Nevertheless sentences about heights would be quite empirical whichever system they belonged to. There would be exceptions like "The height in centimetres of the Duke of Edinburgh = the height in centimetres of the Duke of Edinburgh", which follows from the axioms of identity, together with the small empirical assumption that the Duke of Edinburgh exists and that he *has* a height (he is not a prime number, for example). Indeed for the system to work he must have a height in centimetres which is other than zero, but the assumption that this is so is also a very small one. Apart from the trivial existential assumptions connected with them, identity statements fall under the notion of logical truth, which (unlike analyticity) Quine finds clear enough.

The arbitrariness in a coordinate system which we have been discussing is that of picking particular particle-events as the basis of the coordinate system. According to Quine's method, described in Section II above, the coordinates are just distances from the particle events. The notion of distance, however, contains within itself a new possibility of arbitrariness: it depends on that of a *metric* and according to Grünbaum it is here that a non-trivial sort of conventionality enters in. Grünbaum holds that this sort of conventionality is not a mere trivial arbitrariness, save in so far as the choice of the unit of length or of space-time interval is an arbitrary one. We could go over to a new coordinate system in which the new coordinates are arbitrary functions of the old ones, and define space-time intervals in terms of these new coordinates so that previously equal intervals are no longer equal. Here we would be "remetrizing" the space-time manifold. (It should be remembered, of course, that there are infinitely many changes of coordinate system which can be effected *without* changing the metric: as for example when in Euclidean geometry we change from rectangular Cartesian coordinates to oblique coordinates or to polar coordinates.) The notion of remetrization can be illustrated by means of the following example, which Grünbaum has given for the sake of a more special purpose.[30] (This special purpose is to show that in some cases a change in the metric will not lead to a change in the geometry, in the sense in which, say, a space of constant negative curvature has a "different geometry" from flat Euclidean space. Of course *in general* a change in the metric will lead to a change in the geometry.)

Suppose that we have a rod on a plane Π which is at an angle θ to a plane Π'. Let us suppose that the metric for Π is the usual one according to which the rod keeps the same length no matter what its orientation on Π is. Let us now remetrize Π so that the length of a rod AB (which is confined to Π) is taken to be the length (according to the usual metric) of the projection of Π on to Π'. Thus the length of AB will vary between ℓ and $\ell \cos \theta$, where ℓ is the length of AB according to the usual metric. If the old metric of Π is given by $ds^2 = dx^2 + dy^2$, then the new one will be given by $ds^2 = dx^2 + dy^2 \cdot \sec^2\theta$. (Taking appropriate directions for dx and dy.) With suitable changes in the laws of nature for Π it is clear that the remetrization would lead to no difficulty in theorizing about the behaviour of rods moving about on Π.

Notice, however, that this remetrization leads to the existence of a favoured direction in the plane Π, and all laws of nature relating to Π would now have to make explicit or implicit reference to this direction. With more complicated sorts of remetrization there would be a reference not only to a *direction* but also to a *distance* from an origin. It would seem, therefore, that if we think that a simple theory is more likely to reflect reality than is a more complicated theory, and if we think that reference to a particular point of, or direction in, space-time constitutes a complication, then surely we have some reason to think that certain metrizations reflect reality better than others do. In fact, if we take this line (contrary to that of Grünbaum) and regard the differently metrized theories as properly different theories from one another, then probabilistic considerations may support this appeal to simplicity: since there are an uncountable infinity of different origins or directions, surely any theory which makes reference to any one such must have zero probability, even though (what is no doubt hard to justify) some well tested scientific theories have non-zero probability.

As against this Grünbaum has taken the view that if we remetrize and appropriately alter the laws of nature so as to preserve the empirical content of our theory then any added complexity in the new theory is merely descriptive complexity, not an inductive or factual complexity.[31] Those of us who are convinced by Quine's critique of the analytic-synthetic distinction will probably not be able to make sense of this distinction between two kinds of complexity. The issue between Quine and Grünbaum here is a very deep rooted one which I cannot discuss in detail now, but it is worth noting that, in order to argue against Quine's Duhemian thesis that parts of a theory can always be retained if we make drastic enough alterations elsewhere, Grünbaum has distinguished "trivial semantic conventionalism" from his own more meaty conventionalism. In making this distinction he has made use of concepts of "intension" and "semantic stability",[32] which Quine would regard as suspect.

Grünbaum tends to describe physical geometry as a theory which explains the coincidence behaviour of rigid rods, but it is pretty clear that this is for expository reasons only and that he is willing to allow factual content in more theoretical ways, for example by basing the metric on the constancy throughout space-time of some theoretically derived wavelength. We must not foist a crude instrumentalism on to Grünbaum. Now why should we not go even further in the direction of theoretical realism and think of the so-called "congruence conventions" as hypotheses about certain relations between theoretically postulated physical entities (space-time points)? We can still agree this far with Grünbaum: that if we give up simplicity as one of our constraints on theory construction then alternative physical geometries are possible and the choice between them is arbitrary. From the realistic point of view, which I wish to advocate, we may hold that descriptive simplicity, no less than empirical confirmation, is one of our touchstones of reality.

Grünbaum sees his thesis of geochronometric conventionalism as intimately bound up with his thesis that space-time has no intrinsic metric. This thesis is complicated by the fact that Grünbaum distinguishes three kinds of metric: measure metrics, distance metrics and Riemannian metrics.[33] Measure metrics assign numbers to sets of points, and in the physically most important case to sets of points in an interval. Distance metrics assign numbers to a relation between two points (which may indeed be end points of an interval). The notion of a Riemannian metric may be regarded as a generalization of that of a distance metric. Speaking a little bit loosely, we can say that a Riemannian metric assigns a "distance" along a path which unlike ordinary distances may be not only real but zero or imaginary and which is the sum of infinitesimal differences between nearby points along the path. However, the main point seems to be that if the measure of a set of points or the distance between two points A and B is determined only by the cardinality of the set of points between A and B then the metric (measure metric or distance metric) is intrinsic. (In the case of measure metrics the converse of this statement requires qualification because of the existence of pathological measure metrics, pointed out by G. J. Massey.[34] Thus if one unit set of an n-tuple of unit sets of points is given measure $1 + \frac{1}{3}$ and the remaining $n - 1$ are given measure 1, then the measure of a k-tuple of points will depend not only on k but also on whether it contains the special point.) Thus in the case of a measure metric, if we give the measure zero to every unit set of points, then any finite or denumerably infinite set of points will have measure zero, though a non-denumerably infinite set of points can have non-zero measure. Similarly in the case of a distance metric, the distance along a path between points A and B in a discrete space (made up of indivisible chunks of space) can be defined as one plus the number of chunks between A and B. However this metric would still be conventional in the sense that there would be nothing to prevent us defining the distance between A and B in terms of a variety of suitable functions of the number of points between A and B.[35] It would appear, therefore, that when Grünbaum says that space-time has no intrinsic metric he is getting at something else which has no special connection with the question of conventionality. This is that if space-time were a discrete manifold we would be able to define either a distance metric or a Riemannian metric in a non-relational manner, but if space-time is continuous then measure-metrics, distance-metrics and Riemannian metrics need to be defined in relation to something else (for example the period of a certain type of radiation). In the case of dense but not continuous spaces it would seem that the notion of a Riemannian metric does not apply, and that the measure metric can be intrinsic though (according to the usual theory) always zero, and that distance metrics need to be defined in relation to something else. Consider then the ''conventionality'' which arises from the fact that a continuous space does not have an intrinsic metric. This extrinsicality or relationality surely reduces to something to which Quine could well agree, namely arbitrariness: the arbitrariness of which of all the objectively existing and suitable relations we should select for attention.

Moreover, it is not clear that we can make a distinction between absolute and relational properties which would be acceptable to Quine. (Even though the notion of ''property'' itself were to be made acceptable.) Suppose that one philosopher says that he defines the distances between A and B as the number of wave crests of a certain sort of radiation between A and B. He says that this is just (as a matter of convention) what he *means* by talking of the distance between A and B, and that he adopts this convention because it makes physics simpler. Suppose now that another philosopher says that he *postulates* that the *amount of space-time* between A and B is equal to the number of wave-crests between A and B and that he says that he believes in the truth of his postulate because of the way in which his physics becomes simpler if he adopts it. Then he needs to observe wave crests (or something from which he can make calculations about wave crests) in order to *find out* the amount of space-time between A and B. There is no reason, as far as I can see, why Quine should not take the viewpoint of this latter philosopher, in which case the relationality of our determinations of space-time intervals need not imply a relational definition of the metric itself. Indeed in Quine's philosophy the distinction in question is not a clear one, since according to Quine definitionality is not a semantic property of sentences but a trait of their use at some time in their history.[36] The fact that Grünbaum can give a non-essentialist definition of "intrinsic metric" perhaps does not save him from the essentialism implicit in his reliance on the definition itself *qua* definition. I therefore have a lingering suspicion that, despite the clarity or relative clarity of "intrinsic" as defined by him, the *use* of the definition implies that "intrinsic" is after all in the same box as words like "necessary" and "essential".

Similarly we can say that metrical predicates which we apply to space-time such as "is curved at point P" or "is flat at point P" are non-relational, even though we need relational predicates in our theories in order to test the hypothesis that they apply. (If we want to give numerical values, say to the curvature at a point, then relationality and conventionality do enter in, in the harmless sense of arbitrariness, because we need a relation to a standard of length or interval.) This choice is open to us if we reject, on Quinean grounds, Grünbaum's distinction between factual simplicity and mere descriptive simplicity, and if we allow simplicity, no less than testability by observation, to be an inductive canon in its own right.

In order to try to make my point of view a little clearer, I shall now consider an argument put forward by Roman U. Sexl,[37] who extends Grünbaum's thesis of geochronometric conventionalism. Sexl holds that not only the metric[38] but also the topology and the number of dimensions of space-time are conventional. In discussing the question of the topology of space-time Sexl wittily illustrates his point by considering the hollow world theory, according to which the earth is a solid comprising the infinite exterior of a sphere so that we live in its interior. In its usual form[39] this theory is of course easily disproved. However Sexl points out that no observation will disprove it if we choose a suitable coordinate system with its origin in the centre of the (hollow) earth and adjust the laws of nature appropriately. (For the purposes of the example he assumes that the earth is a perfect sphere and that space is Euclidean.)

Let (x_1, x_2, x_3) be the coordinates of a point P according to the system of

Cartesian coordinates whose origin is the (old) centre of the earth. Map this on to a point P' which has coordinates (x_1', x_2', x_3') as follows

$$x_i' = \frac{R^2}{r^2} x_i \quad , \quad i = 1, 2, 3$$

where R is the radius of the earth, 6370 km, and $r^2 = x_1^2 + x_2^2 + x_3^2$.

The mapping preserves angles, and straight lines are transformed into circles which pass through the (new) centre of the (hollow) earth. A light ray will never reach the (new) centre because light travels slower and slower as it approaches this point, (and rods become shorter and shorter). The sun is rather near this centre and has a radius of 10^{-17} cm. Light rays can never reach a part of the interior spherical surface which is on the other side of the centre from the sun and this explains night and day. Stars of course are even closer to the centre, and the galaxies are very close indeed (and very tiny). Sexl points out that we need to impose a symmetry condition on the laws of nature[40] when they are modified so as to accord with the new geometry. Thus if we drilled a hole through the (old) centre of the earth we could drop a particle which would fall through the hole, passing through the centre and coming up to the antipodeal point (at least if we can neglect air resistance). In the new theory the particle goes off to infinity in one direction and reappears from infinity in the other direction.

The imposition of such a symmetry condition is what Reichenbach described as a breach of the principle of causality. In his book *The Philosophy of Space and Time*[41] Reichenbach discussed ways in which we could alter the topology and still preserve the same empirical content in a theory, thus holding, as Sexl did after him, that the topology is conventional. However Reichenbach seems to have held that the topology is *less* conventional than the metric.[42] Grünbaum generally speaks as though the topology is not conventional at all (though this may perhaps be no more than a difference in emphasis). As against Sexl and Reichenbach, I want to say that neither the topology nor the metric is conventional. But I can agree with Reichenbach and also with Grünbaum in saying that it would be a much more profound change in a physical theory if we changed the topology than it would be if we merely changed the metric. In Sexl's example the topology is changed without a change in the cardinality of the set of points of space-time. A change from a compact to a merely dense or to a discrete space-time would of course lead to even more profound changes. If we reject the suspect notions of "empirical content" and "conventionality" we can say what we need to say by talking in terms of the way in which giving up a principle makes either a large or a small change in a theory. A principle whose abandonment makes a small change in a theory has no difference in *semantic* status from a principle whose abandonment causes a large change. We can have a Tarskian theory of truth, which is in the spirit of the correspondence theory, though the relation to the world is not between sentences and facts but between predicates and sequences of objects,[43] and we can also have a coherence theory of warranted assertibility. (I think that this is indeed Quine's position.) We must not confuse semantic and epistemological concepts, as did coherence theorists like H. H. Joachim, who spoke of "Truth-or-knowl-edge".[44]

In Sexl's example the causal anomaly involved in a particle disappearing to infinity in one direction and reappearing from infinity in the opposite direction might in itself be taken to constitute a complication in the hollow world theory, but the theory involves other much more serious complications. Neither the velocity of light nor the average dimensions of stars and galaxies are the same everywhere and they depend on the particular centre of the universe. Martians, Venusians and Alpha Centaurians would all doubtless have their own special forms of the hollow world theory.

Different people will have different reactions to the hollow world theory. Most will (I think) say that they just *know* it to be false. This may of course be because they do not fully understand it and they mistakenly think that there is an observational falsification of it. However, it may also be because they do understand it and yet reject it on account of its complexity and the importance which it puts on one particular region of space, the (old) centre of the earth. However, others will take a different view and will hold that there is no factual difference between the old theory and the new one. I think that to take this line would be wrong. It comes from a verificationist theory of meaning which we should reject, or what is perhaps the same thing, a confusion of semantic and epistemological matters. Undetectable differences can still be differences. I have found that mathematicians sometimes say that the two theories are differ-ent "representations". Well, they are indeed representations of each other in the sense of being two structures isomorphically related to one another. From this we should not be tempted to go on to say that they are both representations of some underlying reality "behind" both the usual theory and the hollow world theory. (The difficulty is to see what could be meant by this.)

The main reason for rejecting the hollow world theory lies in the impor-tance which it attaches to the (old) centre of the earth. Apart from the objec-tionable particularity in this it leads to great complexity in the laws of nature. For this reason it seems to me that there is a right and wrong in the matter and that the hollow world theory is wrong. It is unclear to me how this relates to Quine's thesis of indeterminacy of translation.[45] In the case of indeterminacy of translation there is, according to Quine, no question of one translation being right and the other wrong (when there are two languages which can be mapped into one another, or one language which can be mapped into itself). Even though one might prefer one translation manual to another on the grounds of simplicity, I think that Quine would not allow that one translation was more correct than another, there being no objective fact in question. But I do want to talk of objective right and wrong in the case of the choice between the hollow world theory and its normal alternative.

If we think of the metrical, as well as the topological, properties of a space as hypothesized, then the so-called congruence definitions of physical geometry lose their apparently analytic or conventional character. That a metre stick remains a metre stick when it is moved from A to B is something deducible from the theory and is part of a network of propositions which is tested as a whole. If need be we can give up the so-called congruence definition in just the same way as we can give up any other sentence. After all, as Hilary Putnam has pointed out,[46] if the laws of nature are statistical (as according to quantum theory they indeed are) it is possible (though of course overwhelmingly improbable) that a metre stick should spontaneously double in length. The defender of a sharp concept of analyticity might say that if we gave up or modified a "congruence definition" we should merely have moved from one convention to another. In reply we could say that this was an unrealistic way of looking at the matter, and we could say this for familiar Quinean reasons. We still would have a place for a certain insight which Grünbaum (I think misleadingly) expresses when he says that the metric of space-time is not intrinsic (and is conventional). This insight seems to me to be as follows: there are fewer mathematical constraints on our use of the hypothetico-deductive method in physical geometry than we might be prone to think, and that a change in the metric alone can be made with less difficulty than a change in the topology. (Though certain distinctions may still need to be made. A change in the topology which was made by postulating a denumerable cardinality for the points of space-time would be a very drastic change, and it would force us to take an instrumentalist view of most of the mathematics used in physics. But it would not be such a peculiar or idiosyncratic change as a change to the hollow world theory!)

Sexl's position seems to be at the other extreme from Quine's: he holds to the conventionality not only of the metric but also of the topology. Grünbaum's position is intermediate. If he does not want to go all the way with Sexl, then his reasons against doing so should be reasons for moving to Quine's end of the spectrum.[47]

IV

Space-Time Language and Indexical Expressions

Let us now pass on to Quine's discussion of indexical expressions and its relevance to the philosophy of space-time. An important class of indexical expressions consists of tensed verbs. The tense indicates position in time in relation to the time of utterance of the word in question, or in the case of pluperfects and future perfects, in relation to some reference point which is dated as earlier or later than the utterance in question.[48] Quine excludes indexical expressions from canonical notation, which of course is based on the logic of quantification and contains only predicates, variables, truth-functional connectives, and quantifiers. In such notation all verbs (i.e., predicates) are tenseless and the "$\exists x$" must be read as a tenseless "there is a": any temporal reference must be made explicitly by means of temporal predicates.[49] Canonical notation is designed not for everyday use but in order to encompass total science, and Quine sees a consilience between quantification theory on the one hand and the theory of relativity on the other hand, since it is already natural to speak tenselessly when theorising about the relativistic space-time world.[50] Against this P. T. Geach has objected[51] that quantification theory is perfectly able to deal with tensed language and that Quine himself has shown how to do it in his *Methods of Logic*.[52] Despite this I shall try to defend Quine's preference for tenseless notation.

It is indeed perfectly possible for logic to deal with arguments in a language containing indexical expressions provided that certain precautions are taken. However the semantics of such a language will be more complicated than the semantics of Quine's canonical notation. My objection to tenses and other indexical expressions is partly this: that they conceal in their semantics notions which are made explicit in a language without such expressions. A comparison with the case of ordinary modal logic may help to clarify the issue. Consider a semantics for a theory which is expressed in terms of quantified modal logic. I shall assume that the theory quantifies over non-denumerably many entities, as normal scientific theories do, and that a substitutional semantics for the quantifiers will not work. I shall assume that David K. Lewis is right in holding that in this semantics there must be reference to possible worlds, as well as to the actual world, and to counterparts in the possible worlds to things in the actual world.[53] We have to think of the possible worlds as full blooded realities, at least if we are to believe in the semantics and to understand a theory which is based on quantified modal logic. As Lewis has nicely suggested, "actual" is an indexical expression: the actual world is that world in which our utterance "actual" occurs, and in each possible world denizens of that world will hold their own world to be the actual one. (I am aware that Saul Kripke has contested this interpretation of "possible world",[54] but I think that there are great difficulties in his own recent proposals for the semantics of modal logic. However as my discussion of modal logic here is illustrative only, I shall not go into this matter here.) Thus to believe in quantified modal logic you have to believe in a vast metaphysics of possible worlds, and also you need to have a notion of "counterpart" which is not very precise. Now if one is going to do this sort of thing, how much better it would be to do it *openly* within quantification theory, quantifying in the object language over possible worlds, as David Lewis has done in his "counterpart theory". This brings into the open the ontic commitments which are hidden behind the modal operators. Using modal logic is concealing skeletons in cupboards, whereas using counterpart theory is displaying them in the drawing room. (Lewis would doubtless contend that what I think of as skeletons are really beautiful sculptures.) Moreover, counterpart theory has greater expressive power than modal logic, because though to any sentence of the latter there is a sentence of the former, the converse is not true.

Now tenses do not commit us to a vast and questionable ontology in the way in which modal operators do, though they need modification to take account of the relativity of simultaneity in the theory of relativity. The semantics of tensed verbs, and of words like "past", "present", "future", and "now" can be fixed up fairly easily. The semantics of Quine's canonical notation is done in terms of satisfaction according to Tarski's method.[55] If we wish to extend this to a language containing indexical words we need (following Donald Davidson[56]) to replace ". . . satisfies . . ." by ". . . satisfies . . . for *P* at *t*", where *"P"* stands for a person who utters the sentence and *"t"* stands for a time of utterance. (And similarly, in consequence, for "true".) Thus "He will be hungry" as uttered by John Smith at 9.00 a.m. on 1 April 1973 is true if and only if the person referred to by John Smith at 9.00 a.m. on 1 April 1973 is (tenselessly) hungry at a time later than 9.00 a.m., 1 April 1973. If our only indexical expressions are tenses then the *"P"* may be left out, except for the fact that (because of special relativity) if we want to communicate with someone in a fast space-ship we have to mention a frame of reference, which might well be taken to be the rest system of the utterer of the sentence. For other indexical expressions, such as "I", "you" and "here", the introduction of *"P"* is more obviously needed. Now the introduction of *"P"* and *"t"* may suggest an Aristotelean or Strawsonian metaphysics of persons and the permanent in change, but this appearance is deceptive. If we take the velocity of light as unity (or comparable to unity) then we can think of a person (or if you prefer, his body) as approximately lying along a line in space-time. Now if we think of *P* as determining a line in space-time, then in effect this settles three coordinates with *t* settling the fourth.

As Quine has remarked, "Logic chases truth up the tree of grammar."[57] When we have a contextualist semantics we still have one tree but we have a whole mob of possums to chase up it. (One possum for each *"P* at *t"*.) So in order to apply quantification theory to testing an argument in ordinary language we need to assume that the *"P* at *t"* are held constant for all the sentences in the argument. In his *Methods of Logic* Quine puts the matter in terms of "ambiguous reference".[58] Indeed tenses and other indexical expressions are not the only causes of this. Consider Yehoshua Bar-Hillel's example of "the box was in the pen". We interpret "pen" as "play pen" not "fountain pen" because of our background knowledge of the small dimensions of fountain pens.[59] Davidson has discussed this example[60] and has suggested that we expand "for P at t" to "for P at t in circumstances c". Quantification theory can be applied to arguments provided that the "for P and t in c" is constant for all sentences in the argument.

However in the semantics for a language in Quinean canonical notation we do not need the "for P at t in c". This is all to the good because we do not want to have reference to persons and times in the semantics for science. (In so far as scientific language is embedded in ordinary language, then the reference to persons and times does occur in the semantics for scientific sentences, but only as harmless idle wheels.[61]) Though tenses do not commit us to a questionable ontology, as modal operators do, they do commit us (as can be seen when we look at the semantics) to a particularity which is contrary to the spirit of science. The advantages of the tenselessness of Quinean canonical notation are all the greater since the advent of the theory of relativity. The tenses of ordinary languages imply the uniqueness of the present, and hence of simultaneity. This uniqueness is denied in special relativity. Suppose that in future there are very fast space-ships. It may be natural for the inhabitants of each space-ship to use a coordinate system in which they are at rest. How could tensed language be modified so as to be usable by such space voyagers, even when signalling from one space-ship to another? A natural convention would be that the present tense as used by space-traveller Smith would be used to indicate simultaneity with respect to Smith's rest system, whereas the present tense as used by Brown would indicate simultaneity with respect to Brown's rest system. Such conventions would be clumsy to use, and it would be easier for theoretical purposes at least, to eschew tenses altogether. (I must concede that in practical life tenses are often useful. If at 12.00 a.m. I shout "someone is drowning" I give useful information to someone who does not know what the time is, save in so far as he knows that it is the time of my shouting. But this is no argument for admitting tenses to the canonical notation of theory.)

A reason for avoiding tenses when doing philosophy is that misunderstanding of them can lead to bad metaphysics. (In this respect they are not so bad as the operators of modal logic, which imply objectionable metaphysics even when they are *not* misunderstood!) Misunderstanding of tenses can lead to Bergsonian notions of the process or flow of time. Again, it is sometimes said that the tenselessly described Minkowski world of special relativity is a "static" one. This is to forget that change can be perfectly pictured in the Minkowski theory. Instead of saying that a substance changes we say that one temporal stage of a thing is (tenselessly) different from another temporal stage of it. A world without change would be one in which all the world lines of particles were parallel to one another.

It is sometimes argued that indexical expressions are needed in order to fix the origin of a coordinate system. This is not so because in fact we can pick out a unique origin, say the centre of the sun, by means of a conjunction of predicates which is so detailed that it is unlikely to be instantiated by more than one object. It might still be objected that a Quinean canonical language would not be enough for metaphysics, because in metaphysics we need at least to be able to talk about a possible universe in which individuation by means of predicates is not possible. The short Quinean answer to this of course is that in good metaphysics we do not talk about possible worlds. However let us nevertheless consider the objection a little further. Suppose that the universe is perfectly symmetrical with respect to a central point O so that corresponding to the object A there will be an exactly similar object A' on the other side of O. It is clear that in such a universe even the relational predicates applicable to A will be the same as those applicable to A', so that A could not be distinguished from A' (or Quine from anti-Quine), though they could be individuated by indexical expressions. (Quine and anti-Quine could both use the word ''I'' and in so doing they would refer to different objects.) I cannot see that Quine need be worried by such metaphysical anxieties. As I have noted, he does not believe in possible universes anyway, and his metaphysical interests are subserved so long as we can talk about the one and only actual universe, for which he has good empirical evidence that it is not a perfectly symmetrical one and that there is no anti-Quine. But for the sake of argument let us go along with a contrary to fact supposition, and suppose that there are Quine and anti-Quine in a perfectly symmetrical universe. We would have: $(\exists x)\ (\exists y\ (x\ \text{quines} \cdot y\ \text{quines} \cdot x \neq y)$. Why should the one Quine worry about which of the two quiners he is? If one is happy or hungry then so is the other. Everything needful for science can still be said. One thing that could be said would be that every instance of the following schema would be true (restricting quantification to a universe of space-time objects, since presumably there would be uniqueness in the case of abstract objects): $(x)\ (\exists y)\ (Fx \equiv Fy \cdot y \neq x)$. Very odd it would be if there were such a law of nature, but everything which ought to be scientifically sayable would still be sayable.

J. J. C. SMART

PHILOSOPHY DEPARTMENT
AUSTRALIAN NATIONAL UNIVERSITY
MARCH 1974

NOTES

1. I prefer to say ''philosophy of space-time'' rather than ''philosophy of space and time'' because modern physics has shown that the common sense dichotomy between space and time is untenable.

2. See W. V. Quine, *Word and Object* (Cambridge, Mass.: M.I.T. Press, 1960), §49.

3. See W. V. Quine, "Ontological Reduction and the World of Numbers", *Journal of Philosophy* 61 (1964): 209–216, reprinted in W. V. Quine, *The Ways of Paradox and Other Essays* (New York: Random House, 1966).

4. See W. V. Quine, "Mr. Strawson on Logical Theory", *Mind* 62 (1953): 433–451, reprinted in *The Ways of Paradox*. See especially p. 145 of the latter.

5. See W. V. Quine, *Mathematical Logic,* Revised Edition (Cambridge, Mass.: Harvard University Press, 1951), p. 279.

6. See *Word and Object,* p. 251.

7. *Word and Object,* pp. 255–257.

8. See the reference to curved space-time on p. 303 of Quine's reply to Chomsky in Donald Davidson and Jaakko Hintikka (eds.), *Words and Objections, Essays on the Work of W. V. Quine* (Dordrecht: D. Reidel, 1969).

9. J. A. Wheeler, *Geometrodynamics,* (New York: Academic Press, 1962). A philosophical discussion of Wheeler's geometrodynamics may be found in J. C. Graves, *The Conceptual Foundations of Contemporary Relativity Theory,* (Cambridge, Mass.: M.I.T. Press, 1971).

10. See report of a lecture by Wheeler, *Nature* 240 (1972): 382.

11. A. Einstein, "Zur Elektrodynamik bewegter Körper", *Annalen der Physik* 17 (1905): 891–921. An English translation of this may be found in H. A. Lorentz, A. Einstein, H. Minkowski, and H. Weyl, *The Principle of Relativity, A Collection of Original Memoirs on the Special and General Theory of Relativity* (New York: Dover, 1952).

12. Nevertheless a theologically based (and non-verificationist) argument of Leibniz could be easily adapted to his own purposes by a verificationist philosopher. See §5 of Leibniz's third paper in reply to Samuel Clarke's second reply, in H. G. Alexander, *The Leibniz-Clarke Correspondence* (Manchester: Manchester University Press, 1956).

13. See W. V. Quine, *Ontological Relativity and Other Essays* (New York: Columbia University Press, 1969), p. 149.

14. *Word and Object,* p. 253.

15. Ernst Mach, *The Science of Mechanics: A Critical and Historical Account of its Development* (La Salle, Illinois: Open Court, 1960), Chapter II, Section VI.

16. *Word and Object,* pp. 256–257.

17. For a theory of conditionals based on a theory of possible worlds see David K. Lewis, *Counterfactuals* (Oxford: Blackwell, 1973).

18. For such a theory, see W. V. Quine, "Necessary Truth", in *The Ways of Paradox,* pp. 48–56.

19. Saul Kripke, "Naming and Necessity", in G. Harman and D. Davidson (eds.) *Semantics of Natural Language* (Dordrecht: D. Reidel, 1972), pp. 253–355 and 763–769.

20. *Critica* 2 (1968): 3–22, reprinted in *Ontological Relativity and Other Essays.*

21. *The Ways of Paradox,* pp. 199–207; *Ontological Relativity and Other Essays,* pp. 55–68.

22. See *Ontological Relativity and Other Essays,* p. 58.

23. Leslie H. Tharp, in his "Ontological Reduction", *Journal of Philosophy* 66 (1971): 151–165, has argued that Quine's criteria for reduction (e.g., the specification of a proxy function) need to be supplemented by informal ones.

24. On the referential opacity of ". . . is explained by . . ." and for the suggestion that we should take explananda to be sentences (or the truth of sentences), see

W. V. Quine and J. S. Ullian, *The Web of Belief* (New York: Random House, 1970), pp. 74–75.

25. *Ontological Relativity and Other Essays*, pp. 139–160.

26. On abstract algebra and the like, see W. V. Quine, *Mathematical Logic*, Revised Edition, p. 279.

27. But perhaps instrumentalism is part and parcel of contemporary quantum theory anyway. On this worrying matter see P.K. Feyerabend, "A Recent Critique of Complementarity", *Philosophy of Science* 35 (1968), 309–331, and 36 (1969), 82–105.

28. Adolf Grünbaum, *Philosophical Problems of Space and Time*, Second, enlarged, edition (Dordrecht: D. Reidel, 1973).

29. Roman U. Sexl, "Universal Conventionalism and Space-Time", *General Relativity and Gravitation*, 1 (1970): 159–180.

30. Grünbaum, *Philosophical Problems of Space and Time*, pp. 98–100.

31. See Grünbaum, *Philosophical Problems of Space and Time*, near bottom of p. 151, where the contrast is made between "inductive" and "descriptive" simplicity, and also pp. 66–67. Near the top of p. 144 Grünbaum contrasts the "factual commitments" of a theory with its "linguistic trappings".

32. *Philosophical Problems of Space and Time*, p. 111.

33. See Adolf Grünbaum, *Philosophical Problems of Space and Time*, Second, enlarged, edition, 468–474.

34. For a discussion of Massey's pathological metrics see Grünbaum, *Philosophical Problems of Space and Time*, Second, enlarged, edition, pp. 487–488.

35. See Lawrence Sklar, "The Conventionality of Geometry", in Nicholas Rescher (ed.), *Studies in the Philosophy of Science, American Philosophical Quarterly Monograph Series* No. 3, (Oxford: Blackwell, 1969), pp. 42–60.

36. See W. V. Quine, *The Ways of Paradox*, pp. 112–113 and 124.

37. Roman U. Sexl, "Universal Conventionalism and Space-Time". [Added in February 1977, and after seeing a typescript of Quine's 'Reply'. My article has now been a good few years in the press, and in the meantime Graham Nerlich has pointed out to me what seems to be a flaw in Sexl's argument. Where does the point at the centre of the earth go under Sexl's transformation? Or for that matter where would a particle or point mass at the centre of the earth go? Yet to "take out" this point is already to change the topology, and even though it might not alter the observational consequences of the theory, it can make an ontic difference to the theory. On this matter see Graham Nerlich, *The Shape of Space* (London: Cambridge University Press, 1976), p. 101 (footnote) and p. 146 (footnote). Nerlich and I agree of course (as against Sexl) that the topology is not a matter of convention.]

38. Sexl's conventionalism about the metric goes further than Grünbaum's in that Sexl allows non-Riemannian metrics.

39. For a readable account of the origins of this eccentric theory see Martin Gardner, *Fads and Fallacies in the Name of Science* (New York: Dover, 1957), Chapter 2.

40. As Sexl puts it, on all wave functions.

41. Hans Reichenbach, *The Philosophy of Space and Time*, (New York: Dover, 1958).

42. See Reichenbach, *The Philosophy of Space and Time*, p. 285.

43. See Donald Davidson, "True to the Facts", *Journal of Philosophy* 66 (1969): 748–764.

44. H. H. Joachim, *Logical Studies* (London: Oxford University Press, 1948).

45. W. V. Quine, *Word and Object*, p. 27 and pp. 72–79, and "Ontological Relativity", in *Ontological Relativity and Other Essays*, pp. 26–68.

46. Hilary Putnam, "An Examination of Grünbaum's Philosophy of Geometry", in B. Baumrin (ed.), *Philosophy of Science, The Delaware Seminar,* Vol. 2, (New York: John Wiley, 1963), pp. 205–255. See especially p. 229.

47. In an interesting article, "Topology, Cosmology and Convention", *Synthese* 24 (1972): 195–218, Clark Glymour gives examples of alternative but observationally indistinguishable cosmologies. They are of more physical interest than Sexl's simple but fanciful example. I think that Glymour and I are philosophically in agreement in wanting to take a realistic attitude to alternative topologies, but there are doubtless subtleties in his views which I have missed.

48. See H. Reichenbach, *Elements of Symbolic Logic* (New York: The Macmillan Company, 1947), §50–51.

49. See Quine, *Word and Object,* §36.

50. W. V. Quine, "Mr. Strawson on Logical Theory", in *The Ways of Paradox,* pp. 135–155. See especially p. 145.

51. P. T. Geach, "Some Problems about Time", *Proceedings of the British Academy* 51 (1965): 321–336, especially pp. 322–323. This paper has been reprinted in P. F. Strawson (ed.), *Studies in the Philosophy of Thought and Action* (London: Oxford University Press, 1968).

52. W. V. Quine, *Methods of Logic,* Revised Edition (New York: Holt, Rinehart and Winston, 1959). See p. 43.

53. David K. Lewis, "Counterpart Theory and Quantified Modal Logic", *Journal of Philosophy* 65 (1968): 113–126.

54. Saul Kripke, "Naming and Necessity", in G. Harman and D. Davidson (eds.), *The Semantics of Natural Languages* (Dordrecht, Holland: D. Reidel, 1972), pp. 253–355.

55. For a very readable exposition of Tarski's theory of truth see W. V. Quine, *Philosophy of Logic* (Englewood Cliffs: Prentice-Hall 1970), Chapter 3.

56. See Donald Davidson, "Truth and Meaning", *Synthese* 17 (1967): 304–323, and "Semantics for Natural Languages", *Linguaggi Nella Societá e Nella Technica* (Milan: Edizioni di Communitá, 1970), pp. 177–188. In Davidson's treatment of tenses these are not treated as operators and there is no "tense logic". Moreover the semantics for non-tensed expressions does not depend on that for tensed ones.

57. W. V. Quine, *Philosophy of Logic,* p. 35.

58. W. V. Quine, *Methods of Logic,* p. 43.

59. Yehoshua Bar-Hillel, *Language and Information* (Jerusalem: Hebrew University, 1964), p. 182.

60. Donald Davidson, "Semantics for Natural Languages". See p. 182.

61. Davidson has suggested that a language without indexicals would not be learnable. It is not clear to me that this is so, but if it is so, then we do need a reference to persons and times in the semantics for even canonical notation, which would be a substructure of a natural language. But even so, the reference to persons and times, so far as canonical notation is concerned, would be mere "idle wheels" in the semantics.

REPLY TO J. J. C. SMART

Smart rightly represents me as having espoused a relational theory of space-time. But he goes on to say that in a later publication I seem to lean toward an absolute theory. Puzzled, I looked up the source (*Words and Objections*, p. 303) and found a misleading remark. By "my fully realistic attitude toward electrons and muons and curved space-time" I meant only my literal acceptance of physicists' testimony on these topics. I meant acceptance of their doctrine that space-time is curved rather than Euclidean, but I continued to regard this as a doctrine about the distances and relative motions of particles and other bodies.

He reports my treatment of physical space-time coordinates in *Word and Object*, and remarks that in "Propositional Objects" I took the further step of identifying space-time points with their coordinates. Actually this was my intention already in *Word and Object*, and indeed it fits with my early doctrine about pure geometry which Smart cites from *Mathematical Logic*. I have held what Smart calls the "quasi-absolute" theory early and late. What is relational about it is that no one choice of coordinate axes is theoretically pre-eminent.

He had not seen my paper "Whither Physical Objects?", which was still at press when I received his. In it I adduced reasons from microphysics for rejecting the notion of particle and speaking rather of the distribution of various quantitative states over regions of space-time. The regions would be identified with sets of coordinates, hence sets of quadruples of numbers. A state would be ascribed to a region by applying an appropriate functor and equating the result to a real number. Pure set theory, without ground elements, would thus serve as the ontology. The vocabulary would consist of symbolic logic, the epsilon of set theory, and a finite lexicon of physical functors.

What then of our dependence on one arbitrary system of measurement and frame of reference? Smart reports my suggestion in "Propositional Objects" of how to transcend this limitation in the case of a Newtonian universe. He expresses reasonable doubt as to whether the same sort of thing can be done for modern physics.

I can rationalize the adherence to a single system of measurement and a fixed frame of reference. The units of measurement can be selected with a view to minimizing the use of constants of proportionality in the basic laws. As for the fixed frame of reference, it would simply not show itself in strictly theoretical physics; laws would quantify over quadruples of numbers and pick none specifically. The particularity of the frame of reference would emerge in astronomy, geology, geography, and history, where it belongs. It would figure as an exalted indexical; and indeed it probably would have been specified with help of ostensively learned terms in the first place. The contrast suggests a demarcation between physical law and casual matter of fact, between the causal and the casual.

Even though quantifying indiscriminately over quadruples of numbers, theoretical physics would still—Smart feels—be making "implicit reference to particulars" because of our tacit frame of reference, I do not find this objectionable. The physical theory would still look the same if we changed the underlying frame of reference; and this, I feel, is aloofness enough.

Smart is unusual in sharing my distrust of a distinction between factual truth and truth by convention; hence between differences of language and differences of doctrine. Yet one must sympathize with the dissident multitude on this issue when one considers an extreme example of the following sort, suggested by Barbara Humphries: two physics texts that agree *verbatim* except that one of them uses the respective words 'electron' and 'molecule' wherever the other uses 'molecule' and 'electron'. The two are in surface contradiction: the one affirms things about electrons, so called, that the other denies. Yet both are sustained by the same observations. Are we to say that we have here two alternative theories explaining the observations, and that they disagree regarding the properties of electrons and of molecules? Or are we to say that we have one theory and a terminological difference? The man in the street, stout fellow, will describe the disagreement in the latter way. But Smart and I would seem to be committed to denying any real difference between the two descriptions of the disagreement.

An unobjectionable way of describing the relation between the two imaginary physics texts is as follows. Relative to the homophonic manual of translation—the identity transformation—the two physics texts stand in logical contradiction. Relative to another and better manual of translation, which is homophonic except for translating 'molecule' as 'electron' and vice versa, the two physics texts agree completely. The second manual of translation is better in that it maximizes doctrinal agreement. One of the physics texts is likewise better than the other, and not merely in that it adheres to a more widespread usage. It is better in that the etymologies of 'electron' and 'molecule' hint of electricity and molarity, appropriately in that text and inappropriately in the other.

Again there is the odd cosmology that Poincaré constructed to argue the conventionality of geometry. Space was finite and things shrank as they moved away from center. The same considerations apply to this example as to the trivial example of 'molecule' and 'electron'. Relative to homophonic translation, the odd cosmology conflicts with Newton's; relative to a more elaborate manual of translation the two accounts agree. The more elaborate manual of translation is defensible, despite its complexity, on the score of maximizing agreement. And Newton's cosmology is better than Poincaré's fantasy on the score of simplicity. It is important to note that reconcilability by translation does not mean that two accounts are equally good.

Similar remarks apply to the cosmological fantasy that Smart cites from Sexl. Generalizing, one might like to demarcate fact and convention in terms thus of translation. One might say that two texts agree factually and differ only conventionally if we can see how to bring them into logical equivalence by constructing a translation manual that touches only theoretical sentences and leaves observation sentences undisturbed. I discussed these matters in ''Empirically Equivalent Systems of the World'', but Smart had not seen that paper; it was still at press when I received his.

I was gratified by Smart's defense of the canonical notation in which we banish tense in favor of the four-dimensional view. I was gratified by his scorn for the stubborn notion of the flow of time, the stubborn notion that the four-dimensional world is static, and the stubborn notions of possible worlds and counterparts. In connection with his discussion of indexical expressions, two clarificatory remarks may be in order for some readers (though not for Smart). One is that the elimination of indexical expressions is the least of my motives for eliminating tense. The other is that I have no stake in maintaining that language could be learned, or coordinates fixed, without indexical expressions. I am content to ascend to canonical notation by a ladder of indexicals, which may then be kicked away.

W. V. Q.

19

P. F. Strawson

REFERENCE AND ITS ROOTS

It is impossible to write about reference without referring to Quine. He who does the first does the second. I myself have done both often enough and am now to do both again. But I need have no fear of repeating myself. The appearance of *The Roots of Reference,* packed with fresh thoughts brilliantly phrased, supplies enough, and more than enough, new matter. What follows is concerned solely with that book, is a critique of certain aspects of it. Only of certain aspects. On set theory, for example, the hot-house of reference, I have nothing to say. I am concerned only with the roots and the natural growths, the common or garden flowers.

I begin with (I) a few general reflexions on Quine's reform of epistemology and his shunning of the mentalism that haunted its classical forms; there follows (II) the substance of my critique; I end with (III) a short defence against a possible charge of misunderstanding.

I

Classical empiricist epistemology took the way of ideas and the way branched into different familiar paths. One led to scepticism about the objects of natural science, others to idealist interpretations, others to a laboriously argued realism. A reformed epistemology, Quine suggests, will take science for granted and ask, given its results, how we came to achieve them. The question itself belongs to natural science. Impingements on the human exterior progressively modify the inner constitution in such a way that yet further impingements produce a behavioural output which counts as manifesting command of scientific theory, including, crucially, the apparatus of objective reference. Just what are the mechanisms involved? That is the question.

Or is it? As the story develops, as the explanation of early learning and later elaboration of language and theory gets under way, physiological mechanisms recede into the background. They may, someday, be isolated (27).[1] It is a comfort, perhaps, to be confident they are there, to be assured that all the terms used in the course of the explanation have correlates of enormous complexity in the realm of receptors, neural paths and fibres of striped muscle. But it is the various terms of the explanation that do the explaining, not this perfectly general assurance, invariant in form at all stages. It is the melody, not the ground-bass, we attend to.

When mentalism is forsworn, it is important to be clear just where, and within what limits, it is being forsworn. As theorists we investigate the acquisition of theory, beginning with the acquisition of speech. We are not to speculate about inaccessible goings-on in our subjects' minds. We are to attend to what is observable, including utterances of words, "out where we can see and hear them" (35). Thus the language-learning process is "a matter of fact, accessible to empirical science" (37). So the theorist *observes* the teacher's conditioning of the child to utter an observation sentence in appropriate *observable* circumstances: to utter 'red', say, in the conspicuous presence of red. But how does the theorist come to treat the occasion as one for learning about the learning of 'red'? Surely the theorist of theorising here tacitly credits the observant theorist with the full mentalistic load of perceptual-conceptual experience: with *seeing* what *he* sees *as* red, *hearing* what *he* hears *as* 'red'. And how does the theorist—the first theorist this time, not his meta-half—how does he suppose the teacher knows when to teach? Without the tacit appeal to mentalism at some point, the explanation could never start, could never count as explanation, could never be understood.

However it may be with theorists and teachers, can we not still avoid mentalism in our account of the learning subject, the child? What he goes through falls "within the scope of standard animal training" (42). When we say that "the learning of an observation sentence amounts to determining. . .the distinctive trait shared by episodes appropriate to that observation sentence" (43), this is to be construed as referring to the bringing about in the child, by a combination of impingements, of an internal modification which itself results in a selective response to further impingements. But the child is father of the man, the learner of the teacher and even of the theorist of learning. In the end he must be viewed as mentalistically as his mentor; and *this* end is not far from the beginning. Before long the pupil shares the teacher's understanding; knows when to respond just as teacher knows when to encourage; says as teacher says because he sees as teacher sees.

So much mentalism is elementary, a fairly easy consequence of the emphasis on externality commended as observable. What of the psychogenetic stages that carry us ultimately to "the advancing front of natural science"? Surely it is right to conceive the stages, as Quine does, in terms of "analogical exten-

sion" or "natural if not inevitable continuation of what is already at work at
lower language levels" (121), to think of steps in the development of system
as a "series of short leaps each made on the strength of similarities or analogies" (138). At the advancing front itself we are said to go forward with our
eyes open: "the minds at the advancing front are themselves aware of what
they are doing" (130). Before we reach it, that front, we jump and stumble
forward in the dark, with but a dim consciousness, if any, of the analogies
which guide our steps. But it is the retrospective discerning of the guiding
analogies which yields the understanding of the forward movement; and this
we elicit from ourselves by a variant of that species of self-conscious reflexion
on our own practice and its rationale which is characteristically philosophical.
Certainly we should check with the psycho-linguists; but the categories we use
in submitting the story to check, and in interpreting the psycho-linguists' independently advertised results, these categories belong to logical reflexion. We
need the perspective of minds that know what they're doing to appreciate the
stages by which they reached the point of knowing.

These points have further connexions, connexions, in particular, with the
attempt to understand our *developed* understanding of the semantically significant structural features of language; for a theory of development is an ingredient in a theory of developed understanding. We handle our structural forms
with unreflective expertise just as we handle the items of vocabulary which fill
them with unreflective expertise. Reflexion may suggest principles of handling
which the more reflective handlers may recognize and acknowledge; and they
will be the readier to do so in proportion as they can see more sophisticated
styles of thought as emerging, by analogy and extension, from more basic
styles.

We may perhaps hope, in the end, for a physiology of mental development,
disclosing the underlying mechanisms, the adjustments of micro-functioning;
but the logical reflexion, the critical self-consciousness, comes first.

II

When does objective reference emerge? It stands forth in its clearest, unclut-
tered form, Quine holds, in the apparatus of quantification and variables; and
so he suggests that we could "approximate to the essentials of the real psychogenesis of reference" (100) by a plausible account of the steps which could
lead the child or the primitive to quantification. But "quantification, in the
form in which we have come to know and love it, is less than a hundred years
old" (100). Science is not so young; and even now the knowing lovers form
but a small minority of those whom science would not blush to acknowledge

as her own. So it might be wiser not to confine ourselves to checking the steps of the Quine-child, but rather to allow ourselves and our subject to make free with "the less tidy referential apparatus of actual English" (100).

There is a certain wavering over the characteristics of this last or a certain reluctance, perhaps, even to concede the character of "referential apparatus" to any forms other than the canonical. Predication goes hand-in-hand with reference. The forms 'An α is a β', 'Every α is a β', are put forward as forms of predication on p.66 and firmly denied to be such on p.93; "This is not a predication. It couples two general terms." Again, plural endings are mentioned on p.84 as a feature of the referential apparatus of English, but no single instance of their functioning as part of that apparatus is allowed a mention in these pages; notoriously, 'Many αs are β', 'A few αs are β', etc. are not very easily or simply accommodated in the favoured idiom.

It seems best explicitly to acknowledge the distinction between a wider and a narrower notion of a form of predication. In the narrower notion all predication, whether under quantification or not, joins a general term in predicative position to a singular term in referential position and hence is grammatically singular, creating no role for plural endings. The wider notion allows general terms, with or without plural endings, into subject-position. Shall we say: into *referential* position? or restrict that title to a place occupied only by a singular term, whether name or variable? It hardly matters. It does matter that we should see "the referential apparatus of actual English" as at home with the wider notion. One thing we may helpfully notice as common to both conceptions of predication, a bridge between them: the proper name of the bodily individual, the singular term *par excellence,* is admitted by both as a prime occupant of subject- or referential position. It is not the only thing; some singular pronouns, too, are, on both conceptions, equally admissible occupants of the place.

So what is the path to predication? How does our child, or primitive, make his way to the referential apparatus? Quine envisages a pre-predicative situation of language-learning and language-use, where all sentences are occasion-sentences and all terms observation-terms. He distinguishes, initially, three classes of observation-terms. To the first belong 'red', 'water', 'sugar', 'snow', 'white'; 'Fido' and 'Mama' are examples of the second; 'dog', 'apple', 'buckle', 'woman' of the third. For the learning child all are alike in so far as it is the recurrence of some recognisable circumstance that prompts utterance, or assent to utterance, of any of them. Still, there are general differences, in the bases of his recognition, between the three classes. Red can manifest itself in simultaneous scattered portions, as can water; and shape has nothing to do with the recognisability of either. But Mama is neither scattered nor amorphous; 'Mama' names a body. Terms of both these classes, however, "share a certain semantic simplicity" (55) which does not belong to terms of the third class. These last are more sophisticated. 'Dog', 'buckle', etc. have built-in individuation and to learn them the child must master their individuative force: he can be "confronted by many dogs at once" and has to learn "what to count as one dog and what to count as another". (55)

With later developments in mind (Quine says), we can categorize 'Fido' and 'Mama' as singular terms and 'apple', 'dog', etc. as general terms. But "our categorizing them as such is a sophisticated bit of retrospection that bears little relation to what the learning child is up to" (85); for the terminology of 'general' and 'singular' terms is appropriate only at the level of objective reference and the child has not yet reached that level when the limit of his achievement is utterance, or assent to utterance, of observation terms on appropriate occasions. This holds good whatever the class of the term, although (Quine adds) the learning of terms of the third class brings the child a step nearer to objective reference "because of the individuation" (85).

There is much to pause over in this. Consider first the claim that 'Fido' and 'Mama' are semantically simpler than 'dog' and 'woman', together with the claim that the first pair are nevertheless what in due course we may classify as singular, the second pair what we may in due course classify as general, terms. The simplicity-ordering is backed by the observation that to learn the name 'Fido' the child has only to appreciate the similarity of Fido-presentations whereas to learn 'dog' he "has to appreciate a second-order similarity between the similarity-basis of 'Fido' and the similarity-bases determining other enduring dogs" (56). But the child is said to be learning 'Fido' and 'Mama' *as singular names* or what will eventually qualify as such. If this is so, it is not enough that the child should not in fact encounter, or be confronted by, a plurality of simultaneous but spatially separated presentations sufficiently similar for them all to count for him as Fido-presentations. It must be part of his mastery of 'Fido' that Fido is unique. A plurality of Fidos simultaneously soliciting his attention must be ruled out by his understanding of the term— semantically ruled out. If it is not ruled out, then 'Fido' is semantically on a par with 'dog', deserving just as much as the latter to be called a general term, though doubtless more specific. But if it is ruled out, then what becomes of the claim that 'Fido' is semantically simpler than 'dog'? The answer at least is simple: we just reverse the terms. Fido is not just *any* Fido-like creature, though he is that; he is the one and only Fido.[2] 'Fido' is a more, not a less, sophisticated acquisition than 'dog'. 'Dog' has individuation; 'Fido' has individuation plus.

Let us consider, second, the thesis that the learning of 'dog', for all the built-in individuation and for all that it is a step on the way, has not yet brought the child to the point of objective reference. Why not? What must he do to qualify? Would it be enough if he said 'dogs' in the presence of a plurality? But he is supposed already to have mastered the individuation, to be able to tell one dog from another; 'dog' for him, as occasion sentence, has the force that 'a dog' has for us. Of course he hasn't mastered the *whole* apparatus of objective reference. But why hasn't he wholly mastered a part of it?

It is difficult to find in Quine's text an explicit answer to this question. But the text strongly suggests the following answer: that no one has reached the stage of reference unless he has at least reached the stage of predication. A predication, on any view, must be a joining of terms, capable of yielding truth or falsity according as the terms are aptly or inaptly joined. But the child's primitive observation sentences consist only of one term, of whichever of Quine's three classes. There is, of course, a certain implicit duality about the utterance, a duality which makes it capable of being right or wrong, assessable for truth-value. For we have both what he says and the when-and-where he says it. We can represent this duality to ourselves by tacking on to the term an explicit 'here-now', or we can think of the 'here-now' as implicit in the very utterance of the term. But the implicit 'here-now', an invariant feature of the observation-sentence, does not qualify as a term in a predication. No doubt a grown-up who says 'A dog is here' or 'At least one dog is here' or (more plausibly) 'There's a dog here' may be allowed to have exercised the power of objective reference, in that the adult utterance can be both grammatically and psychologically grouped with others of which the adult is capable but the child is not. But it would be a misrepresentation of the stage of development our child is at to make any such assimilation of *his* one-term observation sentence.

This, then, I suggest, is Quine's answer to the question why the child who has learned the individuative 'dog' has not yet reached the point of objective reference. Given my earlier point about 'Fido', the same question arises, with even greater force, about the child's mastery of that singular name; and it must receive the same answer. That this is the answer Quine would give is strongly borne out by his treatment of what he calls "observational compounds" (59–62); but that treatment also suggests that he is wedded to a very much stronger, and highly questionable, thesis about the conditions for achieving true predication and objective reference. These points I now proceed to develop, beginning with a sketch of Quine's position.

The child who has learned 'yellow' and 'paper' as observation terms, i.e., has learned to utter, or assent to, each as a one-term observation sentence, is well placed to be taught an observation term of a new kind—'yellow paper'. "All our mentor has to do to perfect our training in the compound" is to encourage assent when the yellow and the paper coincide and "to discourage assent in those less striking cases where the yellow and the paper are separate" (60). Given the learning of a few more such compounds, one by one, the child cottons on to the general principle: he learns to form new compounds of his own and to respond correctly to new ones proposed to him. But he is not yet at predication, not even when one of the terms is individuative, as in 'brown dog', or a name, as in 'wet Fido'. He has not learned to couple terms (predic-atively) to make a sentence, he has only learned to couple terms to make a term—which can serve as a sentence. The other element of the duality which yields truth-valuedness is still what it was before, the implicit 'here-now' of the utterance of the observation-sentence-term.

What of 'The dog is brown', 'Fido is wet', uttered or assented to in the conspicuous presence of a brown dog or of wet Fido? These have the gram-matical form of predications and, spoken by an adult, even in these circum-stances, may (doubtless? perhaps?) be accounted such. But for our child, at the present stage of his learning Odyssey, they could only be pointless variants on his pre-predicative one-term observation sentences where the term is a com-pound term; and variants which the teacher would do well to withhold from his pupil if he wants to bring the child to the point of true predication, the point of objective reference (67).

For to reach that point, Quine holds, the child has to cross a gulf—a gulf that separates all the learning he has done so far (the learning of occasion sentences) from the learning of the standing or "eternal predicational construc-tion" (65). This gulf is bridged, Quine suggests, by a quite different mecha-nism of learning from any put to work hitherto. The correct assent to, or asser-tion of, an observation term as occasion sentence requires the presence of the relevant feature or—in the case of an observational compound—the present coincidence of the relevant features. Correct assertion or assent just *is* assertion or assent on an occasion of such presence or coincidence. Correctness or in-correctness is wholly occasion dependent. But correctness of assertion or assent in the case of a standing or eternal sentence is quite a different matter. Cor-rectness is occasion-independent, assent is—subject to actual change of mind—once for all. So the mechanism of learning must be quite a different matter too.

Quine has a suggestion about this new mechanism of learning. In the con-spicuous or ostended presence of snow, the child has already learned occasion-assent not only to 'snow' but also to 'white'; in the presence of Fido, he has learned to assent not only to 'Fido' but also to 'dog'; in the presence of dog, not only to 'dog' but also to 'animal'. The mechanism proposed is that of transfer of conditioning, transfer of response from, e.g., "the snow stimulus to the associated verbal stimulus, the word 'snow'" (65). From the stage at which the presence of snow is sufficient to induce assent to 'white' the child moves to the stage at which the presence of 'snow' is sufficient to induce assent to 'white', irrespective of the presence or absence of snow. From assenting to 'dog' on seeing Fido he moves to assenting to 'dog' on hearing 'Fido'. Thus he learns to assent to queried eternal sentences, 'Snow is white', 'Fido is a dog' (65–6); and thence, by a psychological mechanism of generalisation, he moves to the point of producing such constructions on his own. (One sees why the formally predicative variants on observation-compounds had better not reach the child's ears too soon. Too early an exposure to them would at the very least necessitate a painful process of re-education—if it didn't dish the child's chances of learning predication for ever!)

Quine shakes his head a little over the murkiness of this transition, with its more-than-hint of confusion of sign and object, use and mention. But we should rejoice, he says, in the final outcome, science, rather than dwell on its dubious antecedents (68).

Still, there are other things to pause over in this account; and to pause over, this time, for rather longer. It is not the reputability, nor even the credibility, of such a way of "bridging the gulf" between observation sentence and eternal predication that need detain us. There is a prior question. Predication, for Quine, predication with objective reference at least, is like the soul of Adonais: it beacons from the abode where the eternal (sentences) are; between that abode and the lower regions of occasion-bound utterance there is a gulf to be bridged, or leaped; on the further side of the gulf stands predication, the joining of terms to make a sentence; on the hither side we have, at best, the joining of terms to make a term—an observational compound—which can serve as a sentence. The prior question is whether this picture is realistic.

Surely it is not. Predication does not stand on the further side of such a gulf. There is no such gulf. Several features of Quine's presentation may combine to mask from us, and from him, the realities of the case. One is the extremely confined range of examples of forms of predication considered at the point of transition: the two forms mentioned are the universal categorical 'An (i.e. any) α is a β' and the traditionally associated singular categorical exemplified by 'Fido is a dog'. Another is a striking omission from the range of observation terms considered: with one exception they include no words for types of happening or change. A third is an unrealistically sharp-edged conception of an 'occasion' or an 'occasion-sentence'.

Let us see how these work in together. Recall, first, Quine's account of the learning of attributive observational compounds. 'Yellow' and 'paper', already learned separately, provided good material: all we need is a coincidence of what could also occur separately and be verbally responded to separately, viz., yellow and paper. We need "an intersecting of the pertinent saliences" and the stage is set. Suppose, now, our child has learned 'dog' and 'cat' and, perhaps, 'Fido' and 'Felix'. Before his eyes a dog chases a cat. Perhaps Fido chases Felix. Another teaching opportunity. But what are we teaching him? We can scarcely have taught him 'chase' already, and separately, as an observation term all on its own, the pertinent salience now happily intersecting with dog- and cat-saliences so that we can seize the opportunity to introduce him to the observational compound 'dog chase cat' (or 'Fido chase Felix'). So the standard account doesn't fit. Are we then teaching him a predicational construction already at this tender stage, with full objective reference and no "hanky-panky over use and mention" (68)? Why not?

At one point Quine himself seems to waver, to forswear the theory of the gulf; notably enough, at the point where there figures the one exception or near-exception to my remark about the exclusion of happening-words from the list of observation-terms. Thus he says: "Attributive composition affords access to a rich vein of predications" (61); and immediately afterwards offers 'Mama is smiling' or 'smiling Mama' as an instance of attributive composition. But the wavering is only apparent. The doctrine is that we still have at most a "mere variant" (67) of the observational compound; that there is as yet no need to distinguish a genuinely different mode of composition.

What, then, of the point that the standard account of the learning or framing of observational compound doesn't fit the case of 'dog chase cat' or 'Fido chase Felix'? It doesn't really fit 'Mama smiling' either; much less the contented observation, 'Spoon gone', emanating from the child who has just pitched the instrument off his high chair.

Quine's answer emerges fairly clearly on pp. 61–2. Attributive composition, so clearly exemplified by the case of 'yellow paper', is not the only mode of constructing observation-terms from observation-terms. There are others. Quine mentions the '. . . in . . .' construction, which yields such terms as 'Mama in garden' and the '. . .-like' construction which yields 'dog-like', 'tree-like' etc. as further observation-terms. No doubt the '. . . chase . . .' construction and the '. . . gone' construction could be added to the list. It would be quite a long list. Too long surely. But the doctrine must be that all the phrases that can be formed by means of such constructions are sufficiently like a simple observation term to be themselves classified as observation terms—which can serve as sentences. "They can be viewed indifferently as terms or sentences" (62). Or to put the point negatively: there is as yet no sufficient case for distinguishing any one part of such a phrase as having an essentially predicative role in relation to some other part or parts to which a referential or subject-role can be assigned. A gulf still divides these constructions from predicative constructions proper.

The doctrine rests on a notion of sufficient likeness. But what is the respect of likeness? The answer, like the question, imposes itself. Every one of the complex terms yielded by these modes of composition is available as an occasion-sentence, available for utterance with that implicit 'here-now' which makes them subject to assessment as correct or incorrect, true or false, on any occasion of utterance. The underlying idea is still a little elusive. But it seems to be the thought that it is this combination of a situation-description, in itself truth-valueless, on the one hand, and the implicit 'here-now', on the other, which makes the utterance assessable for truth value in the light of what goes on—so that there is no occasion to find, in the composition of the situation-description itself, a structure which confers assessability for truth-value on the utterance. But how important is implicit 'now' as opposed to implicit 'a moment ago'? implicit 'here' as opposed to implicit 'nearby'? 'dog chase cat' happily murmurs the child when the chase has taken both of them out of sight or 'Cat drink milk' he remarks to Mama as she enters the room to find the saucer indeed empty and the cat licking his fur. Surely the child is not in error; and equally surely he has not, just by the timing of the announcement, taken so portentous a step as that from compound term construction to genuine predicative construction with objective reference.

But if he has not taken it now, when *does* he take it? Observe the formidable ambiguity of the phrase 'occasion-sentence'. Most of the sentences we utter outside our studies and seminars, however complicated their construction, depend, for assessment of their truth-value as uttered, upon account being taken of the *occasion* of utterance. They are sprinkled, you may say, with indicator-words, explicit or implicit. Some of them, numerous enough, yet but a small proportion of the whole, relate to what is within the range of direct observation at the very moment of utterace. These last are occasion-sentences in the narrow sense. I have just suggested that it would be absurd to hold that a structural revolution occurs when the child edges reminiscently (or anticipatorily) outside this narrow range. But if we agree that this is absurd, if we abandon the narrow sense, then we are on a slide which carries us smoothly down the whole range of occasion sentences in the broad sense, i.e., of all sentences which depend for their evaluation, as uttered, on account being taken of the occasion of utterance.

So shall we, after all, make the structural break only when we reach the end of the slide and are deposited on the secure terrain of the eternal sentence? More strictly, perhaps: shall we hold that the child makes *his* structural breakthrough when he steps, at any point, off this slide on to that terrain for the first time—thereafter predicating in occasion-dependent sentences too? But this would be, if possible, even less acceptable. It would seem bizarre to maintain, for example, that no sentence containing the first-person pronoun or possessive really exhibits predicational structure in the fullest sense of that phrase—unless its speaker has mastered some eternal sentence as well. Moreover, some of Quine's claimants for the status of eternal sentence—those which "gain [their] specificity through explicit use of names, dates, or addresses" (63)—are not, on any realistic view of the matter, eternal sentences at all, place- and person-names being what they are. It is quite unrealistic to say of such sentences that "their truth-values are fixed for good, regardless of speaker and occasion" (63). We could, indeed, within the limits of a language, remove or minimise speaker-and-occasion relativity by, e.g., adding dates and places of birth, if we knew them, to personal names. An unpromising route to logical metamorphosis. Better to say straight off that the goal is reached only when the sentences "most characteristic of scientific theory" (63) appear, the completely general sentences. Reviewing his review of the genesis and development of reference, Quine comes near to saying just this: "An early phase of reference, *perhaps the earliest worthy of the name,* was the universal categorical, as in 'A dog is an animal' '' (123).

There is surely confusion of aim here. 'When and how do we achieve objective reference?' is one question. 'When and how do we achieve that complete generality of utterance which frees our sentences, as regards truth-value, from any dependence on utterance-occasion?' is another question. There is no profit in conflating them. Objective reference and context-free, or setting-free, generality are doubtless alike "central to our scientific picture of the world" (89). But the achievement of setting-free generality is not essential to the achievement of objective reference. To legislate to the contrary is to obscure the understanding of both.

Back, then, to the starting-point—painful as it is to retrace one's steps. Back, in particular, to Quine's acknowledgment that the learning of individuative terms like 'dog' is a first step towards objective reference—'because of the individuation'' (85). Make this acknowledgment more generous; allow that step to take the child all the way to objective reference, though not indeed to mastery of all its modes (i.e., of all its apparatus); and the slippery questions we have been toying with appear as spurious as they really are. Let us by all means recognize, or at least allow for, a pre-referential and pre-predicative stage of language-learning. I myself used to call sentences (or terms) which might figure at this stage 'feature-placing' sentences (or terms).[3] There is nothing in that conception which excludes composition of terms to form compound feature-terms. These would correspond, within limits, to Quine's observational compounds. Only within limits; for what the conception of a feature-placing sentence does exclude is individuative terms. The decisive conceptual step, the transition from the pre-referential to the referential stage, is the step to individuative terms. Individuation delivers individuals, and language which relates to individuals is referential. With individuative terms in general, and *a fortiori* with individual names, we have reference. I postpone for a moment the question whether we also have predication.

Consider, first, that the child who has taken the decisive conceptual step, who has learned 'dog', say, as an individuative term, has thereby learned to distinguish one dog from another from a third, to identify a dog as the same again. (Not that he never makes mistakes—the important thing is that he is able to make *such* mistakes.) He is poised, thereby, for the mastery of much of the referential apparatus of ordinary English, and for its employment in what we call noun-phrases containing the individuative term—the apparatus, e.g., of pluralisation, numeration, determiners, more or less vague quantifiers like 'a few', 'several', 'lots of'. I earlier issued a caution against neglecting, or bypassing, this ordinary apparatus in order to construct a speculative path by which the Quine-child could climb to mastery of canonical notation. It is not a path that any of us followed. Instead, we should recognize that wider notion of reference and predication, or subject and predicate, in which subject- or referential position is occupied not only by singular names or variables but also by noun-phrases consisting of general terms together with determiners, vague quantifiers, or number words. When we review our topic from this position, then—however much we may value the notation of logic—we must surely find it misleading to rule *both* that reference requires predication *and* that predication consists solely in coupling general term in predicative position with singular name(s) or variable(s) under quantification in such a way as to yield truth or falsity. Yet at least the hint of such a rule may be thought to underlie the reluctance to concede to the decisive step its full decisiveness.

The subjacent rule would encourage the reluctance in more than one way. 'A dog chases a cat', for example, with its English unreformed, would fail to qualify as referential since the terms in subject-position, the noun-phrases, though grammatically singular, are neither names nor variables. 'Here's a dog' or 'Two dogs are here' are in even worse case; not only do the putative subject-terms, the noun-phrases 'a dog' and 'two dogs' fail to qualify, the second more drastically than the first, but the indicator-word 'here' is at best a dubious candidate for the role of general term in predicative position. Yet it would be strange to maintain that the appropriate utterance of these sentences does not show, whereas utterance of, say, 'Something (here) is such that it is a dog' would show, that the utterer had got hold of the trick of objective reference. The latter, artificial form indeed satisfies the rule's requirement for predication—it has an undoubted general term, 'dog', in predicative position; whereas the ordinary 'A dog is here', with the noun-phrase, 'a dog', as putative subject-term, does not. But surely it matters not a straw whether we *call* 'A dog is here' or 'Two dogs are here' predications or not. Traditional grammar sanctions it; and if we insist that there is no such thing as objective reference without predication, we had better follow traditional grammar.

I have already referred to another way in which the subjacent rule might operate to delay recognition of objective reference. It seems sufficiently important in Quine's thinking to deserve mentioning once more. This is the idea that where there is objective reference, it is the predicative or predicative-cum-quantificational combination of terms *and this alone* which yields as outcome something assessable for truth or falsity. Or rather, since this description is ambiguous, it is the construction put on this condition which is responsible, a construction which turns it into a condition satisfiable by eternal sentences alone, a condition disqualifying all dependence, explicit or implicit, on indicator-words, ruling out any degree of determination of the truth-value-assessable outcome by the circumstances of utterance, including time, place, identity of speaker and other less obvious features of the utterance-setting. A mild symptom of this effect I noted in referring to Quine's readiness to multiply constructions yielding complex observation-terms rather than acknowledge predication and reference at the level of occasion-sentences in the narrow sense. I speculated on his readiness to add the 'chase' construction to the list to deal with 'dog chase cat' or 'Fido chase Felix'. But surely good sense must quickly call a halt. What a complication of term-yielding constructions would be necessary to deny the status of full objective-reference-cum-predication to such a simple observation as 'Fido is fighting two other dogs in the garden'.

III

It may be felt that much of the foregoing misses the essential point of Quine's position; that it is not by any sort of oversight that he defers recognition of the achievement of objective reference; that he really holds that objective reference in the fullest sense (101) is not achieved until we reach the level of general theory and until our theories are couched, in effect, in terms solely of predicates, truth-functions, and quantification (139). But if this is to be more than an idiosyncratic definition, if it is to be a thesis, it needs defence. And how should it be defended? Not on the ground that such is the language of science. The language of science is simply this or that natural language, enriched, sometimes, by the symbolism of mathematics; differing from the language of law reports or Parliamentary debates only in descriptive vocabulary, not in grammatical structure; but when we speak of the apparatus of reference, it is grammatical structure, not descriptive vocabulary, that is our topic.

Is it claimed, rather, that the range of our references stands forth more clearly when we effect (where we can) the paraphrase into the quantificational notation as we now have it? If this is the claim, it should be noted, first, that it is a different claim. It is no longer disputed that we who are content with the ''less tidy referential apparatus of actual English'' are as fully engaged in objective reference as the purist of logical language; it is claimed merely that we are not so clear about what we are referring to.

But there seems to be no reason for conceding even this claim. There is nothing intrinsic to the spare apparatus of variable and predicate which makes it any better an index than the less tidy, i.e., richer, referential apparatus of actual English. It is true that we deploy the referential apparatus of actual English with a lavishness which may offend nominalistic scruple. But, again, there is nothing in the formal structure of quantification which inhibits a quite parallel lavishness in *its* deployment. We may have, or think we have, reasons for wishing to check, or limit, this lavishness. Some may, in particular, insist that no deployment of referential apparatus, rich or spare, tidy or untidy, shall count as comporting objective reference (or even, in strictness, be admitted at all) unless either a general principle of individuation or a general 'criterion of identity' is forthcoming for the sort of thing to which the putative objects of reference belong. This is an issue I have discussed elsewhere,[4] arguing, in effect, that though individuative principles are integral to the birth of reference (to reference to spatio-temporal particulars), it is gratuitous, and would be crippling, to insist that they be forthcoming at every stage through which, by logical analogy, reference evolves. The issue itself is not now to the point. The point is that whatever stand we take on the issue we must take on its own philosophical merits. The referential forms themselves, rich and familiar or spare and strange, make no metaphysical claims and impose no ontological limitations. It is we who do these things, if we do them at all—and for diverse reasons. What can be conceded, perhaps, is a certain harmony between a taste for spareness in the forms of reference and a distaste for luxuriance in the range of categories of items referred to. But now we are outside the range of reasons. As Quine remarks in another connexion, *de gustibus non disputandum est* (50).

P. F. STRAWSON

MAGDALEN COLLEGE
OXFORD UNIVERSITY
DECEMBER 1975

NOTES

1. Numerals in parentheses refer to pages in *The Roots of Reference* (La Salle, IL.: Open Court, 1974). Quotations proper are in double quotation marks. Single quotation marks are used for mention of words or phrases.

2. It is worth recalling here an experiment recorded by Bower in the course of his studies of the intellectual development of very young children. With the help of mirrors the child is surrounded with a plurality of Mama-presentations, moving and smiling together. The very young child is unbewildered, indeed delighted, at being confronted with many mamas at once. It is the somewhat older child who shows signs of distress. (Bower, *Scientific American*, October, 1971).

Doubtless the result admits of more than one interpretation. My argument, of course, is quite independent of it.

3. See *Individuals*, (London: Methuen, 1959) Chapter 6, section 6; also "Particular and General", *Proceedings of the Aristotelian Society*, 1953–4, reprinted in *Logico-Linguistic Papers* (London, Methuen, 1971).

4. See "Entity and Identity", in H. D. Lewis, (ed) *Contemporary British Philosophy*, Fourth Series, London: Allen and Unwin, New York: Macmillan.), pp. 93–120.

REPLY TO P. F. STRAWSON

Strawson begins with a plea for the mental, which he sees my naturalism as repudiating. I shall try to clarify my attitude toward the mental. Feeling pain, thinking about Vienna, understanding French, and the like, are in my view states of a physical organism. I do not repudiate them, nor do I envisage defining them in neurological terms, nor even in terms of behavior. The place of behaviorist strictures is in marshaling the symptoms by which these states can be recognized in persons other than ourselves. Introspection works nicely in ourselves, but even here we are indirectly dependent on the behavioral symptoms, for it is through them that we acquire our mentalistic vocabulary from our elders in the first place. Let me add that I do not insist on full behavioral criteria; see, e.g., *Roots of Reference,* p. 22, on perceptual similarity. Here, as in any natural science, full operational definition is too much to ask. A concept can play a central role in a good scientific theory and admit only very partial observational criteria. The more effective the concept is in unifying and simplifying the theory, or in suggesting plausible mechanisms, the more tolerant it behooves us to be of paucity of empirical criteria.

Now I turn to what Strawson says about me on reference. He interprets me as holding that reference requires variables and quantifiers and that nobody refers who has not mastered these esoteric devices. It never occurred to me to disavow such an absurd position until, to my surprise, I found myself suspected of it. Of my subsequent disavowals, the most recent is "On not Learning to Quantify." My essay "The Variable and Its Place in Reference", in Strawson's own *Festschrift,* is another. In it I hail the relative pronoun as the crucial referential particle in ordinary language, and the variable as its mathematical version. Note however that Strawson's present essay was written in 1975, thus antedating both of these pieces of mine.

My position is not subtle. Variables *become* the vehicle of reference *if* we switch to a regimented notation embracing only quantifiers, truth functions, predicates, and variables. To be is *then* to be the value of a variable—or, equivalently, to be among the denotata of a predicate or its complement. What counts as reference in some other notation, say ordinary language, hinges on how we choose to translate that notation into this regimented one. If we leave that choice open, as well we may, we leave the referential question hanging; for the choice of such translation is simply a choice of how to interpret one's notation in respect of reference and ontology. The reason for taking the regimented notation as touchstone is that it is explicit referentially, whereas other notations, having other aims, may be vague on the point.

There is nothing special about regimentation into variables and quantification, as against any other notations that are intertranslatable with that one in accepted ways—for instance predicate-functor logic. I add this reluctantly, because it is so glaringly redundant to do so. If translation into regimented notation A affords a touchstone of reference, and we are agreed on intertranslation of regimented notations A and B, then *of course* translation into B affords a touchstone of reference as well.

In my essay in Strawson's *Festschrift* I deplored the neglect of the relative clause in his writings on reference. In the relative clause we have the analogue and indeed the prototype, in H.M. English, of the bound variable. This is why in speculating on the ontogenesis of reference in the learning of language I have treated the mastery of the relative clause as its culmination.

Strawson supposes wrongly that I regard reference as suddenly coming into being. There is no thought of a "structural revolution." I see reference as emerging in degrees. In *Roots of Reference* I have speculated on the development, and in the first eight pages of *Theories and Things* I stress the degrees.

Strawsons finds that I neglect plurals. Whatever is accomplished by the contrast between singular and plural in English is accomplished along other lines in the regimented logical notation. No purpose is found for a distinction between 'Every A is a B' and 'All As are Bs', or between 'Some A is a B' and 'Some As are Bs'. In the fourth edition of *Methods of Logic*, though, I am finding it convenient to distinguish between 'A excludes B' and 'As exclude Bs' as readings of 'A $\subseteq$ $\bar{\text{B}}$'; on the one reading the capitals stand for abstract singular names of classes, and on the other reading they stand for general terms. As for his examples 'many' and 'few', they are of little scientific utility because of their vagueness; but there is no special problem here of plural endings. 'More than half the As are Bs' goes readily into the regimented notation of set theory.

Strawson writes that I envisage "a pre-predicative situation . . . where all sentences are occasion sentences and all terms observation terms." Sentences, yes; terms, no. Terms for me are emergent with predication. It is only with the advent of terms, moreover, and the individuation of their denotata over time, that we can properly recognize reference to Mama. Prior to all that, the observation *sentence* 'Mama' was associated with recurrent stimulation patterns no less scattered in time and varied in visual outline than those with which the observation sentence 'Water' is associated.

Strawson finds me multiplying grammatical constructions, assuming a new one for each transitive verb or preposition. This is not my analysis. I recognize *dyadic predication,* a single triadic construction that joins subject, verb, and direct object to form a sentence. I recognize the verb as a general term denoting each of various ordered pairs of objects.

W. V. Q.

20

Manley Thompson

QUINE'S THEORY OF KNOWLEDGE

The interpretation of Quine's theory of knowledge presented here differs considerably, especially in emphasis, from any I have seen. It is an interpretation I have come to gradually in rereading his work. I develop it gradually here, suggesting in the early sections tentative conclusions that are qualified in later sections. I hope my prejudices have not led me to push Quine much further in a certain direction than he wants to go. I have tried to show that he has a theory of knowledge and theory of language (the two being inseparably intertwined) and not merely, as some of his critics hold, a physics of stimulation and response. I have been led by my own interests and by limitations of space to slight, and in some cases even to pass over without mention, important points that many would consider essential to Quine's theory of knowledge. But I do not believe that the omissions affect my interpretation.

I

A person is "prompted" by sensory stimulation to assent to an "observation sentence," say the one-word sentence 'Red'. His assent, Quine says, "serves to attest to the presence of red".[1] But what is meant by 'presence of red'? A ready answer is that the phrase is short for 'the presence of something red'. But the trouble with this answer is that it is not always easy to specify just how assenting to 'Red' is attesting to the presence of *something* red. One may say, for instance, 'There is nothing red on the floor; only red light reflected from the stained glass window'. Such a remark, rather than specifying what the something is that is red, provides a causal account of why it looks as if there is something red on the floor. In order to understand the account one must have some minimal knowledge of the physics of color perception. There is nothing red on the floor in the sense of something that can be picked up, or rubbed off, or painted over. There is only the reflection of red light from a small area on the floor. Yet one need have no understanding of this causal account in order to attest to the presence of red. One may have the erroneous belief that there is something tangible and red on the floor. But this belief does not prevent one from being prompted to assent to 'Red' and thereby to attest to the presence of red.

It may seem more reasonable to take 'the presence of red' as short simply for 'the presence of red light'. In a typical stimulatory situation that we would construct for testing whether one uses 'red' as a color word as we normally do, there would be the presence of red light. Why not say that in all such cases the person in assenting to 'Red' is attesting to the presence of red light? The objection here is that we thus impute to the person our own theory of color perception. But when we say of a three-year old child that he knows his color words we do not mean that he knows anything at all about the role of light in color perception. We may say that the presence of red light is a causal antecedent of the sensory stimulations that prompt his assent to 'Red', but not that in assenting he is attesting to the presence of red light.

In an effort to explicate 'the presence of red' as a phrase specifying what is attested to we may be tempted to take it as short for 'the presence of a red sense datum'. But this appeal to sense data is just as theoretical and just as little applicable to a child who has just learned color words as our appeal to red light. The child's assent to 'Red' can be taken as attesting to the presence of a red sense datum only if he understands a certain amount of sense-datum theory and is able to follow instructions for picking out (recognizing) sense data in his own experience. We might think the difficulty here lies in our persistence in viewing 'the presence of red' as calling for the specification of something red—if not red light or a red sense datum then something else. Why not simply say that in assenting to 'Red' one attests to nothing more than that one is seeing redly? True, we do not expect the child to understand the phrase ''seeing redly', but unlike 'red light' and 'red sense datum', 'seeing redly' characterizes only what we may be sure the child is doing when he assents correctly to 'Red'. He may assent correctly without in any sense *recognizing* that he is stimulated by red light or has a red sense datum, but he cannot assent correctly unless he is *seeing* redly. In attesting to the presence of red the child is attesting merely to the fact that he is seeing redly. We thus seem to have an explication of 'the presence of red' that is in accord with Quine's contention that observation sentences are epistemologically prior to any reference to objects.

But this explication is only apparently in accord with Quine and is at best a parody of what he holds. We who observe the child and decide he has learned to use 'red' correctly as a color word are in a position to say that whenever he assents he is seeing redly. But we are equally in a position to say that whenever he assents his brain is stimulated in the way it normally is when his retina is

stimulated by red light. The two statements differ only in the degree of specificity with which they characterize the conditions that prompt the child's assent
to 'Red'. But in order for the child *himself* to be in a position to attest to the
fact of his seeing redly, and *a fortiori* to the fact that his brain is stimulated in
a certain way, he must be able to think of his seeing as something that may
occur independently of the object he sees. Yet before we have any reason to
say the child has acquired this ability we must find him capable of far more
complicated verbal behavior than any we ordinarily expect from a three-year
old who has just learned color words. In saying that in assenting to 'Red' a
person is attesting to the presence of red, Quine is not to be understood as
saying that what is attested to are the conditions that prompt the assent, even
if these conditions are specified only with the utmost generality by a phrase
such as 'seeing redly'. Quine is concerned ultimately with questions of reference, and he wants to begin with an account of assent to 'Red' which neither
presupposes nor precludes that with the assent there is a referential use of 'red'.
If this point is overlooked any attempt to expound Quine's theory of knowledge
can result only in a parody of it.

It will help at this point to note two different uses of 'attest'. With one use
'attest' has the force of 'demonstrate', 'reveal', 'make clear', as in 'His works
attest his industry', 'His manners attest his upbringing'. In another use it has
the force of such expressions as 'certify', 'declare to be true', 'vouch for',
'acknowledge'. In general, with this second use the attesting is something done
by a person intentionally, while with the first use the attesting need not be done
intentionally nor need it be done by a person. (E.g., 'The height of the waves
attest to the severity of the storm'.) The attesting with the second use, moreover, is usually done by a use of words, and we may speak (as Quine does) of
what a word "serves to attest to" when it is used in a certain way. The important thing to note here is that the attesting is done *by the person* through his
use of words and not *by the fact* of his utterance of words on appropriate
occasions. The fact that a person utters 'Red' (or a sound indicating assent to
it) on appropriate occasions attests to the fact that on such occasions he is
seeing redly, but this may very well not be what the person himself is attesting
to—not what 'Red' for him serves to attest to. We undercut Quine's philosophical stance if we simply rule out the question of what the person himself is
attesting to and insist that the only proper question is what the facts of the
person's verbal and other behavior in certain situations attest to.

Quine wants, we noted, to begin with an account of assent to 'Red' which
neither presupposes nor precludes that with the assent there is a referential use
of 'red'. Two persons may agree in assenting to 'Red', yet for one of them
'red' may always serve to attest to the presence of the quality red while for the
other it serves to attest to the presence of red light. Each then has a different
referential use of 'red', although in view of their common assent we may say

that 'Red' as a one-word sentence calling for assent or dissent serves for each to attest to the presence of red. The phrase 'the presence of red' is thus unavoidably vague. It is not in general replaceable by 'the presence of the quality red', 'the presence of red light', 'the presence of the experience of seeing redly', or by any other phrase more specific or more precise than itself. On particular occasions it may be replaceable by one or another such phrase, though not always (probably not in the case of a child who has just learned color words). Its use thus neither presupposes nor precludes its replaceability by a more specific phrase. However, if it is used to specify only what the facts of stimulation and behavior attest to, its use either presupposes or precludes its replaceability, depending on the theory in terms of which the facts are interrelated. With this second use of 'the presence of red' we do not have a context in which we can ask the questions about reference Quine wants to ask. These questions arise only when we begin with some statement, however vague, about what 'Red' *for a person* serves to attest to.

Yet the contexts are not as neatly divided as these remarks suggest. In the course of developing his theory of reference Quine says much that seems to belong entirely within a context of facts of stimulation and behavior. His account of "stimulus meaning" seems to afford just the sort of explication of 'the presence of red' that I have said undercuts his philosophical stance. It is for this reason that an attempt to develop a theory of knowledge in terms of such an explication may afford a parody of Quine's theory rather than an obviously opposed theory.

I turn now to some details of Quine's theory of reference. I consider them primarily as they bear on his theory of knowledge, and in the light of the distinction I have tried to mark by the two uses of 'attest'.

II

Specification of reference always rests, according to Quine, on "analytical hypotheses". These hypotheses provide a basis for the analysis of meaningful utterances (others' and our own) into smaller meaningful segments. They are not, Quine claims, strictly "genuine" hypotheses since they are not subject to inductive confirmation in any ordinary sense.[2] That is, they are not tested ultimately by appeal to empirical nonlinguistic data. We cannot test the hypothesis that a person uses 'rabbit' to refer to rabbits simply by noting the stimulatory conditions that prompt his utterances of 'rabbit'. We must also analyze his utterances in which 'rabbit' is a segment, and the reference we assign to 'rabbit' will be a function of how we break down the rest of the utterance into segments and of the meaning we give to these further segments. Whether, for example, we give a further segment S the meaning of 'is the same as' or of 'belongs with' will in general determine whether we can assign to 'rabbit' reference to rabbits or to temporal slices of rabbits and remain in agreement with all the facts of stimulation and behavior. But which meaning we should give S and hence which reference we should assign to 'rabbit' cannot be determined by these facts. They support equally well either choice of meaning and consequent assignment of reference. Analytical hypotheses—the hypotheses by which we fix meaning and reference—are thus not hypotheses that certain facts are interrelated thus and so but rather hypotheses concerning what various words for certain persons serve to attest to.

In effect, then, analytical hypotheses are an articulation of certain basic assumptions about another person one makes in the course of communicating linguistically with that person. Linguistic communication as we commonly understand it is possible only to the extent that one feels at least some of one's referential apparatus is substantially the same as another's. This sameness, Quine remarks, is "the sameness that is tested by smoothness of dialogue".[3] It is not tested by facts of stimulation and behavior although facts of this sort are always present whenever it is tested. Communicating linguistically with another is not the same as trying to predict his linguistic or other behavior under certain stimulatory conditions. It makes no difference for the success of our prediction whether we take another's utterances of 'Rabbit' as serving to attest merely to the presence of a rabbit or to the presence of a temporal slice of a rabbit. But it may make a great deal of difference to smoothness of dialogue in a philosophical discussion. Insofar as one pleads inability to understand another's use of S for 'belongs with' there is interruption of dialogue and failure of communication, but not necessarily failure of prediction regarding another's utterances of 'Rabbit' under certain stimulatory conditions.

Quine's theory of knowledge requires a fundamental distinction between the hypotheses by which we fix the stimulus meaning of an expression and those by which we fix its reference. As he develops the distinction, hypotheses of the former sort in contrast to the latter seem to be genuine hypotheses. Even though two people assign different references to 'rabbit', the stimulus meaning for each is the same if the stimulatory conditions under which they both assent to and dissent from 'Rabbit' are the same. The sameness here is tested by induction and the hypothesis proclaiming the sameness is thus "genuine". But with this induction we seem to determine only what the facts of the person's stimulation and behavior attest to and not what 'Rabbit' for the person serves to attest to. Quine's account of stimulus meaning thus seems to create just the predicament that I argued above undercuts his philosophical stance. The fact that a person's utterance of 'Rabbit' attests to his being stimulated in the way he normally is by the presence of a rabbit provides no basis for assuming that 'Rabbit' for the person serves to attest to the presence of anything. We may just as well assume that it serves to attest to the presence of red. To be sure, with such an assumption any linguistic communication with the person on the basis of his utterances of 'Rabbit' will no doubt be impossible. But then we are not trying to achieve linguistic communication with the person. We are concerned only with predicting his utterances of 'Rabbit', and any relation between these utterances and the reference we assume the person assigns to 'rabbit' is entirely fortuitous. "Inscrutability of reference" and "ontological relativity" obviously obtain in this case, but not in the way Quine proclaims them. They hold only in the trivial sense that insofar as we stay solely with facts that we in no way relate to a person's references, we are free to fix his references as we please, and any ontology we impute to him is relative to our choice of references.

With this view of Quine we obtain an invidious distinction between, on the one hand, genuine hypotheses that fix stimulus meanings by induction from facts of stimulation and behavior, and, on the other hand, analytical hypotheses that yield arbitrary assignments of reference. We cannot make the distinction less invidious by claiming that analytical hypotheses are tested by smoothness of dialogue. If we are free to assign meaning and reference as we please (to take 'Rabbit' as serving to attest to the presence of red, or to whatever else we want) we can easily achieve the semblance of smoothness of dialogue. But in actuality, of course, there is only a monologue, or a dialogue with oneself; the other person's references are only a figment of our imagination. We have now either reduced Quine's theory to the absurdity of linguistic solipsism—to a world in which there is only one's own private language—or we have confused his theory with a parody of it.

It is not hard to find passages in Quine that seem to draw the invidious distinction just mentioned, but some of the passages contain an important qualification. Having spoken of the stimulus meaning of 'Rabbit' as "inductively well established", Quine adds in a footnote, "Strictly speaking, even this induction presupposes something like an analytical hypothesis in a small way: the decision as to what to take as signs of assent and dissent."[4] Not even the modification suggested by the phrase 'something like in a small way' occurs in the following.

> The linguist's decision as to what to treat as native signs of assent and dissent is on a par with the analytical hypotheses of translation that he adopts at later stages of his enterprise; they differ from those later ones only in coming first, needed as they are in defining stimulus meaning. This initial indeterminancy, then, carries over into the identification of the stimulus meanings.[5]

According to this passage there is more to the definition of the affirmative stimulus meaning of a sentence than identifying the range of stimulations that prompt assent. In terms of the distinction I have tried to mark by two uses of 'attest', the identification of a stimulus meaning is a question both of what an utterance by a person serves for that person to attest to and of what is attested to by the stimulatory conditions and by the fact that the person makes the utterance. The presence of the first question makes an appeal to signs of assent and dissent necessary. With the second question alone there is no need to take the sound emitted as a linguistic utterance at all, let alone a sentence. We may take it simply as a sound sometimes emitted by an organism that has been stimulated in a certain way, and hence a sound sometimes attesting to the presence of this type of stimulation. With the first question we have the problem that what a person may attest to in response to a certain stimulation is infinitely varied. There is an infinite totality of English sentences any one of which might on some occasion be appropriate and perhaps true if uttered by a person who is stimulated as one normally is by the presence of a rabbit. In order to determine another's stimulus meaning of 'Rabbit' we must query him about his use of 'rabbit' and not just passively observe his verbal responses in the presence of a rabbit.[6] But in order to query a person thus we must be able to identify his signs of assent and dissent.

There is more to the indeterminacy in the identification of these signs than the fact that a language may not have any standard expression for assent and dissent. There is in addition the indeterminacy as to whether the other person even assents or dissents at all or whether he merely emits sounds. With this indeterminacy an invidious distinction seems to be implied also at the level of stimulus meaning. On the one hand, there are analytical hypotheses that identify (perforce arbitrarily) signs of assent and dissent and make possible an identification of acts of assent and dissent and hence of stimulus meaning. On the other hand, there are genuine hypotheses that correlate an organisms's emission of sounds with its stimulations. The distinction here covers more than in the previous case where the analytical hypotheses had to do only with the arbitrary assignment of reference. In this latter case, the indeterminacy was only in the assignment of reference and not in the determination of stimulus meaning, which we supposed was settled by genuine hypotheses. But now there is indeterminacy even in the determination of stimulus meaning. Even the fact of assent or dissent as well as what serves as the sign of one or the other is indeterminate and seems to be a question of analytical hypothesis. Yet here where the distinction covers more Quine places it in a different perspective.

"We have", Quine remarks, "a sympathetic way of putting ourselves in the other fellow's place and sensing how the world would look from where he sits. . . . We see what way he is looking when he says 'Water' or assents to it." When we "find ourselves similarly oriented" we can check whether the stimulus meaning we attach to 'Water' is similar to his.[7] We must assume, of course, that the other person received stimulations similar to ours when he was similarly oriented. As Quine puts it elsewhere, we "mete out" stimulations like our own to "our epistemological subject".[8] I will turn shortly to the question of whether this crucial assumption is itself a genuine or an analytical hypothesis. I want first to consider briefly how the assumption properly construed places the distinction we are considering in a new perspective. By 'properly construed' I mean that we must take 'having stimulations like our own' as implying not merely that another has stimulations that prompt assent and dissent as ours do, but also that another's stimulation and behavior attest to his assent or dissent in much the same way as in our own case.

III

The distinction, ultimately, let us recall, is between analytical hypotheses concerning what an utterance for a person serves to attest to and genuine hypotheses concerning what that person's stimulation and behavior attest to. We obtain a different perspective when we assume that what another's stimulation and behavior attest to about his assents and dissents is similar to what our own stimulation and behavior attest to about our assents and dissents. When we are looking at a rabbit plainly in view and respond to the query 'Rabbit?' with a sign of assent, we regard the obvious condition of our stimulation (we are looking) together with our response as attesting to the fact that we assented to 'Rabbit?'. We assume the same is true of another person. With this assumption we take it as a matter of fact that a person's response to our query is sometimes one of assent or dissent, though our ability to identify either sort of response depends on our prior identification of signs of assent and dissent. While this prior identification is a question of analytical hypothesis, it is not without relation to a question of fact. One's signs of assent and dissent (another's and our own) normally occur in conjunction with the fact of assent or dissent and are thus related to conditions of stimulation and behavior. The distinction between analytical and genuine hypotheses in this case does not have the invidious implication that the former are to be separated from the latter as the arbitrarily chosen from the inductively established.

There is thus in our identification of another's signs of assent and dissent something approaching genuine hypotheses concerning facts of stimulation and behavior. But the hypotheses are not genuine in the radical sense of being concerned solely with correlating an organism's emission of sounds with its stimulations. They are concerned also with conditions of stimulation and behavior as attesting to acts of assent and dissent, since we have assumed that such conditions attest to assent and dissent in another's case much as they do in our own. This assumption, we should now note, is itself neither a genuine nor an analytical hypothesis. It is, rather, this assumption that gives rise to a distinction between the two kinds of hypotheses. Without this assumption we have only an invidious distinction between genuine hypotheses and arbitrary assignments of meaning and reference. We have then no language, properly speaking—no communication, but only linguistic solipsism. But with the assumption, we can distinguish hypotheses that assign meanings attested to by facts of stimulation and behavior from hypotheses that simply interrelate facts. Hypotheses of the first sort are analytical in that they are concerned with analyzing meaningful utterances into their smaller meaningful segments and not, as are hypotheses of the second sort, with establishing causal connections. In a theory of language and a theory of knowledge the two sorts of hypotheses come into subtle interplay. That a certain type of sensory stimulation prompts a person to assent to 'Rabbit?' is a causal hypothesis. But its confirmation requires an analytical hypothesis by which a sign of assent can be identified, since acts of assent are identified by signs of assent. Yet it does not follow that in being prompted to assent one is prompted to utter a sign of assent. Such an utterance is usually in response to a query, and in Quine's terms it is then *elicited* and not prompted: "to prompt . . . is not to elicit. What elicits . . . is a combination: the prompting stimulation plus the ensuing query."[9]

An utterance serving as a sign of assent or dissent, then, is an elicited and not a prompted response. The response, in other words, has linguistic meaning; it occurs in the course of linguistic communication and is not merely a sound emitted in response to a stimulation. Yet the sound is not elicited in a vacuum but in conjunction with a prompting stimulation. One assents to a query because one is prompted to assent by a stimulation one receives prior to or at the same time as the query. Analytical hypotheses identifying signs of assent and dissent are tested, like all analytical hypotheses, by smoothness of dialogue. Refusal to respond to a query with a sign of assent or dissent may interrupt or even terminate a dialogue. When the prompting stimulation is clearly evident and the other person appears to share our desire for communication, we expect our query to elicit a sign of assent or dissent. As Quine observes, we may be guided in our decision as to which of two signs is for assent and which for dissent by noting which when repeated after the other's remarks "is the more serene in its effect"[10]—which, in other words, does not disrupt the flow of dialogue with indications from the other of surprise and annoyance and perhaps elicit repetition of his remarks in a vexed tone.

While in practice we may have no doubt as to another's signs of assent and dissent, our identification of these signs is subject to an indeterminacy that does not affect genuine hypotheses. The indeterminacy arises because we are concerned with another's meaning as attested to by his stimulation and behavior and not just with his behavior as caused by his stimulations. We cope with the indeterminacy by assuming that another's stimulation and behavior attest to his meaning much the same as ours attest to our meaning. With this assumption we do not remove the indeterminacy, but, rather, recognize it and agree to live with it. That is, we do not assume that hypotheses identifying a person's meaning are reducible without remainder to hypotheses interrelating his stimulations and behavior. We recognize both that meaning is never wholly determined by stimulation and behavior and yet that another's stimulation and behavior are all we have to go on when we try to determine his meaning. We reconcile ourselves to the fact that no matter how much smoothness of dialogue we may seem to achieve and no matter how successful our predictions of another's responses to stimulations, there is still the possibility, however remote, that our communication is an illusion. What we take to be another's signs of assent and dissent may not be that at all, but only sounds the emission of which happens to accord with our expectations of assent and dissent.

While the indeterminacy here is without practical import it reveals the theoretical impossibility of completely equating hypotheses that fix meanings with those that merely interrelate stimulations and behavior. Yet once a field linguist decides on the identification of the native's signs of assent and dissent and waives any question of indeterminacy, he "is in a position to accumulate inductive evidence for translating" the native's 'Gavagai' as the sentence 'Rabbit'. "The general law for which he is assembling instances is roughly that the native will assent to 'Gavagai' under just those stimulations under which *we, if asked, would assent to 'Rabbit?'*; and correspondingly for dissent."[11]

Hypotheses equating the stimulus meanings of another's sentences with those of our own are thus very much like genuine hypotheses. But they are not entirely so. The initial indeterminacy regarding signs of assent and dissent "carries over into the identification of the stimulus meanings".[12] The identification thus rests on the assumption that another has stimulations prompting assent and dissent as ours do and that his stimulations and behavior attest to his assent or dissent in much the same way as in our own case. This qualification does not affect the central contrast Quine draws between hypotheses identifying stimulus meanings and those segmenting utterances and fixing assignments of reference. In this contrast the former hypotheses appear as genuine and the latter as analytical. The contrast looms large in Quine's theory of knowledge and the qualification we have noted is easily overlooked. Much that Quine says is readily taken as suggesting that the contrast is between genuine and analytical hypotheses without qualification. When he does mention the qualification he may be led by the context to underplay its importance, as when he remarks in a footnote that an induction establishing a stimulus meaning "presupposes something like an analytical hypothesis in a small way: the decision as to what to take as signs of assent and dissent."[13] Yet if the qualification is ignored, one ends with the sort of parody of Quine's theory that is summed up in Ziff's remarks: "Quine's concept of stimulus meaning is cast in a causal mold; thus it faces the wrong way: it looks from conditions to speakers instead of from speakers to conditions. And it is inflexible. In consequence, it is useless."[14]

I will begin consideration of Quine's contrast between stimulus meaning and reference by relating our present discussion to some epistemological considerations.

IV

We may say that one is prompted to assent to 'Rabbit?' when one is aware of the presence of a rabbit. But what do we mean by 'awareness'? We become aware of our external environment through the stimulation of our nerve endings. Then is the identification of one's awareness, unlike one's stimulus meaning, entirely a matter of genuine hypothesis? Quine's answer is negative. Nerve endings and awareness are on different "levels."

> The nerve endings, on the one hand, are the place of unprocessed information about the world. The stage where this information has become processed to the point of awareness, on the other hand, is the basic level for conceptualization and vocabulary . . . At the one level we do well . . . to speak not of sense data but of nerve endings. At this other level we do well to speak not of sense data but of observation sentences.[15]

The point is not that sense data prior to awareness are identical with nerve endings and after awareness, with observation sentences. Sense data are not assumed in the first place and hence the question of their identity at the two levels does not arise. There is no need to posit sense data or entities of any other kind in order to bridge the gap between the two levels. The first level comprises only facts of stimulation and behavior, and nerve endings are posited in the course of framing genuine hypotheses to account for the mechanism by which stimulatory forces impinge on bodily surfaces and trigger various reactions. The bridge to the second level is provided, not by positing entities with an identity on both levels, but by specifying the first level in relation to the second.

We would create a gap if we spoke of nerve endings as merely certain areas of bodily surfaces sensitized to various stimulatory forces. But we say more than this. We say that nerve endings are "the place of unprocessed information about the world". We thus specify the first level as the potentiality for the second level—for the processing of this information "to the point of awareness". Information processed to this point issues in stimulus meaning—in an awareness of being prompted to assent to a certain observation sentence when that sentence is put as a query.

Awareness, then, is simply the possession of this processed information, the completion of the process that begins with the input of unprocessed information and ends with an observation sentence. When one receives the processed information equivalent to the observation sentence 'Rabbit', one is prompted to assent to 'Rabbit?'. Though of course one can always withhold assent—refuse to utter a sign of assent. The concept of being prompted to assent, then, is causal. It "looks from conditions to speakers". One does not decide to be prompted to assent—one is simply aware of being prompted. But one is not thereby causally determined to assent—to utter a sign of assent in response to a query. The response is elicited, not prompted; it occurs in the course of linguistic communication—of dialogue—in which information about the world is communicated and acknowledged. If the response is contrary either to the prompting stimulation (if one tells a lie) or to the ensuing query (if one mistakes it), there is failure of dialogue. The response must be elicited by the combination of the prompting stimulation and the ensuing query. The first is necessary if there is to be information about the world; the second, if the information is to be communicated.

Quine's concept of stimulus meaning is thus not inflexible, "cast in a causal mold". It "looks from conditions to speakers" only to the point of a speaker's awareness of being prompted to assent. But at this point there is no definition of stimulus meaning. A definition attempted here would yield something like the concept of a sense datum rather than of a stimulus meaning. Meaning presupposes dialogue and must be defined intersubjectively. One's responses of assent and dissent (another's as well as our own) attest to one's stimulus meanings. It would be pointless to define the affirmative stimulus meaning of a sentence S as the class of all stimulations that would prompt assent to S, if we had no way of deciding except in our own case which stimulations prompt assent. In order to have language and not linguistic solipsism we must regard another's responses as attesting to his acts of assent and dissent. But then we "look from speakers to conditions". We assume that the conditions (the sounds emitted) occur because the speaker intended assent or dissent and not because the speaker was causally determined by his stimulations to emit sounds. Our identification of signs of assent and dissent is thus via analytical hypotheses, and the indeterminacy peculiar to these hypotheses carries over into the identification of stimulus meanings.

While with this account of stimulus meanings we thus in one respect "look from speakers to conditions", in a more fundamental respect we look from ourselves to others. We learn from our own case that one may be prompted to assent and yet withhold any response of assent. The effect of the prompting stimulation alone is thus not a response of assent but rather of an awareness of being prompted to assent. We need no evidence of the awareness in our own case—we simply have it. But we recognize that the conditions of our stimulation (we are looking directly at a rabbit plainly in view) plus our normal responses to queries (we assent to 'Rabbit?') attest to our awareness. We assume that another's stimulation and behavior attest likewise to his awareness—to his possession of processed information that issues from the stimulation of his nerve endings.

V

We have now pushed Quine's theory to the point where it might seem that we can no longer maintain his separation of stimulus meaning from reference. Awareness in our own case hardly seems just an awareness of being prompted to assent. We say that we are aware of the presence of a rabbit. To say that we are aware of being prompted to assent to 'Rabbit?' seems at best a back-handed way of saying the same thing. In assenting we acknowledge that the object of our awareness is a rabbit and not merely that 'Rabbit' is true. Reference thus seems inseparable from stimulus meaning. We have said that awareness is processed information about the world. But then surely it is information about objects in the world. If we say rather that it is information as to what expressions are true of the world, it is still information that the objects of which these expressions are true are objects in the world. 'Rabbit' is true on just those occasions in which this expression is said of something in the world that is a rabbit.

With the line of thought sketched above we arrive at what Quine calls "mentalistic semantics". The point is not that the objects of reference are then mental entities. They may be simply "denoted concrete objects". The point is rather that "Semantics is vitiated by a pernicious mentalism as long as we regard a man's semantics as somehow determinate in his mind beyond what might be implicit in his dispositions to overt behavior".[16] With mentalistic semantics as Quine conceives it, then, we reject the claim that one's awareness (another's and our own) is no more than what is attested to by the conditions of one's stimulation and behavior. We assume rather that awareness is a determinate mental grasp of objects in the world, even if this grasp as attested to by facts of stimulation and behavior is not determinate.

Thus when we assent to 'Rabbit?' we may claim that we are aware of the presence of a relatively enduring spatiotemporal object with rabbit properties. That we have this awareness, we may contend, is indeed attested to by further verbal responses we are prepared to make. If queried a moment later with the rabbit still plainly in view, we would assent to 'Same rabbit?'. If another rabbit appeared we would assent to 'Two rabbits?'.

But on reflection we may wonder whether these further responses do attest to the awareness we claim to have. We can imagine that instead of thinking of a rabbit as we do we had come to think of it as a series of rabbit stages belonging together to comprise a rabbit history. We would then say that we were aware of the presence of a momentary object comprising a stage in a rabbit history. We would understand 'same rabbit' as, in effect, 'rabbit stage belonging with another stage in a rabbit history'. Similarly, we would understand 'two rabbits' as 'two rabbit stages not belonging together in a rabbit history'. The conditions of our stimulation and behavior would then be the same though the awareness we contend they attest to is quite different.

We may be tempted to dismiss this sort of reflection as idle fancy. After all, our awareness is processed information about the world. It is not merely information that might be guessed from our stimulation and behavior by one who does not have (as we assume all persons do) essentially the same input of unprocessed information and essentially the same means of processing it that we have. Any one thus constituted as we are and sharing our language will recognize our stimulation and behavior as attesting to the awareness we claim to have.

This retort in behalf of mentalistic semantics begs the question. It assumes that we have a means of processing information that produces a determinate awareness of an object. What needs to be shown is that when we are stimulated as we normally are by the presence of a rabbit we obtain processed information that constitutes a determinate mental grasp of a definite kind of object—of a rabbit and not, say, of a rabbit stage or of anything else. But we cannot show this as long as we stay with what is attested to by the conditions of our stimulation and behavior. We have just noted that these conditions may be taken as attesting to an awareness either of a rabbit or of a rabbit stage. Our only recourse is to argue that unless we assume a determinate awareness we are driven to absurdities in a theory of language and a theory of knowledge.

We encounter the absurdity of linguistic solipsism noted above in Section II if we take total arbitrariness of reference as the alternative to assuming a determinate awareness. But it should now be clear that this is not the alternative provided by Quine's theory. Assignment of reference is not independent of stimulus meaning, as we assumed at the outset of Section II. We are not free to say that 'Rabbit' serves for a person to attest to the presence of red if the stimulus meanings of 'Rabbit' and 'Red' for that person are different. Indeterminacy (arbitrariness) enters when we ask the meaning of expressions like 'same rabbit' and 'same red'. To answer such questions we need analytical hypotheses of translation and not merely those by which we identify signs of assent and dissent. In particular we need analytical hypotheses serving to identify predicates of identity. Are we to understand (translate) 'x is the same rabbit as y' as 'x and y are one and the same rabbit' or as 'x and y are different rabbit stages belonging together in a rabbit history'? We can understand it either way provided that we make the appropriate assignment of meaning to other expressions. In particular, which way we take it will determine the reference we can assign to 'rabbit' and maintain smoothness of dialogue. If we understand another's 'x is the same rabbit as y' as signifying a two-term relation holding between different rabbit stages, we cannot keep smoothness of dialogue if we also take him as using 'rabbit' to refer to a relatively enduring spatiotemporal object with rabbit properties. We would then have the person, with regard to his use of 'is the same rabbit as', dissenting from 'One Rabbit?' at the same time that, with regard to his referential use of 'rabbit', he assents to it. There is thus indeterminancy (arbitrariness) only in our initial choice of analytical hypotheses of translation. Once a choice has been made the rest is by no means arbitrary. Smoothness of dialogue is not achieved by translating another in any way we please. Our translations must make consistent sense of one's stimulus meanings as they are revealed by one's stimulations and acts of assent and dissent, or linguistic communication fails. Indeterminacy in the assignment of references is thus limited by previous assignments of stimulus meanings and is not a matter of complete arbitrariness.

From this point of view, assignments of stimulus meaning and assignments of reference may be contrasted as genuine and analytical hypotheses. Once we have identified signs of assent and dissent we fix stimulus meanings by induction, while our assignments of reference are then arbitrary within the limits of stimulus meaning. But these limits fail to obtain if there is nothing more to the determination of stimulus meaning than correlating an organism's emission of sounds with its stimulations. There is nothing more if we forget the need for analytical hypotheses at the start identifying signs of assent and dissent. This need, we saw, becomes clear when we note that linguistic communication requires the assumption that another's stimulation and behavior attest to his assents and dissents much as our stimulation and behavior attest to ours.

With this assumption we look from ourselves to others. If we still want to argue for a determinate awareness we must show first that the failure to acknowledge such awareness in our own case leads to absurdity. The central point seems on first thought rather obvious. With no determinate awareness we can never know what we are talking about. If we are aware only of being prompted to assent to 'Rabbit?', we do not know what we are acknowledging the presence of when we assent. Falling back on some such vague phrase as 'the presence of rabbit' or 'a rabbit presence' will not help. We may say that a child who has just learned color words acknowledges the presence of red because we do not believe that the child is fully aware of what he is attesting to. He has learned to respond correctly with 'red' but he has not yet acquired a concept of red. To deny that we ever achieve a determinate awareness thus seems equivalent to denying that we ever advance beyond the position of the child and know what we are attesting to—what we are talking about.

When we assent to an observation sentence, then, we know what we are talking about only when we have a concept of the object whose presence we acknowledge. But it by no means follows that having a concept of an object makes one's awareness of it determinate. Conceptualization is fundamentally a discursive (linguistic) activity. It involves interrelating words and parts of words and presupposes an apparatus of pronouns, pluralization, identity, numerals, and the like. Awareness thus precedes conceptualization. Information "processed to the point of awareness . . . is the basic level for conceptualization and vocabulary."[17] We first become aware at this level and then con-

ceptualize our awareness. That alternative conceptualizations are equally tenable does not imply that we can never know what we are talking about. We
cannot ask what we are talking about without presupposing some apparatus of
pluralization, identity, etc. It makes no sense to ask whether we are talking
about rabbits or about rabbit stages if we do not know what we mean by 'same
rabbit'—whether 'one and the same rabbit', 'rabbit stage belonging with another stage in a rabbit history', or neither of these. Alternative conceptualizations are equally tenable insofar as they accord equally well with our awareness—with the observation sentences we are prompted to assent to, i.e., to
accept as true. We may conceptualize our awareness when we are prompted to
assent to 'Rabbit?' as the awareness either of a rabbit or of a rabbit stage. It
does not matter which as long as we are prompted to accept 'Rabbit' as true
and to reject it as false always under the same conditions. The further question
'But what *really* are the objects of our awareness, rabbits, rabbit stages, or
something else?' makes no sense except relative to a scheme of conceptualization. An answer is always provided by the scheme relative to which the question is posed. We know what we are talking about once we have the conceptualization necessary for raising the question.

There is thus no absurdity, even in our own case, in denying that we ever
achieve a determinate awareness. Recognition that we can form alternative conceptualizations forces us to admit that even our own references in an absolute
sense are inscrutable. 'What really are the objects?' taken absolutely has no
answer. Yet we know what we are talking about in the only sense in which
such knowledge is possible. Having admitted the inscrutability of reference in
our own case we admit it in the case of others as well.[18] We can have no more
absolute knowledge of another's references than we can have of our own. We
assume that another's stimulation and behavior attest to his references as well
as to his stimulus meanings as ours do.

Stimulus meaning differs sharply from reference, however, in that its identification requires analytical hypotheses only to determine signs of assent and
dissent. The identification of reference, on the other hand, requires analytical
hypotheses to determine predicates of identity and thus to provide a scheme of
conceptualization. Awareness arises with stimulus meaning and is thus not an
awareness of objects. Information processed to the point of awareness is information determined by what impinges on our nerve endings and by the mechanism of our nervous system. In terms of traditional epistemology it is information we are "given" and not information we "construct" or "infer" from
what we are "given". Quine's theory of knowledge differs radically from traditional theories in holding that what is "given" is not an awareness of definite
sorts of objects but rather an awareness of being prompted to assent to observation sentences.[19] Alternatively, we may say 'an awareness of a presence'—
'the presence of rabbit' or 'the presence of red'. Though of course we are not

to take such phrases as implying the presence of a definite kind of object. The vague phrase 'the presence of p' represents no more than whatever one attests to when one assents to 'P?'.

Observation sentences, then, and not simple terms (names or predicates) represent final objectivity, i.e., information not subject to conflicting yet equally tenable interpretations. The stimulus meaning possessed by 'Rabbit' as an observation sentence remains invariant through all tenable interpretations of 'rabbit' as a name or a predicate. This stimulus meaning alone is absolute. All tenable interpretations are relative to it and to a particular scheme of conceptualization. Inscrutability of reference and ontological relativity are inevitable consequences. But they do not produce the absurdity that we never know what we are talking about—that we never advance beyond the position of a child who has just learned color words. The child does not ask 'But what really are colors?'. We do. We are then far beyond the position of the child.

I want now to consider how Quine's theory as I have interpreted it contrasts with certain other theories and how it can cope with some rather obvious dialectical objections that may be urged against it.

VI

We noted that according to Quine mentalistic semantics rejects the claim that one's awareness is no more than what is attested to by the conditions of one's stimulation and behavior. Yet I have argued that with Quine's theory we must assume that such conditions attest to assent and dissent in another's case much as they do in our own. But why, then, do these conditions not attest also to a determinate awareness of an object? If we regard our affirmative response to 'Rabbit?' when we are looking at a rabbit plainly in view as attesting to our assent to 'Rabbit?', why do not these same conditions attest to our determinate awareness of a rabbit? If we assume that they do and that the same holds for others, we generally have no difficulty maintaining smoothness of dialogue. In fact this seems to be how we usually proceed. But then we have embraced mentalistic semantics without rejecting the claim that one's awareness is no more than what is attested to by the conditions of one's stimulation and behavior.

The argument overlooks a fundamental point in Quine's theory. We can vary what we take to be our determinate awareness represented by 'rabbit' without varying our assents to and dissents from 'Rabbit?'. But we cannot in general vary our assents and dissents without varying what we take to be our determinate awareness. We may take our determinate awareness as that of a rabbit or of a rabbit stage without varying in the least our assents to and our dissents from 'Rabbit?'. But we cannot change our assent to dissent when we are looking at a rabbit plainly in view and claim that our response still attests to the same determinate awareness. It makes no difference if the sentence in question contains a referential use of 'rabbit'. If we assent to 'The same rabbit?' and then dissent, we cannot claim that the awareness attested to by our response is the same in both cases. On the other hand, we can still vary what we take to be our determinate awareness without varying any of our assents or dissents. Though in this case, of course, when we vary the awareness we also vary the meaning we assign to 'same' as well as to 'rabbit'.

My remark four sentences back that "it makes no difference" has limited application. It makes no difference as far as variations in awareness vs. variations in assents and dissents are concerned. But if the sentence we consider contains a referential use of an expression it makes quite a difference with regard to what we say the awareness is. When we take the sentence holophrastically, in effect as 'Rabbit' or 'Red', we can hardly say more of the awareness than that it is an awareness of being prompted to assent. When we add that it is the awareness of a presence, we do no more than emphasize that we are not precluding a referential use for the expression we are taking holophrastically. The important point is the implication of objectivity carried by the expressions 'being prompted to' and 'presence'. The awareness here, as we have noted, is for Quine the epistemological "given". On the other hand, when we take 'Rabbit' with the force of 'This is a rabbit' the awareness represented is a conceptualized awareness. The determinate awareness claimed by mentalistic semantics is of this sort. Though conceptualized, it is not relative to a scheme of conceptualization. It is supposed to be fixed by a determinate epistemological "given", however that may be specified.

I said earlier, in presenting Quine's theory, that conceptualization is fundamentally a discursive (linguistic) activity and that awareness thus precedes conceptualization. With mentalistic semantics, on the contrary, conceptualization is in effect fused with awareness in determining the epistemological "given". In assenting to 'Rabbit?' one may be taken as being aware of the presence of a rabbit—of the existence of an object falling under a concept. There is then no distinction between the awareness and the conceptualization of the object. There is only a distinction between the conceptualized awareness and its verbal expression. With this Aristotelian mentalistic semantics the verbal expression is not merely a predicate. It is also a "common name" identifying the objects of a certain kind.[20] With this approach we regard the conditions of stimulation and behavior in our own case as attesting to our determinate grasp of the identifying reference of the common name, and we assume the same for others. We give no thought to whether we might vary what we take as our grasp of the reference of 'rabbit' without varying our assents to and our dissents from 'Rabbit?'.

The fusion of conceptualization and awareness is concealed by packing the effects of both into the one word 'rabbit'. The holophrastic 'Rabbit' is fused with 'This is a rabbit' not taken holophrastically. With Quine's theory, the second sentence represents a conceptualization and thus does not represent an epistemological "given." In canonical idiom it becomes 'There is something such that it is here and it is [a] rabbit'.[21] Whether this something is then an enduring object, an object stage, or something else is relative to a scheme of conceptualization. But if 'rabbit' is a common name, the generic identity of the objects it names is determined by the conceptualized awareness attested to by a correct use of the name—even if the use is no more than an utterance of 'Rabbit' or an assent to it when a rabbit is plainly in view. There is thus no conceptualization to be represented discursively as an addition to the awareness. The reference of 'rabbit' is purportedly fixed by awareness alone and the addition of conceptualization is thus concealed.

The identificatory role of common names is eliminated in Quine's theory. As regimented through paraphrase in canonical idiom substantives (common names), adjectives, and verbs are represented simply as predicates.[22] Hence in the paraphrase of 'This is a rabbit' given above the indefinite article may be bracketed as extraneous matter. Simply as predicate, 'rabbit' is on a par with other predicates. The identificatory role of proper names (singular terms) is of course also eliminated in Quine's theory.[23] Singular terms are first assimilated to singular descriptions and then eliminated à la Russell in favor of general terms (predicates) and variables of quantification.[24]

Quine holds that his elimination of singular terms (and by implication, of common names) is "epistemologically neutral".[25] The elimination can be maintained "at the level strictly of logical grammar, without prejudice to epistemology or ontology".[26] But the neutrality here seems to me questionable. At least since the time of Kant philosophers have turned to logic as an independent science for aid in the development of epistemology and ontology. Kant claimed to find in logic the clue for a correct list of categories. Quine also: "The quest of a simplest, clearest overall pattern of canonical notation is not to be distinguished from a quest of ultimate categories".[27] But then if the notation permits the elimination of all names, common and proper, is it epistemologically and ontologically neutral?

Russell saw logic as permitting the elimination of "indefinite" descriptions (hence of common names) and of "definite" or singular descriptions.[28] But he insisted that logic had to retain some form of proper names. The bearing of this retention on his epistemology and ontology is not hard to discern. A logically proper name is a "simple symbol" whose meaning simply is the object it names.[29] One can know the meaning of a name only through direct acquaintance with the object named and not through a description of it. The distinction between knowledge by acquaintance and knowledge by description thus becomes fundamental in epistemology.[30] On the ontological side, objects named

by logically proper names are the only true individuals—absolutely simple objects in no way complex and hence incapable of description. For a time at least
Russell was prepared to recognize a kind of ontological relativity. It "may be
the case" that whatever we take to be an individual "is really capable of further analysis". We can then speak only of "relative individuals" (relative to
"the context in question") and have only "relative names."[31] But this is not
Quinean ontological relativity. It obtains, if it does, because of what is contingently true of objects in the world and not because of the nature of our references to objects. Russell later came to consider simple sense qualities as the
most likely candidates for individuals—for simple nameables. He proposed to
take 'red' as a name and not a predicate. His paraphrase of 'This is red' in
canonical idiom then becomes 'Redness is here',[32] a paraphrase one would
hardly come to if one were not in quest of simple nameables.

In the light of this comparison with Russell it is hard to see how Quine's
claim of neutrality for his elimination of all names can be sustained. Comparisons with other philosophers quite different from Russell yield a similar conclusion. The philosophical question such comparisons raise is how far logical
grammar, insofar as it comprises a quest of ultimate categories, has a bearing
on what we assume about how we know and about what there is to know.
Quine presumably would answer that it has no bearing as far as the elimination
of names in favor of predicates is concerned. I believe a different answer is
suggested by his theory of knowledge.

If names are not to be eliminated we can hardly take information processed
to the point of awareness as adequately represented by a Quinean observation
sentence. The awareness will comprise more than just being prompted to assent
to such a sentence. It will comprise in addition something like either a conceptualized awareness fixing the reference of a common name or a Russellian
acquaintance with an individual.[33] Quine no doubt would reply that either addition goes beyond anything attested to by conditions of stimulation and behavior. But he would hardly make this reply if he retained a logical grammar in
which names could not be eliminated. For he would then be obliged to account
for the references of names as an epistemological "given," and hence as independent of any scheme of conceptualization we may impose on the "given".

One may claim that "given" references are strictly private and therefore
not attested to by anything in the conditions of stimulation and behavior. But
this claim in effect concedes Quine's point. What is strictly private cannot be
communicated. You can never know what reference if any I am privately
"given" for 'red'. You can only guess what my reference is by observing my
assents to and dissents from 'Red?' under various stimulatory conditions. Your
guess will be your own conceptualization of what you take to be the awareness
attested to by my assents and dissents. Your conceptualization will comprise
your fixing the use of 'red' in relation to other predicates, specifically predicates of identity. You thus pass from the sentence 'Red' to the predicate 'red'

and do not consider 'red' as a name. You construe it as a name, if you do, subsequent to your conceptualization—as a common name if you conceive of red things as constituting a kind, as a proper name if you take 'red' as a predicate true of but one object. But any private reference I may claim for 'red' has no place in the picture. The success of our communication depends on the references each of us conceptualizes from the awarenesses attested to by the conditions of stimulation and behavior, the other's and his own. Neither of us is ever sure his conceptualization is the same as the other's. But as long as we keep in agreement with conditions of stimulation and behavior and maintain smoothness of dialogue, we may discourse about objects in the only sense humanly possible.

For a genuine alternative to Quine, then, one must claim "given" references that are intersubjectively ascertainable. But if logical grammar permits the elimination of all names, common and proper, it conflicts with such a claim. 'There is something such that it is here and it is red' may often suffice as a paraphrase of 'This is red'. One often does not think of 'red' as a name. But an analogous paraphrase of 'This is a rabbit' is another matter. One would hardly ask 'What is it that it is a rabbit?'. The object there right before one *is* a rabbit. The question implies that one has missed the force of 'rabbit' as a term generically identifying an object. Such a question, however, may be quite appropriate in response to 'This is red'. The object before one may be plainly red, and yet one may be unable to identify it. Then one sensibly asks 'What is it (this object) that is red?'. But there is no absolute answer if logical grammar permits the elimination of all names—if answers like 'This is a red book' and 'This is the color red' both have in paraphrase the same form as Quine's 'This is red'. There are no "given" references intersubjectively ascertainable. All references are relative to conceptual schemes in terms of which awarenesses attested to by facts of stimulation and behavior are conceptualized.

With these considerations against Quine's claim of neutrality for his elimination of names, we are left with the question of how far our logical grammar dictates and how far it is dictated by our epistemological and ontological prejudices. But the question is beyond the scope of this paper. In conclusion I turn to some very general considerations, which may have some bearing on the question, and which I believe are helpful in obtaining an overall picture of Quine's theory of knowledge—in particular its intimate connection with his theory of language and his philosophy of science.

VII

I trust enough has been said already to show that Quine's rejection of "given" references intersubjectively ascertainable does not lead to a pernicious relativism—to a blanket Protagoreanism according to which each man is the measure of what is true for him. Stimulus meanings are "given" in one's promptings to assent or dissent—to accept sentences as true or false. They are intersubjectively ascertainable on the assumption that conditions of stimulation and behavior in another's case attest to assent and dissent much as they do in our own. This assumption, I have argued, plays a unique and crucial role in Quine's theory of knowledge. It is not a genuine hypothesis and hence it has no place in scientific theory. Quine thus admits inability to give anything he can accept as a theoretical (scientific) formulation of the conditions for an intersubjective equating of stimulations that will guarantee sameness of stimulus meaning. But he notes that in practice there is "no evident practical problem".[34] We usually accept similar orientation toward a source of stimulation as sufficient sameness of stimulatory conditions when we are communicating with another.[35] But then the crucial assumption in question seems justifiable only on practical grounds. Yet if this is the case we may ask again, Why assume that conditions of stimulation and behavior attest only to assent and dissent? Why not assume that they attest also to a determinate awareness of an object? The latter seems clearly what we assume in practice, and the assumption creates no evident practical problem.

The reply, that this expanded assumption overlooks the variability of any supposed determinate awareness even when there is not variation in assents and dissents, seems highly theoretical. It seems to me unquestionably so. Quine wants to keep the intrusion of the practical (the nonscientific) to an absolute minimum. Assents and dissents are enough to assure linguistic communication, even though not the sort that comprises speaking of objects. Generalizations as to what holds of all linguistic communication (of all languages) must therefore be restricted to communication that comprises only assents and dissents.[36] Even predication, the distinction between the general and the singular, is parochial.[37] It is not attested to by anything objective—by conditions of stimulation and behavior. It is marked in canonical notation by the distinction between terms in predicative position and variables of quantification. But it is not explained theoretically. Yet, parochial though it may be, it is for us, practically speaking, a trait of all languages. It is conspiciously present not only in our ordinary language, it "is expressly tailored to a full-size language adequate for science".[38] Unlike Carnap's distinction between analytic and synthetic sentences, it is not parochial to the point where it is clear only "within some artificial diminutive language" and has no clear application "to our own language, nor yet to any full-size language adequate to science".[39] However, unlike "stimulus synonymy" and "stimulus analyticity" predication lacks "applicability to all languages".[40]

Quine speaks of his epistemology as "only science self-applied".[41] In another context he says it "becomes semantics," and adds two sentences later that it "merges with psychology as well as with linguistics."[42] But he is at pains to see that in the process of self-application science does not become science misapplied—a "parascientific"[43] account of what defies scientific explanation. Scientific theories, Quine holds, are undetermined by all possible data.[44] Yet epistemology and linguistics are faced with an additional indeterminacy.[45] Their data are not merely facts attesting to the presence of further facts, but rather facts attesting to the presence of linguistic activity, to acts of assent and dissent and of reference.[46] The additional indeterminacy is minimal when what is to be attested to is merely the *sine qua non* of linguistic activity, stimulus meanings as defined through acts of assent and dissent. The indeterminacy arises because the scientist in this case can obtain his data only by actively querying and not merely passively observing another person. The querying here is querying in the literal sense of interpersonal communication and is not querying in the metaphorical sense in which an experimental scientist may be said to query nature. The indeterminacy is banished by the assumption that conditions of stimulation and behavior attest to assent and dissent in another's case much as in our own. If this assumption is a step toward a parascientific account, it is, with one exception, the only such step Quine countenances. The exception concerns the fact that even if the indeterminacy in identifying signs of assent and dissent is passed over, there is still some indeterminacy in the identification of truth functions.[47] Quine is willing to pass over both indeterminacies when he develops his theory of stimulus meaning and related concepts that apply to all languages.[48] But it is another matter when he comes to the question of reference. Any attempt to pass over the indeterminacy here results in a parascientific theory of mentalistic semantics. Such an attempt, I have argued, presupposes a logical grammar (a canonical notation) in which names are not eliminable. And it may leave the way open, I would add, for a logic with *de re* modalities and other concepts that have no place in Quine's austere idiom.

The indeterminacy that infects reference looms large in Quine's philosophy. One may question his preference for logical austerity and scientific purity when these can be purchased only at the price of this indeterminacy. But if I am right, one cannot object that he has indulged his preference to the point where he has neither a theory of knowlege nor a theory of language, but only a physics of stimulation and response.

MANLEY THOMPSON

UNIVERSITY OF CHICAGO
SEPTEMBER 1973

NOTES

1. W. V. Quine, *The Roots of Reference* [hereafter RR], (La Salle, IL: Open Court, 1974), p. 83. The exact phrase "serves to attest to the presence of red" occurs only in an early manuscript of this work.

2. Cf. W. V. Quine, *Word and Object* [hereafter WO] (Cambridge, Mass.: M.I.T. Press, 1960), §§ 15, 16.

3. RR, p. 84. The quotation is from the early manuscript.

4. W. V. Quine, "On the Reasons for Indeterminacy of Translation", [hereafter RI], *Journal of Philosophy*, 67 (1970): 181.

5. W. V. Quine, "Replies", in D. Davidson and J. Hintikka (eds.), *Words and Objections* [hereafter WsOs] (Dordrecht, Holland: D. Reidel Publishing Co., 1969), p. 312.

6. Quine (WO p. 29) mentions only the overlap of expressions (e.g., 'Animal', 'White', and 'Rabbit') as the reason for querying a person and not just passively observing his utterances in the presence of a rabbit. In WsOs p. 308 he remarks, "Passive observation cannot give reasonable evidence even of stimulus meanings of observation sentences, because of an overlap problem." An infinite variability of possible responses arises only if we assume the other person has a full-size language like English. But in a context of radical translation we need at the start only the minimal assumption that the jungle native has stimulus meanings. Then querying is necessary only because of possible overlapping expressions. The important point, which I emphasize in my interpretation of Quine, is that even this minimal case requires dialogue—interpersonal communication between linguist and native. Quine's restriction to the minimal case in which communication turns only on "stimulus synonymy" and not sameness of reference is essential for generalizations about all languages. I comment briefly on this point below in Section VII.

7. W. V. Quine, "Grades of Theoreticity" [hereafter GT] in L. Foster and J. W. Swanson (eds.), *Experience and Theory* (University of Massachusetts Press, 1970), p. 6.

8. W. V. Quine, *Ontological Relativity* [hereafter OR] (New York and London: Columbia University Press, 1969), p. 83.

9. WO p. 30.

10. WO p. 29.

11. WO p. 30; my italics.

12. WsOs p. 312.

13. RI p. 181.

14. Paul Ziff, "A Response to 'Stimulus Meaning' ", *Philosophical Review* 79 (1970); 74.

15. GT p. 3.

16. OR p. 27.

17. GT p. 3. I pass over the question of whether belief involves conceptualized awareness, except to remark that as I read WO §45, Quine's answer is in the negative only when belief is considered solely within the limits of observation sentences. In this case, to say that a person believes a rabbit is there is to say no more than that he would, if asked, assent to a sentence that has the same stimulus meaning for him as 'A rabbit is there' has for us. But once we go beyond observation sentences we need more than stimulus synonymy in specifying another's belief. We need analytical hypotheses in terms of which we assign 'rabbit' a reference. We then make one's belief that a rabbit is there involve a conceptualization of one's awareness of being prompted to assent to 'Rabbit?'. Cf. my remark about one's "erroneous belief" at the close of the first paragraph of Section I.

18. Cf. OR p. 47.

19. This view of an observation sentence as the epistemological "given" raises a problem for Quine. He begins with the statement that a sentence "queried for our assent

or dissent . . . is an observation sentence if our verdict depends only on the sensory stimulation present at the time" (OR p. 85). The problem comes when he goes on to observe that "a verdict cannot depend on present stimulation to the exclusion of stored information" (Ibid.). He suggests the qualification that "a sentence is an observation sentence if all verdicts on it depend on present sensory stimulation and on no stored information beyond what goes into understanding the sentence" (OR p. 86). But the distinction between "information that goes into understanding the sentence" and "information that goes beyond" is in effect the distinction between analytic and synthetic truth. Quine proposes to replace analyticity with the "straightforward attribute of community-wide acceptance" (Ibid.). He then defines an observation sentence as "one on which all speakers of the language give the same verdict when given the same concurrent stimulation" (OR pp. 86–87).

Quine's resolution of his problem here points up clearly a central difference between his theory of knowledge and any version of mentalistic semantics. If the stored information that goes into understanding a sentence is viewed as consisting of analytic truths, the awareness that constitutes the epistemological "given" must be an awareness that is fused with conceptualization, i.e., an awareness of the presence of an object and not merely an awareness of being prompted to assent. I argue below in Section VI that this fusion of conceptualization and awareness is characteristic of mentalistic semantics. Cf. also my comments on Russell, footnote 33.

20. For a recent defense of common names, cf. P. T. Geach, *Reference and Generality* (Ithaca, N.Y.: Cornell University Press, 1962), pp. 25–46. The crucial point is the claim: "A name may be used outside the context of a sentence simply to name something—to acknowledge the presence of the thing named" (p. 26). Geach defends this claim for common as well as for proper names. Russell, as I note below, defends it only for proper names.

21. In canonical idiom the demonstratives 'this' and 'that' are construed as the "indicator words" 'here' and 'there' and thus become predicates. Cf. WO p. 163. Cp. Geach's construal of a sentence like 'That is gold' or 'That is a man' as representing "a simple act of naming" and not an "asserted proposition" (*Reference and Generality,* pp. 26–27, 40–41). I comment below on the reason for bracketing the indefinite article in the Quinean paraphrase.

In GT p. 8 Quine speaks of construing 'Rabbit' (or 'That is a rabbit' taken holophrastically) as an observation *term* rather than sentence, and adds that "as an observation term it should be taken only as a mass term, applying collectively to so much of the world as is made up of rabbit. It is only thus that the stimulus meaning suffices to fix the designatum. The stimulus meaning of 'rabbit' consists, in its affirmative and visual part, of just those scenes that give noticeable evidence of rabbit presence." Observation terms thus arise at "the primitive conceptual level" (Ibid., p. 9). But then at this level is there ontological relativity? Is there any alternative to conceptualizing one's awareness of rabbit presence as the determinate awareness of an object consisting of just that stuff of the world that is made up of rabbits? In an earlier paper Quine seems wary of the problem. He comments that treating 'mama' and 'red' on the model of the bulk (mass) term 'water' provides an "imperfect" formula, "for it unwarrantedly imputes an objectification of matter, even if only as stuff and not as bits" (OR p. 7).

22. Cf. WO, p. 96.

23. Cf. WsOs p. 321.

24. Cf. W. V. Quine, *Methods of Logic* [hereafter ML] (3rd ed. New York: Holt, Rinehart and Winston, 1972), pp. 230–234; also, WO pp. 181–86.

25. WsOs p. 327.

26. ML p. 229.

27. WO p. 161.

28. Cf. Bertrand Russell, *Introduction to Mathematical Philosophy* (2nd ed. London: George Allen & Unwin, 1920), ch. 16.

29. Ibid., p. 174.

30. Cf. Bertrand Russell, *The Problems of Philosophy* (London: Williams & Norgate; and New York: Holt, 1912), ch. v.

31. *Introduction to Mathematical Philosophy,* pp. 173–174.

32. Bertrand Russell, *An Inquiry into Meaning and Truth* (London: George Allen & Unwin, 1940), p. 97. Russell of course would not allow 'Redness is here' to be paraphrased à la Quine as 'There is something such that it is-Redness and it is-here'. 'Redness' remains irreducibly a name. I ignore the further paraphrase Russell gives (Ibid., p. 128) in his efforts to eliminate 'this' as an "egocentric particular", since his point here in no way qualifies his denial of the eliminability of names.

33. It might be questioned whether Russellian acquaintance is conceptualized awareness. In *The Problems of Philosophy* Russell holds that we are acquainted with universals, and he says that "awareness of universals is called *conceiving*" (p. 52). Acquaintance merely with sense qualities (sense data) is common to animals and men (Ibid., p. 49) and presumably does not involve conceptualization. But animals do not name their sense data. Naming (unlike assenting and dissenting) presupposes awareness conceptualized as the awareness of an object—of something that can be the subject of predication. In other words, it presupposes the *conceiving* that constitutes awareness of the universal represented by 'object'. In its epistemologically relevant sense even Russellian acquaintance thus seems to be a form of conceptualized awareness.

34. OR pp. 158–60.

35. As Quine spells it out, "In practice we usually assure adequately similar stimulation of two subjects by seeing to it that their bodies are reached by similar barrages of outside forces and that the subjects are oriented alike to the stimulus sources and, perhaps, that their eyes are open" (OR p. 159).

36. Chomsky regards Quine's restriction to assents and dissents as an arbitrary selection from the "totality of speech dispositions" (WsOs p. 58). Quine replies, "I am free to pick, from that totality, whatever dispositions are most favorable to my purpose of distinguishing ostensive meanings" (Ibid., p. 308). With my interpretation of Quine, the reason in turn for beginning with ostensive meanings is that they are the meanings necessary and minimally sufficient for linguistic communication. Such meanings can be intersubjectively determined only through assents and dissents. Quine can thus conclude his reply with the retort that for his purpose restriction to assents and dissents is "less arbitrary than judicious" (Ibid.).

37. WsOs p. 321. One is thus not forced to choose between assuming that the other person has only assents and dissents and assuming that he also has reference to objects via predication. "We saw in our consideration of radical translation that an alien language may well fail to share, by any universal standard, the object-positing pattern of our own; and now our supposititious opponent [who rejects translation into canonical notation] is simply standing, however legalistically, on his alien rights. We remain free as always to project analytical hypotheses . . . and translate his sentences into canonical notation as seems most reasonable; but he is no more bound by our conclusions than the native by the field linguist's." (WO p. 243).

38. WsOs p. 322.

39. Ibid.

40. Ibid.

41. Ibid., p. 293.
42. OR pp. 89–90.
43. My word.
44. WsOs p. 303; RI p. 179.
45. WsOs pp. 303–05; RI pp. 179–80.
46. This sentence, of course, is a consequence of my interpretation of Quine and is not a paraphrase of anything he explicitly says.
47. Cf. OR pp. 103–04.
48. Cf. WsOs p. 317.

REPLY TO MANLEY THOMPSON

Thompson would like to translate my naturalistic and behavioristic idiom back into the more mentalistic style of traditional epistemology, so as to clarify my relation to that tradition and show that my theory of knowlege is not "merely, as some of [my] critics hold, a physics of stimulus and response", that being "at best a parody." The occasional mentalistic passages that are already to be found in my writings consequently command his primary attention. Those, however, are subordinate passages where I sketch some topic lightly so as not to divert emphasis from concerns that are more central on that occasion. Thus the least firm footing invites his heaviest tread.

'Attesting', 'assenting', 'prompting'—these terms admit of dry and meager behavioristic uses and of rich mentalistic uses. Thompson's interpretations favor the latter, my intentions the former. Thus take 'attest', which I used in one of those subordinate passages. I meant it in the sense in which blue litmus paper attests to the presence of acid. Granted, when the native says 'Gavagai' and thereby attests to the presence of a rabbit, he is in some sense aware of the rabbit. But my use of 'attest' was not meant to connote that.

Thompson devotes much attention to the other interpretation, connoting awareness. Here in turn there are senses to distinguish. There is awareness in an ontologically neutral sense: one hears a rustling in the grass which, if the truth were known, is caused by a rabbit. There is also an ontologically determinate sense: one observes a rabbit and recognizes it for what it is—an object and, specifically, a rabbit. Such is the difference, we might say, between mere "awareness of" and "awareness of as". Awareness in the latter sense is, in Thompson's words, "a determinate mental grasp of objects in the world". He writes:

> Awareness in our case hardly seems just an awareness of being prompted to assent. We say that we are aware of the presence of a rabbit. . . . In assenting we acknowledge that the object of our awareness is a rabbit.

Awareness is a dominant theme for Thompson, a recessive one for me. Awareness of being prompted to assent is pivotal, he thinks, to my philosophy. The above passage is illustrative, and so are the next two.

> Why assume that conditions of stimulation and behavior attest only to assent and dissent? Why not assume that they attest also to a determinate awareness of an object?

> Quine's theory of knowledge differs . . . . in holding that what is "given" is not an awareness of definite sorts of objects but rather an awareness of being prompted to assent to observation sentences.

He faces inward, I outward; hence the failure to communicate. When I wrote of being prompted to assent I was not referring, as he supposes, to a felt urge to assent in one's heart. I was describing a routine for tapping the reservoirs of verbal disposition. The notion of prompting was defined without mention of awareness, and served only the technical purpose of settling whether a stimulation was entitled to a place in the stimulus meaning that was being explored by query and assent. Nor did I regard assent as a mental act that was somehow fundamental to thought. Professed assent was what was needed, and it was needed simply in order to accommodate verbal behavior to experiment. In "Mind and Verbal Dispositions," which was still at press when Thompson's paper came, I wrote as follows (p. 91):

> It is objected that assent is no mere mindless parroting of an arbitrary syllable; utterance of the syllable counts as assent only if there is the appropriate mental act behind it. Very well, let us adopt the term *surface assent* for the utterance or gesture itself. My behavioral approach does indeed permit me, then, only to appeal to surface assent . . . . This behavioral notion has its powers, however . . . . For the syllable or gesture of assent . . . is not identified at random.

Thompson ascribes especial importance to the indeterminacy that attends the recognition of the native's signs of assent, because he is intent on the mentalistic notion of an act of assent. He sees the indeterminacy as attaching to the question whether a proposed sign does in fact express that act. This is not my way. Underlying the indeterminacies of translation there is for me, as he notes elsewhere, no fact of the matter; and the indeterminacy of assent and dissent, what little there is of it, has the same status.

Indeterminacy admits of degrees. It will be recalled that even the behavioral criteria for truth functions left a little zone of indeterminacy to await analytical hypotheses. (*Roots of Reference,* p. 76 f.) In the case of the signs of assent and dissent, the indicators on which their recognition depends are generous though incomplete. A stimulation that would sometimes prompt the native to volunteer a sentence should also prompt him to assent to that sentence if queried; here is one indicator. Other indicators are cited from *Word and Object* by Thompson. If we guess wrong, our continuing program of radical translation is pretty sure to bog down, requiring us to guess again. However, let us imagine the fantastic case of two independent radical translators who differ in their identifications of assent and end up with unlike manuals of translation, both of which provide successful training in the language as judged by smoothness of dialogue and influence on behavior. Is the native really performing an act of assent when he uses the word that was hit upon by the one translator, and some mental act other than assent when he uses the word that was hit upon by the other translator? I say there is no fact of the matter. Both manuals are successful, and the native's two mental acts, however unlike, are equally deserving of the name of assent.

Returning now to the last two of the three passages that I quoted from Thompson, I would answer that it was only the probing of speech dispositions from outside that called for stressing assent. What then is, for me, the "given"? To face this question I would have to quit my naturalistic stance. If I were to do so, the mentalistic ground elements that would strike me as more to the point are the *Elementarerlebnisse* of Carnap's *Logischer Aufbau*. Each of these is the total unanalyzed experiential content of one or another specious present—hence the mental counterpart of a stimulation as stimulation is defined in *Word and Object*. The basic relation of these ground elements would be subjective similarity, again as in Carnap; for subjective similarity as a behaviorally testable relation is basic to my account of ostensive learning, as it must be to any. In "Epistemology Naturalized," *Word and Object,* and elsewhere, however, I have expressed my adverse attitude toward a mentalistic approach.

The rest of my reply to Thompson will concern three separate topics. Readers have sometimes objected to my notion of stimulus meaning, protesting that the native cannot be expected even to know about stimulations, especially if they are defined in my way as sets of receptors. The answer is, of course, that stimulus meanings are the business rather of those who are investigating the native's discourse about those other things that are the native's business. Thompson did not make this mistake, but there is a hint of something like it where he concludes regarding my phrase "serves to attest to the presence of red" that

> the phrase 'the presence of red' is thus unavoidably vague. It is not in general replaceable by 'the presence of the quality red', 'the presence of red light', or by any other phrase more specific or precise than itself.

I disagree. We may be as precise as we please, saying in our own terms what the native's assent attests to (in my aseptic sense of 'attest'). We can say it attests to the presence of red light, or of light of wave length 640 nm, or of a red helicopter, without thereby crediting the native with one or another of these notions any more than we credit the litmus paper with the notion of acid.

I turn next to the matter of my elimination of names. Thompson is not convinced that this elimination is epistemologically and ontologically neutral. Perhaps he would see the matter differently if I called my predicates common names, as I should be glad to do. I make no semantic distinction between common noun, adjective, and intransitive verb. I see 'is a', 'is', '-ing', and '-or' as mere grammatical adapters for converting common nouns and adjectives into verbs and verbs into adjectives and common nouns, for adjustment to various grammatical constructions. Thompson sees my assimilation of these parts of speech as an elimination of common names, but it is better seen as an assimilation to common names. 'General terms', after all, is what I usually called them in *Methods of Logic* and *Word and Object*. A general term denotes things; it names them jointly; it is true of them; they satisfy it. No ontology is lost.

Nor is my elimination of singular terms relevant to epistemology. Proper names come to be viewed as differing from common names only in their uniqueness of denotation; and this is almost common sense. Russell's epistemological distinction between logically proper names and other singular terms is not lost; it goes over, nearly enough, into the distinction between general terms that can be learned by acquaintance and those that depend on description. This distinction is important for me, for it distinguishes observation terms from others. For me, unlike Russell, it applies to terms generally; but this is a gain. It was a fault of Russell's distinction between logically proper names and others that it was limited to singular terms. This limitation had ontological consequences, for it impelled him to turn a concrete general term into an abstract singular one in order to take account of its being learned by acquaintance. This meant positing abstract objects before the stage where there is real need of them.

An ontological matter worth taking up in conclusion is raised by Thompson in a long footnote. I have argued that stimulus meaning does not determine what expressions to count as terms. I have argued further that given an observation sentence and given an analytical hypothesis that reckons this observation sentence as a term, we still cannot determine its denotation by ostension; I argued this from deferred ostension. Further analytical hypothesis is needed to settle the denotation. Now Thompson wonders how to reconcile all this negativity with my suggestion, elsewhere, that various observation sentences be viewed as mass terms.

The indeterminacy leaves us free to choose; this is the answer, in a word. We must choose some analytical hypothesis in order to get on with translation, and in so choosing we shall be deciding what objects to construe the native as referring to. Our doing so does not run counter to some ineffable preconception in the native's mind. The indeterminacy means rather that there is no ulterior fact of the matter.

A uniform policy might be laid out for imputing ontologies in radical translation. It is a convention to help guide the choice of analytical hypotheses of translation in an otherwise indeterminate domain. Consider, to begin with, observation sentences that can be taught with help of pointing. Some of them can be taught by single pointings—persistently repeated, perhaps, but single each time. Examples are 'Water' (or 'Here is water'), 'Mama', 'Fido'. Others call for paired pointings—thus 'Here is darker than here'. Now we might simply agree to translate all short observation sentences of that first kind as names of physical objects, accountable to the speaker's ontology. The physical object thus named comprises just so much of the spatiotemporal world as might properly be pointed at when affirming the sentence. Thus the objects named by the sentences 'Fido', 'Mama', and 'Water' are Fido, Mama, and the scattered totality of the world's water.

Such a convention could afford a helpful though arbitrary restraint on the choice of analytical hypotheses. It fixes a part of the ontology of a language and a part of the vocabulary of singular terms. (Of course my elimination of singular terms has no place here; that was a matter of canonical notation.) A further convention in the same spirit can be devised for the recognition and translation of many general terms; for these can be associated with various observation sentences of the second kind, the kind requiring paired pointings. The basic idea is evident from *The Roots of Reference*, pp. 55–58.

W.V.Q.

21

Joseph S. Ullian

QUINE AND THE FIELD OF MATHEMATICAL LOGIC

I

The mathematical logic of *Principia Mathematica*[1] was an infant science. Its maturation has been the work of many: deep and startling discoveries by Gödel and Tarski, brilliant insights of Skolem and Herbrand, vital contributions from Mostowski and Kleene, and the fruitful dedication of Church. The names can be multiplied. But few single figures have done more to bring the science to full growth than Quine. He weaned the infant from its ontological and notational excesses, bathed it in clarity, and clothed it in elegance. For more than two-thirds of the years since *Principia's* appearance he has been teaching us how the field of mathematical logic is to be seen and how what is seen is to be expressed.

As we know, the science has spurted well away from its roots, particularly in mathematical dimensions. Quine's main work has been in the foundations of the science. It has been inseparable in many ways from his philosophical work. To draw a distinction whose time has come, he has served both mathematical logic and the philosophy of mathematical logic. He has never ceased to ask the philosopher's questions about logic nor, as logician, has he ever compromised his commitments as philosopher. Always there has been interplay between his philosophical concerns and scruples and the steps he takes in his logic. You might say that his philosophy and his logic have served to reinforce and to celebrate each other. Indeed, he has blended major philosophical insights with technical work in the field as no one else since Russell.

Much of Quine's focus in logic has been on its underlying principles and

I gratefully acknowledge the valuable suggestions of Hilary Putnam, Teddy Seidenfeld, Lon A. Berk, and especially Burton S. Dreben that aided in the preparation of this article.

the development of smooth, responsible language for their study and employment. It is of course no surprise that Quine should focus on language. His work in its philosophy and his investigations in the foundations of linguistics are among his major achievements. He revels in both the study and the use of language. The quality of his own writing is rarely matched, I think, by modern writers of philosophy, and even more rarely by writers of logic. Language for logic centers on notation, and Quine gives notation especial emphasis. He underscores the importance of respecting it and of being purposeful in its selection. His own basic notation has undergone almost as little change through the decades as his philosophy of logic; you will be in familiar surroundings if you open one of his early papers to a central page. He has thus served the purpose of keeping us in mind of both the unified character of his subject and his own uniform orientation toward it.[2]

Quine has innovated widely. He has given us fresh techniques, novel devices, radical economies; he has contributed substantive results, proposed new theories and recrafted old ones. He has all the while been a master of exposition, both of his own ideas and of the results of others. In my mind what stands out is that he has done so much to give mathematical logic its moorings and to set standards for work in the field.

II

Principia was the standard from which Quine started. His doctoral dissertation was called "The Logic of Sequences: A Generalization of *Principia Mathematica*". More than once in the thirties he wrote of "mathematical logic, as measured, e.g., by *P.M.*"[3] But as we well know, Quine's respect for the Whitehead-Russell work was far from uncritical. On the one front he assailed the confusions about propositional functions and attributes. On another he saw overindulgences in notation: ". . . portions of *Principia* would have been shorter and better if every new notation had been required to pay its way or suffer deletion. . . . algorithmic power turns not on assorted occurrences of many signs, but on repeated occurrences of a few."[4] Further, there seemed room for improvement in the substance of the system.

A System of Logistic developed out of the dissertation, as Quine describes in his "Autobiography". It may be less fluid than his later writings, but there is much in it that could pass as vintage Quine. "Instead of the inefficient membership copula, only a part of whose notationally possible interpositions are significant while the rest yields notational refuse, there now stands the versatile comma, all possible interpositions of which yield expressions significantly denotative of sequences, which latter may or may not be sequences of the kind called propositions."[5] Already we find a motivation for Quine's later treatment of individuals as those objects x such that $x = \{x\}$; occurrences of 'ϵ' prior to terms denoting individuals are wasted if 'ϵ' is always construed as meaning "is a member of". The book presents a system from which that of *P.M.* may be deduced. In his review B. P. Gill[6] stated "At every turn appear novelties of notation and frequently of deeper significance." Gill caviled about Quine's treatment of propositions as sequences, and regretted that "extralogical considerations find almost no mention in the book." The only other review I know of is by J. Bronstein,[7] who was more unreservedly impressed. "Dr. Quine's work is a distinctive accomplishment because he achieves a greater generality as well as a greater precision than *P.M.* He has succeeded in removing many imperfections in the latter work, by a considerable improvement in the technique used." Among the improvements Bronstein cited was Quine's treatment of propositions as sequences.

Several of Quine's early papers were directed toward sharpening the apparatus of *P.M.* or proposing alternatives for it. "On the Theory of Types" employed general variables as means of ridding type theory of its tiresome reduplication of classes. "Set-theoretic Foundations for Logic" (hereafter "STFL") gave a system Γ whose axioms were cast in the Zermelo mold; Γ was a subtheory of Zermelo's that was seen as adequate for the needs of standard mathematical logic. Truth-functional and quantificational axioms were explicitly included; beyond them were only extensionality *for nonempty classes* and a scheme differing from *aussonderung* only in that its yield is the class of all *subsets* of a given set that satisfy a specified condition. Quine gave detailed proof that his Γ sufficed for derivation of an earlier system due to Tarski.

"Logic Based on Inclusion and Abstraction" showed that pair of primitives to be sufficient for logic and set theory; Quine's quest for economy was on the move. "On Ordered Pairs" gave a definition under which the ordered pair of x and y was "of the *same type* as 'x' and 'y'"; "On Relations as Coextensive with Classes" noted that that definition *"makes everything an ordered pair"*. Quine acknowledged that he had not realized that latter fact when he submitted the former paper. Indeed the second paper missed by only one day arriving at the *J.S.L.* a year after the first.

Mathematical Logic may be seen as the culmination of Quine's efforts to rework and recast what was of value in *P.M.* and to incorporate it into a coherent whole. In much the manner of *P.M.* it develops a full system of logic including arithmetic, setting out definitions and proofs in full detail. It is of course a very different development from that of *P.M.*, yet it is clearly rooted in that work's tradition. One matter it treats of that *P.M.* could not is Gödel's Incompleteness Theorem, which Quine proves anew in the book's last chapter from carefully built results about protosyntax.

Remarkably, a trait of *Mathematical Logic* that was seen as novel was its treatment of truth-functional validity. *P.M.* had offered axioms from which further tautologies were to be derived; that had been the way. Quine saw the pointlessness of the approach and took instead among his axioms the closures of all tautologies whatever. He freed this part of logic from slavish adherence to the pattern of longwinded proof from axioms. He had, it might be noted, paid his own dues by performing just such proofs in "A Note on Nicod's Postulate", *System of Logistic,* and "Completeness of the Propositional Calculus". Indeed today we not only see no need for truth-functional axioms, we assume the entire apparatus of quantification theory when we set sail beyond it. Such is the attitude of *Set Theory and Its Logic.* Still, the quantificational situation is unlike the truth-functional, there being no decision procedure. In a 1940 book that sought—like *Principia*—to provide a full axiomatic development for the subject, it was appropriate to give quantificational axioms as part of the system and to work out proofs explicitly in terms of them; and Quine did. In fact his logical axioms had a novel ring, since they were the *closures* of formulas of familiar kinds.

The book was hailed by White and Black alike, and also by Nagel. White[8] called it "a clear, exact, and exhaustive treatment of the subject . . . an excellent systematic presentation. It is a model of careful attention to the distinction between using and mentioning expressions. . . . Quine's discussion of the meaning of the word 'implies' and its relation to the conditional-sign is very enlightening." As all who have seen it know, the book is the finest hour for the device of quasi-quotation. Nagel[9] emphasized that the "treatise is based squarely on the central distinction between the *use* and the *mention* of signs." He observed that "Quine did not aim to write a 'Mathematical Logic Without Tears', and partly because he has striven after elegance, logical economy, and precision, his book makes large demands upon the concentrated attention of its readers." Black[10] too spoke of the "novelty" of "the emphatic introduction and observance of the distinction between the use and mention of symbols." He saw the book as "concerned with the rehabilitation of the 'logistical thesis' that mathematics is reducible to logic" and as one which "will . . . bear comparison with its distinguished predecessors in respect of precision and sustained excellence of presentation." Black worried, though: "it is impossible to end without wondering how much competence it is desirable for the philosopher to have in this difficult and still controversial field." Generations of graduate students have worried too.

Fitch[11] cited the book's system's easy proof of an infinity axiom as evidence of dangerous strength. I will discuss that system "ML" in a later section. Philosophical matters troubled Fitch. "It is hard to see how questions of empirical methodology could be adequately treated within a symbolic logic that makes no provision for classes of propositions." Forty-one years later (1982:231)[12] finds Fitch still voicing related troubles about Quine's philosophical framework.

Church (1940:163) reported on the book's contents, dwelling on Quine's proof of Gödel's Theorem and seeing "Quine's major original contribution . . . [as] the method which is adopted in order to avoid the logical paradoxes." But he too cautioned prophetically against "hasty conclusions" about this method. He agreed that the use-mention distinction was "rigidly maintained throughout"; this is by now a familiar theme. It is something of a shock, then, to find that in his review (1958:208) of Quine's "Logic, Symbolic" Church chides Quine for "many confusions of use and mention" stemming from his use of schematic letters in lieu of predicate letters. Church cites the context 'Writing '*Fx*' to indicate application of the predicate '*F*' to '*x*' ',[13] saying that this "invites the objection that '*F*' is by his account not a predicate letter but a schematic letter." In fact Church goes on to complain about Quine's use of 'implication', not that it is different here from what it had been in Quine's previous writings. "Because it violates long-established terminology, this usage is in the reviewer's opinion objectionable in a way which the unusual use of 'predicate' is not." Church later (1975:472) chided Quine for lesser sins that he saw in Quine's piece on incomplete symbols in the van Heijenoort volume.[14] The class of those chided by Church, particularly on matters of use and mention, has some very distinguished members. In fact Church is one himself (1976:752, fn. 17).[15]

Elementary Logic was Quine's first published primer on the subject. In its brief compass can be found forerunners of portions of *Methods of Logic*. The style is somewhat similar, but with much less mention of metatheory and with less scope than even the first edition of *Methods*. It is a patient text, with polyadic predicates arriving on the scene quite late. In interests of economy negation, conjunction, and the existential quantifier are called upon to bear the full burden of quantificational logic. Verbal examples are plentiful. Baylis (1941:99) found it a "clear and concise work" that succeeded especially in showing how to interpret "English idioms involving composite statements" symbolically. Still, he could not resist saying that "Pedagogically, the book seems a better introduction to *Mathematical Logic* than to mathematical logic." Stanley (1970:166) praised the revised edition of the book without reservations: "As the text for an undergraduate course in modern logic, the book seems well suited to philosophy's purposes, especially for its treatment of ordinary-language usages. . . . The book is an elegant and highly suitable resource for . . . [those] who 'need a bit of logic' " (the inner quote coming from Quine).

III

Quine's Portuguese book, *O Sentido da Nova Logica*, was a less high-powered treatise than *Mathematical Logic* but covered almost the same ground. The set theory in it was that of "Element and Number", the stopgap system that lived briefly between the two editions of *Mathematical Logic*. Quine made his first use of the virtual class device, and his efficient decision procedure for monadic schemata surfaced in one of his books for the first time. Berry (1947:16) saw it as "set apart from most elementary texts by its attention to relevant philosophical issues, its rigor, and its scope."

The text *Methods of Logic,* now about to see its fourth edition, finally emerged from its mimeographed precursors. It incorporates Quine's best as a teacher of logic, smoothly interweaving techniques for dealing with truth-functional and quantificational schemata, canons of translation into and out of notation, and substantial morsels of metatheory. Since the second edition the book has contained an elegant proof of quantificational completeness. The book's emphasis is revealed by the title: *methods* of proof, of symbolic manipulation, of application. It steps briefly into underlying philosophical questions: 'to be is to be the value of a variable' finds its place. Late chapters offer a glimpse of the ascent to set theory, mainly exhibited as tiered into types with different style variables for each. The first two editions used a natural deduction system as the chief vehicle of proof; the third emphasizes rather the semantic tableaux method, which is then called upon to deliver completeness in the manner of Herbrand. The third edition offers several variant proof procedures for quantification theory and looks briefly to axiom systems.

Very much in contrast to *Mathematical Logic,* which was not aimed at the typical beginner, *Methods* encourages informality early. Statement letters and their double negations are identified, being alike in import. The operation of conjunction is treated as n-ary for all $n \geqq 2$, and so is alternation. Putnam has suggested that Quine was reacting to the stiff syntactic presentations that were the rule thirty-odd years ago in logic texts. He wanted to show that the subject and its syntax were safely separable, and that basic logic could be accurately set forth and brought to life all in the same breath. Distinctions that matter are carefully observed: Quine's doctrine of schematic letters is adhered to, allowing us to proceed without commitment to propositions, attributes, or even classes; the distinction between use and mention is very carefully drawn. The book's prose shows Quine at his best. And it is replete with wit: one meets the full sweep, the fell swoop, and the full swap, finds a schema said to "wear its meaning on its sleeve", and is graced with a footnote addressed to "Readers less gifted than yourself". Of course one must advance to another of Quine's books to experience 'the shell game of redefinition', which may be my own personal favorite.

Ambrose[16] feared that *Methods* "presuppose[s] a maturity in the subject that the elementary student lacks", but found "the book a genuine pleasure". Cooley[17] praised the text highly, but shared Ambrose's fear. Turquette (1950:203) mentioned "the emphasis which it places on methods for discovering proofs" and concluded that "for its specified purpose Quine's book is at present one of the best English works in the field." But he demurred at some of Quine's philosophical comments. He found Quine's discussion of "existence" too metaphysical, and he wondered why the book harps on how the sign '⊃' is to be read. "After all, what is important is not the verbal issue concerning the name of a sign, but the real issue of the importance of a distinction like 'use' and 'mention'." Raymond Smullyan (1959:219) had no such reservations about the second, or "revised" edition: "This excellent text is to be highly recommended both as a formal introduction to quantification theory and as an informal exposition of further topics such as class theory and metamathematics. The style is lucid throughout, and much of the standard material in formal logic is treated in a strikingly novel fashion."

Quine has made contributions to logic on a variety of topics; many will not even be mentioned here. "A Basis for Number Theory in Finite Classes" gives an ingenious method of inverting the usual definition of 'natural number'. Here, x is a natural number just in case 0 belongs to every class containing x and closed with respect to *predecessor*. The gain is that the definition works even without infinite classes. There are several theorems on reductions of interpreted theories, most notably the result of "Implicit Definition Sustained" which shows, much to Quine's taste, the lameness of the line between true postulate and definition. In four fruitful papers he wrestled with the problem of simplifying truth-functional formulas efficiently; his main findings are recorded in the third edition of *Methods*. There are his many papers regarding modal logic, uniformly oriented toward unmasking its disutility as philosophical tool. Recently there has been a spate of papers on predicate functors in which Quine revives his interest in algebraic logic that reaches back to "Toward a Calculus of Concepts" and even further. He shows how a meager battery of predicate functors, together with predicates themselves, provide an idiom neatly intertranslatable with the ordinary stock of sentences couched in terms of quantification and identity. The bound variable, which plays such a substantive role in Quine's philosophy, disappears upon translation into predicate-functor logic. That is the point for Quine, who sees that the reduction "should be theoretically significant as an analysis of the idea of the bound variable."[18]

Quine's brilliance as an expositor is widely appreciated. His "Logic, Symbolic", spanning just five encyclopedia pages, telescopes practically the entire technical content of *Methods* and still has room left for invectives against intuitionism and modal logic. His papers on the Löwenheim-Skolem and Church Theorems are masterful distillations. In another paper he shows what is really reflected by the trait of ω-inconsistency. For a result or topic to "meet its Quine" has come to be synonymous with its being accorded clear, accurate, and elegant exposition.

IV

In his 1937 paper "New Foundations for Mathematical Logic" Quine introduced his system NF. It was a liberalization of type theory; type indices were
not demanded for the variables and type violations did not banish expressions
to meaninglessness. A *stratified* formula is one that could, if type indices were
added, be squared with the theory of types. It is a formula whose variables
could be given indices in such a way that 'ϵ' is "always flanked by variables
with consecutive ascending indices".[19] Along with extensionality NF offers but
a single axiom scheme of comprehension:

$$(\exists x)(y)(y \in x \; . \; \equiv Fy),$$

where 'Fy' is stratified and lacks free 'x'. The restriction to stratified formulas
blocks the routine derivation of paradox that type theory avoided at greater
cost. Moreover, there are sets determined by unstratified conditions whose existence is nonetheless provable, by indirect means; thus the power of NF "outruns that of *Principia*".[20] The system is obviously more syntactically pleasing
than type theory. But also, by eschewing any division of its sets into types, it
overcomes the distasteful reduplication of standard sets, such as the natural
numbers, from level to level. And there is but one empty set.

Quine stated NF; he did not develop it. In his review (1937:86) Bernays
saw it as a modification of the system of STFL. Hailperin (1944:1) showed that
NF is finitely axiomatizable, which is to the good. In his review of Hailperin
(1944:73) Berry proclaimed that "the requirement of stratification is more liberal than any other method of avoiding the paradoxes not yet proved unsuccessful." But that very liberality has caused problems. Almost everything else
that has been discovered about NF has made it look like a questionable foundation for set theory and mathematics. It has escaped proof of inconsistency,
despite attempts by Rosser (1939:15) and others. But Rosser and Wang
(1950:113) did show that it admits of no standard models, models in which
'$=$' has its usual sense and both the natural numbers and the ordinals are well-
ordered by $<$. Mathematical induction is in general forthcoming only with respect to stratified conditions;[21] this blocked any easy proof of what had been
regarded as the axiom of infinity for NF: that successor is 1–1 on the natural
numbers (N), or equivalently, that $\Lambda \notin N$. These theorems did follow from a
result of Specker,[22] but they were costly. What yielded them was Specker's
proof that the axiom of choice is inconsistent with NF, since $<$ does not well-
order its cardinals.

The development of NF was mainly carried out by Rosser in *Logic for
Mathematicians (LM)*.[23] Rosser called NF "a greatly simplified version of the
theory of types",[24] adding that "It has been possible to amputate the known
paradoxes with remarkably little injury to the main body of mathematics."[25]

The natural numbers were of the Frege-Russell variety, as Quine had intended. Taking the natural numbers as the intersection of all sets containing 0 and closed under successor assured existence of N, since a stratified condition determines it. Rosser used the Quine device for ordered pairs; it was useful because it caused no increase in "type". Indeed Rosser even remarked that "we know no way to construct a less artificial ordered pair,"[26] which is surely more than Quine himself had claimed for the device. Oddly, Rosser did not exploit or even mention the consequence that $V \times V = V$ (the universe), though it would have enabled some simplification in his treatment of relations. Ordinals and cardinals received natural basic treatment along *Principia* lines. But there were anomalies aplenty, some of which had been pointed out by Quine in "On Cantor's Theorem". With Rosser, write '$SC(x)$' for the power set of x and '$USC(x)$' for the set of one-membered subsets of x. Cantor's Theorem is easily defeated, since both V and I (the identity function) are sets for NF and $V = SC(V)$. We settle for this substitute: $USC(x) \prec SC(x)$. So in particular, $USC(V) \prec V$, which seems anomalous. A set x that is correlable (by a 1–1 function that is itself, of course, a set) with $USC(x)$ is called *Cantorian;* a set that is so correlable by the natural correlation function is *strongly Cantorian.* Thus V is not Cantorian. And by further argument, neither is USC(V) (which is the natural number 1 here). Nor USC(USC(V)), and so on out. Each set in the sequence so generated has smaller cardinal number than its predecessor, which is a sign of trouble. Skolem[27] offered this sequence as argument for Specker's result about the failure of the axiom of choice in NF, but it is less than that inasmuch as the members of the sequence are not known to compose a set.[28] Curry, in his review of *LM*,[29] cited the same sequence but wrote more cautiously: "Informally, Specker's conclusion can be made plausible. . . ." Curry admitted that "NF is of great logical interest. Its promulgation was a major help to deepening our understanding", but added "NF is a strange choice for a logic for mathematicians," in view of "the system's anomalous and dangerous character."

Rosser assumed the cited axiom of infinity in *LM*'s first edition; it may now be dropped. His second edition[30] contains its proof, based on Specker's argument. But still needed is something to take up the slack left by mathematical induction. Rosser adopted the "axiom of counting", which says in effect that a natural number n has exactly n predecessors. This amounts to a single case of the induction schema, one which is not provable outright unless NF is inconsistent (by a result of Orey[31]). And it is strong, allowing proof that such sets as N, the reals, and the set of countable ordinals are strongly Cantorian. Rosser speculates that "Probably adequate for most mathematical uses would be an assumption that all Cantorian sets can be well-ordered."[32] So Rosser sees NF plus the axiom of counting plus a restricted form of choice as a system adequate for mathematics—if it is consistent. At any rate, addition of the axiom of counting seems safer than adding full mathematical induction as an axiom scheme.

Scott[33] provided an ingenious proof that NF, if consistent, fails to decide whether or not there are individuals in Quine's sense, that is, whether or not $(\exists x)$ $(x = \{x\})$. It is Henson who has extracted the broadest array of interesting new results about NF. *Inter alia,* he has stretched Scott's result to certain extensions of NF, for which he has shown it consistent to assume each of the following: that the individuals do not constitute a set; that every well-ordering of a strongly Cantorian set is order-isomorphic to the standard order on a von Neumann ordinal; that there is a finite set whose cardinality exceeds that of its power set (!) (1969:589, 1973:69). The last of these is ruled out by the axiom of counting, which seems a recommendation for that axiom. Henson also proves that the cardinal exponentiation function 2^λ is not 1–1 in NF (1973:59). In another finding that speaks for NF's nonstandardness, Petry[34] proves that if it is consistent NF does not prohibit the existence of a set x that is cardinally comparable with neither USC(x) nor SC(x).

V

It was partly to overcome NF's difficulty with induction that Quine turned to the system ML in *Mathematical Logic.* Here there are classes of two kinds: those that may be members of classes *(elements,* or just *sets)* and those that may not. The logic is still one-sorted; variables range over all classes. In its original version Quine took as axioms extensionality, an impredicative comprehension scheme for classes whereby for every articulable condition (including those with bound class variables) there is a class consisting of all the *sets* that fulfill it, and a comprehension scheme for sets (*200) whereby every stratified condition with parameters restricted to sets determines a set. Outwardly the last scheme is just what NF had, except for the restriction on parameters; without *that* restriction, though, it would at once follow that every class is a set, an evident disaster. But now, among the stratified conditions, there are those with bound class variables. And this led to trouble: Rosser (1942:1) and, independently, Lyndon showed that the Burali-Forti paradox was derivable. ML was thus inconsistent. The argument did not apply to NF.

Quine's hasty repair was given in "Element and Number". Stratification was abandoned as a means of providing for sets. A small number of special axioms of sethood was adopted, a method Quine called "elementhood in driblets". "It seems advantageous to adhere thus to a minimum of elementhood axioms adequate to purposes at hand, rather than running the risk of something like *200."[35] The neatness and elegance of the original family of axioms had been sacrificed in interests of safety; of course *some* sacrifice had been demanded. Black[36] grumbled about the "piecemeal postulation" and called this a "reversion to the formalist programme of Hilbert and his school". Further, he insisted that "once we abandon recourse to our intuitions and 'resort to myth making' . . ., the need to bolster our myths by some justification other than the pragmatic consideration of convenience for the technical needs of mathematics and the sciences becomes imperative." Fitch (1942:121) complained too: "This plan . . . leaves his treatment of mathematics in the perpetually precarious position of being liable to give birth to an unforeseen contradiction."

Wang moved to help. First he offered "A New Theory of Element and Number" (1948:129) with but a single elementhood axiom. But soon after (1950:25) he offered a sweeping and beautiful revision: he simply replaced *200 in ML by a scheme whereby every stratified condition in which not only parameters but also all *bound* variables are restricted to sets determines a set. "Indeed, we may even guess that [this] is the system Quine originally intended to present," Wang wrote. For this, but not the unrevised system, is one where the elements are exactly the sets of NF. Beneš (1952:149) called it an "elegant emendation". This new ML, embraced in the book's revised edition, is precisely the impredicative enlargement of NF. ML's new classes cause there to be no new sets. The enlargement is impredicative because of the comprehension scheme for classes. It is in this regard like the Kelley-Morse (KM) enlargement of ZF, rather than like the predicative enlargement that is von Neumann-Bernays (VB). The new system, to which the name 'ML' is to be transferred, is safe from the earlier route to paradox, and has so far resisted all others. "Quine's way out" worked better than Frege's, as Quine himself has noted.

In fact Wang proved the equiconsistency of ML with NF. That NF is consistent if ML is is immediate; consistency of NF is indeed provable in ML (see Rosser 1952:241). In third-order number theory Wang was able to establish the converse. Further he showed that a formula of NF is provable in NF if and only if its obvious translation into ML (gained by relativizing to sets) is provable in ML. Shoenfield (1954:25) improved this by giving a canonical method for getting a proof in NF from a proof of the translation in ML.

How can ML be an improvement on NF if its sets are just those of NF? What the added classes do is to allow improved *definitions*. The natural numbers may now be defined as the intersection of all *classes* containing 0 and closed under successor, a sharper characterization than was available in NF. Mathematical induction is then provable in ML for all conditions. For every condition determines a class; hence if a condition is fulfilled by 0 and the successor of whatever fulfills it, the *class* determined by the condition must include the natural numbers. Thus ML fares even better than VB with induction, since VB falters on conditions involving quantifications not restricted to sets.

Relations of cardinality benefit too. The 1-1 correlation function need now only be a *class,* so equinumerosity, newly defined, obtains where it was previously impeded by stratification requirements. Gone, under the definitions appropriate to ML, are non-Cantorian classes. Cantor's Theorem holds generally. Specker's proof no longer applies, so the axiom of choice is not thus refuted. The Rosser-Wang result precluding a standard model is also overcome in ML. Moreover, given ML's sharper definition of the natural numbers, it is conceivable that NF is ω-inconsistent without ML's being so.

At what cost is all this gained? A minor price is surrender of finite axiomatizability. ML is not finitely axiomatizable if it is consistent. A more serious matter is development of a theory of ordinals for ML. *Mathematical Logic* stops short of such development; Orey has stepped into the breach (1955:95). If ordinals are cast as in NF there is a difficulty with counting, though now only at transfinite levels. We should like to be able to prove that for ordinal α the set of smaller ordinals, ordered by $<$, has ordinal α itself, but if this is to be provable in ML the ordinals must receive fresh treatment. The natural first move is to strengthen the requirement for well-orderings so that every nonempty sub*class* must have a least member. This sharpened redefinition would be exactly in keeping with those already cited. It would provide a class of ordinals "ORN" for ML that is a proper subclass of the ordinals of NF, and it would overcome the difficulty with counting. Further, it would allow full transfinite induction, which would be lacking if the NF account were imported. But the rub is that on such toughened definition ML cannot prove *existence* of any transfinite members of ORN, unless ML is inconsistent. Orey recommends the further axiom:

$$(\alpha)(\alpha \in \text{ORN} \; . \; \supset \; . \; \omega_\alpha \in \text{ORN}),$$

which allows full standard development of ordinal arithmetic. The choice thus lies between accepting unprovability of desired results about ordinals and adopting a supplementary axiom.

Even so, ML's difficulties here are no worse than NF's. But there is one feature of ML that is worse than NF; ML, if consistent, cannot prove that its class of natural numbers is a *set* (Rosser 1952:240). This obstructs the development of analysis in ML. Indeed, if ML is consistent something *had* to obstruct analysis. For if ML were adequate for third-order number theory it would yield proof that if NF is consistent so is ML.[37] Coupled with provability of NF's consistency in ML, this would have ML proving its own consistency, which Gödel's Theorem precludes if ML is consistent.[38]

So if ML is to furnish adequate foundation for mathematics some further axiom is necessary; Quine acknowledges the need to "acquiesce . . . in the inelegance of an added axiom".[39] Unless otherwise provided for, an axiom of sethood for ML's class of natural numbers is itself the most obvious candidate.[40] Thus strengthened ML can no longer be proved consistent relative to NF, but the additional risk of inconsistency seems slight.

NF has many more anomalies than ML, but permits a foundation for analysis as it stands. Both theories need supplementary axioms for some of the purposes we would have them serve. Lévy[41] favors NF over ML. He cites its greater elegance and the fact that ML's comprehension scheme for classes has no effect on what sets there are, even conditionally. "If the proper classes do not affect the sets at all, perhaps one could do without the proper classes at all?" is his summation. Perhaps he undervalues the role that the classes play in ML's definitions. Quine, in sharp contrast, strongly favors ML to NF. In fact he sees Wang's relative consistency proof as furnishing the main reason for continued interest in NF.

For it would seem a lesser task to find a model for NF in another theory than to find one for ML. So far little has been forthcoming. Quine,[42] in an attempt to show NF consistent relative to type theory, established that NF is consistent if and only if "PM4" is—where PM4 has exactly NF's axioms but rules out unstratified formulas as meaningless. Beneš (1952:212) rightly protested that "PM4 is a version of *P.M.* by courtesy only. . . . PM4 is a set theory rather than a type theory." The strongest result along this line is due to Specker:[43] NF is consistent if and only if the simple theory of types plus an axiom scheme of typical ambiguity is consistent. Axioms of typical ambiguity are all sentences $\ulcorner S \equiv S^{+} \urcorner$, where S^{+} results from S by raising all type indices of its variables by 1.

Rosser gained some results about models of ZF in extensions of NF (see 1957:294); so did Orey (1956:280). As Beneš noted (1958:41), the other direction would be the more interesting one. Boffa (1977:215) reports on assorted consistency results for NF, including his own and Grišin's. Let NF_k be the theory whose axioms are all those of NF that could be squared with the theory of types without using more than k distinct indices, where both 'ε' and '=' are regarded as predicates of the language. Grišin proved that NF_3 is consistent and that $NF = NF_4 = NF_3 +$ existence of $\{\{\{x\}, y\} : x \in y\}$.[44] More recently, Crabbé (1982:131) has added consistency proofs for further fragments of NF and shown that already in the "predicative fragment" '$\Lambda \notin N$' is a theorem. None of these results takes us far toward what we would really like to learn: that NF is consistent if ZF or some plausible extension of it is. But the volume of work surely testifies to the interest that the NF consistency problem continues to generate.

While it is more a curiosity than a useful positive result, it should be noted that Jensen,[45] remarkably, proved what can be called the outright consistency of a system NFU that differs in only one detail from NF: the extensionality axiom is weakened, identifying only *nonempty sets* that have the same members. It turns out that NFU is even provably consistent with the statement that V has finite cardinality! But Jensen shows that NFU plus one or both of the axiom of infinity and the axiom of choice is consistent if the simple theory of types, similarly supplemented, is. Quine[46] seemed astonished at how Jensen's weakening of extensionality affected NF. He should have recognized the weakened axiom, by the way, as precisely his own extensionality postulate Γ6 of STFL.

VI

I see *Set Theory and Its Logic (STL)* as a real *tour de force* on set theory.[47] Its title is carefully chosen; it examines exactly what beyond quantification theory is needed for the subject's development and exactly how that development might proceed. Kneebone (1972:768) wrote that it "caters to the needs of both mathematicians and logicians". It is for the philosopher as well. It continually explores alternative courses, interspersing penetrating discussions of rationale. The single system that it sets forth is unlike any other in the literature. It must be emphasized that this is *not* a system that Quine is proposing as a viable foundation for mathematics, as he had once guardedly proposed NF and has with more enthusiasm endorsed ML. The system of *STL* is designed to provide a framework for the study of set-theoretic foundations. In large measure it remains neutral with respect to issues on which known set theories diverge, yet it gives a thoroughgoing development of everything through ordinal numbers and transfinite recursion. The book's last third offers a comparison of five set theories (type theory, NF, ML, ZF, and VB) greatly illuminated by what has been brought out in the building of the book's own system. It teems with insights and with lucid précis of deep relative consistency arguments. E. J. Cogan[48] saw the book as "an attempt to describe . . . the intuitive and logical forces leading to the development of the variety of theories of sets we now know."

Much of the neutrality of the book's system stems from what is really a notational device: the device of "virtual classes" that Quine first used in *O Sentido*. Class abstracts are contextually defined so that "we can enjoy a good deal of the benefit of a class without its existing."[49] The device had been used elsewhere, but nowhere so scrupulously and profitably. Its use was and still is implicit in a host of writings where notation is allowed to mushroom without official sanction; probably due to *STL* it has been gaining increased explicit exposure of late.[50] It is by far the smoothest device that allows unrestricted use of abstracts without threat of meaninglessness, without regard to existence assumptions, and without unwelcome reduction to some entity like Λ in recalcitrant cases. It makes for truth of '$y \in \{x{:}Fx\}$' whenever Fy, which is a boon. And we find that it facilitates our realizing exactly how much that has passed as set theory is really nothing but quantificational logic fancily dressed.

The book's system embraces only a meager battery of axioms: extensionality, existence of Λ and unordered pairs, replacement on certain finite sets (among them the Zermelo natural numbers), and replacement on ordinals. The last of these was absent in the book's first edition; the development is smoother with it, but was not altogether strapped without it. There is no axiom—nor indeed even a *theorem*—of infinity. Quine exploits his inversion trick to define the natural numbers and gain the theory of the ancestral without assumption of infinite classes. There is neither power set nor sum, nor even *aussounderung*. And of course there is no regularity, since Quine clings to his usual treatment of individuals and is not moved to rule them out. Obviously, many standard theorems cannot be proved in such a system. No transfinite ordinals can be shown to exist, though it can be shown that there is no *last* one thanks to an improvement due to Parsons (1964:179). Neither the set of natural numbers nor any real number other than 0 is forthcoming outright. But, with the aid of virtual classes, the theory of these realms can be built nonetheless. And where existence is needed it is available through the medium of *comprehension premises*, since there is no bar to proving that *if* some conjunction of existential hypotheses is fulfilled *then* certain further statements hold. Quine uses this technique very extensively.[51] We are used to seeing the axiom of choice and the continuum hypothesis relegated to the status of special assumptions, not to be embraced unconditionally. Here we find that treatment accorded assumptions that are normally contained in more modest axioms. Not only does this allow maintenance of considerable neutrality, it keeps us uncommonly aware of just which assumptions are required for which results. We never forget that set theory is a first-order theory and we are kept in mind of how comfortably it may be seen as a lengthy exercise in what Putnam[52] has called "if-thenism".

Martin[53] objected that the system of *STL* is not really neutral at all, since only ZF among major set theories allows proof of Quine's axioms. Further, he argued that in the presence of the axiom of choice Quine's scheme of replacement on ordinals becomes equivalent to full replacement. Quine refuted the latter claim by observing that the numeration theorem, which is equivalent in ZF to the axiom of choice, is not provable from it in the weak system of the book; thus a needed step in Martin's argument is blocked.[54] So the system is somewhat less like ZF than Martin had thought. That it shares features with ZF that it does not share with rival theories is true enough; this is in part a consequence of Quine's "maxim of minimum mutilation". At any rate, it has been emphasized how weak *STL*'s system is.

VII

Doing set theory nowadays all but means working in ZF or some extension of it. The subject has become a sophisticated and beautiful part of mathematics. For many it is underlain by what is regarded as a highly intuitive concept, the iterative notion of set.[55] This issues in the "generation" of sets rank by rank, up into the transfinite. Martin calls it "the standard concept of set" and says that "Perhaps the most serious defect in the book is. . .that. . .[it] is never discussed." But it was not Quine's purpose in *STL* to ride any intuitive concept. It was his purpose to stand back and see what, beyond quantificational logic, is needed for a foundation of mathematics. For Quine this means what formal apparatus is needed, not what "concepts" are needed. He sees the logician's task as one preeminently of formal construction and proof—of "syntactic exploration", in Dreben's phrase.[56]

Thus seen, Quine is not "doing set theory" at all by modern lights. He is doing rather the philosophy of set theory, or, as in his title, its logic. He has emphasized that our conceptions are a fallible guide: "Intuition is in general not to be trusted here." In an early paper he wrote "Common sense is bankrupt, for it wound up in contradiction. . . . The logician has had to resort to mythmaking. That myth will be best that engenders a form of logic most convenient for mathematics and the sciences; and perhaps it will become the common sense of another generation."[57] Martin and others might argue that that best "myth" is already with us, and is none other than the iterative conception of set. One is reminded of disputation elsewhere.

It is not surprising, then, that Quine has shown little warmth for intuitionist logic. Quine has acknowledged that he too has intuitions, but that they are not "the intuitionists' intuitions". Indeed Quine has made few references to intuitionism in his writings. In "Logic, Symbolic" he dismissed it with "An extreme variant of constructionalism is *intuitionism*. . ., which even revises elementary logic."[58] In *Philosophy of Logic* he summed up his attitude with "Intuitionist logic lacks the familiarity, the convenience, the simplicity, and the beauty of our logic." He went on to suggest that the usual explanations of the intuitionist connectives "go dim when one tries to respect the distinction between saying a sentence and talking about it" and that one would be better off "to bypass these explanations and go straight to Heyting's axiomatization."[59]

Though mathematics has its own special needs, Quine holds that the criteria of adequacy for mathematical theories are not different in kind from those for theories in other realms of science. Mathematics is but one component of science, not a breed purely apart; what one is after is "simplicity in one's overall system of the world".[60] As Dreben has put it, for Quine mathematical truth is not *sui generis*. Nor, he has also noted, does Quine draw the sharp distinction between mathematical problems and epistemological problems that can be found in Gödel.[61] In a recent paper Quine writes "I look upon mathematics. . .in its relation to natural science." He goes on to make an ontological point: "to view classes, numbers, and the rest in this instrumental way is not to deny having reified them; it is only to explain why."[62]

For Quine "Choice among. . .alternative foundations of set theory hinges on relative naturalness, elegance, convenience, power, and likelihood of consistency."[63] Simplicity and economy are vital aspects of elegance and convenience; throughout his writings Quine emphasizes their importance for theories generally, all across science. In a phrase, his quest in set theory is to find, within the bounds of consistency, the smoothest way to derive the most from the least. Naturalness is to be hoped for only up to a point; Quine writes in response to Geach "when we. . .pursue general set theory, we must grapple with the paradoxes, whether by von Neumann's method of non-elements, or by Russell's hierarchy of types, *or by some other probably equally artificial device*" (1951:138, italics mine). Syntactic exploration is exploration free from external restraints, exploration that need not answer to intuition. Quine's view is clearly as far from what Lakatos[64] condemns as "Euclideanism" as you can get; antecedent claim to truth is not to be demanded of a set-theoretic axiom, and much less is claim to anything like self-evident truth. Truth accrues to an axiom, if at all, from the success of the system in which it participates; and even then, there may be alternatives. Quine closed *STL* hoping "to leave the reader with a sense of how open the problem of a best foundation for set theory remains."[65]

We have observed that there are technical difficulties with NF and, to a lesser extent, with ML. We saw that NF admits of no standard model, in the Rosser-Wang sense, and that it has some highly nonstandard consequences. Granted Wang's proof, the two theories are equiconsistent; but we have no arguments that reduce their consistency to that of any standard set theory. Both are certainly elegantly axiomatized, though both seem to require *ad hoc* supplementation if they are to serve as foundations for mathematics. Now to worry about *these* features of NF and ML is to worry about them from a point of view consonant with Quine's. Much of the disparagement they have received, however, has been of another kind. NF has been the target mainly, though what has been argued would seem to apply to ML *a fortiori*. The attitude is pithily summed in Myhill's scornful query, "What is a new foundation?" It is recorded in Martin's "New Foundations is not the axiomatization of an intuitive concept."[66] It is voiced by Drake[67] when he says "Since. . .[NF] cannot have an intuitive basis in the cumulative type structure,. . .we cannot regard it as being a set theory, in our sense, at all. . . .[ML] is equally difficult to consider as a set theory, although the results of Rosser and Wang do not apply to it."

Even Henson, who has contributed so much to what we know about NF, acknowledges that the " 'surprising' results concerning NF serve to emphasize the fact that there is no informal or intuitive idea of 'set' which leads to the axioms of NF" (1975:242). From Henson this is not disparagement. It can be regarded as discouraging, however, that NF does not seem to lend itself to the development of intuitions that might facilitate work in it; by any practical measure there is something to be said for theories that may be intuitively grasped, whether the intuitions involved are common coin or not. Convenience, if nothing else, is thereby served.

There are related further objections to NF and ML. Neither accommodates a rank function. The main obvious reason for this lies in the symmetry between large and small: complements of sets are again sets in both NF and ML, and in particular, the universe V is a set for each with itself as member.[68] Lack of a rank function inhibits natural routes—like that available for KM—toward establishing consistency relative to extensions of ZF. A kindred limitation is the difficulty in seeing how to apply the notion of "constructible set" to NF or ML, though Rosser (see 1957:294) obtained some results about the modeling of the constructible universe in a (rather vast) extension of NF.

How much force is to be given objections like these depends on what demands are to be placed on a set theory. Clearly we would require that set theory provide for arithmetic and analysis. Also, we want some theory of ordinals and cardinals, though their theory is surely less entrenched in mathematics than is analysis. How much of the "standard" theory of ordinals and cardinals need be forthcoming? Do NF's anomalies, ranging from non-Cantorian sets on up, speak for its inadequacy? Or are we rather to take them as suggesting that there can be a viable alternative to the standard development? Quine remarked that "One could look upon NF as merely more general. . .than set theories where everything is Cantorian."[69] How vital is accommodation of ranks and constructible sets? *Now* we are inquiring about machinery, itself spawned by ZF and VB, whose application is wholly internal to set theory and foundational studies. It has certainly proved highly fruitful there. But to *demand* of a set theory that such machinery be incorporable into it is to have what is now the standard theory laying down conditions of adequacy for its competitors. That seems more of a right than a resident theory should be granted; it far exceeds the conservatism that Quine has looked on with favor in other contexts. Indeed, a demand that inhibits the growth of new theories takes a step toward stifling the quest for knowledge.

JOSEPH S. ULLIAN

WASHINGTON UNIVERSITY
ST. LOUIS, MISSOURI
JUNE 1982

NOTES

1. Alfred N. Whitehead and Bertrand Russell (Cambridge, vol. 1, 1910; vol. 2, 1912; vol. 3, 1913).

2. Even his uncommon clinging to '⊃' and '≡' in set-theoretic contexts may be seen to have its point, in that it underlines the role that logic plays there. When unqualified, 'logic', for Quine, usually denotes no more than quantification theory with identity; that is the sense intended here.

3. See *Selected Logic Papers*, pp. 85, 100.

4. *Selected Logic Papers*, p. 28.

5. *A System of Logistic*, p. 27.

6. *Scripta Math.* 4(1936), 75–79.

7. *Philosophical Review* 45(1936), 416–418.

8. *Philosophical Review* 51(1942), 74–76.

9. *Journal of Philosophy* 37(1940), 640–642.

10. *Mind* 52(1943), 264–275. Black's review appeared well after the original system's inconsistency had been discovered; I cite further parts of it in section 5.

11. *Scripta Math.* 8(1941), 177–178.

12. References to the *Journal of Symbolic Logic*, of which there are many, are almost always incorporated in the text. Any pair of numerals separated by a colon is a reference to that *Journal*, with the former entry giving the year and the latter the first page or the pertinent page of the article or review cited. Standard designations for volumes of the *J.S.L.* may uniformly be obtained by subtracting 1935 from the year and expressing the result in Roman numerals.

13. See *Selected Logic Papers*, p. 43.

14. Jean van Heijenoort, ed. *From Frege to Gödel: A Source Book in Mathematical Logic* (Cambridge, Mass.: Harvard University Press, 1967), 216–217.

15. I learned of this from Teddy Seidenfeld.

16. *Philosophical Review* 60(1951), 595–597.

17. *Journal of Philosophy* 50(1953), 350–366.

18. *Ways of Paradox* (1976 revised ed.), p. 284.

19. *Set Theory and Its Logic* (revised ed.), pp. 287f. The characterization assumes that 'ε' is the sole predicate symbol of the language. If ' = ' is regarded as primitive it commands an obvious additional clause.

20. *From a Logical Point of View*, p. 93.

21. This and other special features of the systems NF and ML are discussed at length in Chapter XIII of *Set Theory and Its Logic*. For valuable further treatment, see also A.A. Fraenkel, Y. Bar-Hillel, and A. Lévy, *Foundations of Set Theory*, second revised ed. (Amsterdam: North-Holland, 1973), pp. 161–171.

22. E. Specker, "The Axiom of Choice in Quine's New Foundations for Mathematical Logic", *Proc. of the National Academy of Sciences* 39(1953), 972–975.

23. J.B. Rosser, *Logic for Mathematicians* (New York: McGraw-Hill, 1953).

24. Ibid., p. 5.

25. Ibid., p. 207.

26. Ibid., p. 281.

27. T. Skolem, *Abstract Set Theory* (Notre Dame Math. Lectures No. 8, 1962), pp. 51f. Teddy Seidenfeld called this to my attention.

28. Wang noted that "such a set is not definable in NF, the condition being unstratified." H. Wang, *A Survey of Mathematical Logic* (Peking and Amsterdam: Science Press and North-Holland, 1963), p. 414.

29. *Bull. of the Amer. Math. Soc.* 60(1954), 266–272.

30. *Logic for Mathematicians,* second ed. (New York: Chelsea, 1978).

31. "New Foundations and the Axiom of Counting", *Duke Math. Journal* 31(1964), 655–660.

32. *LM,* second ed., p. 541.

33. "Quine's Individuals", in E. Nagel et al. (eds.), *Logic, Methodology, and Philosophy of Science* (Stanford: Stanford Press, 1962), pp. 111–115.

34. "On Cardinal Numbers in Quine's New Foundations", *Set Theory and Hierarchy Theory V* (New York: Springer-Verlag, 1977), Lecture Notes in Math., vol. 619, pp. 241–250.

35. *Selected Logic Papers,* p. 127.

36. *Mind* 52(1943), 274.

37. See Fraenkel et al, *Foundations of Set Theory,* second revised ed., p. 170.

38. See Rosser's warning about carelessly combining the cited consistency arguments, 1952:241.

39. *Mathematical Logic,* revised ed., 9th printing, 1981, p. iv.

40. This axiom is implied by Orey's axiom for ordinals. In turn, it implies existence of at least one transfinite member of Orey's ORN.

41. *Foundations of Set Theory,* p. 169.

42. "On the Consistency of 'New Foundations' ".

43. "Typical Ambiguity", in Nagel et al., *Logic, Methodology, and Philosophy of Science,* pp. 116–124.

44. See Boffa's paper in *Set Theory and Hierarchy Theory V,* p. 98.

45. "On a Slight (?) Modification of Quine's *New Foundations*", in D. Davidson and J. Hintikka (eds.), *Words and Objections: Essays on the Work of W.V. Quine* (Dordrecht: Reidel, 1969), pp. 278–291.

46. In "Replies", *Words and Objections,* p. 349.

47. See my reviews of the first edition in *Philosophical Review* 75(1966), 383–385, and of the revised edition in *L'Age de la science* 4(1970), 350–355.

48. *Scripta Math.* 28(1967), 68–69.

49. *STL,* revised ed., p. xii.

50. See, for example, A Lévy, *Basic Set Theory* (New York: Springer-Verlag, 1979), p. 9.

51. But Quine argues in his "Reply to D.A. Martin": "Let it not be supposed. . .that systems are easily weakened just by conditionalizing the desired theorems with the missing axioms as antecedents. It is in the missing axiom schemata that the rub comes." This observation is crucial when it is theorem *schemata* that are in question. When it is some individual theorem, on the other hand, the conditionalization device is always in principle available, unwieldy though it may be in some cases.

52. See "The Thesis that Mathematics is Logic", in Hilary Putnam, *Mathematics, Matter and Method* (Cambridge: Cambridge University Press, 1975), pp. 12–42. I discuss related matters in "Is Any Set Theory True?" *Philosophy of Science* 36(1969), 271–279.

53. *Journal of Philosophy* 47(1970), 111–114.

54. "Reply to D.A. Martin".

55. See, for example, J. Shoenfield, *Mathematical Logic* (Reading, Mass.: Addison-Wesley, 1967), pp. 238f.

56. Dreben observes that whereas contemporary work in set theory exhibits *both* consideration of "intuitive models" *and* concern with systematic construction and

proof, only the latter is discernible in Quine, for whom the syntactic aspect *is* the subject.

57. *Selected Logic Papers*, p. 27.

58. *Selected Logic Papers*, p. 50.

59. *Philosophy of Logic*, p. 87.

60. *Theories and Things*, p. 10.

61. See Gödel's "What is Cantor's Continuum Problem?" reprinted in P. Benacerraf and H. Putnam (eds.) *Philosophy of Mathematics* (Englewood Cliffs: Prentice-Hall, 1964), esp. pp. 262 and 270.

62. *Theories and Things*, p. 15.

63. *Selected Logic Papers*, p. 49.

64. See "Infinite Regress and Foundations of Mathematics", in I. Lakatos, *Mathematics, Science and Epistemology* (Cambridge: Cambridge University Press, 1978), pp. 3–23.

65. *STL*, p. 329.

66. *Journal of Philosophy* 47(1970), 113.

67. F. Drake, *Set Theory*. (Amsterdam: North-Holland, 1974), pp. 19f.

68. In his *Lectures on Set Theory*, p. 52, Skolem writes that NF "does not seem to have many adherents among mathematicians. The reason for this is presumably the existence of such sets in it as V which are elements of themselves, pathological sets as they are called." But he goes on to say "I don't think, however, that this circumstance ought to worry mathematicians, because it is not necessary to take these abnormal sets into account in the development of the ordinary mathematical theories."

69. *STL*, revised ed., p. 296.

REPLY TO JOSEPH S. ULLIAN

Ullian's generous and perceptive survey of my work in logic gives me nothing to rebut, but it offers some welcome tangents on which I shall take off.

From *Set Theory and Its Logic* and *The Roots of Reference* it is perhaps clear that I do not single-mindedly espouse ML, let alone NF. In *The Roots of Reference* I plumped for the theory of types on psychogenetic grounds. I speculated on the steps of analogy and extrapolation that might plausibly lead to the positing of abstract objects, and I found the theory of types to be the system of set theory that could be made intelligible along such lines. One can then slip easily into Zermelo's system by successive deliberate refinements of the theory of types, as seen in *Set Theory and Its Logic*. A hierarchy of cumulative types lingers still in the intuitive background. A familiar further improvement, the admitting of ultimate classes, yields the von Neumann-Bernays system. NF and ML are a more radical and artificial departure, in which the preferential treatment of stratified formulas survives as the merest fossilized trace of the primordial hierarchy of types.

The gains in power and simplicity that motivate this radical departure are undeniable, but there are losses. Abandonment of the hierarchical intuition is a heuristic loss that could hamper discovery. The need of an added axiom to assure sethood of the class of natural numbers, in ML, is a grievous mar to elegance and simplicity. A third drawback philosophically may be seen in the rejection by NF and ML of the axiom of regularity, or *Fundierung;* for, as I noted in "On the Individuation of Attributes," ungrounded classes have an individuation problem. The celebrated principle of individuation of classes, namely that they are identical if and only if their members are identical, serves to individuate them only insofar as their members are already individuated; and on this score an ungrounded class totters over an infinite regress.

There is an exception to *Fundierung,* however, that is worth safe-guarding by an *ad hoc* rider to that axiom. It is my identification of individuals with their singletons, or unit classes. This maneuver is advantageous for set theories generally, those in the Zermelo succession no less than NF and ML. It spares us the distinction between the null class and other memberless objects, a distinction that has otherwise to be assumed as primitive. It likewise spares us a restrictive clause in the axiom of extensionality. Commonly these benefits are bought at the cost of repudiating ground elements and retreating into pure set theory, thereby segregating set theory from its applications in a general language of science. Individuation of classes, dependent generally on *Fundierung*, can tolerate this exception, for individuals are presumably already individuated by criteria independent of set theory. See further my reply to Parsons, last paragraph.

Turning now to another matter, let me supply the background of one of Ullian's quotations from Beneš. By the *prima-facie consequences* of a formula I shall mean the formulas that follow from it according to predicate logic when the variables are taken at face value as unrestricted in range. In PM—the theory of types with typical ambiguity—the variables are not thus viewed; each variable of a formula is tacitly restricted, rather, to some one type. Some prima-facie consequences are consequently disqualified as consequences, in PM, even though stratified. They are ones whose step-by-step deduction, according to some familiar systematization of predicate logic, would involve unstratified steps. Now the theorems of NF are simply all the prima-facie consequences of PM. What was called PM4 comprises the stratified prima-facie consequences of PM. What I remarked in my note "On the Consistency of NF," obvious by now, is that if PM4 is consistent, so is NF. What Beneš was pointing out is that this is small comfort, for PM4 is no minor variant of PM; it abandons type restrictions in favor of a single comprehensive universe. True enough. It was worth stressing.

What Beneš actually wrote, we saw, was that "PM4 is a set theory rather than a type theory." This distinction in terminology, frequently encountered, is the topic of my next tangent. It springs from a wrong philosophy. The orthodox terms 'first-order predicate logic' and 'higher-order predicate logic' have the same deplorable source. I welcome this occasion to deplore it, out of concern not with the terminology as such but with the distorted vision that gave rise to it.

Consider the three formulas:

(1) $\forall x \, (Fx \lor Gx)$,
(2) $\forall F \, \exists G \, \forall x (Fx \lor Gx)$,
(3) $\forall y \, \exists z \, \forall x (x \in y \lor x \in z)$.

In the distorted vision that I deplore, more affinity is seen between (2) and (1) than between (2) and (3). (1) and (2) are seen as logic, of lower and higher order, while (3) is seen as set theory. Or, if the variables in (3) are taken as typically ambiguous rather than as unrestricted, then even (3) is seen as logic rather than as set theory, because it retains the hierarchy of orders exemplified by (1) and (2). Yet when (3) is taken in Zermelo's way, with general variables but against an intuitive background still of hierarchical nature, it is seen as set theory. Why?

The source of the trouble is a blurred view of two distinctions: the distinction between schematic letters and variables, and the distinction between use and mention. Dimness of the first distinction dims one's awareness that (2) assumes new objects as values of the newly quantified variables. Dimness of the second distinction leaves one thinking that these objects, which one is indeed dimly aware of assuming, are anyway just the good old predicates. It is not appreciated that they have rather to be abstract objects which the predicates must be newly regarded as naming. They are perhaps properties, and might well be sets—indeed might better for the sake of clarity of individuation as well as simplicity and economy.

Evidently the one distinction that shines clearly through this murk is the difference between general and restricted variables. General variables boast concrete individuals among their values, so it is sensed that all their values pretend to the same robust reality as the concrete individuals. Abstract objects thus boldly assumed are called sets, in contrast to the hazy values of the quantified predicate letters. But epsilon and quantified lower-case letters also turn up, embarrassingly, in PM. Because of the hierarchical restrictions of ranges, the robustness of individuals is not felt to carry over to the values of these variables; so sets, one feels, they are not. Nor predicates, at this point, nor indeed properties, what with the axiom of extensionality. Very well, *classes;* emphatically not sets. Yet how easy it is, as in *Set Theory and Its Logic,* to transcribe PM in terms of genuinely general variables, and how nearly inevitable are the ensuing simplifications that issue in Zermelo's set theory!

My line, of course, is to shun the notation (2), rewrite so-called higher-order logic as set theory, recognize PM as set theory, and reckon only first-order logic to logic.

The term 'class' has figured conspicuously in set theory also apart from PM. In Cantor on one interpretation, and in some work of Bernays, it has been used for what Gödel called notions and I called virtual classes. Classes in this sense are not values of variables; they are a mere and eliminable manner of speaking. In the fourth edition of *Methods of Logic* I have abandoned the manner of speaking and glossed the erstwhile notation of virtual class abstraction rather as an innocent 'such that' clause, a general term amounting to a relative clause.

In Cantor on another interpretation, and in some set theories from von Neumann onward, the classes lose their innocence; they get quantified over and thus reified. Under this usage they were seen in the same dim status, presumably, as were the classes of PM. They were still distinguished from the sets, if any, with which they were coextensive. Those coextensive with no sets were the so-called proper classes, better *ultimate* classes.

To quantify over classes is to assume them as real, I say, and no hedging. Identify them with the coextensive sets if such there be. 'Class' and 'set' become redundant terminology, but with some residual utility in systems that recognize ultimate classes. Sets are then those classes that are members of classes.

Substitutional quantification, in Charles Parsons' relativized form,[1] offers a latter-day rationalization of (2) to some degree, and even of an interpretation of the theory of types without sets. It does not make a clean sweep of abstract objects, but it gives them a shadowy status in a clear sense. However, as Parsons recognizes, this line is not tenable if impredicative classes are to survive, as they do in PM.

Ullian forges an interesting link when he points out that Jensen's weakened extensionality axiom is precisely mine as of "Set-theoretic Foundations for Logic," 1936. I was none the less astonished that so seemingly slight a weakening should have enabled Jensen to prove within elementary number theory that the resulting system is consistent if PM is consistent.

W. V. Q.

NOTE

1. "A Plea for Substitutional Quantification", *Journal of Philosophy* 68 (1971), pp. 231–237.

22

Jules Vuillemin

ON DUHEM'S AND QUINE'S THESES

The "Duhem–Quine thesis" says that isolated hypotheses are not severally verifiable by experience, only the whole body of a theory being able to be subjected to the test of experiment.

I shall first examine the rather divergent meanings this thesis takes, when it is replaced in the different contexts of Duhem's and Quine's philosophies.

Secondly, questions will be asked about the acceptability of the thesis, its logical strength and its historical soundness.

Finally, the consequences of some doubts raised by this inquiry will be examined especially with respect to Quine's philosophy.

I

The meanings of "the" thesis

I am going to note the kernel of agreement between Duhem and Quine, before showing that their general common conception is nevertheless tinged with shades of difference, which turn out in the end to be fundamental explicit disagreements.

The criticism of positivism furnishes the common starting point. According to Comte, science was born when people, dismissing all metaphysical speculations about the alleged nature of things, decided to accept only empirically tested laws. Similarly, for the Vienna circle, concepts and propositions receive their meanings and therefore their acceptability from their empirical interpretability or testability. Quine, like Duhem, dissents: scientific experiments are

I thank Mr. Thomas F. Morran for his help in translation. I am also grateful to the *Grazer philosophische Studien* and its director, Dr. Rudolf Haller, for permission to republish here this article, which appeared in his journal in 1979 (Vol. 9: 69–96).

so much theory-laden that it is impossible, even in principle, to isolate which part in them belongs to theoretical constructions and which to empirical findings.

Comte insisted indeed on the mathematical form of the physical laws. From this symbolic outlook Duhem draws the consequences. Since physics knows only "theoretical facts" the empirical foundations relied on by empiricists to justify induction are not enough. Interpolations and extrapolations for instance introduce into the laws the real numbers to which empirical data give no application. As for the modern positivists, they sought for atomic and empirically meaningful concepts and "Protokolsätze", to which logic, being thought tautologically valid, should not add anything new. Quine faced them on two fronts. He took seriously the ontic commitments tied to the real use of quantification. On the other hand, he said, as soon as we try to connect our dispersed occasion sentences in order to explain and predict, one-to-one coordinations of concepts and even of propositions with empirical data are lacking and we must introduce posits into our universe which are never severally determinable by our sensations, nor eliminable by directly empirically interpretable conditions.

Duhem maintains secondly that scientific laws are neither true nor false, but only approximate. Since instead of depicting nature they merely symbolize it, we cannot expect them to give an absolutely exact and definitive picture of things, but only a relative and revisable formula for them. Likewise Quine's posits and theoretical existences receive the status of provisory myths, eliminable, if at all, solely in favor of other more basic or more convenient myths by a reduction (e.g., by a 'proxy-function') or by a 'correspondence' (e.g., Newton's as a limit case of Einstein's law).

This being so, the Newtonian concept of inductive generalization and the positivist hopes invested in isolated empirical tests lose much of their appeal. The interdependent sentences of science are built into a truly organic theory. Except for some very concrete sentences then belonging to the physiological or observational field, there is no hope that empirical meanings could be determined by the so called crucial experiments. Between experience and theory or between surface irritation and theoretical constructs, there are too many interconnections for us to single out through empirical decision the several hypotheses of a theory.

The comparison may be pushed still further. To this "second" dogma of empiricism, Quine links a "first" one, which takes for granted a clear-cut distinction between analytic and synthetic truths. The intermingling of theory and experience makes it as difficult to test empirically a would-be synthetic sentence as to insulate a would-be analytic one from all contact with experience. In point of fact, Poincaré's conventions were for Duhem what Carnap's analytic truths are for Quine. According to Poincaré, because the geometrical axioms and the mechanical principles are conventional, they have nothing to fear from a possible adverse experience. They provide precisely the framework without which experience makes no sense. To this extent the conventions were conceived of as a priori, although not belonging to the class of true sentences. Although Duhem agreed that these sentences were more protected against revision than other more superficial ones, he situated them in the general fabric of physics, making their validity too dependent ultimately on the universal but collective verdict of experience. By taking exception to the autonomy of Poincaré's conventions he anticipated, within his restricted horizon,[1] Quine's criticism of the "first dogma".

There seems to be a complete agreement between Duhem and Quine from a philosophical point of view. Both of them are pragmatists. Both admit a statement of physics as true if the theory to which it belongs is globally confirmed by experience and is the most simple among its then known rivals. Some minor differences, nevertheless, can already be detected within this common conception.

For Duhem, a truly acceptable physical theory must not only meet the requirements of empirical confirmation and relative simplicity but must be minimal as well, i.e., refraining from explanations concerning the hidden behavior of things. In the history of science, he distinguishes four types of rival theories: Peripateticism which admits irreducible qualities, Newtonianism which accepts matter and forces, atomism which considers as real only ultimate particles of matter, and Cartesianism which reduces matter to space. The order of this classification shows theories becoming more and more exacting and arrogant. Peripateticism makes do without explanation: hypotheses, unavoidable as they are, confine themselves to predicting phenomena. At the extreme opposite, Cartesianism, mocking the *qualitates occultae,* fathoms the secrets of nature: an "idea" is "true" if it is clear and distinct. Since extension is the one attribute of matter which we conceive of clearly and distinctly it must be considered to be its "principal" attribute, only verbally discernible from material substance. For Duhem the history of science illustrates the triumph of the Peripatetic method. The three other theories made only heuristic contributions whose presence is never found in the final scientific statements. They can be eliminated since their concepts have a provisional and always dispensable status in conformity with the contemporary program of "Als ob" philosophy.[2]

Such a distinction results inevitably in an instrumentalism from which Quine's pragmatism is immune. Corporate testability and internal simplicity select theories without interfering with any phenomenological preferences in Mach's and Ostwald's sense. Since abstract posits are unavoidable, why should we burden our freedom with choosing only descriptive theories? Quine rightly protested against anyone's confusing his own pragmatism with instrumentalism. Phenomenological thermodynamics has thus no methodological advantage as compared with statistical mechanics, and since Boltzmann's hypotheses are fewer for more predictions, they are to be preferred in spite of, or perhaps even for, their explanatory ambitions.

Still the core of the agreement between Duhem and Quine seems to remain. It might be thought that historical circumstances could be invoked to explain the differences away. Duhem wrote before relativity and quantum mechanics restored Cartesianism and atomism. Had he been alive in the 1930's, he would have amended his own thesis in Quine's sense.

There are nonetheless more fundamental reasons to account for this apparently local dissent. These may be divided into four classes regarding 1) the methodological foundations of "the" thesis, 2) the width of its scope, 3) the kind of articulation it introduces into the body of scientific laws, and 4) the nature of the resulting ontic commitments which dictate in turn the relation between philosophy and science.

Duhem taught physics at Bordeaux University, but he owes his fame to his historical and philosophical studies on natural science. His thesis is then an historical one.[3] Let us recapitulate the two principal steps science had to take. It had first to break with the world of our perception as expressed by the statements of natural language and espouse mathematical symbolism. This latter must not be too narrowly conceived. Qualities, as essential to Peripateticism and instrumentalism, must figure in the equations as well as the quantities. Thus arithmetic is subordinated to algebra. Yet symbolism and approximation inevitably entail a discontinuity between the two worlds of science and common sense. The birth of mechanics shows how much our natural intuitions, better called prejudices, actually resisted the making of science. Witness the difficulties involved in the discovery of inertia.

This first step, Duhem says, is often immediately and mistakenly followed, as in the case of Galileo, by a second one which leads and misleads from description to mechanistic or atomistic explanation. Comte had believed that positivism, i.e., a science without hypotheses, would succeed in eliminating all metaphysical speculation. Thus Fourier's equation for the diffusion of the flux of heat by translating phenomena excludes all metaphysics such as Stahl's caloric, but it also excludes Bernoulli's kinetic speculations. Duhem indeed disputes Comte's right to deprive Fourier's equation of its theoretical character, but, like Rankine, he distinguishes abstract or phenomenological and explicative or "hypothetical" theories. He agrees essentially with Mach in disregarding all theories which might pretend to be anything but simple economies of thought. He thus restores Comte's ideal of the autonomy of science against all metaphysical dreams or authorities.[4]

On the contrary, Quine, indifferent as Americans often are concerning history, starts from the sciences as they are now given. To Carnap's method of rational reconstruction, he objects that his framework is neither empirically genuine nor ontologically innocent. But let us use at once logic, set theory, and psychology. According to Quine, science starts from perception, which the logical operators and the constructs of our natural languages give form to, and gradually emerges into the more abstract constructs of physics. Quine's thesis is then nothing but the most general scientific hypothesis, which unifies science without departing from its present state and its available methods. It results in showing the inextricable connections between science's most abstract schemes and most concrete applications, between logic and psychology.

But as soon as we reject the clear-cut division between perception and language and science, we have no more ground to condemn metaphysics. As Comte recognized, ancient metaphysics, like all *Weltanschauungen* embodied in each natural language, amounted to primitive scientific theories or even primitive forms of truly modern views and questions within science. Reciprocally, it is misleading to believe with Comte and Duhem that science can be sharply insulated from metaphysics. Scientific theories do not only dislodge the old metaphysics, they introduce into living science a new one which is perhaps nearer the true metaphysical spirit in being more unpicturable than its ancestors. That is why Quine bluntly accepts theories which are not phenomenological and which Duhem like Comte would have classed among the relics of ancient ages.

This methodological opposition entails a dissent concerning the scope of the thesis. Duhem's thesis ('D-thesis') has a limited and special scope not covering the field of physiology, for Claude Bernard's experiments are explicitly acknowledged as crucial.[5] Quine's thesis ('Q-thesis') embraces the whole body of our knowledge. Mathematics and logic on one hand, linguistics on the other, are here on a par with the physical theory which thoroughly exhausted the D-thesis.

One then expects that the Q-thesis should receive different expressions corresponding to its different applications. From the mathematical point of view, it means that sentences are not severally translatable, even only *salva veritate,* from one theory into another. There are, e.g. in von Neumann's set theory, theorems whose translations diverge on truth values when expressed in the sister theory of Zermelo-Fraenkel. Similar phenomena are met with in the classical translations of metrical geometries endowed with spaces of constant curvatures.[6] Between the two extremes of physics and mathematics natural languages partake of the empirical underdeterminacy of the first and of the indeterminate translatability of the second. At the same time there are continuous transitions joining all the sciences. Mathematics, language, and physics belong to the same fabric of human knowledge.

There is yet a more radical opposition tied to those differences concerning the scope of the thesis. Being limited to physics, the D-thesis involves a strict demarcation between science using mathematical language and the domain of common language (including physiology) which does not fall under the thesis.

Comte[7] distinguished from the metaphysical, i.e., the untestable hypotheses, the "philosophical" ones, which only aim at measuring and coordinating phenomena with numbers and so "anticipate" experience without guessing the causes. Comte's philosophical hypotheses became Duhem's truths of physiology and common sense. As opposed to Comte, Duhem still retains as unavoidable, hypotheses which are not directly testable, condemning only their exuberance as soon as they go beyond phenomenology. His distinction though remains clear-cut and essentially backed up by the history of science.

By virtue of its universality, the Q-thesis eradicates Duhem's sharp distinctions. Its "gradualism" truly connects the criticisms addressed to the two dogmas. It fuses the analytic with the synthetic as it fuses theory with experience. Leibniz had shown such a propensity. Virtue was for him nothing but the refinement of pleasure, and God's intellect perceived truths of fact like truths of reason, their differences pertaining not to their real nature but to our imaginative and finite understanding. Quine has taken the place of a Leibnizian devil for whom the truth of "$2+2 = 4$" should be lowered to the truth of Caesar's crossing the Rubicon. But in challenging his adversaries to find a discontinuity in our knowledge, he puts the burden of theological dogmatism upon them. More than that, he would also dismiss any accusations of ignorance of the history of science. As ontogeny recapitulates philogeny, history, he would say, spreads psychology, and neither one makes jumps. The so-called scientific revolutions would disappear if we were to give a more thorough picture of the fluctuation of ideas.

The last and most important contrast of the D- with the Q-thesis concerning the relations between science and ontology can now be understood.

Duhem's science conquered its autonomy with respect to common sense in the same way that the French State did with the "lois de séparation" as regards the Church. In return, science is neutral. The physical hypotheses are deprived of all "physical" meaning. As in the case of ancient astronomy, they only aim at saving the phenomena and giving them "ex suppositione"[8] the most natural, i.e., the simplest classification. Faith and metaphysics are "physical" in the full meaning of the word. They must indeed agree with scientific statement, but only in order to justify its symbolic approach analogically on the level of reality. Although he believed that science prepares the ways of the Lord, Duhem agreed with Comte and Carnap that science was foreign to metaphysics. Internal to science are questions to be decided by neutral instrumental criteria. And there are external questions as to the choice of our language: Ptolemy or Copernicus? Sainte-Claire Deville or Dalton? Brouwer or Hilbert? Heisenberg or Schrödinger? If Duhem countenances choices by resorting to a metaphysics which Carnap spurns, both of them agree in taking science by itself to be tolerant and unable to decide on metaphysical questions.

Quine would recognize in Duhem's dualism some remnant of the first positivist dogma. For him, an appeal to abstract posits and eventually to the whole apparatus of set theory forces someone into ontological commitments. To take the *tertium non datur* either as an analytic statement or as a synthetic one is a convention, but a convention upon which experience will finally decide. Quine's pragmatism is thus a realistic one. The relativity of his ontology has in any case nothing to do with an alleged opposition between science and "transcendental metaphysics." It results rather from the infinite regress by which we go from theory within which we quantify to background theory "with its own primitively adopted and inscrutable ontology".[9]

II

Critical examination of the common core of the D- and the Q-theses.

Because of its scope, the Q-thesis cannot be fully appreciated by its physical bearing, without taking account of its feedback to mathematics and linguistics. But even from Quine's point of view, physics being the ultimate language of our knowledge, we can examine the common core of the D- and the Q-theses as "limited" to physics (let us call it the "D'-thesis"), neglecting for the moment the collateral subtheses.

I shall restrict my examples to the field of physical geometry and I am going to make the following points. 1) It is disappointing to attack a trivially true or inductively falsifiable D'-thesis by contrasting it with Poincaré's conventionalism. 2) It is as disappointing to defend the D'-thesis against counter-evidences by alleging that seemingly compelling hypotheses are merely recommended by their simplicity. 3) An historical analysis, e.g. of the theoretical development of physics just before special relativity, affords grounds for settling an otherwise undecidable issue. 4) What was then at stake against the D' thesis was nothing less than the ethics of science. 5) The pertinence of this last depends on some empirical circumstances.

1) Everybody agrees on the impossibility of disentangling geometry and physics when assuming the hypothesis of a physical geometry.

Now, according to Grünbaum,[10] there are two very different ways of interpreting this impossibility.

The first interpretation is linguistic and completely foreign to the D'-thesis. Suppose, e.g., that parallax measurements showed the paths of light not to be straight in the Euclidean sense. We could either name these paths geodesics and thus choose non-Euclideanism, or save Euclideanism by choosing new optical geodesics. Such an interpretation of the connection between geometry and physics is linguistic since if we take the second option, we merely rename certain physical laws by "recasting the same factual content in Euclidean language rather than revising the extralinguistic content of optical and other laws".[11] Naturally, as soon as the metric has been chosen by a purely semantical convention, the nature of our physical geometry is determined.

The second interpretation, which corresponds to the D'-thesis, would be an inductive one. The impossibility of testing in isolation the hypothesis of a physical geometry would be ascribed to the nature of experience, which only selects the whole of geometry and physics. Against any observational evidence, the validity of any geometry might then be saved by modifying the laws of the collateral field of physics.

Grünbaum attributes the first of these interpretations to Poincaré. He accepts it as valid. As to "Duhem's" interpretation, he discards it. Either it is seen to be trivially true by suitably changing the semantical rules within the system, or, if the semantical stability shelters a non-triviality, it is a *non sequitur,* for new observations falsifying the whole system do not by themselves warrant the possibility of saving a given geometry by modifying some of the physical laws. Grünbaum claims even to give a counterexample to the D'-thesis.

Without dwelling on these points,[12] let us reconsider whether geometrical conventionalism can be as pure as assumed by Grünbaum from any inductive sin. The conventions we adopt have two different senses accordingly as we choose a spatial metric in differential geometry (the "Absolute" in projective geometry) or the physical objects we have to consider as straight and rigid. There are, in the first case, 3^3 distinct possible metrics for space considered as a group of rigid motions. But our choices are much more limited in the second case, since, as soon as we adapt our geometry to the real behavior of the physical solids, we exclude all metrics of angles which are not elliptic.[13] *Sub specie aeterni* we are free to select any body for our standard of measurement. On the other hand, when we are invited to name non-Euclidean a surface measured with rigid rods (in the Euclidean sense) or to name it Euclidean while measuring it with the squirming shadows of those rods, an imperious convenience confirmed by the whole history of physics leaves us indeed no hesitation. We select light rays as straight and solid bodies as rigid. These rules of coordination reflect a double physical fact: all solid bodies, perturbations being duly taken into account, define the same metric which is Euclidean to a very good approximation.[14] Since a linguistic convention about space metrics and the kind of inductive convention about standards of measurement are both indispensable to a physical geometry, it seems very dubious that this science should confirm the dogmas of empiricism and show us how to separate the burden of language from the burden of experience.

Two special circumstances account for the situation which favored a linguistic conventionalism in geometry at the end of the 19th century. First, the alleged experiments (parallactic measurements) which should have occasioned a modification of our geometry remained speculative.[15] Secondly, all the alternative geometries among which we were supposed to choose embodied groups of rigid motions, which amounts to making space the form of phenomena and the locus for motion. Since congruence is possible with many spaces, space was seen to be no longer a priori; it became conventional through playing with names. These games however exclude any mixing of content and form, i.e., any physical magnitude appearing inside the geometrical expression of the metrics. It was the supposed isotropy and homogeneity of space which invited us to divorce language and experience.

If, under the pressure of real experiments, we should relinquish the isotropy at least of the space-time of the special theory of relativity, or its homogeneity by endowing it with the variable curvature of general relativity, the interdependence of the content of geometry and physics would appear at once. The expression for the ds^2 contains now, in one case, an electro-optical constant, in the other, a gravitational one. Geometry has done with being either a form or a language for physics. Science's modern context would therefore have justified Duhem[16] had he extended to the geometrical axioms his critical examination of Poincaré's conventionalism concerning the principles of physics.

2) The difficulty of distinguishing Poincaré's alleged linguistic from Duhem's inductive interpretation of physical geometry still settles nothing for the D'-thesis. Is it then only the inseparable unity of a geometry G' and a physics F which is tested by experience? Would all isolated tests be circular, since, e.g. the corrections required by variations of temperature in order for a rigid rod to be definable, cannot be determined without an implicit geometry?

Reichenbach[17] answered this question by distinguishing between "universal" physical effects which are the same for all materials and "differential" effects which depend on their peculiar constitution.

At least three times[18] now history has borne out how fruitful is Reichenbach's rule according to which we must incorporate universal effects into geometry itself, while the geometrization happens to be impracticable for differential effects like temperature correction. When faced with the whole G' + F of geometry and physics, we are selectively bound, despite the D'-thesis, in the first case to choose a new geometry G, where the effects for F are cancelled out, in the second case to keep G' and F apart.

To save the D'-thesis could this forced decision be explained by considerations of simplicity, elegance, theoretical unity and beauty? Should we oppose to the mathematically simpler Newtonian theory the physically simpler Einsteinian one?[19] But the concept of simplicity is as elusive as the concept of convention. How are we to weigh respective simplicities? Between two theories, one is often called simpler when for the same empirical predictions it allows us to reduce the number of *ad hoc* and of collateral hypotheses. But it is doubtful that such situations are met except in the fancy of apologetics. Simpler theories seem rather always to have predicted *new* unexpected experiences, the simplicity being measurable by the empirical vulnerability[20].

We run indeed no risk of logical inconsistency if, in the face of a recalcitrant experience, we preserve the validity of a hypothesis by resorting to such diverse stratagems as pleading hallucination or amending our logical laws. Our concept of simplicity still lacks all determinateness[21]. As Kant[22] remarked when describing the birth of science: to get laws man has to put nature to the question instead of trying to save the appearances of his old world image. And as this "Copernican revolution" is not answerable to logic (witness the logical perfection of Aristotle's metaphysics as the principal obstacle to the new sciences!) but to conventions ruling our behavior regarding experience, only an historical, not a logical, analysis of knowledge can settle on the validity of the D'-thesis.

3) A good example would be the theoretical developments in physics just before the special relativity theory. How did they in fact come to pass? The difficulty was with the three principles governing the classical relations between mechanics and electro-magnetism: 1) The principle of relativity of Galileo-Newton is valid in mechanics (R); 2) The classical transformation between Galilean referentials supposes absolute duration and distance (C); 3) Maxwell's laws of electro-magnetism are true (E). Now, since these last laws are not invariant with respect to (C), it would be possible to detect the absolute magnitude of the velocity of a Galilean frame through the ether by means of electro-magnetic experiments (0).[23]

The most direct effect of the motions of the sources and the receptors, the aberration and the Doppler-effect, are effects of the first order relative to the velocities. As these terms only involve the relative source-receptor velocity, they were easily accounted for by the classical theory of optics, which supposed the ether. The ether drift, however, was expected to manifest itself at the first order, when light is transmitted in transparent media such as glass or water. Effects of first order would be unavoidable, were the ether drag by such a material medium total or null. As all experiments (Arago, Mascart) turned out to be negative, the following theoretical situation:

$$(R. \ C. \ E. \rightarrow 0), \ \sim 0$$

was to be explained.

Fresnel had shown that the necessary and sufficient condition for annulling the ether drift to the first order was to admit a partial drag. This *ad hoc* hypothesis—Fresnel's law being equivalent to the complete annulment of any first order effect due to the ether drift—was supported by direct experiments (Fizeau, Michelson, Zeeman).

Lorentz succeeded in making Fresnel's convection coefficient a necessary consequence of his own theory, the apparent partial drag resulting from the electronic constitution of moving matter. Now as an auxiliary hypothesis turned into an organic element of the theory, the gain in simplicity and in falsifiability foretold new experiments conducted to a higher order of precision which would yield positive results. The merit of Lorentz, after having accounted for Fresnel's coefficient, and thus for the first order of approximation in the negative experiments, is to have made the ether static again and to have predicted second order positive effects, i.e., different velocities of light according to the different directions of the earth's motion. This prediction amounted to restricting the validity of the principle of relativity to mechanics. The Michelson-Morley experiment disavowed this prediction.

In such a situation, either we have to extend the principle (R) to electromagnetism and optics and to postulate that the distinguished equivalence between Galilean referentials is a law valid not only in dynamics, but in the whole of physics; or we leave (R) as it is, but we must imagine compensating mechanisms, i.e., *ad hoc* hypotheses according to which the supposed existence of the ether is made inaccessible to experiment. The first solution is often and misleadingly identified with Einstein's discovery; the extension of (R) would have had as a direct consequence a change in (C). History chose the other, more indirect way: (R) was preserved and the doubts were forced to focus on (C) or (E).[24]

As for (E), suppressing the mathematical terms which caused Maxwell's equation to be non-invariant in respect of (C) would have led to a rejection of the well established theory of electro-magnetic induction. A modification of the electro-magnetic conception of the waves of light, assumed by Ritz, could have explained, on the other hand, the Michelson-Morley results, but failed to resist the test of Stark's experiments. More generally, in a conflict between cinematics, considered as being part and parcel of rational mechanics, and optics, we are obliged to prefer optics because of its incomparably superior precision.[25]

In this detective story only (C) could now be guilty. A new hypothesis had been afforded to explain the stubborn constancy of the speed of light *in vacuo* by assuming an appropriate contraction of matter in the direction of the Earth's motion; but no trace could be found of the modification which this Fitzgerald-Lorentz contraction was supposed to make in the optical and electrical properties of bodies, which were attached to the Earth. Lorentz then extended the *ad hoc* hypothesis and made it into his celebrated principle of correlation, according to which nature regulates her course in such a way that an absolute velocity must always be beyond our reach. In other terms, (C) must be changed into new transformations whose group leaves Maxwell's equations invariant. From here on the slowing down of clocks is on a par with rod contractions. It saves the phenomena *ex suppositione* and does not unify mechanics and electromagnetism. To build Lorentz' transformations into an organic theory, Einstein had to generalize (R), to give up (C), and to change the laws of mechanics.

Our description already suffices to suggest how science indicts the suspected hypotheses and tracks down one responsible one. Einstein seems to be right when he speaks of crucial experiments in physics and cites Michelson-Morley's as well as Rumford's[26] or Hertz-Lenard's.[27] The history of science is seen to accuse the D' thesis more than a logical analysis did.

4) The D'-thesis predicted the possibility of saving (strong or positive D'-thesis) and the impossibility of verifying (weak or negative D'-thesis) any isolated hypothesis in the face of experience. Against the first prediction, our historical sketch has suggested that successes did occur in falsifying such hypotheses. Did they occur in confirming as well? All crucial experiments have been found to be negative. Physical hypotheses indeed, as clothed in their mathematical symbolism, forbid any crucially positive experiment because their accuracy and completeness preclude any possible verification. When observations have been translated into a coordinate language in terms of points, these points, once margins of error are taken account of, can be situated only inside or outside the width of a "band curve".[28] Unsound as it is for the hopes it promises, the D'-thesis is thus, like many ideas, sound for the hopes it prohibits.[29]

Progress in science means calling for more organically tied theories by falsifying more finely separated hypotheses. That sounds like a paradox, but it vanishes as soon as we remember that the scientific enterprise obeys an ethical law: interrogate nature by bringing out hypotheses in such a way that your predictions, being more precise, are more easily falsified. Were we to reject this imperative because of being tired of an endless, aimless, risky struggle, and were we to feel content with where we are, our theories could be kept compatible with experience by managing some *ad hoc* hypotheses. Is it not so today in our enlightened age that psychology and history often flirt with such a regression to the Dark Ages, not to speak of recent cosmology, genetics, and even physics?

But let us accept the value of science. While nothing supports a sharp cut between inductive and linguistic conventionalism, Duhem's ambiguous concept of simplicity fails to warrant salvaging any hypothesis. With Popper,[30] we disallow the isolated unfalsifiability of hypotheses while accepting the collective verification even of geometry.

This disentanglement has consequences for our conception of the history of science. Duhem opposed Comte's and Kant's idea of a simple and linear progress, which supposedly leads from abstract, simple, mathematical sciences to concrete, complex and dynamical ones.[31] He rightly brought up frequent feedbacks from the complex to the simple: even the most abstract hypotheses are always subjected to the thread of revision. But do these revisions entail that hypotheses enjoy a perennial revival and that Peripateticism always ends up triumphant over rivals whose sole destiny is to pave its way? Should not history rather be compared to a cemetery of hypotheses which need a thorough transformation before resurging? To say with Duhem that Peripateticism revives in phenomenological thermodynamics seems to be more relevant to the philosophical analogy than to the historical truth.[32]

The D'-thesis remains valuable however for two negative consequences. 1) An experiment can only verify an undetermined set of theories, as an infinity of curves can be made to pass through a finite number of given points. So, when some hypothesis is shown to resist falsification, we may not be sure that it does not, in spite of appearance, contain several subhypotheses, which other tests will eventually separate out. The simplicity of concepts and sentences is thus merely relative to a given theory. Absolute simplicity eludes us despite a dogma which nourished rationalism (see Descartes) as well as empiricism. 2) Even if we are told to specify our new theory in order to account for cases provided for by the discarded hypothesis, we are never sure that a successful generalization will be ''the'' good one. There are hollow generalizations deprived of any predictive virtue which are nothing more than mathematical games devoid of physical meaning.[33] But even while being fecund, two generalizations can occur which have no common proper part. Physical geometry affords an example. There have been two ways of getting new geometries from Euclid. Either the concept of congruence was extended by considering all groups of rigid motion or the concept of distance was taken as fundamental and defined by a quadratic differential form whose coefficients, instead of being constants, are functions of the coordinates and their derivatives. The first extension excludes spaces of variable curvature, the second one groups of congruence. Not only is there feedback from more abstract to more simple structures, but, for want of any clear chain of inclusion between admissible structures, physics splits into parts and no universal language is, for the time being, able to reorganize the *disjecta membra*.[34]

5) If discarding separate hypotheses depends on an ethical choice and often occurs in the history of science, it remains to ask nature herself why the scientific enterprise has been so successful.

To fit with the whole of the then available experiments, the theory of special relativity was required to account for the classical laws of mechanics as invariant within the old margins of approximation. The Lorentz transformations merge into the classical ones as soon as the velocity of the moving body is negligible as compared with the velocity of light. The approximate annulment of a coefficient v/c makes henceforth possible the approximate validity of classical mechanics.

The recurrence of such a situation in physics has its cause in objective traits of nature according to which special circumstances give certain coefficients in our equations so low a value that we are entitled to neglect them. The analysis of nature into simple parts is thus made easy by well determined properties of things and especially by a strong spacing in the order of magnitude of determined effects. Owing to the minuteness of effects bound to small proportional numbers, we are able to study gravitational fields by neglecting second order effects due to general relativity,[35] to develop chemistry without looking at nuclear physics and also to manage with nonrelativistic mechanics by splitting motion from radiation. Conversely, one could construct models as alterations of reality which would perhaps give a precise meaning to the modal concept of possible worlds. By assigning high values to the considered proportional numbers, we could for example generate situations where matter would no longer be made of atoms and chemistry would be considerably changed.[36] World analysis and partial theories would eventually be forbidden and the D'-thesis would rightly claim the impossibility of falsifying a separate hypothesis.

It is then an empirical fact that Nature, even if she is not compartmentalized, admits degrees of compartments. I mean by "compartments" the existence of quasi closed and self-contained systems, independent to a good approximation from any external intrusion. Science was made possible, as the history of taxonomy, astronomy, statics, and dynamics shows, because some of such compartments were frequent and elementary enough—inasmuch as they contained few constants and variables tied by linear or at most by quadratic relations—to become an easy object of theoretical reconstruction. Such are the simple static machines. If we are to give a picture of these compartmentalized situations, we must first exclude from our examination every event which is not clearly involved in the compartment, i. e., we must, as Descartes said, proceed to a "complete enumeration". A simple lever, for instance, affords only three elements: the fulcrum and the two weights, the fulcrum playing through its respective distances to the weights. So we refrain from any intervention by an "irrelevant" statement. Not only do we cut as sharply as possible our theoretical system from the whole fabric of sentences which confuse our ordinary discourse, but we systematically neglect the perturbations due to the influences of specific agents from which the system can and must be insulated on a first approximation. Only such compartments can then be subjected to tests of falsification and to determinate revisions, inasmuch as we reintroduce into the system the minute neglected efforts.

Holism is a logically consistent representation of science. A compartmentalized, discontinuous, approximate representation seems, however, more faithful to history and to nature herself. It could indeed be explained by the compensatory interplay of our subjective theoretic interests, simplicity and conservation, which would again restore the strong D' thesis. But Quine leaves us in ignorance of why this interplay has been objectively successful, as Hume left us in ignorance of how Nature makes our subjective habits possible. Above all this, idealism of theory retains a subjective simplicity identified with a maximal theoretical conservation, while it neglects the objective simplicity which we found bound to compartmentalized nature as the objective conservation which has to do not with a regulatory likeness between the old and the new theories, but with a constitutive respect for the until now acquired laws.[38]

The D'-thesis is then logically irrefutable since it would become true in some possible worlds. After all, nothing but the contingent vanishing of some coefficients justified Einstein when he wrote : "The historical development has shown that among the imaginable theoretical constructions there is invariably one that proves to be unquestionably superior to all others. Nobody who really goes into the matter will deny that the world of perceptions determines the theoretical system in a virtually unambiguous manner, although no logical way leads to the principles of the theory."[39]

III

The D- and Q-theses in their philosophical contexts.

The positive part of the D'-thesis as restricted to physics has raised doubts whose consequences remain to be examined by replacing the thesis in its philosophical context. The analysis of Duhem's and Quine's philosophies has now led to two kinds of differences. a) While the D-thesis—in its general meaning— arose from historical considerations and only physics fell under its scope, metaphysics and science being kept completely distinct, Quine justified his thesis by using all the available methods of science, psychology included, extended its scope to the whole of our knowledge and refrained from drawing any sharp distinction between science and mataphysics. b) To Duhem's neutral science purged of metaphysical claims Quine opposed a realist science merging into metaphysics by its ontological commitments. The question is thus what light, or shadow, doubts about the possibility of keeping any hypothesis in the face of negative experience throw upon the dualism and instrumentalism versus the gradualism and realism case.

Consistently enough, the D-thesis aimed at eliminating science's pretention of deciding on ontological questions. Since there is no ultimate scientific explanation, and keeping any hypothesis means that only description can be obtained, physics deals merely with phenomena, i.e., with the things inasmuch as they are accessible to our symbolic knowledge. The way is then open for another knowledge which would reveal the things in themselves, on the unique condition that they agree with science by an otherwise obscure analogy.[40] So, when Duhem spoke of "saving the phenomena," he actually intended tran-

scending science in favor of metaphysics. We should not find it surprising then
to see this first rate historian lapse into more and more acrobatic mechanical
and chemical "equivalentism".[41] And when Poincaré[42] protested against the
misappropriations of some aspects of his own philosophical work by "all the
reactionary French Journals" which deformed it in the sense of a sceptical
evaluation of science, there is some evidence that Duhem's voice was not missing from this right-minded choir.

This pre-Comtian and pre-Kantian retrogradation to a kind of new
"Schwärmerei" needs no thorough examination. More subtle and intricate is
the Q-thesis in its two very different connections with the system of knowledge.

The first has to do with Quine's rebuttal of meaning, which is even said to
be "identical" with the D'-thesis.[43] A sentence of physics has the same under-
determined relation to experiments as a sentence of natural language has to the
things and events which it is about. Only meanings might remove the under-
determination, since the relation a natural language sentence has to things or
events is nothing else than the class of interpretations it receives when it is
translated into other natural languages. Such was the stand taken by the verification theory of meaning which involved crucial decisions about the province
of signs and the province of things. Now people obey one and the same prejudice when they assume a one-to-one translatability of sentences by hypostatiz-
ing meanings or when they call a statement "analytic" because of its being
vacuously verified.

Would doubts about the validity of the positive D'-thesis then entail the
acknowledgement of meanings in science? Such a consequence is not at all
unavoidable. First, science is indeed extensional. As soon as it attains a reasonable growth, at least, it quite differs from natural languages, because of not
tolerating any nonreferential occurrences of terms. But, then, we do not have
to bother with meanings in science. With Popper[44] we can, for example, discard the verification theory of meaning in favor of a "demarcation" theory of
empirical extensions. Secondly, in so far as natural languages are concerned
there are two ways open. Either we maintain with Quine the ideal of a scientific
extensional linguistics from which actual linguistics is far removed. Then, because of lack of behavioristic criteria which would here play the role of the
negative experiments to distinguish shades of sense, we should have to accept
for this field the positive D'-thesis. Or we could, as the working linguists indeed do, keep on with the concept of meaning and give up the scientific character of term-to-term or sentence-to-sentence translatability by classing linguistics among the arts rather than the sciences.

There is, however, a second connection. Once scientific language has been
purged of meaning and made extensional, the Q-thesis is still supposed to be

valid. It is thus connected with a universal trait of languages, even of extensional ones. Quine calls this trait the inscrutability of reference.

The apparatus of quantification and of identity is only parochially determined. Thus it remains always somewhat arbitrary and subjective. It is indeed
relative to the choice of the language as inseparable from the choice of the
world we believe we live in.

Quine has defended himself against an imputation of having changed his
mind from instrumentalism to realism.[45] I am not going to examine whether or
not there is a different evolution in his thought from realism to relativism, or
if his realistic ontology implied relativistic consequences from its very inception. It is remarkable though that these consequences are only pointed out in
Quine's last books;[46] but they do seem to be necessary ones, if, to the scientific
realism ("to be is to be the value of a variable"), one adds the holistic gradualism ("to be is determinable only in the whole"). Now this inscrutability
introduces an indeterminacy of reference, and consequently of translatability,
which makes the theory reverberate everywhere across the fabric of our empirical knowledge;[47] and that precisely is the D'-thesis!

Would the doubts concerning the D'-thesis then involve rejecting that intranslatability of scientific languages which is linked with the inscrutability of
reference?

There are two aspects of this question.

The first has to do with how to translate mathematical languages. Quine's
gradualism entails that there are all degrees between the literal intranslatability,
e.g., from one version of set theory into another, and the spiritual intranslatability from one apparatus of quantification into another one. For people speaking within the same framework of objectual quantification logic, the intranslatability remains harmless because axiomatic theory makes it possible to locate
the causes of discrepancies. One clearly sees why two corresponding statements
differ in their truth-value and what limited consequences these differences
have. When Poincaré compared changing a geometry of constant curvature to
changing a coordinate system, he was certainly exaggerating and did not pay
enough attention to literally intranslatable concepts or sentences.[48] He was right
on the whole, though, since here dissent can always be settled by going back
up to arbitrary incompatible choices between adjoined quadrics.

On the other hand, the more we rely upon 'deviant' logics, the more difficult a translator's situation becomes. As long as he moves from objectual into
substitutive quantification, although the situation is often already not so clear,[49]
he seems to be able to manage, e.g. by taking as objects the names which he
quantifies over. When the alien language, however, is the intuitionistic one, he
meets strongly deviant speakers who appeal to intensions[50] and stubbornly contest whatever translation their statements receive in his classical idiom.[51] Mod-

ern mathematics evokes the linguistics of Babel. But the linguistic splitting in classical set theory is mild as compared to the disagreements with and within intuitionism itself. In the latter case at least, there would seem to be an unavoidable radical ontological relativity which would be difficult to reconcile with dismissing the strong, i.e. the positive part of the D'-thesis.

But even in his most sceptical concessions Quine seems to moderate his relativism. 1) Because the classical idiom of quantification, he says,[52] is the most clear and convenient, we have to stick to it until new unforseeable events should bid us to change it. This decision is made for the internal advantages this language offers us ; it is, by Kant's standards, "metaphysical." 2) Even if it is doubtful that the language of physics is of only one piece, there is no doubt that it is the last framework to which we can refer for deciding on the merit of every "posit."[53] But physics seems to need classical mathematics.[54] Are we not then justified in dismissing as a kind of "gibberish"[55] the deviant theories of quantification and of sets ? Are we not bound to relativize our own relativism and, using an argument Kant classed among the transcendental ones, i.e., by the possibility of experience, must we not consider as sound our realistic and committal starting point ?

The classical philosophers and scientists ruled out the inscrutability of reference. They clearly excluded rabbit stages or scattered parts of rabbits in favour of the rabbits themselves by requiring substances to have the proper spatio-temporal connection and continuity.[56] The ideal of physical determinism was born from this requirement. Now Heisenberg's uncertainties do indeed afford an argument for a qualified inscrutability of reference. Because of the limiting condition of the correspondence principle, however, they also justify classical mechanics and scrutability within a limited range of phenomena.

There were thus a mild relativism and a mild intranslatability which Quine's talent for analysis knew how to interpret. Their counterpart is a mild or a negative Q-thesis according to which not all empirical statements can be subjected in isolation to the test because of conjugation of magnitudes. That is not yet a reason to accept a tolerant equivalence of all logics of quantification nor to claim that no physical hypothesis is falsifiable in isolation.

Conclusion

The sound part of the D'-thesis is bound to the symbolic aspect of scientific knowledge. Notwithstanding the verification theory of meaning, no direct empirical test can verify such indirect statements.

The full-blown D-thesis results when the separation mathematical symbolism draws between common sense and science is interpreted as entailing the ontological neutrality of scientific knowledge. Beyond this phenomenalism, classical metaphysics would be justified in resorting to direct intuition. The proper Q-thesis, on the contrary, results when all the symbolic posits, which, in themselves, commit us to ontology, are put on a par or at least on a continuous scale. The symbolic separation is then blurred in favor of a holistic gradualism which relativizes ontology. While being so widely different, the positive D-thesis and Q-thesis agree in claiming that any hypothesis can be sustained in the face of any experience, choices between theories only resorting to pragmatic simplicity.

The difficulty of disentangling the two parts of these theses seems to be due to the neighbourhood of two philosophical concepts.

When Duhem distinguishes scientific symbolism from natural languages and when Quine invests the use of a symbolism with ontological commitments, they do not go beyond a strictly negative interpretation of their theses, since what is forbidden by mathematical symbols or by logical quantification is any straightforward empirical verification. So, Duhem's distinction of symbolisms and Quine's commitments can be said to belong to the concepts of a critical philosophy. On the contrary, both Duhem's phenomenological neutrality and Quine's gradualism are characteristic of a positive interpretation of their theses, which seems to be required as well by descriptions *ex suppositione* as by radical ontological relativity. These last concepts are thus relevant to a sceptical philosophy.

It is in principle not easy to divorce separation from neutrality nor commitments from gradualism. But the history of science seems to have done it.

If instrumentalism is not enough, gradualism seems to be too much. Experimental method developed by appealing to more and more exacting and metaphysical theories in Duhem's sense. But the whole fabric of experience, into which physics, psychology, sociology, and history would enter on a par, is a myth. Duhem ignored the positive sense of Kant's *Ding an sich* by excluding ideas from scientific knowledge. Quine blurs their negative bearing by merging them with positive concepts.

JULES VUILLEMIN

COLLÈGE DE FRANCE
AUGUST 1975

NOTES

1. Duhem has given no explicit views on the aprioristic theories of logic and mathematics.

2. Pierre Duhem, *La théorie physique, son objet, sa structure,* 2e éd. (Paris: Rivière, 1914) p. 14; *Le mixte et la combinaison chimique, Essai sur l'évolution d'une idée* (Paris: Naud, 1902), p. I.

3. Kurt Hübner, "Duhems historische Wissenschaftstheorie und ihre Weiterentwicklung'', 9. Deutscher Kongress für Philosophie, Düsseldorf 1969, *Philosophie und Wissenschaft* (Meisenheim am Glan; Anton Hain,), pp. 319–337.

4. Duhem, *La théorie,* pp. 72, 74, 8.

5. Duhem, *La théorie,* pp. 273–278.

6. Patrick Suppes, *Axiomatic Set Theory* (Princeton: Nostrand, 1960), p. 41, p. 133; Quine, *Set Theory and its logic,* 2d ed., (Cambridge, 1969), § 12, p. 84; Gilbert Harman, "An Introduction to 'Translation and Meaning' '', in *Words and Objections, Esssays on the Work of W. V. Quine,* Donald Davidson and Jaakko Hintikka (eds.), (Dordrecht: Reidel, 1969), p. 18; Felix Klein, *Nichteuklidische Geometrie* (Berlin: Springer, 1927), p. 186 (the subgroup of the similitudes fails in non-Euclidean geometries).

7. *Cours de philosophie positive* (Paris: Bachelier, 1835), Vol 2, p. 337.

8. Duhem, *Sôzein ta phainomena, Essai sur la notion de théorie physique de Platon à Galilée* (Paris, 1908); Duhem, *Le système du monde, Histoire des doctrines cosmologiques de Platon à Copernic,* 10 vol., New edition. 1954–71.

9. Quine, *Ontological Relativity and Other Essays* (New York: Columbia Univ. Press, 1969), pp. 51 and 69.

10. Adolf Grünbaum, *Philosophical Problems of Space and Time* (New York: A. Knopf, 1963), chap. IV, pp. 106–151.

11. Grünbaum, *Philosophical Problems,* p. 119.

12. The first attribution raises three questions : 1) How account for the extension of Poincaré's conventionalism to the principles of mechanics (*La science et l'hypothèse* (Paris: Flammarion, 1968), p. 128) ? Are the relativistic mechanics too a linguistic renaming ? 2) Do Klein's model of hyperbolic Geometry in the Euclidean plane and Poincaré's model of the same in the complex plane belong to physical Geometry (Klein, *Nichteuklidische Geometrie,* p. 299) ? Do they not speak rather in favor of Nagel's "syntactical" interpretation ? 3) Has Poincaré really elaborated Riemann's conception ? Does not Riemann's generalized concept of distance lead to spaces of variable curvature, which are "purely analytic" ones (Poincaré, *La science,* p. 73), since groups of rigid motions lose any sense here (Elie Cartan, *Oeuvres complètes* (Paris: Gauthier-Villars, 1952), Part I, vol. 2, p. 842) ? On the other hand, I was unable to find in Duhem a justification for the second attribution ; at one point, at least, he seems rather to agree with Poincaré on geometry (Duhem, *La théorie,* p. 407). Finally, Grünbaum's counterexample seems to be limited to the case of spaces of constant curvature, which will be seen as more of a ground for dismissing it.

13. Klein, *Nichteuklidische Geometrie,* p. 179, p. 189. Poincaré (*La science,* p. 72) considered a "very strange" pseudo-Euclidean geometry. Minkowski's model in four dimensions has however nothing to do with it in the second sense of the word "convention", i.e., when we choose our standards of measurement, since the exclusion of hyperbolic motions for angles remains valid in space.

14. Olivier Costa de Beauregard, Critical Review of Adolf Grünbaum, "Geometry and Chronometry in Philosophical Perspective", (*L'Age de la Science* (N°4, Oct.-Dec., 1969): 350–362), p. 353; Michael Friedman, "Grünbaum on the Conventionality of Geometry", in Patrick Suppes (ed.), *Space, Time and Geometry* (Dordrecht: Reidel, 1973), pp. 217–233.

15. Because of their inaccuracy, measurements were unable to decide between Lobachevsky's, Euclid's, and Riemann's geometries.

16. Duhem, *La théorie,* p. 328.

17. *The Philosophy of Space and Time* (New York: Dover, 1957), §6 - §8, pp. 24–

37; Rudolf Carnap, *Einführung in die Philosophie der Naturwissenschaft,* translated by W. Hoering, (Munich: Dialog, 1969), pp. 170–171 (The letter "F" indicates that 'forces' are resorted to).

18. Max von Laue, *Die Relativitätstheorie,* 1ère ed., Fr. Vieweg, Braunschweig, 1911.

Henri Poincaré, *Sur la dynamique de l'électron (Ren. Circ. Math. Palermo,* t. 21, 1906, pp. 129–176), *Oeuvres complètes,* Gauthier-Villars, t. IX, pp. 494–586.

Hermann Minkowski, *Die Grundgleichungen für die elektromagnetischen Vorgänge in bewegten Körpern (Nachr.,* Göttingen, 1908, pp. 53–111).

Albert Einstein, *Die Grundlage der allgemeinen Relativitätstheorie,* Annalen der Physik, XLIX, pp. 769–822.

19. Such a distinction is already implicit in Nicod's criticism of Poincaré (Jules Vuillemin, *La logique et le monde sensible* (Paris: Flammarion, 1971), p. 228).

20. "In a general way, it may be said that the fragility of a theory expresses a measure of its coherence" (A. d'Abro, *The Evolution of Scientific Thought from Newton to Einstein,* 2d. ed., (New York: Dover, 1950), p. 409). On simplicity and degrees of falsifiability, K. Popper, *La logique de la découverte* Paris: (Payot, 1973), pp. 140. He justifies (§45, p. 144, see also Klein, *op. cit,* p. 207) Poincaré's claims concerning Euclid, when only geometrical simplicity is concerned.

21. Quine, *From a Logical Point of View,* 2d. ed., (Cambridge: Harvard University Press, 1961), p. 43

22. *Kritik der reinen Vernunft,* BXIII - BXIV.

23. I follow and summarize d'Abro, *op. cit,* pp. 120–128, 131–135; Albert Einstein et Leopold Infeld, *L'évolution des idées en physique,* translated by Maurice Solovine, (Paris: Flammarion, 1948), pp. 124–125; E. Borel, *L'évolution de la mécanique* (Paris: Flammarion, 1943), pp. 179–187; Olivier Costa de Beauregard, *La théorie de la relativité restreinte* (Paris: Masson, 1949), pp. 11–14.

24. A case study by Gerald Holton (*"Einstein, Michelson and the 'Crucial' Experiment,"* Isis 60 (1969): 133–197, reprinted in Gerald Holton, *Thematic Origins of Scientific Thought: Kepler to Einstein* (Harvard, 1973) shows the unlikelihood of the first solution, which is for example clearly stated by Max Laue, when he says (quoted by Holton, p. 143): "The negative result of the Michelson experiment, however, forced it (the Lorentz theory of the stagnant ether) to make a new hypothesis which led over to the relativity theory. In this way, the experiment became, as it were, the fundamental experiment for the relativity theory, just as starting from it (the experiment) one reaches almost directly the derivation of the Lorentz transformation which contains the relativity principle." According to Laue, history showed that, in order to account for ~0, Lorentz had to change (C) and this change is equivalent to the generalization of (R) to the whole of physics. Holton rightly contests the last equivalence; there is a fundamental difference in obtaining and interpreting Lorentz' transformations from Lorentz' *ad hoc* hypothesis or from Einstein's general conception. Three different situations may be contrasted:

1) The Michelson-Morley experiment forced Lorentz to abandon (C), which mathematically but not theoretically is equivalent to generalizing (R), since any effect of the existence of the ether is thus denied.

2) The Michelson-Morley experiment forced Einstein to generalize (R), which entailed abandoning (C). That very probably did not happen. The special theory of relativity does not admit this inductive genesis.

3) Asymmetries of Maxwell's electrodynamics when applied to moving bodies in-

vited Einstein to generalize (R), which entailed abandoning (C), which removed the contradiction with experiments since it made one expect ~0.

The point is that in the three possible situations the doubts were forced on (C). The Michelson-Morley experiment is then not crucial if we mean with Holton by 'crucial' an experiment which would positively prompt the discovery of the generalization of (R) (second, counter-factual situation). But it is crucial in forbidding, directly or indirectly, in all three possible situations, the maintenance of (C).

25. Costa de Beauregard, *La théorie de la relativité restreinte*, pp. 14–15 (the author adds systematic reasons for this preference). Between two hypotheses belonging to a theory informed by experience, we must preserve one of them whenever its precision range of verification is indubitably superior to the precision range of the other, this last one being then designated for a modification.
26. Against the theory of calorics (Einstein-Infield, *op. cit.*, pp. 36–37 and pp. 125 and 128).
27. Against the undulatory theory of light (photo-electric effect) (Einstein-Infield, *op. cit,* p. 186).
28. Felix Klein, "Elementarmathematik vom höheren Standpunkte aus," *Präzisions und Approximationsmathematik*, 3d ed., Vol. 3, (Berlin: Springer, 1969), pp. 13 *ff.;* Felix Klein, *Gesammelte mathematische Abhandlungen* (Berlin: Springer, 1973) Vol. 2, pp. 214–231, esp. p. 217 on "Funktionsstreifen".
29. On the crucial discarding of Newton's *Opticks* by Foucault's experiment and on the failing crucial verification of Fresnel's theory by experiment, see N.R. Hanson, *The Concept of the Positron* (Cambridge: Cambridge Univ. Press, 1973), p. 17. Situations occur where no real working alternative to a given theory seems to be found; witness the "hidden variables" theory, viz the theory of quanta. So even an "epistemological nihilist" *(Ontological Relativity and Other Essays*, p. 87) is forced to avow the existence of crucial falsification).
30. Popper, *La logique*, pp. 145, 107–108.
So far as I know, Quine's work does not contain any allusion to Popper until the article "On Popper's Negative Methodology" written for the Schilpp volume on Popper. In the fundamental essay "Two Dogmas of Empiricism" no reservation seems to have been made in favor of any negative methodology and the complete symmetry between confirmation and infirmation (whatever might detract from the likelihood of a theory) seems to be maintained (see *From a Logical Point of View*, pp. 40, 41). In *Ontological Relativity and Other Essays* Hempel's and Goodman's paradoxes are accounted for in relation to concepts such as projectability and natural kinds, without any reference to the asymmetry between confirmation and infirmation. In *Word and Object* Quine spoke symmetrically of confirming and disconfirming experience (Para. 14).

Now, in the contribution to Popper's volume, he opposes a certain instability in the notion of evidence for laws of the form 'All ravens are black', to the stability in the notion of evidence against such laws, the asymmetry being relevant for both the paradoxes. At the level of multiple quantified theoretical laws, if no direct refutation and no direct confirmation are then possible, the same asymmetry occurs between collective refutation and confirmation, corresponding to the duality between conjunction and alternation of laws.

This new emphasis on the asymmetry between confirmation and infirmation is, however, not completely germane to Popper's intentions. Answering Quine, Popper wrote (p. 991) that negative instances and only they "derive their interest from being crucial experiments or crucial cases. . . . Crucial cases are attempted refutations of the theory.'' In fact the whole theory of *Die Logik der Forschung* was to show how an isolated hypothesis of a scientific theory can be falsified, because, even if the theory has not been completely axiomatized and its several hypotheses have not been shown to be independent, the different parts of physics are clearly enough organized to allow us to decide which subsystems are questioned by a falsifying observation (para. 16). This enterprise, completely adverse to a holistic philosophy, is the real ground for the asymmetry between confirmation and falsification.

31. According to Kant, physical hypotheses are ''mathematical'' if they are 1) mutually independent, 2) directly (intuitively) evident; ''dynamical'' if they are 1) organically interdependent, 2) only indirectly verifiable. The first grasp the surface and the form of nature (e.g., phoronomy), the second its core and content (e.g., mechanics).

32. Duhem, *La théorie* pp. 462–472; Duhem, *Le mixte,* p. 198.

33. Such is the generalization of Newton's law by Laplace: Vuillemin, *Sur la généralisation de l'estimation de la force vive chez Laplace* (Thalés, 1958), pp. 61–75.

34. E being the discarded hypothesis, two generalizations T and T' are met such that T and T' merge into E for some particular value of their respective variables, although there is no known passage from T to T'. Let E be Euclidean geometry, T the pseudo-Euclidean space-time of special relativity, T' Cartan's space of variable curvature where Newton's gravitation has been geometrized. While T has still its place in the *Erlanger Program,* T' excludes the whole of classical group theory. It was by no means evident that a reunification could be effected before, e.g., Cartan's holonomy groups proved it possible (Elie Cartan, *Oeuvres Complètes* III, vol. I, pp. 666–686; 1955, vol. II, pp. 1378–1379). Or consider the actual relations between the theory of quanta and general relativity.

35. Karl Schwarzschild, ''Ueber das Gravitationsfeld einer Kugel aus inkompressibler Flüssigkeit nach der Einsteinschen Theorie'', *Sitzungsberichte der königlich preussischen Akademie der Wissenschaften,* 1916, p. 433.

36. Friedrich Hund, ''Denkschemata und Modell in der Physik,'' *Studium generale,* 18 (1965): 181. Similar considerations, applied to astronomy, can already be found in Comte, *op. cit.,* Vol. 2, p. 100, 158.

37. Aristotle, *Mechanics,* 3, 850 a–b.

38. Quine, *The Roots of Reference* (LaSalle: Open Court, 1973), p. 137. On p. 7 Quine says that, for moderate velocities, the Newtonian mechanics retains its utility. That is the subjective conservation: it is still useful to think in Newtonian terms. But the fact that the laws of relativity merge into Newton's laws for moderate velocities is objective and completely independent of a subjective conservation of Newton's theory.

39. Einstein's address for Max Planck's sixtieth birthday in 1918; compare with Quine, *From a Logical Point of View,* p. 42: ''A conflict with experience at the periphery occasions readjustments in the interior of the field. . . . Having reevaluated one statement we must reevaluate some others, which may be statements logically connected with the first or may be statements of logical connections themselves. But the total field is so under-determined by its boundary conditions, experience, that there is much latitude of choice as to what statements to reevaluate in the light of any single contrary experience.'' (also pp. 16–17).

40. Duhem, *La théorie,* pp. 453–462.

41. Duhem, *La théorie,* pp. 286–289; Duhem, *Le mixte,* passim, e.g. pp. 160–161; Duhem, *Sôzein ta phainomena,* pp. 128–9, p. 136; Duhem, *Le système,* e.g., II, p. 83. The equivalence of hypotheses justifies Bellarmin against Galileo. On Galileo's realism, M. Clavelin, ''Galilée et le refus de l'équivalence des hypothèses,'' *Revue d'histoire des sciences et de leurs applications,* vol. 17, No. 4, (Oct.-Dec. 1964): 305–

330; on Copernicus' realism, J. Bernhardt, "L'originalité de Copernic et la naissance de la science moderne," *Revue de l'enseignement philosophique*, No. 6, (Aug.-Sept. 1973): 1–35.

42. As quoted by Grünbaum, *Philosophical Problems*, p. 129

43. Quine, *From a Logical Point of View*, p. 41.

44. Popper, *La logique*, 30.

45. Smart, "Quine's Philosophy of Science," in *Words and Objections*, pp. 8–9; Quine's "Reply," pp. 293–294.

46. *Word and Object*, Para. 12; *Ontological Relativity*, p. 30f.

47. Quine, *Ontological Relativity*, p. 16; *The Roots of Reference*, p. 82.

48. Poincaré, *La science*, p. 76; see note 6 above.

49. *The Roots of Reference*, p. 87 (pp. 132–133), p. 116.

50. Physics is extensional. Is the requirement of extensionality necessary for mathematics?

51. Example: Gödel's translations of intuitionism.

52. Quine, *Ontological Relativity*, pp. 112–113.

53. Quine's reply to Chomsky, *Words and Objections*, p. 202f.

54. Could we rewrite all the equations of physics in the language of the equations of finite differences? In any case, the burden of proof is incumbent on the intuitionist.

55. *Word and Object*, p. 254.

56. And by distinguishing the "modes" (e.g., space) from the "substances" (e.g., matter) (*The Roots of Reference*, p. 133).

REPLY TO JULES VUILLEMIN

Since some of what I have written regarding the relation of theory to evidence is conspicuously akin to the holistic doctrine of Duhem, I am glad now to see the differences as Vuillemin has so clearly drawn them; for they seem about as important as the kinship. There is the difference in scope: Duhem's holism just applies to theoretical physics, as distinct from pure mathematics on the one hand and natural history on the other. Mine does not respect these boundaries. This is due on the one hand to my view of common sense as primitive scientific theory. Further there is the difference between Duhem's fictionalistic attitude toward physics and my realistic attitude. This is due to my naturalism, which recognizes no higher truth than what we seek in our aggregate scientific system of the world.

It may seem from these comparisons that my holism is more radical than Duhem's. In other and vaguer ways mine is more moderate, however, as will now appear.

The primary reference for my holism is "Two Dogmas." The holism for which I declared in broad lines in that context exceeded what was needed in controversion of Dogma 2, the dogma that credits each synthetic sentence with a separable empirical content. To controvert that dogma we need only argue that *many* scientific sentences inseparably share empirical content. The holism also exceeded what was needed against Dogma 1, the analytic-synthetic distinction. For the use that I made of it there, it would suffice to argue that *many* sentences that are synthetic by popular philosophical acclaim can be held true come what may, and *many* that are analytic by acclaim can be declared false when a theory is being adjusted to recalcitrant evidence. See further my reply to Hellman.

What, then, of the holistic doctrine that *every* sentence is vulnerable? This claim is tenable in legalistic principle. Even a truth of logic or mathematics could be abandoned in order to hold fast some casual statement of ephemeral fact: "could" in the sense that the thus altered system of the world could still save the appearances. Could be abandoned—very well; but *would* be? Yes, in an extremity; there are the two oft-cited examples, intuitionist logic and the deviant logics that have been proposed for quantum mechanics. In principle, thus, vulnerability is universal. What is more worth noting, however, is that in practice it comes in degrees. It is at a minimum in logic and mathematics, because disruptions here would reverberate so widely through science. (See my reply to Parsons.) Basic laws of physics, such as those of physical geometry or of conservation, are a little more vulnerable. There is a grading off. As we move toward the observational periphery of the fabric of science, vulnerability increases. 'There are brick houses in Elm Street' could be refuted in the space of a short walk.

Holism at its most extreme holds that science faces the tribunal of experience not sentence by sentence but as a corporate body: the *whole* of science. Legalistically this again is defensible. Science is nowhere quite discontinuous, since logic and some mathematics, at least, are shared by all branches. We noted further that logic and mathematics are vulnerable, according anyway to a legalistic holism, along with the rest of science. But the connections between areas of science vary conspicuously in degree of intimacy. Widely separate areas will share only very general laws, notably those of logic and mathematics, which are in practice the least vulnerable: the least likely candidates for revision in the face of recalcitrant experience. Thus it is that widely separate areas of science can be assessed and revised independently of one another. Hence the compartmentalization that Vuillemin rightly stresses. These practical compartments variously overlap and are variously nested, as well as varying in sharpness of outline. Smallness of compartment goes with a higher degree of practical vulnerability of each of the sentences. Smallness of compartment, high vulnerability, proximity to the observational periphery of science: the three go together. An observation sentence, finally, is in a compartment by itself. It, at least, has its own separate empirical content.

The extreme holist can insist still that these compartments and gradations are a matter of practice rather than principle, and that even an observation may sometimes be disavowed to save a theory. Witnesses must agree in their verdict on an observation sentence at the time, but the standing sentence that records the observation is a theoretical sentence and can be reevaluated afterward.

But even the extreme holist cannot hold that *no* single sentence has its empirical content to itself. We can meet legalism with legalism. If the empirical content belongs to the scientific theory as a whole, then it still belongs to a single sentence, the long conjunctive one that states the whole theory.

The practical compartmentalization has of course been essential to progress in science. So has differential vulnerability, and indeed vulnerability beyond what goes with smallness of compartment; for the experimenter picks in advance the particular sentence that he will choose to sacrifice if the experiment refutes his compartment of theory. (See again my reply to Parsons.) He will select the sentence with a view to disturbing the existing theory least, unless strong simplicity considerations intervene. The experimenter means to interrogate nature on a specific sentence, and then as a matter of course he treats nature's demurral as a denial of that sentence rather than merely of the conjoint compartment. This pattern accounts in part for the air of inevitability that Einstein remarked on in Vuillemin's striking quotation. It also accounts for another important effect that Vuillemin remarks upon: the preservation of an old theory such as Newton's, up to a certain margin of accuracy, within the new.

Vuillemin reports Popper as arguing, contrary to holism, that scientific hypotheses are separately falsifiable. The reasoning is akin to what I have been reviewing above, so I am in substantial agreement, slogans aside. But I am puzzled that Popper should find here, as Vuillemin puts it, "the real ground for the asymmetry between confirmation and falsification." To falsify a single hypothesis, after all, is to confirm its negation; symmetry obtains. To my mind the ground for asymmetry is not the separate falsifiability of hypotheses, but just the reverse: the fact that what is falsified is the theory or compartment taken conjunctively. Such falsification is no longer so readily described as confirmation of a negation. Rather, to falsify the theory taken conjunctively is to confirm the negations of the component hypotheses taken in alternation; and to take them thus is alien to our habitual ways of thinking. Or, if we conjoin all the hypotheses as a single long hypothesis, then we are back to the case of a separately falsifiable hypothesis, and symmetry returns: falsification is confirmation of the negation.

Vuillemin raises the perennial question why simplicity is objectively successful. I have guessed at several partial reasons, but I am not satisfied. In "On Simple Theories of a Complex World" I conjectured, following Kemeny, that simplicity affects the way we draw the line between approximate instances and counter-instances. I suggested also that the criteria for some of our terms are biased in such a way that an experiment would have to attest either to a simple law or to nothing. In "On Natural Kinds" I suggested that our subjective standards of simplicity are of a piece with our standards of similarity, and have been partly attuned to nature by natural selection.

Regarding the dogma that credits each synthetic sentence with a separable empirical content, Vuillemin writes:

> Quine, like Duhem dissents: scientific experiments are so much theory-laden that it is impossible . . . to isolate which part . . . belongs to . . . empirical findings.

That is not quite my line of argument, since I think I have a fair working criterion of what to count as an observation sentence and what to count as its stimulus meaning. Observation sentences are indeed theory laden, in the sense that their component terms recur in theoretical sentences. But what impedes the distribution of empirical content over separate theoretical sentences is the fact that most theoretical sentences will not separately imply observation categoricals; they will imply them only in conjunction.

Vuillemin writes of Duhem and me that

> both admit a statement of physics as true if the theory to which it belongs is globally confirmed by experience and is the most simple among its known rivals.

I can assent to this in one sense and not in another; there is a curiously subtle ambiguity. I do not agree that the described conditions are sufficient for truth. I do agree that they are sufficient to induce me, perhaps mistakenly, to admit a statement of physics as true.

Vuillemin refers to

> degrees between the literal intranslatability, e.g., from one version of set theory into another, and the spiritual intranslatability from one apparatus of quantification into another one.

There are degrees of indeterminacy of translation; see my reply to Thompson. But indeterminacy of translation is not intranslatability; it is multiple translatability. In set theory and elsewhere in mathematics there are also cases of intranslatability: cases where we can prove that one theory cannot be modelled in another because of essential difference in strength.

Vuillemin senses a tension between my professed realism and my seeming relativism and instrumentalism. The reconciliation is to be sought in my naturalism, which, as noted at the beginning of this reply, recognizes no higher truth than what we seek in science. For a little more in this vein see an early portion of my reply to Lee. Regarding inscrutability of reference, which Vuillemin also discusses, I might mention my reply to Thompson.

W. V. Q.

23

Hao Wang

QUINE'S LOGICAL IDEAS IN HISTORICAL PERSPECTIVE

In 1970 Quine said: "Carnap is a towering figure. I see him as the dominant figure in philosophy from the 1930s onward, as Russell had been in the decades before" (*Ways of Paradox,* 1976, p. 40). Those who share Quine's conception of philosophy as "scientific philosophy" are likely to amend the statement by adding Quine as the dominant figure from the 1950s on. Others may wish to mention, for the extended period suggested, Peirce, Bergson, James, Croce, Husserl, Dewey, Whitehead, Wittgenstein, Lukacs, Heidegger, Gramsci, Sartre, and of course more.

The title of this paper was originally proposed to me many years ago by P. A. Schilpp. At that time I wished more to talk about philosophy and proposed to insert after "logical ideas" also "and philosophical presuppositions." Schilpp agreed to my suggestion and the matter stopped there. In 1981 the new editor returned to the project and I wrote a long paper of about forty thousand words. This was too long for the purpose so that I have recently decided to expand it into a small book. Since the parts relating to logic are short enough for my contribution, I have revised those parts and returned to the original title. This is probably just as well since the points which are definite enough for Quine to wish to consider replying to are presumably all included. In order to offer the reader a global view of Quine's more technical work in historical perspective, I shall also devote considerable space to a summary exposition of his contributions to non–elementary logic and mention related works by others.

It is familiar that Quine studied and reacted against Russell's work in logic (particularly the famous *Principia Mathematica,* briefly *PM*) and Carnap's work in philosophy. Most of his influential ideas can be traced back to the half decade up to 1940. "Truth by Convention" was completed in 1935, and by 1940 he was voicing, in discussions with Carnap, those qualms over analyticity which later received a persuasive formulation in his "Two Dogmas" (1951).

[Detailed references can be found in the bibliography of Quine's work in this volume.] NF ("New Foundations") and its predecessor were worked out in 1936; these were followed by an inconsistent enlargement in *ML* (*Mathematical Logic*, 1940). The error was corrected by me in 1949 and the correction was incorporated into the revised edition published in 1951. The corrected version is known as ML in the literature. By the way, his only other book on higher logic, *SL* (*Set Theory and Its Logic*, 1963 and 1969) also grew out of a comparison of NF and ML with standard systems of set theory, which is quite similar to but more polished than my monograph with R. McNaughton (*Les systèmes axiomatique de la théorie des ensembles*, 1953). Two papers on existence and "ontology" were published in 1939 (one of them with preprints only at that time) which to a large extent anticipated the more definitive proposal in "On What There Is" (1948). This and the two papers on dogmas and on NF (with added notes on ML) were all reprinted in *LP* (*From a Logical Point of View*, 1953).

My considerations will center around NF and ML. But I shall begin with two philosophical issues related to analyticity and existence: the nature of logic and set theory; and the relation of reference to predicative (or ramified) set theory (particularly a system proposed by me in 1953). These issues are quite central to Quine's outlook and my discussion will illustrate more general differences between his preferences and mine in a relatively definite context.

I

Objects and Predicative Set Theories.

As early as 1939, Quine posed the question to which he returns over and over again (*Ways of Paradox*, 1966, p. 68): "How economical an ontology *can* we achieve and still have a language adequate to all purposes of science?" His answer at that time amounts to physical objects and sets (as in set theory). Something like this persisted over the years. It was probably in 1976 that the physical objects were also "eliminated" (e.g., *TT* or *Theories and Things*, pp. 1–23). What remains are the pure sets of set theory. Hence, it is of central importance to Quine's philosophy to find out what sets are needed to get enough mathematics to do physics (and consequently also other sciences according to his outlook).

Given this fact plus his familiarity with *PM*, and his emphasis on "virtual classes," it is surprising that Quine for many years did not seem to have paid much attention to predicative set theory as a way of getting ordinary mathematics. In addition, some of his considerations of "substitutional quantification" in 1974 seem to me to bring to completion a conceptual framework within which the system I am about to describe is exactly what he wants. Let me first describe this system and then relate it to Quine's extended study of reference and ontology.

In the second edition of *PM* (1925) Russell attempts to develop mathematics from predicative type theory (or, as he says, type theory without the axiom of reducibility). He is even willing to give up Cantor's set theory, but he cannot even get real numbers (more exactly, Dedekind cuts). He thought he could get arithmetic (of natural numbers) but his proof of mathematical induction is mistaken. In 1953 I came upon the idea of using general variables, much as moving from type theory to Zermelo set theory (without the axioms of replacement but with the first order axiom of separation as made explicit by Skolem). In other words, I propose to use one style of variable which ranges over sets of all (finite) orders.

Russell's difficulty with induction is that a principle is needed for each order. The definition of identity of two sets has the same problem. The use of general variables removes these obstacles outright. A more interesting question is with the Dedekind cuts. The least upper bound of a bounded set of real numbers of order n is a real number of order $n + 1$. Hence, no single order suffices. Here the use of general variables is elegant: each x (say a bounded set of real numbers) is of some fixed finite order (say n); therefore, $n + 1$ is also of a finite order and a set of order $n + 1$ also falls within the range of a general variable. Hence, we are able to get a form of the central parts of mathematics in such a system which, moreover, is demonstrably consistent.

Let Σ_ω be the system obtained from the empty set by iteration of the formation of predicative sets to order $\omega + \omega$ (see *Survey*, i.e., my *A Survey of Mathematical Logic*, 1962, pp. 571 and 619). This suffices for the theory of natural and real numbers and more. For a detailed formulation of and philosophical support for this system, see C. Chihara, *Ontology and the Vicious-Circle Principle*, 1973. A remaining problem is to find a natural stopping place in thus moving to infinite orders. And I suggested a device that has come to be known as "autonomous progressions". These ideas were presented to the Association for Symbolic Logic in December 1953 at Rochester, New York and published in *JSL* (i.e., *Journal of Symbolic Logic*), vol. 19 (1954): 241–266. A good deal of work along this general line has appeared in the literature since that time (in particular, I have devoted pp. 559–651 of my *Survey* to this subject).

In December 1966 there was a session on Russell in the APA meeting with Carl Hempel and me commenting on Quine. For this purpose I listed eight comments on Quine's criterion for ontological commitment. Since the length of the abstract was severely restricted, no elaboration was included (*Journal of Philosophy*, vol. 63, pp. 670–673). Quine took the comments rather ill. Some of the comments are probably asking for too much from the criterion. Recently

Quine observes that the connection between ontology and referential quantification is trivially assured by the very explanation of the latter. "The solemnity of my terms 'ontological commitment' and 'ontological criterion' has led my readers to suppose that there is more afoot than meets the eye, despite my protests" (*TT*, p. 175). But in reading *The Roots of Reference* (*RR*, 1974), I now feel that some of my vague comments can be made clearer in terms of some of the relevant passages in it.

I argued there that the ramified type theory does not commit us to the existence of sets in any opaque way because the range of variables is quite transparent. I am now gratified to see that Quine indeed makes a similar point in terms of substitutional quantification which works for predicative definitions of sets. Indeed, as I see it, the ramified theory is more or less a repeated enlargement in the manner of what Quine calls virtual theory of classes. Hence, I feel that systems like Σ_ω should be congenial to Quine.

I do not fully understand Quine's relevant observations in *RR* and elsewhere. He seems to say that substitutional quantification and substitutional truth conditions are clear when impredicative definitions of sets are absent. "As long as we adhere to predicative class abstracts, the circularity we just now observed does not occur" (p. 112). Moreover, in terms of psychogenesis, "abstract objects owe their acceptance to what is essentially substitutional quantification, cast in natural language" (pp. 112–113). What confuses me is what appears to me to be a different attitude toward substitutional quantification when he comes to number theory (p. 119). My conjecture is that he seems to say different things at different places because he has in mind also the different matter of the relation between abstract objects and infinity. Before turning to these points, permit me to make some historical remarks.

Both Ramsey and early Wittgenstein used to talk about the nature of quantifiers and about whether they can be replaced by conjunctions and disjunctions (see Moore's notes in *Mind*, 1954 and Ramsey's *Foundations of Mathematics*, p. 237 ff). Recently I have found passages in the introduction to the second edition of *PM* which seem quite relevant to what is being considered here. I give just two examples. "A function can only appear in a matrix through its values" (p. xxix). "Theoretically, it is unnecessary to introduce such variables as ϕ_1, because they can be replaced by an infinite conjunction or disjunction" (p. xxxii). As I see it, the distinction between predicative and impredicative is clearer than that between substitutional and objectual quantification. The distinction between finite and infinite is clearer than that between the concrete and the abstract. It seems to me artificial in these cases to reduce the clearer to the less clear or to discuss issues that can be done in terms of the clearer distinctions, in terms of the less clear ones.

Of course the matter of infinity is crucial, as I have often argued. Most of us find quantification over natural numbers quite clear. But according to Quine, "A substitutional explication of arithmetical quantification brings no ontological economy to elementary number theory; for either the numbers must run short or the numerals are infinitely numerous" (p. 119). Quine's point is that numbers are abstract and numerals, if infinitely many, are too. He refers back to the 1947 nominalist construction by Goodman and him in *JSL*. What about large numbers? Would $10^{9^{9^{9^9}}}$ numerals be concrete or acceptable for substitutional quantification? This may also be compared with the following paradox: 1 is a small number, $n + 1$ is a small number if n is; therefore, all numbers are small. I should like to suggest that the choice to stay with a finite universe rather than the choice to stay with the concrete is what is determinative. Once I argued this point at length in connection with Goodman's nominalism (*Philos. Rev.* 62 (1953): 413–420) and I have never been satisfied with his replies.

What I find confusing is the mixing of the matter of substitutional quantification with the question of concreteness. I suppose we could imagine the universe infinite in space-time so that there would be every numeral. We would then presumably be justified in using the substitutional explication of arithmetical quantification. Would we then have avoided abstract objects? We would agree that envisaging infinitely or finitely many objects commits to different ontologies. Quine seems to say that when there is an infinite range substitutional explication yields no ontological economy. If that is so, does economy require restricting ourselves to finite ranges and to the question whether members of such ranges have names? In this regard, Quine's brushing away numerical coordinates (*RR*, p. 140) seems unconvincing if he is dealing with a finite range.

Perhaps Quine is not unhappy with natural numbers but merely saying that we are still committed to objects, and abstract objects at that. This interpretation would seem to agree with what he says elsewhere. "If I could see my way to getting by with an all-purpose universe whose objects were denumerable and indeed enumerated, I would name each object numerically and settle for substitutional quantification. . . . Where substitutional quantification serves, ontology lacks point" (*Ontological Relativity*, p. 107). This is followed by a footnote saying in part: "On the pointlessness of ontology at the denumerable level see also my *Ways of Paradox*, p. 203." For example, the denumerable universe of Σ_ω mentioned above may arguably serve the required all-purpose universe. How does Quine view this possibility? In other words, Σ_ω does yield ordinary mathematics on the college level and can take care of the physical objects in the manner Quine recently suggested (*TT*, op. cit.). Would this then suffice as the desired universe for Quine? If so, what importance does such a result have?

II

Logical Truth and Set Theory

An extended consideration by Quine on logical truth is "Carnap and Logical Truth", written in 1954 and published (among its various forms) in 1963 with Carnap's reply. In this paper Quine includes set theory in logic (e.g., "The further part of logic is set theory," p. 388). He argues that the linguistic doctrine (of conventionalism) is less empty for set theory than for elementary logic. He offers as support for this view his widely influential and highly controversial opinion that in set theory we find ourselves "making deliberate choices and setting them forth unaccompanied by any attempt at justification other than in terms of elegance and convenience" (pp. 394 and 396). (This is often called "the bankruptcy theory.") A distinction is mentioned between logical truth (in a narrower sense) and a broader sense which includes truths by "essential predication" and might as well retain its familiar label of "analytic". The conclusion is that logical truth (in the first sense, which is Quine's own usage, followed here) is well enough definable, but analyticity calls for some "accounting of synonymies throughout a universal language" (p. 404). The monograph *Philosophy of Logic* (1970) sets down Quine's views on the nature of logic in a systematic way. Here we find a change of mind on the relation between logic and set theory: Does set theory belong to logic? "I shall conclude not" (p. 64).

With regard to set theory I shall take as a known fact that mathematics is reducible to set theory, a conclusion which, I believe, Quine also accepts. I wish to argue for three propositions which seem to be contrary to Quine's views of 1970. First, set theory is one; there are different systems of set theory only in the same sense as there are different systems for the theory of natural numbers which, incompletable as they are, invite further and further extensions (e.g., the arithmetic part of increasingly stronger systems of set theory). This proposition is contrary to Quine's belief expressed on pp. 65 and 45. Second, set theory is a part of logic. This agrees with Quine's statement in 1954 but is contrary to his 1970 statement, as mentioned above. Third, set theory and mathematics are analytic and necessary. This proposition is probably contrary to Quine's opinion not so much because he denies it but rather because he finds it unclear. This difference reflects what might be called metaphilosophical issues on which it is harder to reach agreement.

The position is that we have a stable enough concept of set to enjoy agreement not only in believing that the familiar axioms of ZF are true of this concept but even on many stronger axioms of infinity. In most cases we have a pretty good idea how high a "rank" we have to go to in order to satisfy the axiom under consideration. In a few unsettled cases, it is believed that the matter will be clarified in a manner that preserves agreement. Hence, the paradoxes represent "misunderstandings" of the concept rather than prove its bankruptcy. The meaning of the concept of set is certainly not obvious in the sense that given a proposition we can easily see whether it is true of the concept. The most spectacular example is of course the continuum hypothesis which has passed its hundredth anniversary. All these and more have been discussed at great length in Chapter VI of my *From Mathematics to Philosophy* (1974) and in the first part of "Large Sets" (mentioned below in Section V). I would only like to add some historical explanation and suggest that Quine has, undoubtedly as a result of more reflections, come closer to this view since 1970.

The concept of set just mentioned is known in the literature as the iterative (or Cantor's) concept of set. It is debatable how clearly Cantor did have such a concept. For others this concept seems to have taken quite some time to emerge more and more clearly. In other words, it had taken time and effort before the "misunderstandings" got corrected and therefore the paradoxes were then said to be misunderstandings. In Zermelo's case, he wrote in 1908 much as Russell did on this matter. But in 1930, he expounded the iterative concept in an exemplarily lucid manner in his "Über Grenzzahlen und Mengenbereiche" (*Fundamenta mathematicae* 16: 29–47).

Of course the iterative concept is essentially just the simple type theory extended to higher and higher infinite types (or "ranks"). Quine says in his *RR* of 1974, "Thus I do not see Russell's theory of types as dormant common sense awakened. Still I do see it as somewhat akin to that" (p. 121). In the 1980 foreword to *LP,* Quine is more explicit. He criticizes NF and ML "for allowing self-membership, which beclouds individuation". He continues, "Russell's theory of types has an epistemological advantage over NF and ML: it lends itself to a more plausible reconstruction of the genesis of the high-level class concepts. From the theory of types to the set theories of Zermelo and von Neumann, in turn, a natural transition can be made." In fact, I feel that Quine's elaborations of the several sentences just quoted offer an alternative account of the iterative concept of set which may be more congenial to many professional philosophers.

Quine's appeal to the concept of individuation in evaluating NF and his use of the idea of substitutional quantification in placing predicativity suggest to me an illustration of different attitudes toward the formal and the intuitive. Many people who are familiar with set theory achieve an "intuition" that predicative set theory, having much in common with number theory, is more transparent than the impredicative, and that ZF is more "natural" than NF; but they often have difficulty in adequately articulating these differences. In con-

trast, Quine's appreciation and categorization of relatively indefinite ideas seem
to go together. This sort of difference must be the source of many disagreements.

The explanation so far may also be viewed as an argument for the conclusion that set theory (hence also mathematics) is analytic and therefore necessary. To Quine's possible objections to this conclusion, I want to say that if
we do not wish to abandon the terms like "analytic" and "necessary" altogether, I do not see that anything can be found which is better qualified than
mathematics (including set theory this time) for being (said to be) necessary.
Relative to our present knowledge the iterative concept is the best concept of
set (at least for developing mathematics) we have got. For me one most interesting part of philosophy is to understand the richest concepts we currently
possess. We have no assurance that the iterative concept will not someday turn
out to be inconsistent but in speculating idly over such a possibility I cannot
find anything nearly as attractive as the work of elaborating and sharpening the
existing concept to speed up its evolution.

The arguments for excluding set theory from logic in Quine's *Philosophy
of Logic* do not appear convincing to me. For example, Quine points out that
truth (even of the axioms) in set theory is not obvious nor "potentially obvious" in his special sense (bottom of p. 82), set theory has no complete axiomatization, and set theory has strong existence axioms. But I do not see these
as reasons for excluding set theory from logic, nor did they seem so to Quine
in 1954. On the other hand, Quine notes important common traits between
logic and mathematics (and therefore set theory): their relevance to all science
and their neutrality (p. 98). Among the advantages of including set theory in
logic I may mention: a greater continuity with the tradition of Frege and early
Russell, a better conformity with actual practice, as well as making Quine's
framework more coherent by bringing what he calls "the locus of ontology"
(the pure sets) closer to his home ground.

III

The Historical Perspective

Of course the word logic has many different meanings. For example, I. M.
Copi and J. A. Gould have collected together various pieces in two volumes
(*Reading on Logic* and *Contemporary Readings in Logical Theory*). A glance
at the tables of contents would give an idea of the diversity of material which
has been put under the heading logic. Hegel and Engels tend to construe logic
in a broad sense. In a related sense Galvano Della Volpe develops *Logic as a
Positive Science* (1969, English translation 1980). H. Scholz considers various

senses of logic in his *Concise History of Logic* (1931, English translation 1961). There is the familiar contrast of deductive logic with inductive logic and perhaps also scientific method. Also formal logic is contrasted with (dialectical, transcendental, etc.) logic. The older chair of logic at Oxford means something quite different from the recently created chair of mathematical logic. In their *Development of Logic* (1962), W. and M. Kneale include much which others would put under philosophy of logic. In some of these broader senses of logic, more if not all of Quine's work would be thought to be in logic.

In the present context, I shall confine my attention to Quine's work in logic in the more definite sense of mathematical logic. Even within this limited domain, I shall not consider his various elegant formulations of elementary logic but discuss primarily his work in constructing formal systems of set theory.

Before concentrating on Quine's treatment of set theory and its relation to Russell, I should like to list some of Quine's other contributions to logic. What has struck me for many years and seems to have drawn little attention is the formal perfection of *ML*. It has often been remarked that in a strictly formal system, a machine should be able to check the proofs. I have seen this goal stated and aimed at. But as far as I know, *ML* is the only extended development which satisfies this stringent requirement. Here, we have, so to speak, the last word on whatever is being covered in the book. If I remember rightly, once the eminent logician R. B. Jensen told me that the reading of *ML* contributed to his making the decision to switch from economics to logic. To attain a more practical rigor, I wrote programs in 1958 to prove all theorems of elementary logic in *PM* by computers (see my *Survey,* pp. 224–268).

There is also a treatment of Gödel's first incompleteness theorem in *ML* by way of the first order theory of concatenation, probably for the first time. Later in a paper of 1946 in *JSL,* Quine shows that this theory is equivalent to first order arithmetic (with addition and multiplication as primitive functions). More detailed considerations by others on concatenation have appeared since then, for instance, by R. Smullyan in his *Theory of Formal Systems* (1961). In particular, there is an interesting analogue of Hilbert's tenth problem first proposed independently by H. B. Lob and A. A. Markov around 1955. Take an alphabet with two symbols (say a and b) and make up equations by concatenating strings of these symbols with variables to get terms; e.g., one solution of the equation $axb = yaab$ is $x = aa$, $y = a$. The problem is: is there a decision procedure for solvability of any finite set of such equations? The problem remained open for many years. Only recently did G. S. Makanin give an elaborate positive solution to this problem, in his "Equations on a Free Semigroup" (Russian), *Proceedings of the 1978 International Congress of Mathematicians,* Helsinki, 1980, pp. 263–268.

In the 1950s contact with computer engineers led Quine to publish several papers on the quick simplification of truth functions. These results are frequently cited and his terms such as ''core'' and ''prime implicant'' are widely used. Quine's considerations are related to more recent studies of feasible computability. In fact, since S. A. Cook's work of 1971, the problem whether P = NP has emerged as a central open problem in mathematics. And it is equivalent to the ''tautology problem,'' i.e., the problem whether there is a feasible method (viz. one that can be done in polynomial time) to decide whether an arbitrary truth functional formula is a tautology. It is also equivalent to many other familiar problems in graph theory, algebra, number theory, etc. A whole book has recently appeared just to summarize the results on the general problem: M. R. Garey and D. S. Johnson, *Computers and Intractability*, 1979. I have also written a joint paper with B. Dunham on this problem (in *Annals of Mathematical Logic*, 1975).

Quine is careful in choosing his notation and terminology to reflect what he sees as the correct usage. He has introduced and made fashionable among philosophers a number of terms which often depart from common usage among mathematical logicians. Sometimes the difference reflects divergence of philosophical views such as Quine's preference of ''truth function theory'' over ''propositional calculus.'' Sometimes Quine is simply more careful in cases such as his distinction between implication and conditional, equivalence and biconditional, his use of ''denial'' instead of ''negation,'' ''alternation'' instead of ''disjunction,'' etc. Quine's term ''quantification theory'' leaves out identity, while the more familiar usage today is to include identity and speak of the first order logic (or just elementary logic). There is of course a minor dilemma in deciding how far one is willing to conform to common usage, especially when nothing substantive is at stake.

A convenient point to begin an examination of the place of Quine's work relative to the history of logic is 1940. For one thing, the interruption of logic by war came around this time. For another thing, the bibliographical references given in the original edition of *ML* in this year help to determine Quine's range of familiarity in logic at this time. Moreover, I feel that since 1940 Quine has tended to limit his attention to refining and deepening his understanding of those parts of logic which had interested him before 1940. By 1940 most of the important directions which have dominated logic for the last half a century have already received their solid beginnings. But Quine, even at that time, restricted his attention to elementary logic and a single aspect of set theory (namely its alternative formulations), undoubtedly because (at least partly) these are the areas of philosophical interest according to Quine's conception of philosophy. What I find unfortunate is that on account of Quine's great influence among philosophers, most philosophers get a distorted view of what logic is about.

Up to 1900 the most consequential work in logic was done by Frege and Cantor, and to a lesser extent by Dedekind and Peano. Frege introduced (roughly speaking) the first order logic and attempted to reduce mathematics to logic. Cantor developed a powerful concept of set and introduced infinite numbers. Recently I have argued in my *Popular Lectures on Mathematical Logic* (1981) that many central results in logic have been obtained by the interplay of first order logic with (infinite) ordinals, Gödel's constructible sets and much of model theory being the most conspicuous examples. From 1900 to 1930, we see the emergence of L. E. J. Brouwer's intuitionism; Zermelo's set theory and its refinements; *PM* and its simplifications; Hilbert's program of "formalism" and proof theory; seminal contributions by Löwenheim and by Skolem; the first edition of Hilbert-Ackermann; and certain isolated results by others (such as Paul Bernays, J. Lukasiewicz, W. Ackermann, J. v. Neumann, E. L. Post, L. Chwistek, M. Schönfinkel, F. P. Ramsey).

In the history of science, we encounter here and there a relatively brief period when a subject makes spectacular advances. This happened to quantum theory in the 1920s, to molecular biology for a decade or more since the early 1950s. In logic the period was the 1930s. Gödel discovered the completeness theorem (of elementary logic), the incompleteness theorems (for arithmetic and set theory), an interpretation of classical arithmetic in intuitionistic arithmetic, and the constructible sets. J. Herbrand brought out some fine structures of elementary logic. Zermelo 1930 (op. cit.) contains a persuasive description of the concept of set underlying standard set theory. Skolem constructed an elegant nonstandard model of arithmetic. G. Gentzen perfected "natural deduction" for elementary logic and gave two consistency proofs of arithmetic. Gödel tightened a suggestion by Herbrand to introduce a definitive general concept of recursive functions. A. M. Turing produced a neat model of idealized computers and gave convincing arguments to show that it captures the intuitive concept of computability, Carnap and Tarski independently made a closer study of truth and validity as they are, for example, employed only intuitively in Hilbert-Ackermann (1928).

In 1934 Gödel lectured at the Princeton Institute and interacted with Alonzo Church, S. C. Kleene, and Barkley Rosser who have all extended Gödel's results in several different directions and continued to exert important influence by their work and their teaching. In contrast, Quine's interactions in the 1930s were with Russell, Carnap, and Tarski. In terms of books, the most remarkable one was the monumental two-volume work by Hilbert-Bernays (1934 and 1939). Also an extensively revised second edition of Hilbert-Ackermann appeared in 1938. The first edition of Gödel's surprisingly formal monograph on the continuum hypothesis (and constructible sets) appeared in 1940. These books contain a majority of the results listed in the preceding paragraph.

Looking back to 1940 after more than forty years, one who studies logic today must envy those good old days when only so little and such attractive material needed to be digested to get to the frontier of the whole (now vast) field of logic. But of course even in those days most logicians tended to select only a few parts from the short list of directions given above. Quine's interest then and later seems to stay away from proof theory as well as what has come to be known as recursion theory, model theory, and computation theory. Within set theory he does not seem to enter deeply into the tradition represented by Cantor and Gödel. He is of course very much at home with *PM* and sympathetic toward certain earlier work from Poland. Frege's work is important to Quine but, I conjecture, Quine probably knew in 1940 more of Peano's work than of Frege's. Since 1940 or 1950 Quine must have made a more thorough study of Frege's work. Indeed, I believe, Frege rather than Russell or Carnap is the model for Quine's own work. I recall vaguely that at one time a copy of Frege's photo was the only displayed portrait in his study at Harvard. I have certainly heard him speak of Frege with veneration.

Quine's interest is not to discover new theorems in set theory (or "new facts about sets") or to find new axioms which conform to an evolving yet somewhat fixed concept of set. He is not even much concerned with deriving standard results of set theory. Rather he looks for an elegant set of axioms from which "ordinary mathematics" can be deduced. This was the goal of Frege and to a slightly less extent that of Russell who was also interested in recovering Cantor's infinite numbers. But both Frege and Russell (most of the time) also looked for true or even obvious axioms (without complete success of course). For Quine, certainly until a few years ago, the task is rather to find neat axioms which are not demonstrably inconsistent and from which ordinary mathematics can be derived comparatively smoothly. The concluding paragraph in Chapter Six of *ML* expresses this view in a somewhat old fashioned manner (with regard to the scope of mathematics). Similar views have also been expressed by others before Quine.

It is a little complex to evaluate the influence of Quine's work in logic. Viewed in a narrow way, one is inclined to say that the direct influence has been rather slight. His system NF has certainly provoked much ingenious work. His influence on his students takes different forms but I believe it fair to say that those who have broadened their viewpoint beyond Quine's have done more interesting work in logic. Quine himself is not interested in inventing special systems for special purposes but those who do so (mostly with philosophical orientations) probably often learn their skill from Quine's books. Of course if we come to what are called logical theory and philosophy of logic, Quine's influence is conspicuous. Moreover, I believe that Quine's books in logic are helpful to the training in computer programming in that they help to cultivate the habit of (sometimes rather artificial) formal precision. Presumably a number of students are prevented from specializing in philosophy by requirements in logic for which Quine's books set the tone.

A more substantive issue is that generally as a subject develops, concerns and even styles tend to change. This phenomenon is especially striking for logic since it has over the last few decades grown from a young discipline into a mature one. In particular, it has become more and more like older parts of mathematics in its style of work. Among other things, this means that concern for formal precision is pushed into the background. As a result, for the working logicians much of Quine's work is thought to be off the main stream.

IV

From NF to ML to SL

Anyone who has struggled with *PM* (as I did in 1939–40 as a freshman in Kunming) would find the basic apparatus of *ML* amazingly simple and elegant: a single style of variable ranging over all things, with only three primitives (one for truth functions, one for quantification, and one for membership). Admittedly it was known before *ML* that set theory can be developed with such a simple notation, but nobody had carried out such a project. If we begin with *PM*, we can trace simplifications to Leon Chwistek (in 1921 and 1922) and F. P. Ramsey in 1925 (for details, see Church's review in *JSL* 2 (1937): 168–170). In Gödel's celebrated paper of 1931, we can find a similar formulation of the simple theory of types, which is commonly used today. The use of a single style of variable goes back to Zermelo (1908).

In 1936 Quine completed his term as a Junior Fellow and began to teach as a Faculty Instructor. To prepare his courses he "tried to settle on a sanest comprehensive system of logic—or, as I would now say, logic and set theory." The first interesting attempt is "Set-Theoretic Foundations for Logic." *JSL* 1 (1936): 45–57. [By the way, in this paper the reference to Skolem 1930 is a mistake (surprisingly uncorrected even in 1966); the correct reference is to Skolem's familiar "Remarks on Axiomatized Set Theory" of 1922 (included in the collection *From Frege to Gödel*).] In 1936 Quine published eight articles, all but one in logic. Moreover, for the first three years of *JSL*, he probably published more material in it than anybody else.

This early system S uses membership as the only primitive predicate, defining = and $\subset$ in familiar manner. Apart from a form of the axiom of extensionality, the only axiom (scheme) is (1) $EyAx[x\epsilon y \equiv (x \subset z \ \& \ Fx)]$. It is shown that counterparts of the basic axioms (i.e., leaving out the axioms of infinity and choice) of the simple theory of types can all be derived. Roughly speaking we can derive the power set axiom from (1) and also prove that the empty set exists. Hence, beginning with the empty set, we can move from each type n to the next type by using as z in (1) the power set of the universal set of type n and obtain all sets of the next type.

Several comments can be made on this system. It is a proper subsystem of Zermelo's system Z (as made more explicit by Skolem 1922). First, (1) is an easy theorem in Z. Next, it is easy to verify that the familiar finite sets built up from the empty set make up a model of S. Hence, the axiom of infinity is demonstrably underivable in S. Of course, we can add some form of an axiom of infinity to S. But in that case, we just move toward Z and its further extensions. A subsidiary matter suggested by S is the possibility of playing with neat alternative (equivalent) formulations of the axioms of set theory. For example, I did some of this many years later in *Zeitschrift f. math. Logik* 13 (1967): 175–188.

A more mysterious and more interesting development of the ideas in S was the introduction of NF a few months later. It was presented to the Mathematical Association of America in December 1936 and published in February 1937. In place of (1), Quine now drops the clause $x \subset z$ and imposes some restrictions on Fx, namely, it must be *stratified*. In other words, it must be possible to put numerals for variables in it in such a way that ϵ comes to occur only in contexts of the form $n\epsilon n + 1$. Thus, for example, $x\epsilon x$ and $x\epsilon u$ & $u\epsilon x$ are not stratified. This device of course reminds one of type theory. In fact, it sounds very much like what Russell calls typical ambiguity which he introduces more as a mere convenience than as a serious strengthening of type theory. Ernst Specker shows (1958 and 1962) that NF is indeed equivalent to type theory plus suitable axioms of typical ambiguity. This incidentally offers an intuitively better motivated formulation of NF in the sense that it brings out more clearly in what way NF enlarges type theory. Specker's construction which makes this reformulation possible is employed, for example, in Jensen's surprising result that NFU, seemingly a slight modification of NF, can be proved consistent in elementary number theory. NFU differs from NF only in a weaker axiom of extensionality which adds the condition that x is not empty to the usual form: if x and y have the same members, then $x = y$. The modification is reasonable in that it leaves room for non-sets or urelements. By coincidence, this weakened extensionality is the one Quine uses in S.

The story of NF forms a strange chapter in the history of logic. On the one hand, NF is off the main stream and results limited to it are of only isolated interest. On the other hand, some of the cleverest mathematics are brought out in attempts to meet the seductive challenge from such a deceptively simple system either to derive a contradiction or to prove it consistent (relative to standard systems).

It is Quine's habit to combine his book-writing with his course-teaching. The book *ML* of 1940 was the first fruit of this practice. The axiom of infinity had not been available in NF until 1953 when Specker disproved the axiom of choice in NF and thereby derived the axiom of infinity. Partly for this reason Quine constructed and taught an enlargement of NF. As he says in the preface to *ML*, "The material presented is substantially that covered in my course Mathematics 19 at Harvard." Shortly after the appearance of the book, Rosser derived the Burali-Forti paradox from its axioms. Quine promptly published repairs which introduce sets "in driblets" and are sufficient for the limited development of his book. "I arranged with the publisher to paste a corrigendum slip into the remaining stock of the book, indicating a makeshift repair of the system. The text of this slip was inserted in the second printing (1947)." In 1947 I managed to use even weaker axioms and develop much more mathematics than *ML* (see my *Survey*, pp. 515–534). In 1949 I discovered that there is a natural alternative to the troublesome axiom (scheme) *200 and proposed the alternative system ML. I also gave with my proposal a proof that ML is consistent if NF is (*JSL*, vol. 15, 1950, pp. 25–32).

The situation is of some general interest. Let S be a given system. For convenience, we assume that S uses a single style of (set) variable x, y, etc. and that S is a set theory with membership as the only primitive predicate. Thus S could be a Zermelo type set theory or NF or the system S described above or even ML. There were two familiar ways of enlarging S before 1949: the predicative and the impredicative. In both cases we add a new type on top of S using, say, another style of (class) variable X , Y , etc. so that x ϵ Y , etc. can also be formed. We add an axiom of extensionality for the classes. The original variables of S are said to be ranging over sets.

A predicative enlargement PS of S is formed if we add the axiom scheme:

(P) If Fx contains no bound class variables, EYAx (x ϵ Y $\equiv$ Fx).

This has the advantage that we can not only reduce (P) to a finite number of special cases but also replace the familiar axiom schemes of S (e.g., the axioms of separation and replacement) each by a single axiom (e.g., Fx by x ϵ X). This is the sort of enlargement developed by J. v. Neumann and Bernays.

An impredicative enlargement IS of S is just a second order theory of S or roughly the adjunction of the next higher type in a truncated part T_n (for some n) of the simple theory of types. More explicitly, what we do is to add the unrestricted axiom scheme (in the enlarged notation):

(I) EYAx (x ϵ Y $\equiv$ Fx).

But then we also strengthen the axiom schemes of S by allowing bound class variables. For example, if S is NF, then the axiom scheme EyAx (x ϵ y $\equiv$ Fx), where Fx is stratified becomes in IS:

*200Q. If Fx is stratified and contains no free class variables, EyAx (x ϵ y $\equiv$ Fx).

When we straighten out notational differences, this is the troublesome axiom in the original edition of *ML*. The restriction on free variables is necessary because otherwise every class is a set: EyAx (x ϵ y $\equiv$ x ϵ Y). This restriction is not needed in type theory because it is not cumulative. In other words, INF is Quine's system in the original edition of *ML*.

What I did in 1949 was to introduce a new type of enlargement, which may be said to be weakly impredicative. More explicitly, such an enlargement WIS of S is obtained by adding (I) as in IS but not strengthening the axiom schemes in S. Thus, if S is NF, then the old axiom scheme remains as in NF:

*200W. If Fx is stratified and contains no class variables, then EyAx (x ∈ y ≡ Fx).

In fact, ML is just WINF. And for my proof of the relative consistency of ML to NF, the above restriction on *200 is essential.

A puzzling thing about NF is that when S is one of the standard systems in the Zermelo tradition, the enlargement to IS introduces no contradiction and indeed adds little new content to any moderately rich S. Hence, the inconsistency of INF points to some peculiar property of NF which, I believe, is not yet fully understood (but compare next section). Moreover, the enlargement of a system S to WIS is less natural than IS because the sets (e.g., the set of natural numbers or the set of real numbers) do not benefit from the added power in WIS as they do in IS.

Before examining the various strong results on NF (and derivatively on ML), let me briefly outline the actual content of *ML* (1940 and 1951) and *SL* (1963 and 1969).

ML leaves out transfinite numbers altogether, derives the axioms of Peano arithmetic and a few elementary theorems, and gives a few definitions for ratios and real numbers. Curiously a system of set theory includes practically nothing from set theory. This is also why much weaker axioms suffice for the material developed. In 1953 Rosser published a more extensive development of NF in his *Logic for Mathematicians* which is not nearly as precise as *ML*. Moreover, much of the original elegance of the system NF is lost through the ad hoc introduction of complex formulations of the axioms of infinity and choice which are needed for the derivation of more mathematics.

Quine's primary effort from spring 1950 to spring 1959 was devoted to the composition of *Word and Object*. He returned to logic in the summer of 1959 and wrote *SL*, which was completed in January 1963. An extensively revised second edition was prepared in 1967 and published in 1969. The book divides into three parts. Part I covers more briefly and in a different way the body of *ML*; Part II deals with real numbers, cardinals and ordinals; Part III compares alternative axiom systems for set theory. The last part embodies the origin of the book which grew out of a short lecture course Quine gave at Oxford in 1953–54. In writing up the lectures he got new ideas regarding the preliminary part and decided to expand it to occupy more than two-thirds of the book.

One special feature is what Quine calls the virtual theory of classes and relations, which is closely related to some work of Bernays; *JSL* 2 (1937): 65–77. A second feature is a new definition of the set of natural numbers which dispenses with an appeal to the axiom of infinity. The earliest definition with such a property goes back to Zermelo 1909 (*Acta math.* 32: 185–193). A definition closer to Quine's was proposed by Michael Dummett in 1957 to answer my question of finding such a definition more akin to Frege's (see my *Survey*, pp. 440 and 52). But Quine's is simpler.

The most pervasive feature is the emphasis on restricting to weaker axioms as far as possible (mostly existence statements) and "neutrality" toward axiom systems "largely incompatible with one another." I am sure most working set theorists are not in sympathy with this attitude. Moreover, no clear intuitive picture emerges as to what axioms are sufficient for what purpose. There is no surprising new result in the sense that axioms formerly not known to be sufficient for the purpose on hand are now shown to be enough. The revised edition removes some defects in the treatment of transfinite recursion, prompted by Charles Parsons; and it brings the section on infinite cardinals closer to common usage, following a suggestion by Burton Dreben. A special case of the axiom (scheme) of replacement is singled out for attention: the image of an ordinal is a set. If we assume the axiom of constructibility (which, by the way, is mistakenly listed as the axiom of constructivity in the index on p. 353), I believe this is equivalent to the axiom of replacement.

As far as I can determine, Quine has published no technical papers in set theory since this book. In fact, I am under the impression that since 1963 Quine's work has been mostly in philosophy. The two editions of *SL* contain a survey of work done on NF and ML up to the beginning of 1963. In the 1980 foreword to *LP*, we find some brief comments on more recent contributions.

V

The career of NF (and ML).

Forty-seven years have elapsed since NF was first introduced. As recently as October 1981 a meeting devoted to NF was held in Louvain. The chief challenge is to determine whether NF is consistent relative to standard set theory based on the iterative concept of set. Over the years a consensus has developed that neither NF nor ML is a serious contender for being the basic system of set theory. In the 1980 foreword to *LP*, Quine remarks on the difficulty with natural numbers and mathematical induction in NF and ML, as well as their "allowing for self-membership, which beclouds individuation". True, Quine still emphasizes the "real" advantages of their "convenience and elegance". But this is a debatable point in view of the lack of an intuitive picture comparable to the iterative concept and the necessity to add ad hoc axioms and concepts to actually develop mathematics in them.

Soon after the publication of NF, Rosser published two papers to consider definitions by induction in it and explain how the familiar paradoxes seem to be blocked in it (*JSL*, 1939). The first definite results on NF and INF (viz. the system in the original *ML*) are:

T1.   The Burali-Forti paradox is derivable in INF (Rosser, *JSL* 7 (1942): 1–17).
T2.   There is a finite axiomatization of NF (Theodore Hailperin, *JSL* 9 (1944): 1–19).

Since NF is a descendant of the theory of types, the theory of (finite and infinite) cardinals and ordinals is developed in the manner of *PM* rather than in the more convenient fashion that is customary in axiomatic set theory. To derive the Burali-Forti paradox Rosser carried out some of these developments. As we noted before, since the inconsistent system is a natural enlargement INF of NF, there must be something strange about NF. Part of this unnaturalness is brought out in the following result (Rosser-Wang, *JSL* 15 (1950): 113–129):

T3.   NF has no standard model: no interpretation of the membership predicate (with the right identity relation) compatible with the axioms of NF could make well-orderings of both the less-than relation among ordinals and that among finite cardinals. (Compare *SL*, p. 294)
T4.   If NF is consistent, so is ML; or Con(ML) if Con(NF). (Wang 1950, op. cit.).

At that time I also noted a general argument by which we can prove the consistency of S in WIS (S is related to WIS as NF is to ML), provided WIS contains a reasonable amount of arithmetic. In January 1950 I communicated this argument to Rosser in a larger context. Applied to NF, the argument shows:

T5.   The consistency of NF is provable in ML; or, Con(NF) is provable in ML.

If now we combine T4 and T5, we seem to arrive at the result that Con(ML) is provable in ML. Hence, by Gödel's second incompleteness theorem, ML would be inconsistent. The subtle gap in this astonishing argument is, as pointed out by Rosser in the spring of 1950, that there is an ambiguity in the arithmetic statements expressing consistency because natural numbers behave differently in NF and ML. In other words, even though we can give formally a similar definition (say, Frege's version) in NF and ML (i.e., WINF), the two definitions mean different things. The class Nn of natural numbers in ML is the intersection of all classes (not just all sets) containing zero and closed with respect to the successor operation. Hence, we get the following undesirable result (Rosser, *JSL* 17 (1952): 238–242; *SL*, pp. 306–307; and the 1980 foreword to *LP*):

T6.   If NF is consistent, the class Nn of ML is not a set.

This, as noted by Quine, points to an unattractive feature of ML because for any substantial development of mathematics, Nn needs to be a set.

Specker told me that he had got interested in NF through a lecture of mine during my visit to Zurich in 1950–51. Moreover, he said on several occasions that he found a note of mine, "Negative Types" (*Mind* 61 (1952): 366–368), suggestive. (H. M. Sheffer also liked this simple note.) It is a sort of midway station between type theory and NF. Add to the types 0, 1, 2, . . . of type theory also the negative types -1, -2, etc. and use formally the same axiom schemes of comprehension and extensionality. For each type m and each positive n, it can then be shown that the type m includes more than n sets. On the other hand, one can prove in ordinary arithmetic that the system is consistent. This system is more homogenous than type theory because every type is like every other type to the extent that each type has infinitely many types above and below. Hence, there is a somewhat stronger "typical ambiguity."

A decisive advance in the study of NF was made by Specker in 1953 (*Proc. Natl. Acad. Sci.,* briefly, *PNAS* 39: 972–975). It not only settles the outstanding question on the axiom of infinity in NF but brings out more sharply the complications with well-orderings in NF.

T7.   The axiom of choice is refutable in NF.
Since the axiom of choice for finite sets is provable in NF, this implies that there must be infinite sets in NF.
T8.   The axiom of infinity is derivable in NF.

Before the publication of these results, I had reflected on Hailperin's finite axiomatization of NF (T2 above). By a suitable axiom of choice, we seem able to enumerate a model required by the finitely many axioms by a formula in NF. In this way we can formulate an axiom of limitation which says that only the sets thus enumerated exist. But then by the diagonal argument we can also define a set distinct from the enumerated ones. We would seem to get an alternative refutation of the axiom of choice in NF, except that the new set is not defined by a stratified formula. The situation remains unclear despite T7 because a different axiom of choice is employed (*Math. Zeitschr.,* vol. 59, 1953, pp. 47–56). Since it is hard to obtain an intuitive grasp of stratification, making natural deviations in NF often turns out to violate the stipulated restrictions.

The next interesting result with ingenious constructions again came from Specker (*Dialectica* 12 (1958): 451–465 and *Logic, Methodology, and Philosophy of Science,* edited by E. Nagel et al., 1962, pp. 116–124; *SL,* p. 292):

T9.   NF is consistent if and only if the theory of types has a typically ambiguous model, i.e., a model such that for any sentence p without free variables and p* obtained from p by raising all indices by 1, $p \equiv p^*$ is true in the model.

As I have mentioned above Jensen produced a surprising result in 1969, using a whole battery of powerful tools. Let NFU be obtained from NF by slightly weakening the axiom of extensionality to require x having some members (as specified before):

T10.   The consistency of NFU can be proved in ordinary arithmetic (i.e., elementary number theory). (*Words and Objections,* edited by Davidson and Hintikka).

Further refinements of the results listed above have appeared in recent years; for a summary see, e.g., M. Boffa, *JSL* 42 (1977): 215–220; see also his paper in *Bull. Soc. Math. Belg.* 33 (1981): 21–31, which proves the consistency of some more subsystems of NF. At any rate, it is clear that everyone implicitly uses the Zermelo kind of set theory in studying properties of NF or any other novel system.

In this regard it is of interest to compare the unresolved situation of NF with the fairly quick clarification of Ackermann's system of 1956, *Math. Annalen* 131: 336–345. This is usually tidied up by adding the axiom of foundation. Let the resulting system be AS. Soon afterwards, A. Levy shows that AS is no stronger than ZF, in JSL 24 (1959): 154–166. W. N. Reinhardt then showed in his thesis that ZF is no stronger than AS. This last result and a review of previous work is published in *Annals of Math. Logic* 2 (1970): 189–249. Here the question of relative consistency is not the main concern. Rather the relationship between the two systems is brought out more explicitly by interpreting sentences and theorems of each in the other.

Ackermann's set theory leads to interesting principles of reflection and stronger systems which are thought to be philosophically attractive. For an extended discussion relating to these issues, the reader is referred to my "Large Sets," in R. E. Butts and J. Hintikka (eds.), *Logic, Foundations of Mathematics, and Computability Theory,* 1977, pp. 309–333; in particular, there is a contribution by Gödel on p. 325.

Let me conclude with a few observations about work which I have done in directions closely related to Quine's interests.

With regard to the enlargement of NF, it seems, as noted before, equally natural to use INF or WINF. Yet in one sense Quine did make a mistake in using INF at first because he says explicitly that he wants the sets of ML to be the same as those of NF (*ML,* p. 165). As we saw before, in that case he wants ML to be WINF rather than INF. It is in this sense that the revised edition uses not just "a better repair" but rather a correction. From this viewpoint it is also easy to hit upon the relative consistency proof of ML to NF as mentioned before.

Related to this work was my attempt to arrive at a sharper formulation of the Löwenheim-Skolem Theorem and an ambitious project to generalize the argument for proving relative consistency. The first attempt led to a strengthening of a result in Hilbert-Bernays to the following: If S is consistent, then arithmetic predicates can be written down so that substituting them for the predicates of S in the theorems of S , we obtain arithmetic statements derivable from Con(S) in ordinary arithmetic (*Methodos* 3 (1951): 217–232). Related to this work is my attempt to devise a theory of the relative strength of axiom systems in terms of "translatable." Thus, S is stronger than T if T is translatable into S but not conversely (*Trans. AMS* 71 (1951): 283–293).

In the process of trying to carry out an exact consistency proof of S in IS or WIS , I noticed also a sharp distinction between giving a truth definition and giving a consistency proof. Roughly speaking, in order to give a truth definition in Tarski's sense for a system T (say one of the Zermelo type), we only need to handle the language of T ; how strong the axioms of T are makes no difference. On the other hand, in order to give a consistency proof (or a *normal* truth definition), all the theorems of T must come out true. Hence, Tarski's assertion in his 1936 paper is false: "In this way we are able to produce a proof of the consistency of every science for which we can construct the definition of truth." (*Logic, Semantics, Metamathematics* (1956): 236). I remember writing to Quine on this point but, greatly to my surprise, Quine was not convinced by my simple observations. I often think this is connected with Quine's tendency to use "theory" and "language" interchangeably. (Compare *Words and Objections*, pp. 308–311). At any rate, Tarski did make an admission of his mistake in an added footnote (ibid., p. 237) with a reference to my paper in *PNAS* 36 (1950): 448–453. Tarski concedes, "it is seen that in some cases, having succeeded in constructing an adequate definition of truth for a theory T in its metatheory, we may still be unable to show that all the provable sentences of T are true in the sense of this definition." But the explanation of this phenomenon which he proceeds to give seems to miss the point. He does not seem to appreciate that, for a consistency proof by way of a truth definition, the metatheory has to contain in some form all theorems of T as theorems.

Since Tarski's work on defining truth is so well known, it may be of some interest to mention Gödel's related idea. In 1976 he told me that in the summer of 1930, he had first realized that truth for number theory is not definable in number theory before moving further to get the stronger result of his first incompleteness result. (For more details, see my report in JSL 1981: 653–659.) In fact, an explicit proof of the indefinability of truth in the original language was given in a letter from Gödel to Zermelo, dated October 12, 1931 (two years before Tarski's first publication of the result), which has recently been published in *Historia Mathematica* 6 (1979): 298–302 (the proof is on p. 299).

HAO WANG

ROCKEFELLER UNIVERSITY
JANUARY 1984

REPLY TO HAO WANG

"It [was] Quine's habit", Wang rightly notes, "to combine his book-writing with his course-teaching." It is an understatement; the pedagogical motive has dominated my work in logic. Wang takes insufficient account of this motive when he wonders that my "interest is not to discover new theorems in set theory" and that I seemed "to stay away from proof theory as well as . . . recursion theory" and "restricted [my] attention to elementary logic and a single aspect of set theory."

Let me then sketch the pedagogical motivation of my work in logic. I wanted to enable every undergraduate to grasp a complete proof procedure for the predicate calculus in the space of an introductory semester course and to be able to apply it by recasting ordinary language in logical notation. In 1936 there was no book to the purpose in English, nor did any in German come close enough to warrant translation. Techniques had to be simplified and streamlined. The relation between formal logic and its applications needed clarification too, for students and colleagues alike; and so did the nature of variables and schemata. The fog that enshrouded these matters is hard to visualize in today's clear light.

My project was one of pedagogical engineering, and I progressed in it through two editions of *Elementary Logic,* four of *Methods of Logic,* and a string of interim articles, not to mention *O Sentido da Nova Lógica.* Even my papers on simplification of truth functions, so pertinent to computer engineering, began as an abortive strategy in logic teaching, as recounted near the end of section 11 of the Autobiography. Granted, I slipped back into the topic on later occasions rather as a relief from less tidy philosophical undertakings.

I was pedagogically motivated in set theory as well, from 1935 on; see Autobiography, section 7. Here I had graduate students in mind, budding professionals who should be given a clear and organized conception of the logico-mathematical strands of our system of the world. "New Foundations," to which so much high-powered mathematical thought has since been devoted, was my attempt at an efficient foundation of the subject for my course Mathematics 19; and it is characteristic that I have not felt impelled to try my mettle in those subsequent researches on NF, impressed though I am with what others have done and are now continuing to do in the circle around Boffa and Crabbé at Louvain.

Pedagogically my preferred approach to the subject in later years is embodied in *Set Theory and Its Logic*. Wang's disappointment over there being "no surprising new result" in that book is due again to his not grasping my pedagogical or expository objectives: clarity, elegance, and congenial philosophical perspective.

Even my work on concatenation, issuing in a theorem of which Wang speaks well, was primarily expository in inception. I wanted to get Gödel's incompleteness theorem down to clear and minimal essentials for inclusion in *Mathematical Logic;* and concatenation entered as a device for accommodating certain recursions, or ancestrals, without recourse to set theory.

Understandably, Wang has judged my goals by his own. Given that initial error, he has judged my work in logic as generously as I could ask. The fact is that early and late I have seen myself no more in the role model of a Tarski or a Gödel than in that of an Einstein. But I yield to no one in my admiration of their achievements.

My pedagogical drive in logic has been coupled with a philosophical drive. My work on concatenation came of both, through separate channels; the philosophical channel was the ill-starred project touched on in section 6 of the Autobiography. At other points the philosophical drive was inseparable from the pedagogical, for the drive for clarity partakes of both. So it was with my eschewing of propositions and properties in favor of sentences and classes; also my emphatic distinction between implication and the conditional, and between use and mention generally; also my stress on the variable as the touchstone of ontology, and on the associated contrast between variable and schematic letter. Inculcation of a sound philosophical attitude toward logic has been a major purpose of mine. I accordingly find wry amusement in Wang's remark:

> What I find unfortunate is that on account of Quine's great influence among philosophers, most philosphers get a distorted view of what logic is about.

Does logic include set theory, or does logic leave off where set theory sets in? Wang finds me construing logic inclusively, after the precedent of Frege, Russell, and Carnap, until my *Philosophy of Logic* (1970), and he deplores this latter-day change of heart. He does not notice that I approvingly entertained the narrower usage already in *Mathematical Logic* (1940, pp. 127–128), *Elementary Logic* (1941, pp. 165–166), and *Methods of Logic* (1950, p. 244). Actually it was sometime in the fifties, well before *Set Theory and Its Logic,* that my philosophical considerations in favor of the narrower usage prevailed unequivocally over my inertia or piety toward the broad usage of Frege, Russell, and Carnap; but documentation is sparse, for occasion arises only occasionally for drawing the distinction.

The word 'logic' is as may be; what exercises me is the importance of the boundary between predicate logic and set theory. It is nicely marked terminologically, I feel, by terminating logic and initiating extra-logical mathematics at that boundary. Wang mentions some of the differences between predicate logic and set theory that I find so vital. One of them is that predicate logic is ontologically neutral and set theory is not; another is that predicate logic is completable and set theory is not; a third is that set theories are multiple as predicate logic is not. Wang denies the third point and concedes the first two, but is unswayed by them. I have especially stressed the first of the three points because it has long been obscured by playing fast and loose with schematic letters and variables; see my reply to Ullian. An error of that kind even occurs in Wang's first section, where he mentions my virtual classes; what are really in point, there, are ultimate classes.

Wang's insistence on reckoning set theory as logic is based evidently on their sharing the quality of necessity. Would he then by the same token reckon all mathematics to logic? Perhaps so, following Frege, Russell, and Carnap. For my part, I grant the necessity, in some sense, of logical and mathematical truth; see my reply to Hellman. I am prepared, accordingly, to group them under a single important heading, and it is not far to seek: *mathematics*. I do not count set theory as logic, but I am prepared to count them both as mathematics.

I remarked just now that Wang rejects the last of my three points of contrast between predicate logic and set theory. It was a question of the multiplicity of set theories; and the issue, which Wang makes rather much of, is one that I find hard to draw. He cannot deny that there are incompatible alternative systems of set theory, for he has contributed notably to one and another of them himself, and in his monograph with McNaughton he surveyed various of them. The most he can do is plump for the primacy of the iterative concept, but he recognizes that I have plumped for it too, in *Set Theory and Its Logic* and *Roots of Reference*. See the last page or two of my reply to Parsons.

Wang toys with the notion, which has had its latter-day backers, that the iterative intuition was intrinsic to the notion of set from the start and the paradoxes were mere misunderstandings. This view presupposes a dissociation, from the outset, of the notion of set from that of class; for there is no blinking the age-old and fatal intuition that reifies a class for every membership condition, or the analogue for properties. If sets are indeed dissociated from classes, one's philosophical concerns tend to linger with the classes. See again my reply to Ullian.

I just cited the 1953 monograph of Wang and McNaughton as a comparison of set theories, as is *Set Theory and Its Logic*. Wang remarks on their similarity, but I find little further in common. It pleases me to read that in that same year he hit upon the transition from the theory of types to Zermelo's system through translation of the theory of types into general variables; for I in that year was hitting upon the same idea, thousands of miles away, and presenting it in my lectures at Oxford. It was a major factor in inspiring the project that issued in *Set Theory and Its Logic;* see the Autobiography, section 12.

In the last two sections of his essay Wang provides an informative survey of work in logic by me, him, and others. He slips up at one point: T6. What Rosser proved is not that consistency precludes sethood of Nn, but that it precludes proof of sethood of Nn without additional postulation. This result mars the elegance of ML, but the stronger result would in my view utterly vitiate the system.

A point may be made in mitigation also of T3. The oddities of NF there noted can be put down to extra coverage: what Rosser called non-Cantorian sets, not covered in other systems. The usual sets behave in NF much as usual, and the non-Cantorian ones lend auxiliary service.

Wang writes that I was unconvinced by his correction of Tarski. If so, I no longer know why. In my correspondence with Wang, which began in China in 1942 and has run to 106 letters, I find his letter about Tarski but no response of mine on the point.

Midway in his essay Wang conjectures that in 1940 I knew more of Peano's work than Frege's. I did know Peano's work much earlier: 1930. By 1939 I was catching up on Frege's logic, though not his semantics, for the small-print historical paragraphs in *Mathematical Logic*. See Autobiography, section 8. Wang is right in that what I thus learned of Frege got into my small-print credits without having influenced the text, which was already written.

Elsewhere in his essay Wang touches on ontological issues. My usual attitude toward mathematics, he notes, has been to accept it so far as needed as an integral part of the scientific system of the world, and to accept set theory as its foundation. What then is my ontological policy, he asks, regarding the empyrean of higher set theory? My answer, in three words, is "Round smoothly off." See the middle of my reply to Parsons.

The most vital issue in Wang's essay is constructivism, in one or another sense of the term. One sort of constructivism is afforded by substitutional quantification. Wang is puzzled by my statement that "a substitutional explication . . . brings no ontological economy to elementary number theory." My point is just that explication of the substitutional quantification in turn involves appeal to numerals, which in their infinitude are no improvement over the numbers. I can put my point more strongly: when names are at hand for all the values of the variables, I see no distinction between substitutional and objectual quantification.

I agreed with Parsons, toward the end of my reply to him, that the substitutional interpretation of quantification over abstract objects is attractive because of the shadowy status that it accords them— a becomingly tenuous existence, parasitic on language. The one obstacle to this course, Parsons and I agreed, was impredicative classes, or impredicative sets. In his present essay Wang urges that this obstacle can be lifted without prejudice to the uses of mathematics in natural science.

The move would have sweeping consequences for ontological relativity. Proxy functions would cease to matter to abstract objects in their newly shadowy status. As for concrete objects, the ones that are amenable to ostension can be pinned down by waiving deferred ostension and imposing some conventions along lines hinted toward the end of my reply to Parsons.

Wang rightly suggests that a predilection for predicativity would have been in keeping with my philosophical temper. Though never tempted to embrace constructivism at the cost of trading our crystalline bivalent logic for the fog of intutitionism, I have indeed wished that I could see my way to following Hermann Weyl in settling for classical logic and a predicative set theory without compromising the needs of science. The idea appealed to me on grounds of economy and clarity long before I was aware of the considerations set forth in the above two paragraphs. I looked hopefully into Lorenzen, but had trouble sorting out sign from object and seeing what was achieved. Bishop's ponderous work appeared only after my concerns had shifted to less austere domains.

Why had I not already risen to Wang's system Σ? Partly I was put off by the arbitrariness of where to terminate the hierarchy. Mainly I was put off by lack of detail on how to recover the continuity of the real numbers and on where to delimit the mathematical needs of natural science. Wang now offers a gratifyingly sharp and conservative cut-off point for the hierarchy and a reassuring expression of confidence that the needs of science are met. Hope shines forth of a firm and down-to-earth ontology.

                                                                    W. V. Q.

24

Morton White

NORMATIVE ETHICS, NORMATIVE EPISTEMOLOGY, AND QUINE'S HOLISM

In this paper I make some comments and raise certain questions about what Quine has called his epistemological "holism".[1] My chief aim is to persuade Quine to agree with me that we may include sentences containing expressions such as "ought", "ought not", "may", "has a right to", and "is entitled to" in certain bodies of sentences that may be tested in a holistic manner that I shall soon characterize. In my view such sentences appear in normative ethics as well as in normative epistemology. For example, I regard the sentence "Newton had a right to defend his life" as a sentence in normative ethics whereas I regard "Newton had a right to accept the principle of universal gravitation" as a sentence in normative epistemology; and I hope to persuade Quine to agree that heterogeneous conjunctions of such normative sentences and descriptive sentences may be tested holistically. In my view these heterogeneous conjunctions of sentences are not tested for their capacity to link sensory experiences alone—as systems consisting of purely descriptive sentences do according to Quine—but rather for their capacity to link sensory experiences with feelings or emotions. In sum, I hope that Quine will accept two views of mine: the view that holistically testable systems of belief may contain normative beliefs of ethics and epistemology, and the view that such heterogeneous systems may link sensory experiences with emotions.[2]

I must admit that I have a suspicion that Quine may not agree with me, a suspicion prompted by certain things he has written about ethics and epistemology. Thus, in the one piece on ethics that Quine has published—so far as I know—he writes of what he calls "the methodological infirmity of ethics as compared with science" and then goes on to say: "The empirical foothold of scientific theory is in the predicted observable event; that of a moral code is in the observable moral act. But whereas we can test a prediction against the independent course of observable nature, we can judge the morality of an act only by our moral standards themselves. Science, thanks to its links with observation, retains some title to a correspondence theory of truth; but a coherence theory is evidently the lot of ethics''.[3] Quine has also maintained that when empiricism reached its fifth and most recent milestone it assimilated epistemology to empirical psychology.[4] So, on the basis of Quine's sharp separation of science and ethics as well as his insistence that epistemology is a branch of empirical psychology, I have some reason to think that Quine may not agree that normative ethics and normative epistemology as I conceive them may be tested holistically. But if he should not agree with my views before reading what follows, I hope that I can persuade him here to accept certain views that I advance in *What Is and What Ought To Be Done*. And if I do not succeed in persuading him, I hope that he will be good enough to say why.

One of my main purposes in this paper is to persuade Quine to abandon a dualism between the methods of testing normative and descriptive statements which is as untenable as that between analytic and synthetic statements. I also want to say that if Quine thinks that his assimilation of epistemology to empirical psychology requires epistemologists to refrain from making normative statements about what they ought to believe or have a right to believe, and therefore to limit themselves to description, then I disagree. I believe that we properly make normative statements in epistemology which are not assimilable to purely descriptive statements, that we test systems which contain these normative statements holistically, and that nothing to which we appeal in this process or in the process of testing systems that contain normative ethical statements should frighten Quine the empiricist or Quine the naturalist. There are no supernatural cards up my sleeve and I set up no suprascientific tribunals, to use his phrase,[5] when I urge him to recognize that we may make ethical as well as epistemological statements about what we ought or have a right to do and that we appeal to feelings along with sensory experiences when we test the systems that contain such statements.

Before I begin my efforts to persuade Quine, I want to say something about his more recent comments on his holism in publications that appeared after my aforementioned book was published—comments that I had not known about while I was writing that book. First of all, I note with pleasure that he no longer insists—as he seemed to in his deservedly famous paper "Two Dogmas of Empiricism"—that "the *totality* [my emphasis] of our so-called knowledge or beliefs," or "the *whole* [my emphasis] of science",[6] is what is tested by experience according to his version of holism. In my book I had taken him to espouse that view and had dissented from it, but upon reading his essay "Five Milestones of Empiricism" I now see that he has changed his mind in a direction that I applaud. That essay of his was first published in October of 1981 in his *Theories and Things,* the preface to which he had signed in February of 1981. In that essay Quine writes that "it is an uninteresting legalism . . . to think of our scientific system of the world as involved *en bloc* in every prediction. More modest chunks suffice . . .''.[7] Although I do not fully grasp the reference to legalism, I infer from this passage that I should no longer dissent from Quine's views on this point as I did in my book, the preface to which I signed in August of 1980, well before I had learned of what he had said in "Five Milestones of Empiricism". I am pleased to find that Quine qualifies his view that our whole scientific system is involved *en bloc* in every prediction; I am also pleased to see that Quine says something else in "Five Milestones of Empiricism" that accords with something that I had written while I was understandably ignorant of what Quine had said in an unpublished version of "Five Milestones of Empiricism". I have in mind Quine's statement that we can make a conjunctive sentence of a whole theory and therefore regard a modest chunk of science as a single sentence even while subscribing to his holism.[8]

With these preliminaries behind me, I now want to begin my efforts at persuasion. Readers of Quine know that he acknowledges his debt to Pierre Duhem on the subject of holism,[9] but neither Duhem nor Quine discusses what I call normative sentences or normative beliefs in this context. Both are preoccupied with descriptive sciences such as physics and therefore do not focus on the testing of heterogeneous systems or conjunctions that consist of normative as well as descriptive sentences. But, impressed as I am by Quine's use of Duhem's holism to bridge the traditional epistemic gap created by the distinction between the analytic and the synthetic, I try to use my own version of holism to bridge the equally traditional epistemic gap between the normative and the descriptive. In developing his version of Duhem's approach, Quine has sometimes distinguished (a) the descriptive scientific thinker, (b) the body of purely descriptive science that such a thinker uses as a tool for organizing or linking sensory experiences, and (c) those sensory experiences themselves.[10] By analogy, when I deal with normative belief, I distinguish (a') the normative thinker, (b') the body of descriptive *and* normative beliefs that the normative thinker uses as a tool for organizing or linking sensory experiences with each other *and with emotions,* and (c') those experiences and emotions themselves.[11]

To anyone who might say that normative sentences are reducible to descriptive sentences and would therefore try to assimilate the second element in my triad to the second in Quine's, I should reply that I cannot accept such reductionism if it rests on saying that all normative sentences are synonymous with descriptive sentences. Like Quine, I find the notion of synonymy excessively obscure; and no matter what other philosophers might maintain, I should certainly not expect Quine himself to use this route in assimilating my triad to his. Furthermore, because I include emotions in (c'), the third element in my triad is not the same as the third element in Quine's. And if someone criticized my triad by denying that there are normative beliefs to be included in (b'), I should have to disagree. It seems obvious to me that many people not only believe that Newton had a right to defend his life but also that Newton had a right to, or was entitled to, accept the principle of universal gravitation; and I do not agree that they are mistaken when they say that they have such singular normative beliefs. Nor do I agree that they are mistaken when they say that they have beliefs such as those expressed by the normative ethical principle ''One ought to keep one's promises''; or that philosophers are mistaken when they say that they have beliefs such as those expressed by the normative epistemological principle ''One ought to (or has a right to) accept a system of descriptive belief that organizes one's sensory experiences in the simplest way and in a way that disturbs one's previously held system of belief less than any rival system''. In what may be an untypical statement, Quine himself expresses a normative epistemological principle when he writes as follows of an ''ultimate duty'': ''. . . the purpose of concepts and of language is efficacy in communication and in prediction. Such is the ultimate duty of language, science, and philosophy, and it is in relation to that duty that a conceptual scheme has finally to be appraised''.[12] That there are ethical and epistemological normative beliefs is as evident to me as it is that physicists hold the descriptive belief that all bodies attract each other. I am aware that some philosophers may try to defend the view that people do not have such normative beliefs by arguing that the sentences which allegedly express them lack cognitive meaning. But here, as in the case of the appeal to synonymy construed as the relation of having *the same* cognitive meaning, appeal is made to a notion that cannot support so bold a philosophical claim. At any rate, I should not expect Quine, who has inveighed so effectively against philosophically tendentious use of synonymy and cognitive meaning, to employ such notions in an effort to refute my view of the testing of heterogeneous systems of belief.

Assuming that normative ethical sentences do express beliefs, I want first of all to present an example of ethical reasoning (that I have used elsewhere) and then to offer some comments on it.[13] I ask Quine to suppose that the following argument is presented by a critic of abortion, bearing in mind that it does not make explicit any assumed logical truth that might be added by a holist who wanted to dramatize the fact that such logical truths were also elements of the system of belief in question:

(1) Whoever takes the life of a human being does something that ought not to be done.
(2) The mother took the life of a fetus in her womb.
(3) Every living fetus in the womb of a human being is a human being.

Therefore,

(4) The mother took the life of a human being.

Therefore,

(5) The mother did something that ought not to be done.

I now ask Quine to imagine that the mother who is criticized does not have the feeling of being obligated *not* to have done what she did. In my view, she might be justified under certain conditions in denying statement (5). In denying (5) she would, I contend, do something analogous to what a descriptive scientist, say a chemist, might do upon failing to have a sensory experience that was predicted by some chunk of purely descriptive belief. The chemist might deduce from a set of premises the statement that a certain piece of litmus paper was red and add that any normal person in a normal state who looked at a red object in white light would have the sensory experience of redness. But then the chemist might go on to say that although he was normal, in a normal state, and looking at the piece of paper in white light, he did not experience redness but greenness. Thus the chemist would, to use Quine's language, have a recalcitrant sensory experience whereas I would say that the mother mentioned in my ethical example would have a recalcitrant feeling. Quine says that a descriptive scientist having such a recalcitrant experience might plead hallucination—in other words, plead that he was not in a normal state—but then he might not so plead.[14] If he did not, and therefore denied that the litmus paper was red, other alternatives would be open to him, alternatives that have their analogues in those open to the mother. As soon as we grant that after denying (5) the mother may deny the conjunction that implies it, we may say that the mother, or anyone else engaged in such thinking, may amend or surrender a law of logic such as that which gets us from (2) and (3) to (4); an ethical principle such as (1); or a descriptive statement such as (2), (3), or (4). Any one of these moves will bring about what may be called a Duhemian alteration of the original body of beliefs in response to a recalcitrant feeling.

Because we need not deny or alter (1), our normative principle, we may deny or alter some other statement. If we deny (3), we exchange our conjunction of beliefs for a new one by denying a descriptive belief; but it should be emphasized that we deny that descriptive belief because we reject a normative conclusion that follows from our former assumptions. Thus the denial of (5), which denial expresses a normative belief, may play a part in determining what descriptive beliefs appear in our chunk of beliefs, since the denial of descriptive statement (3) is also descriptive. We have changed our chunk by adopting the descriptive statement that not every living fetus in the womb of a human being is a human being because we have adopted the normative statement that in killing the fetus the mother did not do something that ought not to be done. And this is similar in a certain crucial respect to a physicist's amending or rejecting a previously accepted logical belief because of certain data of quantum mechanics—an example mentioned by Quine. In my view, the right to alter one's description of an act in response to certain feelings about an act is anologous to the right to alter one's logic in response to certain sensory experiences arising from physical experiments. Here we see an analogy between Quine's permitting a recalcitrant experience to lead to the abandonment of a logical statement and my permitting the abandonment of a descriptive statement because of a recalcitrant feeling.

Of course, I am not saying that the denial of (5) logically implies the denial of (3) and therefore do not hold that descriptive (3) itself logically implies normative (5). The statement "Every living fetus in the womb of a human being is a human being" does not imply "The mother did something that ought not to be done". The latter is implied by the conjunction of premises in the illustrative argument and not by any one of them taken by itself. Because some philosophers, for example, Hume, think it fallacious to deduce an "ought"-statement from an "is"-statement, I want to say that I do not license such a deduction. I merely assert that if a conjunction containing descriptive and moral statements logically implies a moral conclusion which is denied, we may alter the conjunction by surrendering *either* a moral or a descriptive statement. Just as a logical statement is rarely recanted in the light of the rest of one's theory, I am prepared to admit that a descriptive statement is rarely recanted in the light of a moral statement. Nevertheless, I want to emphasize that, rarity aside, such recantation is *permissible* according to my view and that its very permissiblity is of great philosophical significance.

If Quine should grant the permissibility of such recantation, I think he should be led to reconsider a statement of his that I quote earlier in this paper. It will be recalled that after granting that the empirical foothold of scientific theory is in the predicted observable event and that of a moral code is in the observable act, Quine says that whereas we can test a prediction against the independent course of observable nature, we can judge the morality of an act only by our moral standards themselves; adding that science "thanks to its links with observation, retains some title to a correspondence theory of truth; but a coherence theory is evidently the lot of ethics".[15] However, if Quine should accept my earlier comments about ethical reasoning, I think he would have to acknowledge, first of all, that even though our moral standards (principles) play some part in guiding us to singular statements such as (5) about the morality of an act, those moral principles do not do so without the help of descriptive statements. Secondly, he would have to acknowledge that heterogeneous chunks of belief are to be tested by seeing whether they organize sensory experience-cum-feeling. In that case he would have to withdraw his remark that a coherence theory is the lot of ethics. For if science—that is to say, descriptive science—retains some title to a correspondence theory of truth "thanks to its links with observation'', then ethics should retain some title to a correspondence theory of truth thanks to its links with *observation and feeling*. Like Quine, I think ethics has a foothold in the observable act which corresponds to descriptive science's foothold in the predictable observable event; however, just as we ought to test chunks of descriptive science by appealing to what is observed, we ought to test chunks of what I am prepared to call normative science by appealing to what is observed and what is felt. Once we let feeling play the part that I assign to it, a coherence theory is *not* the lot of ethics, and it does not suffer from the "methodological infirmity" of which Quine speaks. It may well have ills, but I do not think that the disease known as the coherence theory of truth is one of them.

Having assured Quine that I believe nothing that should scare a naturalist or empiricist, I should point out to other philosophers that I have not tried to reduce normative ethical statements to allegedly synonymous descriptive statements. My view may be termed naturalistic not because I advocate such reduction but rather because I do not assert or imply the existence of anything beyond the confines of nature as usually conceived. And yet, although I avoid naturalistic reductionism in ethics, I maintain that there are rationally testable ethical beliefs whereas I think that Quine sharply distinguishes between rationally testable beliefs and moral valuations. I think he holds that the typical moral situation is one in which a person believes scientifically that a certain action will cause a certain effect which the person merely values while not asserting anything scientific about that effect. Moreover, Quine accepts "the deep old duality of thought and feeling, of the head and the heart, the cortex and the thalamus, the words and the music".[16] He appears to hold that we may value furthering our neighbor's welfare and that we may learn in a scientific way how to further our neighbor's welfare while we deny that the sentence "We ought to further our neighbor's welfare" expresses a belief.

In that case, what does Quine, an epistemologist who is anxious to present a general theory of how beliefs should be tested, say to people who believe that in asserting normative moral principles they express beliefs? Presumably that they are mistaken. But what reasons would he give them for saying that they are mistaken? I am not sure, but, believing as I do that Quine could not successfully argue for the non-existence of such beliefs, I think that it would be better for him to recognize that moral normative beliefs appear in systems which are holistically tested, and also to broaden the flux that normative thinking is supposed to organize by recognizing that such a flux contains feelings. In this way he would help us to hold on to the deep old belief that we have ethical beliefs and thereby disturb our view of the world as little as possible. Here I might remind Quine, who once abandoned nominalism because he thought that arithmetic was something to reckon with, that rational normative ethics is something to conjure with. It permits us to defend singular moral beliefs about what we should do on specific occasions by appealing to heterogeneous conjunctions of beliefs.

Having said what I hope is enough on the subject of normative ethics, I now turn to normative epistemology. I believe that I make a statement in normative epistemology when I say that one who denies statement (5) is entitled to accept the denial of (3) and thereby to alter the body of statements from which (5) is deduced. I also make a statement in normative epistemology when I say that an ethical thinker ought to accept a system of belief which organizes his sensory experiences *and* his feelings with due regard to the demand for scientific simplicity and the demand that we disturb a prior system of belief as little as possible. Moreover, I think that Quine makes a statement in normative epistemology when he says: "A recalcitrant experience can . . . be accommodated by any of various alternative reëvaluations in various alternative quarters of the total system".[17] I regard this "can"-statement as normative because I do not think it is a statement in formal logic or natural science. I think that Quine is here telling us that we *may*, that is to say, *have a right to*, accommodate a recalcitrant experience in different ways. I do not wish to discuss at length the question whether he is asserting a *moral* right. I have argued elsewhere that the generic notion of a duty or that of a right is neutral, thereby allowing that we may use the words "duty" and "right" univocally in moral and epistemological contexts even though moralists and epistemologists usually focus on different sorts of acts.[18] This, in my opinion, is analogous to the univocal use of the word "exists" by mathematicians and physicists who assert the existence of things as different as numbers and electrons. But whatever view we take of an epistemic right or duty to accept a body of belief under certain conditions, I believe that a statement that every thinker has such a right or duty does not describe what every thinker in fact does under those conditions. For this reason I question Quine's statement that epistemology may be assimilated to empirical psychology if he thinks that empirical psychology does not contain normative statements of ethics or epistemology. Moreover, I think that the "assimilation" of normative epistemological statements to statements in descriptive psychology might require the use of the discredited notion of synonymy just as an analogous assimilation of normative ethical statements would. The unassimilated epistemological principle that a scientist *should* check a body of beliefs against experience is normative. It tells us what a scientist should do, as Quine seemed to think when he said that the "ultimate duty" of language, science, and philosophy is to communicate and predict efficaciously. It is a general normative principle to which we must appeal when we say that we ought to accept a given body of belief. We cannot justify such a singular epistemic statement without appealing to epistemic normative principles that contain the word "ought". We cannot answer the question whether a given body of scientific beliefs ought to be accepted by fallaciously reasoning as follows: "This is a scientific theory; scientific theories *are* accepted if and only if they have characteristics A, B, and C; this has characteristics A, B, and C; therefore, this *ought to be* accepted". How can we defend deducing that a scientist ought to accept a given theory, or that he has a right to accept it, without deducing our singular normative epistemic statement from a conjunction which contains at least one normative epistemic rule as a conjunct?

After having asked this rhetorical question, I may well be asked how normative epistemic rules are to be tested so as to allay Quine's fear that I may be setting epistemology on too high a pedestal, converting it into a "supra-scientific tribunal". And my answer is that I view normative epistemology much as I view normative ethics because I believe that there are systems of normative epistemological reasoning which are analogous to the argument from (1) through (5), and that there is a flux of sensory experiences *and* emotions which may be organized by a normative epistemologist who argues in a manner that is analogous to the manner in which the moralist argues in statements (1) through (5). Accordingly, I think that Einstein the determinist believed that no physicist *ought* to accept as final a chunk of belief that is non-deterministic in the way that modern quantum mechanics is. And in stating this normative epistemic belief Einstein did not describe how twentieth-century physicists *do* think, for he was quite aware that they did not think as he believed they *should* think. By analogy with the ethical argument presented earlier, Einstein's reasoning might be represented as follows:

(6) No physical system which is non-deterministic ought to be accepted as final.

(7) Quantum theory is a physical system which is non-deterministic.

Therefore,

(8) Quantum theory ought not to be accepted as final.

Now if (8) should be rejected, it is open to us to reject (6), (7), or the unexpressed logical principle of the above argument. Furthermore, the basis on which we may accept or reject (8) is analogous to the basis on which we may accept or reject (5) in our earlier illustration. In other words, we have what may be called epistemic feelings of obligation to accept or not to accept certain physical theories which are analogous to our moral feelings of obligation to perform acts of the kind treated in ethics. Moreover, one who describes a body of physical beliefs as deterministic or non-deterministic has sensory experiences that are analogous to the sensory experiences of a normative moralist who describes acts as mendacious. We must look at theories to discover whether they are deterministic. Therefore, the normative epistemological system represented by (6) through (8) should itself be tested by seeing whether it organizes a relevant flux of experience-cum-feeling. For this reason, an opponent of Einstein who has a recalcitrant epistemic feeling may, like the mother in our ethical example, reject or alter a normative principle such as (6), a descriptive statement such as (7), or a principle of formal logic. To increase the likelihood that Quine will agree, I point out that, so far from making normative epistemology a "first philosophy" or a "supra-scientific tribunal",[19] I let its acceptability depend in part on its capacity to organize such sensory experiences and feelings of obligation as Einstein might have had upon contemplating a nondeterministic system and deciding that he ought not accept it as final. In other words, one who is faced with deciding whether to accept a heterogeneous body of belief such as that represented by (6), (7), and (8) must do something analogous to what a moralist must do when faced with deciding whether to accept the set of premises used in the earlier discussion of abortion. When testing a hypothetico-deductive argument in ethics or in epistemology, we ought to appeal to sensory experience and feelings of obligation or entitlement.

In trying to persuade Quine, I have not used such terms of his as "surface irritations", "sensory receptors", and "nerve endings". I hope that Quine will not object to this in spite of a statement by him that his "non-committal term 'experience' " in "Two Dogmas of Empiricism" awaited his later theory that invoked surface irritations and other such entities.[20] I feel no qualms in not using the language of neurological psychology because I believe that the terms "sensory experiences" and "feelings of obligation" refer to things that I have, that Quine has, and that other human beings have. Since he has managed to his own satisfaction to construct a theory which avoids "phenomenalistic interpretation" by invoking surface irritations rather than experiences, he might—if he were to accept what I have said so far—be able to work a similar transformation on "feelings of obligation" if he finds that term too non-committal or subject to some defect of the kind he finds in "experience" because of its association in his mind with phenomenalism. Naturally, I am not urging Quine to direct his psychological talents toward this end if he does not find it desirable or possible to do so, but I hope that he will not reject my assumption of the existence of feelings of obligation merely because they are not incorporated in his neurological scheme of surface irritations or the triggering of sensory receptors.

I say this for a number of reasons of different kinds. For one thing, I think that an epistemologist should take account of what I shall call the typical situation of a thinker who seeks guidance from normative epistemology, just as a moralist should take into account the typical situation of a thinker who seeks guidance from ethics. When one is faced with the question whether to accept a certain body of beliefs, one asks: "Should I accept this body of beliefs", and one may rightly expect an answer that does not depend on one's knowing anything about neurology. Quine himself writes that when he referred to surface irritation in *Word and Object,* he was not supposing "that people are on the whole thinking or talking about the triggering of their nerve endings; few people, statistically speaking, know about their nerve endings".[21] Obviously, therefore, Quine would not require a physicist who is trying to decide whether to accept a physical theory to examine his nerve endings as well as the objects dealt with in the theory. And even if Quine were to discover neurological counterparts of the epistemic feelings of obligation that an Einstein might have in defending (8), Quine would not require Einstein to examine those neurological counterparts. Nor should I expect Quine to insist that the mother in my moral example engage in analogous neurological inquiry before deciding whether she should or should not have committed an act of abortion. Whatever merit Quine sees in moving to neurology, such a move would not—if I understand him correctly—eliminate the duty of Einstein and the moralist-mother to test their heterogeneous bodies of belief by discovering whether those bodies organized their sensory experiences and feelings.

However, even if Quine were to insist that the language of neurology produces much improvement in our description of the process of thinking, I should insist that the use of such language would not eradicate the difference between saying that one *ought to* accept a body belief under certain conditions and saying that one *does* accept it under those conditions. If Quine thinks that my reference to feelings is too noncommittal, he is welcome to handle my feelings by doing something analogous to what he does when he replaces his experiences by surface irritations. That is to say, he is welcome to produce a neurological term that would stand to the term "feeling of obligation" as "triggering of sensory receptors" stands to "experiences". But producing such a term would not assimilate normative epistemology to descriptive psychology, any more than it would reduce ethics to descriptive psychology. The production of such a neurological term might lead us to replace the word "feeling" by that neurological term in normative epistemological statements but it would not force us to eliminate the terms "ought" or "may" from such statements. If Quine's pre-neurological epistemological thesis was that scientists have a duty to accept only bodies of belief that link *experiences* to each other, his newer neurological thesis, as I see it, would be that they have a duty to accept only bodies of belief that link *sensory stimulations* to *sensory stimulations*. The survival of the word "duty" after Quine's move to neurology is related to the fact that there is a difference between saying that a thinker *does* accept a body of belief only if it has certain characteristics and saying that he *ought to* or *may* accept it only if it has those characteristics. I venture to say that even if every physicist were *in fact* to stop accepting bodies of statements that linked sensory stimulations to sensory stimulations according to Quine's view, and were to begin accepting only those bodies of statements that they were told by Ronald Reagan to accept, Quine would not revise his philosophy by surrendering some of his epistemological statements even though he might well revise his descriptive psychological account of how scientists do behave. Why? Because I think that Quine's fundamental principles of epistemology express norms or standards which should be formulated in statements containing such words as "duty", "ought", and "may"; and such statements are not to be rejected merely by pointing out that physicists *in fact* support their theories on presidential authority.

I view Quine's epistemology as one that might conceivably be pitted, for example, against the view of those who advocate what Peirce called the method of authority. In other words, I believe that Quine's holism might be viewed as taking the following form: "Bodies of belief ought to be accepted if and only if they satisfy condition Q", in which case authoritarian holism would take the form: "Bodies of belief ought to be accepted if and only if they satisfy condition A", where "A" refers to a condition other than Q. Of course, this way of depicting the issue between two such epistemologies allows for the *possibility* that authoritarian holism is true whereas Quine's holism is false; and since Quine regards his own epistemology as a fallible and corrigible inquiry into reality, he would not be fazed by this consequence of my view of the contest between his holism and authoritarian holism. As I understand Quine, however, his own view of such a contest would involve pitting his fallible and corrigible *description* of the conditions under which bodies of belief *are* accepted against other fallible and corrigible *descriptions* of such conditions. Insofar as Quine regards his epistemology as fallible and corrigible, I agree with him; but I doubt that he can, by examining the activity of accepting beliefs in which all persons called scientists engage, establish that all these persons in fact accept bodies of belief if and only if such bodies satisfy condition Q. The point is that there are scientists who accept bodies of belief which do *not* satisfy condition Q. And, of course, if Quine were to reply that he is describing the behavior of scientists who do what they ought to do as scientists, he would import a normative element into his enterprise.

Furthermore, even if Quine were able to show that *all* scientists do accept those and only those bodies of belief that satisfy condition Q, he would leave open the question whether beliefs that are accepted on these grounds ought to be accepted on these grounds. And that open question, I believe, is the one to be answered by a philosopher who advises us to use the method of science rather than some other method in testing bodies of belief. Although Peirce did not attain the highest degree of clarity when he discussed this issue, he appears at times to see that what he presents as alternative methods of fixing belief— the method of tenacity, the method of authority, the a priori method, and the scientific method—are being assessed by him with the following question in mind: "Which of them ought to be used in the fixation of belief?". True, Peirce seems to think that he can describe the method of science by examining the behavior of scientists, but he does not stop after he has supposedly described that method; he seems to think that he should say why he thinks that it *ought* to be used as the method of fixing beliefs.[22] Now I do not urge Quine to accept the specific views that Peirce presents when singing the praises of the so-called scientific method. But I do urge Quine to recognize that even if he were able to tell us what scientific method is on the basis of an examination of the behavior of all scientists, there would be a further question to answer, namely, "Why should we use scientific method in fixing our beliefs?". If Quine were to adopt this view of at least one problem of epistemology, he would see himself as asserting principles explicitly couched in normative terms; and when testing heterogeneous bodies containing such principles he would, I hope, appeal to emotions as well as sensory experiences.

By now it will be evident that I do not advocate the abandonment of the distinction between normative and descriptive sentences. On the contrary, I advocate its retention insofar as I question the reducibility of ethical or episte-mological "ought"-sentences to "is"-sentences. However, although I retain this distinction, I use holism to avoid drawing an epistemological distinction between the *testing* of normative statements and the *testing* of descriptive state-ments. In this way I do something analogous to what I think Quine does when he retains a distinction between logical statements and non-logical statements while using holism to avoid drawing an epistemological distinction between the testing of logical statements and the testing of non-logical statements. That is why I have conceived my task as two-fold: to show on the one hand that holistically testable systems of belief may contain normative beliefs of ethics and epistemology; and on the other to show that such systems ought to be tested by referring to their capacity to link sensory experiences and feelings.

If Quine were to agree with me, he could do so without any fear that he would be viewing the epistemologist as an infallible inquirer whose views are incorrigible. In my view moral principles are not a priori truths, not necessary truths, not analytic truths, not intuitively known. Nor can they be extracted by reflection on the so-called essence of man or on the so-called meaning of "man". By parity of reasoning, the normative principles of epistemology as I view them are not to be extracted by reflection on the so-called essence of science nor on the so-called meaning of "science". Chunks of belief contain-ing them are to be tested holistically, just as chunks containing moral principles and physical principles are. If Quine were to accept my view of holism as applied to normative belief, he would travel to a new milestone of empiricism at which the deep old duality of thought and feeling is no longer used to sup-port the deep old untenable dualism between the normative and the descriptive; he would help strike yet another blow for methodological monism.

MORTON WHITE

THE INSTITUTE FOR ADVANCED STUDY
PRINCETON, NEW JERSEY
MARCH 1982

NOTES

1. I have in mind the view advocated by Quine in section 6 of "Two Dogmas of Empiricism" as reprinted in his *From a Logical Point of View* (Cambridge, Mass.: 1953), pp. 42–46. See also the remarks on holism in his "Five Milestones of Empiricism", *Theories and Things* (Cambridge, Mass.: 1981), pp. 71–72.

2. The views to which I seek Quine's reactions are defended in my book *What Is and What Ought To Be Done: An Essay on Ethics and Epistemology* (New York: 1981), esp. Chapters II–IV.

3 W. V. Quine, "On the Nature of Moral Values", *Theories and Things*, p. 63.

4. *Theories and Things*, p. 72.

5. Ibid.

6. *From a Logical Point of View*, p. 42.

7. *Theories and Things*, p. 71.

8. Ibid.

9. See Duhem's *La Théorie physique: son objet, sa structure* (2nd edition, Paris: 1914) pp. 278–89; also Quine, *From a Logical Point of View*, p. 41.

10. *From a Logical Point of View*, p. 44.

11. *What Is and What Ought To Be Done*, pp. 29–35.

12. *From a Logical Point of View*, p. 79.

13. *What Is and What Ought To Be Done*, pp. 30–35.

14. *From a Logical Point of View*, p. 43.

15. See note 3 above.

16. *Theories and Things*, p. 55.

17. *From a Logical Point of View*, p. 44.

18. *What Is and What Ought To Be Done*, pp. 82–83.

19. In "Five Milestones of Empiricism" Quine regards the fifth milestone as one at which empiricism abandons the goal of a "first philosophy" and sees natural science as not being answerable to any "supra-scientific tribunal". See note 5 above.

20. *Theories and Things*, p. 40.

21. Ibid.

22. See "The Fixation of Belief", *Collected Papers of C. S. Peirce*, edited by C. Hartshorne and P. Weiss (Cambridge, Mass.: 1931–1935), Volume V, paragraphs 358–387. This is a convenient place at which to note that when Duhem discusses the alteration of theories that face recalcitrant experiences, he says: "Le bon sens est juge des hypothèses qui doivent être abandonnées", op. cit., p. 329. Note the explicitly normative part of this statement. Furthermore, he says that our choice here is dictated by Pascalian "raisons que la raison ne connaît pas", ibid., p. 330. I do not cite these statements by Duhem in order to endorse obscurantism in epistemology but merely to show that the Ur-holist recognized not only the normative element in epistemology but also the role of feeling in it.

REPLY TO MORTON WHITE

White's concern to accommodate value judgments within epistemology dates back nearly three decades, to *Toward Reunion in Philosophy*. He would accomplish this by consulting the testimony of the emotions along with that of the senses. In my account of moral indecision, the bemused subject held various moral tenets which, along with his descriptive ones, formed an inconsistent conjunction. The descriptive part was supported ultimately, if at all, by the senses. What of his moral tenets? Some were singular, perhaps, others general; some innate, perhaps, others inculcated by precept or example, birch rod or sugar plum. But in any event, White observes, the substance of these moral evaluations—what they consist in, apart from lip service—is the subject's emotional response of approval or revulsion in each singular instance. Now White points out that if we pool these emotions with the sensations, we can view the inconsistent conjunction of descriptive beliefs and moral evaluations just as we might view an inconsistent conjunction purely of descriptive beliefs. In either case we restore consistency by casting out some component, chosen by considerations perhaps of simplicity, perhaps of minimum mutilation, and perhaps of direct experiential input, sensory or—now—emotive.

The reasoning is plausible in its own terms, but turns problematic when set over against a background of naturalized epistemology. We are saddled with three incompatible beliefs, say, two of them descriptive and one moral, and must eliminate one. White suggests treating all three as empirical, by treating emotions on a par with sensations. Ideally, then, we should critically assess the ultimate empirical evidence for each of the three. Holism warns us that none of the three will have its own isolable empirical evidence, but we might combine each with some adequate cluster of trusted kindred beliefs so as to get three critical masses, each capable of implying observable consequences. (See my reply to Vuillemin.) Schematically each such consequence would take the form of a conditional joining two observation sentences, one stating an experimental condition and the other a prediction. Some of the observation sentences to which we would be thus driven, in the situation now imagined, would be moral ones. This is what I find problematic, as I shall explain.

Note first that my definition of observation sentence does not explicitly favor sensation over emotion. It mentions neither, and is predicated rather on publicly shared stimulation. An observation sentence is an occasion sentence that commands the same verdict from all witnesses who know the language. Consider, then, the moral occasion sentence 'That's outrageous'. In the hope of getting it to qualify as an observation sentence, let us adopt an unrealistic "best-case" assumption about our linguistic community, to the effect that all speakers are disposed to assent to 'That's outrageous' on seeing a man beat a cripple or furtively snatch a wreath off a door or commit any other evil that can be condemned on sight without collateral information. (The malefactor would be foreign, since our fellow speakers are assumed to deplore all such acts.) Would 'That's outrageous' then qualify as an observation sentence? It would still not, simply because it applies also and indeed mostly to other acts whose outrageousness hinges on collateral information not in general shared by all witnesses of the acts.

The sentence 'It's raining', in contrast, almost never hinges on information not shared by present witnesses, and the sentence 'That's a rabbit' does so only seldom. These two consequently qualify well enough as observational, a status that is somewhat a matter of degree. 'He's a bachelor', at the other extreme, depends on collateral information that is seldom widely shared. 'That's outrageous' is intermediate between 'That's a rabbit' and 'He's a bachelor'. Even our best-case assumption is insufficient, we see, to qualify it as an observation sentence. Moral judgments differ thus from cognitive ones in their relation to observation.

The difference is due to a difference between sensation and emotion, despite the aloofness of my definition of observation sentence. Sensation is nicely coordinated with concurrent, publicly accessible stimulation. Impacts on a certain range of surface receptors produce the sensation, and conversely, apart from occasional illusion, the sensation occurs only when thus produced. It is not so with emotions. The emotion of revulsion matches up only half way even under the best-case assumption, for the converse condition still fails: revulsion is commonly aroused also by acts that are visibly evil only in the light of collateral information not generally shared. Hence the lack of moral observation sentences. Natural science owes its objectivity to its intersubjective checkpoints in observation sentences, but there is no such rock bottom for moral judgments.

A word now about the status, for me, of epistemic values. Naturalization of epistemology does not jettison the normative and settle for the indiscriminate description of ongoing procedures. For me normative epistemology is a branch of engineering. It is the technology of truth-seeking, or, in a more cautiously epistemological term, prediction. Like any technology, it makes free use of whatever scientific findings may suit its purpose. It draws upon mathematics in computing standard deviation and probable error and in scouting the gambler's fallacy. It draws upon experimental psychology in exposing perceptual illusions, and upon cognitive psychology in scouting wishful thinking. It draws upon neurology and physics, in a general way, in discounting testimony from occult or parapsychological sources. There is no question here of ultimate value, as in morals; it is a matter of efficacy for an ulterior end, truth or prediction. The normative here, as elsewhere in engineering, becomes descriptive when the terminal parameter is expressed. We could say the same of morality if we could view it as aimed at reward in heaven.

Moral values do occasionally intertwine with epistemological norms, but not inextricably. Falsification of an experiment is immoral, and also it is epistemologically inefficacious, however rewarding in respect of fame and fortune. When in a passage quoted by White I referred to "the ultimate duty of language, science, and philosophy" I was using the word somewhat as when we speak of a heavy-duty cable or tractor. It was what language, science, and philosophy are for, as eyes are for seeing.

W. V. Q.

PART THREE

A BIBLIOGRAPHY OF THE PUBLICATIONS OF W. V. QUINE

COMPILED BY W. V. QUINE

PUBLICATIONS OF W. V. QUINE

BOOKS

1934: *A System of Logistic*. Cambridge: Harvard, xii + 204 pp.

1940: *Mathematical Logic*. New York: Norton, xii + 344 pp.
Emended 2d printing: Harvard, 1947.
Revised edition: 1951.
Paperback: New York: Harper, 1962; Harvard, 1981.
Translations:
Spanish by H. Pescador, Madrid: Ocidente, 1972.
Polish by L. Koj, Warsaw: Państwowe Wydanictwo, 1974.
Excerpts reprinted: 1968: pp. 27–33 in Iseminger;
1971: pp. 23–33 in Manicas;
1974: same in Zabeeh et al.

1941: *Elementary Logic*. Boston: Ginn, vi + 170 pp.
Revised edition: Harvard, 1966.
Paperback: Harper, 1965; Harvard, 1980.
Translations:
Italian by F. Gana, Rome: Ubaldini, 1968.
French by J. Largeault and B. St.-Sermin, Paris: Colin, 1972.
Japanese by R. Tsueshita, Tokyo: Taishukan, 1972.
Spanish, Mexico: Grijalbo, 1983.

1944: *O Sentido da Nova Lógica*. São Paulo: Martins, xii + 190 pp.
Translation: Spanish by M. Bunge, Buenos Aires: Nueva Visión, 1958.
Excerpts translated: 1943: pp. 140–144, 146–158, 179–183 in "Notes on existence and necessity," below.

1950: *Methods of Logic*. New York: Holt, xxii + 272 pp.
Revised edition: 1959 and London: Routledge, 1962.
3rd edition, revised and enlarged: Holt, 1972, and Routledge, 1974.
Paperback: Routledge, 1974.
4th edition; revised and enlarged: Harvard, 1982. Also paperback.
Translations:
Italian by M. Pacifico, Milan: Feltrinelli, 1960.
Japanese by S. Nakamura and S. Ohmori, Tokyo: Iwanami, 1962. 3rd ed. 1978.
Spanish by M. Sacristán, Barcelona: Ariel, 1963. 3rd ed. by J. J. Acero and N. Guasch, 1981.
Hungarian by Urban J., Budapest: Akademiai Kiado, 1968.
German by D. Siefkes, Frankfurt: Suhrkamp, 1969.
French, 3rd ed., by M. Clavelin, Colin, 1973.
Excerpts reprinted: 1971: Introduction in Manicas;
1973: same in MacKinnon.

1953: *From a Logical Point of View*. Harvard, vii + 184 pp.
Revised edition: 1961.
Paperback: Harper, 1963; Harvard, 1980.
Translations:
Spanish by M. Sacristán, Ariel, 1963.
Italian by E. Mistretta, Rome: Astrolabio, 1966.

Polish by B. Stanosz, Państwowe Wydanictwo, 1970.
Japanese by E. Mochimaru and K. Nakayama, Iwanami, 1972.
German by P. W. Bosch, Frankfurt: Ullstein, 1979.
Excerpts reprinted: 1961: pp. 47–64 in Saporta;
     1964: same in Fodor and Katz;
     1969: same in Olshewsky;
     1971: pp. 139–157 in Linsky;
     1974: same in Zabeeh et al.
Excerpts translated: 1969: pp. 139–157 in Pasquinelli;
     1973: pp. 47–64 in Eisenberg et al.;
     1975: pp. 102–129, 139–159 in Stegmüller.
For further excerpting see under component articles.

1960: *Word and Object*. Cambridge: MIT, xvi + 294 pp.
 Paperback: 1964.
 Translations:
  Spanish by M. Sacristán, Barcelona: Labor, 1968.
  Italian by F. Mondadori, Milan: Saggiatore, 1970.
  French by P. Gochet, Paris: Flammarion, 1978.
  Portuguese by P. Alcoforado, Rio de Janeiro: Alves, 1978.
  German by J. Schulte; Stuttgart: Reelam, 1980.
 Excerpts reprinted: 1960: pp. 5–8 in *Sat. Review of Lit.*, Aug. 6.
     1964: pp. 170–176, 251–257 in Smart;
     1967: pp. 270–276 in Rorty;
     1968: pp. 157–161 in Iseminger;
     1971: pp. 26–79 in Rosenberg and Travis:
     1974: pp. 176–186 in Davidson and Harman.
 Excerpts translated: 1973: pp. 214–216 in Simpson. (For further excerpting see under
 "Meaning and translation.")

1963: *Set Theory and Its Logic*. Harvard, xvi + 359pp.
 Revised edition: 1969 and Taipeh: Mei Ya, 1969.
 Paperback: Harvard, 1971
 Translations:
  Japanese by A. Ohe and T. Fujimura, Iwanami, 1968.
  German by A. Oberschelp, Brunswick: Vieweg, 1973.

1966: *The Ways of Paradox and Other Essays*. New York: Random House, x + 257 pp.
 Paperback: 1968.
 Translation: Italian by M. Santambrogio, Saggiatore, 1975.
 Revised enlarged edition: Harvard, 1976.

1966: *Selected Logic Papers*. Random House, x + 250pp.
 Paperback: 1968.

1969: *Ontological Relativity and Other Essays*. New York: Columbia, x + 165pp.
 Paperback: 1977.
 Translations:
  Spanish by M. Garrido, J. L. Blasco, and M. Bunge, Madrid: Tecnos, 1974.
  German, Stuttgart: Reklam, 1975.
  French by J. Largeault, Paris: Aubier, 1977.
  Portuguese, São Paulo: Abril, 1975.

1970: *The Web of Belief* (with J. S. Ullian). Random House, v + 95pp.
 Revised edition: 1978.

1970: *Philosophy of Logic*. Englewood: Prentice Hall, xv + 109pp.
    Paperback: 1970.
    Revised edition: Harvard, 1986.
    Translations:
        Portuguese by T. A. Cannabrava, Rio de Janeiro: Zahar, 1972.
        Japanese by M. Yamashita, Iwanami, 1972.
        Spanish by M. Sacristán, Madrid: Alianza, 1973.
        German by H. Vetter, Stuttgart: Kohlhammer, 1973.
        French by J. Largeault, Paris: Aubier, 1975.
        Polish by H. Mortimer, Państwowe Wydanictwo, 1977.
        Italian by D. Benelli, Saggiatore, 1981.
    Excerpts reprinted: 1972: pp. 35–43, 47–60 in Davidson and Harman *(Logic of Grammar)*;
    1974: pp. 35–46 in Moravcsik.
    Excerpt translated: 1970: "Sur la tâche de la grammaire," below.

1974: *The Roots of Reference*. La Salle, Ill.: Open Court. xii + 151pp.
    Translations:
        German by H. Vetter, Suhrkamp, 1976.
        Spanish, Madrid: Occidente, 1977.
    Excerpt translated: 1972, "Reflexiones sobre el aprendizaje del lenguaje," below.

1981: *Theories and Things*. Harvard, xii + 219 pp.

1982: *Saggi Filosofici 1970–1981*. M. Leonelli, ed., Rome: Armando, 238 pp.

1985: *The Time of My Life: An Autobiography*. MIT, xii + 40 + 499 pp.

ARTICLES

1932: A note on Nicod's postulate," *Mind* 41: 345–350.

1933: "The logic of sequences," *Summaries of Theses 1932* (Harvard), pp. 335–338.
    "A theorem in the calculus of classes," *Jour. London Math. Soc.* 8: 89–95.

1934: "Ontological remarks on the propositional calculus," *Mind* 43: 472–476.
    Reprinted 1966 in *The Ways of Paradox*.
    "A method of generating part of arithmetic without use of intuitive logic," *Bull. Amer. Math. Soc.* 40: 753–761.
    Reprinted 1966 in *Selected Logic Papers*.

1936: "Concepts of negative degree," *Proc. Nat. Acad. Sci.* 22: 40–45.
    "A theory of classes presupposing no canons of type," ibid.: 320–326.
    "A reinterpretation of Schönfinkel's logical operators," *Bull. Amer. Math. Soc.* 42: 87–89.
    "Definition of substitution," ibid.: 561–569.
    Reprinted 1966 in *Selected Logic Papers*.
    "On the axiom of reducibility," *Mind* 45: 498–500.
    "Toward a calculus of concepts," *Journal of Symbolic Logic* 1: 2–25.
    "Set-theoretic foundations for logic," ibid., pp. 45–57.
    Reprinted 1966 in *Selected Logic Papers*.
    "Truth by convention," *Philosophical Essays for A. N. Whitehead* (O. H. Lee, ed., New York: Longmans), 90–124.

Reprinted 1949 in Feigl and Sellars;
      1964 in Benacerraf and Putnam;
      1966 in *The Ways of Paradox.*
Translated 1969 in *Cuadernos de Filosofía* (Buenos Aires).

1937: "New foundations for mathematical logic," *Amer. Math. Monthly* 44: 70–80.
Reprinted 1953 with additions in *From a Logical Point of View.*
Translated 1969 in Pasquinelli.
"On derivability," *Journal of Symbolic Logic* 2: 113–119.
"On Cantor's theorem," ibid.: 120–124.
"Logic based on inclusion and abstraction," ibid.: 145–152.
Reprinted 1966 in *Selected Logic Papers.*

1938: "Completeness of the propositional calculus," *Jour. Symbolic Logic* 3: 37–40.
Reprinted 1966 in *Selected Logic Papers.*
"On the theory of types," *Jour. Symbolic Logic* 3: 125–139.
Reprinted 1970 in Klemke.

1939: "Designation and existence," *Jour. Philosophy* 36: 701–709.
Reprinted 1949 in Feigl and Sellars;
      1953 partly in *From a Logical Point of View;*
      1969 in Olshewsky.
Translated 1972 in Sinnreich.
"Relations and reason," *Technology Review* 41: 299–301, 324–332.
"A logistical approach to the ontological problem," *Jour. Unified Science* 9: 84–89 (preprints only).
Reprinted 1966 in *The Ways of Paradox.*

1940: "Elimination of extra-logical postulates" (with Nelson Goodman), *Jour. Symbolic Logic* 5: 104–109.
Reprinted 1972 in Goodman.
1941: "Element and number," *Jour. Symbolic Logic* 6: 135–149.
Reprinted 1966 in *Selected Logic Papers.*
"Russell's paradox and others," *Technology Review* 44: 16ff.
"Whitehead and the rise of modern logic," *Philosophy of A. N. Whitehead* (P. A. Schilpp, ed., LaSalle: Open Court) 125–163.
Reprinted 1966 in *Selected Logic Papers.*

1942: "Reply to Professor Ushenko," *Jour. Philosophy* 39: 68–71.
"On existence conditions for elements and classes," *Jour. Symbolic Logic* 7: 157–159.

1943: "Notes on existence and necessity," *Jour. Philosophy* 40: 113–127. Translation of part of *O Sentido da Nova Lógica.*
Reprinted 1952 in Linsky;
      1953 partly in *From a Logical Point of View.*
Translated 1972 in Sinnreich;
      1973 in Simpson.

1945: "On the logic of quantification," *Jour. Symbolic Logic* 10: 1–12.
Reprinted 1966 in *Selected Logic Papers.*
"On ordered pairs," *Jour. Symbolic Logic* 10: 95ff.
Reprinted 1966 in *Selected Logic Papers,* combined with next:

1946: "On relations as coextensive with classes," *Jour. Symbolic Logic* 11: 71f.
"Concatenation as a basis for arithmetic," ibid.: 105–114.
Reprinted 1966 in *Selected Logic Papers.*

"Os Estados Unidos e o ressurgimento da lógica," *Vida Intellectual nos Estados Unidos* (R. Amorim, ed., São Paulo: U.C.B.E.U.), 267–286.

1947: "The problem of interpreting modal logic," *Jour. Symbolic Logic* 12: 43–48.
Reprinted 1953 partly in *From a Logical Point of View;*
1968 in Copi and Gould;
1974 in Zabeeh et al.
Translated 1978 into Hungarian.
"On universals," *Jour. Symbolic Logic* 12: 74–84.
Reprinted 1953 partly in *From a Logical Point of View.*
Translated 1975 in Stegmüller.
"Steps toward a constructive nominalism" (with Nelson Goodman), *Jour. Symbolic Logic* 12: 97–122.
Reprinted 1969 in Bobbs-Merrill Reprint Series;
1972 in Goodman.
Translated 1967 in Cellucci.

1948: "On what there is," *Review of Metaphysics* 2: 21–38.
Reprinted 1951 in *Aristotelian Soc. Suppl.* Vol. 25, appendix;
1952 in Linsky;
1953 in *From a Logical Point of View;*
1964 in Benacerraf and Putnam;
1965 in Nagel and Brandt; partly in Baylis;
1968 in Copi and Gould; in Iseminger; in Margolis;
in Bobbs-Merrill Reprint Series;
1970 in Myers; partly in Loux;
1971 in Manicas;
1972 in Landesman; in Feigl, Sellars, and Lehrer;
1975 partly in Beck;
1978 in Copi and Gould.
Translated 1958 in Krzywicki;
1966 in Krishna (Hindi);
1971 in Bar-On (Hebrew);
1972 in Pereira;
1975 in Porchat de Assis;
1977 in Jánoska and Kauz;
1978 in Stegmüller; also into Hungarian;
1980 in Baudouri.

1949: "On decidability and completeness," *Synthese* 7: 441–446.

1950: "On natural deduction," *Jour. Symbolic Logic* 15: 93–102.
"Identity, ostension, and hypostasis," *Jour. Philosophy* 47: 621–633.
Reprinted 1953 in *From a Logical Point of View.*
Translated 1975 in Porchat de Assis.

1951: "Ontology and ideology," *Philosophical Studies* 2: 11–15.
Reprinted 1953 partly in *From a Logical Point of View;*
1972 in Feigl, Sellars, and Lehrer.
"On Carnap's views on ontology," *Philosophical Studies* 2: 65–72.
Reprinted 1966 in *The Ways of Paradox;*
1972 in Feigl, Sellars, and Lehrer.
"Semantics and abstract objects," *Proc. Amer. Acad. Arts and Sci.* 80: 90–96.
Reprinted 1953 partly in *From a Logical Point of View.*
Translated 1978 in Stegmüller.

"The ordered pair in number theory," *Structure, Method, and Meaning* (P. Henle et al., eds., New York: Liberal Arts), 84–87.

"[Rejoinder to Mr. Geach] on what there is," *Aristotelian Soc. Supp. Vol.* 25: 149–160.

"A simplification of games in extensive form" (with J. C. C. McKinsey and W. D. Krentel), *Duke Mathematical Journal* 18: 885–900.

"On the consistency of 'New foundations'," *Proc. Nat. Acad. Sci.* 37: 538–540.

"Two dogmas of empiricism," *Philosophical Review* 60: 20–43.

    Reprinted 1951 in small part in "Semantics and abstract objects";

        1953 in *From a Logical Point of View;*

        1962 in Aiken and Barrett;

        1963 in Lewis;

        1964 in Ammerman; in Benacerraf and Putnam;

        1965 partly in Nagel and Brandt;

        1966 in Rorty;

        1968 in Tillman, Berofsky, and O'Connor; in Bobbs-Merrill Reprint Series; partly in Margolis;

        1969 in Olshewsky;

        1970 in Harris and Severens;

        1971 in Rosenberg and Travis; partly in Arner; partly in Munsat;

        1972 in Morick; in Feigl, Sellars, and Lehrer;

        1974 in Berlinski; partly in Fodor, Bever, and Garrett; in Zabeeh et al.;

        1976 in Harding;

        1983 in Klemke.

    Translated 1964 in Marc-Wógau;

        1966 in Krishna (Hindi);

        1972 in Sinnreich;

        1974 in Pârvu;

        1975 in Porchat de Assis;

        1980 in Jacob; in Boudouri.

1952: "On an application of Tarski's theory of truth," *Proc. Nat. Acad. Sci.* 38: 430-433.

    Reprinted 1966 in *Selected Logic Papers.*

Preface to Joseph Clark, *Conventional Logic and Modern Logic* (Woodstock), pp. v-vii.

    Reprinted 1971 in Bynum.

"The problem of simplifying truth functions," *Amer. Math. Monthly* 59: 521-531.

    Reprinted 1973 in Swartzlander.

"Some theorems on definability and decidability" (with Alonzo Church), *Jour. Symbolic Logic* 17: 179-187.

"On reduction to a symmetric relation" (with William Craig), ibid: 188.

1953: "On ω-inconsistency and a so-called axiom of infinity,"ibid. 18: 119-124.

    Reprinted 1966 in *Selected Logic Papers.*

"On a so-called paradox," *Mind* 62: 65-67.

    Reprinted 1966 in *The Ways of Paradox.*

"Mr. Strawson on logical theory," *Mind* 62: 433-451.

    Reprinted 1966 in *The Ways of Paradox;*

        1968 in Copi and Gould.

    Translated 1979 into Hungarian.

"On mental entities," *Proc. Amer. Acad. Arts and Sci.* 80: 198–203.

    Reprinted 1966 in *The Ways of Paradox;*

        1969 in O'Connor.

"Two theorems about truth functions," *Boletín Soc. Matemática Mexicana* 10: 64–70.

    Translated 1953 ibid.

    Reprinted 1966 in *Selected Logic Papers.*

"Three grades of modal involvement," *Proc. XI International Congress of Philosophy* 14: 65–81.
Reprinted 1966 in *The Ways of Paradox.*

1954: "Interpretations of sets of conditions," *Jour. Symbolic Logic* 19: 97–102.
Reprinted 1966 in *Selected Logic Papers.*
"Quantification and the empty domain," *Jour. Symbolic Logic* 19: 177–179.
Reprinted 1966 in *Selected Logic Papers.*
Translated 1976 in Bencivenga.
"Reduction to a dyadic predicate," *Jour. Symbolic Logic* 19: 180–182.
Reprinted 1966 in *Selected Logic Papers.*

1955: "A proof procedure for quantification theory," *Jour. Symbolic Logic* 20: 141–149.
Reprinted 1966 in *Selected Logic Papers.*
"A way to simplify truth functions," *Amer. Math. Monthly* 62: 627–631.
Reprinted 1973 in Swartzlander.
"On Frege's way out," *Mind* 64: 145–159.
Reprinted 1966 in *Selected Logic Papers;*
1969 in Klemke.

1956: "On formulas with valid cases," *Jour. Symbolic Logic* 21: 148.
"Unification of universes in set theory," ibid.: 267–279.
"Quantifiers and propositional attitudes," *Jour. Philosophy* 53: 177–187.
Reprinted 1966 in *The Ways of Paradox;*
1971 in Linsky;
1972 in Marras;
1974 in Davidson and Harman;
1985 in Martinelli.
Translated 1973 in Simpson.

1957: "Logic, symbolic," *Encyclopedia Americana.*
Reprinted 1966 in *Selected Logic Papers.*
"The scope and language of science," *Brit. Jour. Phil. of Sci.* 8: 1–17.
Preprinted 1955 in Leary with corruption of text.
Reprinted 1966 in *The Ways of Paradox.*
Translated 1969 in Pasquinelli;
1973 in Diánoia (Mexico);
1979 in AMR Info (Vienna);
1980 in Jacob.

1958: "Speaking of objects," *Proc. and Addresses Amer. Phil. Assn.* 31: 5–22.
Reprinted 1959 in Krikorian and Edel;
1960 partly in *Word and Object;*
1964 in Fodor and Katz;
1966 in Kurtz;
1969 in *Ontological Relativity and Other Essays.*
Translated 1960 in Bunge;
1969 in Pasquinelli.
"The philosophical bearing of modern logic," *Philosophy in the Mid-Century* (R. Klibansky, ed.; Florence: Nuova Italia), 3f.
Translated 1969 in Pasquinelli.

1959: "Meaning and translation," *On Translation* (R. A. Brower, ed., Harvard), 148–172.
Reprinted 1960 in large part in *Word and Object;*
1964 in Fodor and Katz;
1969 in Olshewsky;

1971 partly in Rosenberg and Travis;
1972 in Morick;
1974 in Berlinski.
Translated 1973 in Bonomi;
1977 in Sukale.
"On cores and prime implicants of truth functions," *Amer. Math. Monthly* 66: 755–760.
Reprinted 1966 in *Selected Logic Papers*.

1960: "Posits and reality," *Basis of the Contemporary Philosophy* 5 (S. Uyeda, ed., Tokyo),
391–400.
Translated 1960 ibid.;
1964 in *Rivista di Filosofia*.
Reprinted 1966 in *The Ways of Paradox;*
1969 in Landesman;
1973 in Grandy.
"Variables explained away," *Proc. Amer. Phil. Soc.* 104: 343–347.
Reprinted 1966 in *Selected Logic Papers*.
"Carnap and logical truth," *Synthese* 12: 350–374.
Preprinted 1956 partly in Hook.
Reprinted 1962 in Kazemier and Vuysje;
1963 in Schilpp;
1966 in *The Ways of Paradox;*
1979 in Benacerraf and Putnam.
Translated 1957 in *Rivista di Filosofia*.

1961: "Reply to Professor Marcus," *Synthese* 13: 323–330.
Reprinted 1963 in *Boston Studies in Philosophy of Science;*
1966 in *The Ways of Paradox;*
1968 in Copi and Gould;
1978 in another Copi and Gould.
"Logic as a source of syntactical insights," *Proc. of Symposia in Applied Math.* 12: 1–5.
Reprinted 1966 in *The Ways of Paradox;*
1974 in Davidson and Harman.
Translated 1966 in *Langages* (Paris).
"A basis for number theory in finite classes," *Bull. Amer. Math. Soc.* 67: 391f.

1962: "Paradox," *Scientific American* 206, no. 4: 84–95.
Reprinted 1966 in *The Ways of Paradox;*
1968 in Kline.
Translated 1969 in Pasquinelli.
"Le mythe de la signification," *La Philosophie Analytique* (Cahiers de Royaumont IV,
Paris: Minuit), 139–169.

1963: "On simple theories of a complex world," *Synthese* 15: 107–111.
Reprinted 1964 in Gregg and Harris;
1966 in *The Ways of Paradox;* in Foster and Martin.
Translated 1984 in *Literatura na Świecie* (Warsaw).

1964: "On ordinals" (with Hao Wang), *Bull. Amer. Math. Soc.* 70: 297f.
"Implicit definition sustained," *Jour. Philosophy* 61: 71–74.
Reprinted 1966 in *The Ways of Paradox;*
1968 in Bobbs-Merrill Reprint Series.
Translated 1964 in *Rivista di Filosofia*.
"Ontological reduction and the world of numbers," *Jour. Philosophy* 61: 209–216.
Reprinted 1966 in *The Ways of Paradox*.
"Necessary truth," *Voice of America Forum Lectures, Philosophy of Science Series*, no. 7;
7 pp.

Reprinted 1966 in *The Ways of Paradox;*
 1967 in Morgenbesser.
"The foundations of mathematics," *Scientific American* 211, no. 3: 113–116, 118, 120, 122, 124, 127.
Reprinted 1966 in *The Ways of Paradox;*
 1968 in Kline.
"Henry Maurice Sheffer," *Harvard University Gazette* 60, no. 14.
Reprinted 1965 in *Proc. and Addresses of Amer. Phil. Assn.*
"Frontières dans la théorie logique," *Etudes Philosophiques:* 191–208.

1965: "J. L. Austin, comment," *Jour. Philosophy* 62: 509f. (A résumé; see 1969.)
 Translated 1977 in Muguerza.

1966: "Russell's ontological development," *Jour. Philosophy* 63: 657–667.
Reprinted 1967 in Schoenman;
 1968 in Klibansky;
 1970 in Klemke;
 1972 in Pears;
 1981 in *Theories and Things.*

1967: "On a suggestion of Katz," *Jour. Philosophy* 64: 52–54.
Reprinted 1970 in Woods and Sumner.
"Thoughts on reading Father Owens," *Proc. VII Inter-Amer. Congress of Philosophy* 1, pp. 60–63.
Introductory notes, *From Frege to Gödel* (J. van Heijenoort, ed.; Harvard), 150–152, 216f., 355–357.

1968: Comments, *Problems in the Philosophy of Science* (I. Lakatos and A. Musgrave, eds.; Amsterdam: North-Holland), 161–163, 200f., 223.
Reprinted 1981 in part in *Theories and Things.*
Replies, *Synthese* 19: 264–321.
Reprinted 1969 in Davidson and Hintikka.
Translated 1973 partly in Simpson.
"Ontological relativity," *Jour. Philosophy* 65: 185–212.
Reprinted 1969 in *Ontological Relativity and Other Essays;*
 1971 partly in Steinberg and Jakobovits.
"Propositional objects," *Critica* 2, no. 5: 3–22.
Reprinted 1969 in *Ontological Relativity and Other Essays.*
"Existence and quantification," *L'Âge de la Science* 1: 151–164.
Reprinted 1969 in Margolis and in *Ontological Relativity and Other Essays.*

1969: "Natural kinds," *Essays in Honor of Carl G. Hempel* (N. Rescher et al., eds.; Dordrecht: Reidel), 5–23.
Reprinted 1969 in *Ontological Relativity and Other Essays;*
 1977 in Schwartz.
"Linguistics and philosophy," *Language and Philosophy* (S. Hook, ed.; NYU Press), 95–98.
Reprinted 1972 in Morick;
 1975 in Stich;
 1976 in *Ways of Paradox.*
Translated 1977 in Stanosz.
"Existence," *Physics, Logic, and History* (W. Yourgrau, ed.; New York: Plenum), 89–98.
Reprinted 1976 partly in *Ways of Paradox.*
Foreword to D. K. Lewis, *Convention* (Harvard), pp. ix-x.
"Stimulus and meaning," *Isenberg Memorial Lecture Series 1965–66* (East Lansing:

Michigan State), 39–61.
Reprinted 1971 partly in "Epistemology naturalized."
"On Austin's method," *Symposium on J. L. Austin* (K. T. Fann, ed., Routledge), 86–90. For résumé see 1965.
Reprinted 1981 in *Theories and Things*.
"The limits of decision," *Akten des XIV. Internationalen Kongresses für Philosophie* 3: 57–62.
Reprinted 1981 with expansion in *Theories and Things*.

1970: "Philosophical progress in language theory," *Metaphilosophy* 1: 2–19.
Reprinted 1970 in Kiefer.
Translated 1977 in Stanosz;
1982 in *Saggi Filosofici*.
"Methodological reflections on current linguistic theory," *Synthese* 21: 386–398.
Reprinted 1972 in Davidson and Harman *(Sem. of Nat. Lang.);*
1974 in Moravcsik and in Harman;
1975 partly in Davis.
Translated 1976 in Dascal;
1977 in Stanosz;
1982 in *Saggi Filosofici*.
"Sur la tâche de la grammaire," *L 'Âge de la Science* 3: 3–15. Author's translation of part of a draft of *Philosophy of Logic*.
"On the reasons for indeterminacy of translation," *Jour. Philosophy* 67: 178–183.
Reprinted 1976 in Davis.
"Reply to D. A. Martin," *Jour. Philosophy* 67: 247f.
"Grades of theoreticity," *Experience and Theory* (L. Foster and J. W. Swanson, eds.; Amherst: U. Mass.), 1–17.
Reprinted 1976 partly in *Ways of Paradox*.
Translated 1982 in *Saggi Filosofici*.

1971: "Epistemology naturalized," *Akten des XIV. Internationalen Kongresses für Philosophie* 6: 87–103.
Preprinted 1969 in *Ontological Relativity and Other Essays*.
Reprinted 1972 in Royce and Roozeboom;
1973 in Chisholm and Schwartz.
Translated 1984 in *Literatura na Świecie* (Warsaw).
"Predicate-functor logic," *Proc. II. Scandinavian Logic Symposium* (North-Holland), 309–315.
"Algebraic logic and predicate functors," pamphlet (Indianapolis: Bobbs-Merrill), 25 pp.
Reprinted 1971 in Rudner and Scheffler;
1976 in *Ways of Paradox*.
Homage to Carnap, *Boston Studies in Philosophy of Science* 8: xxii-xxv.
Reprinted 1976 in *Ways of Paradox*.

1972: "Remarks for a memorial symposium," *Bertrand Russell* (D. Pears, ed., New York: Doubleday), 1–5.
"Reflexiones sobre el aprendizaje del lenguaje," *Teorema* 6: 5–23. Author's translation of part of a draft of *Roots of Reference*.

1973: "Vagaries of definition," *Annals N.Y. Acad. of Sci.* 211: 247–250.
Reprinted 1976 in *Ways of Paradox*.

1974: "On Popper's negative methodology," *The Philosophy of Karl Popper* (P. A. Schilpp, ed., Open Court), 218–220.
"Paradoxes of plenty," *Daedalus* 103, no. 4: 38–40.
Reprinted 1981 in *Theories and Things*.

"Truth and disquotation," *Proc. 1971 Tarski Symposium* (Providence: Amer. Math. Soc.), 373–384.
Reprinted 1976 in *Ways of Paradox.*
Comments on Davidson and Dummett, *Synthese* 27, nos. 3–4: 325–329, 399.

1975: "Mind and verbal dispositions," *Mind and Language* (S. Guttenplan, ed., Oxford: Clarendon), 83–95.
Translated 1982 in *Saggi Filosofici.*
"The nature of natural knowledge," ibid.: 67–81.
Translated 1975 in *Rivista di Filosofia,* by author.
Translation reprinted 1982 in *Saggi Filosofici.*
"The variable," *Logic Colloquium* (Lecture Notes in Mathematics 453, New York: Springer), 155–163.
Reprinted 1976 in *Ways of Paradox.*
Letter of 1964 to Robert Ostermann, *The Owl of Minerva* (C. J. Bontempo and S. J. Odell, eds., New York: McGraw Hill), 227–230.
"On the individuation of attributes," *The Logical Enterprise* (R. M. Martin, ed., New Haven: Yale), 3–13.
Reprinted 1981 in *Theories and Things.*
"On empirically equivalent systems of the world," *Erkenntnis* 9: 313–328.
Respuestas, *Aspectos de la Filosofía de W. V. Quine* (R. Garrido, ed., Valencia: Teorema), pp. 149–168.

1976: "Grades of discriminability," *Jour. Philosophy* 73: 113–116.
Reprinted 1981 in *Theories and Things.*
Comments, *Norbert Wiener: Collected Works* 1 (P. Masani, ed., MIT), 225, 233.
"Whither physical objects?" *Boston Studies in Philosophy of Science* 39: 497–504.
Preprinted 1976 partly in *Ways of Paradox.*
Translated 1982 in *Saggi Filosofici.*
"Worlds away," *Jour. Philosophy* 73: 359–364.
Reprinted 1981 in *Theories and Things.*
Translated 1982 in *Saggi Filosofici.*

1977: "A closer look," *Jour. Philosophy* 74: 415f.
"Intensions revisited," *Midwest Studies in Philosophy* 2: 5–11.
Reprinted 1979 in French et al.;
1981 in *Theories and Things.*
Translated 1982 in *Saggi Filosofici.*
"Facts of the matter," *American Philosophy from Edwards to Quine* (R. Shahan, ed., Norman: University of Oklahoma), 176–196.
Reprinted 1979 in *Southwestern Jour. Philosophy* and in Shahan and Swoyer.
Translated 1982 in *Saggi Filosofici.*

1978: "Reply to Lycan and Pappas," *Philosophia* 7: 637f.
Translated 1982 in *Saggi Filosofici.*
"The ideas of Quine," *Men of Ideas* (B. Magee, ed., London: BBC Pubs.), 168–179.
Abridged in *Listener,* March 23: 367–369.
"Use and its place in meaning," *Erkenntnis* 13: 1–8.
Reprinted 1979 in Margalit;
1981 in *Theories and Things.*
Translated 1977 in *Deucalion;*
1982 in *Saggi Filosofici.*
"On the nature of moral values," *Values and Morals* (A. I. Goldman and J. Kim, eds., Reidel), 37–45.
Reprinted 1979 in *Critical Inquiry;*
1981 in *Theories and Things.*

"Postscript on metaphor," *Critical Inquiry* 5: 161f.
Reprinted 1979 in Sacks;
1981 in *Theories and Things*.
Translated 1984 in *Literatura na Świecie* (Warsaw).

1979: "Comments" (on Davidson), *Meaning and Use* (A. Margalit, ed., Reidel), pp. 21f.
"Comments on Newton-Smith," *Analysis* 39: 66f.
"On not learning to quantify," *Jour. Philosophy* 76: 429f.
"Cognitive meaning," *Monist* 62: 129–142.
Translated 1982 in *Saggi Filosofici*.
"Kurt Gödel," *Amer. Phil. Soc. Yearbook* 1978, 81–84.
Reprinted 1981 in *Theories and Things*.
"Clauses and classes," *Bulletin d'information* 6 (Soc. Franç. de Logique, Méthodologie, et Phil. des Sci.) 23–39.
"Has philosophy lost contact with people?" *Newsday*, Nov. 18, Part I, § 2, pp. 5, 13.
Rewritten by editor.
Original printed 1981 in *Theories and Things*.

1980: "Sellars on behaviorism, language, and meaning," *Pacific Phil. Qtrly.* 61: 26–30.
Reprinted 1981 partly in *Theories and Things*.
"Soft impeachment disowned," ibid., 450–452.
Reprinted 1981 in *Theories and Things*.
"What is it all about?" *Amer. Scholar* 50: 43–54.
Reprinted 1981 with amplification in *Theories and Things*.
"The variable and its place in reference," *Philosophical Subjects: Essays on the Work of P. F. Strawson* (Z. van Straaten, ed., Oxford), 164–173.
Reprinted 1981 partly in *Theories and Things*.

1981: "What price bivalence," *Jour. Philosophy* 78: 90–95.
Reprinted 1981 in *Theories and Things*.
"Grammar, truth, and logic," *Philosophy and Logic* (S. Kanger and S. Ohmann, eds., Reidel), 17–28.
"Predicate functors revisited," *Jour. Symb. Logic* 46: 649–652.
Reprinted 1981 in *Theories and Things*.
"Replies to the eleven essays," *Philosophical Topics* 12: 227–243.
Reprinted 1981 partly in *Theories and Things*.
Replies to Stroud and Chihara, *Midwest Studies in Phil.* 6: 453f, 473–475.
"The pragmatists' place in empiricism," *Pragmatism* (R. J. Mulvaney and P. J. Zeltner, eds., U. of S. Carolina Press), 21–39.
Preprinted 1981 partly in *Theories and Things*.

1982: "Burdick's attitudes," *Synthese* 52: 531f.
"Respuestas," *Análisis Filosófico* (Buenos Aires) 2, 159–173.

1983: "Ontology and ideology revisited," *Jour. Philosophy* 80: 499–502.
"Gegenstand und Beobachtung," *Kant oder Hegel?* (D. Henrich, ed., Stuttgart: Klein-Cotta), 412–422.
"Donald Cary Williams," *Proc. and Addresses Amer. Phil. Assn.* 57: 245–248.
Reprinted 1983 in *Harvard University Gazette*.

1984: "Relativism and absolutism," *Monist* 67: 293–296.
"What I believe," *What I Believe* (M. Booth, ed., London: Waterstone), 69–75.
"Sticks and stones; or, the ins and outs of existence," *On Nature* (L. S. Rouner, ed., Notre Dame), 13–26.

1985: "States of mind," *Jour. Philosophy* 82: 5–8.
"Events and reification," *The Philosophy of Donald Davidson* (E. LePore, ed., Oxford: Blackwell).

Translated 1984 in *Revista de Filosofía* (Chile).
"Carnap's positivistic travail," *Fundamenta Scientiae* 5: 325–33.

ANTHOLOGIES WHERE ARTICLES HAVE REAPPEARED

1949: Feigl and Sellars, *Readings in Philosophical Analysis* (New York: Appleton).

1952: Linsky, *Semantics and the Philosophy of Language* (Urbana).

1955: Leary, *The Unity of Knowledge* (New York: Doubleday).

1956: Hook, *American Philosophers at Work* (New York: Criterion).

1958: Krzywicki, *Filozofia Amerikańska* (Boston Univ.).

1959: Krikorian and Edel, *Contemporary Philosophic Problems* (New York: Macmillan).

1960: Bunge, *Antología Semántica* (Buenos Aires).

1961: Saporta, *Psycholinguistics* (New York: Holt).

1962: Aiken and Barrett, *Philosophy in the Twentieth Century* (New York: Random House).
Kazemier and Vuysje, *Logic and Language* (Dordrecht: Reidel).

1963: Lewis, *Clarity is Not Enough* (London: Allen and Unwin).
Schilpp, *The Philosophy of Rudolf Carnap* (LaSalle: Open Court).

1964: Ammerman, *Classics of American Philosophy* (New York: McGraw Hill).
Benacerraf and Putnam, *Readings in the Philosophy of Mathematics* (Englewood: Prentice Hall).
Fodor and Katz, *The Structure of Language* (Prentice Hall).
Gregg and Harris, *Form and Strategy in Science* (Reidel).
Marc-Wogau, *Filosofin Genom Tiderna, 1900-talet* (Stockholm).
Smart, *Problems of Space and Time* (Macmillan).

1965: Baylis, *Metaphysics* (Macmillan).
Nagel and Brandt, *Meaning and Knowledge* (New York: Harcourt Brace).

1966: Foster and Martin, *Probability, Confirmation, and Simplicity* (New York: Odyssey).
Kurtz, *American Philosophy in the Twentieth Century* (Macmillan).
Rorty, *Pragmatic Philosophy* (Doubleday).

1967: Celucci, *La Filosofia della Matematica* (Bari: Laterza).
Morgenbesser, *Philosophy of Science Today* (New York: Basic Books).
Rorty, *The Linguistic Turn* (Cambridge: MIT).
Schoenman, *Bertrand Russell: Philosopher of the Century* (Allen and Unwin).

1968: Copi and Gould, *Contemporary Readings in Logical Theory*. (Macmillan).
Iseminger, *Logic and Philosophy* (Appleton).
Klibansky, *Contemporary Philosophy* (Florence: Nuova Italia).
Kline, *Mathematics in the Modern World* (San Francisco: Freeman).

Margolis, *Introduction to Logical Inquiry* (New York: Knopf).
Tillman, Berofsky, and O'Connor, *Introductory Philosophy* (New York: Harper).

1969: Davidson and Hintikka, *Words and Objections* (Reidel).
Klemke, *Essays on Frege* (Urbana).
Landesman, *Readings in the Foundation of Knowledge* (Prentice Hall).
Margolis, *Fact and Existence* (Oxford: Blackwell).
O'Connor, *Modern Materialism* (Harcourt Brace).
Olshewsky, *Problems in the Philosophy of Language* (Holt).
Pasquinelli, *Neo-Empirismo* (Turin: UTET).

1970: Harris and Severens, *Analyticity* (Chicago: Quadrangle).
Kiefer, *Contemporary Philosophical Thought* (Albany: State Univ.)
Klemke, *Essays on Bertrand Russell* (Urbana).
Loux, *Universals and Particulars* (Doubleday).
Myers, *The Spirit of Analytical Philosophy* (New York: Putnam).
Woods and Sumner, *Necessary Truth* (Random House).

1971: Arner, *Readings in Epistemology* (New York: Scott Foresman).
Bynum, *Frege* (New York: Oxford).
Linsky, *Reference and Modality* (Oxford: Clarendon).
Manicas, *Logic as Philosophy* (Princeton: Van Nostrand).
Munsat, *The Analytic-Synthetic Distinction* (New York: Wadsworth).
Rosenberg and Travis, *Readings in the Philosophy of Language* (Prentice Hall).
Rudner and Scheffler, *Logic and Art* (Indianapolis: Bobbs-Merrill)
Steinberg and Jakobovits, *Semantics* (Cambridge Univ.).

1972: Davidson and Harman, *Semantics of Natural Language* (Reidel).
Feigl, Sellars, and Lehrer, *New Readings in Philosophical Analysis* (Appleton).
Goodman, *Problems and Projects* (Bobbs-Merrill).
Landesman, *The Problem of Universals* (Prentice Hall).
Marras, *Intentionality, Mind, and Language* (Urbana).
Morick, *Challenges to Empiricism* (Wadsworth).
Pears, *Bertrand Russell* (Doubleday).
Pereira, *Significação e Verdade* (São Paulo: Perspectiva).
Royce and Roozeboom, *The Psychology of Knowing* (London: Gordon and Breach).
Sinnreich, *Zur Philosophie der idealen Sprache* (Munich: Deutscher Taschenbuch).

1973: Bleikasten and Birnbaum, *Versions* (Paris: Masson).
Bonomi, *La Struttura Logica del Linguaggio* (Milan: Bompiani).
Chisholm and Schwartz, *Empirical Knowledge* (Prentice Hall).
Eisenberg, Bense, and Haberland, *Linguistische Reihe* (Munich: Hueber).
Grandy, *Theories and Observation in Science* (Prentice Hall).
MacKinnon, *The Problem of Scientific Realism* (Appleton).
Simpson, *Semántica Filosófica* (Buenos Aires: Siglo XXI).
Swartzlander, *Computer Design* (New York: Hayden).

1974: Berlinski, *The Cutting Edge* (New York: Alfred).
Davidson and Harman, *The Logic of Grammar* (Encino: Dickenson).
Fodor, Bever, and Garrett, *Psychology of Language* (McGraw Hill).
Harman, *On Noam Chomsky: Critical Essays* (Doubleday).
Moravcsik, *Logic and Philosophy for Linguists* (Hague: Mouton).
Pârvu, *Epistemologie: Orientari Contemporare* (Bucharest).

1975: Beck, *Perspectives in Philosophy*.
Porchat de Assis, *Os Pensadores* 52 (São Paulo: Abril).
Stich, *Innate Ideas* (Berkeley).

1976: Bencivenga, *Logiche Libere* (Turin: Boringhere).
Dascal, *Metologia da Linguística* (São Paulo: Atica).
Davis, *Philosophy of Language* (Bobbs-Merrill).
Harding, *Can Theories Be Refuted? Essays on the Duhem-Quine Thesis* (Reidel).

1977: Jánoska and Kauz, *Metaphysik* (Darmstadt: Wissensch. Buchges.).
Muguerza, *Lecturas de Filosofía* (Madrid: Alianza).
Schwartz, *Naming, Necessity, and Natural Kinds* (Ithaca: Cornell)
Stanosz, *Lingwistyka a Filozofia* (Warsaw: Państwowe Wydanictwo).
Sukale, *Moderne Sprachphilosophie* (Hamburg: Hoffman).
Zabeeh, Klemke, and Jacobson, *Readings in Semantics* (Urbana).

1978: Copi and Gould, *Contemporary Philosophical Logic* (New York: St. Martin's)
Stegmüller, *Das Universalienproblem* (Wissensch. Buchges.)

1979: Benacerraf and Putnam 1964, 2nd ed.
French et al., *Contemporary Perspectives in the Philosophy of Language* (Minneapolis: University of Minnesota)
Margalit, *Meaning and Use* (Reidel).
Sacks, *On Metaphor* (Chicago: University of Chicago).
Shahan and Swoyer, *Essays on the Philosophy of W. V. Quine* (Oklahoma).
Tucker, *The Critical Temper* (New York: Ungar).

1980: Boudouri, *Metaphysike* (Athens).
Jacob, *De Vienne à Cambridge* (Paris: Gallimard).

1981: Casari, *La Logica del Novecento* (Torino: Loescher).
Ulivi, *Gli Universali e la Formazione dei Concetti* (Milano: Communità).

1983: Klemke, *Contemporary Analytic and Linguistic Philosophies* (Prometheus).

1985: Martinelli, *Philosophy of Language* (Oxford).

ABSTRACTS

1935: "A unified calculus of propositions, classes, and relations," *Bull. Amer. Math. Soc.* 41: 338.

1937: "Is logic a matter of words?" *Journal of Philosophy* 34: 674.

1940: *Mathematical Logic, Year Book of Amer. Phil. Soc.*, 230f.

1947: "On the problem of universals," *Journal of Symbolic Logic* 12: 31.

1950: "Information patterns for games in extensive form" (with W. D. Krentel and J. C. C. McKinsey), *Proc. Internat. Cong. of Math.* 1.

1951: "Some theorems on definability and decidability" (with Alonzo Church), *Journal of Symbolic Logic* 16: 239f.

1952: "The problem of simplifying truth functions," ibid. 17: 156.

1956: "Unification of universes in set theory," ibid. 21: 216.

1959: "Eliminating variables without applying functions to functions," ibid. 24: 324f.

1970: Comments on Belnap, *Noûs* 4:12.

1971: "Predicate-functor logic," *Journal of Symbolic Logic* 36: 382.

MISCELLANEOUS

1934: Report on Whitehead, "Logical definitions of extension, class, and number," *Amer. Math. Monthly* 41: 129–131.

1946: Translation (with introduction) of Löwenheim's MS "On making indirect proofs direct," *Scripta Mathematica* 12: 125–134.

1947: Letter in Carnap, *Meaning and Necessity* (Chicago), 196f.

1951: "It tastes like chicken," *Furioso* 6: 37–39.

1954: Letter on Griggs, *Atlantic Monthly* 194: 21.

1976: Comment on Croddy, *Erkenntnis* 10: 103.
Letter to Grünbaum in Harding (above), 132.

1979: Reply to Prof. Seidel, *New York Review of Books* 25, no. 22: 49.
"Word of advice," letter, *Boston Herald American,* Jan. 22: 15.

BOOK REVIEWS

1930: Of Nicod, *Foundations of Geometry and Induction; Amer. Math. Monthly* 37: 305–307.

1933: Of Peirce, *Collected Papers,* vol. 2; *Isis* 19: 220–229.

1935: Of same, vols. 3–4; *Isis* 22: 285–297, 551–553.
Of Carnap, *Logische Syntax der Sprache; Philosophical Review* 44: 394–397.

1936: Of García Baca, *Introducción a la Lógica Moderna; Journal of Symbolic Logic* 1: 112f.

1937: Of Weinberg, *Examination of Logical Positivism;* ibid. 2: 89f.
Of Jeffreys, *Scientific Inference; Science* 86: 590.

1938: Of Tarski, *Einführung in die mathematische Logik; Bull. Amer. Math. Soc.* 44: 317f.
Of Ushenko, *Theory of Logic; Philosophical Review* 47: 94.
Of Hilbert and Ackermann, *Grundzüge der theoretischen Logik; Journal of Symbolic Logic* 3: 83f.

1941: Of Russell, *Inquiry into Meaning and Truth;* ibid. 6: 29f.
Of Serrus, *Essai sur la Signification de la Logique;* ibid.: 62f.
Of da Silva, *Elementos de Lógica Matemática;* ibid.: 109f.

1946: Of Godinho, *Esboços sobre Alguns Problemas da Lógica;* ibid. 11: 126.

1947: Of Toranzos, *Introducción a la Epistemología y la Fundamentación de la Matemática;* ibid. 12: 20f.

1948: Of Reichenbach, *Elements of Symbolic Logic; Journal of Philosophy* 45: 161–166.

1951: Of Goodman, *Structure of Appearance;* ibid. 48: 556–563.

1952: Of Ferrater Mora, *Diccionario de Filosofia; Journal of Symbolic Logic* 17: 129f.

1963: Of *National Geographic Atlas; New York Review of Books* 1, no. 3: 8.

1964: Of Mencken, *American Language;* ibid., no. 9: 7.
Reprinted 1981 in *Theories and Things.*
Of *Atlas of Britain;* ibid. 2, no. 2: 17.
Of Smart, *Philosophy and Scientific Realism;* ibid., no. 11:3.
Reprinted 1981 in *Theories and Things.*
Of Geach, *Reference and Generality; Philosophical Review* 73: 100–104.

1965: Of Bagrow, *History of Cartography; New York Review of Books* 5, no. 4: 18f.

1967: Of Russell, *Autobiography,* vol. 1; *Boston Globe,* April 9, p. B-43.

1968: Of *Times Atlas of the World; Book World* (in *Washington Post* and *Chicago Tribune*), May 5, p. 7.
Reprinted 1981 in *Theories and Things.*

1969: Of *American Heritage Dictionary* and *Random House Dictionary,* College Edition; *New York Review of Books* 13, no. 10, pp. 3f.; see also no. 12, p. 38, and vol. 14, no. 1–2, p. 54.

1972: Of Munitz (ed.), *Identity and Individuation; Journal of Philosophy* 69: 488–497.
Reprinted 1981 partly in *Theories and Things.*

1977: Of Evans and McDowell (eds.), *Truth and Meaning;* ibid. 74: 225–241.
Reprinted 1981 partly in *Theories and Things.*
Of Lewis Carroll, *Symbolic Logic; Times Lit. Suppl.* (London), pp. 1018f
Reprinted 1981 in *Theories and Things.*
Of Lakatos, *Proofs and Refutations; Brit. Jour. Phil. Sci.* 28: 81f.

1978: Of Goodman, *Ways of Worldmaking; N.Y. Rev. of Books* 25, no. 18: 25.
Reprinted 1981 in *Theories and Things.*
Of Smullyan, *What is the Name of This Book?; N.Y. Times Book Rev.,* May 28, pp. 6, 17.

1983: Of Bickerton, *Roots of Language; Quaderni di Semantica* 4: 403f.

1984: Of Parsons, *Mathematics in Philosophy; Jour. Phil.* 81: 783–794.

1985: Of Strawson, *Skepticism and Naturalism; N.Y. Rev. of Books* 32, no. 2: 32.
Of MacHale, *George Boole: His Life and Work; Times Lit. Suppl.,* July 12: 767.

REVIEWS OF ARTICLES

1936: Of Tarski, "Grundzüge des Systemenkalküls"; *Journal of Symbolic Logic* 1: 71f.
Of Russell, "On order in time"; ibid.: 73f.
Short ones (under 400 words): ibid.: 43, 68, 113.

1937: Of Saarnio, "Zur heterologischen Paradoxie"; ibid. 2: 138.
Of Stone, "Note on formal logic"; ibid.: 174f.
Short ones; ibid.: 37, 46f., 59, 83f.

1938: Of Chwistek and Hetper, "New foundation of formal metamathematics"; ibid. 3: 120f.
Short ones: ibid.: 47–49, 56, 94, 121f.

1939: Of Hermes, "Semiotik"; ibid. 4: 87f.
Short ones: ibid.: 102, 125.

1940: Of Bröcker, "Antinomien und Paradoxien"; ibid. 5: 79.
Of Lésniewski, "Einleitende Bemerkungen"; ibid.: 83f.
Of Church, "Formulation of theory of types"; ibid.: 114f.
Short ones: ibid.: 30, 71, 84, 157, 168f.

1941: Of Rosser, "Independence of Quine's axioms"; ibid. 6: 163.

1942: Short one: ibid. 7: 44f.

1946: Of Barcan, "Functional calculus based on strict implication"; ibid. 11: 96f.

1947: Of Nelson, "Contradiction and existence"; ibid. 12: 52–55.
Of Barcan, "Identity of individuals"; ibid.: 95f. [Correction in 23 (1958): 342.]
Of Schröter, "Was ist eine mathematische Theorie?"; ibid.: 136f.
Short ones: ibid.: 55, 95.

1948: Short ones: ibid. 13: 122, 158.

1949: Of Fraenkel, "Relation of equality"; ibid. 14: 130.
Of Saarnio, "Der Begriff der Hierarchie"; ibid.: 131.
Short ones: ibid.: 59f., 64, 257.

1950: Of Feys, "Simple notation for relations"; ibid. 15: 71f.
Short ones: ibid.: 139, 149f, 215.

1951: Of Myhill, "Complete theory of numbers"; ibid. 16: 65–67.
Of Geach, "Subject and predicate"; ibid.: 138.
Of Myhill, "Report of investigations"; ibid.: 217f.
Short ones: ibid.: 138f., 214, 273.

1952: Of Ajdukiewicz, "On the notion of existence"; ibid. 17: 144f.

1958: Short one: ibid. 23: 41.

INDEX

(by S. S. Rama Rao Pappu)